Medieval
Studies
Library

PUBLICATIONS OF THE NEW CHAUCER SOCIETY

THE NEW CHAUCER SOCIETY

Studies in the Age of Chaucer, the yearbook of The New Chaucer Society, is published annually. Each issue contains a limited number of substantial articles, reviews of books on Chaucer and related topics, and an annotated Chaucer bibliography. Articles explore such concerns as the efficacy of various critical approaches to the art of Chaucer and his contemporaries, their literary relationships and reputations, and the artistic, economic, intellectual, religious, scientific, and social and historical backgrounds to their work.

Manuscripts, in duplicate, accompanied by return postage, should follow the *Chicago Manual of Style*, fourteenth edition. Unsolicited reviews are not accepted. Authors receive free twenty offprints of articles and ten of reviews. All correspondence concerning manuscript submissions for Volume 19 of *Studies in the Age of Chaucer* should be directed to the Editor, Lisa J. Kiser, Department of English, Ohio State University, 164 West 17th Avenue, Columbus, OH 43210-1370. Subscriptions to The New Chaucer Society and information about the Society's activities should be directed to Christian Zacher, Center for Medieval and Renaissance Studies, Ohio State University, 256 Cunz Hall, 1841 Millikin Road, Columbus, OH 43210-1229.

Studies in the Age of Chaucer

Studies in the
Age of Chaucer

Volume 18
1996

EDITOR

LISA J. KISER

PUBLISHED ANNUALLY BY THE NEW CHAUCER SOCIETY

THE OHIO STATE UNIVERSITY, COLUMBUS

The frontispiece design, showing the Pilgrims at the Tabard Inn, is adapted from the woodcut in Caxton's second edition of *The Canterbury Tales*.

ISBN 0-933784-20-1

ISSN 0190-2407

CONTENTS

Studies in the Age of Chaucer

Chaucer Reading Langland:
The House of Fame

Frank Grady
University of Missouri, St. Louis

T his essay begins not, as it probably ought to, with a dream, but with a series of voices.[1] They are the voices of critics discussing a late-fourteenth-century Middle English poem, an allegorical dream vision—although one critic has called the poem an "apocalypse" by virtue of its mixing of other genres, and another has called attention to how these various genres are constantly "undercut" and found lacking, especially in the early part of the poem. The structure of this *visio* has often been cause for criticism; divided into "irregular parts and discontinuous sequences," the poem's "narrative movement tends to be abrupt and spasmodic rather than smoothly flowing as the poem moves from one self-contained unit to the next." To one reader the "poem is all process."

Such observations, unsurprisingly, are mirrored on the level of interpretation. Thus one critic claims that the "pervasive presence of skepticism, irony, and parody renders the meaning of narrated events uncertain and makes the fictional narrative subject to a continuous project of evaluation." "Too many tantalizing motifs . . . recur, but do not add up," claims one reader, and another observes that the poet responsible for this text "repeatedly builds up the standard devices for assuring the truth of a medieval narrative, only to draw back from them, leaving the issue of truth for his readers to judge." On the other hand, certain readers find this indeterminacy the poem's most engaging feature: "Much of its fun is in its contradictions, its sudden shifts of focus, and its creation of significant tensions, and part of its peculiar pleasure lies in the fact that it ends . . . with these tensions intact and unresolved."

At the center of this poem stands the figure of the narrator, "oscillating

---

[1] In my own voice I'd like to thank Anne Middleton, Steven Justice, David Wallace, George Kane, and Ralph Hanna III for their valuable comments on this essay, and Mark Scapicchio for technical assistance.

3

between roles, now the autonomous, self-conscious maker of fictions, now the limited, fictive persona made by the author." This persona sometimes finds himself in disputation with the other characters in the poem; in the words of one critic they "confront one another as embodiments of two apparently incompatible ways of knowing." Although occasionally given to self-doubt, the narrator remains resolute: "Disappointment after disappointment has not daunted him: he has pressed on despite our growing surety that his search for stability amid contingency will be a failure."

Curiously this male dreamer—who at one point is described as being like a hermit of insufficiently ascetic habits—is known by his first name, which happens also to be the first name of the poet. Early on in the poem the dreamer is caught up in, even ravished by, the story of a woman— a queen—and her ultimately unsuccessful marriage plans. Later the dreamer's progress comes to a halt that threatens to derail the narrative (in so far as it can be said to exist): unable to learn the necessary tidings, he is rescued and put back on track only by the sudden, unexpected arrival of an apparently authoritative guide specifically suited to the next phase of progress. In this poem the narrator is sharply if comically rebuked by his guide for his intellectual incapacity and misguided aims; in this poem the dreamer finds himself the observer of a large, busy crowd of pilgrims, pardoners, and others, bustling about on the world's business; and finally, in this poem the geography of a tower on a hilltop and a considerably less attractive building in a valley below figure prominently in the representation of crucial epistemological concepts.

This poem is Chaucer's *House of Fame*.[2] But it could just as easily have been another great allegorical dream vision of fourteenth-century English

---

[2] The quotations at the beginning of the essay are drawn from the following criticism: "apocalypse": Lisa Kiser, *Truth and Textuality in Chaucer's Poetry* (Hanover, N.H.: University Press of New England, 1991), pp. 25–26; genres "undercut": Robert W. Hanning, "Chaucer's First Ovid: Metamorphosis and Poetic Tradition in *The Book of the Duchess* and *The House of Fame*," in Leigh A. Arrathoon, ed., *Chaucer and the Craft of Fiction* (Rochester, Mich.: Solaris Press, 1984), p. 151; "irregular parts," "narrative movement": Robert M. Jordan, "Lost in the Funhouse of Fame: Chaucer and Postmodernism," *ChauR* 18 (1983): 113, 111; "all process": Robert Burlin, *Chaucerian Fiction* (Princeton, N.J.: Princeton University Press, 1977), p. 51; "pervasive . . . skepticism": Jordan, "Lost in the Funhouse," p. 108; "tantalizing motifs": Burlin, *Chaucerian Fiction*, p. 46; "standard devices": Karla Taylor, *Chaucer Reads "The Divine Comedy"* (Stanford: Stanford University Press, 1989), p. 38; "much of its fun": Larry Benson, "'The Love-Tydynges' in Chaucer's *House of Fame*," in Julian Wasserman and Robert J. Blanch, eds., in *Chaucer in the Eighties* (Syracuse, N.Y.: Syracuse University Press, 1986), p. 9; "oscillating": Jordan, "Lost in the Funhouse," p. 108; "confront one another": Burlin, *Chaucerian Fiction*, p. 51; "disappointment": J. Stephen Russell, *The English Dream-Vision: Anatomy of a Form* (Columbus, Ohio: Ohio State University Press, 1988), p. 194.

literature, *Piers Plowman*. In that poem, of course, the narrator, Will (who starts out "In habite as an heremite, vnholy of werkes"), is captivated not by the story of Dido, Queen of Carthage, but by the spectacle of Lady Meed: "Hire Robe was ful riche, of reed scarlet engreyned, / Wiþ Ribanes of reed gold and of riche stones. / Hire array me rauysshed; swich richesse sauʒ I neuere."[3] Meed's doomed affair with False is the matter of passus 2, and Meed's fate at the hands of a divinely underwritten, state-oriented authority—the King, Conscience, and Reason, not Virgil—concerns the narrator through passus 4. In passus 5, the dreamer and the throng of pilgrims with whom he has thrown in his lot find themselves not lost in a featureless desert (as is the case with Chaucer's Geffrey outside the temple of Venus) but blundering over hills, interrogating a palmer who claims never to have heard of St. Truth. The day is saved—and the pilgrimage irrevocably changed—by the unexpected appearance of Piers the Plowman, who claims to know truth "as kyndely as clerc doþ his bokes" (5.538), and whose introduction into the poem is no less an act of willful artistic license than the abrupt, lightninglike descent of Dante's golden eagle into Chaucer's text.

If Chaucer's windy eagle abuses poor Geffrey for his lack of success in love, his hermitlike lifestyle, his timidity, and his portliness (with its threatening susceptibility to the force of gravity), Langland's Will is thrice-cursed, rebuked by Holichurch for having forgotten his catechism, scorned by Dame Study for his intellectual pretensions, and contradicted by Scripture for his incomplete grasp of theology. And of course, Langland's poem begins with a tableau that suggests—or looks forward to—the end of Chaucer's: "a tour on a toft trieliche Ymaked; / A deep dale byneþe, a dongeon þerInne / Wiþ depe diches and derke and dredfulle of siʒte," with a field full of folk in between, "Werchynge and wandrynge as þe world askeþ" (B.Prol.14–16, 19). Is it too much to find in this picture an image analogous to that evoked when Geffrey goes out of Fame's castle and sees "in a valeye, / Under the castel, faste by, / An hous, that Domus Dedaly, / That Laboryntus cleped ys, / Nas mad so wonderlych, ywis, / Ne half so queyntelych ywrought,"[4] a house which we soon find to be full of pilgrims and shipmen and pardoners and messengers and couriers, all bearing tid-

---

[3] *Piers Plowman* B 2.15–17; all citations from this version of the poem are drawn from *Piers Plowman: The B Version*, ed. George Kane and E. Talbot Donaldson, rev. ed. (Berkeley: University of California Press, 1988); further citations will appear in the text.

[4] *House of Fame* 1918–23; all citations from Chaucer's works are drawn from Larry D. Benson, gen. ed., *The Riverside Chaucer*, 3d ed. (Boston: Houghton Mifflin, 1987); further citations will appear in the text.

ings of the world, whispers and gossip "Of werres, of pes, of mariages, / Of reste, of labour, of viages, / Of abood, of deeth, of lyf, / Of love, of hate, acord, of stryf" (*HF* 1961–64)?

My answer to the question of whether these two scenes echo one another is an unsurprising yes, or rather, "Yes, and more." To demonstrate that *Piers Plowman* and *The House of Fame* have lived parallel lives in the experience of readers and critics is to tell only half the story. In this essay I will argue that they were also separated at birth—that is, that Chaucer composed *The House of Fame* after his first encounter with the B-version of Langland's poem at the end of the 1370s. For generations most students of Middle English literature have assumed, remarkably, that these two poems of the same essential genre, lively examples that demonstrate many of that genre's most striking features (authorial signatures and self-reference, formal experimentation, incompleteness and irresolution), written in the same decade in the same city—possibly even in the same neighborhood—had nothing whatsoever to do with one another. It is time to reexamine that assumption.

I

That the two poems were virtual contemporaries can easily be shown, though the priority of the B-text cannot be absolutely demonstrated. *The House of Fame* is usually dated 1379–81;[5] that the poem precedes both *The Parliament of Fowls* and *Troilus and Criseyde* has been generally accepted since Lowes, Tatlock, and Kittredge reached that conclusion at the turn of the century.[6] We know Langland was working on what we traditionally

---

[5] Benson, "Love Tydynges," p. 10; see also John Fyler's notes to the poem in the *Riverside Chaucer*, p. 978, where he follows Robinson's dating and provides further citations. For an alternate view, see Derek Pearsall, *The Life of Geoffrey Chaucer* (Oxford: Blackwell, 1992), pp. 109–10.

[6] See J. L. Lowes, "The Prologue to the *Legend of Good Women* Considered in its Chronological Relations," *PMLA* 20 (1905): 749–864, esp. pp. 854–60; J. S. P. Tatlock, *The Development and Chronology of Chaucer's Works*, Chaucer Society, 2d ser., vol. 37 (London: K. Paul, Trench, Treubner, 1907), pp. 34–40; and G. L. Kittredge, *The Date of Chaucer's Troilus and Other Chaucer Matters*, Chaucer Society, 2d ser., vol. 42 (London: K. Paul, Trench, Treubner, 1909 [for 1905]), pp. 53–55. Pratt argues ("Chaucer Borrowing from Himself," *MLQ* 7 [1946]: 259–64) that *Parliament* borrows from *House of Fame* in its invocation of Venus, using material that Chaucer had already lifted from Boccaccio—though the question of Boccaccio's presence in *HF* is still unsettled.

call the B-revision in the early 1370s, thanks to the reference to the London mayoralty of John Chichester (1369–70) and a likely allusion to the Dominican William Jordan (d. 1368?), both in B.13;[7] the "latest unmistakable reference" in the poem is to Richard II's July 1377 coronation at B.Prol.112–45.[8]

The *terminus ad quem* for B is harder to establish; Kane offers both 1379 and 1381, though Steven Justice has recently promised arguments in favor of 1376–77.[9] The earlier date better supports the argument of this essay, though perhaps more relevant is Justice's remark that "all this is complicated by the real ambiguity of what it means to date a work in a manuscript culture, where copies could be made and circulated with or without the author's approval, while the process of composition was still going on."[10] That is, for the B-text—and for Langland's poem in general—the matter of composition is inextricably bound up in matters of circulation, a fact that quickly turns the hardest evidence for the former into fodder for speculation about the latter.

The conflation of these two fields of inquiry is most obviously reflected in the recent renewed attention to the place of the A-text in the sequence of versions of *Piers Plowman*. In a critique of the Athlone editions of *Piers*, Robert Adams has called into question our traditional assumptions about the order of publication of the poem's versions, arguing that while the order of composition was probably ABC, the B-version was perhaps the first "officially" circulated version.[11] Anne Middleton has suggested to me that what we call the A-version of *Piers Plowman* may not have been a completed authorial effort but rather a large piece of a work-in-progress (that is, the B-version) that somehow "got away" and out into circulation. Alternately Jill Mann and others have argued recently that A is part of a "Reader's Digest" version of the poem, prepared late for a less Latinate

[7] Ralph Hanna III, *William Langland*, Authors of the Middle Ages, vol. 3 (Aldershot, U.K.: Variorum, 1993), p. 13.

[8] George Kane, "The Text," in John A. Alford, ed., *A Companion to* Piers Plowman (Berkeley: University of California Press, 1988), p. 184. Hanna, *William Langland*, pp. 12–13, following Gwynn ("The Date of the B-Text of *Piers Plowman*," *RES* 19 [1943]: 1–24), suggests that the incorporation of later allusions toward the beginning of the poem indicates a two-stage process of revision in which Langland completed the amplification of the poem before returning to revise the early passus.

[9] Kane, "The Text," p. 185; Steven Justice, *Writing and Rebellion* (Berkeley: University of California Press, 1994), p. 232 n.130.

[10] Justice, *Writing and Rebellion*, p. 232 n.130.

[11] Adams, Editing *Piers Plowman* B: The Imperative of an Intermittently Critical Edition," *Studies in Bibliography* 45 (1992): 59–63.

7

audience.[12] What Adams calls the "slim and ambiguous" evidence of the order of *Piers Plowman*'s publication suggests that the status of the publication or release or escape of the A-version is likely to remain an open question for some time, and it further reminds us that assertions about B's circulation ought to be offered tentatively as well. A substantive acquaintance with *Piers Plowman* need not require, or imply, personal possession of a full manuscript copy of the poem, as any teacher who has assigned excerpts of *Piers* ought to recognize.

Demonstrating Langland's influence on Chaucer does require some proof that the poem, in whatever form, circulated in London, where Chaucer leased the Aldgate house from 1374–86. This is quite likely. We can now point to medieval owners of *Piers Plowman* who lived in London, the earliest of whom—the cleric William Palmere—died in 1400.[13] Moreover, dialect study indicates that around half of the sixteen surviving B-manuscripts show signs of having been copied in or around the city.[14] Finally, the poem itself provides evidence that Langland meant to reach a London audience. Even if we accept the entirely reasonable hypotheses of Langland's West Country origin and a West Country retirement for the completion of the C-revisions,[15] we can nevertheless argue that Langland was well and even intimately acquainted with the capital. Caroline Barron's recent essay "William Langland: A London Poet" impressively documents the poem's extensive references to the geography of the city and its environs.[16]

[12] Jill Mann, "The Power of the Alphabet: A Reassessment of the Relation between the A and the B Versions of *Piers Plowman*," *YLS* 8 (1994): 21–50. The "Reader's Digest" phrase is Adams's; he attributes the suggestion to Ian Doyle; "Editing *Piers Plowman* B," p. 61 n.50. As Mann notes (p. 48n), John Bowers has also suggested that A might be the last of the versions; his paper and Mann's were both presented at the Cambridge Langland Conference in 1993.

[13] Other known London owners include the mercer Thomas Roos (d. 1434); Sir Thomas Charleton, Speaker of the House of Commons (d. 1465); and Thomas Stotevyle, a member of Lincoln's Inn who owned a copy in 1459. For Palmere—rector of St. Alphage, Cripplegate, probably from 1397 until his death in July 1400—see Robert A. Wood, "A Fourteenth-Century London Owner of *Piers Plowman*," *MÆ* 53 (1984): 83–90; for the others, see Anne Middleton, "The Audience and Public of *Piers Plowman*," David Lawton, ed., in *Middle English Alliterative Poetry and Its Literary Background* (Cambridge: D. S. Brewer, 1982), pp. 103, 148.

[14] Hanna, *William Langland*, p. 14. See also M. L. Samuels, "Langland's Dialect," *MÆ* 54 (1985): 232–47, and "Dialect and Grammar," in Alford, ed., *Companion to* Piers Plowman, pp. 201–21; and I. A. Doyle, "Remarks on Surviving Manuscripts of *Piers Plowman*," in Gregory Kratzmann and James Simpson, eds., *Medieval English Religious and Ethical Literature: Essays in Honour of G. H. Russell* (Cambridge: D. S. Brewer, 1986), pp. 35–48.

[15] Samuels, "Langland's Dialect," p. 240; see also John Bowers, "Piers Plowman and the Police: Notes Toward a History of the Wycliffite Langland," *YLS* 6 (1992): 15.

[16] In Barbara Hanawalt, ed., *Chaucer's England: Literature in Historical Context* (Minneapolis: University of Minnesota Press, 1992), pp. 91–109. Barron's essay is paired suggestively with David Wallace's piece on the relative invisibility of London in Chaucer's poetry, "Chaucer and the Absent City," pp. 59–90.

The host of citations adduced by Barron; the fact that Chichester, a former mayor, is the only contemporary person mentioned in the poem; and indeed the inexorable move towards the city at the beginning of the poem all contribute to the impression that Langland was for at least part of his career a London poet. Indeed, Derek Pearsall suggests that London—particularly the modern perversities of London commerce—"is the problem of the poem."[17]

Not that satire of London ought to be confused with circulation in it—but no one has ever suggested that Langland's knowledge of the city, its commercial and spiritual practices, and the discourses of civic government and litigation is based on extensive reading rather than some kind of relevant experience. And the converse claim—that its urban field of reference makes *Piers Plowman* peculiarly legible and accessible to readers in and around the capital—cannot be disputed. Whatever relationship we imagine existed between Langland and his audience, it is reasonably clear that he meant to have one in London, and his potential audience there certainly included Geoffrey Chaucer, whose Aldgate dwelling stood no more than a quarter-mile from Cornhill, where Langland's Will claims to reside (C.5.2).

II

It has long been a critical cliché that the end of *The House of Fame* looks forward to *The Canterbury Tales*, either as a sign of Chaucer's embrace of "realism" and rejection of the "conventions" of his Continental models—in the older view—or as an acknowledgment of the potential for the generation of tales out of a welter of tidings. But the end of *The House of Fame* also looks backward, or at least laterally, to Langland's poem, where at intervals various members of various estates are given their own tidings to tell, in their own voices. J. A. W. Bennett pioneered this claim, suggesting over twenty years ago not only that Chaucer may have first seen the "literary potentialities" of pilgrimage in Langland's poem but that Langland's account of the estates and of the mendacity of pilgrims and pardoners recalled nothing so much as the "wicker suburb" at the end of Chaucer's poem.[18] Indeed, it is in these passages that the most irresistible verbal parallels reside; certainly Langland's "bidderes and beggeres" that "faste

---

[17] "Langland's London," in Kathryn Kerby-Fulton and Steven Justice, eds., *New Historical Studies of* Piers Plowman (forthcoming).

[18] J. A. W. Bennett, "Chaucer's Contemporary," in S. S. Hussey, ed., Piers Plowman: *Critical Approaches* (London: Methuen, 1969), p. 320. See also, more briefly, James Simpson, Piers Plowman: *An Introduction to the B-Text* (London: Longman, 1990), pp. 217 n.4 and 251.

aboute yede / Til hire bely and hire bagge were bretful ycrammed" (B.Prol.39–40) should make us think of Chaucer's pilgrims and pardoners, bearing "scrippes bret-ful of lesinges" and "boystes crammed ful of lyes" (*HF* 2122, 2129). In fact, it was such an echo that first suggested to me the topic of this essay. When Chaucer's eagle appears for the second time to aid Geffrey, who desires to hear tidings but cannot make his own way into the House of Rumor, he begins his offer of assistance with the same interjection—"Petre"—that Piers Plowman uses in his striking first appearance, when he offers his aid to the assembled pilgrims who are looking for tidings of Truth's whereabouts and who cannot make their own way to his abode. Here Chaucer may be recalling Langland both in his choice of interjection and in his return to the eagle, an allegorical guide who had apparently vanished from the poem a thousand lines earlier.[19]

The accumulation of such instances, however, does not add up to an argument, as Jill Mann cautions in her own remarks on Langland's and Chaucer's prologues. In warning us away from echo-hunting, Mann invokes the phrase that John Fisher invented to describe Gower's relationship to Chaucer—"stimulus diffusion"—which, while it somewhat coyly allays the anxiety about influence that seems to haunt every account of Chaucer's relationship to his English contemporaries, nevertheless also points us to the broader issues of genre and poetic practice.[20] Thus we can move from suggestive lexical resonances to more compelling formal and structural ones—not just the fact that Chaucer and Langland both draw on the commonplace devices of the fourteenth-century allegorical dream vision (personifications, pilgrimages, debate, instructive dialogues, allegorized land-

---

[19] The echo is probably fortuitous, although its inclusion here shows that I haven't quite discarded the possibility that it is significant. The *MED* cites nine instances of "Peter" used as an interjection: three in later romances (*Eglamour* 919, *Perceval* 933, *Amadace* 119), two in the stressed position in alliterative poems (*William of Palerne* 681, *Sir Gawain and the Green Knight* 813), two in Chaucer (the instance I cite, *House of Fame* 2000, and *CT* 3.1332, the Summoner's interruption of *The Friar's Tale*), and two in Langland. Neither of those two instances really stands up to scrutiny: at A.7.3, "seint poul" is the more regularly attested reading, while at B.6.3 it is "by seint Peter of Rome"; at A.8.118/B.7.115, "Peter" is used by the priest in direct address to Piers, not as an interjection. The *MED* omits Piers's first appearance at A.6.25/B.5.537, the one I find so striking. There are at least three other similar uses in *The Canterbury Tales*: 7.214 (*Shipman's Tale*), 8.665 (*Canon's Yeoman's Prologue*), and 3.446 (*Wife of Bath's Prologue*). Chaucer's heavy representation in this sample—five of twelve instances—is doubtless due to his facility in representing dialogue, which is also a frequent strength of Langland's.

[20] Jill Mann, *Chaucer and Medieval Estates Satire* (Cambridge: Cambridge University Press, 1973), esp. p. 212. See also Helen Cooper, "Langland's and Chaucer's Prologues," *YLS* 1 (1987): 71–81, where Cooper argues for the influence of the A-version of *Piers* on *The General Prologue*.

scapes)[21], but rather that they both interrogate these devices and the representative and hermeneutic power of the genre, its authoritative figures, and its characteristic species of narrative. Beyond similarities in vocabulary, Chaucer and Langland both use the grammar of the dream vision in the same way.

Critics have long known this, though they haven't always known that they've known it. Lisa Kiser calls *The House of Fame* an apocalypse, without reference to Morton Bloomfield's well-known if not well-accepted characterization of *Piers Plowman*.[22] Robert Hanning points out how books 1 and 2 of *The House of Fame* undercut their genres, the "love narrative" and the "symbolic heavenly journey," by revealing that such forms lack "any verifiable connection to the reality" they claim to embody; Steven Justice shows how the Visio tries out and progressively discards genres that prove inadequate to the poet's search for an authoritative mode: estates satire in the prologue, Boethian dialogue in the encounter with Holichurche, debate in the Meed episode, penitential manual in the confession of the sins, and finally a biblical genre (which Justice calls "Exodus") encompassing the crazy wanderings of the pilgrimage, the plowing of the half-acre, and the Mosaic tearing of the pardon.[23]

In one sense this interrogation of authorities and authoritative discourses can be seen as the constitutive mode of the late-medieval dream vision. Certainly in the second part of the *Roman de la Rose* a slew of claimants to regulatory, amatory, marital, ecclesiastical, and intellectual power are relentlessly prodded, mocked, and questioned. Moreover, the dream vision is, in Jacqueline T. Miller's lucid formulation, not only "a genre particularly suited to, and even generated by, the attempt to locate an authoritative perspective or interpretation with which the author may associate himself or from which he may speak," but also one in which conventional authorities are often exposed as either inadequate or fundamentally in conflict with the speakers' own self-assertive claims.[24] The relevance of this definition of the genre to the practice of Langland and Chaucer will be immedi-

[21] Stephen A. Barney, "Allegorical Visions," in Alford, ed., *Companion to* Piers Plowman, p. 127; George Kane, *The Autobiographical Fallacy in Chaucer and Langland Studies* (London: Chambers Memorial Lecture, 1965), p. 11.

[22] Morton W. Bloomfield, Piers Plowman *as a Fourteenth-Century Apocalypse* (New Brunswick, N.J.: Rutgers University Press, 1962).

[23] Steven Justice, "The Genres of *Piers Plowman*," *Viator* 19 (1988): 291–306. Langland's continual generic shifts and his rejection or deconstruction of different genres' authoritative premises are ongoing concerns of Simpson's Piers Plowman: *An Introduction to the B-Text*.

[24] Jacqueline T. Miller, "The Writing on the Wall: Authority and Authorship in Chaucer's *House of Fame*," *ChauR* 17 (1982): 95.

ately clear to anyone familiar with the conventional account of Will's iras-cible nature, or the surprising self-possession of Geffrey, who can somehow still manage to say after 1800-odd lines of adventure, "I wot myself best how I stonde" (*HF* 1878). On the level of narrative, such outbursts are the sign of a submerged tension between the desire to seek out and confirm authority and the desire to constitute it anew.

But for both Langland and Chaucer these negotiations go deeper and can be apprehended at the level of practice that precedes and enables narrative. Thus, while Robert Jordan calls attention to the fits and starts by which *The House of Fame* proceeds, and Robert Burlin to the often comic confron-tation between characters who represent different and potentially irrecon-cilable modes of knowing, Anne Middleton has convincingly shown how similar traits in *Piers Plowman* derive from the poet's very method, his way of creating the stuff of narrative out of one animus-filled encounter after another.[25] Chaucer, too, understands and employs this mode—turgidly at times in *The House of Fame*, with considerably more verve in *The Parliament of Fowls*, and finally with unprecedented (or almost unprecedented) audac-ity and success in *The Canterbury Tales*.

In "Langland and Chaucer II," the sequel to "Langland and Chaucer: An Obligatory Conjunction," George Kane speaks directly to the two poets' complex and ironic use of the dream vision genre: both poets, he writes, "evidently understood the dream-vision to be a mode of meaning, its ge-neric features not prescriptions but serviceable devices to that end"; each also took advantage of "the invitation implicit in the genre to identify dreamer and poet as a means of engagement."[26] The visible sign of that engagement is the signature passage, and in her recent work on Langland's signature strategy Middleton has noted the similarity of Langland's early and less occulted signatures to Chaucer's in *The House of Fame*: both are "openly referential, and largely discrete, using the baptismal name alone in close proximity to 'pointing' remarks about the dreamer-author's distinc-

---

[25] Anne Middleton, "Narration and the Invention of Experience: Episodic Form in *Piers Plowman*," in Larry D. Benson and Siegfried Wenzel, eds., *The Wisdom of Poetry: Essays in Early English Literature in Honor of Morton W. Bloomfield* (Kalamazoo, Mich.: Western Michigan University, Medieval Institute Publications, 1982), pp. 91–122, 280–83. The charge of lack of unity in Langland's poem extends back to the late eighteenth century, as Vincent DiMarco has recently shown in his essay "Godwin on Langland," *YLS* 6 (1992): 125–35.

[26] Both essays are printed in Kane's *Chaucer and Langland: Historical and Textual Approaches* (Berkeley: University of California Press, 1989); the quoted passages are on pp. 144 and 146.

tive physical characteristics and social habits"[27]—i.e., long, lean, and lazy Will, and chubby, timid, "daswed" Geffrey. In another essay Middleton claims that Langland's signatures occur "at joinings of sections, as one venture yields to another," implying that the signatures mark those transitions and perhaps enable them poetically.[28] Chaucer's signatures in *The House of Fame* do the same thing.

The most famous example of a poet's "open" signature at a moment of transition is probably Dante's use of his own name "di necessità" in *Purgatorio* 30 as he stands across the river from the Earthly Paradise and exchanges one guide, Virgil, for another, Beatrice. Closer in space and time to our poets is the spectacle of Amans becoming John Gower, an old man unfit for Venus's court, at the end of the *Confessio amantis*. Langland and Chaucer are less dramatic overall than this. Signatures (at B.5.60–61, 8.70–74, and 8.117–31) occur as the poem moves from Conscience's sermon to the confession of the Sins and from the waking search for Dowel among the friars to the third vision's inner interrogation of Thought and Wit. These transitions are certainly not the most dramatic moments in the poem; at the same time, long familiarity makes it possible to underestimate their abruptness. Truth's affording of the pardon is greatly desired but hardly predictable, anticipated only by the final line of passus 6, which closes with an apocalyptic prophecy of Hunger's imminent return (new in B):

> Whan ye se þe mone amys and two monkes heddes,
> And a mayde haue þe maistrie, and multiplie by eiȝte,
> Thanne shal deeþ wiþdrawe and derþe be Iustice,
> And Dawe þe dykere deye for hunger
> But if god of his goodnesse graunte vs a trewe. (lines 327–31)

The movement from the Friars to Thought, about which I will have more to say below, is scarcely a natural one according to the canons of narrative or oneirology, however much it has been naturalized for us by repeated rereadings of the poem.

The most striking instance of this motif is the point at which what we call the B-continuation commences, the fall into the dream-within-

---

[27] Middleton, "William Langland's 'Kynde Name': Authorial Signature and Social Identity in Late Fourteenth-Century England," in Lee Patterson, ed., *Literary Practice and Social Change in Britain, 1380–1530* (Berkeley: University of California Press, 1990), p. 37.

[28] Middleton, "Narration," pp. 119–20.

a-dream and the Land of Longing, persuasively identified as a signature by Middleton.[29] This is most obviously a point where the poem is stalled and needs to get moving again. Traditionally it is taken as marking the transition from the A-version's final impasse to the first provisional steps of the B-continuation; even leaving aside the succession of versions, in B alone it is clear that the dreamer, reduced to tears by Scripture's scorn, has reached a dead end. To get the poem moving again, Langland makes two formal gestures that come so near to contradicting one another that they seem inextricably linked—linked by necessity and mutual implication. One is the inclusion of a signature passage that points in the complex ways Middleton describes to the truth-value and life-reference of his enterprise, and that governs the moment of transition, as in the other instances. The second gesture is paradoxically an indication of the explicit fictionality of his undertaking, a dream-within-a-dream, which further interrogates his initial exploration of the genre and undermines the conflicting, explanatory pieties of one dream with the self-revealing scrutiny of another in the mirror of Middle Earth.

Chaucer's narrator confronts similar impasses in *The House of Fame*. Towards the end of book 3, for example, Geffrey is accosted by an anonymous friend who questions him closely about his attendance at Fame's court. The questions cause Geffrey to adopt a self-revealing and self-reflexive stance, and to use twenty-nine first-person pronouns in thirty lines. Although Geffrey refuses to divulge his name—a strategic gesture employed to help distance himself from the spectacle of haphazard arbitration just witnessed before Fame's throne—the passage is nevertheless certainly a species of signature, because by the end of the encounter Geffrey's interlocutor very definitely knows *him*: "wel y see," says the friend (in a speech whose abrupt change from the interrogative to the declarative has always troubled critics), "What thou desirest for to here" (lines 1910–11). And the passage (lines 1868–1915) clearly governs an important transition for the poem (and, one could argue, for Chaucer's poetic), as the action subsequently moves from the palace of Fame to the House of Rumor.[30]

The more celebrated signature in *The House of Fame* is, of course, the one embedded in the eagle's speech at the beginning of book 2; "Geffrey" is

---

[29] Middleton, "'Kynde Name,'" pp. 44–52.

[30] The passage offers an interesting (inverse) parallel to Will's encounter with Thought at B.8.70ff.: there it is the narrator's companion who knows his name but the narrator himself who knows what he wants. Each passage, however, leads to the discovery of a new and relevant body of information.

named here in an extended review of his occupation, habits, disposition, and bodily form. Here as in the B-text a signature and a more conventional formal marker exist in close proximity. The former functions to smooth over and naturalize the flow of the episode, which begins with the narrator's panicked prayer at the end of book 1, by submerging into idle and mildly insulting chatter the abruptness with which the eagle, with the subtle agency of a "dynt of thonder," quite literally moves the poem forward and upward from the sterile desert to the eponymous House of Fame. Simultaneously, the formal marker represented by the end of book 1 and the beginning of book 2 (complete with invocation) calls attention to the explicitly fictive status of the experiences being portrayed. Real dreams do not divide themselves into books.[31]

Both Langland and Chaucer are drawn to the dream vision because of its promise as a mode for self-conscious fiction-making rather than for its potential for representing psychological realism, and consequently both poets are relatively uninterested in the interpretation of dreams. This may seem like a strange claim to make, given the one's lifelong devotion to the genre and the other's obsessive enumeration of the types and causes of dreams in the proem to *The House of Fame*. But it is a defensible claim nonetheless; each poet uses the dream not to suspend disbelief but, in A. C. Spearing's words, "to evade the whole question of authenticity, of belief and disbelief" altogether,[32] and to force from his readers an acknowledgment of the power of fiction, not dreams. The influence of the one upon the other for which I am arguing also helps to explain Chaucer's movement from the relatively conventional dream-theory of *The Book of the Duchess* to the intentionally frustrating proem of *The House of Fame*.

In the earlier poem the dreamer describes how he

> . . . mette so ynly swete a sweven
> So wonderful that never yit

[31] One might suggest, to press the case further, that Chaucer further anticipates the B-text here because his use of the eagle already represents a dream-within-a-dream. The eagle is drawn not just from *Purgatorio* 9 but from the pilgrim Dante's dream within that canto; according to Virgil, it is not the eagle that the sleeping Dante imagines but St. Lucy herself who lifts him from the vestibule to the gate of Purgatory. Thus the dream of the eagle is already marked as a fiction, an allegory, within Dante's poem, which means that in *The House of Fame* it is twice-removed from consciousness. Here if anywhere is what we normally see as Chaucer's advantage over Langland: his reading of other explicitly literary texts is assumed to be so much wider that he can do by creative borrowing what Langland must presumably do by invention—though Langland certainly may have inspired the gesture.

[32] A. C. Spearing, *Medieval Dream-Poetry* (Cambridge: Cambridge University Press, 1976), p. 75. See also J. A. Burrow, *Langland's Fictions* (Oxford: Clarendon Press, 1993), pp. 6–7.

> Y trowe no man had the wyt
> To konne wel my sweven rede;
> No, not Joseph, withoute drede,
> Of Egipte, he that redde so
> The kynges metynge Pharao,
> No more than koude the lest of us;
> Ne nat skarsly Macrobeus
> (He that wrot al th'avysyoun
> That he mette, kyng Scipioun,
> The noble man, the Affrikan—
> Suche marvayles fortuned than),
> I trowe, arede my dremes even. (*BD* 276–89)

The narrator's dream is more marvelous than the dreams of kings, and he suspects that it would stymie the efforts of Old Testament and classical interpreters alike. He does not suggest, we should note, that the dream is not susceptible to interpretation—only that the usual suspects would prove ineffective in elucidating it. Perhaps they are too suited to deciphering political allegories to be of any use in reading the more personal vision to follow, or perhaps the narrator's hyperbolic aggrandizement of his dream's complexity is simply a space-clearing gesture designed to carve out for his account a place in the canon of celebrated dream visions. Either way, the dream is not described as beyond interpretation, and in fact the narrator's exaggeration here serves only to sharpen the reader's hermeneutic sensibilities—which will turn out to be considerably more acute than the narrator's in this poem. The dream is presumed to be open to a reading that, by its correctness, will retroactively vindicate the authenticity and authority of the vision.

In *The House of Fame*, the idea of authorizing a dream by pointing to a correct interpretation is aggressively abandoned in the proem. In the guise of "skeptical fideism"[33]—"God turne us every drem to goode!" (line 1)—the narrator displaces the problem of interpretation onto a class of "grete clerkys" (line 53) who are implicitly distinguished from both the narrator ("But why the cause is, noght wot I" [line 52]) and his readers. This will turn out to have been an eminently logical way to open a poem dedicated to deconstructing authoritative texts from literary and philosophical tradition, and when Geffrey does lapse into a hyperbole reminiscent of *The Book of the Duchess*, as he does in the proem to book 2 ("Isaye, ne Scipion, / Ne

[33] The best exploration of this theme in the poem is of course Sheila Delany's *Chaucer's House of Fame: The Poetics of Skeptical Fideism* (Chicago: University of Chicago Press, 1972).

16

kyng Nabugodonosor, / Pharoo, Turnus, ne Elcanor, / Ne mette such a drem as this" [lines 514–17]), he is quickly rebuked by the eagle's comic counterpoint. "Thow demest of thyself amys," he says (line 596) when Geffrey mentions Enoch, Elijah, Romulus, and Ganymede; later, his thoughts of Boethius, Martianus Capella, and Alan de Lille are banished by the eagle's "Lat be . . . thy fantasye!" (line 992). Book 3, significantly, has no proem, simply an invocation of Apollo's aid in correctly describing the House of Fame.

Concern for the authentication and authorizing of the dream vision is thus displaced in the later poem. But it has not disappeared. Legible in the Invocation that follows the proem to book 1 is a new interest in what might broadly be called the performative rather than the interpretive status of dreams. The narrator calls upon "he that mover ys of al" to send joy and all good things to those readers that "take hit [the poem] wel and skorne hyt noght, / Ne hyt mysdemen in her thoght / Thorgh malicious entencion" (lines 81, 91–93). Alternately, those who "thorgh presumpcion, / Or hate, or skorn, or thorgh envye, / Dispit, or jape, or vilanye, / Mysdeme hyt" should experience "every harm that any man / Hath had syth the world began" and hang like Croesus (lines 94–97, 99–100). The effect of a dream is thus tied not to correct interpretation but to the moral state and intention of the reader. Dreams, that is, are to be taken as texts, as fictions, and their significance is not to be traced to the predispositions, obsessions, or digestion of the dreamer but to the ways in which readers are moved to respond and to act.

An intervening acquaintance with *Piers Plowman* would help to explain this change in orientation between *The Book of the Duchess* and *The House of Fame*. In Langland's poem, visions arise not out of the dreamer's disposition or diet, but existentially, simply out of going "wide in þis world" (B.Prol.4) aware of its wonders. And while the dream is a conventional "merueillous sweuene" (B.Prol.11), it is not described as "so marvelous that . . ." or "more marvelous than. . .". The dream is given no context beyond itself, and all efforts toward interpretation are internalized, a practice made manifest at the beginning of passus 1, where the still-dreaming narrator assures us that "What þe mountaigne bymeneþ, and þe merke dale, / And þe feld ful of folk I shal yow faire shewe" (B.1.1–2). Langland's great technical innovation in the dream vision form is his practice of simply dreaming and, when one dream is done, of simply following it with another one.[34] When the dreamer awakes at the end of the first vision, he

---

[34] Burrow, *Langland's Fictions*, p. 8, makes a similar observation.

is filled with woe, not because he lacks the key to understand aright his dream but because it has ended, because he "ne hadde slept sadder and yseiȝen moore" (5.4). This desire to dream again is almost immediately fulfilled, and the problem of the authority of the visionary experience—the conventional preoccupation of a waking dreamer—is implicitly diminished, made to bow before the importance of the stuff of the vision itself.

This is not to say that Langland is unconcerned with the problem of authorization for his text; indeed, it is in some ways his fundamental interest. His experimentation with genres; his use of academic, legal, and clerical models of disputation; and the very episodic and dialogic structure of the text all show him to be obsessively concerned with the practice of wielding authority. But it is a concern largely played out within the dreams themselves, and not in the terms of dream-theory but ultimately in terms of "making," or the creation of poetic fictions. As Middleton observes, "What is pursued in every encounter is not knowledge but power: the power to wield the text that 'makes' the world as a world."[35] What interests Langland is not the interpretation of dreams but their performative power as fictions, an issue that in his poetic is most fruitfully explored within the boundaries of the vision itself.

A brief look at the B-version's longest waking episode will help to confirm these claims. The passage runs from the end of the second vision at B.7.145 to the beginning of the third at B.8.70, a total of about 130 lines. At first the narrator moves into that kind of speculation about the significance of dreams that he has so far eschewed. The end of his second dream and the disagreement of Piers and the Priest over the terms of the Pardon have left him "pencif in herte" and doubtful about interpretation: "Ac I haue no sauour in songewarie for I se it ofte faille" (7.154). Should he follow the advice of Cato and the canonists, "*sompnia ne cures*"? Or should he look instead to the example of how both Daniel and Joseph successfully "diuinede þe dremes of a kyng" (7.158)? This conventional dilemma, here conventionally staged, is resolved rather unconventionally with a return to the moral matter and imperatives of the recently ended vision. Thinking of Piers, the Pardon, and the Priest's impugning of it, the narrator concludes that "Dowel at þe day of dome is digneliche vnderfongen; / He passeþ al þe pardon of Seint Petres cherche" (7.177–78). The victory achieved here by Langland's semi-Pelagian theology of works over the constraining gestures of documents representing ecclesiastical power is enabled by his refusal to

[35] Middleton, "Narration," p. 104.

get bogged down in questions about the interpretation of dreams; after raising that issue he quite startlingly (though quite consistently) discards it and moves at once to the question of the performative power of his fiction. For Langland at this point, a correct reading of *Piers Plowman* ought to issue not in our understanding but in our prayer "þat god gyue vs grace er we go hennes / Swiche werkes to werche, while we ben here, / Þat, after oure deeþ day, dowel reherce / At þe day of dome we dide as he hiʒte" (7.204–6). "God turne us every drem to goode," indeed.

In passus 8 Langland makes this point again through Will's waking encounter with the Friars. In this episode the whole process of interpretation in the interest of moral instruction—specifically here the allegorical exegesis of the Friar's "forbisene"—is shown to be a sterile one, productive of no "kynde knowyng." The literal tale of a man stumbling around on a rocking boat holds no interest in itself, and produces no meaning without the kind of conventional clerical explication that Will has previously rejected. He prefers to learn better "if I may lyue and loke" (9.49), and "living and looking" is Langlandian shorthand for "dreaming," as we learned in the Prologue. The third vision quickly ensues, in circumstances that explicitly recall the beginning of the poem. The place to learn is in dreams, and waking hours are better spent doing than interpreting; the latter is the pastime of "grete clerkys," in Chaucer's words.

In Chaucer's dream visions his narrator's waking moments are generally spent reading, which we might consider the literate equivalent of Langlandian living and looking. Each poet seeks to demonstrate the permeability of the boundary between "dreaming" and "not-dreaming," as indeed it is the premise of the poetic dream vision to elide the dream and the book. And with this observation we can see finally the difference between the two: for Langland, writing a masterpiece without ever having read one (in the memorable phrase of the teacher who introduced me to his poem), "not-dreaming" means the life; for Chaucer, scandalously fluent in multiple literary traditions, it means the library.

III

In "Langland and Chaucer II" Kane closes with a reference to both poets' final inconclusiveness. "An unfinished revision of *Piers*, and an incomplete *Canterbury Tales*," he claims, "symbolize the condition of English poetry in their time."[36] A similar observation could be made about the state of

[36] Kane, *Chaucer and Langland*, p. 149.

English poetry in 1380, judging by the evidence of the incomplete *House of Fame* and a version of *Piers Plowman* that, if not unfinished, is certainly unresolved. Each poet stages within the explicitly fictive allegorical dream vision his search for a stable ground on which to found a philosophically serious vernacular poetry; each poem is authentically exploratory; and each poet resigns in what looks like frustration.

It may be better, however, to avoid the formalist neoplatonism involved in measuring "incomplete" against "unfinished" and to turn instead to what might be called both poems' potential endlessness, and the infinitely generative possibilities of the dream vision form as understood by both Chaucer and Langland. Once again, the key to this potential is Langland's innovation of piling dream upon succeeding dream, sometimes to enable the further exploration of salient issues (as in the inner dreams of *Piers Plowman*) and sometimes to move from one allegorical register to another (and sometimes to do both). Once you've decided you can go back to sleep, abandoning the one conventional, formal constraint limiting the poetic dream vision (and substituting one kind of verisimilitude for another), you are theoretically "capable of going on forever," as Jill Mann observes about Langland.[37] Indeed, the last half-line of the poem—"til I gan awake"— scarcely differs from Langland's standard formula, "and I awakede þerwiþ," employed six times elsewhere.[38]

Chaucer does something similar in the three books of *The House of Fame*—each is sort of a different dream—but at this point in his career lacks either Langland's stamina or his singlemindedness. Realizing that his "man of gret auctorite" can say nothing authoritative or conclusive in the situation into which he has been introduced,[39] or figuring that, by making him a thing of seeming only, he has said enough for those who have ears to hear, Chaucer simply stops his poem, leaving his "man" the voiceless center of a place where voices murmur and whisper and shout endlessly. He refuses to explore any further the bind he has gotten himself into while searching for a mode sufficiently authoritative for the transmission of tidings *and* history, love *and* truth. The dream vision is evidently not it, and the ever-hopeful narrator is left in mid-sentence.

Neither poet ever really finds a way past this impasse, though each

[37] Mann, "The Power of the Alphabet," p. 46.

[38] The phrase appears (twice as "and þerwiþ I awakede") at B.11.406, 13.1, 14.335, 16.167, 17.355, and 19.481; "Thus I awaked" is used at 19.1. All of these instances are in the Vita portion of the poem.

[39] Donald Fry, "The Ending of the *House of Fame*," in R. H. Robbins, ed., *Chaucer at Albany* (New York: Burt Franklin, 1975), p. 38.

returns to the dream vision genre, Langland with apparent lifelong devotion and Chaucer with the spurious harmony of the roundel that concludes *The Parliament of Fowls*. There, where the clash of genres merges with a comic vision of class divisions—topics Chaucer would continue to explore together in *The Canterbury Tales*—the issue of desert and desire are left unresolved too, though the poem is forced to a conclusion by the *fiat* of an increasingly exasperated Nature.[40] To judge by the evidence of these two poets, achieving an appropriate sense of an ending for a long vernacular poem was a continuing problem. In Chaucer's case, we can point not only to the incomplete Canterbury project but to the convoluted conclusion of *Troilus and Criseyde*, where the narrator awakens from his dream of Trojan history to face the supervenient claims of his own Christian culture, and where the ultimate resolution arrives only after a half-dozen false starts, or rather, false conclusions.[41] And no one would dispute that even the most "complete" version of *Piers Plowman* ends with its most important issue, the earthly realization of spiritual renewal, essentially unresolved.

George Kane writes that the first result of studying Langland and Chaucer in conjunction as opposed to isolation "is likely to be an adjustment of attitudes."[42] The aim of this essay is to facilitate two such adjustments, two attitudes that are perhaps best expressed metaphorically. I borrow the figure of speech from Robert Hanning, who says this of the relations of the House of Rumor to the House of Fame:

Perhaps we can best think of the whirling house as Chaucer's version of the grimy kitchen beneath the fancy restaurant in George Orwell's *Down and Out in Paris and London*: a place where, hidden from public view, the dirty work is done that, once known, tarnishes the repute of the establishment it supplies. That is, Chaucer's expansion of the Ovidian model of Fame's dwelling place effectively imparts to Fame an extra measure of ill-fame.[43]

This image can be repositioned in two ways. First, imagine if you will Langland as Chaucer's kitchen, the kitchen where the dirty—read textual—work goes on all the time but seldom spoils the stylish presenta-

[40] For an argument that the roundel is spurious textually as well, see Ralph Hanna III, "Presenting Chaucer as Author," in Tim William Machan, ed., *Medieval Literature: Texts and Interpretation*, Medieval and Renaissance Texts and Studies, vol. 79 (Binghamton, N.Y.: Center for Medieval and Renaissance Studies, 1991), pp. 29–35.

[41] For an accounting, see E. T. Donaldson, "The Ending of Chaucer's *Troilus*," in *Speaking of Chaucer* (New York: Norton, 1970), pp. 84–101.

[42] Kane, *Chaucer and Langland*, p. 124.

[43] Hanning, "Chaucer's First Ovid," p. 149.

21

tion of the main course. Few of us get the chance to see Chaucer's verse, as Kane says, "in the raw,"[44] with the thorns and yoghs and orthographic and metrical irregularities that make *Piers Plowman* look so foreign—so medieval—to our students. Chaucer comes to us clean, "with the signs of his medievalism expunged so far as possible"[45]—not only expunged but also, I would argue, displaced onto other writers, Langland chief among them. And if the search for a theory of Langland's meter is finally beginning to receive adequate attention, the very way in which that statement is phrased calls attention to the lateness of the hour, which is itself related to the perceived prestige of the task.[46]

Acknowledging this fact has consequences not only for textual criticism but also for literary history, as Lee Patterson and Ralph Hanna have recently argued.[47] Thus, second, we should try to imagine the House of Rumor as the place where what's cooking is a species of poetic eloquence in Chaucer's own vernacular, of which *Piers Plowman* is the exemplar. Kane—who has spent more time in the kitchen with Langland than anyone since Skeat—has suggested that Chaucer would have found much in Langland's poem to remind him of Dante—poetic sublimity, seriousness, and an "uncompromising dedication" to its particular values.[48] The comparison between *Piers Plowman* and the *Divine Comedy* is not unusual; it is a theme that runs throughout T. P. Dunning's *Interpretation of the A Text*.[49] But in regard to *The House of Fame* and the argument of this essay, the comparison takes on special significance. Dante looms large in *The House of Fame*, particularly in the *ars poetica* reading of the poem that highlights Chaucer's negotiations with his varied poetic heritage. Ninety years ago, Kittredge felt able to assert that "the composition of the *House of Fame* was directly preceded by a time of reading and study, during which Chaucer, busy at the custom-house in the daytime, spent evening after evening over French, Latin, and Italian books."[50] However, if *The House of Fame* is to be seen not

[44] Kane, *Chaucer and Langland*, p. 136.

[45] Hanna, "Presenting Chaucer," p. 19.

[46] Recent work on this topic is surveyed by one of its chief architects, David Lawton, in "The Idea of Alliterative Poetry: Alliterative Meter and *Piers Plowman*," in Míćeál F. Vaughan, ed., *Suche Werkis to Werche: Essays on* Piers Plowman *In Honor of David C. Fowler* (East Lansing, Mich.: Colleagues Press, 1993), pp. 147–68.

[47] See Hanna, "Presenting Chaucer," pp. 19–20, and Patterson's essay on the Kane-Donaldson edition of *Piers Plowman* B in his *Negotiating the Past: The Historical Understanding of Medieval Literature* (Madison: University of Wisconsin Press, 1987), esp. pp. 108–9.

[48] Kane, *Chaucer and Langland*, p. 25.

[49] T. P. Dunning, Piers Plowman: *An Interpretation of the A Text*, 2d ed., rev. and ed. T. P. Dolan (Oxford: Clarendon Press, 1980). See also Howard Schless, "The Backgrounds of Allegory: Langland and Dante," *YLS* 5 (1991): 129–42.

[50] Kittredge, *The Date of Chaucer's* Troilus, p. 54.

only as Chaucer's preliminary attempt to mediate between authority and tradition on the one hand and the "preve by experience" on the other, but also as an attempt to reconcile or manage the multiple traditions that had become his literary inheritance, then the conventional description of that inheritance ought to be amended. It includes not only Virgil, Ovid, and other philosophical and scientific Latin texts, French dream visions and court poetry, and the newer Italian influences of Dante, Boccaccio, and Petrarch. It also includes a native English tradition represented by—and represented to him by—Langland. What was Geffrey reading, till "fully daswed" was his look? Why, *Piers Plowman.*

A Voice for the Prioress: The Context of English Devotional Prose

Richard H. Osberg
Santa Clara University

From the initial line of her invocation—"O Lord, oure Lord"—to the first line of the final stanza—"O yonge Hugh of Lyncoln"—the Prioress apostrophizes with incantatory zeal; fourteen instances of the trope are compressed into 237 lines, a density of rhetorical color unmatched elsewhere in *The Canterbury Tales*.[1] Apostrophe is only one of a number of tropes in the tale, but even without underscoring rhetorical strategies like *comparatio*, *sententia*, *determinatio*, or *circumlocutio*, almost everyone who comments on the tale notes its salient stylistic features: the frequency with which certain words are repeated, its rhyme royal stanza,[2] and the character

---

[1] The Prioress's fondness for apostrophe in her tale and the exquisite table manners of her portrait in *The General Prologue* may be opposite sides of the same coin. Geoffrey of Vinsauf remarks: "Take delight in apostrophe; without it the feast would be ample enough, with it the courses of an excellent cuisine are multiplied. The splendor of dishes arriving in rich profusion and the leisured delay at the table are festive signs"; in Alex Preminger, O. B. Hardison, and Kevin Kerrane, eds., *Classical and Medieval Literary Criticism: Translations and Interpretations* (New York: Ungar, 1974), p. 392. Apostrophe occurs elsewhere in *The Canterbury Tales*, of course, most notably in *The Man of Law's Tale*: see discussions of the trope in Joseph E. Grennen, "Chaucer's Man of Law and the Constancy of Justice," *JEGP* 84 (1985): 498–514, and Kevin J. Harty, "The Tale and Its Teller, the Case of Chaucer's Man of Law," *American Benedictine Review* 34 (1983): 361–71. All citations of *The Prioress's Tale* are from Larry D. Benson, gen. ed., *The Riverside Chaucer*, 3d ed. (Boston: Houghton Mifflin, 1987), unless otherwise noted.

[2] Rhyme royal in Chaucer's hands is always, as Charles Muscatine remarks, "an implement of seriousness"; *Chaucer and the French Tradition* (Berkeley: University of California Press, 1957), p. 192. G. H. Russell describes the rhyme royal stanzas in *The Prioress's Tale* as "statuesque, formal stanzas which recall an earlier, 'courtly,' phase of Chaucer's creative work," and he also characterizes the tale's vocabulary as "simple and undemonstrative"; "Chaucer: *The Prioress's Tale*," in D. A. Pearsall and R. A. Waldron, eds., *Medieval Literature and Civilization: Studies in Memory of G. N. Garmonsway* (London: Athlone, 1969), pp. 213, 216. Stephen Knight observes of rhyme royal in *The Prioress's Tale* that "it is by no means a highly worked stanza; rather it is the easy, varied rhyme royal stanza that . . . Chaucer seems to be able to produce without strain"; *Rymyng Craftily: Meaning in Chaucer's Poetry* (London: Angus and Robertson, 1973), p. 29. Carolyn Collette characterizes the style of *The Prioress's Tale* somewhat differently: "It is as if she [the Prioress] meant us to experience the

of its syntax.[3] Dorothy Guerin, for instance, argues that verbal repetition serves many purposes: to heighten emotions through liturgical and biblical associations; to elicit pathos through reiteration of the child's sweetness and littleness; to suggest a sincere and simple piety through a limited vocabulary; and to replicate "the boy's single-minded innocence."[4] C. David Benson, following Alan T. Gaylord, argues that repetition in the tale means that "childlike innocence . . . characterizes its artistry."[5]

Against the grain of critical estimation that reads the tale as the expression of a naive and untutored piety, I would like to explore the implications

---

religious significance of her tale through the same intense, emotional reaction she obviously has to the action of her own story. In this effect the rhyme royal stanza, intensely expressive in its inherent periodicity, works as part of the story, not just as form, but as form become content"; "Sense and Sensibility in *The Prioress's Tale*," *ChauR* 15 (1980): 138–50. Martin Stevens pushes the stylistic implications of the stanza further than anyone, suggesting it is "an implement of characterization" and a "vehicle to explore literary concepts": it reveals the Prioress as a person given to the external form of things; "The Royal Stanza in Early English Literature," *PMLA* 94 (1979): 62–76.

[3] See G. H. Roscow, *Syntax and Style in Chaucer's Poetry* (Cambridge: D. S. Brewer, 1981), pp. 34–35. Dorothy Guerin cites Margaret Schlauch, "Chaucer's Colloquial English: Its Structural Traits," *PMLA* 67 (1952): 1103–18, and notes "the anticipation with repetition of 'this litel child . . . / Ful murily . . . wolde he synge' and the parataxis of the two sentences"; "Chaucer's Pathos: Three Variations," *ChauR* 20 (1985): 90–112, and n. 17).

[4] Guerin, "Chaucer's Pathos," pp. 95–96. The liturgical aspects of the style have been analyzed by many critics, among them Marie P. Hamilton, "Echoes of Childermas in the Tale of the Prioress," *MLR* 34 (1939): 1–8, and Beverly Boyd, *Chaucer and the Liturgy* (Philadelphia: Dorrance, 1967), pp. 67–69. Derek Pearsall refers to "a semi-liturgical style full of echoes of the offices of the Church . . . unexaggerated in tone and loftily orthodox in its statement of her [Mary's] role in the Trinitarian scheme"; *The Canterbury Tales* (London: G. Allen and Unwin, 1985), p. 247. So too Alfred David: "More than any of the other of the tales the Prioress's has a liturgical flavor, not only in echoes of the liturgy but in the dialogue and description"; "An ABC to the Style of the Prioress," in M. Carruthers and E. Kirk, eds., *Acts of Interpretation: The Text in Its Contexts, 700–1600: Essays on Medieval and Renaissance Literature in Honor of E. Talbot Donaldson* (Norman, Okla.: Pilgrim Books, 1982), pp. 147–57. The connection between style and pathos is invoked by a number of critics. George Keiser, for instance, considers the poem composed in the pathetic mode; "The Middle English Planctus Mariae and the Rhetoric of Pathos," in T. Heffernan, ed., *The Popular Literature of Medieval England* (Knoxville: University of Tennessee Press, 1985), p. 167. Ralph W. V. Elliott points to the pathos achieved by "repeated use of evocative adjectives, some of them reiterated with powerful cumulative effect." Particularly, Elliott notes the Italianate doubling and post-positioning of adjectives ("his litel body swete," "the white Lamb celestial"); "Chaucer's Clerical Voices," in G. Kratzmann and J. Simpson, eds., *Medieval English Religious and Ethical Literature, Essays in Honour of G. H. Russell* (Cambridge: D. S. Brewer, 1986), pp. 146–55. Pearsall also discusses the repetition of "litel" as invoking "a sentimental pathos so piercing as almost to verge on mawkishness"; *The Canterbury Tales*, p. 248. C. David Benson sums up: "In the Prioress's Tale, all the resources of the poet's art are employed to evoke strong emotion in an audience"; *Chaucer's Drama of Style: Poetic Variety and Contrast in* The Canterbury Tales (Chapel Hill: University of North Carolina Press, 1986), p. 139.

[5] Benson, *Drama of Style*, p. 136.

of reading *The Prioress's Tale* as an appropriation of the stylistic mannerisms of devotional prose written for women religious. I will argue that Chaucer constructs a voice for the Prioress from a textuality that is feminized but not gendered female, a textuality whose stories of women and their spiritual lives are social constructions constituted by men.[6]

First, I will show that recurring in the surface of *The Prioress's Tale* are tropes of repetition familiar to readers of devotional prose, tropes that create an impression of a style spontaneously oral and naive. I will then argue that the stylistics of repetition point to larger patterns of recurrence, the similarity of certain elements signaling larger oppositions.[7] For instance, in the *Prologue*, praise of the divine is "parfourned . . . by the mouth of children . . . on the brest soukynge" (*PrP* 456–58). In the tale, however, the allusion to St. Nicholas, who "so yong to Crist dide reverence" (*PrT* 515), echoes ironically, subverting the earlier assertion; for the infant Nicholas honored Christ by fasting, refusing his mother's breast on Wednesdays and Fridays.[8] Rhetorical oppositions—particularly in the representations of time and space and in the association between revulsion toward the body (cesspits, torture), anti-Judaism, and the theme of virginity—present serious distortions in the narrative voice. *The Prioress's Tale* represents itself in a series of oppositions, social and spiritual, natural and supernatural, in which mutilation and magical transformation, dung and salvation, scatology and eschatology are the polarities of a self-cancelling fiction. These oppositions suggest that the chief rhetorical strategy by which the verse

---

[6] See Elizabeth Robertson, *Early English Devotional Prose and the Female Audience* (Knoxville: University of Tennessee Press, 1990), p. 43. The present essay is deeply indebted to Robertson's work.

[7] Robert O. Payne suggests that "the whole stylistic texture is permeated with a coloration of opposed but not at all equally balanced sentiments. Chaucer uses a limiting adjective with a substantive about seventy times in the tale; principle groupings of repeated or very similar adjectives are as follows: the group 'litel, smale, yonge' provides seventeen of the adjectival constructions, about one-fourth of the total; the opposed group, 'grete, chief, large,' gives five; similarly a large but semantically tightly knit group 'tendre, sweet, blissful, free, sely, innocent, meek, kinde, pitous, deere, cleere, merciable' is used for sixteen constructions (nearly another quarter of the total) as against ten uses from the group 'cursed, foul, harmful, yvel, sinful, unstable'"; *The Key of Remembrance* (New Haven, Conn.: Yale University Press, 1963), p. 169. Payne's major point here is that the narrative is less important than style to the final effect: "In the Prioress's tale, the story is in effect frozen into a kind of basic situation and the major effort is in the theoretical elaboration of its emotional implications"; p. 166. See Louise O. Fradenburg, "Criticism, Anti-Semitism, and the Prioress's Tale," *Exemplaria* 1 (1989): 85–88. Denise L. Despres has suggested that such polarities are inherent in the eschatological vision permeating post-Lateran (1215) theology; see her article, "Cultic Anti-Judaism and Chaucer's Litel Clergeon," *MP* 91 (1994): 413.

[8] This episode is reproduced in a fine, twelfth-century carved ivory crosier-head now at the Victoria and Albert Museum.

27

identifies its provenance as a feminine "voice" also functions as the language by which it subverts itself and its claims to authenticity, laying bare the absence of a voice, an absence that, ironically, the rhetoric of apostrophe attempts to obscure.

A number of critics have suggested other formal literary parallels for the Prioress's style. Peggy Knapp, for instance, sees the Prioress as "awkwardly constituted by two discourses, that of feminine aristocratic nicety and that of religious vocation."[9] Hope Weissman and Dorothy Guerin look to the tradition of *sermo humilis* for stylistic affinities with the Prioress's tale.[10] Verbal repetition has been connected with affective piety,[11] and recently Elizabeth Robertson has linked affective piety particularly with the construction of a feminine voice in *The Prioress's Tale*.[12] As Alfred David suggests, religious language may be by its very nature repetitious, and he construes the Prioress's voice as a response to another literary tradition, Chaucer's *An ABC*: "Its repetitiousness may make it tedious to the modern reader, but that is, of course, what makes it a prayer. Repetition is the fundamental structural principle in prayer, and so it is in *An ABC*; the poem never goes anywhere because prayer never goes anywhere. The ulti-

---

[9] Peggy Knapp, *Chaucer and the Social Contest* (New York: Routledge, 1990), p. 49.

[10] Guerin, "Chaucer's Pathos," p. 91 n. 3.

[11] Payne's analysis of the tale's affective elements is seminal: "The Prioress's Tale is the summation of an effort, running through five of the twenty-three tales, to write a purely affective narrative in which irony, characterization, and complexity of action all give way to a very rigidly controlled stylistic artifice"; *The Key of Remembrance*, pp. 162–69. Payne identifies such rhetorical devices as apostrophe or exclamation, *determinatio*, *circumlocutio*, and *epithetum*. Other critics have followed Payne's lead. Benson, for instance, calls the tale "a lyrical exercise in affective piety" and notes that the literary presentations of affective piety "generally ignore narrative and intellectual complexity in favor of extreme expressions of love, praise, and gratitude prompted especially by the spectacle of unmerited suffering"; *Drama of Style*, pp. 131, 140. David notes that "such an art of affective piety seeks to arouse a corresponding emotion in its audience, to move the audience to tears of sympathy and repentance. Weeping thus manifests an appropriate religious and aesthetic sensibility"; "An ABC," p. 153. Leonard Koff, quoting David, argues that "the Prioress's Tale is historically an example of 'sentimentalized' religion that 'worships beauty as a version of truth,' characteristic of the 'new and fashionable religiosity' of Chaucer's day that 'combines gentility with emotion, decorousness with enthusiasm' and anticipates the aureate style of the fifteenth century"; *Chaucer and the Art of Storytelling* (Berkeley: University of California Press, 1988), p. 216. Arguing especially against such analyses of style and lay piety and responding to the repetition of "litel," Ruth Ames remarks that "if all that remained of medieval Christianity were *The Prioress's Tale*, we would deduce a 'little' religion, suitable for tribal children and their maiden aunts"; *God's Plenty: Chaucer's Christian Humanism* (Chicago: Loyola University Press, 1984), p. 200.

[12] Elizabeth Robertson, "Aspects of Female Piety in the *Prioress's Tale*," in C. David Benson and Elizabeth Robertson, eds., *Chaucer's Religious Tales* (Cambridge: D. S. Brewer, 1990), pp. 145–60.

mate effect is no different from that of a series of Hail Marys except that the poem seeks to express its worship in a richly decorated style."[13]

What the pairing of *The Prioress's Tale* with the religious texts of the Katherine Group, the Wooing Group, and the late-fourteenth-century compilation of earlier devotional materials, *A Talkyng of þe Loue of God*, will illuminate, I hope, is that the Prioress's style, although it has elicited frequent comment in passing, has not been treated in the way that Robert Jordan invites us to examine the text: "We shall find the primary evidence of Chaucer's views, of his poetics, not in the mouths or the heads of characters reified by interpretive criticism but in the verbal figures and formal structures of Chaucerian texts."[14] Such reification is an interpretive fate, I would add parenthetically, that the character of the Prioress seems particularly to have attracted.[15] The Prioress is, as far as I am aware, the only pilgrim for whom an early childhood has been invented,[16] and for whom a fine education, a dower-pinching father, and an aborted love child have been postulated.[17] In the context of the English devotional prose tradition, however, the details constructing the impersonated voice in the Prioress's tale may seem less than striking as evidence for a diseased psyche. In seconding Maurice Cohen's assertion that the Prioress's fastidiousness and kindness are reaction-formations, "attempts to mask the Prioress's interest in sex, which she associates with dirt and punishment,"[18] Judith Ferster, for instance, notes that "the mention of the whiteness of the lamb, emphasizing cleanness and purity, is the Prioress's addition to her Scriptural source."[19] The association of sexuality with filth, and purity with clean-

[13] David, "An ABC," p. 150. Noting that all of Chaucer's religious tales have women at their centers, Robertson suggests "that to Chaucer women and Christian spirituality occupy the same marginal space" and suggests that religious language, taken altogether, is linked with the female and the feminized; "Aspects of Female Piety," p. 146.

[14] Robert Jordan, *Chaucer's Poetics and the Modern Reader* (Berkeley: University of California Press, 1987), pp. 18–19.

[15] For recent psychoanalytic criticism, see, for instance, Fradenburg, "Criticism," p. 52, who posits "the formal intricacy of phobic language [that] expresses the desire for dissolution"; Judith Ferster, "'Your Praise is Performed by Men and Children': Language and Gender in the Prioress's Prologue and Tale," *Exemplaria* 2 (1990): 149–68, who argues that "penis envy" here becomes "envy of privilege in the world of religious discourse" (p. 154); and Thomas Hahn, "The Performance of Gender in the Prioress," *Chaucer Yearbook* 1 (1994): 113–34, who suggests that "for the Prioress, the masquerade [of gender] consists in a studied (if not labored) performance of the most conventional male-devised roles for women" (p. 121).

[16] See Maurice Cohen, "Chaucer's Prioress and Her Tale: A Study of Anal Character and Anti-Semitism," *Psychoanalytic Quarterly* 31 (1962): 232–49.

[17] See Wolfgang E. H. Rudat, *Earnest Exuberance in Chaucer's Poetics: Textual Games in the Canterbury Tales* (Lewiston, N.Y.: Edwin Mellen Press, 1993), p. 86ff.

[18] Ferster, "Language and Gender," p. 151.

[19] Ibid., p. 166 n. 34.

ness, however, is a standard trope of the clerical tradition and reveals much more about the misogyny of male-scripted texts for women than it does about the Prioress's tale as the record of an imagined psychosis. Likewise, Edward Condren and Wolfgang Rudat both find, for different reasons, the image of suckling infants invoked in the *Prologue* "gratuitous";[20] Thomas Ross finds it " 'obscene' in some special sense."[21] In addition to the allusion from Psalms, the image of suckling, it should be noted—indeed, of Christ's wound as the teat—is one of the more striking tropes of the devotional prose, also surfacing in *A Talkyng of þe Loue of God*:

Heo ȝeueþ him hire pappe ꞏ and stilleþ his teres. Þat pappe beo my lykyng.my mournyng.my longyng. swete Ihesu heuene kyng ꞏ to souken of my fulle.þat þorw þe speres openyng.in feole mennes gounyng.wiþ dewing of þi deore blood.stilleþ alle bales.And wher eny mon wene þat he schal.haue part of þat ilke sok.of þi deore herte.in heuene riche blisse.[22]

Impersonating the female voice in such texts, male clerical writers brought to bear what they thought women's experience was. Constructing the feminine from a differentiation of male and female rooted in Aristotelian categories, as Robertson has shown, these authors thought women were "suited by nature to two kinds of experience: an identification with Christ's suffering and an expression of that experience through tears."[23]

The figure of the "litle clergeon," the Prioress's humility *topos*, and especially the syntax of the Prioress's tale have suggested to a number of critics a naive, colloquial, and oral style; G. H. Roscow, for instance, takes the separation of sentence elements as distinctive of idiomatic speech, noting that aspects of idiomatic expression include "the use of personal pronouns and demonstrative adjectives in noun phrases referring to people (*PrT* 688). The construction enables the speaker to identify himself or his listener(s) as belonging to a particular group, but it tends also to have an emotive force that registers his attitude towards the group."[24] So too the

---

[20] Edward I. Condren, "The Prioress: A Legend of Spirit, a Life of Flesh," *ChauR* 23 (1989): 192–218, and Rudat, *Earnest Exuberance*, p. 87.

[21] Thomas W. Ross, *Chaucer's Bawdy* (New York: Dutton, 1972), p. 48.

[22] M. Salvina Westra, ed., *A Talkyng of þe Loue of God* (The Hague: Martinus Nijhoff, 1950): 6/19–24.

[23] Robertson, *English Devotional Prose*, pp. 8–9.

[24] Roscow, *Syntax and Style*, pp. 61–62. Discussing lines 555–56, in which "a verb taking an object of complement may come between the genitive phrase and its noun," Roscow observes that "Chaucer appears to use this construction on some occasions to create an impression of difficulty." Comparing this line to a similar construction in *The General*

possible anacoluthon in *PrT* 567–68 represents another example of disjunctive speech.[25] Diverging from Guerin's assertion that "the narrator's first-person comments in the Prioress's Tale are . . . sparse, consisting of an occasional 'as I have seyd,' 'I seye,' or a brief pious wish,"[26] Benson makes much of the presence of the narrator's voice and contrasts a suspicion of direct speech with the power of song.[27] In fact, "seye" is the most frequently repeated word in the poem, underscoring the performative character of the tale. Benson develops particularly the association of orality and childishness: "This concentrated use of an aspect of oral style (doublets) does not produce the dignified effect of repetition in the *Knight's Tale* because the noble vocabulary of the romance is missing, but instead these doublets well represent the slow, modest, and childish style of the *Prioress's Tale*"[28]—an analysis furthered by Robertson: "Adopting Mary's humility as her own, the Prioress is able to overcome her own sense of inferiority and find her own voice. The tale both embodies and investigates the nature of the power of that voice, for the Prioress describes herself as speaking like a child in her Prologue and then tells a tale that is an explicit analysis of the nature and effects of childish voices."[29]

The reading of the Prioress's voice as childish, naive, and untutored is a response, I will argue, to particular stylistic features and rhetorical strategies indebted to a tradition of devotional prose still current in Chaucer's day[30] and perhaps most clearly seen in *A Talkyng of þe Loue of God*, which

---

Prologue, Roscow continues, "The length of separation is about the same in both sentences (*GP* 343; *PrT* 555) and in both there is the characteristic enjambment; yet the second seems more disjunctive. This is possibly because a descriptive genitive, as in the first example, may have the force of an appositive construction and therefore seem less radically separated from its antecedent than does the possessive genitive in the second."

[25] As edited by Beverly Boyd; *The Prioress's Tale, A Variorum Edition of the Works of Geoffrey Chaucer*, vol. 2, *The Canterbury Tales*, pt. 20 (Norman: University of Oklahoma Press, 1987).

[26] Guerin, "Chaucer's Pathos," p. 92.

[27] Benson, *Drama of Style*, p. 137.

[28] Ibid., p. 40.

[29] Robertson, "Aspects of Female Piety," p. 151.

[30] A good deal of evidence for the influence of the *Ancrene Riwle* on later prose has been adduced: see Hope Emily Allen, "On some 14th Century Borrowings from the *Ancrene Riwle*," *MLR* 19 (1924): 95, and "Further Borrowings from the *Ancrene Riwle*," *MLR* 24 (1929): 1–15; S. J. Crawford, "The Influence of the *Ancrene Riwle* in the Late Fourteenth Century," *MLR* 25 (1930): 191–92; A. C. Paues, "A Fourteenth Century Version of the *Ancrene Riwle*," *Englische Studien* 30 (1902): 344–46; and J. R. R. Tolkien, "*Ancrene Wisse* and *Hali Meiðhad*," *Essays and Studies* 14 (1929): 104–26. Particularly germane to this argument is Margery M. Morgan's "*A Talking of the Love of God* and the Continuity of Stylistic Tradition in Middle English Prose Meditations," *RES*, n.s., 3 (1952): 97–116; and Elizabeth Zeeman, "Continuity in Middle English Devotional Prose," *JEGP* 55 (1956):

survives in the Vernon[31] and (in part) the Simeon manuscripts, a prose written initially for women religious, although later adapted to a generalized audience.[32] A peculiar feature of the "affective" style of some English devotional prose is its embrace of the colloquial, suggesting both syntactically and lexically an oral style, a speaking voice.[33] The *Ancrene Riwle*, for instance, employs rhetorical figures like *polysendeton*, by means of which "thoughts are so ordered as to create an impression of spontaneous

417–22. Evidence for the continuity of this tradition well into the fifteenth century has also recently become available. English translators of Brigittine tracts in the fifteenth century, for instance, often amplify, develop, or correct such stylistic features as *epanalepsis*, *epistrophe*, and *anadiplosis* from their Latin models; Domenico Pezzini, "Brigittine Tracts of Spiritual Guidance in Fifteenth-Century England: A Study in Translation," in Roger Ellis, ed., *The Medieval Translator 2* (London: Centre for Medieval Studies, Queen Mary and Westfield College, University of London, 1991), pp. 175–207.

[31] The Vernon MS begins, "Here byginnen þe titles of þe book þat is cald in latyn tonge salus animae and in englisch tonge sowlehele." The manuscript contains saints' lives, organized by the liturgical calendar, and a large number of Miracles of Our Lady. See Mary S. Serjeantson, "The Index of the Vernon Manuscript," *MLR* 32 (1937): 222–61. *A Talkyng* is found toward the end of the manuscript where its "purpose evidently was to prepare the meditating soul for affective prayer, or to make it attune its feelings to those suggested by the text" (Westra, ed., *A Talkyng*, p. xxviii). There is some evidence of female ownership of the Vernon manuscript: both N. F. Blake, "The Vernon Manuscript: Contents and Organisation," pp. 45–59, and Carol M. Meale, "The Miracles of Our Lady: Context and Interpretation," pp. 133–35, in Derek Pearsall, ed., *Studies in the Vernon Manuscript* (Cambridge: D. S. Brewer, 1990) offer arguments for a female readership of the Vernon MS. See Susan Groag Bell, "Medieval Women Book Owners: Arbiters of Lay Piety and Ambassadors of Culture," in Mary Carpenter Erler and Maryanne Kowaleski, eds., *Women and Power in the Middle Ages* (Athens, Ga.: University of Georgia Press, 1988); originally printed in *Signs* 7 (1982): 168. For the evidence of wills and book inscriptions for women's book ownership in late medieval England, particularly books in the vernacular with religious subject matter, see Carol M. Meale: "' . . . alle the bokes that I haue of latyn, englisch, and frensch': laywomen and their books in late medieval England"; in Carol M. Meale, ed., *Women and Literature in Britain, 1150–1500* (Cambridge: Cambridge University Press, 1993), pp. 128–58. Meale notes that Bell's emphasis on mother-daughter relationships is misleading.

[32] As early as 1911, it had been pointed out that the first part of *A Talkyng* (2/21–10/14) is a loose and somewhat amplified version of *On wel swuðe god ureisun of God Almihti*; the third part (26/14–62/24) is mostly indebted to *þe Wohunge of ure lauerd* for its main theme. Like its predecessors, *A Talkyng* is ultimately indebted to St. Anselm's *Prologue* to the *Liber Meditationum et Orationum*, whose importance to the affective tradition Robertson has demonstrated; *English Devotional Prose*, p. 184. Eugen Einenkel asserts that *On Ureisun* and *þe Wohunge* and similar pieces were written both for and by women. Though attributing the authorship of such texts to men, William Vollhardt agrees with Einenkel that they seem to have been specially meant for nuns; in Westra, ed., *A Talkyng*, p. xxx. See Anne Eggebroten, "*Sawles Warde*: A Retelling of *De Anima* for a Female Audience," *Mediaevalia* 10 (1984): 27–47. As Westra observes, however, "the fact that in the 'Sowlehele MS.' *A Talkyng* is put together with the works of Walter Hilton, Richard Rolle and the *Ancrene Riwle* (which immediately follows it), seems to prove that it ranked with the most popular devotional works of the 14th century"; *A Talkyng*, p. xxxi.

[33] See, for instance, Cecily Clark, "'With Scharpe Sneateres': Some Aspects of Colloquialism in *Ancrene Wisse*," *NM* 79 (1978): 341–53.

utterance in artless succession."[34] So too the figure of *paregmenon* "suggests to the modern mind a naivete which is lost in translation."[35] For an earlier generation of scholars, "naive" is, in fact, the word invoked most often to describe the style of the *Ancrene Riwle* generally. J. W. H. Atkins, for instance, writes, "Above all it is naive"; Bernhard Ten Brink observes, "*Naive and spontaneous* as it seems [italics mine] we are charmed by this language which already contains so much of art"; and James Morton states, "The *Ancrene Riwle* is written in a plain, unambitious style, and with scarcely any attempt at rhetorical ornament . . . the style is simple and free from decoration."[36] Even the rubric—"Heer is.a Tretys. A *Talkyng* of þe Loue of God" [italics mine]—suggests that text's oral character.

That *The Prioress's Tale* and devotional prose like the *Ancrene Riwle* should share a perceived oral style and a characteristic naivete is not altogether surprising. In the clerical writings of the late Middle Ages, the association between oral style and the female voice is frequently sounded: "The stress on feminine persuasive power, however, remained constant: from the time of Ermengard to the time of Thomas of Chobham male clerical writers persistently emphasized the ability of women to use spoken language—sweet words and eloquence—to soften men's hearts."[37] The power of women's voices to affect others is noted in *A Talkyng*: "As Moder doþ hire deore sone.þat hereþ hit wepen.Takeþ hit in hire Armes. and askeþ him so sweteliche.Ho leof.Ho lef heo doþ him.hire bi twenen.Ho wole be bi clupped.and cusse me swete.who haþ do my deore.who haþ do þe so."[38] In effect, Chaucer has given the Prioress a voice that some clerical English authors adopted when addressing a female audience largely untrained in the Latin tradition and particularly when impersonating the lyrical prayers and devotions of such an audience.[39] The voice thought

[34] See Sister Agnes Margaret Humbert, *Verbal Repetition in the* Ancrene Riwle (Washington: Catholic University of America Press, 1944), p. 85.

[35] Ibid., p. 89.

[36] Quoted in ibid., pp. xv–xvii.

[37] Sharon Farmer, "Persuasive Voices: Clerical Images of Medieval Wives," *Speculum* 61 (1986): 517–43.

[38] Westra, ed., *A Talkyng*, 6/15–19.

[39] I do not mean to imply that all religious prose in Middle English is written in a single voice or style or to suggest that English devotional works were composed exclusively for Latin *illitterati*; I am concerned here mainly with those texts Norman F. Blake has categorized under "Affective Works" as those designed "to emphasize the emotional affinity for Christ or Mary felt by the listener" and those written "to assist the listener's devotions"; "Varieties of Middle English Religious Prose," in Beryl Rowland, ed., *Chaucer and Middle English Studies in Honour of Rossell Hope Robbins* (Kent, Ohio: Kent State University Press, 1974), pp. 348–56. Although the affective writings of Richard Rolle could well be included in this study, I rely mostly on the *Ancrene Riwle* and related texts, the so-called "Katherine

appropriate for addressing religious women—rhythmical and alliterative, highly descriptive and concrete, creating strong affective responses—becomes the voice in which the Prioress answers back.

Symptomatic of its rhetorical naivete, repetition—phonemic, lexical, phrasal, syntactical—characterizes that voice. A number of critics have remarked on the tale's alliteration[40]—a form of phonemic iteration, as in the opening three stanzas where repeated *l*, *p*, *s*, and *b* suggest a number of extra-syntactical connections. The hallmark of devotional prose, however, is lexical repetition, an attribute, of course, of the rhyme royal stanza in general—it comes as no surprise that the first thirty-four stanzas of *Troilus and Criseyde* repeat twenty-two times in various morphological variants the word "love." Words repeated more than ten times in thirty-four stanzas, however, are rare (*MLT*, "man" 10 times, "Custance" 11 times; *ClT*, "markys" and "wed" 12 times, "Lord" 14 times; *Tr*, "Troy" 13 times). *The Second Nun's Tale* and *The Prioress's Tale* run counter to this pattern; both taper off at words repeated between five and ten times, following the pattern of other rhyme royal stanza poems. However, words repeated between eleven and twenty times are surprisingly numerous (*SNT*, "Valerian" 11 times, "Cecile" and "say" 13 times, "right" 15 times, and "man" 18 times). *The Prioress's Tale* uses repetition even more dramatically: "song" 11 times; "litle," "Crist," and "Jew" 12 times; "Child," "O," and "sing" 14 times; "moder" 15 times; and "sey" 17 times.

Furthermore, morphological iteration is seconded in *The Prioress's Tale* by other patterns of reduplication: apposition (also *anadiplosis*), simple reduplication (also *epanodos*), morphemic iteration (*paregmenon*—"swete swotnesse"—and also *polysyndeton*), larger patterns of reduplication (over three lines, within or between stanzas), and expressions of reduplication such as "eek" and "also."

Group" and "Wooing Group" and the fourteenth-century *A Talkyng of þe Loue of God*—texts that "clearly draw upon each other to a considerable extent"; see Margery M. Morgan, "*A Talking of the Love of God* and the Continuity of Stylistic Tradition in Middle English Prose Meditations," *RES* 3 (1952): 97–116.

[40] See Sumner Ferris, "A Hissing Stanza in Chaucer's 'Prioress's Tale,'" *NM* 80 (1979): 164–68. So too the devotional prose, particularly *A Talkyng*: Westra notes that "the treatise appears to have a very strong rhythmical character. The cases of alliteration are far more numerous in the parts based on *On Ureisun* and *þe Wohunge* than in those for which no original has been found" (Westra, ed., p. xxii). However, whereas the twelfth-century treatises show alliteration only, *A Talkyng* has a good deal of rhyme as well, which Westra lists (see p. xxiii). Bella Millett, "The Saints' Lives of the Katherine Group and the Alliterative Tradition," *JEGP* 87 (1988): 16–34, quotes the late twelfth-century writer Giraldus Cambrensis on the popularity of alliteration among contemporary English writers because of "its power to please the ear and insensibly arouse the emotions of the hearers"; p. 34.

Rather than labor this point, I have listed below those stylistic devices in *The Prioress's Tale* that I find occurring frequently as well in *A Talkyng* and elsewhere in earlier, related devotional prose. It is less the discovery of parallel figures than it is the accumulation in a relatively short poem of so many stylistic features shared with the Katherine Group and later, associated devotional works that occasions in *The Prioress's Tale* the echo of this affective, devotional tradition.

Patterns of Repetition in *The Prioress's Tale* and Devotional Prose

I. Apposition (*epanados*, also *anadiplosis*)

PrT

O Lord, oure Lord (line 453)
O mooder Mayde, O mayde Mooder free! (line 467)

DP

Ihesu ⁊ swete Ihesu (*Talkyng* 2/23)
A Þou Blisful moder.þat art vr oune Moder (*Talkyng* 24/14)
and leuen þe my lemmon.my derlyng my dere. ⁊ A ⁊ my deore lemmon.
   (*Talkyng* 40/13–14)
anadiplosis: swinkeð | to biȝeotene, biȝeoteð forte leosen, leoseð forte sorhin
   (*HM* 14/35–15/1)[41]

II. Simple reduplication (also *antistrophe*,[42] *epanodos*)

PrT

Nat that I may encressen hir honour, / For she hirself is honour and the roote
   (lines 464–65)
That lerned in that scole yeer by yere (line 498)

---

[41] See Dennis Rygiel, "A Holistic Approach to the Style of *Ancrene Wisse*," *ChauR* 16 (1982): 270–81. The texts cited are as follows: *AW*: J. R. R. Tolkien, ed., *The English Text of the Ancrene Riwle: Ancrene Wisse, Edited from MS. Corpus Christi College Cambridge 402*, Early English Text Society [hereafter EETS], o.s., vol. 249 (London: Oxford University Press, 1962); *HM*: Bella Millett, ed., *Hali Meiðhad*, EETS, o.s., vol. 284 (London: Oxford University Press, 1982); *Lofsong*: "On lofsong of ure louerde," in W. Meredith Thompson, ed., *þe Wohunge of Ure Lauerd*, EETS, o.s., vol. 241 (London: Oxford University Press, 1958), pp. 10–15; *Ureisun*: "þis is on wel swuðe god ureisun of God almihti," in Thompson, ed., *þe Wohunge*, pp. 5–9.

[42] Antistrophe ranks third in order of frequency among figures of verbal repetition in the devotional prose; Humbert, *Verbal Repetition*, p. 22.

That day by day to scole was his wone (line 504)
This litel child, his litel book lernynge (line 516)
And as he dorste, he drough hym ner and ner (line 520)
Wherfore I synge, and synge moot certeyn (line 663)

DP

Þou þat ӡiuest hire liht.and al þat liht haueþ.Lihte my þester herte. (*Talkyng* 4/11–12)
& þou my leof so pore.as þi self weore pore. (*Talkyng* 42/31–32)
Meiden . ӡ moder . Meiden . hwas . moder (*Ureisun* 9/138–39)
antimetabole: as brude ne nimeð gumè′ ne brudgume brude (*HM* 6/14); cleane ouer alle þing, ant ouer alle þinge luueð cleannesse (*HM* 5/30–31)
epanalepsis: schaweð in ham his ahne troden þ me trudde him in ham. ifinden hu he wes totreden as his trode schaweð. (*AW* 194/9–11)

III. Morphemic reduplication (also *paregmenon, polyptoton*)

PrT

O bussh unbrent, brennynge in Moyses sighte (line 468)
Thurgh thyn humblesse, the Goost that in th'alighte, / Of whos vertu, whan he thyn herte lighte (lines 470–71)
As smale children doon in hire childhede (line 501)
Up taken was, syngynge his song alway (line 622)
That of his mercy God so merciable / On us his grete mercy multiplie (lines 688–89)

DP

Ihesu my saueour.þat me schalt sauen (*Talkyng* 4/4–5)
ӡit art þou so louelich.Louelich and louesum. (*Talkyng* 4/7–8)
Allas Allas nou fynde I me grisloker in my gultes.þen þe grislihed of him.þat helle gryseþ offe. (*Talkyng* 14/5–6)
ӡ þi dereowurðe dead from þene deað ðet neuer ne deieð . þ ði dead adeadie þe deaðliche lustes of mine licame. (*Lofsong* 11–12/59–61)

IV. Reduplicating doublets (also *polysyndeton*)

PrT

Wherfore in laude, as I best kan or may (line 460)
But as a child of twelf month oold, or lesse (line 484)

For foule usure and lucre of vileynye (line 491)
Ful murily than wolde he synge and crie (line 553)

DP

Ihesu my weole.& al my wynne. (*Talkyng* 4/6)
Ac I. was.war þer bi.and bi moni oþere.Bi warnyng.and wissyng (*Talkyng*
   12/24–25)
he was so feir and so briht an Angel (*Talkyng* 12/27)
Summe freodam & largesse.þat leuere is menskeliche to ȝiuen þen
   quedliche.to wiþ holden. ❡ summe wit.and wisdam ᛫ and hap of þe world.
   ❡ Summe miht and strengþe. to ben kud kene in fiht.his riht to defenden.
   ❡ Summe nobleye.& hendelek ᛫ and gentrise of kuynde. ❡ Summe gret
   cortesye ᛫ and loþles leetes. ❡ Summe mylde. and Mekenesse. & deboner
   herte ᛫ wiþ swete louereden.and godliche dedes. (*Talkyng* 26/25–31).
to wite me.and were me.in gostliche weorre (*Talkyng* 38/24)
Þer weore þou.for my loue.wiþ harde knotti scourges.swongen and beten.so
   smart and so sore ᛫ so þat þi louely leor. þat was so briht and so cleer.was
   al to fouled.and I.schent.þi skin to riuen and to rent. (*Talkyng* 48/9–12)
Iesu teke þ tu art se softe . ⁊ se swote . ȝettet to swa leoflic . swo leoflic and
   swa lufsum . (*Ureisun* 1/6–8)

V. Expressions of reduplication ("eek," "also")

PrT

And eek also, where as he saugh th'ymage (line 505)
Hire to salue, and eek hire for to preye (line 533)

DP

Ihesu al so.þat þou art. so feir and so swete. (*Talkyng* 4/7)
And also þat þou for me.ȝaf so þy seluen (*Talkyng* 32/15)
Also þei seiden.þe envyous Iewes (*Talkyng* 44/30)
in bodi & in soule ᛫ and eke in deite. (*Talkyng* 62/16)

VI. Larger patterns of reduplication (over three lines, within or between stanzas)

PrT

Amonges Cristene folk a Jewerye . . . / Hateful to Crist and to his
    compaignye . . . / A litel scole of Cristen folk ther stood . . . / Children an
    heep, ycomen of Cristen blood (lines 489–97)
His felawe taughte hym homward prively . . . / To scoleward and homward
    whan he wente (lines 544–49)
This abbot, which that was an hooly man / As monkes been . . . / This hooly
    monk, this abbot (lines 642–70)

DP

A.swete lord Ihesu.whi wiþ armes of loue.ne cluppe I.þe so faste ꞉ þat no
    þing from þi loue.departe myn herte ꞉ ❡ Whi ne cusse I.þe lord.
    sweteliche in soule ꞉ wiþ a lykinge cos.of a swete menyng.& hertliche
    þonkyng.of þi gode dedes ꞉ // whi nas me vnworþ vche worldliche
    þing.aȝeyn þe muchele delyt.of þi swetnesse ꞉ ❡ whi ne fele I.þe lord.in
    my brest roote. ❡.whi art þou me so fremde. þow þat art so swete. ❡ whi
    ne con I. loue þe.and loueueliche wouwe þe.wiþ sweete loue wordes.and
    lykynge þouȝtes.Aller þing swettest. (*Talkyng* 8/3–12) {7 "sweets" in 100
    words}
And make me lyuen in þe liuinde lord.þat I.be to þe world ded.and a lyue to
    þe.so þat I.mai verreyliche.sigge wiþ þe apostle.Paulus. *viuo ego.iam non
    ego.viuit autem in me Christus*.I.liue not Ich.but crist lyueþ in me.þat is
    poules wordes.And þus for to siggen. In liue not in lyue þat I.liuede ꞉ but
    crist liueþ in me þorw wonyinde grace.þat from deþ of sunne.me torneþ
    and quikneþ to lyf þat is blisful.of gostliche hele.From alle worldliche
    loue.& fleschliche lustes.al one forto lyuen.in likyng of crist. (*Talkyng*
    10/7–15) {11 "lives" in 87 words}
repetitio: A folc tolaimet ⁊ totoren. A folc he seið fearlich. schal makien to ure
    lauerd present of him seoluen. Folc tolaimet. ⁊ totoren wið strong liflade ⁊
    wið heard ꞉ he cleopeð folc fearlac. (*AW* 185/21–24)

In short, in creating a feminized, religious voice, Chaucer develops a narrative style in the manner of this devotional prose tradition, whose salient
rhetorical characteristics remain fairly constant from the twelfth through

the fourteenth century. Not simply a response to "late affective piety,"[43] nor a reflection of a childish, naive, or untutored rhetoric,[44] the voice of *The Prioress's Tale* echoes a long-standing, widely distributed high-style tradition composed for women religious in English.

The stylistics of repetition point to larger patterns of iteration and reduplication: figures of repetition, seeming to advance the narrative by adding words but simultaneously seeming to force the narrative to circle back over and over the same words, suggest both motion and cessation, opening and enclosure. In the tale's phenomenology of time and space,[45] markers of time contrast narrative linearity with lyric stasis; representations of space juxtapose confinement—grammatical "structures of sequestration"[46]—with freedom—openness, liminality, transmutation. Embedded in the smallest linguistic units of the narrative, these oppositions of space and time are consistent with tensions in the devotional prose, written for religious women to articulate, marking the feminization of the speaking voice and simultaneously underscoring its fictive character.

The paradox of space for the religious woman is summed up by Rob-

---

[43] Collette argues that "concern with emotion, tenderness, and the diminutive are part of the late fourteenth-century shift in sensibility, which, following the so-called triumph of nominalism, produced the flowering of English mysticism, a highly particularized, emotional style in the arts, and the ascendancy of the heart over reason in religious matters"; "Sense and Sensibility," 138.

[44] One might take the Prioress's disclaimer that she speaks "But as a child of twelf month oold, or lesse, / That kan unnethes any word expresse" (lines 484–85) to be nothing more than the "modesty topos," an echo of *Sapientia* 9.5: "Quoniam servus tuus sum ego, et filius ancillae tuae; Homo infirmus, et exigui temporis, Et minor ad intellectum iudicii et legum." Julian of Norwich too has frequent recourse to the modesty topos: in chapter 2, "a simple creature that cowde no letter" (p. 39, line 41); chapter 7, "to shew me that am so simple" (p. 47, line 263); and chapter 9, "I cannot ne may not shew it as hopinly ne as fully as I wolde" (p. 50, lines 342–43); The Shewings *of Julian of Norwich*, ed. Georgia Ronan Crampton (Kalamazoo, Mich.: Western Michigan University, Medieval Institute Publications, 1993).

[45] This idea is related to what E. D. Blodgett has elsewhere characterized as "Chaucerian Pryvette and the Opposition to Time," *Speculum* 51 (1976): 477–93.

[46] See Barrie Ruth Straus, "The Subversive Discourse of the Wife of Bath: Phallocentric Discourse and the Imprisonment of Criticism," *ELH* 55 (1988): 527–54. The polarities of sequestration and liminality may in fact signal an anxiety about representing gender in *PrT*, if we see gender "as a theory of borders that enables us to talk about the historical construction and maintenance of sexual boundaries, both intra- and intercorporeal, through powerful historical processes of repetition and containment"; Kathleen Biddick, "Genders, Bodies, Borders: Technologies of the Visible," in Nancy F. Partner, ed., *Studying Medieval Women: Sex, Gender, Feminism* (Cambridge, Mass.: The Medieval Academy of America, 1993), pp. 87–116. For a study of the way in which a clerical male text written for a female audience establishes physical, spiritual, and theological limits, and so "overtly and covertly encloses the female reader within those boundaries, and restricts and regulates her spirituality," see AnneMarie Fox, "The Boundaries of Sainthood: The Enclosed Female Body as Doctrine in *Seinte Margarete*," *Medieval Perspectives* 8 (1993): 133–42.

ertson: "The English religious woman who in particular wished to replicate the spiritual quest of the desert fathers in the wilderness could do this only in a small and enclosed place, in the anchorhold."[47] Julian of Norwich also provides the terms of this paradox: "Our good Lord shewid Him in dyvers manners, both in Hevyn, and erth; but I saw Him take no place but in mannys soule. . . . And in other manner He shewid Him in erth, wher I sey I saw God in a poynte. And in other manner He shewid Him in erth, thus as it were in pilegrimage."[48] Pilgrimage, then, the journey out from center, is paradoxically a continual drawing in; or, as Linda Georgianna reminds us in her study of the *Ancrene Wisse*, the anchoress focuses insistently on the boundary between inner and outer experience.[49] The polarities of these two movements provide one set of oppositions in *The Prioress's Tale*.

The movement toward interiority is announced in the series of concentric circles beginning with "in this large world" (*PrT* 454). The narrative then narrows its perspective, moving rapidly from "in Asye" to "in a greet citee" (line 488), limiting its horizon further to "amonges Cristene folk a Jewerye" (line 489), narrowing again to a street, and finally restricting itself to "a litel scole of Cristen folk. . . . Doun at the ferther ende, in which ther were / Children an heep" (lines 495–97). Prepositions indicating interiority, inwardness, or restrictions of space account for twenty-five of the prepositional phrases in the tale.[50] Typical of this discourse of enclosure is the stanza recounting the widow's wanderings. "With moodres pitee *in* hir brest *enclosed*," yet "*out* of hir mynde" (lines 593–94; italics mine), the widow ranges as if "to every place" (line 595); yet the search throughout the city is recounted, paradoxically, in a stanza almost entirely composed of prepositional phrases of enclosure: "in thilke place" (line 601), "in that place" (line 605), "in hir thoght inwith a litel space" (line 604), "in

[47] Robertson, *English Devotional Prose*, p. 13.

[48] *Shewings*, chap. 81, p. 150, lines 3290–94.

[49] Linda Georgianna, *The Solitary Self: Individuality in the* Ancrene Wisse (Cambridge: Harvard University Press, 1981), p. 54. There was a good deal of ambivalence in the Middle Ages regarding clerical pilgrimage, particularly that of nuns; St. Bernard suggests that the true pilgrimage for a religious person is to be made through the feelings (*affectus*) rather than by foot, pilgrimage having as its goal the heavenly city rather than the earthly Jerusalem. See Giles Constable, "Opposition to Pilgrimage in the Middle Ages," *Studia Gratiana* 19 (1976): 123–46.

[50] A good number of these restrictions of space, introduced by "in" or "within," may also be seen as oppositions: "in this large world" (line 454) against "in an aleye, at a privee place" (Boyd, line 568); "in Jues herte" (line 559) against "in hir [the mother's] brest enclosed" (line 593); and "in a pit bisyde" (line 606) against "in a tombe of marbul stones" (line 681), for instance.

a pit" (line 606). The lines of an external space necessary for narrative development are continually being shifted, redrawn, withdrawn, and subverted by the rhetorical insistence on interiority.

In opposition to this pattern of sequestration is a group of eighteen prepositional phrases and modifiers suggestive of exteriority, free passage, and transformation: the street of the ghetto, "free and open at eyther ende" (line 494), where the child "cam to and fro" (line 552). In this constellation of phrases one discovers a set of parameters that are constantly violated— "out of hir mynde" (line 594), "mordre wol out" (line 576), "blood out crieth" (line 578), "out of this world to chace" (line 566), a world in which things hidden and secret are revealed, in which confines are destroyed and limits are transcended, culminating in the eternal procession of the 144,000 virgin martyrs.

The way in which repetition underlines a central confusion about space is illustrated in the first translation of the "clergeon" from singing in the privy to singing in that procession (lines 579–85; italics mine):

A	O martir, *sowded to virginitee*,
B B¹	Now maystow *syngen, folwynge evere in oon*
C	The *white Lamb celestial*—quod she—
	Of which the grete evaungelist, Seint John,
B¹	In Pathmos wroot, which seith that *they that goon*
CB	*Biforn* this *Lamb* and *synge* a song al newe,
A	That *nevere, flesshly, wommen they ne knewe.*

If stanzas may be conceived as a space through which one moves, then a number of stanzas in *The Prioress's Tale* create an enclosed space, ending where they begin. This stanza, for instance, folds back upon itself in recursive symmetry.[51] The first and last lines state the principal idea of virginity (A); the second line and last half of the sixth line describe the procession (B¹) singing (B); the third and first half of the sixth lines phrase the lamb motif (C); and the two middle lines overdetermine the evangelist, St. John. Such recursion underlines a spatial confusion. In the first three lines, the virgin martyrs follow "evere in oon / The white Lamb." In the restatement, they go "Biforn this Lamb and synge." This vagueness about the spatial relationships of the virgin procession and the Lamb, about who is following

[51] Fradenburg observes of lines 495–501, "The language of the Prioress's tale differs, folds, alters just enough to show us that we have not really gone anywhere and nothing has really happened to us"; "Criticism," p. 95.

41

whom, is underscored by the tension between "quod she" and "Seint John, / In Pathmos wroot," an anxiety about oral and written discourse, fluidity and fixedness.[52]

Larger patterns of repetition also point to contradictions that subvert the authority of the voice. The narrative passes easily from the child's confinement "in a wardrobe" (line 572) in one stanza to his mobility, "folwynge evere in oon" (line 580), in the next; from enclosure in the ultimate symbol of the alienated world[53] to the liturgical and ritual procession of the virgin martyrs. This antithesis, to which I will return, does not provide closure (even though it represents the "end" of the narrative in eschatological terms, emphasizing the ways in which ordinary sequential patterns are disrupted or unsettled through the intercession of the divine); three stanzas later the narrative returns the boy to the "pit" and, in this second redaction of the opposition between society's waste products and chastity, replaces the fleeting eschatological vision with "this gemme of chastite" (line 609), ruby and emerald—a transmutation to be sure, but one whose materiality may remind us more of the reliquary than the relic. Finally, the fleeting vision of the virgin martyrs is supplanted at the end of the tale by the martyr's tomb in which his body remains,[54] not otherworldly in the end, as in "out of this world to chace" (line 566) but rather an image of enclosure "in a tombe of marbul stones cleere" (line 681), the sequestration of the body rather than a triumph of the spirit. That is, against muck and mutilation, the agents of decay and degeneration, the poem offers images of a material world that fail to transcend earthly mutability, and the contingent image of the heavenly procession, associated with liminality and transformation, is replaced at the end of the poem by an image of enclosure.

---

[52] As Farmer observes, "The association of feminine weakness and seduction with the power of persuasion sometimes suggests an inherent distrust of spoken language." Even though spoken language was an implement of evangelization, "medieval authors often asserted that by itself speech could not bring about conversion, the desired effect of evangelism"; "Persuasive Voices," p. 540.

[53] See Gerhart B. Ladner, "*Homo Viator*: Mediaeval Ideas on Alienation and Order," *Speculum* 42 (1967): 233–59.

[54] Robertson's analysis of devotional prose argues that male writers conceived of women's spirituality as experienced through physicality, in the flesh. The oppositions I am suggesting here run counter to Condren's analysis of a movement from a condition of corporality to one of spirituality: Condren argues that the "religious life culminates in formal orders and a virginal apotheosis; femininity leads to physical consummation and motherhood. . . . Whereas God originated the process from his eternal state in spirit to become flesh in Christ, the Prioress begins in the flesh. She must diminish, deny, rarefy out of existence, the flesh in which she originated to become the pure spirit to which she aspires"; "The Prioress," pp. 43, 192–93.

It is, of course, the Virgin's intercession that allows dead matter—subject to the corruption, filth, and decay of flesh—to sing hymns of praise. The condition of the little clergeon—enclosed in a privy, dead to the world, but singing nevertheless in praise of Mary—might be thought to bear some resemblance to that of an anchoress. Even the ceremony by which the abbot undertakes to "conjure" the clergeon resembles the mass for the dead used to immure anchoresses:

Female anchorholds most often consisted of a room or rooms attached to a church. Usually the women were boarded up or bricked into these rooms and the mass for the dead was said over their door. Warren describes the following, probably typical, twelfth-century pontifical service for enclosure: "The barefoot postulant lies prostrate in the church (in the west end if female, at the entrance to the choir if male, and in mid-choir if a cleric). Two clerks recite the litany while the bishop (or his appointed delegate) and his entourage bless the candidate with holy water and incense. The postulant then receives two lighted tapers. One is given to him by a priest, the other by someone he himself has chosen. The tapers and their bestowers represent the love of God and of one's neighbor. There is a scriptural reading. Then, while the sponsors of the postulant lead him to the foot of the altar, the clergy chant the *Veni creator*. Kneeling at the altar the postulant recites the verse *Suscipe me Domine* three times and then places his tapers in a candelabra on the altar. Following an explication of the scriptural text by a priest, the congregation is invited to pray for the individual who is about to become enclosed, the *recludendus*. A mass of the Holy Spirit is then celebrated. If the postulant is himself a priest, he may be the celebrant. After the mass the recluse is conducted to his *reclusorium* while the entourage chants antiphons and psalms drawn from the Office of the Dead, the *reclusorium* is sanctified with holy water and incense. The officiant then proceeds with the Office of extreme unction followed by prayers for the dying. Now the recluse enters the house; the officiant sprinkles him with a little dust to the continued singing of the antiphons and psalms; all then withdraw save the priest, who remains with the recluse to tell him to rise and to live by obedience . . . two final prayers are said and all then depart in peace." In one enclosure ceremony, the anchoress is carried into the anchorhold in a coffin while the mass for the dead is sung for her.[55]

Such male-scripted rituals of sequestration emphasize the parallels between renunciation of the world and death, both enclosing and silencing the

---

[55] Robertson, *English Devotional Prose*, pp. 26–27. The citation is from Ann K. Warren, *Anchorites and Their Patrons in Medieval England* (Berkeley: University of California Press, 1985), pp. 97–98.

anchoress as the abbot silences and entombs the little clergeon. The Prioress's tale exists in the space created between procession and sequestration.

That spatial opposition—concentric circles of confinement contrasted with figures of passage—is paralleled in the poem's chronology by the opposition between narrative stasis (*always*, *ay*) and narrative development (*and after that*), so that patterns of repetition underscore an opposition between time described as typological (recurrent moments of vision associated with the sempiternal) on the one hand and the sequential and serial time of narrative causality on the other.[56]

Temporal confusion is perhaps only to be expected in a poem in which the Virgin is apostrophized "er men praye to thee, / Thou goost biforn" (lines 477–78), and medieval narratives are rarely concerned with strict chronology in any case.[57] From the very start of the poem, however, eschatological, sacramental, and historical time are presented as simultaneous; in the *Prologue*, Mary is sequentially a figure of time past, the burning bush; time present, the mother of Christ; and time future, Queen of Heaven; while Christ is Lord, Son, and Sapience, a sequence that suggests both the stasis of sacramental time and the linearity of historical time. Nonetheless, duration in *The Prioress's Tale* is singularly perplexing; what might strike an anxious auditor as a present promise, "My litel child, *now* wol I fecche thee" (line 667) turns out to be future conditional, "Whan that the greyn is fro thy tonge ytake" (line 668). Likewise the exclamatory "*Now* maystow syngen, folwynge evere in oon / The white Lamb celestial" (lines 580–81) as a statement of the clergeon's present condition seems radically undercut by the assertion that in "a tombe of marbul stones cleere. . . . Ther he is *now*" (lines 681–83) [all italics mine]. On the one hand the reported martyrdom of Hugh of Lincoln, an episode already 200 years past by the fictional date of the pilgrimage to Canterbury, is nonethe-

---

[56] A characteristic of devotional prose seems to be inattention to direct causation and sequentiality. Westra, for instance, observes of *A Talkyng*, "Whereas all that precedes presents no structural difficulties, here both thought and construction are often not quite clear. The same ideas are repeated over and over again in rambling sentences devoid of originality"; pp. xxi–xxii. In addition, the structure of Julian's work, as Barry Windeatt has demonstrated so persuasively, "violates expectations of linear narrative, being repetitious, contradictory, and fundamentally experiential"; Robertson, *English Devotional Prose*, p. 195. Perhaps temporal confusion is native to all hagiography.

[57] See Clifford Davidson, "Space and Time in Medieval Drama: Meditations on Orientation in the Early Theater," in Clifford Davidson, ed., *Word, Picture, Spectacle* (Kalamazoo, Mich.: Western Michigan University, Medieval Institute Publications, 1984), pp. 39–93. Alfred David notes some elements of the pervasive typology: "this newe Rachel" (line 627) and the "villainous Jews' typological status as 'cursed folk of Herodes al newe'" (line 574); "An ABC," p. 156.

less reported as "but a litel while ago" (line 686). Conversely, the child reports that without the miraculous "greyn" upon his tongue, he would "have dyed, ye, longe tyme agon" (line 651). Confusion regarding duration is symptomatic of the linguistic tension in the tale between markers of time that deny temporal sequentiality and those that insist on it.

One set of adverbial patterns resists time, flux, change, and exposure by positing recurrence. Expressions like "day by day," "Fro day to day," and "yeer by yeer" establish that nothing changes; the insistent typology sounded in "this newe Rachel" (line 627) to describe the grieving mother, or in the "cursed folk of Herodes al newe" (line 574) to describe the Jews, intimates that whatever seems new is really just the same old thing over and over. Associated with recurrence are expressions of time that posit stasis, particularly the adverbs "ay" (in such phrases as "ay, whan I remembre" [line 513], "To worshipe ay" [line 511], "And herkned ay" [line 521]), "alwey" (in phrases like "wol alwey soone lere" [Boyd, line 512], "is a mayde alway" [line 462], "I loved alwey" [line 657]), and "evere" (as in "stant evere in my presence" [line 514]). The cumulative effect of such adverbs is a scale of time stretched out to the sempiternal.

Against this pedal bass of "always," "ever," and "ay" sounds the counterpoint of narrative sequentiality, insisting on both process and speed: "and after that" is repeated five times, varied with "and at the laste," and "Fro thennesforth." The impression of narrative impetus and ineluctability is reinforced by expressions suggesting how time flies: "anon withouten tariyng" (line 617), "And hastily" (line 616), "and that anon" (line 630), and "sped . . . ful faste" (line 638), at least two of which are themselves reduplicative.

Further confusion with regard to time and duration may be seen in the confusion of tense in a passage like the description of the mass (lines 635–38; italics mine):

> Upon this beere *ay* lith this innocent
> Biforn the chief auter, *whil the masse laste*;
> *And after that*, the abbot with his covent
> *Han sped* hem for to burien hym *ful faste*. . . .

Here "lith" is present (a use of the historic present that links it with classical Latin),[58] "han sped" is past, and the adverb "ay" (forever, always) is

[58] I am indebted to the anonymous reader for *Studies in the Age of Chaucer* for this observation.

45

undercut by the adverbial clause "whil the masse laste." Even syntactical incompleteness in an anacoluthon like "An homycide therto han they hired, / That in an aleye, at a privee place"[59] can be seen as the refusal, on the level of sentence structure, to create movement through time.

Repetition in a stanza's final line of words from the first line frequently creates an impression of stasis or anti-narrative circularity in the poem.[60] The stanza detailing the Provost's punishment of the Jews illustrates the opposition between a serial narrative of causality[61] and a rhetorical circularity that runs counter to narration (lines 628–34; italics mine):

A   With *torment* (1) and with shameful *deeth* (2) echon
    This provost dooth thise Jewes for to sterve
    That of this mordre wiste, [*and that anon*].
B   He *nolde no* swich cursednesse observe.
    "Yvele shal have that yvele wol deserve";
A¹ *Therfore* with wilde hors he dide hem *drawe*, (1)
    [*And after that*] he *heng* (2) hem by the lawe.

Collette argues that "the description of the Jews' punishment creates the impression of reason, deliberateness, and inevitability. 'He nolde,' 'therefore,' 'and after that' are the three phrases which encapsulate the sequential nature of the summary justice they receive."[62] In tension with these assertions of sequentiality, however, is a series of reduplications radiating out from the tautological repetition of "yvele" in the stanza's central line to

[59] See Boyd, *The Prioress's Tale*, p. 143, n. to lines 1757–58. G. H. Roscow, in *Syntax and Style in Chaucer's Poetry*, lists the following: "The swetnesse hath in his herte perced so / Of Cristes mooder" (line 555); he observes, "A verb taking an object or complement may come between the genitive phrase and its noun. . . . Chaucer appears to use this construction on some occasions to create an impression of difficulty"; p. 35.

[60] Guerin observes that verbal repetition occurs as a form of stanza linking, clusters of words that sketch the development of the plot: stanzas 2–5 are linked by "scole" and "litel"; stanzas 6–11 by "song"; stanzas 16–20 by "pitee" and "pitous"; and stanzas 22–27 by "hooly"; "Chaucer's Pathos," p. 95.

[61] Davidson observes that "direct causation can exist only in a world which has been successfully subjected to desacralization and in which a separate secular order has been established"; "Space and Time," p. 60.

[62] Collette, "Sense and Sensibility," p. 147. In discussing the Conversion of St. Paul, Davidson remarks of Saul that he "is obsessively concerned with the ordering of actions in time in order to comply with the minutest aspects of Jewish law"; "Space and Time," p. 56. The Jews and the Provost may be thought to act entirely within the sphere of civil authority and the temporal; the apocalyptic imagery of the transfigured martyr is beyond their comprehension. Dismemberment by wild horses was a punishment accorded traitors; following the loss of Guînes in January 1352, for instance, King John of France had Sir William Beauconray, deputy commander of the garrison, torn to pieces by wild horses. See *The Poems of Laurence Minot*, ed. Richard H. Osberg (Kalamazoo, Mich.: Western Michigan University, Medieval Institute Publications, 1996), p. 112.

underscore the perfectly circular structure of the stanza, which ends exactly where it began by specifying the torment and shameful death. Such circularity runs directly counter to the markers of sequentiality, and the irony of a language of linear sequence that returns to where it started is reinforced by the confusion of time ("and that anon" / "and after that") in which present and past are conflated.

Words associated with place and time, that is, with location (*out*, *in*) and narrative progression (*therefore*, *then*, *now*, *next*, *after*), point toward oppositions of freedom and enclosure, and to a confusion of time and duration, suggesting the subversion of a consistent fictive voice. Such stylistic oppositions at the linguistic level, embedded in but not contained by the narrative, mirror conceptual oppositions—unconverted Jews and transfigured martyrs, bodily wastes and virgin purity, physical dismemberment and gemlike entombment—by which the tale is structured into irreconcilable polarities. This set of conceptual oppositions, particularly the alliance between revulsion toward the body and the scatology of English anti-Judaism, has certain resonances within the devotional prose tradition. Ready at hand in the medieval period was a conventional belief in the desecrating and desacralizing consequences of contact with excrement ("shryned in an hogges toord" [*PardT*, line 955], for instance). References to dung as proximate cause of desecration derive most probably from the numerous biblical uses of the image, as in Lamentations 4:5: "Qui nutriebantur in croceis, Amplexati sunt stercora" ("they who were brought up [dressed] in purple have embraced dung"); [63] or in what may stand as the ur-desecration of a false god in 2 Kings 10:27: "et comminuerunt eam. Destruxerunt quoque aedem Baal, et fecerunt pro ea latrinas usque in diem hanc" ("Thei distroyeden the hous of Baal, and thei maaden for it wardropis" [Wyclif, 1382; "priuyes," 1388]). A comparable desecration in a Christian context is related by Ranulph Higden, who describes how the Emperor Julian the Apostate and his steward deliberately defiled a church in Antioch by defecating and urinating on the sacred vessels and cloths of the altar:

Also at Anthiochia he gadred togiders þe holy vessel and towaylls of þe auter, and defouled hem wiþ þe filþe of his ers. . . . Also his steward pissed uppon the vessel of þe chirche, and seide, 'Loo in what vessel Mary sone is i-served. . . .'[64]

[63] R. P. Alberto Colunga and Laurentio Turrado, eds. *Biblia Sacra*, Nova editio. (Madrid: Biblioteca de autores cristianos, 1946). Translation from Alexander Jones, ed. *The Jerusalem Bible* (Garden City, N.J.: Doubleday, 1966).

[64] *Polychronicon Ranulphi Higden Monachi Cestrensis*, ed. Joseph R. Lumby, Rolls Series, no. 41, vol. 5 (London: Longman, 1874), pp. 170–71.

As Velz observes, "Dunghill language and dunghill behavior in medieval religious literature are potentially marks of alienation from God both in their implication of a finite corporeality and in their connotation of the rejected, the no longer valued, the insalubrious."[65] Langmuir notes the "medieval association of Jews with privies," by which the cesspit motif, a seemingly obligatory gesture in Miracles of Our Lady, enters even the earliest historical accounts of the English "ritual murder libels," the Anglo-Norman ballad of William of Lincoln.[66] Although not as frequent as in the miracles of the Virgin, anti-Judaism is certainly a staple theme in the devotional prose, e.g., in A Talkyng: "schendful spittyng.of vn worþi men heþene houndes. . . . Also þei seiden.þe envyous Iewes ꝰ he is worse þen a þef."[67] In The Prioress's Tale, the Jews' moral pollution is imaged as human dirt and excrement, and their resistance to the felt truth of the anthem is symbolized by the mutilation of the throat that produces it. The wardrobe is an image of both an obdurate corporeality that resists transformation and an obdurate spirituality that resists conversion (the effect of the anthem on the uncomprehending boy is contrasted with its effect on the learned and law-conscious Jews). At the heart of the Prioress's tale is an image—the irredeemable and intractable nature of the human body as waste product, mutilated, encased in ordure.

In discussing the Lives of St. Katherine, St. Margaret, and St. Juliana, Robertson remarks that the "lives' almost obsessive interest in physical torture" is coupled with "the obsession of male religious writers with female sexual sin. Their portrayal of torture is excessive if not sexually perverse."[68] Likewise in The Prioress's Tale, the fate of the Jews, dismemberment, is analogous to the scatology of human waste—corruption, formlessness, and dissolution. In tension with this imagery of disintegration, the tale presents images of gemstones and a marble tomb in which, respectively, the clergeon's virginity and his body are preserved.

The juxtaposition of the privy and the procession of the 144,000 virgin martyrs, particularly the introduction of the theme of virginity in this

---

[65] John W. Velz, "Scatology and Moral Meaning in Two English Renaissance Plays," South Central Review 6 (1984): 4–21.

[66] Gavin Langmuir, Toward a Definition of AntiSemitism (Berkeley: University of California Press, 1990), p. 247. Typical is the Assumption of Our Lady, in Joseph R. Lumby, ed., King Horn with Fragments of Floriz and Blauncheflur, and of The Assumption of Our Lady, EETS, o.s., vol. 14 (London: Trübner, 1866), in which the Jews attempt to desecrate Mary's body: "That bodi þat þei bere nyme we it / And cast we it in a foule pit, / Or brenne we it & do it somme where / Or cast we it in a foule sere" (p. 94, lines 701–7). Note the reduplication of "foule pit" and "foule sere."

[67] Westra, ed., A Talkyng, 44/24–30.

[68] Robertson, English Devotional Prose, pp. 96–97.

stanza, has puzzled a number of critics,[69] but it reveals most radically, I believe, the construction of the feminized "voice" of the Prioress and, simultaneously, the subversion of that fictional voice. Linda Georgianna initiates her study of the *Ancrene Wisse* with a citation from Abbess Herrad of Hohenberg: "Despise the world, despise nothing; Despise yourself, despise despising yourself; These are four good things."[70] The oppositions commended here are particularly germane to the English tradition in which the physical body, described in scabrous and scatological language, gives rise to revulsion. In the late medieval period, associations between excrement and licentious sexual behavior were commonplace. Writing about scatological manuscript drolleries, Karl Wentersdorf, for instance, reports, "Sometimes the depiction of defecation or exposure of the buttocks symbolizes sin or the intention of sinning—again a usage that is hardly surprising in view of the fact that medieval preachers and moral theologians often referred to excrement or to the evacuation of faeces as an image for mortal sin."[71] Two grotesqueries Wentersdorf discusses speak directly to issues of excrement and sexual license. Cambridge, Trinity College, MS B.11.22, fol. 73 depicts a courtly young gentleman defecating into a bowl, and a servant carrying a bowl of faeces to an elegant courtly lady, who herself holds a third bowl. One thinks of the owl's indictment of the nightingale—the bird who sings of courtly love builds her nest by the privy—or the more oblique fate of Damien's *billet-doux* in *The Merchant's Tale*. Even more telling is a drollery from Oxford, Bodleian Library, MS Bodley 264, fol. 56, presenting a man bent over and defecating in front of a nun, who holds up her hands as if to ward off the sight. Defecation, dung, and the cloaca had a long tradition of association with sex and sin in the medieval period,[72] an association that Odo of Cluny, echoing John Chrysostom, elaborates:

[69] Condren, for instance, sees this relationship in sequential rather than oppositional terms; "The Prioress," p. 208.

[70] Georgianna, *Solitary Self*, p. xi.

[71] Karl P. Wentersdorf, "The Symbolic Significance of *Figurae Scatologicae* in Gothic Manuscripts," in Clifford Davidson, ed., *Word, Picture, and Spectacle* (Kalamazoo, Mich.: Western Michigan University, Medieval Institute Publications, 1984), pp. 1–19, esp. p. 7.

[72] Wentersdorf notes: "In a long series of religious works, from the *Ancrene Riwle* to *The Pilgrimage of the Soul*, there are many denunciations of sinners who 'wer falle and ley defouled in the dong of synne'; and since it is human frailty that leads to mortal sin, the author of *The Vision of Philibert* (c. 1475) could apostrophize the 'wrecheyd fleche' of mankind with the outcry 'O thou stynkynge donge!' In the morality play of *Mankind*, the protagonist Mankynde likewise laments his soul's association with his flesh, 'þat stynkyng dungehyll.' A similar attitude is revealed by Chaucer's Parson, who uses the image of 'ordure' several times to characterize 'thilke stynkynge synne of Lecherie.' And the image survived into the late Renaissance: in a comedy by Middleton and Rowley, *A Fair Quarrel* (II.i.127), unchastity is referred to as 'sin's dunghill'"; ibid., pp. 7–8.

49

In fact, if men saw what lies beneath the skin . . . the sight alone of women would nauseate them: that feminine grace is nothing but phlegm, blood, bile, rheum, and waste. Consider what is hidden in the nostrils, the throat, the belly: filth everywhere. And we who shrink from touching even a fingertip in vomit or dung, how can we then wish to embrace this bag of excrement.[73]

In a bizarre twist of this misogynist hysteria, the female audience of the English devotional prose tradition is instructed to regard their own bodies with revulsion. The mere sight of a beautiful face unveiled, they are cautioned, can become the occasion of sin, and Robertson discerns in the devotional prose, unlike "men's stories of their own experience," "a thematic emphasis on sexual temptation and bodily weakness."[74]

Examples of revulsion in the devotional prose are numerous and betray in a crude and paradoxical way the misogynistic tendencies of the male writers who celebrate the fair nobility of their female audience and yet revile and vilify their beauty. Again, Robertson notes of *Seinte Marharete*, "Although in these passages the man and woman are equally susceptible to sexual sin, the author's association of the concrete images of flesh, filth, and dung solely with the woman's fall reinforces the impression that his picture of female sexuality is negative."[75] Although many passages might be cited from devotional prose from the twelfth through the fifteenth century,[76] I will cite one in which the oppositions of beauty and filth are particularly striking:

I þe licome is fulðe ʒ unstrengðe. Ne kimeð of þ vetles swuch þing as þer is in? . . . Amid te menske of þi neb. þ is þe fehereste deal. bitweonen muðes

---

[73] Cited by Nancy Huston, *Dire et interdire: Elements de jurologie* (Paris: Payot, 1980), pp. 53–54.

[74] Robertson, *English Devotional Prose*, p. 43.

[75] Ibid., pp. 109–10.

[76] The devotional prose offers many examples. See, for instance, *A Talkyng*: "Pese me ladi for þi muchele merci. . . . Mi sunnes ben so gastliche.grisliche and grete.makeþ me so wlatsum. and stinkinde foule ꞏ/ þat I.ne dar him neihʒen.ne folwe my neode" (10/29–33); also, "And more was a schomet to don in monnes siht. and eþeliche truifle.of vn sittyng þing ꞏ/ þen mony a ful sunne.in siht of god almiʒti. ⊄ More him delyted forte enbrace Mock.And styngk of Worldliche Mok.þat gyleþ so foule ꞏ/ þen baþen in þe lykyng.& in þe loue cluppyng.in þe brennynge loue of þe holygost" (Westra, ed., *A Talkyng*, 14/30–16/1). See also Millett, ed., *Hali Meiðhad*: "þet bestelich gederunge, þet scheomelese sompnunge, þet ful of fulðe, stinkinde ant untohe dede" (4/27–28). In *Seinte Marharete*, the devil leads maidens "lutlen + lutlen into se deope dung et ha druncnið" ("little by little into the deep dung in which they are swallowed up"); Francis M. Mack, ed., *Seinte Marharete þe Meiden ant Martyr*, EETS, o.s., 1934; vol. 193 (rpt. London: Oxford University Press, 1958), p. 36, lines 5–6. Elsewhere, the maiden "falleð fule + fenniliche i flescliche fulðen . . . for a lust þet alið in an hondhwile, leoseð ba þe luve of Godd + te worldes wurðscipe" ("she falls foully and filthily into fleshly filth. . . ."); p. 36, lines 15–17.

smech. ⁊ neases smeal. ne berest tu as twa priue þureles? Nart tu icumen of ful slim? nart tu fulðe fette.

[In the body there is uncleanness and weakness. Does there not come out of a vessel such stuff as is in it? . . . In the middle of your face, which is a noble part of you and the fairest, between the mouth with its taste and the nose with its faculty of smelling, have you not as it were two privy holes? Have you not come from foul slime? Are you not a vessel of filth?][77]

Revulsion toward the body in the devotional prose arises because sin, sexual license especially, is associated with filth, foul odor, and bodily functions; its opposite then, the state of virtue, is conceptualized as cleanliness and whiteness. In *A Talkyng*, for instance, Christ and his mother are petitioned: "But siþen onliche in ow & in non noþer ⁀ Is welle of alle Merci.þat euermore floweþ.For þat muchel Merci.clanse my soule.and wasch hit of. þat fulþe⁀ þat hit is fuyled wiþ."[78] To some degree, all the devotional prose intended for the female reader focused on the issue of desire, particularly, as Robertson notes, desire transformed into desire for Christ.[79] The texts dramatize a woman's literalized marriage to Christ and her place as virgin in the procession of the Lamb, where, as the author of *Hali Meiðhad* put it, her reward is

to singe þet swete song ant þet englene drem vtnume murie, þet nan ha[lh]e ne mei, bute meiden ane, singen in heouene; ant folhin Godd almihti, euch godes ful, hwider se he eauer wendeð, as þe oðre ne mahe nawt, þah ha alle beon his sunen, ant alle hise dehtren.[80]

[to sing that sweet song and that angelic melody surpassingly joyful, that no saint may, except a virgin only, sing in heaven; and follow God almighty, full of

---

[77] Tolkien, ed., *Ancrene Wisse*, pp. 142–43. The translation is from M. B. Salu, *The Ancrene Riwle* (Notre Dame, Ind.: University of Notre Dame Press, 1956), p. 123.

[78] Westra, ed., *A Talkyng*, 26/6–9. Another example may be found in *A Talkyng*: "He wusch me wiþ cristendam.of Adames sunne ⁀ and I me fuylede siþen mony fold worse" (12/12–13).

[79] Robertson, *English Devotional Prose*, p. 63.

[80] Millett, ed., *Hali Meiðhad*, p. 9/14–19. This passage, addressed specifically to a woman, "Wite þe, seli meiden," (8.26) and alluding to the heavenly procession, "ant folhin Godd almihti, euch godes ful, hwider se he eauer wendeð" (9.17), makes it clear that women are not excluded from the procession of the Lamb, as Ferster would have it: "The little boy is recruited into a company of followers of Christ as the Lamb from which the Prioress is excluded. He outstrips his author by joining a society she cannot join" ("Language and Gender," p. 158).

every virtue, wheresoever he goes, as the others may not, though they all are his sons and all his daughters.]

Like the Pearl-maiden, the little clergeon is both *sponsa* and holy innocent, a "mayden" in the procession of the Lamb, so that the refusal of the world, the flesh, and the devil is presented in direct opposition to the scatological presentation in the preceding stanza of the visible, historical world.

This antithesis between revulsion toward the body mired in the world's filth and desire of the spirit as *sponsa*, as Bride of Christ, is a commonplace of the devotional literature of the period. If I am right in thinking that the style of *The Prioress's Tale*, developed from that prose, betrays the absence of a constituted fictive voice, then the moment at which the narrator asserts most insistently the speaker's presence may well reveal the greatest lacunae in the fictional "voice." It is not coincidental, I think, that the stanza celebrating the clergeon's virginity, immediately following the wardrobe imagery, is one of only two places (the other is in the second line of the *Prologue*) at which the male narrator insists on the presence of a female voice. The insistence on the feminized text, "quod she," underlines a narrative anxiety about the potentially destabilizing juxtaposition of images: on the one hand a social and material event—the filthy and mutilated corpse enclosed in waste; on the other a ritual and mystical eschatology—the white, sacrificial Lamb leading a ritual procession of those who refused the flesh and its consequences.[81]

In the final ambiguous exclamation of the poem, "And in a tombe of marbul stones cleere / Enclosen they his litel body sweete. / Ther he is now, God leve us for to meete" (lines 681–83), the three themes of time, place, and eschatology find a paradoxical confluence. What meaning does "now" have in relation to the tale or to the audience? Is the body "there" in the tomb or somewhere else, to be revealed in a dream? Is the earlier vision of the procession of the holy innocents called into doubt by the reservations inherent in "God leve us for to meete"? Inconsistencies, ambiguities, and contradictions suggest that the fictive voice constantly subverts itself and that the story it has to tell cannot contain the stylistic impetus to contradiction and opposition.

The Prioress is a persistent, though shadowy, figure in the critical esti-

---

[81] At least two fifteenth-century scribes (Chetham 6709, Harley 2251), copying *The Prioress's Tale* into anthologies of religious literature independent of *The Canterbury Tales* frame, were disturbed enough by the "quod she" to change it to "quod he," apparently attempting to conflate the speaker with "Seint John."

mation of her tale. The voice we hear is not hers, however, but that of a
textuality which conceptualized her as its audience. The Prioress has been
characterized as a Woman of Style; I have argued here that the Prioress is
simply a style, a style recognizably feminized for its largely female audience, but one constituted nonetheless of a masculine textuality. The style
itself, in its recursiveness and its incremental repetitions and oppositions,
subverts its implicit claim to represent a consistent fictive voice. In the
Prologue, the Prioress does not claim to speak as a child, as so many critics
would have it, but rather she claims to be unable to speak at all, as a child
of less than one is unable to utter a comprehensible word. Indeed, the
poem opens by contrasting the speech of men ("men of dignitee," i.e.,
hierarchy) with the speechlessness of children suckling on the mother's
breast, a paraphrase of Psalm 8, from the Mass of the Holy Innocents, but
one that establishes the major contrasts of the poem—that is, speech is
equated with masculine power whereas silence is equated with the powerlessness of children and mothers.[82] The miraculous song of the clergeon
is in fact silenced by the figure of masculine authority—the local abbot—
but the ironic result of the miracle is to silence the abbot himself ("And
gruf he fil al plat upon the grounde, / And stille he lay as he had ben
ybounde" [lines 675–76], where "stille" plays ambiguously as silent or
motionless). The ultimate effect in the Canterbury frame of the Prioress's
tale is to silence all the pilgrims.

Set against the voicelessness that the Prioress claims for herself is the
rhetorical posture of the tale, particularly its characteristic apostrophe. Beyond mere ornament, beyond a simple outpouring of emotion, apostrophe
plays a principal role in Chaucer's realization that the social construction of
the self in all its contradictory postures leaves an absence of identity at the

---

[82] The Prioress is perhaps not, like her little clergeon, *illitteratus*, but religious works in
the vernacular certainly had as an important audience religious women, as the northern
metrical version of the Rule of St. Benedict suggests: "Monkes & als all leryd men / In latyn
may it lyghtly ken . . . / Bott tyll women to mak it couth, / Þat leris no latyn in þar ȝouth /
In ingles is it ordand here"; in Ernst A. Kock, ed., *Three Middle-English Versions of the Rule of
St. Benet*, EETS, o.s., vol. 120 (London: Kegan Paul, Trench, Trübner, 1902), p. 48. By no
means were all female religious Latinless, however. See, for instance, Jocelyn Wogan-
Browne, "Wreaths of Time: The Female Translator in Anglo-Norman Hagiography," in *The
Medieval Translator 4*, Medieval & Renaissance Texts and Studies, vol. 123 (Binghamton,
N.Y.: State University of New York, 1994). For the status of anchorites particularly as
having an intermediate position between *laici* and *clerici*, *illitterati* and *litterati*, and hence
being influential in the development of a vernacular devotional prose, see Bella Millett,
"Women in No Man's Land: English Recluses and the Development of Vernacular Literature
in the Twelfth and Thirteenth Centuries," in Carol M. Meale, ed., *Women and Literature in
Britain, 1150–1500* (Cambridge: Cambridge University Press, 1993), pp. 86–103.

Chaucer's Canterbury Poetics: Irony, Allegory, and the *Prologue* to *The Manciple's Tale*

Warren Ginsberg
SUNY, Albany

F or a long time, irony and allegory have occupied prominent, but opposing, places in the lexicon of criticism on *The Canterbury Tales*; recently, however, readers of Chaucer have grown suspicious about granting either one the status of a first principle that governs the organization and reception of the *Tales* and the pilgrims who tell them. New Critical and exegetical interpretations virtually defined themselves according to the ways in which they deployed these tropes; commentators such as Lee Patterson have demonstrated how adherents of one or the other approach, by burying their political commitments in what they assumed were unchanging operations of language or belief, presented a Chaucer strangely detached from the social and material conditions of late medieval England.[1] From a different quarter, textual critics have interrogated the use of these or any concepts to promote ideas of order and unity the manuscripts will not sustain. To see in the disposition of tales indications of Chaucer's global intentions becomes highly problematic: whether *The Parson's Tale*, for instance, was meant to be the last tale told, or whether Chaucer even intended it should be part of the *Tales*, much less provide a retrospective gloss for them, are questions scribal evidence warrants asking.[2]

---

[1] Lee Patterson, *Negotiating the Past* (Madison: University of Wisconsin Press, 1987), pp. 3–39; see also Derek Pearsall's comments, *The Canterbury Tales* (London: George Allen & Unwin, 1985), pp. 318–19.

[2] A number of critics have relied on the uncertainty of textual evidence to call into question the assumption that the Parson's rejection of fiction in his *Prologue* and emphasis on penance in his tale coincides with Chaucer's final vision of the scope and purpose of *The Canterbury Tales*. See Charles Owen, *Pilgrimage and Storytelling in the Canterbury Tales* (Norman: University of Oklahoma Press, 1977); A. J. Minnis, *Medieval Theory of Authorship* (London: Scolar Press, 1984); and especially David Lawton, "Chaucer's Two Ways: The Pilgrimage Frame of *The Canterbury Tales*," *SAC* 9 (1987): 3–40. More generally, Norman Blake especially has argued against basing critical assumptions on the Ellesmere order; *The*

It is an irony of history that allegory and irony should have become identifying characteristics of antagonistic approaches to Chaucer, since in
medieval rhetorical theory both figures were closely related. Because it
simultaneously negates what it asserts, irony in fact was considered a kind
of allegory, which was the name for any language that said more than one
thing at once. It is equally ironic that these figures should have been disso-
ciated from history, since, as I hope to demonstrate, irony and allegory virtually constitute the style of the social and the historical in the *Tales*. And
though tales and blocks of tales are fragmentary, the prologues and end-
links to them show that Chaucer did conceive of them as parts of a whole.
While we cannot in many cases say a particular order is his, *The Canterbury
Tales* do subscribe to the idea of order, an idea that irony and allegory—the
tropes that join negation and plenitude together—help to determine.

I want to argue these propositions by examining the *Prologue* to *The
Manciple's Tale*. Many feel the performance of the thieving steward Chaucer
describes in *The General Prologue* hastens what James Dean has called the
dismantling of the Canterbury book.[3] In the Manciple's tale, not only
irony but speech itself yields to a cynicism so desolating, words clot and
sour on the tongue; with its closing injunctions to silence, Chaucer seems
to disengage from his fiction and confront "the limits of poetic utterance."[4]
Chaucer's renunciation of his craft then becomes unequivocal in the affect-
less prose of the Parson's tale of penance and the repudiations of the *Retraction* that follow: all poetry that is not part of the discourse of the spirit is
explicitly revoked.

Although the Manciple's tale does indeed move toward "alienation and
silence,"[5] the portrait of the man and the *Prologue* to his tale do not. In *The
General Prologue*, Chaucer explicitly links the Manciple to irony; in the
Prologue to his tale, the Manciple seems to embody it, first when he excuses
the Cook from telling a tale, then when he offers him his gourd of wine. In
each case, however, ironic negations and reversals rehabilitate and vindicate
Chaucer's fiction. They do so in two ways: first, by evoking a host of voices

---

Textual Tradition of the Canterbury Tales (London: Edward Arnold, 1985). I argue below that
the Parson's monological view of language dialectically engages the dialogic style of *The
Manciple's Prologue* and *Tale*, in which allegory and irony collide; together the tales
constitute a satisfying sense of ending for Chaucer's book, even if we cannot say that this
sequence represents his final intention.

[3] James Dean, "Dismantling the Canterbury Book," *PMLA* 100 (1985): 746–62.

[4] The quotation is from Stephen Knight, "Chaucer and the Sociology of Literature," *SAC*
2 (1980): 51.

[5] Dean, "Dismantling the Canterbury Book," p. 753.

related to the Manciple's, whose polyphony counters his desire to reduce language to his own denial of its truthfulness; and second, by evoking allegorical contexts, through which the antinomies and rivalries that give the material world its structure at the same time herald the advent of the spiritual. As the pilgrimage comes ever closer to Canterbury, Chaucer increasingly makes the style of his own fiction his subject; in his poetics, the final silence that completes repentance ironically refutes all the chatter of the world, and allegorically justifies it.[6]

I

The portrait of the Manciple in *The General Prologue* is striking, less for his brand of venality than for the pilgrim Chaucer's attitude toward it. Of this noble "achatour" Chaucer says (lines 567–86),

> A gentil MAUNCIPLE was ther of a temple,
> Of which achatours myghte take exemple
> For to be wise in byynge of vitaille;
> For wheither that he payde or took by taille,
> Algate he wayted so in his achaat
> That he was ay biforn and in good staat.
> Now is nat that of God a ful fair grace
> That swich a lewed mannes wit shal pace
> The wisdom of an heep of lerned men?
> Of maistres hadde he mo than thries ten,
> That weren of lawe expert and curious,
> Of which ther were a duszeyne in that hous
> Worthy to been stywardes of rente and lond
> Of any lord that is in Engelond,
> To make hym lyve by his propre good
> In honour dettelees (but if he were wood),
> Or lyve as scarsly as hym list desire;

---

[6] In the following argument, it is clear that I accept the linkage of *The Manciple's Tale* to *The Parson's Tale* and am convinced that together they bring *The Canterbury Tales* to completion. As the editor of the *Variorum* edition of *The Manciple's Tale* says, the textual evidence "strongly suggests that the earliest scribes" thought Fragment 9 should immediately precede Fragment 10. See Donald C. Baker, ed., *The Manciple's Tale, A Variorum Edition of the Works of Geoffrey Chaucer*, vol. 2, *The Canterbury Tales*, pt. 10 (Norman: University of Oklahoma Press, 1984), p. 44. Even in Hengwrt, whose order constitutes the chief challenge to Ellesmere, the word "Maunciple" seems to have been written, in the scribe's hand, over an erasure at the beginning of the *Prologue* to *The Parson's Tale*. The tales are joined and always stand last in all complete manuscripts.

> And able for to helpen al a shire
> In any caas that myghte falle or happe.
> And yet this Manciple sette hir aller cappe.[7]

Chaucer acknowledges the Manciple's malfeasance with something like bemused irony, which imparts to the portrait the flavor of a disagreeable aftertaste. The man's cunning is given its due, but at the same time his thievery is made a mean thing. Chaucer produces this double effect by structuring the portrait as an analogy. As a procurer of provisions, the Manciple's perspicacity makes him an ideal practitioner of his profession, since manciples were charged with overseeing the domestic affairs, especially the table, of a college or inn of court. But this particular Manciple pulls the cap over the eyes of the lawyers for whom he procures, masters whose potential stewardship in principle makes them manciples to the lords they would serve.[8] By itself the Manciple's conniving is the dishonesty of a shrewd but small mind; in the context of the portrait, however, it seems to acquire outsized implications, as if his chicanery threatens to turn inside out the relations that link and regulate all levels of English society. Were stewards to discharge their obligations to their lords, and lords their duty to the shire, the way the Manciple discharges his, every social transaction, from the buying of food to the governing of the realm, would become a commodification of deceit.

The Manciple's vigilance in grocery shopping, therefore, is something more than preparation for his quarrel with the Cook; the repetition of "achatours/achaat" is more than a stylistic forecast of the repetitions of his tale ("Whit was this crowe as is a snow-whit swan" [*ManT* 133], etc.). By superimposing his petty fraud against the larger ideas of stewardship, law, and the maintenance of the well-ordered community, Chaucer has implied that, no matter how private, the Manciple's dealings still are part of the public discourse of professions, and that his intentions, no matter how contrary, still are comprehended by the civic function they subvert. Yet for all this emphasis on the social formation of the Manciple's character, he is

---

[7] All citations of *The Canterbury Tales* are from Larry Benson, gen. ed., *The Riverside Chaucer*, 3d ed. (Boston: Houghton Mifflin, 1987).

[8] According to the *MED*, a steward was "an official or servant in charge of the domestic affairs of a household"; the term came to be applied to a "noble appointed to supervise at a feast; also an officer in charge of provisions." The duties of manciple and steward overlap; at least some of the contempt for the aristocracy that Chaucer's Manciple shows may derive from his envy of better born men who do what he does. More particularly, his contempt perhaps stems from his association with the lawyers of his temple, who probably were members of the aristocracy. (See below, note 39.)

chiefly defined by Chaucer's ironic reaction to him. This is not easy to describe precisely. In his own voice the narrator seems to admire the Manciple's guile even as he deliberately distances himself from it: "Now is nat that of God a ful fair grace" (*GP* 573). In its double-edgedness, its approving disapproval, the narrator's irony becomes a correlative to those sly but fraudulent acts that provoke it.[9]   *How ridiculous!*

See rhetorical question in MLi's Pro.

The temptation is strong to see this response as personal, Chaucer's peculiar displeasure for the Manciple's kind of duplicity. But complex as it is, Chaucer's stance here is not really his own; it is Luke's, when he tells the parable of the wicked steward (16:1–9):

There was a certain rich man who had a steward: and the same was accused unto him, that he had wasted his goods. And he called him, and said to him: "How is it that I hear this of thee? give an account of thy stewardship: for now thou canst be steward no longer." And the steward said within himself: "What shall I do? for my lord taketh away from me the stewardship: to dig I am not able: to beg I am ashamed. I know what I will do, that when I shall be put out of the stewardship, they may receive me into their houses." Therefore calling together every one of his lord's debtors, he said to the first: "How much dost thou owe my lord?" But he said: "A hundred barrels of oil." And he said to him: "Take thy bill, and sit down quickly, and write fifty." Then he said to another: "And how much dost thou owe?" Who said: "A hundred quarters of wheat." He said to him: "Take thy bill and write eighty." And the lord commended the unjust steward [villicum iniquitatis], forasmuch as he had done wisely: for the children of this world are wiser in their generation than the children of light. And I say to you: make yourselves friends of the mammon of iniquity [de mammona iniquitatis], that when ye shall fail, they may receive you into everlasting dwellings.[10]

Chaucer's Manciple has a portion in the special irony of Jesus' commendation. The wicked steward in the Bible does act wisely in a difficult situation; by remitting part of the debtors' liability, he purchases their good

---

[9] Unlike other instances in *The General Prologue*, Chaucer's words here seem to be an instance of irony in the technical sense; we imagine him conveying the opposite meaning of what he says through vocal pronunciation. For this definition of irony, a commonplace of classical rhetorical tradition, see Isidore of Seville, *Etymologiarum libri XV*, 1. 37,25: "ironia est sententia per pronuntiationem contrarium habens intellectum." Quoted in Hennig Brinkmann, *Mittelalterliche Hermeneutik* (Tübingen: Niemeyer, 1980), pp. 217–18; for further medieval elaboration, see pp. 218–19.

[10] All biblical quotations are from *The Holy Bible: Douay Rheims Version* (Rockford, Ill.: Tan Books, 1971).

will, and with it, future entrance to their houses. Nevertheless, the wisdom of this world is silly-wise: the steward's charity to those in debt is one final defrauding of his lord. Thus, as the commentaries explain, when the lord praises the steward's wisdom, he commends not the deception but the shrewdness that prompted it.[11] The steward has forfeited the right to dwell with his master, but the cunning way he has assured admittance to the houses of his lord's debtors nevertheless is an object lesson to those who would walk the path to light.

At the same time, however, Jesus' final embrace of the steward's conduct obliterates it. In his own voice he offers wily, practical counsel, counsel that the faithful instantly reject. "Make friends with the mammon of iniquity," Jesus advises, "enter into the economy that determines social relations on earth, so that when you fail at the end of days you may find dwelling in eternal tabernacles" ("aeterna tabernacula"), by which presumably he means the tabernacles of Hell.[12] In the face of the eschaton, the success of all worldly maneuvering becomes utterly ironic.

Jesus can damn with real, not faint, praise here because his talking at cross-purposes, instead of producing an impasse in meaning, becomes part of allegory's project to speak otherwise. If irony negates the subject it posits, if by saying "I and Not-I" at once it creates a rift of contradiction no logic can repair, allegory transforms such oppositions into analogies of difference.[13] Luke's parable in particular exemplifies the biblical method of taming irony's impulse toward nihilism, toward what Gordon Teskey has called "the absolute, nondialectical oppositions of antiphrasis," which is the form of irony that "derives its name from negation."[14] In one utterance,

[11] See, for instance, Hugh of St. Cher, *Evangelii super Lucam*, pp. 208–9, in *Biblie cum postilla domini Hugonis Cardinalis* (Basel: Amerbach, 1484). His comment reflects a long tradition, but, as we shall see, it by no means is the only reading of the steward's foresight.

[12] This is Ambrose's reading: "pecuniae uilis usura tabernacula defunctis adquirit aeterna"; *Expositio Evangelii secundum Lucum*, 7.122–23, in G. Tissot, ed., *Traité sur l'Évangile de S. Luc*, 2 vols. *Sources chrétiennes* 45, 52 (Paris: du Cerf, 1952): 2:255. Most commentators, however, influenced by the positive overtones of "tabernacula," see the eternal dwellings as a metaphor for heaven. I explain the divergence below.

[13] In these characterizations of irony and allegory I follow Gordon Teskey, "Irony, Allegory, and Metaphysical Decay," *PMLA* 109 (1994): 397–408. Drawing on de Man's "The Concept of Irony," Teskey offers a powerful analysis of the inevitable linkage and fundamental incompatibility of irony and allegory in the rhetorical tradition. See also Larry Scanlon, "The Authority of Fable: Allegory and Irony in the *Nun's Priest's Tale*," *Exemplaria* 1 (1989): 43–68. Scanlon also briefly treats the connection of irony to allegory; like me he sees in the association a justification of Chaucer's fiction.

[14] On antiphrasis, see Quintilian, *Institutio oratoria*, vol. 3, trans. H. Butler, Loeb Classical Library (Cambridge, Mass.: Harvard University Press, 1920), 9.2.47. Quintilian's discussion epitomizes the rhetorical tradition's classification of irony as a species of allegory "in which opposites are shown" (8.6.54). For the medieval transmission of this tradition, see Brinkmann, *Mittelalterliche Hermeneutik*, pp. 214–19, and Teskey, "Irony," p. 399.

Jesus twice bespeaks himself. He endorses the lord's commendation of the steward by impersonating him: in the voice of worldly expediency, he says, "Make friends with the mammon of iniquity." But though he can speak as steward, the steward does not speak for him. In a voice not the steward's— above the steward's—Jesus invokes an apocalyptic context, which immediately cancels the literal, opportunistic sense of his words by identifying it as a rhetorical deflection from proper (indeed ultimate) significance. Like the leaves scattered through Dante's universe that are gathered into one volume bound by love, even contrary antagonisms have been made part of an unfolding proliferation of forms already and always unified in the mind of God. Through impersonation Luke has domesticated irony's oppositions by extending them into a metanarrative in which the economies of this life are both cancelled by those of the next and reformed in their image. "I" negates "Not-I" and becomes convertible with it; the steward is wise and corrupt; his foresight is and is not a model for the children of light. Instead of being a principle of annulment, contradiction has been transformed into a postulate of simultaneous continuity and fracture between the historical world and the timeless realms of the spirit.[15] Irony's negations have been subsumed by allegory's concurrent swerve from propriety and promise of return to a truer form of it; singleminded inversions have become sites of doubled vision, wherein acts that undermine the social ideal are immoral because they undo the sanctioned material order, and commendable because they proclaim every earthly community the shadow of a different, higher sodality that will finally replace it.

Depending on whether one regards this life or the next, therefore, Luke's parable altogether endorses or completely does away with the emphasis classical ethics had placed on the relative and the mean. Formally, however, by joining irony and allegory, the parable is entirely conventional. Because irony says one thing but implies the opposite, in ancient and medieval rhetorical theory it was always considered a species of allegory, which was defined as that general category of language wherein proper meaning is deflected. Whether created through intonation or by verbal means, from Quintilian to Isidore, through Bede and Gervais of Melkey, all forms of linguistic contrariety, rather than bringing discourse to a halt, were seen as a way of doubling it.[16]

[15] Jesus' impersonation in fact makes irony the appropriate trope to mirror the paradoxical, but not self-negating, epistemology of parables in general, which couch the profoundest truth in forms so simple they confound the wise.

[16] For medieval discussions of irony and the other tropes of rhetorical allegory, which include *aenigma* (riddle), *charientismos* (euphemism), *paroimia* (proverb), and *sarcasmos*, see Brinkmann, *Mittelalterliche Hermeneutik*, pp. 214–19.

61

In the Middle Ages, parables were the ideal form to exhibit the connection between allegory and irony. By definition, parables sustain a comparison between dissimilar kinds of things.[17] To the extent that one foregrounds the comparison, parables therefore *were* allegories in the rhetorical sense of the word: extended metaphors that say one thing and mean another. Indeed, because they were spoken by Jesus, the Gospel parables were even thought to partake of the mysteries that characterize theological allegory: from the earliest times many details were interpreted spiritually. But Jesus also announced a time when there would be no need to speak in parables (e.g., John 16:25); to the extent, then, that one foregrounds dissimilarity, the parables would tend toward irony, juxtaposing things whose incompatibility increasingly borders on pure opposition.

Medieval commentators recognized the contrary pull of these impulses and did their best to make them companionable; they acknowledged that the literal can have an extended or allegorical sense, but at the same time they emphasized the difference between this kind of polysemy and divine discourse. Parables provided the pattern that demonstrated how human speech could house multiple meanings: by the time of Aquinas, in fact, figurative meaning generally had been given the name *parabolic* ("parabolicus seu metaphoricus").[18] But because this proliferation of senses was generated by overstepping the bounds of the proper, it could never be more than a rhetorical trope; the resemblance parabolic language bore to the anagogic unity of spiritual allegory was of the lowest order.[19]

Medieval interpretations of the parable of the wicked steward are exemplary in this regard.[20] Not surprisingly, a fault line runs through the logic

---

[17] "Parabola est rerum genere dissimilium comparatio"; the definition comes from Cicero. For a discussion of the range of meanings parable had in the Middle Ages, see Brinkmann, *Mittelalterliche Hermeneutik*, pp. 164–68.

[18] De Bruyne's model of the senses that were ascribed to the literal is still useful. Words can have both proper and figurative meaning; under proper meaning, one understands the denotative definition of words (the "historical" sense), the meaning they bear by reason of their cause ("secundum aetiologiam"), and the meaning they bear by virtue of their proportionate relationship to other elements in the work, through which the unity of thought is conveyed ("secundum analogiam"). Under figurative meaning, one understands the "typical" ("typicus"), that is, the individual representing the universal; the parabolic or allegorical in the rhetorical sense; and the moral, in the sense that beast fables contain a moral that is not conveyed by what they literally say. See Edgar de Bruyne, *Études D'Esthétique Médiévale*, 3 vols. (Bruges: De Tempel, 1946), 2:312. On the relation of beast fables to parables, see below, note 27.

[19] Aquinas makes these points in the *Summa Theologiae*, 1.1.10. Thomas Aquinas, *Opera Omnia*, ed. S. E. Fretté and P. Maré, vols. 1–4 (Paris: L. Vivès, 1874–89).

[20] For a complete summary of medieval commentary on this as well as the other biblical parables, see Stephen Wailes, *Medieval Allegories of Jesus' Parables* (Berkeley: University of California Press, 1987). Wailes documents the pronounced tendency to allegorize details from the parables throughout the Middle Ages.

of the commentaries. Some take the lord's commendation of the steward literally, but in order to do so, they read the steward's actions metaphorically, nearly to the point of allegory: by forgiving our neighbor's debts, we make friends with the angels and saints (Ambrose); by modifying the accounts, the steward shows that a life of penance requires the release of our debtors and almsgiving (Haimo of Auxerre).[21] Others read the commendation metaphorically; to do so, they take the steward's fraud literally, and ironically find moral substance by rejecting it.[22] These inconsistencies create little tension, even if the distance they interpose between cause and effect seems to widen almost to the point of contradiction. As Bonaventure explains, the parable obviously mixes literal and parabolic teaching: the lord's praise of prudent behavior is literal, since it speaks to the steward's liberality and mercy, but his detestable fraud is something Christ would never have supported; it teaches only parabolically, by means of contraries.[23]

Such accommodations, however, cannot entirely put to rest the fundamental struggle between irony and allegory over the nature of figurative language itself. According to Quintilian, whose account, though modified, set the terms of discussion throughout the Middle Ages, language becomes figurative when what is said bends away or deviates from what is meant, much the way nouns in the oblique cases were thought to decline from the "uprightness" of the nominative. Allegory is the home and source of all such expressions; it operates by ordering the divergence of meanings it creates as parts to the whole. Allegory simultaneously produces and repairs the tilt away from the nominative by presupposing an original, "linguistically omnipotent self," a self "that both intends and deflects its intentions in a language that it 'uses.'"[24] Under such a dispensation, even irony's opposition of same and different will participate in one unifying truth and thereby become a form of likeness.

But if, as Teskey says, the essence of irony is antiphrasis, it, rather than allegory, is the site of the genesis of tropes. Since irony "speaks not from an angular but from an opposite position," it must be part of allegory's arc of

---

[21] Ibid., pp. 249–50.

[22] St. Augustine is a good example of this reading. He comments that the parable teaches by contraries: not all aspects praised by the lord are to be imitated; *Quaestionum evangeliorum libri duo, Patrologia Latina* 35:1348. See Wailes, *Allegories*, p. 247.

[23] As Wailes says, Bonaventure therefore allegorizes some elements of the story: the steward's inability to dig, for instance, shows that the weak of spirit will not accept the corporal labor that the perfection of penance requires. Other elements he accepts as literal, such as the adjusted debts; *Commentarius in Evangelium S. Lucae*, cited in Wailes, *Allegories*, 247–48.

[24] Teskey, "Irony," p. 399.

deflection, but what is posited there is posited as absolute, nondialectical negation, as I and Not-I at once. Divergence thus is genetically closer to contradiction than to similitude; once it takes noncoincidence rather than identity as its limit, however, no interpretation can return us to a prior "uprightness." On the contrary, "speaking *against* now comes before, and enables, speaking *other*,"[25] for it is in the space irony creates that juxtaposition is infinitely possible, and all forms of deflected language are born. Allegory emerges out of irony, which haunts from within every attempt to construct a polysemous system of correspondence. In the primal scene where irony and allegory meet, figuration, which is the result of their encounter, now looks more toward the meaningless noise of chaos than toward the transcendental silence of a logos singular to itself.

Far more than medieval commentators perceived, the parable of the wicked steward dramatizes what is at stake in the clash between irony and allegory. Unlike other instances, such as the parable of the mustard seed, allegory and irony here arise from the same utterances. Within the narrative, the lord's commendation of the steward's cunning begets a complementary declaration, which like it is both praise and rebuke: "For the children of this world are wiser in their generation than the children of light." Interpreting these words is difficult, not so much because we need to decide whether they are straightforward or meant to refute what they posit, but because we cannot read the sentence allegorically without reading it ironically at the same time. The figurative language—"the children of this world" and "the children of light"—invites us to take allegorically the opposition these terms suggest between this world and the next. But if we do, the assertion cancels itself: in the last analysis, when all generations have passed away, only the children of light are wise. So where do these children of light come from: are they begotten from the irony or from the allegory of the statement?[26]

Outside the narrative, interpreting it, we find an exhortation that, instead of drawing a clarifying (and therefore reductive) lesson from the story, repeats its inhering ambiguity: "And I say unto you: make yourself friends of the mammon of iniquity, that when ye shall fail, they may receive you into eternal tabernacles." In most parabolic utterances, the hermeneutic

---

[25] Ibid.

[26] The commentaries reveal the *aporia* in interpretation very nicely: both the children of this world and the children of light are variously interpreted. Most often, as one might expect, they are contrasted, to the benefit of the latter. But other exegetes reversed the valency (Peter Chrysologus); Innocent III takes both groups negatively! See Wailes, *Allegories*, pp. 252–53.

64

imperative is to establish the hidden likeness that enables the differences to be compared. Here no similarity brought in from beyond the text seems to reconcile those differences; irony runs unchecked, to the point that Jesus seems to turn heaven into hell. Yet even here, as we have seen, Luke does work to limit the effect of the irony by doubling the language from which it arises. In repeating the lord's commendation, Jesus' counsel also subordinates it; the reversals both statements occasion have been situated in the domain of the same, and (ironically, of course) an order (inside and outside, contained and container) has been established between them.

Because Chaucer saw the Manciple's cunning subversion of his office as a corruption of the entire social order, he fashioned his déclassé steward, who, like Luke's, defrauds the masters he serves by cooking his records of purchase, after that equally sly "villicus iniquitatis."[27] More important, Luke's parable furnished Chaucer a set of traditionally connected rhetorical figures to associate with the Manciple, which between them define the range and power, as well as the dangers, of poetic language. Most of all, however, Luke demonstrated how through impersonation these tropes can coexist without cancelling each other. When Chaucer wrote the *Prologue* to *The Manciple's Tale*, he extended his meditation on the inevitable linkage of polysemy and negation, and on impersonation as a means of representing them simultaneously. The Manciple will speak, both for himself and for the Cook, with all the irony an alienating cynicism can command, but what he says does more than deny, because he has been otherwise involved in allegories of conversion. *Making the simple impossibly complex*

II

The *Prologue* to *The Manciple's Tale* begins with a question that asks readers to locate themselves (lines 1–9):

---

[27] There is a formal link between the parable in general and the Manciple as well: to the extent that his tale is a beast fable, it is first cousin to parables. In discussing *homoiosis*, which is the demonstration of something less known by drawing an analogy between it and something similar but better known, medieval rhetoricians classified both the *apologus* and the *parabola* as kinds of *paradigmae* or *exempla*, that is, exhortatory or warning examples. The *apologus* introduced its analogies from the beast world; the *parabola* drew them from human interaction; Brinkmann, *Mittelalterliche Hermeneutik*, pp. 165–66.

Chaucer certainly thought the Manciple a child of this world, wise in his generation: in the *Tale* he endlessly reinforces the association through his exhausting recitation of his mother's injunctions to keep quiet: "My sone, thenk on the crowe, a Goddes name! / My sone, keep wel thy tonge, and keep thy freend" (*ManT* 318–19), and so forth. These strictures have rightly reminded many readers of Proverbs. *Parabola* and *proverbium* were also synonyms: The Book of Proverbs itself was called *Parabolae Solomonis*.

> Woot ye nat where ther stant a litel toun
> Which that ycleped is Bobbe-up-and-doun,
> Under the Blee, in Caunterbury Weye?
> Ther gan oure Hooste for to jape and pleye,
> And seyde, "Sires, what! Dun is in the myre!
> Is ther no man, for preyere ne for hyre,
> That wole awake oure felawe al bihynde?
> A theef myghte hym ful lightly robbe and bynde.
> See how he nappeth! See how, for cokkes bones,
> That he wol falle fro his hors atones!

The straggler, of course, is the Cook, whom the Manciple besmirches while excusing him from telling a tale. In response,

> . . . the Cook wax wrooth and wraw,
> And on the Manciple he gan nodde faste
> For lakke of speche, and doun the hors hym caste,
> Where as he lay, til that men hym up took. (lines 46–49)

This is both roadside drama and a drama that points to the road beside it. At Bobbe-up-and-doun, the Cook and Manciple travel in two directions at once; as they quarrel, they mark out one path for their souls and a contrary path for the spiritual pilgrimage to Canterbury, for their actions recall and parody Paul's conversion.

Soon after his persecution of Stephen, Saul asked the high priest for letters to the synagogues at Damascus,

ut si quos invenisset huius vie viros ac mulieres vinctos perduceret in hierusalem. et cum iter feceret contigit ut appropinquaret Damasco et subito circumfulsit eum lux de celo et cadens in terram audivit vocem dicentem sibi Saule Saule quid me persequeris. (Acts 9:2–4)

[that if he found any men and women of this way, he might bring them bound to Jerusalem. And as he went on his journey, it came to pass, that he drew near to Damascus: and suddenly a light from heaven shone round about him. And falling on the ground, he heard a voice saying to him, "Saul, Saul, why dost thou persecute me?"]

In the Vulgate account, it is not clear whether Paul went by horse or by foot: medieval iconography of the incident in fact accommodated both possibilities. In the majority of scenes, however, Paul is on horseback, or was just before he falls: his horse appears either to have stumbled, or has been blinded and has thrown him.[28] With the Host's cry that "Dun is in the mire" ("the horse is in the mire"), Chaucer announces that this game in his fiction is played in "ernest."[29] The sleepy Cook of London rides the (Pilgrim's) "*Weye*" to Canterbury, an easy prey for a thief to "robbe and *bynde*": the kind of man a persecutor like Saul would catch on the *way* ("huius vie") and bring *bound* ("vinctos") to Jerusalem. The metaphorical mire, the actual "slough" Harry wants the Cook's horse to avoid (*ManP* 64), the heaviness that has overcome Roger (line 22), the real weight of his "dronken cors" (line 67), even his admission that he would rather sleep now than drink, whereas the night before he drank rather than slept (lines 22–24): literally and figuratively the scene seems to point to the need for spiritual rebirth.

But as Chaucer stages this allegory of the soul's conversion on the way to the "Jerusalem celestial" that the Parson sees the nearer he gets to Canterbury [*ParsP* 51], his Saul splits into two: one the object, the other the agency, of the nullifying spirit of irony. As object the sodden Cook embodies irony's propensity toward noncoincidence by powerfully countering any movement toward change or reformation. Unlike his confreres, whom the Pardoner claims "stampe, and streyne, and grynde / And turnen substaunce into accident" (*PardT* 538–9), this mormal-ridden maker of blankmanger fixedly remains what he was. Now hung over, his anger at the Manciple will soon reduce him to witless "lakke of speche," but the night before, when drunk, he was also something less than the creature God made in the image of his word: the comparison of various grades of inebriation to animals (the Manciple says Roger has "dronken . . . wyn ape" [*ManP* 44]), if nothing else, rests on wine's wresting from humans their distinctive power to speak meaningfully.[30] As the Manciple implies, the Cook has fallen away from the place people occupy in God's order: accident has become substance in him; hung over now, he will drink merely to be drunk again. By himself, the Cook resists incorporation into larger communities because, not being himself, he is incapable of being

[28] In the Princeton Index of Christian Art, there are thirty-four depictions of Paul on horseback in illuminated manuscripts, four paintings, two frescoes, three sculptural portrayals, two in glass, and an ivory diptych, all before 1400.

[29] For a description of the game of "Dun is in the mire," see Baker, *Variorum*, p. 81.

[30] See the helpful note in ibid., pp. 87–88. Compare the Summoner, who would "speke and crie as he were wood" after he had drunk "strong wyn" (*GP* 635–36). This religious figure debases language to the point of stupidity and unintelligibility; he is the other side of the Friar, who perverts language for sexual and monetary ends. Both are presented as adulterers of God's word.

like anyone else. He resists allegory's compulsion toward synecdoche; instead he stands as the emblem of the fall into matter, the ironic end-product of what Teskey calls "metaphysical decay," that dropping off from the polysemous unity of God into its counterpoint, a morass of matter nearly exhausted of its form, which defies intelligibility.

The thief who catches and binds the Cook is the Manciple. He is ironic in a more insidious way than Roger, since he is the efficient cause, the agent who intentionally would set the Cook apart from the other pilgrims, the man who, in speaking for Roger, will render him the speechless, "hevy dronken cors" (*ManP* 67) he becomes. Indeed, the Manciple cynically forecloses the very possibility of conversion by levelling its contraries. For him, "before" and "after" not only do not mark an essential difference in condition, they disguise the fact that nothing has changed. Thus the Manciple politely releases Roger from telling a tale on the one hand (lines 25–29), but immediately defames the Cook's character on the other (lines 30–45). Though this seems a reversal in behavior, the Manciple is never less than malicious, even when his malice has been cloaked as politesse (lines 25–29):

> "Wel," quod the Maunciple, "if it may doon ese
> To thee, sire Cook, and to no wight displese,
> Which that heere rideth in this compaignye,
> And that oure Hoost wole, of his curteisye,
> I wol as now excuse thee of thy tale."

Considering how it purchases the audience's complaisance at the expense of excluding one of its members, what is ironic in this "captatio benevolentiae" is its apparent lack of irony. Similarly, in retrospect, because we know the Manciple holds aristocratic values in contempt—for him "degree" is nothing more than high-toned language that gilds the basest acts (*ManT* 212–22)—the sarcasm of his "sir-ing" the Cook becomes impossible to separate from his uttering it.[31] Just as sarcastic are the Manciple's nods to the Host's "courtesy" and the company's welfare. As in the portrait in *The General Prologue*, the Manciple's purview is comprehensive. It extends from the individual to the community as he traduces, oh so mannerly, not only the Cook but the very means—performing penance by telling a tale— Harry Bailly has offered Roger so that he might again become a member of the pilgrimage he has fallen behind.

---

[31] The fact that the Manciple uses the familiar "thou" to Roger also is a verbal indication of the irony of the title.

Thus the actual maligning of the Cook, which begins with the Manciple's next word, does not contradict the spirit of what he has just said but continues it. The Manciple's denunciation meticulously follows the same order that his absolving of the Cook had: as before, he moves from Roger himself—focusing on his eyes, which are half-shut; his mouth, which is too open; and his breath, which poses a danger to the company ("Thy cursed breeth infecte wole us alle" [*ManP* 39])—to a mocking reprisal of the Host and his courtesy. The Manciple mimics Harry's call of "Dun in the mire" by referring to the equally popular game of fan jousting: "wol ye justen atte fan" (line 42); unlike Harry, however, in his desire to humiliate the Cook, to see him muddied, the Manciple again would soil highborn pursuits by dragging them down to the lowest level.[32] In him graciousness is indistinguishable from venom, and calumny a kind of service to the well-being of the community: a consistent mean-spiritedness enables the Manciple to make bad and good, true and false, versions of each other.

III

In the first part of the *Prologue*, the Manciple's irony imperils allegory's capacity for weaving opposition into the fabric of the universe. Like Jesus in Luke's parable, the Manciple seeks to speak in two voices: out of seeming concern for the Cook, he would become Roger's mouthpiece, yet in his own voice he never stops vilifying him. But unlike Jesus' steward, whose voice is affirmed even as what it says is rejected, the Manciple nullifies Roger *by* impersonating him. His "I" negates its "Not-I," however, not because the Manciple recognizes the Cook as his inimical opposite, but because he eliminates all space for him to speak. In the Manciple's manner of speaking, "Not-I" never speaks for itself; it exists only as the denial that it can say something other than what "I" does. The Manciple's irony cancels whatever differs from himself: it un-makes character.[33]

Even before Roger falls speechless from his horse, the Manciple has silenced him, left him behind in the unintelligibility of the slough, denied

---

[32] On the popularity of the game, see again Baker, *Variorum*, pp. 86–87. Clearly, I would argue that the Manciple's snide swipe at a game that prepares squires to become knights is set in context by Paul's call to arm the soul with the breastplate of faith and charity, and with the helmet of hope for salvation.

[33] In a fascinating article, Louise Fradenburg also comments on the Manciple's appropriation of Roger's voice; she sees in it a complex reflection of Chaucer's position as court poet; "The Manciple's Servant Tongue: Politics and Poetry in *The Canterbury Tales*," *ELH* 52 (1985): 85–118.

him the possibility of conversion. The pilgrimage itself as a polysemous event, as a scene of divergent subjectivities joined by social play and the possibility for spiritual reform, has thus been put in jeopardy by a spirit of negation that deprives its object of the potential to exist, much less to change, because it refuses to give it the chance to say something different. If allegory operates by establishing likeness even between opposites, the Manciple has struck at its heart; his irony makes all similarity alternate forms of emptiness. As his tale of the crow's transformation will make clear, for the Manciple black and white are contraries only in illusion; in truth, the difference means nothing.

For Chaucer, however, it is precisely because the Manciple would make every peripety an occasion for more of the same, because he levels opposites and makes them able to substitute for one another, that his irony has prepared the ground for allegory. The way this watchful, sober child of the world, who steals from the lawyers he serves, suddenly falls on the crapulous Cook both associates the Manciple with the thief Harry mentions and recalls Jesus' coming as a thief in the night, an event, Paul says, of great significance for the children of light (1 Thess. 5:2–8):[34]

. . . the day of the Lord shall so come, as a thief in the night. . . . But you, brethren, are not in darkness. . . . For all you are the children of light, and children of the day: we are not of the night nor of darkness. Therefore, let us not sleep, as others do; but let us watch and be sober. For they that sleep, sleep in the night, and they that are drunk, are drunk in the night. But let us, who are of the day, be sober, having on the breastplate of faith and charity, and for a helmet the hope of salvation.

To enable the Thessalonians to understand the second coming, Paul must turn earthly structures upside down. Though he comes to bring day and establish the kingdom of God, Jesus will return not in triumph but in stealth, like a thief in the night. Though the children of light who await him would gladly give him all they have, they must arm themselves as adults to protect themselves from attack by the reprobate who might assault them like highwaymen, whether it is day or night. As if in response to these reversals, after Roger has fallen from his horse, the Host, Cook, and Manciple replay their encounter in reverse. Instead of the hollowness of barren repetition, however, their actions acquire a second sense that inverts the demeaning intent that had impelled the Manciple's previous engineer-

---

[34] These allusions to Paul were first noted by Rodney Delasanta, "Penance and Poetry in the *Canterbury Tales*," *PMLA* 93 (1978): 240–47.

70

ing of them. This incarnation of cynicism now ironically becomes the pilgrim through whom Chaucer unifies oppositions in a discourse of full-ness. This advocate of silence in others becomes the means whereby Chaucer demonstrates and vindicates the meaningfulness of his fiction of impersonation fiction one last time.

Once the Cook has been remounted through the efforts of the other pilgrims, Harry excuses Roger from telling a tale (*ManP* 57–64):

> "By cause drynke hath dominacioun
> Upon this man, by my savacioun,
> I trowe he lewedly wolde telle his tale.
> For, were it wyn or oold or moysty ale
> That he hath dronke, he speketh in his nose,
> And fneseth faste, and eek he hath the pose.
> He hath also to do moore than ynough
> To kepen hym and his capul out of the slough. . . ."

The Cook is drunk, and therefore would talk to no one's profit ("lewedly"), because he would spout gibberish: he speaks through his nose, wheezes hard, and seems to have a head cold. For Roger's own well-being, and for the good of the other pilgrims as well, it is enough that he concentrate on staying in his saddle without having to manage the additional burden of telling a tale. Point for point and in the same order followed by the Manci-ple, Harry focuses first on the Cook and then on his relation to his fellow wayfarers. Harry also speaks in two voices, as did the Manciple; but whether he speaks for himself or as the pilgrims' Host, when Harry talks of Roger's sorry state the Cook is part of the group, not split off from it. Just as Jesus' reformulation of the lord's commendation in the parable of the wicked steward allowed Luke to turn the oppositions of irony into the polysemy of allegory, Chaucer's formal doublings act to repair the Manci-ple's uncouplings.

Yet if the Host can say with the Manciple to the Cook, "Of me, certeyn, thou shalt nat been yglosed" (*ManP* 34), neither will he flatter the Cook's detractor. He reproves the Manciple's too open reproof of the Cook; Roger could "reclayme" the Manciple and bring him "to lure" by raising doubts about the honesty of his reckonings in supplying victuals to his Inn (*ManP* 73–75):

> I meene, he speke wole of smale thynges,
> As for to pynchen at thy rekenynges,
> That were nat honest, if it cam to preef.

71

Harry upbraids the Manciple in exactly the way the Manciple had called the Cook to account. He impersonates Roger, but unlike the Manciple, Harry lends the Cook words that expose the fraud of the man who has defamed him. And as before, the irony of the situation opens to allegory. Even as Harry catches and binds the Manciple, he reminds us of another wily master of provisions who was not quite wary enough, the evil servant whom Jesus, coming suddenly, will separate from the righteous (Mt. 24:43–51; italics mine):

Who, thinkest thou, is a faithful and wise servant, whom his lord hath set over his family, to give them meat in season. [In the Vulgate the word is the more general "cibum."] Blessed is that servant, whom, when his lord shall come, he shall find so doing. . . . *But if that evil servant shall say in his heart: My lord is long a coming, and shall begin to strike his fellow servants, and shall eat and drink with drunkards*, the Lord of that servant shall come in a day that he hopeth not, and at an hour that he knoweth not, and shall separate him, and appoint his portion with the hypocrites. There shall be weeping and gnashing of teeth.

By weighing the actions of both the good and the wicked servant, whose hidden thoughts are brought to light by being given a voice, Matthew frames this tableau of justice as a question, as if it were a case at law. By using this as a model for both the interchange between Harry and the Manciple and, as we shall see, the Manciple's subsequent offer of wine to the Cook, Chaucer counterbalances his recordkeeper's every negation. Despite the Manciple's efforts to portray himself as a faithful steward, in his attempt to quarantine Roger and keep the pilgrims safe from his "infection" he has become one with the servant he persecutes. This pairing of servants does not result solely in their mutual condemnation, however, as would happen if they had been disposed of according to the Manciple's sense of equity. Rather, both men have been made players in a different, exhortatory drama: judge not, lest ye be judged. Even as the clever Manciple, who steals from the lawyers of his temple, and the dull Cook are assigned the same portion, a real difference is opened between them and the truly wise master of provisions. The Manciple's antiphrastic derogations have been "infected" with a likeness that opens into allegory.

Similarly, the Host's metaphor of falcon and lure, pointedly aristocratic in its provenance, rescues the Manciple's contempt for the nobility, not only metaphorically in its suggestion that the Cook will be able to turn the tables on the Manciple, but socially by being a figure of justice.[35] Though the image is common, if Chaucer remembered Dante's striking use of it in the *Purgatorio* his transposition of it here would be apt. As Dante is about to leave the terrace on which envy is repented, Virgil upholds the justice of the form the penance takes—the sewing shut of the sinners' eyelids—by categorizing envy as a kind of misdirected seeing.[36] The devil tempts us with worldly goods, Virgil says, and we take the bait (14.147–51):

> e però poco val freno o richiamo.
> Chiamavi 'l cielo e 'ntorno vi si gira,
> mostrandovi le sue bellezze etterne,
> e l'occhio vostro pur a terra mira;
> onde vi batte chi tutto discerne.[37]

[And therefore rein or lure (literally "recall") is of little effect. The heavens call you and circle about you, showing you their eternal splendors, and your eye looks only on the ground; wherefore he who sees all smites you.]

For all the resemblances—the Cook certainly is a man who looks only to the ground, where he falls as if struck by the Manciple's malice, which one can easily believe is fueled by his envy—Chaucer may well have been most drawn by the allegorized irony of Dante's figure.[38] The heavens themselves

---

[35] "The Manciple, who, like the falcon, has been flying free and "stooping" upon the helpless Cook, is to be "reclaimed" when the Cook sobers up"; Baker, *Variorum*, p. 92. Of course, the figure also proleptically associates the Manciple with the crow of his tale; more important, it suggests that the Cook and Manciple are birds of a feather.

[36] Virgil here and throughout cantos 13 and 14 plays on a very common but false etymology of *invidia* as a form of lack of vision.

[37] I quote from Dante Alighieri, *The Divine Comedy: Purgatorio*, trans. Charles Singleton (Princeton, N.J.: Princeton University Press, 1973). I have altered Singleton's translation slightly to make it more literal.

[38] One should note in this regard that Virgil explains on this terrace the system of scourge and curb, the oppositions that govern penance throughout Purgatory. The scourge goads the penitents toward the virtue that is the contrary of the sin they must repent; the curb deters from the sin itself and so must be of contrary sound to the scourge. Since envy is purged here, "the cords of the whip are drawn from love" ("tratte d'amor le corde de la ferza" [*Purg.* 13.39]). The irony that makes love a whip is thus an allegory for those acts of envy that had perverted love in the first place; and the system of scourge and curb an allegory of the "connemsuration" that, for Aquinas, restores the balance that is justice.

Chaucer offsets the Manciple's advocacy of silence with the Parson's penitential meditation and its insistence on confession. As the greatest book on penance the Middle Ages produced, the *Purgatorio* would be an appropriate work for Chaucer to remember here, especially in light of the fact that, as Thomas Bestul says, penance itself "and the satisfaction for sin fulfill the divine requirement for justice," and Harry's metaphor of "reclamation" is essentially a figure of justice: "Chaucer's Parson's Tale and the Late-Medieval Tradition of Religious Meditation," *Speculum* 64 (1989): 600–19. Moreover, the example of charity that

here correspond to the spirals of the falcon, but in reverse. On earth the bird would descend in ever tighter swoops down to the lure or recall ("richiamo": compare Chaucer's "reclayme" [*ManP* 72]), but this is precisely the opposite way the soul should move. It should spiral upward as it journeys through the ever-increasing ambit of the spheres until finally it rests in the infinite point which is God. Instead we look at the earth. Dante simultaneously inverts the earthly valency of down and up and transcends direction and geometry entirely in locating the "richiamo" in God, whose center is everywhere and circumference nowhere. But one need not claim Chaucer took the image from Dante to see that it counterbalances the Manciple's hoodwinking of the masters of his temple, many of whom would have been members of at least the gentry, if not the upper aristocracy.[39] The very class whose efficacy as instruments of equity and truth the Manciple has called into question provides both the practice and the language whereby the Manciple's hypocrisy may be uncovered and rightfully judged.

Though the cunning Manciple would strike his fellow servant to the earth with his tongue, he is brought up short; in the face of the Host's challenge to his own probity, he now attempts a volte-face and would "eat and drink with the drunkards." The Manciple implies he would cancel his previous slander of the Cook by maintaining he was joking—"I seyde it in my bourde" (*ManP* 81)—and as if to prove this, offers the Cook a propitiatory pourboire of wine. But the antiphrastic spirit never sleeps in him: here's "a good jape," (line 84) he says, as he calls for the pilgrims to witness how the Cook, despite his earlier avowal that he would rather sleep than drink, will become the butt of his joke by drinking again.

In offering Roger his gourd, the Manciple, both in his professional identity and as a man, acts most like himself. Again he speaks in two voices apparently at odds with each other. The man who slandered Roger, he claims, was not really he; yet the man who speaks now is the man he has

---

prompts Virgil's explanation is the miracle at Cana, which will figure in the Manciple's offer of wine to the Cook.

[39] The Inns of Court were a "frequent source of education for the aristocracy"; Christopher Dyer, *Standards of Living in the Later Middle Ages* (Cambridge: Cambridge University Press, 1989), p. 75. From the twelfth century on, lawyers increasingly were members of the gentry; see E. W. Ives, *The Common Lawyers of Pre-Reformation England* (Cambridge: Cambridge University Press, 1983), pp. 322–29. The great stewards mentioned in *The General Prologue* might well have been royal retainers; see J. R. Maddicott, *Law and Lordship: Royal Justices as Retainers in Thirteenth- and Fourteenth-Century England*, *Past and Present, Supplement* 4: 1978. We can imagine that the Manciple developed his scorn for the upper classes from his contact with the lawyers of his Inn.

just denied—if he was joking before, he will joke again now. Again the Manciple cynically stages a conversion in which nothing is converted; as in his first intervention, his mocking oblation here is one in which a false show of charity for the Cook becomes an occasion for public ridicule of him. And yet again, the Manciple's sarcasm evokes an allegorical context: his actions recall Jesus' first miracle, the transformation of water into wine at the wedding in Cana.

After Mary told Jesus that the wine had failed, Jesus ordered six stone jars, used in Jewish rituals of purification, to be filled with water. He then commanded some liquid be drawn from them and brought to the steward of the feast ("architriclinus," or "chief steward" in the Douai-Rheims translation), who did not know what it was. When the steward tasted it, he went to the bridegroom and said (John 2:10):

Every man at first setteth forth good wine, and when men have well drunk, then that which is worse. But thou hast kept the good wine until now.

This event receives its gloss in Jesus' famous admonitions about the proper times to indulge and to fast (Mt. 9:15, 17; cf. Mark 2:22, Luke 5:37):

Can the children of the bridegroom mourn, as long as the bridegroom is with them? But the days will come, when the bridegroom shall be taken away from them, and then they shall fast.

Neither do they put new wine into old bottles. Otherwise the bottles break, and the wine runneth out, and the bottles perish. But new wine they put in new bottles: and both are preserved.

As in the parable in Luke, John's steward becomes the agent through whom we experience the irony of the eschaton. From Augustine on, this miracle has been read as a mark of temporal continuity and spiritual rupture. The old dispensation remains but is fulfilled by the new, yet as the steward makes clear, if not to himself then to those who understand, the new order turns the old inside out. For in the eternal dispensation, according to Augustine, Jesus is the bridegroom, whose miraculous marriage to the soul redeems it from sin; he is the wine that makes the water of the old prophecies fruitful.[40] The same lesson is taught by the figure of new wine in old bottles: while we still reckon years by history's calendar, it is appropriate to preserve both new and old wine, for it is fitting that now one, now the other be drunk. But when one looks toward the end of days, only the spiritual wine of fasting should be drunk: old bottles and new both will crack, if all they contain is wine.

In *The Canterbury Tales*, the Manciple and Cook ironically repeat each other: they both remain what they are. The gourd the Manciple proffers to make his joke is filled with worse wine, for it is the wine of spite; when the Cook drinks it, he merely will get drunk again.[41] At Bobbe-up-and-doun, however, Chaucer, by impersonating both, writes a narrative of choice, which represents that moment when the soul sinks or swims. Even if the Cook is a man who, muddle-brained, would stumble his way through an epiphany, and the Manciple the man who would shut his eyes to it, their actions outreach their intentions. The kitchen economics that link these servants and perhaps account for their rivalry yield to the economics of redemption, in which true opposites are established forever.[42] Despite their

---

[40] Augustine, *Tractatus in Iohannis Evangelium*, tractatus 8 & 9 (*PL* 35:1450–1466). Augustine explicitly sees the miracle as an allegory of history in the form of language, specifically prophecy. The six jars stand for the six ages of the world; Jesus was foreshadowed as the defining event of each age in the prophetic waters of the Old Testament; the miracle at Cana shows that Jesus' coming is both a natural miracle—in the way that the rain nurturing the vines marvellously becomes wine each year ("Sicut enim quod miserunt ministri in hydrias in vinum conversum est opere Domini, sic et quod nubes fundunt in vinum convertitur eiusdem opere Domini" [8.1])—and a miracle that transcends nature and history, performed to show Jesus is God, outside time and place. Miracles themselves embody the irony of allegory.

[41] As Andrew Galloway has shown, the setting of the miracle, the wedding at Cana, became the event from which writers of marriage sermons throughout the Middle Ages drew their counsels. Wyclif, for instance, repeats Augustine's interpretation, but places it in the context of marriage; *Johannis Wyclif Sermones*, in Iohann Loserth, ed., *Wyclif's Latin Works* (London: Trübner, 1887), pars I, sermo 9, 1:78–86. "Nuptiae factae sunt" sermons in fact were widely disseminated; Galloway has argued convincingly that one sequence by Jacobus de Voragine, which survives in twenty-two late medieval copies of English provenance, closely parallels many features of the Wife of Bath's own discussion of marriage; "Marriage Sermons, Polemical Sermons, and *The Wife of Bath's Prologue*: A Generic Excursus," *SAC* 14 (1992): 3–30. In his tale, the Manciple draws on some of the propositions of these sermons, which uphold the institution of marriage and have good things as well as bad to say about women; but unlike them, the Manciple's points are characteristically all uniformly negative. For him, marriage seems no more than an invitation to adultery, woman's nature (and man's) being no different from the "lewedeste" she-wolf's (*ManT* 183–86).

[42] The Manciple is "wise in byynge of vitaille" (*GP* 569): his vigilance is such that whether he bought with ready payment or on credit, he was "ay biforn" in his purchases (line 572). The Cook, who probably also buys the food he prepares for the parvenu guildsmen who employ him, is "al bihynde" (*ManP* 7) the pilgrims at Bobbe-up-and-doun. Certainly

motives, the wine that the Manciple has brought to the Cook, by establishing amity where there had been wrath, is better than the wine Roger had drunk the night before.

Harry Bailly seems to realize this; like Chaucer he acknowledges the Manciple's joke, but completely inverts the spirit that prompted it (*ManP* 95–100):

> I se wel it is necessarie,
> Where that we goon, good drynke with us carie;
> For that wol turne rancour and disese
> T'acord and love, and many a wrong apese.
> O Bacus, yblessed be thy name,
> That so kanst turnen ernest into game!

Harry's irony is gentle and recuperative; his bemusement at this "miracle" perfectly matches Chaucer's wonder at the Manciple's wit: "Now is nat that of God a ful fair grace" (*GP* 573). The Host, of course, is in a good position to know the goodness of the wine, even if the Manciple, like the chief steward at Cana, does not. Harry, after all, will undertake to be manciple to the pilgrims, who have appointed him to "sette a soper at a certeyn pris" (*GP* 815) to reward the teller of the best tale. So it is appropriately ironic that by recognizing Bacchus as the god of sociability, who provides good spirits that preserve the community as they journey to Canterbury, Harry distinguishes himself from the Manciple, whose service is divisive because it only serves himself. The accord and love the Host ascribes to Bacchus, however, Chaucer's readers might ultimately see as attributes of a different

---

Roger is less the Manciple's opposite than his fraternal twin if he is anything like the cooks Langland accuses, along with brewers, bakers, and butchers, of harming the poor by cheating them through fraud: "For þise aren men on þis molde þat moste harme worcheth / To þe pore peple þat parcel-mele buggen" (*Piers Plowman* B.3.80–81). As Bennett explains, it was easy for these tradesmen "to give short weight or measure on small portions, and as the poor can only buy thus, they chiefly suffer"; *Piers Plowman*, ed. J. A. W. Bennett (Oxford: Clarendon Press, 1972), p. 137.

In this regard, Frederick Tupper, *Types of Society in Medieval Literature* (New York: Holt, 1926), pp. 100–102, argued that the enmity between manciples and cooks was traditional. F. N. Robinson cautiously accepted Tupper's "evidence," which has made the conventionality of the rivalry a staple of criticism ever since; *The Works of Geoffrey Chaucer*, 2d ed. (Boston: Houghton Mifflin, 1957), p. 763. In fact, Tupper's evidence is only his inference. Since citations from the *NED* show that manciples and cooks were both involved with the buying and selling of victuals, Tupper assumed they would cross horns. Professional rivalry almost certainly underlies the quarrel, but the spat seems attributable rather more to Chaucer than to convention.

deity, whose godhead, revealed in an even more miraculous birth, and transubstantiated in a different kind of wine, serves as the foundation of a perfect communion. *Flies off to the Bible at every opportunity*

IV

Harry's grateful observation that Bacchus can turn "ernest into game," of course, pointedly employs terms Chaucer has used throughout *The Canterbury Tales* to define its status as a work of fiction; their appearance here signals that beyond shaping the personal drama of the pilgrims' interchanges, what I will call the parabolic affiliation of irony and allegory in the *Prologue* to *The Manciple's Tale* is a central element of Chaucer's poetic practice. Because irony and allegory enable character and event to speak in more than one voice, to say "I" and "Not-I" as well as "I" and "Other-than-I" at once, they together do constitute a rhetoric of motive and action in the *Tales*, a rhetoric that Chaucer foregrounds when his poem nears its end. As an agency of impersonation, irony is explicitly associated with the Manciple in *The General Prologue*; in the *Prologue* to his tale, it becomes a principle of negation, the Manciple's trope of self-affirmation through the annulment of others. But in Harry Bailly's mouth, as in Chaucer's, irony does otherwise: it is transformed into a principle that draws concord out of discord, community out of rivalry. Irony likewise generates a structure for what the pilgrims do, as it has for what and how they speak: the Manciple's censure of the Cook would unknit the pilgrims as a group; the Host's censure of both Manciple and Cook reunites them. These moments, though contradictory, also complement each other, for between them the Cook has toppled from his horse and has been remounted through the common efforts of the pilgrims. In this fall and rise, all oppositions of blood and mire cease merely to oppose; the Cook, Manciple, Harry, all the pilgrims, have become more than themselves by becoming figures in allegories of conversion. Beyond composing events that run counter to one another, irony has been extended into a narrative of its own. The Manciple's desire to alienate and make dumb becomes the occasion for Chaucer to demonstrate that in the "book of the tales of Caunterbury," writing all along has been filled with the plenitude of polysemy.

As much as any pilgrim, the Manciple exemplifies what H. Marshall Leicester has called the disenchanted self; indeed, in an irony Max Weber could have appreciated, it is precisely the Manciple's corrosive, calculating cynicism that encourages us to think him less the representation of an autonomous human being than an agency of disillusionment per se.[43] He tricks his masters not so much for self-gain as to pit his "lewed" wit against their "lerned" wisdom, levelling the difference between honest stewardship and fraudulent service in the process. When accused of keeping crooked accounts, he admits the charge in order to imply it is false: with the Manciple, truth-telling becomes a way to maintain a lie; confession is made the accessory of secrecy. He is the kind of man who, in his tale, would make a fabliau the occasion for a sermon, and a sermon the occasion to preach a gospel of silence: he is the kind of man who would say again and again that the truth is better left unsaid.[44] Through the Manciple we see that neither language nor propriety can stand outside the motives of those who use it and are used by it: in his tale he shows how the courtliest terms can camouflage the basest acts, how the most moral-sounding discourse can urge complete disengagement from ethical responsibility. Through the Manciple we discover that every system and institution, however much it

---

[43] H. Marshall Leicester, *The Disenchanted Self* (Berkeley: University of California Press, 1990). In his introduction (pp. 14–28), Leicester significantly expands Max Weber's notion of disenchantment to distinguish selfhood from subjectivity.

[44] *The Manciple's Tale* was I think first characterized as a fabliau by H. E. Ussery, *Chaucer's Physician: Medicine and Literature in the Fourteenth Century*, Tulane Studies in English, no. 19 (New Orleans: Tulane Dept. of English, 1971), pp. 130–34. It has been called a sermon by John Fyler, *Chaucer and Ovid* (New Haven, Conn.: Yale University Press, 1979), p. 155. Both I think are right, in that the *Tale* harnesses the impulses of each genre to cancel the expectations of the other. Richard Hazelton, "The Manciple's Tale": Parody and Critique," *JEGP* 62 (1963): 1–31, has characterized it as a moral fable; this too is right, since, as antiphrastic counterpart to the Nun's Priest's tale, the Manciple's carefully maligns both morality and fable.

Beyond this, it is worthwhile to point out that the Manciple's desire to replace interpretation with silence is directly related to his embodiment of irony. As Teskey says, irony's disposition with respect to interpretation is completely negative: "There is nothing objectively there to interpret"; "Irony," p. 399. In Chaucer, of course, the irony of the Manciple's peroration is its prolixity: the pullulation of authorities who all counsel curbing the tongue turns the call for muteness into the riot of commentary that is the mark of allegory.

Donald Baker ably summarizes the large literature that assesses the *Prologue* and *Tale* to 1981; see *Variorum*, pp. 19–38. Among the essays that deal with language, of special note are the following: Wayne Shumaker, "Chaucer's *Manciple's Tale* as Part of a Canterbury Group," *UTQ* 22 (1953): 147–56; Britton Harwood, "Language and the Real: Chaucer's Manciple," *ChauR* 6 (1972): 268–79; V. J. Scattergood, "The Manciple's Manner of Speaking," *EIC* 24 (1974): 124–46. Since Baker's survey, a number of important studies have appeared: Chauncey Wood, "Speech, the Principle of Contraries, and Chaucer's Tales of the Manciple and the Parson," *Mediaevalia* 6 (1980): 209–27; Louise Fradenburg, "The Manciple's Servant Tongue: Politics and Poetry in *The Canterbury Tales*," *ELH* 52 (1985): 85–118; James Dean, "Dismantling the Canterbury Book," *PMLA* 100 (1985): 746–62; Mark Allen, "Penitential Sermons, the Manciple, and the End of *The Canterbury Tales*," *SAC* 9 (1987): 77–96; John Hill, *Chaucerian Belief* (New Haven, Conn.: Yale University Press, 1991), pp. 63–76.

offers itself as a reflection of an ideal order, always is realized by the social practice of those who constitute it: in the wrong hands, chivalry is nothing more than the exercise of brute force, courtesy an incitement to adultery, and stewardship, instead of being the bulwark of the good society, becomes the means of assuring its corruption from within.

The Manciple's identity is premised on these effects; he becomes a character when we assign them a motive, when we say he is a person who creates contraries in order to cancel one of them. The Manciple indeed embodies irony, but an irony that imperils the entire project of *The Canterbury Tales*, since, as we have seen, it cancels the subjectivity of the character it impersonates by robbing it of its voice. Irony, however, is by nature self-reflexive; because it does not silence the object that it declares null and void without also relocating that denial in the denier, the Manciple cannot escape becoming its victim. If nothing else, the Manciple delivers his moral exhortations at the end of his tale in the belief that his cynicism has freed him from the mystifications it has exposed. But in the *Prologue*, the Manciple has depended equally on mystification to present himself. Like the steward in Luke, the Manciple will no longer be manciple if he is accused unto his masters; he therefore most bespeaks who he is when, to make sure his thieving remains undiscovered, he acknowledges, jokingly to be sure, that Harry's charge of malfeasance is true. As in the portrait in *The General Prologue*, the Manciple's "true self" is the revelation of a concealment that continues to remain concealed, an admission of defects in his accounts that he neither admits nor compensates. Though the Manciple claims he is "noght textueel" (*ManP* 235), we find his personality based not in the "presence" of voice but in the absence and deflections of writing. As befits a man who means the opposite of what he says and does, the Manciple stands in opposition to himself: he has no inner being of his own that can be divulged, for he exists as the record of his deceiving others.

Within the social world of *The Canterbury Tales*, however, Chaucer undoes the Manciple's irony *through* impersonation, by relating his voice to others, both like and unlike his own, to create a discourse in which antiphrasis is a species of polysemy. When the Manciple speaks for the Cook in excusing him from telling a tale, he reduces Roger to speechlessness. After the Cook has fallen, however, Harry Bailly speaks for him, with opposite effect. Yet this is the same Harry who early in the pilgrimage had bickered with the Cook and seemed ready to resume the game here in the Manciple's spirit of mockery. But the words Harry actually says to "reclaim" the Manciple are modeled not only on the steward's exchange with the Cook but on words Roger himself had previously addressed to Harry. After all, it was Hogge of Ware who had said, in response to the Host's baiting, "sooth pley, quaad pley" [*CkP* 4357] ("a true jest is no jest"), and who then promised, as V. A. Kolve says, that if Harry "comes too near the truth about cooks, he may have to hear some home truths about innkeepers before the journey is over."[45]

Indeed, the Cook's horsemanship recalls so vividly the drunken "chyvachee" (*ManP* 50) of the Miller (*MilP* 3120–21) that the quarrel between Robyn and the Reeve seems a country version of the city squabble that the Manciple and Roger replay here. We sense that the end of *The Canterbury Tales* reiterates the beginning: Fragment 9, at least, repeats Fragment 1.[46] Certainly a circle of sinners is joined, leading from the Miller and Reeve to the Manciple, whose portrait stands between theirs in *The General Prologue*.[47] Nor is it accidental that the tales they tell seem as connected to each other as they do. If, as Lee Patterson has argued, *The Miller's Tale* constitutes a critique of the aristocratic construction of chivalric identity,[48] if the Reeve's response puts sex inside and out of marriage in the service of envy and revenge, if the Cook's tale would turn a profit on adultery, the Manciple manages in his *Prologue* and *Tale* to cast a jaundicing eye not only on genteel values and the idea of a stable identity but on the very possibility of faithful relations or a justice that rewards and punishes according to the canons of truthfulness.

Again, however, repetition in Chaucer everywhere generates meaningful, as well as contradictory, oppositions. Both the Miller and the Manciple would exercise Harry's authority to determine who should tell the next tale; but whereas before, the Host in exasperation had yielded to the Miller's drunken insistence, he now successfully retains his prerogative by permitting the Manciple to substitute for the drunk Cook. And whereas the Reeve, who is a bailiff, had tried to call the "thrice-tolling" Miller to

[45] V. A. Kolve, *Chaucer and the Imagery of Narrative* (Stanford: Stanford University Press, 1984), p. 267.

[46] In this regard see Donald Howard, *The Idea of the Canterbury Tales* (Berkeley: University of California Press, 1976), pp. 303–4.

[47] The Miller leads the pilgrims "out of towne" (*GP* 566); the Reeve always "rood the hyndreste of oure route" (*GP* 622); the Cook has fallen "al bihynde" (*ManP* 7), which prompts the Manciple to tell the last tale before the Parson's. With Miller and Reeve, Cook and Manciple, it makes no difference whether the first shall be last, or the last first. In the case of the Manciple and Parson, the last of the fiction-tellers remains last even when he speaks first.

[48] Lee Patterson, *Chaucer and the Subject of History* (Madison: University of Wisconsin Press, 1991), pp. 244–79.

account (*GP* 562) because he wished to prosecute a quarrel between Robyn and himself, the "baillie" named Harry here composes his quarrel with the Cook by calling attention to the Manciple's "rekenynges."[49] As a swindling recordkeeper himself given to preaching ("The devel made a reve for to preche," says Harry [*RvP* 3903]), the hypocritical Reeve is closely related to the moralizing Manciple; in *The Manciple's Prologue*, however, the corrupt steward—who, as his initial words to Harry reveal, would be friends with that not-so-evil-mammon so that he might be received into his inn—finds himself checked by the crafty publican, a child of this world who is equally concerned that his accounts show a profit.[50] Harry is the Manciple's alter ego; he also is his nemesis.

In the frame of the *Tales*, this backward- and forward-looking polyphony of personal relations equates characters who in their particular settings begin and end in the antinomies of rivalry. These antinomies then are reinscribed as the données that propel the fabliaux the Miller, Reeve, Cook, and Manciple tell. As a group these tales circumscribe a large part of the social world of the poem, a world of often contradictory motives that Chaucer represents under the trope of irony; for whatever else it is, the social in *The Canterbury Tales* is never less than the style that simultaneously registers its antagonisms and constructs from them a network of similarities. Even the tales that seem to stand outside this circle, those of the Knight and Parson, are part of its circumference through contrariety. The Miller announces with all the fustian of "Pilates voys" (*MilP* 3124) that he will "quite" the Knight's tale (line 3127), which he does by brilliantly debunking its courtly, aristocratic pretensions. But by tilting with the Knight, the Miller ironically copies the rivalry of Palamon and Arcite in the Knight's tale. Robyn may mock them, but they have established a

[49] On Harry as bailiff, see *MED* s.v. *baillie* and *bailiff*. See further Linda Georgianna, "Love So Dearly Bought: The Terms of Redemption in *The Canterbury Tales*," *SAC* 12 (1990): 85–116. Her remarks on penance in general and on the notion of reckoning in particular are especially pertinent to my argument here. Also relevant is the legal notion of an action of account. As Elizabeth Dobbs says, in the case of a lord and his bailiff, such an action "compels the latter to account for the profits of the manor" (p. 36); "Literary, Legal, and Last Judgments in *The Canterbury Tales*," *SAC* 14 (1992): 31–52. Like the Reeve, the Manciple is in an accountable relationship. The idea of justifying one's accounts is central to the exchange between Harry and the Manciple.

[50] In this regard, it is of interest to note that in the Wycliffite Bible, the steward of Luke's parable is asked to "ȝelde reckynyng of thi baili" (16:2); cited in Georgianna, "Love So Dearly Bought," p. 104. Luke's use of the figure of childhood to describe both the worldly and the spiritual perhaps also lies behind Chaucer's depiction of himself as poet. Lee Patterson has argued that Chaucer's references to himself as "elvyssh" and "a popet" in the *Prologue to Sir Thopas* represent him as a child; "'What Man Artow?': Authorial Self-Definition in *The Tale of Sir Thopas* and *The Tale of Melibee*," *SAC* 11 (1989): 117–75.

paradigm that remains intact, by which we judge his exchanges with the Host and the Reeve.[51] In the same way, even as the Parson sets himself apart from the Manciple and all other fabulists, the affiliations that relate him to his fellow tale-tellers only grow stronger. With perhaps the Miller's fervor, though certainly with precisely the opposite intent, the Parson says that unlike the Manciple's tale of the crow, the pilgrims will get "fable noon" from him (*ParsP* 30–31).[52] But after suffering through the Manciple's sermon, when we "turne over the leef, and chese another tale" (*MilP* 3177), we find that the Parson, who says he is "nat textueel" (*ParsP* 57) and not inclined to "glose" (line 45), is directly related to the Manciple, who has already declared his "untextuality" and disposition not to "glose." The spiritual steward is everything his too worldly counterpart is not. Therefore, it is no surprise at all that by preaching about ultimate reckonings, the Parson provides the final textual gloss not only on the Manciple's defalcations but on Harry's concern that all debts are marked paid as well: on the day of judgment, the Parson says, everyone

". . . shal yeven acountes," as saith Seint Bernard, "of alle the goodes that han be yeven hym in this present lyf, and how he hath hem despended, / [in] so muche that ther shal nat perisse an heer of his heed, ne a moment of an houre ne shal nat perisse of his tyme, that he ne shal yeve of it a rekenyng." (*ParsT* 252–53)

The dissembling Manciple would bring all tale-telling to an end in silence; the Parson believes we will all be forced, like the Manciple's model in Luke's parable, to justify our stewardship.[53] Everywhere, the Manciple is countered by a host of other voices that, sometimes in his own words, speak everything he would leave unconfessed.

This polyphony often gives intertextuality in *The Canterbury Tales* the structure of irony, an irony, however, in which opposites can fully negate one or the other but can also themselves be translated into something else. Of all the voices that intermix with and counteract the Manciple's, therefore, the most powerful, and the one most at risk, should be Chaucer's. With typical effect, the Manciple, by adopting the narrator's stance toward

[51] If the Cook is in fact Roger Knight of Ware, as Edith Rickert has suggested ("Chaucer's Hodge of Ware," *TLS*, 20 Oct. 1932, p. 761), the verbal polyphony I am discussing here becomes that much more complex.

[52] To Harry's demand for a fable, "for cokkes bones," the Parson responds "al atones" (*ParsP* 29–30). Compare the Miller's opening words: "By armes, and by blood and bones" (*MilP* 3125).

[53] The Parable of the Wicked Steward was in fact most often interpreted as an allegory of man's failings as God's steward; Wailes, *Medieval Allegories*, p. 248.

language, does indeed severely threaten to invalidate Chaucer's repeated apologiae for his fiction. If Chaucer has sought to avoid responsibility for the tales he will rehearse by claiming he will be a false "compilator" unless "the wordes . . . be cosyn to the dede" (*GP* 742), the Manciple, who also seeks to avoid responsibility for the false records he reports, similarly claims he is compelled to speak the unvarnished truth.[54] Just as Chaucer had before him, he appeals to a dictum he ascribes to Plato to ask forgiveness for calling an adulterous noblewoman a wench (*ManT* 208–10):

> The word moot nede accorde with the dede.
> If men shal telle proprely a thyng,
> The word moot cosyn be to the werkyng.

Perhaps these resemblances are what made Chaucer reject entirely in the *Retraction* the "synne" and "greet folye" of fictions that

> . . . apeyren any man, or hym defame,
> And eek . . . bryngen wyves in swich fame. (*MilP* 3146–48)

These are the words the Reeve directs against the Miller before he tells his tale, but they apply even more to the Manciple; indeed, they make us recall the similar case of the Miller's proleptic self-exoneration for his performance, which Chaucer immediately repeats, absolving himself of blame for the "cherles tale" of "harlotrie" by making his readers answerable for it (*MilP* 3169, 3184–86):[55]

> Avyseth yow, and put me out of blame;
> And eek men shal nat maken ernest of game.

But just as the Miller's crying in "Pilates voys" had already established a different register in which all possibility of washing one's hands of liability has been eliminated (even as it brilliantly foreshadows the crucial role

[54] The idea of Chaucer as "compilator" everywhere except in the *Retraction*, where he is "auctor," is Minnis'; *Medieval Theory of Authorship*, pp. 206–10. Lawton, "Chaucer's Two Ways," reads *The Parson's Tale* on the supposition that a compiler, who may have been Chaucer, placed it at the end of *The Canterbury Tales*.

[55] The similarities between the Miller and the Manciple are striking. The Miller "unnethe upon his hors he sat," "nolde avalen neither hood ne hat, / Ne abyde no man for his curteisie" (*MilP* 3121–23); of the lawyers he serves, the Manciple "sette hir aller cappe" (*GP* 586), and though he does "abyde" Harry's "curteisie," he does so in order to make the Cook tumble from his horse.

water will play in the *Tale*), Chaucer has created perspectives here that likewise ironically render him more accountable for everything he has written. He admits double responsibility for the Manciple, first by having made his own ironic attitude synonymous with the Manciple's in *The General Prologue*, and then by turning irony into its opposite: by making it, in accordance with rhetorical precept, an allegory in the *Prologue* to *The Manciple's Tale*.

As the pilgrimage nears Canterbury, the covenant Chaucer forges between irony and allegory more and more becomes the subtext of his discourse. We can see how much it preoccupied Chaucer's attention if we accept the Ellesmere order and consider the last tales a sequence. The Second Nun introduces her life of Saint Cecilia, itself a narrative of conversion, by allegorizing the martyr's name. Little wonder, then, that her hagiography is coupled with *The Canon's Yeoman's Tale*, in which alchemy proves to be essentially ironic, both as language and as practice, because it is a failed allegory for the conversion of matter.[56] Indeed, in alchemical treatises, the "multiplication" of technical terms for the "conversion" of the elements was explicitly associated with the hermeneutics of biblical allegory; the language of *The Canon's Yeoman's Tale* thus is the inverted image of the "doubled" speech of *The Manciple's Prologue*, in which irony unfolds into an allegory of conversion.[57] The Parson, of course, would convert even allegory's figurations into the abstract, univocal language of sacramental penance; but as he pursues rationally the goal that the Second Nun had represented in affective terms, his tale makes conversion itself part of a larger allegory of penance. His "meditacioun" is the verbal act of satisfaction that ironically transmutes the Manciple's mockery of confession, and the alchemical Canon's Yeoman's half-contrition of heart before it, into a narrative of salvation.

We might well call this burgeoning of the spiritual out of the material and social Chaucer's Canterbury poetics; it is proper that Chaucer should explicitly foreground the inner and outer constitution of his poetry at the

---

[56] On the linkage of *The Canon's Yeoman's Tale* and *The Second Nun's Tale*, see especially Joseph Grennan, "Saint Cecilia's 'Chemical Wedding': The Unity of the *Canterbury Tales*, Fragment VIII," *JEGP* 65 (1966): 466–81.

[57] On the association of alchemical language and spiritual hermeneutics, see Lee Patterson, "Perpetual Motion: Alchemy and the Technology of the Self," *SAC* 15 (1993): 25–57, esp. pp. 45–46. I would also note that the emphasis on blindness and sight in *The Second Nun's Tale* and on bleary vision in *The Canon's Yeoman's Tale* nicely prepare the ground for Chaucer's reconfiguration of Paul's conversion. As a result of the flashing light, of course, Saul was blinded three days; when he recovered his sight, he was Paul.

end of the *Tales*, because by doing so he simultaneously recovers and re-verses the opening of the poem, where allegory also converges with irony (*GP* 1–4):

> Whan that Aprill with his shoures soote
> The droghte of March hath perced to the roote,
> And bathed every veyne in swich licour
> Of which vertu engendred is the flour. . . .

Here again, but for the first time, the sacramental and natural are insepara-ble. April showers bring May flowers, but the rain, by answering to the metaphorical overtones of "perced" and "veyne," becomes the blood of Jesus, and this blood, which flowed with water after the spear had pierced his side, is, with the mention of "licour," transformed into the wine of Christian communion.[58] In like manner, the showers pierce the drought of March to the root (the word functions both naturally and metaphorically at once) before their virtue brings forth the flower: from death comes life, and the downward and upward motions of rain and flower are also the direc-tions of Christian salvation, of the Incarnation and Assumption. So too the showers' sweetness naturally modulates into the mildness of "bathed," which itself seems to call forth the idea of baptism, of waters giving life.

And what we learn from the first four lines of *The General Prologue*, the subsequent fourteen confirm (lines 5–18):

> Whan Zephirus eek with his sweete breeth
> Inspired hath in every holt and heeth
> The tendre croppes, and the yonge sonne
> Hath in the Ram his half cours yronne,
> And smale foweles maken melodye,
> That slepen al the nyght with open ye
> (So priketh hem nature in hir corages),
> Thanne longen folk to goon on pilgrimages,
> And palmeres for to seken straunge strondes,
> To ferne halwes, kowthe in sondry londes;
> And specially from every shires ende
> Of Engelond to Caunterbury they wende,
> The hooly blisful martir for to seke,
> That hem hath holpen whan that they were seeke.

---

[58] That "liquor" not only means "liquid" but "wine," especially "communion wine," is confirmed by the *MED*.

The syntax of "Whan Zephirus eek with his sweete breeth," which recalls that of the opening line—the repeated "whan," the equating "eek," the clear similitude of "shoures soote" and "sweete breeth"—all this encourages us to read the wind as we have read the rain. There is a spirit, natural and holy at once, that grows the crops, as the waters, and blood, and wine engender the flower. But there is a larger disposition at work here as well. As we move from the waters to the dry land (the "shoures" to the "roote"), from the plants (the "floures" and "tendre croppes") to the lights in the firmament (the "yonge sonne"), from the birds (the "smale foweles") to people ("Thanne longen folk"), Chaucer refashions for us the program of creation almost point for point as we find it in Genesis 1:9–31. *The Canterbury Tales*, in effect, begins with the third day, when the waters under heaven were gathered together and separated from the dry land. The earth then put forth vegetation, plants yielding seed, fruit trees bearing fruit. The next day God made the greater and lesser lights and set them in the firmament as signs for the seasons, days, and years. On the fifth day the waters brought forth living creatures, and God said, "Let birds fly above the earth." The sixth day, after creating creeping things, beasts, and cattle, God made man and woman.

Chaucer begins his book by suggesting there is an analogy between it and what he took to be the beginning of everything. *The Canterbury Tales* opens by invoking an earlier opening; its allegory partakes of both absolute and conditional origins at once. But, as Barbara Nolan has said, once Chaucer locates himself at the Tabard, the poem shifts to "the fallen, historical world, in which chance, change, unpredictability hold sway."[59] This social world is the realm where absolute and conditional stand in ironic opposition; it is the world where the saint's helping the sick becomes the Manciple's offer of "charity" (wine and all) to the indisposed Cook. It is a world whose style is irony, but an irony that at any time can be parabolic, because as deflected speech it is never other than a form of allegory; the Manciple guides the pilgrims precisely the way Luke would have his wicked steward guide the righteous to eternal tabernacles. And it is a world whose end simultaneously differs from and returns to its rhetorical origins, both in *The Manciple's Prologue* and even more in the *Prologue* to *The Parson's Tale*, where the sense of final balance and judgment implicit in Libra, of harvesting and separating the "whete" from the "draf" (lines 35–36), of knitting up the "feeste" (line 47), and being "fructuous, and that in

[59] Barbara Nolan, "'A Poet Ther Was': Chaucer's Voices in the General Prologue," *PMLA* 101 (1986): 159.

litel space" (line 71), all convey the hurry of a fast-approaching Apocalypse even as they harken back to the springtime fertility of the opening vision of *The General Prologue*.[60] *They do indeed*

Only *The Parson's Tale* and the *Retraction* stand apart. As I said earlier, the Parson's insistence that the language of penance be as univocal as the act would seem to make even the doubled speech of allegory an equivocation. But in establishing sin as a violation of the "ratio dei" throughout the entire "ordo" of the universe, the Parson's anatomy of penance cancels neither irony nor the fictive sociality of which I have argued it is the defining trope. Rather the Parson's prose seeks out all antinomies so that they may be incorporated into the univocality of salvation. Heaven is a state of "endelees blisse," the Parson says, "ther joye hath no contrarioustee of wo ne grevaunce" (*ParsT* 1075–76). Nevertheless,

This blisful regne may men purchase by poverte espiritueel, and the glorie by lowenesse, the plentee of joye by hunger and thurst, and the reste by travaille, and the lyf by deethe and mortificacion of synne. (line 1079)

Though set squarely in opposition to the poetry that precedes it, the intellective and nonreferential language of *The Parson's Tale* is neither logically nor stylistically discontinuous with that poetry;[61] indeed, it relies on a rhetoric of irony as much as the Manciple's sarcasm depends on a rhetoric of allegory. Even if it purchases its metaphors from the economics of Christian redemption, the language remains figurative, its sense parabolic. Derek Brewer has rightly said that Chaucer fashions his poetics out of the "collisions" between sacred and secular, learned and popular forms of

---

[60] One might also note in this regard the linkage between the Manciple's portrait, prologue, and tale and the Man of Law, whose tale may well have stood first at an early stage in the construction of the *Tales*. The Manciple is a thieving "achatour" of a temple whose lawyers match the eminence of Chaucer's none-too-honest "Sergeant of the Lawe," who also is a "purchasour" (*GP* 318), whose "purchasyng myghte nat been *infect*" (line 320; italics mine), and whose legal drafts were unimpeachable: "Therto he koude endite and make a thyng, / Ther koude no wight *pynche* at his writyng" (*GP* 325–26; italics mine). The stylistic reminiscences are striking: the Manciple says the Cook's stinking breath "infect wole us alle" (*ManP* 39); Harry cautions the Manciple that Roger will reclaim him if he were "to pynchen at thy rekenynges" (line 74). Moreover, lawyers like Chaucer's, who made money from their knowledge of positive law ("Al was fee symple to hym in effect" [*GP* 319]), were also characterized as children of this world: Richard of Bury (*Philobiblon*, 11) comments that "the more useful [knowledge of positive law] is to the children of this world, the less it assists the children of light"; quoted in D. W. Robertson, *Chaucer's London* (New York: Wiley, 1968), p. 204.
[61] See Lee Patterson, "The Parson's Tale and the Quitting of the *Canterbury Tales*," *Traditio* 34 (1978): 331–80.

knowledge and narrative; in that poetics, the Manciple and Parson represent two countervailing discourses, each of which presupposes the other.[62] In *The Canterbury Tales*, there is no getting around irony and allegory, nor ?
is there need to.[63] *What does this mean?*

Even in the *Retraction*, language hovers between the final silence of rejection and an all-encompassing embrace of speech. "'*Al* that is writen is writen for oure doctrine,'" says Chaucer, again quoting Paul, "and that is myn entente" (line 1082; italics added). Yet Chaucer then revokes those tales "that sownen into synne." Here is a contradiction that is more than contradiction. The repudiation is irrevocable: a fable like the Manciple's would be exactly the kind of "draf" the Parson rejects for the "whete" of "vertuous mateere" (*ParsP* 35–38). Yet by quoting Paul, Chaucer also quotes himself, since the Nun's Priest has used these words to justify another beast fable, similar to the Manciple's, but very different from it as well: "Taketh the fruyt, and lat the chaf be stille" (*NPT* 3443).[64] In the *Retraction*, Chaucer defends his fiction and disowns it in the same breath; the structure of opposition, however, is not ironic, but allegorical, because the oppositions are resolved in the univocality of Chaucer's intention. "'Al that is writen is writen for oure doctrine' . . . and that is myn entente." This is a language where one rejects what one includes, includes what one rejects. It is a language that makes the Manciple not simply the Parson's opposite but his fellow pilgrim as well. It is a language of heaven and earth; it is not at odds with that of *The Canterbury Tales*, but part of it.

---

[62] Derek Brewer, "Towards a Chaucerian Poetic," Sir Israel Gollancz Memorial Lecture, *Proceedings of the British Academy* 60 (1974): 219–52.

[63] See Carol Kaske's sensitive article, "Getting Around the Parson's Tale: An Alternative to Allegory and Irony," in R. H. Robbins, ed., *Chaucer at Albany* (New York: Franklin, 1975), pp. 146–77.

[64] On Chaucer's use of St. Paul here and elsewhere in the *Tales*, see Russell Peck, "Biblical Interpretation: St. Paul and the *Canterbury Tales*," in David L. Jeffrey, ed., *Chaucer and the Scriptural Tradition* (Ottawa: University of Ottawa Press, 1984), pp. 143–70.

The Summoner and the Abominable Anatomy of Antichrist

Alan J. Fletcher
University College, Dublin

I

The force that lies behind Frederic Jameson's maxim "always historicize," that is, its insistence on the ineluctability of the historical moment in which all cultural products participate, has been taken self-consciously to heart by Chaucer critics of late.[1] If their acts of historically aware interpretation acquire theoretical rigor as a result, so much the better, but still there is no escaping the unavoidable corollary, the spadework that has to be done at the same time the maxim is being applied. If it is left undone, interpretation may find that it marches on an empty stomach.[2] Thus a critic's perusal of a text in isolation is bound to prove relatively fruitless, since from the historicist point of view the interesting aspect of its textual life is seen to inhere less in some notion of its transhistorical value than in its momentary, historically contingent, and evanescent significances, its stance vis-à-vis its contemporary culture and all those other texts through which that culture was mediated.

Bearing in mind the historicist mandate, then (whatever the shortcomings here in my pursuit of it), this discussion will have twin aims. It will attempt to excavate layers of meaning in *The Summoner's Prologue* and *Tale* that would have been more readily available to Chaucer's contemporaries. If

[1] Frederic Jameson, *The Political Unconscious* (Ithaca, N.Y.: Cornell University Press, 1981), p. 9, and invoked by Lee Patterson, ed., *Literary Practice and Social Change in Britain 1380–1530* (Berkeley: University of California Press, 1990), p. 1. The currently prevailing awareness that acts of interpretation, as much as the objects they seek to interpret, are themselves historical products, is to be welcomed.

[2] I take as exemplary, for instance, Michel Foucault's insistent predication of his theoretical inferences upon painstaking surveys of data. A historicizing critic will inevitably need to engage with a wealth of texts, in fact with all those texts that can either be shown or safely assumed to constitute the textual environment of the text for which explication is sought. While this may remain, in practice, an unreachable counsel of perfection, it remains, for all that, an authoritative one.

the requisite spadework unearths results that seem convincing, the second aim will follow automatically. This is to issue a general caution against some recent Chaucer criticism professing itself historicist but which, in being haunted by a certain economy of labor, is reduced in its usefulness. A general case will also therefore be implicit in my commentary on a particular Canterbury Tale: theoretically informed readings of texts are all very well, but they are accompaniments to, not substitutes for, the encounter with the network of writings, many of which are still unpublished, in whose company alone individual texts assume their significance.

II

The working out of the preposterous conceit of the eternal abode of the friars—their infestation of the arse of the devil—preoccupies the narrative space of the *Prologue* to *The Summoner's Tale* almost to the exclusion of all else. There is little doubt but that the *Prologue* is fully absorbed with its joke-telling. Tolerating no narrative digression, its movement toward the anal profanity of its punch line is linear and remorselessly developed. The design of the jest, therefore, if we may regard it for a moment in purely formal terms, draws a singular attention to itself.

There are, of course, many ways in which the emphatic positioning and formal focus on the joke can be resolved into larger readings of the *Tale*. For example, anyone sensitive to the dramatic interplay between the pilgrims may choose to regard it as the vector of the Summoner's antipathy to the Friar, an opening gambit the utter preoccupation of which is an index of the Summoner's depth of feeling; others, interested in the way the joke anticipates concerns in the *Tale* it introduces, may discover in its formal focus a powerful opening salvo of the thematic anality that is to reverberate throughout the *Tale*. Whichever way readers prefer to weight their various responses, the sheer formal emphasis on the *Prologue*'s joke, the common ground from which their various responses stem, is an objective matter that remains beyond question. This emphasis invites reciprocally careful critical attention to the joke's peculiar lineaments; indeed, the attempt of one critic to afford it such attention has therefore every justification.[3] But the joke of the *Prologue*, as I hope to show, while singlemindedly pursued, repays the attention that it may invite with a multiple resonance and interpretative possibilities exceeding the interpretations hitherto framed to contain it.

[3] John V. Fleming, "The Summoner's Prologue: An Iconographic Adjustment," *ChauR* 2 (1967): 95–107.

The conceit of anal residence, as Brusendorff noted, appears in remark-ably few known written versions.[4] The sole parallel that he knew, in fact, in the C Fragment of *The Romaunt of the Rose* (lines 7575–77), finds Dame Abstinence reproving Wicked Tongue with a warning that "thou shalt for this synne dwelle / Right in the devels ers of helle, / But if that thou repente thee."[5] Here, the Old French underlying the Middle English of the *Romaunt* reads "cul d'enfer," which in its French context probably priori-tized the sense "pit" (rather than "arse") "of hell," as indeed other French variants which read the less ambiguous "puis" ("pit," "well"), rather than "cul," imply. It seems conceivable that an awareness of a traditional liaison between those who were especially wicked—hypocrites and heretics in this case—and the devil's arse may already have been in the Middle English translator's mind, nudging him towards his particular translation choice of "ers" for "cul." His translation, with Chaucer's text, may stand as another witness to the existence of some such liaison, if indeed he had not already derived the idea from reading Chaucer.

This single case outside Chaucer provides *The Summoner's Prologue* with slender analogical company, however.[6] Where else was the idea of anal consorting current, if we are to take as having any substance the Sum-moner's claim that his audience has heard about this matter before (*SumP* 1675–77)? Since written analogues have proved so exiguous, recourse has been had to a comparable motif in art.[7] For example, the devil voids damned souls in Giotto's frescoes for the Arena chapel, Padua.[8] For reasons

[4] Aage Brusendorff, *The Chaucer Tradition* (Oxford: Oxford University Press, 1925), p. 411, n. 3.

[5] All citations of Chaucer's works are from Larry D. Benson, gen. ed., *The Riverside Chaucer*, 3d ed. (Boston: Houghton Mifflin, 1987).

[6] And see Theodore Spencer, "Chaucer's Hell: A Study in Mediæval Convention," *Speculum* 2 (1927): 177–200; on p. 196, he observes that the residence of the friars was "pretty familiar to mediæval imagination," though outside Chaucer there are no written examples of it. He cites by way of parallel a case in the vision of Tundale (V.-H. Friedel and Kuno Meyer, ed., *La vision de Tundale (Tnudgal)* [Paris: Champion, 1907], pp. 25–27) where souls of monks and canons are swallowed by a hideous beast, then excreted into a frozen lake; but he notes that the beast is not Satan, nor are the souls permanent residents in its anus. Comparable ingestions of souls, followed by their vomiting or excretion, might also be noted in *Sawles Warde*, where Fear describes how in hell there are "iteilede draken, grisliche ase deoflen, þe forswolheð ham [i.e., souls] ihal ant speoweð ham eft ut biuoren ant bihinden" (Bella Millett and Jocelyn Wogan-Browne, eds., *Medieval Religious Prose for Women* [Oxford: Clarendon Press, 1990], p. 90, lines 34–36). But all these cases are only partial analogues.

[7] Fleming, "Iconographic Adjustment," p. 95.

[8] Giotto's iconography has been thought to have been inspired by the thirteenth-century mosaics of the Duomo's baptistry in Florence (though there defecation seems not in question). Other examples include Francisco Traini's frescoes of the Last Judgment in Pisa.

that will later become clear, speculation on whether Chaucer, in his Italian travels, actually witnessed any of these depictions seems superfluous, but whether or not he was directly inspired by Italian art, the existence there of a hellish punishment loosely comparable to that of *The Summoner's Prologue* suggests again, as the instance in the *Romaunt* perhaps does, that the motif was already at large in medieval European culture, and that the *Prologue* is yet another distillation of it.[9]

But for all that, it distils the motif in a very particular way. The bee-cum-excrement figure is centered upon mendicants, and this naturally enough, some might think, when it is a piqued Summoner who is handling the narrative. Obviously, a focus like his would be avoided in public art as something impossibly tendentious; here, depiction of damned clerics, when it occurs, is normally a less partial and somewhat more sanitized affair.[10] To claim, therefore, as Lee Patterson does, that *The Summoner's Prologue* and *Tale* have connected with weary old antimendicant topoi, begins to look as if it may be wide of the mark; antimendicant they certainly are, but this punishment of the friars seems peculiar, and in its particulars quite unrelated to the few analogues that have so far been adduced to construct contexts from which its range of significances for Chaucer's contemporaries might be hypothesized.

I will approach the question of what I take to be a neglected context from what is chronologically the wrong way around, in a source written some thirteen years after Chaucer's death; but the value of doing so should become clear as I proceed.

On 17 August 1415, John Claydon, skinner, was arrested by the Mayor of London and brought before Henry Chichele, Archbishop of Canterbury, to be examined on grounds of suspected heresy. One of the chief witnesses against Claydon, and which eventually helped to send him to the stake, was his ownership of a book known as the *Lanterne of Liȝt*.[11] Robert Gilbert and William Lyndewode, two of the orthodox theologians appoin-

---

[9] The *Riverside Chaucer*, pp. 876–77, speculates that Chaucer may have seen the Pisa frescoes when he travelled from Genoa to Florence in 1373.

[10] More sanitized in that it is but a still frame, not the moving picture in the mind, with its additional capacity to shock, that written narrative is able to evoke; and less partial in that damned clerics depicted in public art never all belong exclusively to any one identifiable order within the Church. (For a useful commentary on illustrations of the resurrection of the dead, see Meg Twycross, "More Black and White Souls," *Medieval English Theatre* 13 [1991]: 52–63, esp. p. 60, n. 9.) I am grateful to Dr. Eileen Kane of the Department of the History of Art, University College Dublin, for advice on this motif.

[11] See L. M. Swinburn, ed., *The Lanterne of Liȝt*, Early English Text Society [hereafter EETS], o.s., vol. 151 (London: Kegan Paul, Trench, Trübner and Co., and Oxford University Press, 1917), pp. viii–x, for a summary of the evidence.

94

ted to scrutinize the book's contents, determined it to contain fifteen condemned articles. Claydon confessed that he had himself paid for the book to be copied, and that though he could not read, part of it had been read to him. His household servants, under examination, also testified to having heard a book called the *Lanterne of Liȝt* read aloud to Claydon. The fourth of the hereticated articles identified by Gilbert and Lyndewode ran as follows: "That the Court of Rome is the chief head of Antichrist, and the bishops be the body; and the new sects (that is, monks, canons and friars), brought in not by Christ, but damnably by the pope, be the venomous and pestiferous tail of Antichrist."[12] Evidently this article corresponds to the following passage in the sole surviving complete manuscript of the *Lanterne*: "Now bi þe autorite of God & oone accordaunce of hise holi seintis, sueþ an open conclucioun, sadli groundid in trewe bileue, þat in þe court of Rome is þe heed of anticrist, and in archebischopis & bischopis is þe bodi of anticrist. But in þise cloutid sectis, as mounkis, chanouns & freris, is þe venymous taile of anticrist."[13] The composition of the *Lanterne*, known to have occurred after 1409 when the *Constitutions* of Archbishop Arundel, to which it alludes, were promulgated, is necessarily to be dated before this mention of it in the 1415 proceedings against Claydon.[14]

Approximately two years before the Claydon affair, at a far higher end of the social scale but again in London, similar proceedings, if necessarily more cautious and protracted in their prosecution, were in train against Sir John Oldcastle in order to flush out his heresy. On 25 September 1413, he replied to a series of questions that had been put to him, among which was one seeking to elicit his view on papal authority, the establishment of the Church, and the power of the keys. As the Latin text of *Fasciculi zizaniorum* reports it, he answered: "quod papa est verus Antichristus, hoc est, caput ejusdem; archiepiscopi et episcopi, necnon et alii prælati, membra; et fratres cauda ejusdem."[15] This sounds very close to the hereticated senti-

---

[12] George Townsend, ed., *The Acts and Monuments of John Foxe*, 8 vols. (1890; rprt. New York, 1965), 3: 532–33.

[13] Swinburn, *Lanterne*, p. 16, lines 10–15.

[14] Thomas Wright, ed., *Political Poems and Songs*, Rolls Series, 2 vols. (London: Eyre and Spottiswoode, 1859–61), 1:278, prints a poem that he dates to 1388 and that contains the following lines: "Of swche more se he may / in libris ecclesiarum. / The lanterne of lyghtte / non fulget luce serena." Possibly the *Lanterne* either existed in some earlier draft or drew its name from this poem or from some topical reference to "lanterns of light," to which the poem may allude.

[15] The Latin source for Oldcastle's response is contained in the Lambeth Registers; see David Wilkins, ed., *Concilia Magnae Britanniae et Hiberniae*, 4 vols. (London, 1737), 3:356. Another Latin version, contained in the *Fasciculi zizaniorum*, though a little later and possibly copied from the Lambeth Registers, shows similar wording; see W. W. Shirley, ed., *Fasciculi Zizaniorum Magistri Johannis Wyclif cum Tritico*, Rolls Series (London: Eyre and Spottiswoode, 1858), p. 444.

ment of the *Lanterne*, except that for Oldcastle, the pope is singled out from the more general "court of Rome" as Antichrist's head, and the friars exclusively comprise the *cauda Antichristi*. Indeed, an English account of what Oldcastle said survives, which though first published in 1530 quite possibly stems from a lost medieval antecedent. This was taken over by John Bale and issued again in 1544, though now evidently collated with other sources, certain details of which are even more reminiscent of what the *Lanterne* declared on the topic:

> Rome is the verye nest of Antichrist. And out of that nest cometh all his disciples. Of whom Prelates Prestes / and Monkes are the bodye / and these pylde fryers are the tayle which couereth his most fylthye part. Than sayd the pryor of the fryre Augustynes. Alac syr whye do ye say so? That is vncharytablye spoken. And the lorde Cobham sayd. Not onlye is yt my sayinge / but also the Prophete Elayes / longe afore my tyme. The Prophet (sayth he) which preacheth lyes / is the tayle behynde. As you fryers and monkes be lyke Pharysees dyuyded in youre outwarde aparell and vsages / so make ye dyuysyon amonge the people. And thus yow with soche other / are the verye naturall Members of Antichrist.[16]

Not only does Oldcastle compare the structure of the established Church to the abominable anatomy of Antichrist in a way broadly similar to that found in the *Lanterne* (apart from his exclusive consignment of the "pylde fryers" to the "tayle [of Antichrist] / which couereth his most fylthye part"), he is also provoked to use Scripture polemically against one of the interrogators who has regretted his sordid assertion: "Not onlye is yt my sayinge / but also the Prophete Elayes." Oldcastle backs his assertion with an allusion to Isaiah 9:15, a passage also featured in the *Lanterne* just a little before the lines from it quoted above, and which in the *Lanterne* seems to serve as their thematic precursor: "A man of greet agee & worschipful holden to the world, he is heed and cheef Antichrist; a prophete or a prechour techyng lesing, he is þe taile of þis Antichrist."[17] Two possible conclusions follow from this. Either Oldcastle too had been exposed to the

---

[16] Given here from John Bale, *A brefe chronycle concernynge the examinacyon and death of the martyr syr J. Oldecastell* ([Antwerp?], 1544), sig. D [.viij. v]. As Anne Hudson has shown, Bale drew upon the earlier 1530 text for his own account ("'No newe thyng': The Printing of Medieval Texts in the Early Reformation Period," in Douglas Gray and E. G. Stanley, eds., *Middle English Studies Presented to Norman Davis in Honour of his Seventieth Birthday* [Oxford: Clarendon Press, 1983], pp. 153–74; see p. 170, n. 49). The 1530 text is *The examinacion of master William Thorpe preste accused of heresye. The examinacion of syr J. Oldcastell* [Antwerp, 1530], *STC* 24045.

[17] Swinburn, *Lanterne*, p. 14, lines 3–5.

teaching of the *Lanterne*[18]—after all, the tract may already have been circulating in London, since that is where Claydon came across it not very long afterwards—or he had at least been exposed to a web of antimendicant views some of whose particulars were interlinked in a closely comparable way.[19] Whatever the actuality, for Oldcastle friars alone were the basest part of an evil anatomy, twinned with no less than its "most fylthye part," the anus. On this point, the witnesses to what he said essentially agree.

While, as should now be clear, an association of the friars with the *cauda Antichristi* may have been available in Lollard writing (articulated most bluntly by Oldcastle in the course of his own defense) and in London (Chaucer's city), it still remains posthumous as far as Chaucer is concerned.[20] Was the association available *before* he wrote *The Summoner's Prologue* and *Tale*, thus making comparison chronologically justified? It has often been observed that many of the views of the later Lollards may be seen to proceed from ideas encountered in Wyclif's writings, sometimes indeed taken to extremes that the heresiarch himself may not have owned, but found there nevertheless in a seedling form. The explanation of Antichrist's abominable anatomy that surfaces in the vernacular at least by 1413 is no exception.

In 1384, the last year of his life, John Wyclif was engaged in some of his bitterest polemic against the evils he perceived at work in the Church, and especially against those who represented for him the most pernicious traducers of that Church, the friars. Bodily metaphors, developed from patristic sources, had long served him as a means for articulating his understanding of the Church of the *predestinati*, whose head was Christ, and that of the *presciti*, whose head may have been the very pope in Rome: "sic stet quod pretensus Romanus pontifex sit caput membrorum dyaboli."[21] In his last

---

[18] This would, incidentally, require us to regard its composition as falling between 1409–13, and hence close to Swinburn's preference for a date nearer to 1409.

[19] Perhaps he had been exposed to the teaching of a source common both to him and to the compiler of the *Lanterne*. An alternative explanation, that the *Examinacion* is a later construction, fleshed out from other Lollard sources, seems unlikely, since it corresponds in the relevant parts to the proceedings as related in Arundel's Register and *Fasciculi zizaniorum*.

[20] Strictly speaking, of course, "Sathanas" in *The Summoner's Prologue* is not identical with Antichrist, but the pair are closely enough associated for the distinction to be immaterial; in fact, the distinction is evidently confounded in certain of Antichrist's presentations; see R. K. Emmerson, *Antichrist in the Middle Ages* (Seattle, 1981), *passim*.

[21] Iohann Loserth, ed., *Iohannis Wyclif Tractatus De Ecclesia* (London: Trübner and Co., 1886), p. 366. This work was written in stages between the spring of 1378 and sometime early in 1379 (see W. R. Thomson, *The Latin Writings of John Wyclyf* [Toronto: Pontifical Institute of Mediæval Studies, 1983], p. 58).

writings, and notably in the *Liber de Antichristo* (that is, parts 3 and 4 of the *Opus evangelicum*), the metaphors used for discussing the two bodies are worked hard and anatomized, and it is here that a possible point of departure may be found for what later appears in the vernacular in the *Lanterne of Liȝt*. As Wyclif put it in 1384:

Postquam ergo Ysaias prophetaverat de Christo qui est basis huius verbi prophetici, convertit se ad prophetandum de peccato ypocrisis sacerdotum legis gracie. *Disperdet*, inquit, *Dominus ab Israel caudam et caput et incurvantem et depravantem in die una*. Ubi videtur probabiliter prophetare de nequicia et destruccione sacerdotum tempore legis gracie, ita quod per caput intelligat Romanum pontificem et per caudam intelligat sectam fratrum que est novissima sequens papam. . . . Et quantum ad caudam dicit Ysaias *et propheta docens mendacium ipse est cauda*. Sed queso cui potest istud verbum propheticum melius quam fratribus applicari. . . . Et fratres qui sunt cauda huius capitis [i.e., of the head of Antichrist] defamant fideles.[22]

The friars are the tail of the monstrous composite that is Antichrist,[23] that portion of his anatomy covering "his most fylthye part," as Oldcastle uncompromisingly put it. Though Wyclif may have drawn back from naming tail and anus quite as a consortium (something that evidently did not inhibit Oldcastle), by his time they were clearly thought of as a pair, and the association is understandable, given the physiological contiguity of both.[24]

It is therefore reasonable to suppose that the motif in *The Summoner's Prologue* had some Wycliffite resonance and currency by the time Chaucer was writing. It might be thought that arse-infesting friars would have been a natural enough way of depicting a particularly stinking group of heretics, especially when the raw materials from which Chaucer put his offensive conceit together may have already been traditional.[25] It remains the case,

[22] Iohann Loserth, ed., *Iohannis Wyclif Operis Evangelici Liber Tertius et Quartus sive De Antichristo Liber Primus et Secundus* (London: Trübner and Co., 1896), p. 34, lines 30–38; p. 35, lines 16–19; and p. 38, lines 32–33.

[23] "Illa enim est Antichristi persona composita monstruosa"; *Opus Evangelicum*, in ibid., p. 107, lines 29–30.

[24] Moreover, the use of the word *tail* to signify buttocks is well attested; see J. A. Simpson and E. S. C. Weiner, eds., *The Oxford English Dictionary*, 2d ed. (Oxford: Clarendon Press, 1989), s.v. *tail*, 5(a).

[25] For example, Gregory of Tours gave an account of one Leutard, a peasant of Vertus on the Marne, whose infection with heresy was associated with a swarm of bees (*The History of the Franks*, trans. by L. Thorpe [London, 1974]), p. 584; for discussion see Brian Stock, *The Implications of Literacy* (Princeton, N.J.: Princeton University Press, 1986), pp. 101–6. See also V. I. Scherb, "Conception, Flies, and Heresy in Skelton's 'Replycacion,'" *MÆ* 62 (1993): 51–60.

however, that in the decade in which he wrote, the antimendicant polemic most nearly consonant with his chosen antimendicant collocation was coming from Lollard pens. Moreover, in the precise choice of terms in which he couched it in the *Prologue*, some readers would have been liable to perceive an analogy. It will be recalled that the scatalogical revelation is heralded by the command of the angel to Satan (*SumT* 1687–91; italics mine):

> "And now hath Sathanas," seith he, "a tayl
> Brodder than of a carryk is the sayl.
> Hold up thy tayl, thou Sathanas!" quod he;
> "Shewe forth thyn ers, and lat the frere se
> Where is the *nest of freres* in this place!"

The *OED* cites the use of *nest* here as its earliest example of the word in the sense of "a place in which persons of a certain class (especially thieves, robbers or pirates) have their residence or resort." The *MED* cannot substantially better this, since its earliest equivalent sense, "a breeding place of sin or harm; an evil den or lair," again appears first in Chaucer, in *The Man of Law's Tale* (line 364).[26] Next, *MED* cites an example from the *Confessio amantis*, and then the occurrence under review in *The Summoner's Prologue*, which is its last citation safely datable to before the end of the fourteenth century. To judge by these examples, an opprobrious sense of the word *nest* had evidently taken root in the vernacular by the late fourteenth century, notably in Chaucer and in the work of a member of his circle, John Gower. Just a little earlier than Chaucer and Gower's usage, we discover a comparably opprobrious sense available to the equivalent Latin term, *nidus*, and in a very suggestive context. *Nidi* were frequently evoked in precisely those polemical writings that characterize Wyclif's last years and from which some excerpts have already been quoted. His *De Ecclesia* (1378–79), for example, comes out strongly against the pope and his college who, when working contrary to Christ, are a "*nidus hereticorum*, apostema putridum et ydolum desolacionis cum aliis monstrosis nominibus in sacra pagina prophetatis."[27] Or again, the fourth chapter of the *De quattuor sectis novellis*

---

[26] S. M. Kuhn and J. Reidy, eds., *Middle English Dictionary* (Ann Arbor: University of Michigan Press, 1975), p. 936, s.v. *nest*, 2(b).

[27] Loserth, ed., *De Ecclesia*, p. 88, lines 13–19. See also p. 357, lines 19–21: "quis dubitat quin *nidus ille* [i.e., the Roman curia] foret fons veneni ex cuius rivulis scateat toxica in fidelem ecclesiam militantem?" Or again, the supplement to the *Trialogus* (Gotthard Lechler, ed., *Johannis Wiclif Trialogus cum Supplemento Trialogi* [Oxford: Clarendon Press, 1869]), p. 423: "Nam omnes leges predictae iniquae sicut et executiones earum *ab illo nido* [i.e., the Avignon pope] trahunt originem" (all italics mine).

(1383) stigmatizes friars' houses as *"nidi dyaboli."*[28] And part 2, chapter 38 of the *Opus evangelicum* rails against the fraudulence of papal bulls that have proceeded "de illo *nido*" to despoil the people.[29] Just as the credal positions of the heresiarch flowed from his Latin writings into the vernacular of the subsequent Wycliffite derivatives, so too did certain of his lexical preferences, among which we might also now consider including the word *nest*, given the currency of its usage there. The tract *How Satan and his Priests*, the *Tractatus de Pseudo-Freris*, the *De officio pastorali*, the *De papa* and the cause of Claydon's downfall, the *Lanterne of Liȝt*, all feature such nests, whether they be those of Antichrist or of the fiend.[30] Thus Chaucer's *nest of freres* colludes with a typical Lollard turn of phrase for any lair of the limbs of Antichrist.

III

It therefore seems that there are the beginnings here for a historicizing of *The Summoner's Prologue* that would read its antimendicancy afresh, not as being stale and traditional or, as Patterson would have it, historically disengaged, but as something reinvented in accordance with the terms of an antimendicant paradigm prevalent in, and indeed in a few of its aspects

[28] Rudolf Buddensieg, ed., *John Wiclif's Polemical Works in Latin*, 2 vols. (London: Trübner and Co., 1883), 2:253, lines 10–11. The work was written between June and July of 1383 (see p. 236). See also p. 503, lines 14–15: "monasterium seu claustrum huiusmodi male regulatum est *nidus dyaboli*, a quo rapit multas animas ad infernum" (italics mine). This is from the fourth chapter of *De religione privata*, a work that, if not in fact by Wyclif but by a disciple (see pp. 486–88), has caught up and is perpetuating as a Lollard turn of phrase one of the heresiarch's locutions.

[29] Iohann Loserth, ed., *Iohannis Wyclif Opus Evangelicum* (London: Trübner and Co., 1895), p. 383, lines 8–9.

[30] See F. D. Matthew, ed., *The English Works of Wyclif hitherto unprinted*, Early English Text Society, o.s., vol. 74 (London: 1880), pp. 274, 317, 421, and 476–77, and Swinburn, ed., *Lanterne*, p. 19, line 14, respectively. On Lollard sect vocabulary, see Anne Hudson, "A Lollard Sect Vocabulary?" in Michael Benskin and M. L. Samuels, eds., *So Meny People Longages and Tonges: Philological Essays in Scotts and Mediæval English Presented to Angus McIntosh* (Edinburgh: University of Edinburgh, Middle English Dialect Project, 1981), pp. 15–30. The *MED* has noted a few of the metaphorical nests in the Wycliffite derivatives, but there are many more. My searches of the electronic databases of the *Corpus Christianorum* and the *Patrologia Latina* have yielded no significant comparable metaphorical *nidi*, nor have I noticed such usage in William of St. Amour and Richard FitzRalph. (I am grateful to David Howlett of the Medieval Latin Dictionary for alerting me to one comparable usage earlier in the fourteenth century that has been noted in the proceedings of Richard Ledrede, bishop of Ossory in Ireland, against Dame Alice Kyteler of Kilkenny.)

peculiar to, the late 1380s and 1390s, whose terms Wyclif and his immediate successors were largely responsible for dictating and propagating. It
might be objected, however, that the case so far, resting as it does on the
Prologue alone, is not sufficient to be fully convincing: were the tendentious
hints and overtones argued for in the *Prologue* also carried over into the
Tale, as indeed the *Prologue's* obsession with anality undoubtedly is, then
the case might sound more impressive. The objection is a fair one, and
deserves to be addressed, especially when it is also remembered that Arnold
Williams, in a valuable paper published in 1953, spoke so categorically
against the use of Lollard materials as a means of contextualizing Chaucer's
friars.[31]

Anyone reading the annotations on the Summoner in the *Riverside
Chaucer* edition, which is where most people approaching him seriously are
likely to begin, will find only two references there to matters Wycliffite.
One concerns friar John's request for money to help build his friary (*SumT*
2099–2106), which the notes compare with a similar preoccupation found
in the vernacular Lollard materials published in Matthew's anthology.[32]
But criticism of the lavish building projects of the friars was in any case an
old chestnut, already present in the work of William of St. Amour during
the earliest phase of antimendicant writing, and hence there is nothing
novel in citing Lollard parallels, even though they do testify to how this
particular criticism had lost none of its momentum in a later period. The
second reference concerns the letter of fraternity that friar John invokes in
order to tighten his social grip on Thomas and his wife (lines 2127–28).
Here the issue becomes more interesting. The Riverside edition notes that
for Wycliffites, "such letters were but another deceptive way of obtaining
money," and cites two vernacular cases from Arnold's anthology to illustrate the Lollard objection.[33] No one could quibble with this observation,
but it is worth stressing how much a centerpiece the question of letters of
fraternity had become in the Lollard attack on the detested friars, appearing first in Wyclif's Latin polemic, and then, as we might expect, faithfully
followed through into the English derivatives. Of these, the two examples
cited from Arnold by the Riverside edition are the merest tip of an iceberg

[31] Arnold Williams, "Chaucer and the Friars," *Speculum* 28 (1953): 499–513; see esp. p.
504: "There is no evidence of the peculiarly Wycliffite point of view in Chaucer's jabs at the
friars; and it is certainly a mistake to use Wycliffite documents to illustrate Chaucer's friar."
[32] Matthew, *English Works*, pp. 5 and 14.
[33] *The Riverside Chaucer*, p. 878, n. to lines 2126–28. See T. Arnold, ed., *Select English
Works of John Wyclif*, 3 vols. (Oxford: Clarendon Press, 1869–71), 3:377–78, 420–29.

of complaint.[34] Moreover, nowhere does the issue feature in any of the extant writings of William of St. Amour (although that should be conceded as not entirely surprising when we recall that William chose to work by insinuation and nuance, never once naming the friars in the *De periculis novissimorum temporum*, for example, as his intended targets). However, the issue similarly does not feature later on in what survives of the extensive antimendicant campaign of Richard FitzRalph, a campaign that provided Wyclif's own case with so much kindling.[35] It would therefore seem that the refrain-like insistence on the abuse of letters of fraternity, certainly a characteristic Lollard criticism, may also be a comparatively recent and topical addition to the antimendicant arsenal.

There is another mendicant practice clearly alluded to by the Summoner that Wycliffites also vilified, but in this case the fact that they did so has gone entirely unheeded. Trentals were a set of thirty commissioned masses sung for the welfare of a departed soul and sometimes sung all on the same day. Wyclif himself seems not to have targeted trentals by name in his Latin writings, though he frequently excoriated the general abuse of which trentals might so easily prove a local expression, namely, the simoniacal selling of spiritual suffrage.[36] By the time of the vernacular derivatives,

[34] Among the many references to the abuse of letters of fraternity that may be found in both Latin and English Wycliffite writings, the following are a small sample: Matthew, *English Works*, pp. 160, 262, 353; Iohann Loserth, ed., *Iohannis Wyclif Sermones*, 4 vols. (London: Trübner and Co., 1887–90), 3:352–65, and *Opus evangelicum*, 2:40, 41, 248; Buddensieg, ed., *Polemical Works*, 1:35, 143, 193, 222; A. W. Pollard, ed., *Iohannis Wycliffe Dialogus sive Speculum Ecclesie Militantis* (London: Trübner and Co., 1886), pp. 25, 26, 79, 80; Lechler, *Trialogus*, pp. 349, 367; Anne Hudson, ed., *English Wycliffite Sermons* (Oxford: Clarendon Press, 1983), 1:329; Gloria Cigman, ed., *Lollard Sermons*, EETS, o.s., vol. 294 (Oxford: Oxford University Press, 1989), p. 113. Also, see P. L. Heyworth, ed., *Jack Upland, Friar Daw's Reply and Upland's Rejoinder* (Oxford: Oxford University Press, 1968), p. 133, n. to lines 335–41, where he compares the *Fifty Heresies* (Arnold, *Select English Works*, 3:377–78) and *De Blasphemia* (ibid., p. 420 ff.). On letters of fraternity and their abuse, see also C. Erickson, "The Fourteenth-Century Franciscans and their Critics," *Franciscan Studies* 35 (1975): 107–35; see esp. pp. 122–24 and the references given there.

[35] It does not appear in the *Defensio curatorum*, the *De pauperie Salvatoris*, or the London sermons (I have consulted the version of each of these works as represented in Bodleian Library, MS Auct. F. infra 1.2); nor does it appear in FitzRalph's *propositio Unusquisque* (in L. L. Hammerich, ed., *The Beginning of the Strife between Richard FitzRalph and the Mendicants. With an Edition of his Autobiographical Prayer and his Proposition Unusquisque*, Historisk-Filologiske Meddelelser udgivet af Det Kgl. Danske Videnskabernes Selskab 26 [1938]). (I am grateful to T. P. Dolan for access to his list of Bible lemmata used in the *Defensio curatorum*.)

[36] See Anne Hudson, *The Premature Reformation* (Oxford: Clarendon Press, 1988), p. 311. Compare also William of St. Amour in the *Tertia Distinctio* of his *Collectiones*: "Huiusmodi promissores Missarum & Orationum pro aliorum eleemosynis obtinendis merito dici possunt Mercatores, siue Negotiatores, siue Negotiatores Orationum"; *Magistri Gvillielmi de Sancto Amore Opera Omnia* (Constance, 1632), p. 468.

however, trentals *were* being so named and targeted. *Jack Upland*, dated to c. 1390, interrogates its friar as follows on the business of trentals: "Whi make ȝe men bileue þat ȝoure golden *trentale*, soold for a certeyne summe of money—as fyue schylingis or more—may brynge a soule out of helle or of purgatorie?"[37] And both *How Satan and his Children turn Works of Mercy upside down* and *How Religious Men should keep certain Articles* mount comparable attacks of their own: "ȝe, ypocritis of priuat religion maken grete houses & costly & gaely peyntid more þan kyngis & lordis bi sotil beggynge & confessions & *trentalis* & meyntenynge of synne"; the new sects should ensure "þat þey make not comyns so pore bi sotil ypocrisie of gredy beggynge & *trentalis*"; they are also guilty in that they "make worldly festis & wast housis aȝenst here pouert & profession, bi colour of *trentalis* & longe preieris in siȝtte of men."[38] Similarly, the *Fifty Heresies and Errors of Friars* identifies trentals as one of the friars' "sotil meenes" of extortion: "Freris drawen to hom confessioun and birying of riche men by mony sotil meenes, and masse pens, and *trentals*, bot þei wil not cum to pore mennis dirige, ne resseyue hom to be biryed amonge hom."[39] And in *The Grete Sentence of Curs Expouned*, heinous sinners are said to resort to the friars on account of their easy penances and their "*trentalis* and masse pens, and makyng of gaie wyndowis and grete housis," by which the worldly fame of those sinners is bruited.[40]

Thus the Summoner chooses bold strokes for his opening sketch of friar John, portraying him in terms that the Lollards are currently polemicizing (*SumT* 1713–17):

> And so bifel that on a day this frere
> Hadde preched at a chirche in his manere,
> And specially, aboven every thyng,

[37] Heyworth, *Jack Upland*, pp. 62–63, lines 199–201; italics mine. Compare also the Latin Wycliffite text (upon which *Jack Upland* is ultimately based) as reported by friar William Woodford in his *Responsiones*; see E. Doyle, "William Woodford, O.F.M. (*c.* 1330–*c.* 1400), his Life and Works, together with a Study and Edition of his 'Responsiones contra Wiclevum et Lollardos,'" *Franciscan Studies* 43 (1983): 17–187; see esp. pp. 139–40. Heyworth dated *Jack Upland* to *c.* 1390–1420, perhaps to later rather than earlier in the period, but this dating needs revision. A composition anytime between the death of Wyclif in 1384 and 1401 seems likely; see Doyle, "William Woodford," pp. 90–91, and P. R. Szittya, *The Antifraternal Tradition in Medieval Literature* (Princeton, N.J.: Princeton University Press, 1986), pp. 196–97, n. 44.

[38] Matthew, *English Works*, pp. 211, 222, and 224 respectively; italics mine.

[39] Arnold, *Select English Works*, 3:374; italics mine.

[40] Ibid., 3:299. (This is in chapter 11 of the tract.)

> Excited he the peple in his prechyng
> To *trentals*. . . .[41]

Moreover, this trental reference proves too good to let quickly drop, and the Summoner pursues it, having friar John give an account of the redemptive mechanism that trentals trigger: "'Trentals,' seyde he, 'deliveren fro penaunce / Hir freendes soules, as wel olde as yonge,'" so therefore "'Delivereth out,' quod he, 'anon the soules! . . . Now spede yow hastily, for Cristes sake!'" (lines 1724–25, 1729, and 1732). The broader point of this, of course, is to illustrate the venality of friar John's preaching (of which more later), but that has already been established by associating his preaching with trentals; there was no need to go to the extra trouble of interjecting details about how trentals work. Granted, the piteous picture of souls cooking in purgatory chimes well with friar John's sales pitch and its sentimental strategy, but more is at stake than that. By explaining what trentals are supposed to do, another tendentious issue is introduced and annexed. The question of the merit of prayers for the souls in purgatory, let alone that of the simony likely to attend on such prayers, was also currently exercising some Wycliffites. The English sermon cycle, for example, comes out against them:

A greet disseyt in þis mater stondiþ in trist of mennus preyours, as freris and oþere prestis seyen þat þey wolen saue þe soulis and brynge hem hastly into heuene by þe uertu of þer preyer. But heere at þe firste men shulen wite what preyer profiteþ to men. And preyer of good lif profitiþ moost of alle oþere; and þis preyer more to quyke men and to deed. Þou woost neuere wher þis deed man be dampnyde or in purgatorie. And 3if þat he be dampnyd, alle preyeres sauen hym not; 3if he be in purgatory, good lif of þe chirche heere may be medeful to þis man aftir þat Crist acceptiþ it. And þerfore lyue þou wel, and do þou profit to þe chirche, and leeue þis partyng of meede to God, for so mut it nedis be.[42]

---

[41] It might be acknowledged in passing that there is one place in *Piers Plowman* where trentals are mentioned: "Parsones ant parsche prestus preyd here bischop, / For here parsches were so pore sen the pestilence tyme, / To haue a license ant a leue to lauchen annueles / Ant take trentales thereto, to yer togyderus"; A. G. Rigg and Charlotte Brewer, eds., *William Langland Piers Plowman: The Z Version* (Toronto: Pontifical Institute of Mediæval Studies, 1983), p. 41, lines 61–64. However, while Langland's context exposes the unfortunate motives for undertaking trentals, the institution of the trental is not impugned per se, which makes a telling difference.

[42] Anne Hudson, ed., *English Wycliffite Sermons* (Oxford: Clarendon Press, 1990), 3:312, lines 4–15; also, her *Premature Reformation*, p. 309. Compare William of Pagula earlier who, in his *Summa summarum*, attacks *questores* for, among other things, their fraudulent claims to release from purgatory the souls of the parents or friends of those who gave them alms (see Bodleian Library MS Bodley 293, f. 226, col. b).

In addition, and more generally, Lollards execrated mendicant claims for the merit of their special prayers: "Þe thrid heresie of þe thridde askyng sais, þat þei knowe þe wille of oure Lord God to bringe a soule to heven by manere of hor preyyng. But certis we schul trowe, þat God may not be moved but as he has ordeyned bifore þe worlde was made."[43] Consequently, since the introduction here of the function of the trental is supererogatory to establishing friar John as a venal preacher, and since in some Lollard circles that function had been problematized, its elaboration by the Summoner seems mischievous and far from innocent. Indeed, I think we must further conclude that it witnesses to the relative richness of Chaucer's acquaintance with currently contested issues: in isolation, or scattered sporadically through the *Tale*, the appearance of such issues might be taken as nothing especially remarkable, for Chaucer's work, bookish though it largely may be, is by no means entirely cut adrift from contemporary realities.[44] However, from the point of view of Lollard theology, what is of interest as we move from the *Prologue* into the *Tale* is the close overlapping of sensitive material. Radical ideas are concatenated in a way a little reminiscent of Knighton's assessment of the continuity of Lollard doctrine, where one perverse opinion fed inexorably into another.[45]

If we turn from the reprobated institutions of letters of fraternity and trentals to smaller features of the *Tale*'s composition, even here a case may be made for its affiliation with a wider field of contemporary radical texts. Of particular interest in this regard are the terms in which the lord of the manor tries to steady the fuming friar after Thomas has farted on him. Friar John, exasperated, beats his retreat to the manor house where the lord checks him by saying: "Distempre yow noght; ye be my confessour; / Ye been the salt of the erthe and the savour. / For Goddes love, youre pacience ye holde!" (*SumT* 2195–97). Why is the salt of the earth allusion (Matthew 5:13) so especially relevant here? In the circumstances, some Bible lemma on the merits of patience might have seemed more strictly appropriate to the immediate dramatic context: it is evidently friar John's patience that has evaporated, as the lord perceives. But once again, concerns other than mere dramatic appropriateness seem to have supervened. The lord reminds John of his role—he is his *confessor*—before he applies Matthew 5:13. Two

[43] Arnold, *Select English Works*, 3:442.

[44] This point has recently been explicitly emphasized by Alcuin Blamires, "The Wife of Bath and Lollardy," *MÆ* 58 (1989): 224–42, and implicitly by A. J. Fletcher, "The Topical Hypocrisy of Chaucer's Pardoner," *ChauR* 25 (1990): 110–26.

[45] J. R. Lumby, ed., *Chronicon Henrici Knighton*, Rolls Series, 2 vols. (London: Eyre and Spottiswoode, 1889–95), 2:179.

things might be noted about this. First, since Matthew 5:13, *Vos estis sal terrae*, is the opening of the gospel for the feast of a confessor and doctor in Sarum Use, the drafting of it here, given the kind of confessor John is, is a singular irony; but second, and perhaps more important, this particular Bible lemma enjoyed Lollard favor: it is a leitmotif of parts 1 and 2 of Wyclif's *Opus evangelicum*, where it ranks among the most frequently cited Bible lemmata of that work.[46] He also treated it in one of his Latin sermons.[47] Its appeal for him seems to have derived from its elaboration and exegesis in one of the homilies of the *Opus imperfectum*,[48] a work which was to prove something of a favorite with the Lollards.[49] Indeed, the Wycliffite Glossed Gospels turn substantially to this source for their commentary on Matthew 5:13. By contrast, the commentary of the unassailably orthodox *Glossa ordinaria* offered Lollards little on the same verse to suit their purposes: these were more adequately served by the pseudo-Chrysostom.[50] Exposition of Matthew 5:13, now in English, found its way into one of the *Commune sanctorum* sermons of the standard English set, as well as into some of the vernacular derivatives, such as the Lollard sermons for the first Sunday in Advent and the fifth Sunday in Lent, each featured respectively in BL MS Additional 41321 and Oxford, Bodleian Library MS Rawlinson C 751.[51] And in nearly all these places the verse has received its typical Wycliffite skew: it is drafted into the service of the characteristic and reiterated Lollard indictment of abusers of the office of preaching, and notably of those whose morals and message were in contradiction.[52] The Lollard

---

[46] Not every instance of it was noted in Loserth's Index.

[47] See Loserth, ed., *Wyclif Sermones*, 2:376–84.

[48] This is the tenth homily of the *Opus imperfectum*, on the theme *Vos estis sal terrae*.

[49] See Joop van Banning, *Opus Imperfectum in Mattheum: Praefatio*, Corpus Christianorum Series Latina 87B (Turnhout: Brepols, 1988).

[50] I have consulted the three principal recensions of the Glossed Gospels as witnessed in 1) BL MS Additional 41175 (see fols. 13v col. b–14 col. a); 2) Bodleian Library MS Laud Misc. 235 (see fols. 22v col. a–23 col. a); and 3) BL MS Additional 28026 (see fols. 14v–15). (For a summary of the textual criticism of these three recensions, see Hudson, *Premature Reformation*, pp. 249–58.)

[51] See respectively Pamela Gradon, ed., *English Wycliffite Sermons* (Oxford: Clarendon Press, 1988), 2:142–48; Cigman, *Lollard Sermons*, p. 7, lines 249–52: "And þus, for þese two officis (truþe of prechinge and good liyf), clepeþ Crist his true prechoures 'salt of þe erþe' and 'ly3te of þe world'"; and p. 196, lines 42–6: "And for þis same cause also Crist clepid his apostlis 'salt of þe erþe,' by whiche is bitokened ensaumple of good liif. And after he clepid hem 'li3t of þe worlde,' by which is bitokenid þe true preching of her mouþe, meuing hem by þat first þei shulden lyue wel, and after preche truly."

[52] Doubtless this was suggested by its biblical context and by its subsequent patristic exegesis. The emphasis in Lollard writing on compatible life and preaching is exceedingly common; see, for example, Matthew, *English Works*, pp. 55, 104, 116, 163, 178, 225, 240, 245, 279, 363, 374, 408, and 433; also Cigman, *Lollard Sermons*, p. 7, line 250; p. 35, line

fondness for Matthew 5:13 is further emphasized by its utter absence from the extant writings of two of the major detractors of the mendicants in earlier years: William of St. Amour did not commandeer it, nor did Richard FitzRalph.[53] Yet Lollards evidently found it to be a sharp sentence of Scripture, convenient for reminding the clergy of their dominical commission and for reproving those who were lapsing.[54] Thus the use of the lemma at this point in the *Tale*, exceeding as has been argued narrow considerations of dramatic appropriateness, may join the letters of fraternity, the trentals, and the vaunted soul-liberating prayers of the friars in also packing a polemical Wycliffite topicality.

As I have observed, the salt of the earth lemma, in Lollard usage, was normally collected into one of their wider preoccupations: their advertisement of the alarming discrepancy that they often perceived between the message of a preacher and his personal morals. It has already been noted that the issue of venal preaching (and hence by implication the issue of modes and motives of preaching generally) is also conspicuously raised in *The Summoner's Tale*: friar John served the people "with nyfles and with fables" (line 1760), exactly as Wycliffites would have predicted he might, and by his own admission, he has preached "nat al after the text of hooly writ" (line 1790); that is, he has deliberately not preached exclusively *secundum ordinem textus*, a choice that, in Chaucer's day, was no longer a neutral matter.[55] And the reason he gives for doing so, that the simple faithful are

---

162; p. 118, line 456 ff.; p. 191, lines 297–98; pp. 195–97, lines 1–90; p. 205, lines 392–94. The use of Matthew 5:13 is also extended in the vernacular *De officio pastorali* into an attack on prelates whose evil living justifies the withholding from them of the tithes which ordinarily might be their due: "Also crist techiþ in þe gospel þat ȝif salt vanȝsche awey it is not worþ aftir to be castun out & be defoulid of men; & þis salt shulde be þes prelatis"; Matthew, *English Works*, p. 419.

[53] It is absent from all of William of St. Amour's major extant writings: the *Collectiones catholicae*, the *De periculis novissimorum temporum*, the *De Pharisaeo et Publicano*, his *quaestiones*, the sermon for the feast of Sts. James and Philip, and the *Responsiones* (for the latter, see E. Faral, "Les 'Responsiones' de Guillaume de Saint-Amour," *Archives d'histoire doctrinale et littéraire du moyen âge* 25 and 26 (1950–51): 337–94); similarly, it is absent from FitzRalph's works listed above in n. 35. It is impossible to investigate every extant antimendicant source before the 1390s, but none of these major sources, the ones likely to have been foremost in influencing Wyclif, employs Matthew 5:13.

[54] I might mention that John Gower, in book 3 of the *Vox Clamantis*, alludes briefly to priests as "salt of the earth"; G. C. Macaulay, ed., *The Complete Works of John Gower*, 4 vols. (Oxford, 1899–1902), 4:161.

[55] Both these issues were pregnant ones in current debates about the conduct of preaching, yet neither have received the notice they deserve in critical commentary on *The Summoner's Tale*. The accusation that friars stuffed their sermons with such fustian, though an early one, was foregrounded in Wycliffite writings. The very specific description of the content of friar John's sermon, avoiding Scripture, was tendentious at this date. See A. J.

unable to cope with *scriptura sola*, is precisely of the sort that was currently being advanced by those orthodox who advocated the prohibition of a Scripture rendered widely accessible through vernacular translation.[56] Once it is recalled that in the 1380s and 1390s, these (and other) related questions concerning the *officium predicatoris* were also ventillated in the Lollard-versus-orthodox debate, their appropriation by Chaucer, albeit briefly, becomes a correspondingly sensitive matter. Nor should we suppose that he was indifferent to what was being debated in this respect, since preachers of various hues inhabit the Canterbury sequence, and not just for the sake of adding touches of color or a little more breadth to its social panorama. Questions of who may preach, of what may be preached, and how, are integral to the presentation of several pilgrims or, as here, to the presentation of a character within a pilgrim's tale. A modern reader may miss the fact that Chaucer, like the clergy of his day, was also alert to the sensitive social and political implications of preaching, and that preaching issues have been raised in several of his later writings.

Against the case I am making it might be objected that the specter of venal preaching had troubled commentators long before Lollards ever arrived on the scene. To be sure, St. Gregory's famous admonition that "cuius vita despicitur, restat ut eius predicatio contemnatur,"[57] lived on long after him by gaining admission not only to a host of texts destined primarily for clerical consumption but also to texts liable to reach an audience wider still.[58] By the time Chaucer came to write *The Pardoner's Prologue* and *Tale*,

---

Fletcher, "The Preaching of the Pardoner," *SAC* 11 (1989): 15–35, and more recently H. L. Spencer, *English Preaching in the Late Middle Ages* (Oxford: Clarendon Press, 1993).

[56] An instance close in date to the period in which Chaucer is likely to have composed *The Summoner's Prologue* and *Tale* is afforded by the Register of Bishop Trefnant of Hereford. On 29 August 1395, one John Croft, *armiger*, of the diocese of Hereford, swore in the presence of Richard II that "nunquam de cetero legeret vel predicaret publice vel occulte aliquam novam doctrinam dicte fidei catholice reluctantem nec in effectu audiret voluntario set neque libros Anglicos *secundum nudum textum de sacra scriptura* sinistre extractos per quosdam Lollardos vulgariter nominatos fidei catholice ac doctrine Romane ecclesie obviantes"; W. W. Capes, ed., *The Register of John Trefnant, Bishop of Hereford (A.D. 1389–1404)* (Hereford, 1914), p. 148; italics mine.

[57] *Patrologia Latina* 76, col. 1119. The quotation comes from Gregory's twelfth homily on the Gospels, on Matthew 25:1–13.

[58] The influential florilegium *Manipulus florum* recycles Gregory's dictum under *Predicacio*: "Ad regnum eterne beatitudinis peruenire non valet qui non vult opere implere quod docet, nam cuius vita despicitur, restat vt predicacio contempnatur"; Oxford, MS Oriel College 10, fol. 418 col. a. From the *Manipulus* it would have found its way into other *distinctio* collections. (On the *Manipulus* and its influence, see R. H. and M. A. Rouse, *Preachers, Florilegia and Sermons: Studies in the Manipulus florum of Thomas of Ireland* [Toronto: Pontifical Institute of Mediæval Studies, 1979].) William of St. Amour also cites

his most urgent literary shaping of the ancient *scandalum* (forcefully identified by Gregory) to which the rift between precept and practice gave rise,
theologically informed questions about preaching and its conduct were
already being aired by the laity. John Gower, for example, had similarly
interested himself in such questions, and like Chaucer, he too was not
writing for some exclusively clerical coterie. His *Mirour de l'omme* alludes to
discrepancies between preachers and their sermons, and reaches the (orthodox) verdict that such preachers, while they damage themselves, may nevertheless do their audiences good.[59] This point of view recurs in his *Vox
Clamantis*, and here in a context even more elaborately devoted to analysis
of exactly what some of the unworthy motives prompting venal (mendicant) preaching might be and how they were likely to register in the
sermon's style:

> Sunt etenim multi tales qui verba colorant,
> Qui pascunt aures, aurea verba sonant,
> Verbis frondescunt, set non est fructus in actu,
> Simplicium mentes dulce loquendo mouent:
>
> . . . .
>
> Scripta poetarum, que sermo pictus inaurat,
> Aurea dicuntur lingua, set illa caue:
> Est simplex verbum fidei bonus valde meretur,
> Set duplex animo predicat absque deo.
> Despicit eloquia deus omnia, quando polita
> Tecta sub eloquii melle venena fouent:
> Qui bona verba serit, agit et male, turpiter errat,
> Nam post verba solet accio sancta sequi.
>
> . . . .
>
> Sepius aut lucrum vel honoris adepcio vani
> Fratrum sermones dat magis esse reos:

Gregory's maxim in the *Collectiones*; see *Opera omnia*, p. 468. Its echo can be heard in the
antimendicant poem *De supersticione Phariseorum* (*c.* 1360): "Restat, cuius reproba vita
indicatur, / Vt et predicacio sua contempnatur"; A. G. Rigg, "Two Latin Poems against the
Friars," *MS* 30 (1968): 106–18, esp. p. 112, lines 139–40; the dependence on Gregory has
not been noted here.

[59] Macaulay, *Complete Works*, 1:245, lines 21706–20.

Sub tritici specie zizannia sepe refundant,
Dum doctrina tumens laudis amore studet.[60]

Sermons of friars may be occasions for temporal gain or vainglory (accusations already levelled by William of St. Amour), sophistical shows designed to tickle the ears. Gower recycles Petrus Riga on the perils of rhetoric, and displays a concern coinciding with that of many contemporary orthodox churchmen: how to scour rhetoric of moral culpability.[61] Pulpit theoreticians had long been keenly aware of these issues and pitfalls; by the 1380s and 1390s, their awareness, as we have seen, had escaped the rarified confines of *questiones* and the *artes predicandi* to enter a wider lay arena.[62] William Langland's example might serve as a final illustration of this laicizing trend. All versions of *Piers Plowman* identify the problem of the hypocritical preacher, during the time of Lollardy's Advent (*Piers Plowman* A Text) and its Epiphany (*Piers Plowman* B and C Texts): "That ȝe prechen to the peple preue hit ȝowsylue; / Lyue ȝe as ȝe lereth vs—we shal leue ȝow þe bettere."[63] But for the purpose of my argument, one point needs stressing. An important impetus behind the wholesale movement of these debated issues from the clerical province into the lay, and hence ultimately behind Chaucer's concern with them, can be attributed to their strenuous politicizing and democratizing as a result of the orthodox-versus-Lollard contest.[64] When Chaucer, via the Summoner, raises those issues again, including that leitmotif of Lollard polemic, hypocritical preaching,

---

[60] Ibid., 4:195–96, lines 1065–68, 1071–78, 1081–84.

[61] Ideally, preaching had a clear, theologically driven agenda, yet its praxis was necessarily conducted in rhetoric's dangerous domain. Here, that agenda was vulnerable to sundry betrayals and compromises liable to inhere in the very medium of its delivery, either inadvertently, as when preaching fell an unintended victim to the elegance—or *curiositas*, as it was often termed—of its own mediation or, in the case of the unscrupulous, when it was manipulated by their greed or vanity aforethought. Its fictions, ever prone to collapse into the morally perilous category of a feigning that might, moreover, serve as an adjutant to fraud, needed to be carefully policed.

[62] See A. J. Minnis, "Chaucer's Pardoner and the 'Office of Preacher,'" in Piero Boitani and Anna Torti, eds., *Intellectuals and Writers in Fourteenth-Century Europe* (Tübingen and Cambridge: Gunter Narr Verlag and D. S. Brewer, 1984), pp. 88–119.

[63] Derek Pearsall, ed., *Piers Plowman by William Langland* (London: Edward Arnold Ltd., 1978), p. 104, lines 141–42. I cite the C Text, but versions of these lines are already present in Texts A and B.

[64] Wendy Scase takes a broader view when she suggests that devotional literacy in general, by increasing the laity's access to clerical learning, simultaneously lessened their reliance on the clergy as exclusive purveyors of spirituality; *Piers Plowman and the New Anticlericalism* (Cambridge: Cambridge University Press, 1989), pp. 44–45. The consequent diminishing of clerical status might well help to foster the anticlericalism that Scase seeks to establish.

he can only compound what has already been shown in this *Prologue* and *Tale* to be provocative, and spin out further its web of tendentious possibility.

Thus there is good reason for recuperating the immanence of these important historical considerations within both *The Summoner's Prologue* and *Tale*. There is much more here than traditional, throw-away joking at a friar's expense, just as there is more than the equally traditional anal knockabout associated with fabliau modes of writing, however sophisticated and theologically nuanced it may have become in the telling.[65]

IV

This discussion has sought to establish that some of the antimendicant elements of *The Summoner's Prologue* and *Tale* are not traditional and dehistoricized but in fact contemporary, answering to dominant tropes of a controversial and partisan antimendicancy. If, as I have argued, Chaucer's text echoes such tropes, what is the interpretative consequence of this, since it is one thing to identify points of correspondence, but quite another to interpret what they may have meant to his readers? Perhaps one of the least helpful uses to which my attempt to demonstrate correspondences can be put is to use it as an access to biography. For example, while the prospect of Chaucer the card-carrying Wycliffite has rightly receded from sight, it has been replaced with a suggestion, on the face of it more reasonable, that he may have wished to create a forum for the expression of Wycliffite views.[66] Put no more strongly than that, the suggestion may serve its turn, but not if "creating a forum" requires that we also envisage, if not Chaucer the Lollard, then Chaucer the Lollard sympathizer: he has, unquestionably, withheld explicit judgment on Lollard matters, but this reticence should not necessarily be confounded with "sympathy" when other, less committed reasons may lie at the root of it.[67] If anything is to be salvaged of Chaucer the author from all this, what does seem irreducibly true is that he

---

[65] For a recent study of the *fabliau* relations of *The Summoner's Tale*, see John Hines, *The Fabliau in English* (London: 1993), pp. 160–76; the Pentecostalizing of the fart has been explored by Szittya, *Antifraternal Tradition*, pp. 231–46.

[66] See Blamires, "Wife of Bath."

[67] As, for example, self-serving tact, suggested in connection with *The Pardoner's Prologue* and *Tale* by Fletcher, "Topical Hypocrisy," pp. 119–20, and more recently and generally by Derek Pearsall, *The Life of Geoffrey Chaucer* (Oxford and Cambridge, Mass.: Blackwell, 1992), pp. 252–53.

was better acquainted with Lollard thought than has been suspected, a none too surprising conclusion given the place and time of his writing.[68]

Yet since his words share agency with him in the creation of meaning, having a life of their own out in the larger community from which he has borrowed them, it may be appropriate to try to estimate how his contemporaries may have responded to his borrowed Wycliffite nuances, thus shifting attention from authorial intention to questions of reception and of the stance his writings may be considered to have assumed in the textual continuum of the 1390s. Even if, after encountering *The Summoner's Prologue* and *Tale*, "diverse folk diversely they seyde," certain aspects of their plural responses seem not utterly beyond reasonable conjecture. As was noted in the discussion of the use of Matthew 5:13, observation of dramatic appropriateness in the *Tale* was evidently not always supremely incumbent. Lulled by its momentary lapses, the awareness of some readers that it is an irate Summoner who is doing the telling may have slumbered. As a result, their apprehension of the contentious issues raised in the *Tale* would have been at liberty to float free from any anchorage in the ostensible, *parti pris* narrator, and hence from any of the limiting and relativizing of those issues that anchorage in such a narrator might have implied.[69] The issues would have stood as issues in their own right. For these readers, ones for whom issues came to loom largest, the *Tale* may have been received as a complex antimendicant satire with all the bite of a polemic rendered up-to-date by its Wycliffite resonance. To many in Chaucer's audience this resonance would have sounded familiar, and perhaps to some gratifyingly so.

In addition to this, the *Tale's* topical antimendicant polemic finds its narrative culmination in the performance of a very particular set of social relations. These relations had long been the subject of theoretical discussion—and no more so than now in the late fourteenth century—but their practice, by this time, had similarly become topical in the wake of the fresh questioning of their nature that was currently taking place. They can be simply stated as follows. Friar John explicitly introduces the concept of the estate of the Church when he says that not merely he, but via him and his order the Church itself (2189–93), has been assaulted by Thomas, a man who, we repeatedly hear (*SumT* 2205–6, 2218–19, 2227, 2232,

---

[68] Blamires's invitation, "Wife of Bath," p. 237, to investigate the Chaucer canon further from the point of view of Lollard nuance is vindicated.

[69] Also, this is an established medieval mode of reading, as for example in certain sermon exempla, where the issue at stake may sometimes in fact be compromised by a dramatic inappropriateness in the exemplum in which the issue is mediated.

2238–39, 2241, 2267–68, and 2291–92), is a churl, the *Tale's* chief representative of the estate of those who labor. Here we might pause for a moment to locate what is presented in Chaucerian fiction alongside what was occurring in contemporary fact. It was, for example, in no small part his sense of the outrage being offered by the laity, the lowly *pedes* of the body politic, to the inviolable prerogatives of the Church, that powered friar William Butler's Determination against their being given access to vernacular Scripture, and this in the fateful year of 1401, not so very long after the composition of *The Summoner's Prologue* and *Tale*; and not long before it, the Austin canon John Mirk, in his massively popular *Festial*, warned his clerical readers in an aside to be on guard against layfolk "proude in hor wit" who were liable to harass them with vexatious questions about the meaning of the liturgy.[70] So the *Tale's* composition, as these two brief and randomly chosen examples illustrate, was historically sandwiched by a Church defensively aware of lay transgressions of its theological domain. What friar John says, therefore, has in this context a familiar ring to it. His recourse after his assault (in the hope of some redress?) is to the lord, the *Tale's* aristocratic representative, whose introduction now completes the famous three-estates triangle. In a nutshell, by the end of the *Tale* we have been presented with a Church discountenanced by a dissident laity and seeking support for its wounded interests from the secular authorities. Put in these terms, the relations enacted in the *Tale* may soon be seen as a small-time facsimile of the sort of political struggle that in the near future, in the year of Butler's Determination in fact, would result in the Church's successful petition to the State for the enactment of *De heretico comburendo*.

Nevertheless, the potential *seriousness* of the *Tale* as a committed allegory of current political realities may have been belied, as may also the Wycliffite nuances abetting that seriousness, by not only the *Tale's* comic anal entropy but also in proportion as any awareness of its narrator grew.[71] For it is entirely possible to conceive of yet other readers who, conversely, may have been less prepared to pay one of the serious-minded prices (namely, the elimination of the Summoner as a significant mediating presence in the *Tale*) that such responses required. These readers, with equal textual war-

---

[70] For the text of Butler's Determination, see Margaret Deanesly, *The Lollard Bible* (Cambridge: Cambridge University Press, 1920), pp. 401–18.

[71] Just as, too, the seriousness of friar John's complaint is already knocked off course by the lord's attitude, for he sees Thomas's offense less as one against the Church than as one against *ars metrike*. But even his low estimation of Thomas's mathematics is rehabilitated once its feasibility is mockingly demonstrated by the squire.

rant, may have chosen instead to observe the status of the narrator: his motives for speaking are grounded in a malice that, by stridently prefacing his *Tale* as it does, not every reader need necessarily have lost sight of. An awareness of the Summoner as teller of the *Tale* would have entailed, perhaps disconcertingly for Wycliffites or their sympathizers, an awareness that the mediator of their truths was someone whom they would have abhorred. Any reader sympathetic to the Lollard cause perceiving this dislocation would have discovered, strangely enough, the ancient *scandalum* such as St. Gregory identified reinscribed here in another, more sophisticated guise: the articulator of issues that Wycliffites had seized on, making them legitimate game in their (largely antimendicant) campaign, was certainly himself no righteous comrade in arms, but rather a limb of the abominable anatomy of Antichrist.

Consequently, whatever Chaucer's personal investment in the topical issues that his text trades in, at least it cannot be said that his treatment of them has necessarily done much to advance the cause of either side in the debate. Interpretive multiplicity is something that his text has not spurned but actively courted. Such surpluses of meaning, it should be said, would have been inimical to Lollard practices of reading and writing as manifested in their texts, for many of these enshrine a naive belief in the possibility of univocality, of the self-presence of words (most famously, of the self-presence of the Word of Scripture). Thus the substance of Wycliffite writing is typically uncluttered by the pernicious accidents of multiplicity—gloss and ornament—indeed, it is purged of such "nyfles" and "fables" (*SumT* 1760) as were manipulated by the likes of a friar John. To state the ethic of their writing very simply, it could be said that it is frequently sober or angry, but seldom comic; there is much earnest, and very little game.[72] Surpluses of meaning, of course, are also the common condition of many a good joke. Hence when serious Wycliffite possibilities, such as I have tried to illustrate, arise from the outset in the context of the joke that is the Summoner's *Prologue*, they are already introduced on slippery ground. For while the surreal conclusion of the Summoner's *Prologue* may have had some Wycliffite resonance, that is by no means its only interpretive possibility, as a persuasive exploration of its inversion of the traditional *Maria Misericordia* motif has already demonstrated.[73] (According to this motif, earliest recorded in Cæsarius of Heisterbach's *Dialogus*

---

[72] Wyclif's own austere preaching style, one suspects, has been elevated to the point of a principle.

[73] Fleming, "Summoner's Prologue."

miraculorum (*c.* 1223), a Cistercian monk, distraught to see in a vision that heaven looks to be empty of members of his order, is subsequently reassured when the Virgin opens wide her cloak to disclose a clutch of Cistercian souls nestling securely beneath it.) Yet explanation of the *Prologue* simply in terms of its inversion of the *Maria Misericordia* motif is not quite sufficient either, because the inversion is not a symmetrical one. Readers are offered more than a carnivalesque pleasure of watching a hitherto familiar and pious motif of official culture turned on its head, for the friars, not just nestling under Satan's wing, as some straightforward mirror-reversal of the motif might have put it, swarm instead out of his anus like bees. Readers are additionally entertained to a scatalogical surplus, a defecation of apiary mendicants that concludes with the mendicants flying back again to their anal nest and with the devil clapping his tail over it to shut them in. In this bizarre conclusion, Chaucer's rendition of the *Prologue* narrative has complicated its straightforward similarity with the *Maria Misericordia* motif by at once accessing other possible significances, associatively and metonymically.

It was here in the conclusion, also through metonymical association, that the *Prologue*'s possible Wycliffite resonances argued for earlier were introduced. It is also here that parodic reminiscence of yet another famous motif, just as well known as that of the *Maria Misericordia*, can be argued to have taken place. It was the motif of sacred bodily incorporation, and three brief examples may suffice to illustrate its nature and currency. In a meditation on the Passion, Richard Rolle turns various metaphors to express the idea of Christ's wounds as salvific refuge, including the following: "Efte, swet Ihesu, þy body is like to a dufhouse, for a dufhouse is ful of holys: so is þy body ful of woundes. And as a doue pursued of an hauk, yf she mow cache an hool of hir hous she is siker ynowe, so, swete Ihesu, in temptacioun þy woundes ben best refuyt to vs."[74] The wound holes, like roosts in a dovecot, are only a degree of domesticity away from another metaphor, similarly popular, of the wounded side as a dove's nesting place in the crevices of a rock. A passage in Bonaventure's *Soliloquium*, paraphrased somewhat from its acknowledged source in St. Bernard, puts it as follows: "O anima, Christus in cruce te expectans, habet . . . latus apertum, ad te in illud intromittendum. Esto ergo, o anima, iam *columba* nidificans *in foraminibus petrae, in caverna maceriae*, pervola ad manus, pervola ad

---

[74] S. Ogilvie Thomson, ed., *Richard Rolle: Prose and Verse*, EETS, o.s., vol. 293 (Oxford: Oxford University Press, 1988), p. 74, lines 221–24.

pedes, invola lateri, ibi tuta requies, ibi secura quies."[75] These conceits also share the metamorphosis of souls into birds, doves in this case (the Summoner's "bees," we might recall, were thought to have been birds too, according to standard medieval taxonomy).[76] And last, Julian of Norwich testifies to the motif's continuing vigor when she resorts to it in her tenth showing, which as the longer version amplifies it says: "Wyth a good chere oure good lorde lokyd in to hys syde and behelde with joy, and with hys swete lokyng he led forth the vnderstandyng of hys creature by the same wound in to hys syd with in; and ther he shewyd a feyer and delectable place, and large jnow for alle mankynde that shalle be savyd and rest in pees and in loue."[77] As the souls of the righteous had access to the interior of Christ's body through the orifice of his wounds, sometimes flitting in like doves, so the souls of the bee-like friars discover a diabolic version of this all of their own. But while there may be ample warrant for also choosing to read the *Prologue*'s conclusion as a sort of grotesque antitype to that of sacred bodily incorporation, the point is made here simply to help corroborate my broader case for interpretive surplus, a surplus in which Lollard possibilities are simply yet another ingredient. The complexity and layering of Chaucer's writing, its multiple parodic surpluses, thwart the kind of interpretive stability for which Wycliffite texts strove.

At the last, therefore, for some of the "diverse folk" in Chaucer's audience, Lollardy's repertoire too would have been accessed only to be collected finally into Chaucer's varied album of discourses, and Lollardy's ethic entrammeled and compromised there by the multiplicity of his fiction. The Lollard nuances of *Prologue* and *Tale* are mediated by, yet at once absorbed into, the plenitude of a rhetoric that in other contexts, when Lollardy was speaking for itself, it abjured. In this way, while some of Lollardy's serious issues are raised, their serious and pervasive dominion is

---

[75] See *S. Bonaventurae Opera Omnia*, 10 vols. (Quaracchi: 1882–1902), 8:41. The variants of two witnesses used by the Quaracchi edition gloss *in foraminibus petrae, in caverna maceriae* as "id est, in vulneribus Christi." Bonaventure has elaborated an idea that he has found in St. Bernard's sixty-first homily, *In Cantica Canticorum*, "Columba mea in foraminibus petrae" (Cant. 2:14; see *Patrologia Latina* 183, col. 1072).

[76] Bees were classified as birds by Bartholomeus Anglicus; *Bartholomæi Anglici de Genvinis Rervm Coelestivm, Terrestrivm et Inferarvm Proprietatibus* (Frankfurt: Wolfgang Richter, 1601), pp. 520–24.

[77] Edmund Colledge and James Walsh, eds., *A Book of Showings to Julian the Anchoress of Norwich*, Part 2 (Toronto: Pontifical Institute of Mediæval Studies, 1978), p. 394, lines 3–6, and p. 395, line 1. (I have chosen only three examples of the motif when they could easily be multiplied: for example, the well-known fourteenth-century hymn *Anima Christi*, for use in the prayers of thanksgiving after Mass, contains the line "In tua vulnera absconde me.") See also D. Gray, "The Five Wounds of Our Lord—III," *N&Q* 208 (1963): 127–34, esp. p. 129.

refused and never allowed to prevail. Contemporary readers, stimulated by a recognition of contemporary relevance in *The Summoner's Prologue* and *Tale* into active engagement with its issues, were nevertheless also offered freedom, in the terms in which those issues were presented, to judge for themselves: judgment would have been devolved upon them and invited, not thrust upon them ready-made. And in the end, perhaps this was the way in which Chaucer's rhetoric, by remaining abstemiously playful, self-mocking, and *uncommitted*, may most effectively have participated in the social process.

Commentary Displacing Text:
The Nun's Priest's Tale and the Scholastic Fable Tradition

Edward Wheatley
Hamilton College

Although *The Nun's Priest's Tale* is one of the best-known beast fables in European literature, its structure threatens to preclude it from a genre known primarily for its brevity and simplicity. The fabular part of the tale—the fox's capture and release of the cock Chauntecleer—occupies less than half of the tale, while the first three-fifths are devoted largely to the description of the old woman, her rooster, his dream, and the debate surrounding its interpretation. Why is the conventional fable narrative sequestered in the final half of the work? Would Chaucer's medieval audience have been able to make more of the overall structure of the tale than we can?

In a two-part article in *Speculum* Robert A. Pratt found that the fable itself is closely related to one of Marie de France's popular fables, *Del cok e del gupil*,[1] while the earlier portions of the tale come largely from the fourteenth-century *Roman de Renart le Contrefait* and branch 2 of the *Roman de Renart*.[2] Amid numerous similarities to these sources, many significant differences also emerge, three of which provide a starting point for this study:

---

[1] In his editions of Chaucer's work, Thomas Speght clearly categorized *The Nun's Priest's Tale* as a beast fable by choosing the following rubric for the work: "Of a Cocke and an Henne: the morall whereof is to embrace true friendes, and to beware of flatterers"; Derek Pearsall, ed., *The Nun's Priest's Tale, A Variorum Edition of the Works of Geoffrey Chaucer*, vol. 2, pt. 9 (Norman: University of Oklahoma Press, 1984), p. 139. Not only does Speght's rubric provide an all-too-clear fabulistic moral, but it also translates the conventional Latin construction for fable titles, "De . . . et . . . ," into which the names of the animal characters are inserted. Eight manuscripts, including Ellesmere and Hengwrt, give the tale titles including the phrase "of the cock and hen": MSS Bo1, Cn, Ds1, El, Ha4, Hg, Ln, Ma. See Sir William McCormick and Janet E. Heseltine, *The Manuscripts of Chaucer's Canterbury Tales* (Oxford: Clarendon Press, 1933).

[2] Robert A. Pratt, "Three Old French Sources of the Nonnes Preestes Tale," *Speculum* 47 (1972): 1.422–44 and 2.646–68.

1. In both sources, the fox has entered the farmyard before Chauntecleer's dream, thus showing the reader that even as the dream occurs, it is in the process of coming true. In *The Nun's Priest's Tale* the fox first appears after the dream and the chickens' debate.

2. Only in *The Nun's Priest's Tale* does Chauntecleer alone recount his dream; in both Reynardian texts, the narrator recounts it (though in the *Roman de Renart* Chauntecleer later repeats it to his wife, Pinte[3]).

3. In the beast epics, the main conflict unfolds between the cock and the fox, but in *The Nun's Priest's Tale*, Chaucer "has made the rivalry of the cock and hen more important than the rivalry of cock and fox," according to Pratt.[4]

These three differences between the sources and Chaucer's tale intensify the focus upon Chauntecleer's dream, not as the narrator's exploration of a gallinaceous psyche but as a textual paraphrase of a dream that is "written" by a rooster and denied the authority granted it by the narratorial voice in the French text. The dream-text itself, not the early arrival of the fox described in the sources, raises the specter of the predator in Chaucer's tale. Ultimately, the lengthy interpretation of the dream distracts both the characters and the readers from the threat of the fox, at least until the fox begins to act upon that threat.

Alongside Pratt's examination of *The Nun's Priest's Tale*'s fabular and beast-epic source history, some scholars have taken steps toward providing a historical contextualization of the tale as a fourteenth-century beast fable; it has been compared to patristic definitions of fable and examined in relation to aspects of rhetoric generally learned by medieval students.[5] In addition, Peter W. Travis has studied how the fable exemplifies some standard medieval curricular practices and principles. Of the tale's compendious nature, he writes:

Chaucer has designed *The Nun's Priest's Tale* as a palimpsestuous text comprising dozens of schoolboy assignments—not only reading assignments, but transla-

---

[3] Ibid., 1.427.
[4] Ibid., 2.646.
[5] For the tale's relation to patristic writings, see R. T. Lenaghan, "The Nun's Priest's Fable," *PMLA* 78 (1963): 300–307, and Stephen Manning, "Fabular Jangling and Poetic Vision in *The Nun's Priest's Tale*," *South Atlantic Review* 52 (1987): 3–16.

tions, paraphrasings, glosses, applications, imitations, and themes amplifying and defending truths discovered in the master text.[6]

What Travis has begun on a level of considerable generality, I would like to continue here with greater specificity. While he and I agree that Chaucer relies upon "his audience's collective memory, the key to which is old books and old assignments"[7] in order to understand the tale fully, Travis sees the "dozens of schoolboy assignments" as randomly drawn from standard rhetorical and grammatical practices in the grammar-school classroom, resulting in "apothegm, *sententia*, exemplum, and proverb tussl[ing] with fable, history, allegory and riddle for the admonitory center of the literary stage."[8] I hope to show that *The Nun's Priest's Tale* is less a literary wrestling match among assignments than a fully exploited curricular fable whose unique structure, as anatomized by Pratt, resembles a fourteenth-century model for the presentation of fable in the classroom. The tale represents a curricular process of *narratio* and *enarratio*, narration and interpretation, that encompasses the tale in its entirety. Furthermore, Chaucer could have looked no further than curricular practices relating to Aesopic fable as inspiration for many of the apparently "palimpsestuous" elements in the tale. I will base my observations about this fable on a substantial body of manuscript evidence from the fourteenth and fifteenth centuries, largely unstudied, which lies in scholastic fable commentaries from the grammar school curriculum.

Historians of education have long been aware that beast fables were important in the school curriculum from the time of the Roman Empire throughout the Middle Ages, into the Renaissance, and later.[9] In the Mid-

---

[6] Peter W. Travis, "*The Nun's Priest's Tale* as Grammar-School Primer,"*SAC* 9 (1987): 81–91; quotation from p. 82. Travis's other articles on this tale include "Chaucer's Trivial Fox Chase and the Peasants' Revolt of 1381," *JMRS* 18 (1988): 195–220, and "Learning to Behold the Fox: Poetics and Epistemology in Chaucer's *Nun's Priest's Tale*," in Roland Hagenbüchle and Laura Skandera, eds., *Poetry and Epistemology: Turning Points in the History of Poetic Knowledge* (Regensburg: Pustet, 1986), pp. 30–45.

[7] Travis, "Grammar-School Primer," p. 85.

[8] Ibid., p. 87.

[9] Stanley F. Bonner, *Education in Ancient Rome* (London: Methuen, 1977), pp. 254–57; Paul F. Gehl, *A Moral Art: Grammar, Society, and Culture in Trecento Florence* (Ithaca, N.Y.: Cornell University Press, 1993), pp. 122–34; Tony Hunt, *Teaching and Learning Latin in Thirteenth-Century England*, 3 vols. (Cambridge: D. S. Brewer, 1991), 1:70; Nicholas Orme, *English Schools in the Middle Ages* (London: Methuen, 1973), p. 104, n. 1; Clara P. McMahon, *Education in Fifteenth-Century England* (Baltimore: Johns Hopkins University Press, 1947), p. 106; Thomas Noel, *Theories of the Fable in the Eighteenth Century* (New York: Columbia University Press, 1975), p. 14.

dle Ages fables were evidently taught according to the dictates of the rhetorician Quintilian and the grammarian Priscian, who recommended that students memorize and paraphrase fables in abbreviated and/or lengthened versions. Such exercises were generally called *progymnasmata*,[10] and Peter Travis has pointed out that Chaucer's contemporaries would have read *The Nun's Priest's Tale* as a fable amplified according to progymnasmatic precepts.[11]

According to manuscript evidence and records of early printing, most educated readers in the later Middle Ages brought the *progymnasmata* to bear upon an Aesopic collection comprising sixty Latin verse fables now generally attributed to Gualterus Anglicus, who in the late twelfth century had versified a group of the so-called "Romulus" prose fables, themselves redactions of some of the verse fables of the Roman Phaedrus.[12] Today more than 170 manuscripts and evidence of twenty-five printings before 1500 bear witness to this collection's renown in the fourteenth and fifteenth centuries.[13]

Like all "pagan" texts studied in schools, these fables acquired scholastic commentaries. A commentator typically summarized each fable—a practice relating to the *progymnasmata*—and then offered interpretations of the fable's meaning, sometimes leaving the interpretation on a social, earthly level, sometimes providing a Christianizing allegory, and sometimes doing both.[14] Extant manuscripts from the fourteenth century do not indicate

[10] For general discussions of medieval education in relation to *The Nun's Priest's Tale*, see Lenaghan, "Nun's Priest's Fable." A description of the role of beast fables and progymnasmatic practices in the earlier history of European education appears in Jan M. Ziolkowski, *Talking Animals: Medieval Latin Beast Poetry, 750–1150* (Philadelphia: University of Pennsylvania Press, 1993), pp. 21–22.

[11] Travis, "Grammar-School Primer," pp. 86–87.

[12] The complex history of the Phaedrian and Romulan collections, along with texts from some of the compilations, is summarized in Ben Edwin Perry, *Aesopica* (Urbana: University of Illinois Press, 1952), and in Georg Thiele, *Der Lateinische Äsop des Romulus und die Prosa-Fassungen des Phädrus* (Heidelberg: Carl Winter, 1910).

In his article ("Grammar-School Primer") Peter Travis initially misidentifies the most commonly taught fable collection of Chaucer's day as that written by Avianus (p. 83), but later he acknowledges the importance of a collection attributed to "Aesop" (p. 86). By the end of the thirteenth century Avianus had been supplanted in the grammar-school curriculum by the "Gualterus Anglicus" collection as the standard fable collection; see Hunt, *Teaching and Learning Latin*, 1:70; Orme, *English Schools in the Middle Ages*, p. 104, n. 1.

[13] Léopold Hervieux, *Les Fabulistes Latins depuis le Siècle d'Auguste jusqu'à la Fin du Moyen Age*, 5 vols. (1883–94; rprt. New York: Burt Franklin, 1960), 1:472–684; supplemented by Gerd Dicke and Klaus Grubmüller, *Die Fabeln des Mittelalters und der frühen Neuzeit* (Munich: Wilhelm Fink, 1987), pp. lxvi–lxviii.

[14] The fable commentary tradition has received very little critical attention. See Douglas Gray, *Robert Henryson* (Leiden: E. J. Brill, 1979), pp. 124–28, and Aaron E. Wright, Jr., "The 'Nuremberg' 'Aesop' and Its Sources" (Ph.D. diss., Princeton University, 1991), pp. 96–112 and 176–250, for a discussion of fable commentary in German manuscripts.

that any one commentary had ascendancy over others, either in England or elsewhere; rather, almost anyone literate in Latin could summarize and comment upon the fables, as evidenced by a number of puerile attempts at one end of the spectrum (of the type that a young Chaucer might have attempted) and highly learned excurses at the other.[15] Although the academic level and Latinity of most fable commentaries are as elementary as we would expect, they nonetheless helped to familiarize young readers with a variety of forms and levels of allegory in preparation for studying the Bible. The structure and function of fable commentary resemble those of commentaries on more respected, influential texts such as Ovid's *Metamorphoses*, since hermeneutic practices associated with fable served to introduce pupils to forms of interpretation useful for more difficult texts.

Beyond teaching and/or reinforcing acceptable interpretive methodologies, scholastic commentary also defined the field of discursive practice relating to the very act of reading an authoritative text from a manuscript page. In recent years scholars have begun to elucidate the unique textuality of medieval scholastic commentary as both a support and a challenge to its master text. Martin Irvine argues:

Commentary, which was given its own space on the page, had a distinctive textuality, both discursively as a function of interpretive and intertextual relations, and materially in the visual form of the manuscript page.[16]

John Dagenais focuses upon the phenomenology of manuscript reading in terms of the control that a manuscript page exercises over a reader's perception of its contents.

---

[15] In England, commentaries on both the Aesopic fables and an equally popular grammar-school text, the *Ecloga* of Theodolus, have been attributed to no less a figure than Stephen Patrington (d. 1417), Carmelite prior at Oxford, sender of the Oxford friars' anti-Lollard letter to John of Gaunt in 1382, confessor to Henry V from 1413, and bishop, first of St. David's and then of Chichester. Unfortunately no surviving fable commentary has been identified as Patrington's, and otherwise the names of fable commentators remain unknown. See William J. Courtenay, *Schools and Scholars in Fourteenth-Century England* (Princeton, N.J.: Princeton University Press, 1987), *passim*; L. A. Kennedy, "Late Fourteenth-Century Philosophical Scepticism at Oxford," *Vivarium* 23.2 (1985): 124–51, and "A Carmelite Fourteenth-Century Theological Notebook," *Carmelus* 33 (1986): 70–102.

[16] Martin Irvine, "'Bothe text and gloss': Manuscript Form, the Textuality of Commentary, and Chaucer's Dream Poems," in Charlotte Cook Morse, Penelope Reed Doob, and Marjorie Curry Woods, eds., *The Uses of Manuscripts in Literary Studies: Essays in Memory of Judson Boyce Allen* (Kalamazoo, Mich.: Western Michigan University, Medieval Institute Publications, 1992), pp. 81–119; quotation from p. 81. In the same collection, see Christopher Baswell, "Talking Back to the Text: Marginal Voices in Medieval Secular Literature," pp. 121–60.

Marginalia (and interlinealia) help us to measure the pace of medieval reading, the places where it starts and stops, refers, expands, takes note. The text is constantly mediated by glosses, and these glosses, in turn, refer not so much to the text as to the larger and invisible world that is medieval reading itself.[17]

For these critics, commentaries represent a good deal more than scholastic side-dishes accompanying the main course: instead, they control the way that the reader receives and ruminates upon a text.

In the range of recent descriptions of medieval scholastic commentary, the most aggressive belongs to Rita Copeland in *Rhetoric, Hermeneutics, and Translation in the Middle Ages*. To describe the dynamics of scholastic commenting, she uses the metaphor of displacement, implying that the commentary itself takes on a certain agency as it assumes centrality by supplanting the master text.

Latin exegetical practice in the Middle Ages carries the rhetorical force of *hermeneia*, or primary or productive discourse: it works to displace the original text, materially by paraphrase, and conceptually by reconstituting the argumentative structure of the text. . . . Latin commentary substitutes itself for the text in question, inserting itself into the *auctoritas* of that text, hence appropriating that authority, and to varying degrees performing in lieu of text. The dynamic effect of exegesis is to achieve a certain difference with the source.[18]

Copeland's emphasis on displacement (a word that has a range of connotations in her book and that will be allowed similar freedom here) fits scholastic fable commentaries closely, since the very history of fable, especially as a curricular text, is one of appropriation and authorial displacement. Furthermore, in relation to a verse fable collection such as Gualterus's, form itself would have been the first and likeliest aspect of the work to be displaced, as readers would have retained the outlines of each fable much more easily in prose than in the original form—the displacement by paraphrase to which Copeland refers.

Another kind of displacement in scholastic fable commentary results from the collection's standard division into short narrative units between which comments could be intercalated. Most scribes and printers reduced the effect of displacement by positioning the plot summary and commen-

---

[17] John Dagenais, *The Ethics of Reading in Manuscript Culture: Glossing the "Libro de buen amor"* (Princeton, N.J.: Princeton University Press, 1994), p. 27.
[18] Rita Copeland, *Rhetoric, Hermeneutics, and Translation in the Middle Ages: Academic Traditions and Vernacular Practice* (Cambridge: Cambridge University Press, 1991), p. 103.

tary either beside or beneath each fable, as a kind of extended footnote, kissing the foot of the text that it serves while, in a sense, undermining it. But when confronting syntactically tortuous Latin verse fables, would medieval schoolboys have turned to a plot summary only after reading a fable text? It seems much more logical that in presenting a text to lower-level Latin students, a schoolteacher would have used the plot summary and commentary to introduce the fable. Such an introduction would have then allowed pupils to devote less mental energy to comprehension of the plot and to pay more attention to the intricacies of grammar, for which Gualterus was considered a model.[19]

The notion that plot summary and commentary should precede the fable text both temporally in classroom study and spatially on the page is supported by the page layout of some manuscripts and early books that aped those manuscripts. The early exemplars of Gualterus's fables and their commentaries include a few variations on the theme of physical displacement of text by commentary, the most striking in manuscripts that do not reproduce the fable collection at all, but merely provide pages full of plot paraphrases and commentary.[20]

More germane to my discussion of *The Nun's Priest's Tale*, however, are the books in which scribes or printers have given the plot summary and commentary visual priority over the fables. For example, the scribe of British Library MS Harley 2745 first copied the title of a fable, then immediately beneath it, in a small gloss hand, he wrote four or five lines of commentary, and just below the last full line of commentary, he began the fable text. Depending upon the length of the comment, the scribe sometimes completed it in the margin alongside the fable, thus wrapping two sides of the text in commentary. A less conciliatory arrangement of fable text and commentary appears in Milan Biblioteca Ambrosiana MS I.85.supra. Dated July 1415, the manuscript was copied by Johannis Brixianus (i.e., of Brescia in northern Italy). He first copied the *incipit* of each fable, then the fairly lengthy plot summary and its allegorical meanings, and then the fable itself. This page format was popular enough to have been employed

---

[19] Gehl, *A Moral Art*, pp. 122–27.

[20] The most interesting of these that I have studied, Venice Biblioteca Marciana MS 4658, is obviously a teacher's handbook. It provides detailed lesson plans for the fables, telling the teacher the points at which he might appropriately mention a certain rhetorical figure, the declension of a particular noun or adjective, or terms etymologically related to a word in the text. The commentator also revises the fable texts phrase by phrase, taking the words out of their poetic syntax and putting them into a more easily understood order.

In their catalogue Dicke and Grubmüller list four other manuscripts containing fable commentaries but not the fables; *Die Fabeln*, p. lxviii.

in other manuscripts[21] and at least two incunables, one printed by Jean Bouyer in Poitiers in 1490 and one by Bernardinus de Nusintiis in Naples in 1497. In these books, academic plot summaries and commentaries command the attention of the reader by fully displacing the fable texts; the marginal has become both spatially and phenomenologically central.

In the scholastic fable commentaries described above, the progression from the nonauthoritative plot summary to scholastic interpretation(s) to the fable itself bears a striking resemblance to the order of the Nun's Priest's material in his story, a resemblance further strengthened by the changes that Chaucer wrought upon his sources. The dream-text serves as both a paraphrase of Chauntecleer's nightmare and a summary of the fable to come, but, unlike its Reynardian predecessors, it is not recounted in the authoritative narratorial voice that will later tell the fable. Rather, Chaucer textualizes it in the voice of a "reader" within the tale, the cock, who, like a school pupil required to make sense of unfamiliar material, needs help if he is to understand it. The birds' commentary on the abbreviated plot summary both drains authority from the specific dream-text by discussing dreams generally, and displaces the fable, pushing it into the final half of the tale. In spite of these gestures of displacement, experienced readers and, to some extent, Chauntecleer himself know that his dream will ineluctably come true. Chauntecleer implies this knowledge in his exempla about the validity of premonitory dreams, while readers bring the same knowledge to the tale not only because of the laws of nature but also because of the laws of literature: for all its amplifications and embellishments, this tale is recognizably a fable, and members of the audience know that it must follow its preordained course.

The scholastically sanctioned displacement of text in favor of initial commentary could have alerted medieval readers to other aspects of scholastic glossing and curricular practice relating to fable with which Chaucer embellished his tale as he revised his sources. Some borrowings from the classroom are used parodically, some straightforwardly, and others ambiguously, but Chaucer's intentions do not disguise the curricular practices themselves. Studying these markers can help us to understand how

---

[21] Wrocław Biblioteka Uniwersytecka MS 2.Q.33, the so-called "Breslauer-Äsop," a fifteenth-century manuscript that also includes German verse translations of the fables; and Berlin SPK MS Lat. Oct. 87, which formerly belonged to the Benedictine monastery of St. Peter at Erfurt. In *Die Handschriften des Benediktinerklosters S. Petri zu Erfurt* (Leipzig: Otto Harrassowitz, 1920), Joseph Theele asserted that the Berlin manuscript dated from the twelfth century, but on the basis of the scribal hand and the work's condition, I think that it is more likely a product of the thirteenth or even fourteenth century.

Chaucer exploits tension between his contemporaries' expectations about when and how the fable plot would unfold, and the displacement of the plot by delaying the action in order to comment upon it. Even the brief plot is full of what Dagenais calls the starts and stops, references and expansions that typify medieval reading.

The first "stop" in the text occurs before readers can identify the tale as a beast fable, when they meet the old woman who owns the cock and who initially attracts the Nun's Priest's attention so completely that he claims to be telling a tale about her ("This wydwe, of which I telle yow my tale. . . ."[22]). The peasant who owns the Chantecler in *Le Roman de Renart*, Constans de Noes, is introduced in a manner similar to that used by Chaucer in introducing the widow,[23] but retrospectively medieval readers might also have recognized the presence of an animal's owner as an element of scholastic fable commentary. Some prose plot summaries embellish the fables by providing human owners for the animal characters, even though no humans are mentioned in the original Latin texts. In an Italian manuscript of Gualterus's fables, for example, the commentator tells us that the rooster in the first fable is owned by "quidam nobilis homo in quodam rure vel in quadam villa," and that the lamb in the second fable belonged to "quidam pastor nomine Sachomano."[24] Not only are these humans entirely absent from the fable text but they also fail to resurface in the commentator's plot summaries. Their presence serves the same function as that of the widow in the Nun's Priest's story: to validate the life (and in some cases, the death) of the animals by implying that their fate had resonance in the world of humans.

The plot of Chaucer's tale begins with Chauntecleer groaning and waking from a dream to provide a suggestive but incomplete picture of a menacing fox. Interpretation immediately becomes central to the tale as Pertelote asks what her husband's groan signifies ("What eyleth yow, to grone in this manere?" [line 4080]). He replies with the summary of his dream (lines 4086–96):

> "Now God," quod he, "my swevene recche aright,
> And kepe my body out of foul prisoun!

---

[22] Larry Benson, gen. ed., *The Riverside Chaucer*, 3d ed. (Boston: Houghton Mifflin, 1987), p. 253, line 4014. Later references to *The Nun's Priest's Tale* are made by line number within the body of the paper. I have used the Chaucer Society lineation, marked by asterisks in the Benson edition, as it is used exclusively in Pearsall's *Variorum* edition of the tale.

[23] Kate Oelzner Petersen, *On the Sources of the Nonne Prestes Tale*, Radcliffe College Monographs, no. 10 (Boston, Mass.: Ginn, 1898), p. 48.

[24] Treviso, Biblioteca Comunale, MS 156, fols. 71v, 72r.

> Me mette how that I romed up and doun
> Withinne our yeerd, wheer as I saugh a beest[25]
> Was lyk an hound, and wolde han maad areest
> Upon my body, and wolde han had me deed.
> His colour was bitwixe yelow and reed,
> And tipped was his tayl and bothe his eeris
> With blak, unlyk the remenant of his heeris;
> His snowte small, with glowynge eyen tweye.
> Yet of his look for feere almoost I deye."

Chauntecleer prefaces his dream-text with a clear indication that it exists in order to be interpreted ("my swevene recche aright!"). Of course this adumbration of the subsequent conflict, a miniature of the fable, does not provide a full account of what will happen; Chauntecleer does not even elaborate upon how this unidentifiable animal signaled that he wanted the bird dead. The narrative's brevity is typical of scholastic plot summaries, in which most commentators sketched a fable in no more than two sentences. Chauntecleer's recitation of his fable could have reminded Chaucer's early audiences of how the very act of academic paraphrase is bound to result in an abortive version of a text that must necessarily lack not only the authority but also much of the substance of the original.

Significantly Chaucer has not provided a gallinaceous dream vision: as mentioned above, *The Nun's Priest's Tale* differs from its sources in that the dream here is recounted only in the voice of the dreamer, not in the voice of the tale's narrator. Readers are not invited into the rooster's dream for a less mediated description of what happens, as they are in Chaucer's other poems in which the characters dream (e.g., Troilus's and Criseyde's dreams [2.925–31, 5.1233–43] and, more appositely, Cresus's dream of the tree in the final section of *The Monk's Tale*, which directly precedes the Nun's Priest's story). Rather, the dream is summarized by Chauntecleer, and thus taken from the realm of "reality" into textuality. Chauntecleer's dream-text is to his dream as *The Nun's Priest's Tale* is to its sources, since both represent earlier texts. For us, as for Pertelote, the dream only exists as a textual artifact representing another text, which Chaucer has chosen to displace. Rita Copeland has stated that by means of paraphrase, "the com-

---

[25] The Hengwrt Manuscript uses the grammatical variant "say" instead of "saugh" in this line (*Variorum* edition of *The Nun's Priest's Tale*), though Benson fails to mention this difference. The word may represent a pun, since Chauntecleer is "saying" his vision of the beast, thus highlighting the textuality of the picture that he paints.

mentary becomes container of, no longer supplement to, the original text,"[26] and Chauntecleer's recitation of the dream accomplishes such containment, effectively distancing the authority of not only the dream-text but also the Old French texts that Chaucer is translating.

The skewed double interpretation of Chauntecleer's dream-text that follows illustrates Copeland's assertion that the goal of exegesis is to "achieve a certain difference with the source." Even the dullest grammar-school pupil could interpret this text readily: the red, houndlike animal is a fox, and since foxes want chickens dead, Chauntecleer instinctively fears the beast and should continue to do so. However, Pertelote and Chauntecleer are engaged in *hermeneia*, achieving a difference with the source text by interpreting, in this case, not what the dream means, but whether it can mean anything at all.

As some scholars have pointed out, Pertelote is apparently familiar with Macrobius's *Commentarium in Somnium Scipionis*, for she reads the dream as a manifestation of the imbalance of Chauntecleer's humors.[27] In her learned opinion, the dream is an *insomnium* or nightmare, a classification that Macrobius calls "not worth interpreting, since [it has] no prophetic significance."[28] If we also read the dream as beast fable in miniature, we are reminded that Macrobius is equally dismissive of this genre: he writes that Aesopic fables are "inappropriate to philosophical treatises,"[29] simply because a text based entirely upon falsity cannot be interpreted. In light of the scholastic tradition, then, Pertelote implies that fables are the insomnia of literature; although all readers have to live through them, they should move beyond them as quickly as possible into other kinds of reading.[30] For Pertelote, the content of the dream-text itself cannot directly teach any great truth, but it is symptomatic of the truth that Chauntecleer needs a laxative.

In defense of her interpretation she cites one of the *Disticha Catonis*, the Distichs of Cato, a lengthy group of proverbs that were the first canonical

[26] Copeland, *Rhetoric*, p. 83.

[27] Walter Clyde Curry, *Chaucer and the Medieval Sciences*, 2d ed. (New York: Barnes and Noble, 1960), pp. 199–218; Kenneth Sisam, ed., *Chaucer: The Nun's Priest's Tale* (Oxford: Clarendon Press, 1927), p. 35.

[28] Macrobius, *Commentary on the Dream of Scipio*, trans. William Harris Stahl (New York: Columbia University Press, 1952), p. 88.

[29] Ibid., p. 85.

[30] The conjunction of dream and fable is made explicit in the *Roman de Renart*, where Chantecler, skeptical of the prophetic force of the dream, says that it has turned into a fable: "A fable est li songes tornez"; qtd. in Pratt, "Old French Sources," p. 428.

Latin text that medieval European schoolboys studied.[31] Like the fable plot in the dream-text, the distich is drastically abbreviated: Pertelote's paraphrase of the distich achieves a clear difference with its source text. Although she quotes only half of the distich (and thus substantially misquotes it), her incomplete presentation remains unchallenged by Chauntecleer, implying a tacit acceptance that such difference from one's scholastic source is inevitable.

Chauntecleer counters by pointing out Cato's low status among authority figures, perhaps directly attributable to his low place in the curriculum. The cock says (lines 4161–71):

> ". . . as touchyng daun Catoun,
> That hath of wysdom swich a greet renoun,
> Though that he bad no dremes for to drede,
> By God, men may in olde bookes rede
> Of many a man moore of auctorite
> Than evere Caton was, so moot I thee,
> That al the revers seyn of this sentence,
> And han wel founden by experience
> That dremes been significaciouns
> As wel of joye as of tribulaciouns
> That folk enduren in this lif present."

In order to prove that experience shows dreams can come true, Chauntecleer provides a veritable collection of fabulistic exempla in which dream texts are validated by later (textual) reality. Oddly, he refuses to name the author of these exempla, which can be traced to both Cicero and Valerius Maximus. Instead, he simply credits the stories to "oon of the gretteste auctour that men rede" (line 4174). Chauntecleer thereby constructs a conflict between authoritative figures—his against Pertelote's—but then he will not disclose the identity of his chosen ally, in spite of his later ability to cite not only Macrobius and Daniel specifically but also hagiography and Trojan history more generally. His reticence to name his source may represent a misused principle of scholastic commentary: in nearly all fable commentaries Aesop is repeatedly mentioned not by name but simply as *auctor*, a nomenclature that negates the author's identity but adds prestige to his

---

[31] For a discussion of the use of the *Disticha Catonis* in the medieval curriculum, see Ian Thomson and Louis Perraud, *Ten Latin Schooltexts of the Later Middle Ages* (Lewiston, N.Y.: Edwin Mellen, 1990), pp. 52–54, and Gehl, *A Moral Art*, pp. 107–20.

text. Chauntecleer is attempting to displace one authoritative figure with a "greater" one, as the progression through the medieval curriculum did, but his argument is substantially weakened by his substitution of the author's status for his identity, when typically the latter corroborates the former. On the other hand, by leaving the *auctor* unidentified, Chauntecleer forces us as readers to focus on the exempla themselves rather than their author, and he denies Pertelote the opportunity of rebutting his evidence with a figure of even greater authority.

Two of the tales that the cock relates to the dream are longer than the text they purport to interpret, their very length serving to displace both the dream-text in the past and the fable in the future. In the first, one of two pilgrims is murdered by men who hide his body in a dungcart; his ghost, appearing to the other pilgrim, tells him where to find the corpse. The other story develops from a premonitory dream of a shipwreck. Robert Pratt has convincingly argued that the exempla were drawn mainly from Robert Holkot's *Super Sapientiam Salomonis*, a commentary on the biblical Book of Wisdom, though Chaucer may first have known them in Cicero's *De divinatione.*[32] If we look at these possible sources in light of the scholastic background provided by Gualterus's curricular collection, we can see more clearly the significance of the texts as fables brought by Chaucer into the service of his larger fable.

The first exemplum differs from its textual predecessors not only in some general embellishments but also in the conclusion given to the tale. Earlier versions of the story have the living pilgrim finding the dead one in the dungcart, but Chaucer revises the climactic discovery, having Chauntecleer call attention to it as he does so (lines 4236–39):

> "What sholde I moore unto this tale sayn?
> The peple out sterte and caste the cart to grounde,
> And in the myddel of the dong they founde
> The dede man, that mordred was al newe."

The added concluding action of dumping out the contents of the dungcart (displacement of both the corpse and the authority of the original tale) may indicate a more direct link between Chaucer's tale and the fables of the Romulan tradition than we have hitherto seen: this exemplum parodies the first tale in Gualterus's collection and most of the collections related to it,

[32] Robert A. Pratt, "Some Latin Sources of the Nonnes Preest on Dreams," *Speculum* 52 (1977): 538–58.

including that by Marie de France. These begin with the well-known fable of a cock searching for food by scratching in a dungheap; there he finds a jewel, which, according to the moral, represents the gift of wisdom buried in fables. Chaucer effectively turns this story upside down: the scholastic fabulist was a man telling a fable of a cock scratching in a dungheap, but here is a cock telling a fable of humans searching through a dungheap, specially and rather self-consciously created only in Chaucer's version of this exemplum. Both the searching cock in the Latin fable and the searching man in the vernacular exemplum find something that represents wisdom, since in effect the presence of the corpse in the dungheap represents the wisdom inherent in taking dreams seriously; ironically, both creatures also find something that they would rather not find. This reworked tale of Chauntecleer's becomes the parodic jewel in the midst of the heap of authoritative texts that shape *The Nun's Priest's Tale*.[33]

Chauntecleer closes the first exemplum with a conventional marker of scholastic interpretation in the verse, "Heere may men seen that dremes been to drede" (line 4253).[34] The formulaic use of the Latin word *hic* ("here") signals the moment of transition from a text to the commentator's version of its meaning. In a printed *Esopus moralizatus*, for example, every comment begins with the phrase "Hic auctor ponit aliam fabulam cuius documentum est . . . ," after which the commentator paraphrases the moral.[35] The fourteenth-century *Auctores octo* commentary uses such phrases as "Hic auctor dicit quod,"[36] while Biblioteca Comunale MS 156 in Treviso has frequent recourse to "Hic est duplex moralitas" (e.g., 61r) and similar markers. As a well-read student of literature, Chauntecleer has apparently learned that the end of each fable requires this type of clearly marked moralizing statement. What escapes his notice is that all of his exempla could be concluded with the same aphorism (and indeed, the

---

[33] Marie de France began her fable collection with the fable of the cock and the jewel in the dungheap, as most revisers of the Romulan fables did. Furthermore, her *Del cok e del gupil*, clearly one of Chaucer's sources, begins with the image of the cock sitting atop a dungheap ("femer"); *Marie de France: Fables*, ed. and trans. Harriet Spiegel (Toronto: University of Toronto Press, 1987), p. 168. Chaucer's displacement of the dungheap from the animal realm in his source fable to the human realm in the exemplum doubtless serves to reaffirm Chauntecleer's regal nature.

[34] In the *Variorum* edition of *The Nun's Priest's Tale*, Derek Pearsall points out that in the Hengwrt manuscript this line concludes the last verse paragraph in the pilgrimage exemplum, but most modern editors have placed it at the beginning of the next verse paragraph (p. 186). I agree with Pearsall that the Hengwrt paragraphing suits the sense of the passage best.

[35] *Esopus moralizatus* (Cologne: Heinrich Quentell, 1489).

[36] *Auctores octo* (Lyon: Jehan de Vingle, 1495).

second story closes with much the same statement in two slightly different versions [lines 4296–4499]). Of course the "moral" needs no such reiteration, but his amplifying repetition satisfies the generic requirement that a moral follow a short, pithy narrative. Medieval audiences familiar with scholastic practice would have seen here that Chauntecleer, a fable character somewhat too big for his genre, was bound to express himself using the fabulistic terms and structures that validate his textual existence: he works naturally within the parameters of the genre in which he exists. Ultimately the cock's inability to effect a structural synthesis among the exempla here is less important than his inability to synthesize the dream-text and his future, but the problem is the same in both instances.

Although Chauntecleer's exempla demonstrate that dreams can portend terrible mishaps, his final statement about his own nightmare implies a different relationship between dream and subsequent experience. He tells Pertelote, "Shortly I seye, as for conclusioun, / That I shal han of this avisioun / Adversitee" (lines 4341–43). Chauntecleer's unusual turn of phrase indicates the relationship between a fable plot summary and the plot that will follow: the earlier text is inexorably acted out in the later one. In the larger framework of the Aesopic tradition as a whole, such inexorability is the lot of every fable character, destined to repeat the same actions every time a fable is retold.

Medieval readers would have been struck by the parodic intent of the particular tales that Chauntecleer chose for glossing the dream-text, and by the absurdity of a beast telling fables about humans. However, they would not necessarily have been surprised that a tale or two were used to explicate another, for this practice occurred in the scholastic setting. Fable manuscripts include a very similar kind of commentary based upon constructing loose relationships between short narratives and one of the curricular fables. For example, Gualterus's Fable 21 ("Fabula nata sequi," ff. 15r–16v), which tells of the Athenians searching for a king, prompted a commentator to write two fables into his commentary, now Biblioteca Marciana MS 4658. These stories, of some foxes trying to keep flies off their meat, and an unreasonable stag attempting to chase a horse out of his pasture, both reflect the verse fable's central theme of government in the way that Chauntecleer's exempla represent the theme of portentous dreams of death, which his dream-text supposedly exemplifies.

Pertelote's and Chauntecleer's textual interpretations fall into the two most common binary categories of medieval fable interpretation (and indeed, the interpretation of nearly all medieval fiction): the earthly and the

133

spiritual. Pertelote's reading of the text is as mundane as it can be. In her opinion, the text was created by a creature on earth, and it only has meaning for creatures on earth who find themselves in certain unfortunate earthly situations. For Chauntecleer, this dream-text and others, if interpreted correctly, represent supernatural intervention that will help earthbound creatures through potential misfortunes. Two-part, mutually exclusive interpretations like these, in which the secular appears alongside the spiritual, turn up in numerous fable manuscripts and incunables, but the taxonomy for the two types of moral in Biblioteca Ambrosiana MS I.85.supra reflects the interpretive division in *The Nun's Priest's Tale*. In each fable comment the commentator calls the social interpretation of fables *humanum* and the spiritual readings *divinum*. Pertelote's reading of the dreamtext is distinctly human (despite the fact that she is not), while Chauntecleer's concentrates on the divine intervention at work in certain dreams.

In their fervor to strike different interpretive poses, each commentator erases the fact that the dream is really about a fox; and thus the chickens' comments, although marginal to the real import of the dream, have become new centers of attention for us as readers. The coup de grâce in these parallel series of erasures and displacements, however, occurs when the coupling of interpretations is literalized in the coupling of the interpreters: Chauntecleer "fethered Pertelote twenty tyme, / And trad hire eke as ofte, er it was pryme" (lines 4367–68). Even this carnality is significantly bipartite—first feathering as foreplay, and then treading as fulfillment. The action utterly displaces the dream-text, causing the commentators themselves to lose sight of it. Thus the commentary ends, the dream is all but forgotten, and we are finally ready for the fable text.

That the dream-text is so thoroughly displaced as to be driven from Chauntecleer's memory would have made the tale more humorous for Chaucer's early readers, since the medieval curriculum stressed memorization. Other British vernacular fabulists allude to the place of the Aesopic fable in the storehouse of memory. In *Isopes Fabules*, John Lydgate's Middle English renderings of seven of Gualterus's fables,[37] the poet twice connects Aesop's authorial intention with memory (". . . myn auctour remembreþ by wrytyng" [line 102], and "Isophus . . . / This fable wrote for a memoryalle" [lines 827–28]); these lines suggest that although writing ensures a

---

[37] Henry Noble McCracken, ed., *The Minor Poems of John Lydgate, Part 2: Secular Poems*, Early English Text Society, o.s., vol. 192 (Oxford: Oxford University Press, 1934), pp. 566–99.

fable's survival, its proper site is in human memory.[38] The suitability of fable for storage in the memory was made more explicit in Middle Scots poet Robert Henryson's *Morall Fabillis*,[39] in which fable 6, "The Sheep and the Dog," is introduced with the phrase, "Esope ane taill puttis in memorie" (line 1146). Although readers of Chaucer's fable may keep the dream-text in their memories, Chauntecleer does not—and he forgets it at his peril.

In forgetting the primary import of the text requiring interpretation, Chauntecleer is guilty of bad reading, and for medieval readers such misreading had ethical implications. The "translation" of texts into ethical behavior was one of the purposes of reading in the Middle Ages; this goal has been explored at length by Judson Boyce Allen[40] and, more recently, John Dagenais. His paraphrase of Allen provides a guide to how Chauntecleer has misread his dream-text.

According to Allen, the medieval text must be viewed not as verbal icon, not as Letter alone, but as an "event" that actualizes the ethical behavior of a reader, absorbs the reader into its own ethical system, and stimulates, among other ethical acts, its own reenactment (and, I would add, its own retelling and recopying).[41]

Neither the dream-text nor the exempla that Chauntecleer recounts stimulate him to action; rather, the exempla displace the dream-text, since Chauntecleer treats them only as the verbal icons of one of the greatest authors, authoritative texts whose message Chauntecleer can recite but cannot internalize. Although Chauntecleer initially gives voice to his fear of the red creature in the dream, his reenactment of the dream-text shows him overcoming that fear in order to enjoy the fox's flattery. Proper behavior—in this case, simple self-preservation—will fall prey to the vice of pride.

The conclusion of the chickens' commentary liberates the commenting

---

[38] For a discussion of the relationship between memory as the primary site of knowledge and written texts as secondary, see Mary Carruthers, *The Book of Memory: A Study of Memory in Medieval Culture* (Cambridge: Cambridge University Press, 1990), pp. 30–32.

[39] *The Poems of Robert Henryson*, ed. Denton Fox (Oxford: Oxford University Press, 1981). For a discussion of Henryson's extensive borrowings from the scholastic commentary tradition in his fables, see my article, "Scholastic Commentary and Robert Henryson's *Morall Fabillis*: The Aesopic Fables," *Studies in Philology* 91.1 (Winter 1994): 70–99.

[40] Judson Boyce Allen, *The Ethical Poetics of the Later Middle Ages* (Toronto: University of Toronto Press, 1982).

[41] Dagenais, *Ethics of Reading*, p. 21.

voice of the Nun's Priest himself, and he shapes the fable with references to authoritative writers or works of literature apparently meant to help the audience understand the action of the fable. Among these are Augustine, Boethius, Bishop Bradwardyn, *Physiologus*, Geoffrey of Vinsauf, Virgil's *Aeneid*, Saint Paul, and the Bible. Yoking this highly authoritative literature to a beast fable might strike modern readers as only one more aspect of the Nun's Priest's satirical strategy (or perhaps of Chaucer's satire of the Nun's Priest), but the use of such *auctoritates* was not at all uncommon in fourteenth- and fifteenth-century fable commentaries. Nearly every commentary draws in one or two authoritative maxims, and the most learned manuscripts of Gualterus Anglicus's fables include no fewer than ten *auctoritates*, several of which are cited in more than one comment. A late fourteenth- or early fifteenth-century German manuscript in the British Library (MS Add. 11897) glosses the fables with references to Bernard of Clairvaux, Gregory the Great, Horace, Ovid, Aristotle, Henricus Septimellensis, and others. Like the Nun's Priest, this commentator also refers to the Bible, Boethius, and Geoffrey of Vinsauf, but the commentator's favorite, most frequently mentioned *auctor* is Cato, to whom Pertelote and Chauntecleer themselves refer.[42] So while the specific phraseology and context of each *auctoritas* in Chaucer's tale may provide a satirical dimension, the mere presence of most of them in proximity to a fable would not have bespoken satire to an educated medieval audience.

Several of these authority figures are cited in the Nun's Priest's lengthy digression on God's foreknowledge; its position just after the description of the fox entering the farmyard, when the attack upon Chauntecleer is clearly at hand, is an obvious displacement of the inevitable. The first lines of this digression are particularly significant in the context of scholastic commentary displacing the texts that they interpret; they address larger philosophical issues that both foreshadow and delay the conflict of cock and fox (lines 4420–29):

> O Chauntecleer, acursed be that morwe
> That thou into that yerd flaugh fro the bemes!

---

[42] Equally laden with *auctoritates*, the commentary in Biblioteca Marciana MS 4658 includes aphorisms from Peter of Blois, Boethius, Egidius, Augustine, Cato, Seneca, Prudentius, and the Bible; it also cites Aristotle ("Philosophus") and Cassiodorus twice each, and Cicero ten times.

Although his fable commentary has apparently not survived, Stephen Patrington's *Ecloga* commentary cites Boethius, Isidore, Seneca, and Bernardus Silvestris, among other *auctores*; see Thomson and Perraud, *Ten Latin Schooltexts*, pp. 121–22. Patrington may have ornamented his commentary on the fables of Gualterus Anglicus with similar citations.

> Thou were ful wel ywarned by thy dremes
> That thilke day was perilous to thee;
> But what that God forwoot moot nedes bee,
> After the opinioun of certein clerkis.
> Witnesse on hym that any parfit clerk is,
> That in scole is greet altercacioun
> In this mateere, and greet disputisoun,
> And hath been of an hundred thousand men.

The clause questioning whether God's foreknowledge predicates events stands in a purposefully ambiguous relationship to the phrase "after the opinioun of certein clerkis." These lines state literally that according to the opinions of certain clerks, what God foreknows must take place. However, within the world of this text, the lines ask to be read differently: what is foreknown about Chauntecleer's future cannot take place until after the clerk who is the Nun's Priest has aired his "opinioun" about divine prescience and a variety of other subjects. Text comes after commentary.

In the passage above, the Nun's Priest places an odd emphasis upon the cock's cataclysmic decision to fly down from the beams on this fateful day, as if the narrator believes that a rooster might naturally spend full days on his perch. The narrator's extraneous attention to flying from the beams, which does not appear in any of the known source material for this tale, is evidently a detail added by Chaucer. It was also sometimes a detail added to plot paraphrases in scholastic commentaries on the fable of the cock and jewel, mentioned above. Although the curricular Latin fable takes place only in the dungheap, a commentator whose work survives in a handful of fable manuscripts engaged in amplification of the plot by introducing his paraphrase as follows: "Gallus sollicitus de dape mane descendit de trabe et incepit vertere fimum pedibus et rostro"[43] ("A cock desiring a meal early in the morning descended from a beam and began to turn up a dungheap with his claws and beak.") As the fable commentator has rhetorically displaced his source text by adding his own details, Chaucer has taken an available naturalistic detail—that cocks perch on beams and sometimes leave them—and made it central to the "tragedy" that is about to unfold. In making a minor aetiological observation the immediate cause of an

---

[43] Leipzig Universitätsbibliothek MS 1084, f. 115v. The same amplified plot summary appears in Augsburg Universitätsbibliothek MS 2.1.4º.27; Munich Staatsbibliothek Clm. 4409 and 22404; Ottobeuren Stiftsbibliothek 0.82; Freiburg Universitätsbibliothek MS 21; and Prague Statni Knihovna MS 11.C.4. All of these manuscripts date from the fifteenth century.

apocalyptic event, Chaucer's parodic intent is as clear to modern readers as it would have been to their medieval counterparts, but Chaucer's readers in the Middle Ages would have understood that Chaucer was also parodying the rhetorical practice of *amplificatio*, which could clutter the narrative landscape with minutiae.

And so we finally reach the fable: the fox attacks, but the cock escapes. As the Nun's Priest states, this is "destinee, that [may] nat been eschewed" (line 4528).

A fable narrative requires a moral, but at the end of *The Nun's Priest's Tale*, morals displace each other repeatedly, leaving none to dominate. Chauntecleer generalizes about his experience in one couplet ("For he that wynketh, whan he sholde see, / Ay wilfully, God lat him nevere thee!" [lines 4621–22]), and Russell the fox follows suit ("'Nay,' quod the fox, 'but God yeve hym meschaunce, / That is so undiscreet of governaunce / That jangleth whan he sholde holde his pees'" [lines 4623–25]). As if unable to allow the beasts the last word, the Nun's Priest himself adds, "Lo, swich it is for to be recchelees / And necligent, and truste on flaterye" (lines 4626–27).[44] This tripartite moral mirrors the structure of the end of Marie de France's fable; there as here, any one of these morals might suffice as an interpretive gesture to sum up the fable, but instead, no single voice gains dominance.

Although the Nun's Priest gives himself the last word, he finally displaces his own authority, and in so doing he mimics a scholastic practice by raising the possibility of a divine reading after the three earthly, social ones (lines 4628–33).

> But ye that holden this tale a folye,
> As of a fox, or of a cok and hen,
> Taketh the moralite, goode men.
> For Seint Paul seith that al that writen is,
> To oure doctrine it is ywrite, ywis;
> Taketh the fruyt, and lat the chaf be stille.

[44] Chaucer's use of the word "reccheless" in the Nun's Priest's moral has no precedent in his sources, and he may have chosen it as a play on the verb "recche" in line 4086, Chauntecleer's first words in the tale, and indeed, its central concern: "Now God," quod he, "my swevene recche aright. . . ." In the extant corpus of Chaucer's work this is the only use of "recche" to mean "interpret"; Larry D. Benson, *A Glossarial Concordance to the Riverside Chaucer* (New York: Garland, 1993), "recchen," v. (1). Chauntecleer's desire for proper interpretation is flouted by the Nun's Priest in relation to the tale as a whole; the fable, like Chauntecleer's dream, concludes without interpretation that engages the text fully.

The Nun's Priest calls attention to the need to interpret this text, to find its real meaning, as Chauntecleer hoped to do with his dream-text. In asking for interpretation, he unnecessarily raises the Macrobian notion that the fable might be thought meaningless—"a folye," which is what Pertelote believes Chauntecleer's dream-text to be, in effect if not in cause. Like the dream-text within it, this tale will prompt its interpreters to react either like a Pertelote, holding the fable mere folly, or like a Chauntecleer, scratching away at the text to find its transcendent significance.

The closing lines of *The Nun's Priest's Tale* demand another commentary, and in some manuscripts of *The Canterbury Tales*, the fable receives one from the Host (whom we do not assume to represent an educated reader).

> "Sire Nonnes Preest," oure Hooste seide anoon,
> "I-blessed be thy breche, and every stoon!
> This was a murie tale of Chauntecleer.
> But by my trouthe, if thou were seculer,
> Thou woldest ben a trede-foul aright.
> For if thou have corage as thou hast myght,
> Thee were nede of hennes, as I wene,
> Ya, moo than seven tymes seventene.
> See, whiche braunes hath this gentil preest,
> So gret a nekke, and swich a large breest!
> He loketh as a sperhauk with his yen. . . ." (lines 4637–47)

Achieving a difference with his source text, the Host comments not upon the fable itself but upon its relation to its narrator; this is a painfully inappropriate "dramatic" reading of the tale. The Host has heard Chauntecleer textualize his dream for his audience, Pertelote, in order to say something about himself and to ask for commentary, so likewise the Host assumes that the Nun's Priest has textualized himself in his tale for his audience of pilgrims. The hen responds that Chauntecleer's dream-text represented little of value; by calling the Nun's Priest's fable only "a murie tale," the Host expresses a similar unwillingness to read significance into it. Pertelote stated that the dream-text's only real significance was in relation to the body of its narrator, a cock; the Host finds the fable's significance in relation to the Nun's Priest's body, whose physical attributes metaphorically transform him in the Host's eyes to a "trede-foul" or a "sperhauk." In Pertelote's interpretation, the dream-text signified Chauntecleer's need for intestinal catharsis; the Host's reading of the tale leads him to speculate about the Nun's Priest's need for sexual catharsis.

In a reading that is finally neither *humanum* nor *divinum*, the Host fails to interpret the animals in the fable as representative of humans so as to glean a human, moral lesson from the fable; rather, he reads the body of the human before him as an animal's, fantasizing that body back into a fabular setting. But the Host's Pertelotish response to the fable is also quite conventional in terms of scholastic commentary, inasmuch as it threatens to recreate exactly the kind of dialogue of displacing comments that took place between Pertelote and Chauntecleer in the tale, particularly if the Nun's Priest were subsequently to insist upon the divine reading that his citation of St. Paul in the tale's final lines requires. Not surprisingly, no such comment from the Nun's Priest has come down to us, and the Host turns away from the priest in search of a tale from another pilgrim (lines 4651–52).

Since Chaucer elsewhere shows interest in structuring tales around both commentaries and their concomitant gestures of displacement, we might be tempted to see *The Nun's Priest's Tale* as offering only one more instance of a favorite authorial technique. Even if we disregard several prologues, which comment upon the narratives that follow but are separable from them, ostensibly scholastic commentary introduces (and temporally displaces the plots of) other tales. Perhaps the most obvious instance of this structure, *The Merchant's Tale*, begins with the narrator discussing marriage and then passing the discussion to January's brothers, Placebo and Justinus: the argument becomes such a scholarly disputation that January derides Justinus's opinions as "scole-termes" (*MerT* 1569). The Pardoner's rhetorical divisions of the sins to be examined in his tale represent the conventional religious variation upon the same scholastic commenting procedure.

I would argue, however, that in *The Nun's Priest's Tale* Chaucer's use of an overall structure closely akin to that which framed scholastic fable commentary in the classroom and sometimes on the page has a very different effect from the introductory commentaries that he uses elsewhere. In aforementioned tales in which commentary precedes plot, the commentary sketches some possibilities for the tale, but because those tales do not begin with a "master" text to be interpreted, the issues discussed remain more abstract. No other tale begins with a textualized summary of the subsequent conflict provided by one of the characters who will participate in that conflict. As I have suggested, that text, brought to Chauntecleer by some external force, assumes a certain causality in the cock's mind, prescribing rather than describing events in the future.

But if Chaucer's emphasis on the dream-text molds expectations that the dream will come true in the plot, the tale's own history as well as the history of its genre are equally forceful in creating reader expectation. Manuscript evidence such as that cited above shows some important aspects of the interpretive framework within which medieval readers received and situated fable, and Chaucer exploited a number of possibilities in that framework without ultimately privileging any one of them. His most significant gesture, one typical of medieval vernacular poetry based on classical texts, lies in his choice of making conventional interpretive possibilities not external to the tale but integral to it. The proximity of commentary to plot adds to the tale's irony when readers see that physical contiguity cannot guarantee intellectual continuity: the lessons of the former do not influence the course of the latter.

The unification of commentary and plot within the fable is only one of several unifying gestures in the tale. In the medieval classroom, the fable's summarizer, its commentator, and its animal characters were two or three separate entities. Not so for Chauntecleer, who is envisioner of his story, commentator upon it, and participant in it. Significantly, this triad of roles is also played out by "Chaucers" in relation to *The Canterbury Tales*: he is envisioner of a collection of tales mostly inherited from other sources, commentator upon it (particularly at its inception), and participant in it.

If we look at the shape of *The Nun's Priest's Tale* in light of the tripartite nature of the fictionalized Chaucer in his work, we might see the poet Chaucer reacting to the larger question of how a writer can give an inherited text authority and what can deprive it of that status. Obviously mere age and repetition cannot make a text authoritative; rather, the greatest validator of *auctoritas* is experience, as Chauntecleer himself says (line 4168), and he goes on to learn this lesson vividly. Even so, within the framework of this most literary of fables, experience and the texts to which one chooses to give authority (as Chauntecleer gives to his dream) seem closely related. Thus, for educated medieval readers the tale not only parodied their experience of canonical authority in education and the practices it employed, but also showed them that they were ineluctably bound to negotiate within the structures and strictures of education in order to master experience as it attacked them outside the classroom. The world of those readers was as defined and delimited by their epistemologies as ours is for us. Chaucer tacitly suggests that all readers need to learn to negotiate between text and commentary, experience and education, in order to overcome the tendency to allow one to displace the other. Chauntecleer's negotiations nearly fail, but the rest of us readers continue to try.

141

Thomas Berthelette and Gower's *Confessio*

Tim William Machan
Marquette University

Unlike Geoffrey Chaucer, his fourteenth-century friend and fellow poet to whose name his has been inextricably linked in English literary history, John Gower has not been the focus of a great editorial tradition. English works of both poets were printed by Caxton in the 1480s, but there the similarities end. In the 1490s, Richard Pynson, Wynkyn de Worde, and Julian Notary published copies of individual Chaucerian compositions, and in 1526 Pynson compiled a number of poems in a three-volume issue. Six years later William Thynne printed a collected *Works*, which was reissued in 1542 and again about 1550, each time with a few textual supplements. John Stowe added a great deal more material for his 1561 *Works*, while in 1598 Thomas Speght supplemented this edition with two more poems and an elaborate critical apparatus. Speght expanded all of this material in a 1602 revision, which was reissued in 1687. In 1721 yet another, more elaborate collected *Works* was produced under the name of John Urry, and then in 1775 Thomas Tyrwhitt began to issue the five volumes of his *Canterbury Tales* edition, the first edition typically judged to be scholarly by modern standards. Thus, though all of the editors from Stowe through Urry ultimately derived many of their texts from Thynne's 1532 *Works*, by the beginning of the nineteenth century Chaucer's compositions had been treated by at least eight different individuals since Caxton, and the predominant format was the collected *oeuvre* surrounded by an elaborate scholarly apparatus.[1]

The printing history of Gower's *Confessio Amantis* is a story much shorter

---

[1] On the development of the Chaucerian textual tradition, see Eleanor Hammond, *Chaucer: A Bibliographical Manual* (New York: Macmillan, 1908); and Paul G. Ruggiers, ed., *Editing Chaucer: The Great Tradition* (Norman, Okla.: Pilgrim Books, 1984).

to tell.[2] Caxton issued the poem in 1483, but during the period when Chaucer's poems were being edited by Pynson, de Worde, and Notary, no subsequent edition of the *Confessio* appeared, and none would appear until Thomas Berthelette's quarto of 1532, the year in which Thynne issued Chaucer's collected *Works*. In 1554, after two revisions of Thynne's *Works* had been printed, Berthelette's 1532 *Confessio* was reprinted with only minor differences in design and orthography. The 1554 issue is in general also more elegantly laid out than the 1532 one, though the only significant difference may well be the elimination on the title page of reference to Berthelette as "Printer to the Kingis grace." Here, in any case, the early modern editorial history of the *Confessio* stops. During the period in which Stowe nearly doubled the size of the Chaucerian canon, Speght supplemented it with the elaborate apparatus of humanist critical reading, Urry reconceived it from the perspective of an eighteenth-century intellectual, and Tyrwhitt reduced it by empirical means—during this period Gower's *Confessio* remained available only in manuscript, in Caxton's 1483 print, or in Berthelette's two issues, and it is clearly the last two forms that would have been most widely accessible.[3] Another complete text of the *Confessio* would not in fact appear until 1810, when Alexander Chalmers issued it as part of his *Works of the English Poets*, and this edition merely reprinted Berthelette's 1554 issue with minor corrections and alterations. The first truly new edition after Berthelette's was thus not produced until the three-volume effort of Reinhold Pauli in 1857.

The reasons for this relative editorial neglect are complex and varied, involving not only the diminution of Gower's literary status for cultural and political reasons but also the generally low reputation of Middle English literature in the early modern period: Chaucer, it is worth remembering, was the only medieval writer whose works remained continually in print from Caxton's introduction of the medium to England in 1476 until the nineteenth century.[4] Here, in any case, my interest lies less with the

---

[2] G. C. Macaulay, ed., *The English Works of John Gower*, 2 vols., Early English Text Society [hereafter EETS], e.s., vols. 81 and 82 (London: Oxford University Press, 1900), 1:clxviii–clxx. Also see N. F. Blake, "Early Printed Editions of *Confessio Amantis*," *Mediaevalia* 16 (1993 [for 1990]): 289–306.

[3] Robert Watt identifies another edition of Berthelette, printed in 1544, but as there is no other proof of this issue, Watt's identification is likely due to a misreading of the title page of a 1554 copy. See Robert Watt, *Bibliotheca Britannica, or A General Index to British and Foreign Literature*, 4 vols. (Edinburgh: Archibald Constable, 1824), 1:430.

[4] On Gower's reputation see John H. Fisher, *John Gower: Moral Philosopher and Friend of Chaucer* (New York: New York University Press, 1964), pp. 1–36; Neil Gilroy-Scott, "John Gower's Reputation: Literary Allusions from the Early Fifteenth Century to the Time of

reasons for Berthelette's being the only edition of the *Confessio* between the time of Henry VIII and the nineteenth century and more with the consequences of this situation. In particular, since Berthelette's edition constituted a preliminary interpretive frame for most readings of Gower's poem during these three hundred years, how did its critical apparatus, layout, and textual content influence these readings? Inasmuch as readers of any literary works do not access those works intuitively but in specific formats that inescapably (if sometimes imperceptibly) contribute to the character of the works, what does the format of the 1532 *Confessio* indicate about Berthelette's reading of the poem, and how can it help to account for Gower's reputation in literary history?

Physically, the 1532 *Confessio* must be considered a handsome volume. A quarto with leaves measuring a substantial $7^1/_2''$ by $11^1/_2''$ and containing 191 folios, the book is set in a clear and striking black-letter font—the same font Berthelette had used the year before in his printing of Sir Thomas Elyot's *The boke named the gouernour*[5]—with generous margins throughout. On the opening page, the title is framed by a geometric pattern that is attractive though far simpler than the portals and statuary that Berthelette often used in his editions of Elyot's works. Thereafter, the volume proper begins with a two-page dedication to Henry VIII that is set in a single column artfully tapered at the conclusion and followed by a floral woodcut so as to fill up the second page. And after this are a two-page letter to the reader and a detailed ten-page summary of the poem's contents, both of which are set in double columns. In the latter, rubrics announce the "contentes" of the prologue and each of the books, while within these sections every story, designated by a paragraph mark, is itemized, sometimes in detail, and keyed to the appropriate folio number. In this way, a long and complex poem is rendered very accessible to its readers, even more so than in Caxton's 1483 edition, which also itemizes stories and their folio numbers. Verbal parallels indicate Berthelette based his listing on Caxton's, but he both edited individual entries and in some cases increased their total number; in book 8, for example, Caxton itemizes 16 episodes, compared to 27 by Berthelette.

Berthelette's *Confessio* itself, also set in double columns and concluding

'Pericles,'" *YES* 1 (1971): 30–47; and Derek Pearsall, "The Gower Tradition," in A. J. Minnis, ed., *Gower's "Confessio Amantis": Responses and Reassessments* (Cambridge: D. S. Brewer, 1983), pp. 179–97.

[5] Henry R. Plomer, *A Short History of English Printing 1476–1900* (London: Kegan Paul, 1915), p. 51.

LIBER

For thilke vyce, of whiche J mene
Vnkyndshyp where it falleth
The trouthe of mannes herte it palleth
That he can no good dede acquyte
So may he stonde of no meryte
Towardes god, and eke also
Men calle hym the worldes fo
For he no more than the fende
Vnto none other man is frende
But all toward hym selfe alone
For thy my sonne in thy persone
This vyce aboue all other flee
My fader as ye teche me
J thynke to do in this matere
But ouer this J wolde fayn here
wherof J shall me sbryue more
My good sonne as for thy lore
After the reule of couetyse
J shall the propyrte deuyse
Of euery vyce by and by
Nowe herken, and be wel ware therby.

Viribus ex clara res tollit luce rapina
Floribus et iuncta virgine mella capit.

Hic tractat super ista specia cupida que rapina
nuncupatur, cuius mater extorcio ipsam ad de-
seruiendum magnatum curiis specialius commendauit.

In the lygnage of auaryce
My sonne yet there is a vyce
His ryght name it is rauyne
whiche hath a route of his couyne
Rauyne amonge the maysters dwelleth
And with his seruauntes as men telleth
Extorcion is nowe witholde
Rauyne of other mennes folde
Maketh his lardyr, and payeth nought
For where as euer it may be sought
In his hous there shall no thynge lacke
And that fulofte abyeth the packe
Of powre men that dwelle a boute
Thus stant the comune people in doute
whiche can do none amendement
For whan hym fayleth paiement
Rauyne maketh non other skylle
But taketh by strength al that he wille
So ben there in the same wyse
Louers, as J the shall deuyse
That whan nought elles may quayle
Anone

Anone with strength they assayle
And gette of loue the sesyne
when they se tyme by rauyne
For thy my sonne sbryue the here
Jf thou hast ben a Rauynere
Of loue. Certes father no
For J my lady loue so
For though J were as was Pompey
That all the worlde me wolde obey
Or els suche as Alisaundre
J wolde nought do suche a sclaunder
It is no good man whiche so doth
In good seyth sonne thou sayst sothe
For he that woll of purueance
By suche a wey his luste auaunce
De shall it after sore abye
But if these olde ensamples lye
Nowe good father telle me one
So as ye connen many one
Touchende of loue in this matere
Now lyst my son & thou shalte here
So as it hath be befall er this
In loues cause howe that it is
A man to take by rauyne
The preye whiche is feminyne.

Hic ponit exemplum contra istos in amorie
causa raptores, Et narrat qualiter Pandyon rex
Athen.ii. filias vez Progne & Philomená habuit:
Progne autem regi Tracie Thereo desponsata
contigit, quod cum Tereus ad instantiam vxoris
sue Philomenam de Athen in Traciam sororie
visitationis causa secum quadam vice perduceret
in concupiscentiam Philomene tanta seueritate in
Stinere dilapsus est, quod ipse non solum sue vio-
lentia rapine virginitatem eius oppressit, sed et ip-
sius linguam, ne factum detegeret forcipe mutila
uit, vnde imperpetuus memorie cronicam tanti ra-
ptoris austeritatem miro ordine dii postea vindi-
carunt.

There was a ryall noble kynge
A ryche of all worldes thynge
whiche of his propre enheritance
Athenis had in gouernance
And who so thynketh therupon
His name was kynge Pandyon
Two doughters had he by his wyfe
The whiche he loued as his lyfe
The fyrst doughter Progne hyght
And the seconde, as she well myght
was cleped faire Philomene
To

Fig. 1. Berthelette, ed., *Jo. Gower de Confessione Amantis* (1532), fol. 113^v. Reproduced by permission of the Department of Special Collections, Memorial Library, University of Wisconsin-Madison.

with the simple colophon "Thus endeth De confessione Amantis," is attractively and carefully presented, with no obvious errors in composition. The volume has no border decorations, while the running-title is simply "Liber Primus," etc., divided across the gutter. Large woodcut initials are used at the opening of every book, however, and the beginnings of glosses and stories are typically highlighted with a pointing fist, a paragraph mark, or a leaf. If the book lacks the bulk and substance of Thynne's *Works* of Chaucer issued in the same year, thus, its appearance is nonetheless the more elegant, and it is significantly more stylish in this regard than Caxton's 1483 *Confessio* or Robert Crowley's 1550 edition of *Piers Plowman.* The former, for example, utilizes a font far less clean than Berthelette's and contains several signs of hasty composition: The Latin poems are set as prose, though virgules are used to indicate line breaks; woodcuts never replaced the small keying letters left by the compositor in the spaces at the beginning of books and individual stories; and on several pages the text is broken up by large blank spaces due to careless casting off.[6]

One of the ways Berthelette's edition reveals its early modern origins and also shapes interpretive responses to Gower and the *Confessio* is through its definition of the volume's audience, with dedication to Henry VIII alone establishing the seriousness of the enterprise. As formulaic as the fulsome praise of a patron in a dedication could be, invoking Henry's support here may have offered some actual practical utility as a way of deflecting critical responses to one of Berthelette's rare ventures into popular verse. In his dedication to *The gouernour,* similarly, Elyot asks the King to "be patrone and defendour of this little warke agayne the assaultes of maligne interpretours; which fayle nat to rente and deface the renoune of wryters, they themselves beinge in nothinge to the publike weal profitable."[7] But more important, Berthelette's dedication to a monarch imputes the *Confessio* with a political relevance to all of English society, even as it inscribes the King as an arbiter of learning and taste. After asserting that Henry loved learning more than Alexander the Great did, Berthelette maintains that "both the nobuls and commons" will read the book and "beare away the morall doctrines" more quickly when "they shall se hit come forthe vnder your gracis name / whom they with all their very hartes so truely loue 7

---

[6] E.g., Caxton, ed., *THis book is intituled confessio amantis* (London: Caxton, 1483), sigs. xli^v, lxviii^r, and lxxxxi^v. Blake suggests that "Caxton's edition of the *Confessio* exhibits more signs of carelessness in the printing than usual"; "Early Printed Editions," p. 294.

[7] Qtd. in H. S. Bennett, *English Books & Readers 1475–1557* (Cambridge: Cambridge University Press, 1952), p. 50. On dedications in general in the period, see pp. 47–53.

drede, whom they knowe so excellently well lerned / whome they euer fynde so good / so iuste / and so gracious a prince."[8] Reference to the "nobuls and commons" specifies the audience of the book as the whole of England. In turn, when Berthelette notes that Henry customarily accepts gifts not only from "the nobuls and great estates" but also from the "meane subiectes" and then styles himself the King's "mooste humble subiecte and seruaunt," the volume is made to respond to the same socializing forces it initiates.

From this perspective, Gower's *Confessio* is conceptualized as an ethical and moral composition that will edify readers in the way humanist literary paradigms required:

And who so euer in redynge of this warke / dothe consyder it well / shal fynde / that it is plentifully stuffed and fournysshed with manyfolde eloquent reasons / sharpe and quicke argumentes and examples of great auctorite / perswadynge vnto vertue / not onely taken out of the poetes / oratours / history wryters / and philosophers / but also out of the holy scripture. There is to my dome / no man / but that he may bi reding of this warke get right great knowlege / as wel for the vnderstandyng of many 7 diuers autors / whose resons / sayenges / 7 histories are translated in to this warke.[9]

As a veritable cornucopia of eloquence and authoritative doctrine culled from Antique poets, orators, and philosophers, the *Confessio* in effect becomes an English epitome of what we today would call Western culture but Berthelette might simply have labeled "science." And in this regard, the morality of the poem, like the ethical content of Chaucer's writings as Brian Tuke frames them in his preface to Thynne's *Works*, ultimately serves nationalistic as well as moralizing purposes. Gower and Chaucer alike, Berthelette observes in his letter to the reader, "imployed theyr tyme so wel and so vertuously, that they dyd not onely passe forth their lyfes here ryght honourably, but also for their so doyng, so longe (of lykelyhode) as letters shal endure 7 continue, this noble royalme shal be the better, ouer and besyde theyr honest fame and renowme."[10] Dedicated to the King of

---

[8] Berthelette, ed., *Jo. Gower de Confessione Amantis* (London: Berthelette: 1532), sig. aaii[r]. Berthelette's 1554 dedication and letter to the reader are also printed in Alexander Chalmers, ed., *The Works of the English Poets: From Chaucer to Cowper*, 21 vols. (London: Whittingham, 1810), 2:1–5, and in Blake, "Early Printed Editions," pp. 296–301.

[9] Berthelette, ed., *Jo. Gower de Confessione Amantis*, sigs. aaii[r]–aaii[v].

[10] Ibid., sig. aaiii[v].

England, this *Confessio* serves as a testament to the greatness of England itself.

The literary implications of Berthelette's prefatory matter again merge with the political in his discussion of the poem's imitable examples of "englysshe wordes and vulgars." As a model for the way writers ought to use language, Gower becomes a conservative voice speaking against the fashionable coinage of new words and to the broad spectrum of English society. Since throughout the fifteenth century Gower had been praised for the fecundity and eloquence of his rhetoric, this recuperation represents a slight but significant modulation in the reception history of the poet. In recent times, Berthelette notes, writers "beganne to loth and hate these olde vulgars." When they would write English, accordingly, such writers "were constrayned to brynge in / in their writynges / newe termes (as some calle them) whiche they borowed out of latyne / frenche / and other langages." The sarcasm of Berthelette's parenthetical concession to the very idea of "termes" foregrounds a distaste for a style that is in effect exclusionary: "they that vnderstode not those langages / from whens these newe vulgars are fette / coude not perceyue theyr wrytynges," even as Gower's *Confessio*, it should be recalled, offers worthwhile "morall doctrines" to "nobuls and commons" alike. Old writers like Gower, indeed, are said to have coined new words "eyther bycause of theyr metre / or elles for lacke of a feete englysshe worde" and are scarcely therefore a precedent for the indiscriminate "heaping" of neologisms by contemporary writers. Thus, when Berthelette tells the aspiring writer that "this worthy olde wryter John Gower . . . shall as a lanterne gyue hym lyghte to wryte counnyngly / and to garnyshhe his sentencis in our vulgar tonge,"[11] the light Gower casts was decidedly ignited in putatively moderate, democratic traditions of the English past and just as decidedly occludes, in the social upheaval of the 1530s, those motivated merely by elitist fashion or by no principle at all.

Less political but still entirely within early modern literary paradigms are Berthelette's comments on the textual tradition of the *Confessio*. For instance, by telling the reader that in this edition "ye shal your selfe now deme [Gower's learning], whan ye shall see hym (as nere as I can) sette forth in his owne shappe and lykenes,"[12] Berthelette makes the common humanist gesture of equating the poet with his poem. Berthelette also maintains that the previous, printed edition of Caxton omitted authorial

[11] Ibid., sig. aaii\u1d5b.
[12] Ibid., sig. aaiii\u1d5b.

lines, columns, and pages, with the result "that this mooste pleasant and easy auctor coude not wel be perceyued: for that and chaungynge of wordes, and misordrynge of sentences, wolde haue mased his mynde in redynge, that had ben very well lerned."[13] It was in the context of scribal corruption, presumably, that Berthelette understood the existence of the variant dedications of the *Confessio*: an early version, which dedicates the poem to Richard II, and a later one, which cites the future Henry IV. Though the manuscript Berthelette followed evidently contained the early version of the *Confessio* and thus the Richard II preface, Berthelette adapted the revised dedication from Caxton's edition in the body of his text. In the letter to the reader, however, he draws attention to the fact that "the writen copies do not agre with the prynted," notes that the disparity "beganne at the .xxiij. lyne in the prologue," and then prints the whole of the passage referring to Richard II.[14]

While it may be that Berthelette was in fact especially desirous of righting Gower's text,[15] this kind of expression amounted to a topos common among early printers. Caxton, for instance, uses it in the preface to his second edition of *The Canterbury Tales*, where he maintains that he prepared a new edition of the poem after a gentleman drew his attention to the errors of the first edition and offered his father's manuscript as a better text. Berthelette himself had already assumed the posture of the correcting editor a few years prior to the *Confessio* edition. In a prefatory address to a translation of *The table of Cebes*, Berthelette advises the reader that "if any faute be therin, I knowe well it is mistakyng, for my copie was somewhat combrouse, what for the enterlinyng and yll writyng."[16] And he would assume this posture again in 1535, in the preface to his reissue of de Worde's 1495 edition of the English translation of Bartholomaeus Anglicus's *De proprietatibus rerum*: "This worke . . . is newely printed with many places therin amended by the latyne exemplare: wherby ye shalle nowe the better vnderstand it, not onely bycause many wordes 7 sentences / that were here 7 there lefte out, be restored agayne, but also by reson the propre names of men, landes, cites / townes, ryuers, mountaynes / beastes, wodes / foules, 7 fishes, be trewely ortografied."[17] In a 1541 revised edi-

---

[13] Ibid., sig. aaiii^v.

[14] Ibid., sigs. aaiii^r–aaiii^v.

[15] So Bennett maintains in *English Books & Readers*, pp. 199–200.

[16] Qtd. in Bennett, *English Books & Readers*, p. 204. Bennett suggests 1525 as the publication date, which would be three years prior to the earliest of Berthelette's other publications. The *Short-Title Catalogue* offers 1531.

[17] Bartholomaeus Anglicus, *De proprietatibus rerum* (London: Thomas Berthelette, 1535), sig. ii^r.

tion, Berthelette demonstrated his attention to textual accuracy with the very title of *The Castell of helth corrected and in some places augmented, by the first author therof, sir Thomas Elyot knyght.*

Just as Caxton, furthermore, clearly exaggerated his own editorial activities in the second edition of *The Canterbury Tales*,[18] so Berthelette, even though his text of the *Confessio* does represent an improvement over Caxton's, utilizes the alleged textual history of the poem for significant rhetorical purposes. Textual corruption, that is, indexes the antiquity of a poem whose author is inscribed as traditional and conservative, while its correction verifies both the poem's current merit and the reliability of the edition. It is from this rhetorical vein of self-validation that Berthelette's comments about his own efforts, which otherwise might seem pompous vanity, emerge: "And though I shulde saye / that it was not moche greatter peyne to that excellent clerke the morall John Gower to compyle the same noble warke / than it was to me to prynt it / no man wyll beleue it / without conferring both the printis / the olde and myn to gether."[19]

For his actual text of the *Confessio*, Berthelette used an early-version manuscript resembling Oxford, Bodleian Library MS Bodley 294, but he supplemented this manuscript with Caxton's edition of the revised version not only in the dedication but also later in the prologue and in books 1 and 8, including, perhaps most importantly, the Chaucer greeting.[20] Like the majority of the *Confessio* manuscripts and Caxton's edition, it should also be noted, Berthelette's edition integrates the Latin glosses *within* the body of his text. These glosses figure prominently in the *ordinatio* of the manuscripts, where they are often written or underscored in red, so that their authenticity and relevance to the Middle English are generally well accepted.[21] In Berthelette's text, the Latin poems are set in roman, but the glosses appear in a black-letter font that is slightly smaller than that used for the Middle English proper. At the beginning of individual books or

---

[18] See Lotte Hellinga, "Manuscripts in the Hands of Printers," in J. B. Trapp, ed., *Manuscripts in the Fifty Years After the Invention of Printing* (London: Warburg Institute, 1983), pp. 3–11.

[19] Berthelette, ed., *Jo. Gower de Confessione Amantis*, sig. aaii[r].

[20] Macaulay, ed., *Works of John Gower*, 1:clxix. Blake challenges Macaulay's views and, pointing out that "Berthelette said he printed his edition from the earlier print," suggests that the changes between Caxton's and Berthelette's editions of the *Confessio* "are not more than those found between Caxton's first and second edition of *The Canterbury Tales*." Final acceptance or rejection of Macaulay's position, Blake maintains, should await "an examination of Berthelette against the manuscripts"; "Early Printed Editions," p. 306. On the rhetoric of Berthelette's prologue, however, see further below.

[21] Bodley MS 294, for example, displays the glosses in red within the columns of Middle English; Macaulay, ed., *Works of John Gower*, 1:clv.

stories (such as at 1.1 or 1.1235), therefore, the text modulates from roman type for the Latin poem, to small black letter for the gloss, and then to large black letter for the Middle English. In this way, Berthelette's text represents a clear improvement in layout over Caxton's, which sets all of the poems, glosses, and Middle English in the same black-letter font. Black letter was in fact the most common typeface in general for English books until the middle of the sixteenth century, though in the period roman was also used for Latin texts, and for books utilizing both Latin and English it was especially common to use roman for the former and black letter for the latter.[22] While Berthelette's setting of the poems in roman is thus typical of the period, his use of black letter for the glosses is not, although it does typographically identify them closely with the Middle English. Visually, the effect is balanced but striking, so that even though the 1532 *Confessio* is not one of Berthelette's most elaborate productions, it is, again, aesthetically pleasing in a way that Thynne's *Works* and Crowley's *Piers Plowman* are not.

Berthelette's *Confessio* is thus a carefully produced edition that projects a rather conservative conception of Gower and that, while more physically attractive than comparable volumes, demonstrates typical concerns and publishing gestures of the early modern period. But since it remained the most accessible forum for Gower's poem until the nineteenth century, Berthelette's humanist edition physically and conceptually helped to construct Gower's reception in this period as well as the Renaissance. I want now to consider, accordingly, how the reading of the *Confessio* in Berthelette's format helped to shape the poem's reputation before the advent of philology and modern scholarship. Specifically, I want to explore Berthelette's contributions to the almost inevitable linking of Gower with Chaucer and to the judgment of morality as Gower's preeminent characteristic.

Links between Chaucer and Gower are present, of course, in the conclusions to both the *Confessio* and the *Troilus* as well as in the headlink of the *Man of Law's Tale*. These links were solidified in Caxton's edition of the *Confessio*, which relied on a manuscript with a revised version for the first half of the poem but one with an early version for the conclusion and hence the Chaucer greeting. This switch, as John Fisher analyzes it, was at least partly dependent on a desire to make an explicit connection between Gower and Chaucer: Caxton recognized, Fisher maintains, "the publicity value of the Chaucer association and made sure that the lines referring to it

---

[22] R. B. McKerrow, *An Introduction to Bibliography for Literary Students* (Oxford: Clarendon Press, 1927), p. 297.

were included."[23] Even more is this the case with Berthelette's edition, which also includes the valediction to Chaucer. Since Berthelette relied throughout on a manuscript of the early version, this inclusion would seem less significant than it does for Caxton. What is significant is the fact that though Berthelette clearly knew that the *Confessio* survived in differing versions, he did not alert the reader to the existence of a conclusion in which the Chaucer valediction was omitted. If the inclusion of dedications to both Richard II and Henry Bolingbroke facilitated reception of Gower as a political opportunist, failure to acknowledge that the allusion to Chaucer was at some point excised forestalled the myth of the Gower-Chaucer feud that would figure so strongly for later critics.[24]

Even more significant here is Berthelette's letter "To the reder," which inescapably connects the poets before the *Confessio* even begins. Having warned the reader about the poem's textual corruption in transmission and having praised Gower's learning, Berthelette notes that even if Gower's poetry had not survived, "the mooste famous and excellente" Chaucer's words at the conclusion to the *Troilus* (5.1856–59) would testify to "what a clerke" Gower was. In the 1532 (but not 1554) edition, Berthelette foregrounds Chaucer even more with an allusion to Thynne's 1532 *The workes of Geffray Chaucer newly printed* by saying that the *Troilus* "and many other of the sayde Chausers, that neuer were before imprinted, 7 those that very fewe men knewe, and fewer hadde them, be nowe of late put forth together in a fayre volume."[25] Together, these are more than simply gratuitous references to Chaucer: the one links the historical poets through Chaucer's actual testimony on Gower's behalf, and the other does so by relating the editions in which sixteenth-century audiences knew them.[26]

If Berthelette's *Confessio* is in part responsible for the linking of Chaucer and Gower throughout the early modern period, however, it is also in part responsible for the detrimental effects this linking has had on the latter. Certainly, Berthelette implies that the poets are quite alike: Chaucer and Gower "were both of one self tyme, bothe excellently lerned, both gret frendes to gether, and both a lyke endeauored them selfe and imployed

[23] Fisher, *John Gower*, p. 12. Blake has argued that this amalgamation of versions originated not with Caxton but in a single manuscript source; see "Caxton's Copytext of Gower's *Confessio Amantis*," *Anglia* 85 (1967): 282–93.

[24] Cf. Fisher, *John Gower*, pp. 13–14, and Pearsall, "The Gower Tradition," p. 190.

[25] Berthelette, ed., *Jo. Gower de Confessione Amantis*, sig. aaiiiᵛ.

[26] Dating to John Leland's c. 1540 *Commentarii de Scriptoribus Britannicis*, there has been the suggestion that Berthelette may actually have been involved in the production of Thynne's *Works*. While such involvement is doubtful, he certainly did have dealings with Thomas Godfray, Thynne's printer. See Fisher, *John Gower*, pp. 16–17.

theyr tyme so wel and so vertuously, that they dyd . . . passe forthe their lyfes here ryght honourably."[27] But this is all Berthelette says about the similarities between Gower and Chaucer, and it is not enough to counteract the dissimilarities between the printed editions of their respective compositions. Beginning with Thynne's *Works* of 1532 and continuing until Tyrwhitt's *Canterbury Tales* of 1775, for instance, the only Chaucerian editions that were produced were of the collected poetry and prose. If Chaucer thus had to be confronted in the format of his substantial *oeuvre*, Gower continually appeared as the writer of only one (albeit long) work.

This format would in fact seem to reflect a conscious decision by Berthelette. He prints, for example, neither of the two short Latin poems—*Explicit iste liber* and *Quam cinxere*—with which Caxton's edition and nearly all the complete *Confessio* manuscripts conclude. In a few manuscripts, including MS Bodley 294, the *Confessio* is further supplemented with Gower's *Traitié pour essampler les amantz marietz* and *Carmen super multiplici viciorum pestilencia*, neither of which, again, Berthelette incorporates.[28] While such manuscripts are scarcely as ambitious as Chaucerian anthologies like Cambridge, University Library MS Gg.4.27, they do offer a model for a collected works that Berthelette could have but did not follow. Speght's editions of 1598 and 1602 further supplemented the Chaucerian *oeuvre* with an elaborate critical apparatus, including a Life of the poet and a glossary. Berthelette again had and rejected a model: the possibly autobiographical "Quia unusquisque," a Latin prose passage that outlines the contents of Gower's three major poems. This passage concludes Caxton's edition, Bodley MS 294, and many of the other manuscripts, and so it, too, might have been developed into a full-scale Life. Lacking such trappings of humanist editing, Gower's *Confessio* physically could not justify epithets like the Virgil or Homer of English, as Chaucer's *Works* could and did.

What prefatory material Berthelette included did not do Gower's reputation any credit vis-à-vis Chaucer's. For one thing, in the Berthelette edi-

---

[27] Berthelette, ed., *Jo. Gower de Confessione Amantis*, sig. aaiiiᵛ. As Gilroy-Scott points out, editorial differentiation between Chaucer and Gower began as early as Caxton's issues: "A comparison of Caxton's introduction to this edition [*Confessio Amantis*] with his 'Proheyme' to the *Canterbury Tales* (1484?) reveals a remarkable contrast between the uncommitted brevity of the former and the enthusiastic sense of involvement in the latter"; "John Gower's Reputation," p. 35.

[28] Besides these, Cambridge, Trinity College MS R.3.2 also includes Gower's *Carmen super amoris multiplici varietate*. Caxton's edition includes this *Carmen* and the anonymous Latin verses of "quidam Philosophus" in praise of Gower and beginning "Eneidos Bucolis que georgica" (sig. ccxi).

tion Gower was frozen in time as subservient to the author of the *Troilus*, a poet whose worth depended in part on the validation of "the mooste famous and excellente Geffraye Chauser." Nearly every reader who approached the *Confessio* in printed form was thus confronted, before the first line of the poem proper, by a comparison with Chaucer that implicitly held him to be the superior poet. And for another, the religious sentiments of these two poets from "one self tyme" were recuperated quite differently in later ages. At the conclusion of his letter to the reader, Berthelette declares that in the chapel to St. John at St. Mary Overys a daily mass is still said for Gower and that near his tomb there hangs a table "wherein appereth that who so euer praieth for the soule of John Gower, he shal so oft as he so dothe, haue a thousande and fyue hundred dayes of pardon."[29] In 1532, at the advent of the Reformation, such declarations may have been merely problematic, but they remained a religious pretext for readers of the seventeenth, eighteenth, and nineteenth centuries. The religious orientation of Chaucer's *Works*, by comparison, changed considerably during the period. The 1542 edition of Thynne's *Works*, for example, added the spurious and anti-papist *Plowman's Tale*, while Speght's 1602 edition included the equally spurious and anti-papist *Tale of Jack Upland*. Within this textual context, it is scarcely surprising that in his 1563 *Actes and Monuments* John Foxe should consider Chaucer "right *Wicklevian*" and a forerunner of sixteenth-century religious reform. Since Foxe's assessment eventually appeared in the "Testimonies of Learned Men" in John Urry's 1721 *Works*, it, too, came to influence public opinion of Chaucer in a way that was favorable to a Protestant audience, just as Speght did in his Life of Chaucer, where he maintained that Chaucer had studied "by all likelihood in Canterburie or in Merton Colledge, with *Iohn Wickelife*, whose opinion in religion he much affected."[30] In the format of Berthelette's *Confessio*, therefore, Gower remained resolutely Roman, even as Chaucer became increasingly Protestant through the various editions of the sixteenth and seventeenth centuries.

Gower's morality, frequently echoed in the sixteenth and seventeenth centuries, is also well justified by Berthelette's edition.[31] The prefatory material, again, stresses the poet's learning and virtue, with Berthelette's

---

[29] Berthelette, ed., *Jo. Gower de Confessione Amantis*, sig. aaiii[v]. A similar, Latin reference to indulgences to be gained by prayers for Gower occurs at the end of Caxton's edition.

[30] Speght, ed., *The Workes of our Antient and Learned English Poet, Geoffrey Chaucer, newly Printed* (London: George Bishop, 1598), sig. b3[r].

[31] In addition to the references in note 4, see Sylvia Wright, "The Author Portraits in the Bedford Psalter-Hours: Gower, Chaucer and Hoccleve," *BLJ* 18 (1992): 190–201.

first reference to him being, in fact, "that excellent clerke the morall John Gower." But even more important in this regard is the layout of the text itself. With the Latin prose glosses printed within the columns of text, Gower as *commentator* speaks before the stories in order to guide readers' responses to them, much as in *Pericles* Gower as chorus speaks at the beginning of each act to advise the audience what they will see and what it means. In Berthelette's layout, a reader confronts not at all the apologetic and self-deprecating Chaucer *persona* or even merely a poet but an imperious figure who preempts interpretation and who certainly does deserve the label "moral."[32]

Also conducive to the construction of "moral Gower" may well have been the very fact that the printer of the *Confessio* was Berthelette.[33] As the title page of his first *Confessio* issue indicates, in 1532 Berthelette was the King's Printer, a position to which he was appointed in 1530 upon the death of Richard Pynson, to whom he had perhaps once been apprenticed. Berthelette remained in this position until the accession of Edward VI in 1547, and he continued to print, though much less frequently, until his death on 26 September 1555. During this period, Berthelette was far and away the most prolific printer in England: over the course of the last twenty years of his life alone, he printed more than 350 items, while the second most productive printer, William Seres, printed 187.[34] As the work of the King's Printer, furthermore, Berthelette's list is weighted towards the legal and ethical. For example, at least 45 percent of his output was religious or devotional, but he also issued over one hundred legal

---

[32] Blake's assertion that the "Latin notes and verses which occur in some manuscripts and in Caxton's edition are not included" in Berthelette's edition is thus incorrect; "Early Printed Editions," p. 302. For an indication of how the Middle English text and Latin glosses can interact in a reading of the *Confessio*, see R. F. Yeager, "'Oure englisshe' and Everyone's Latin: The *Fasciculus Morum* and Gower's *Confessio Amantis*," *South Atlantic Review* 46 (1981): 41–53. On the function of the Latin in the *Confessio* more generally see Yeager, "English, Latin, and the Text as 'Other': the Page as Sign in the Work of John Gower," *Text* 3 (1987): 251–67; and Pearsall, "Gower's Latin in the *Confessio Amantis*," in A. J. Minnis, ed., *Latin and Vernacular: Studies in Late-Medieval Texts and Manuscripts* (Cambridge: D. S. Brewer, 1989), pp. 13–25. For an account of the printed history of the glosses, see the Appendix.

[33] On Berthelette's career see Plomer, *A Short History of English Printing*, pp. 50–54; E. Gordon Duff, *A Century of the English Book Trade* (1905; rpt. London: Bibliographical Society, 1948), pp. 11–12, and *The Printers, Stationers and Bookbinders of Westminster and London from 1476 to 1535* (Cambridge: Cambridge University Press, 1906), pp. 177–83; and Colin Clair, "Thomas Berthelet, Royal Printer," *Gutenberg Jahrbuch* (1966), pp. 177–81. For a record of the items in the *Short-Title Catalogue* for which Berthelette was responsible, see A. W. Pollard et al., eds., *A Short-Title Catalogue of Books Printed in England, Scotland, & Ireland*, 2d ed. (London: Bibliographic Society, 1991), 3.18–19.

[34] Bennett, *English Books & Readers*, p. 196.

publications, including a two-volume folio edition of collected English statutes from the reign of Henry III to that of Henry VIII.[35] Outside these areas, Berthelette's publications were hardly frivolous. As the exclusive publisher of Thomas Elyot, Berthelette printed translations from Plutarch, Isocrates, Severus, Lucan, and Cyprian, and thereby issued some of the earliest English translations of Greek.[36] And in 1531, after Henry VIII had divorced Catherine of Aragon to marry Anne Boleyn, Berthelette offered Latin and English editions of a small book entitled *The determinations of the moste famous and mooste excellent Vniuersities of Italy and France that it is so unlefull for a man to marie his brother's wyfe that the Pope hath no power to dispense therewith.*[37] Berthelette's seriousness of purpose as a printer is equally apparent in his edition of *De proprietatibus rerum*, which he prefaces with eleven folio pages of an alphabetized table of topics and names, "bycause this werke is so profitable 7 the manyfold thinges therein conteyened soo nedefull to be knowne and had in a redynes."[38]

Berthelette's efforts were stylish as well as ethical, however, with the workmanship of his volumes today recognized as the finest of the period. Though single sheets like proclamations and statutes allowed little elaboration in layout and design, his books are especially renowned for their typeface, ornamentation, and illustration. He may not have been the Royal Bookbinder, as was once thought, but Berthelette did commission numerous sumptuous bindings from various binders. Perhaps the first English printer whose efforts appeared exclusively in calf's leather, Berthelette utilized many bindings that still retain not only their original suppleness and durability but also, as with his gilded white leather bindings, their original beauty. The gold-tooled bindings on his books are among the first such in England, and for their production he is thought to have brought Italian workers to England. Yet Berthelette's decorative flourishes extended beyond commissioned bindings: he also sometimes printed the sides of the closed leaves with legends or had them painted with colored heraldic designs.[39]

[35] Ibid., pp. 65, 196, and 81.

[36] Ibid., p. 164.

[37] Plomer, *A Short History of English Printing*, p. 51. Plomer dates the volume to 1530; the 1531 date is from the *Short-Title Catalogue*.

[38] Bartholomaeus Anglicus, *De proprietatibus rerum*, sig. ii[r].

[39] Duff, *English Book Trade*, pp. 11–12, and *Printers, Stationers and Bookbinders*, pp. 181–82; and Cyril Davenport, *Thomas Berthelet: Royal Printer and Bookbinder to Henry VIII King of England* (Chicago: Caxton Club, 1901). The latter contains several color plates of Berthelette's bindings. On the unlikelihood that Berthelette was Royal Bookbinder—or even that he was a binder at all—see Clair, "Thomas Berthelet, Royal Printer," p. 181.

Berthelette seems to have been known as a learned and judicious individual who was well-liked and familiar to the aristocratic audience of his work as King's Printer. In 1540, for example, in a work issued from a press in Basel, the scholar Nicholas Borbonius praised Berthelette in Latin verse,[40] and already in 1533 Thomas Paynell prefaced his translation of von Hutten's *De morbo Gallico* (which Berthelette printed) with a testament to Berthelette's reputation for judgment, wisdom, and familiarity with public opinion:

Not long agoo, after I had translated into our englysshe tonge the boke called Regimen sanitatis Salerni [1528], I hapned being at London to talke with the printer [Berthelette] and to enquire of hym, what he thought, and how he lyked the same boke: and he answered, that in his mynde it was a boke moche necessarye, and very profitable for them that toke good hede to the holsome teachynges, and warely folowed the same. And this moch farther he added therto, that so far forthe as ever he coude here, it is [by] every man very well accepted and allowed.[41]

This reputation for wisdom and reliability is verified by notices in the Public Records Office that indicate Berthelette was sometimes entrusted with printing tasks so important or confidential that he had not only to swear to secrecy but also to set type himself. In this period he was granted special dispensation from participating in the wars in France, and this military deferment, which had the effect of keeping Berthelette in England, further testifies to his prestige. It should be noted, however, that he was wealthy as well as prestigious. His annual salary as King's Printer was only four pounds, a figure comparable to that of a yeoman or unskilled laborer but less than that of a skilled craftsman. But this sum was supplemented by additional official printing jobs, for which he received separate payment, and by bespoke work for private citizens. The Patent Rolls of Henry VIII indicate that, doubtless as a result of his respectable yearly salary from printing, Berthelette also owned numerous investment properties, from which he would have received still more income.[42]

---

[40] Duff, *Printers, Stationers and Bookbinders*, p. 181.

[41] Qtd. in Bennett, *English Books & Readers*, pp. 42–43.

[42] Davenport, *Thomas Berthelet*, pp. 33, 32, and 50. On wages in the sixteenth century see Sir John Clapham, *A Concise Economic History of Britain* (Cambridge: Cambridge University Press, 1949), p. 208; Henry Phelps Brown and Sheila V. Hopkins, *A Perspective of Wages and Prices* (London: Methuen, 1981), pp. 3, 11; and Maurice Ashley, *The People of England: A Short Social and Economic History* (Baton Rouge: Louisiana State University Press, 1982), p. 77.

Even though Berthelette lost his position as King's Printer in 1547 with the accession of Edward VI, he evidently continued to be respected, particularly in the book professions, until the end of his life. On 1 September 1549, for instance, he was awarded a coat of arms. Dated 23 September 1555, his will indicates that he also remained extremely wealthy to his death, with the property in general being valued at over £125 per annum. The will itemizes assorted gold chains, various land holdings, numerous houses in and around London, and cash grants amounting to a substantial sum, with Berthelette's elder son Edward alone receiving an estate in Hereford and a house in London.[43] Berthelette's funeral, as described in the diary of Henry Machyn, was itself an elaborate and well-attended affair: "The sam day at afternone was bered master Barthelet sqwire and prynter unto Kyng Henry; and was bered with pennon and cote-armur, and IIII dosen of skochyons, and II whytt branchys and IIII gylt candyllstykes and mony prestes and clarkes, and mony mornars, and all the craftes of prynters, boke-sellers, and all stassyoners."[44]

For his personal character, then, as well as for the size of his list, its contents, and their production, Berthelette was a serious, wealthy, respected, and accomplished printer. The conservative and moral portrait he draws of Gower in the Preface to his edition of the *Confessio* might well be one that could image the printer himself. Indeed, Berthelette's list of publications for 1532 epitomizes his career at the same time it establishes a context for his edition of the *Confessio*. In that year, he issued, besides Gower's poem, approximately nineteen items.[45] Several of these were statutes or proclamations, but Berthelette also printed a translation of *De contemptu mundi*, two issues and a French translation of *A glasse of the truthe* (a dialogue between a lawyer and a divine concerning the king's proposed divorce), Elyot's translation *A dialogue between Lucian and Diogenes*, Elyot's own *The educacion or bringinge vp of children*, four issues of Christopher Saint

[43] Davenport, *Thomas Berthelet*, pp. 33, 51–53; Duff, *English Book Trade*, p. 12. Berthelette's coat of arms is reproduced in Clair, "Thomas Berthelet, Royal Printer," p. 178.

[44] Qtd. in Duff, *Printers, Stationers and Bookbinders*, p. 183.

[45] An exact number is difficult to determine since printers sometimes issued volumes without dates or with incorrect ones. The *Short-Title Catalogue* notes, further, that "because of the quantity of Berthelet's undated and repeated-date items, the chronology of his publications is especially provisional" (3.18). It should be noted that the list of works that the revised *Short-Title Catalogue* dates to 1532 differs significantly in individual items (but not in overall character) from that in Paul Guerrant Morrison, *Index of Printers, Publishers, and Booksellers in A. W. Pollard and G. R. Redgrave: A Short-title Catalogue of Books Printed in England, Scotland & Ireland and of English Books Printed Abroad, 1475–1640*, 2d impr. (Charlottesville: Bibliographical Society of the University of Virginia, 1961), pp. 9–10.

German's *A treatise concernynge the diuision betwene the spirytualitie and tempo-ralitie*, a translation of Xenophon's *Economy*, and *Tales and quicke answeres, very mery, and pleasant to rede.*

In several ways Berthelette's edition of the *Confessio Amantis* was for him an exceedingly unusual production: it was vastly longer than his many one-page proclamations; it was a work neither legal nor ecclesiastical; and it offered, by sixteenth-century standards, a kind of popular poetry in which Berthelette otherwise evinced little interest. Yet there was also much in the poem that was consistent with his other printing efforts. As a printer given to lavishing attention on layout and design, Berthelette found in the *Confessio* a poem whose manuscript history also demonstrated such attention in the form of miniatures, illuminations, and general programs of illustration that were characteristically transmitted with the poem.[46] The text of the *Confessio* was itself transmitted with a marked degree of stability in the manuscript tradition, and this textual stability, too, correlates with Berthelette's nominal interest in such matters—which he in fact articulates in his letter to the reader—and with the care he took to stabilize his own text through a table of contents and programs of typographical distinction among Latin poems, Latin glosses, and Middle English stories. The audi-ence of many of the *Confessio* manuscripts, further, was not unlike that of much of Berthelette's list. Given the polish of the illumination programs for the *Confessio*, in the fifteenth century these manuscripts were often owned by aristocracy and rich merchants, the only individuals, quite likely, who could afford them.[47] Berthelette's other published books, similarly, were often expensive productions affordable only by a select audience that may otherwise have known him through his work as King's Printer. And finally, the virtue of Gower and his poem, apparent everywhere in the *Confessio* and rendered a fifteenth-century cliché by Chaucer's reference to "moral Gower," mirrored a quality that dominated much of Berthelette's list. This was the quality that Berthelette emphasized in his dedication to Henry VIII, which, as Neil Gilroy-Scott points out, explicitly aligns the *Confessio* with Berthelette's other virtuous efforts: Berthelette's "main con-cern . . . is to justify and praise the book in terms which place it in a class with which he had already achieved success."[48]

---

[46] Pearsall, "The Gower Tradition," pp. 183–84; Jeremy J. Smith, "Linguistic Features of Some Fifteenth-Century Middle English Manuscripts," in Pearsall, ed., *Manuscripts and Readers in Fifteenth-Century England* (Cambridge: Boydell and Brewer, 1983), pp. 104–12.

[47] Pearsall, "The Gower Tradition," p. 184.

[48] Gilroy-Scott, "John Gower's Reputation," p. 38. Yeager has argued that a moralizing tendency also characterized Caxton's and, to a lesser extent, Thynne's editorial views of

If in the *Confessio* Berthelette confronted a work whose production, audience, and content were consistent with that of his own list, the appearance of the edition from his press, by the same token, not only confirmed the character of its early reception but also stamped the poem with Berthelette's own particular influences. A book issued from Berthelette's house in Fleet Street "nere to ye cundite at ye signe of Lucrece"[49] was a book from a wealthy and well-known man trusted by the King, honored by his peers, and given to publishing deluxe volumes and virtuous works. Just as today specific publishing houses, such as Penguin or The Free Press, are associated with certain kinds of works and therefore invite certain responses and audiences, so, presumably, would have an early modern house whose list and style were as well defined as Berthelette's. Any book from "ye signe of Lucrece," in other words, would by itself likely elicit expectations of edification, so that the virtue of Gower's poem would have been augmented by that of Berthelette's imprint. While it is difficult to speak with certainty about how long Berthelette's reputation remained widespread, it is clear that at his death, eight years after he had lost his position as King's Printer, he was still widely known and respected; that he published nearly twice as many works as the next most prolific printer of the period, providing early modern readers with many reminders of his achievement; and that in a sense he remained an active printer even after his death, since his nephew Thomas Powell continued to print under Berthelette's name until 1563.[50] To the extent that readers of the later sixteenth, seventeenth, and eighteenth centuries remained aware of his career—and at the very least the title page of his 1532 edition was a constant reminder that he had been the King's Printer—Berthelette's name would have continued to surround the printed edition of the *Confessio* with an aura of seriousness, virtue, and expense that was very much at odds with antiquarian productions like Speght's or even Urry's *Works*. Some of the morality in "moral Gower," in other words, may have been Berthelette's.

In the end, the Gower and *Confessio* that Berthelette's edition constructs are decidedly ambivalent. On the one hand, Gower is portrayed as a true

---

Chaucer's works; "Literary Theory at the Close of the Middle Ages: William Caxton and William Thynne," *SAC* 6 (1984): 135–64. Given the impulses of humanist textual criticism, indeed, Berthelette's interest in moral works is not atypical for the period.

[49] Duff, *English Book Trade*, p. 11.

[50] Ibid., p. 124. Powell also seems to have been responsible for books issued from Berthelette's press between 1547 and 1555, though his total list is not large.

voice of the people, noble and common alike: the linguistic and moral traditionalism he is made to articulate against social novelties of the early sixteenth century renders him a bulwark of conservatism. On the other, the textual history of the *Confessio*, including its materialization in Berthelette's editions, could be seen as an index of the poem's limited and elite audience. What shaped the poem's reception history, however, is less this ambivalence than the fact that the printed *Confessio* remained constant over time and thus became, eventually, antiquated. In a comparison between Thynne's 1532 edition of Chaucer's *Works* and Berthelette's *Confessio*, the latter holds up rather well. It is by far the more physically attractive volume in typography, layout, and design, and its editor had the better reputation among contemporaries. What it lacks in appearance, however, Thynne's *Works* makes up in contents, and neither Thynne nor Berthelette could have foreseen how these would develop and affect the reputations of Chaucer and, through their inevitable linking, Gower. In Thynne's *Works*, the nascent apparatus of prefatory poems and Brian Tuke's preface, which opens with consideration of language in general and concludes with the assertion that Chaucer's works will silence those who would challenge the "laude / renoume / and glorie" of England,[51] situates Chaucer far more broadly and intimately in English affairs than Berthelette does Gower and thus provides a basis for the conceptual expansion Speght would effect in 1598. The conception of Chaucer's collected *oeuvre* in the 1532 *Works*, further, portends the direction of not simply Chaucer editions but also of post-medieval literary studies. Ultimately, it is in comparisons with these traditions that Berthelette's *Confessio* suffers, in part because, ultimately, these are the traditions that invented Chaucer as the "father" of English poetry.

Gower, Berthelette's preface repeatedly told readers, was a writer who was important because his language was of great antiquity and for whom daily masses were said, a writer who, in Berthelette's layout, morally interpreted individual stories before they began. Chaucer, on the other hand, remained an elusive poet and a vital figure whose life and canon were adjusted to successive ages' conceptions of themselves and their past. During the initial efforts of the Reformation, for example, Chaucer's alleged authorship of the *Plowman's Tale* could be used for historical justification, just as in Urry's 1721 edition Chaucer could appear as a forerunner of the eighteenth-century intellectual when the Life describes him as "a great

---

[51] Thynne, ed., *The Works of Geffray Chaucer newly Printed* (London: Thomas Godfray, 1532), sig. aiii[r].

Scholar, a pleasant Wit, a candid Critick, a sociable Companion, a stedfast Friend, a grave Philosopher, a temperate Œconomist and a pious Christian."[52] Such material malleability rendered Chaucer ever contemporary, even as Gower was forever conservative. I do not at all mean to deny the differences between Gower's and Chaucer's poetry in subject, style, and quality, nor am I discounting the effect such differences are likely to have on the judgment of individual readers. But I do suggest that given only the developing presentation of their poetry, it is little surprise that it was in the *Canterbury Tales*, not the *Confessio*, that Dryden saw "God's plenty," despite Berthelette's implication that Gower spoke for both the commons and the nobility. In effect, because of the way their reputations were intertwined in critical history, the more Chaucer acquired the status of the "father" of English poetry through the efforts of Thynne, Speght, and Urry, the less the achievement of Gower, as mediated by Berthelette, would have seemed. The simple fact that in the early modern period there were far more printed copies of Chaucer's *Works* than of Gower's *Confessio* is therefore as much a reflection as a cause of Chaucer's reputation.

Throughout this period, indeed, Gower's life and canon never ceased to be consistent with the early Renaissance conception of the Middle Ages. During the sixteenth, seventeenth, and eighteenth centuries, nearly everyone who read the *Confessio* in a printed edition did indeed encounter a poet who was medieval and Catholic and a poem that was resolutely moral. Whatever the specific qualities of Gower's poem, moreover, it remained framed by sixteenth-century editorial concerns and presented in a layout and design that would have seemed increasingly simplistic and quaint in comparison with those of the various Chaucerian *Works*. A useful point of reference here is Tuke's preface to Thynne's 1532 edition, which articulates sentiments about literature, language, and nationalism similar to those found in Berthelette's dedication. Unlike Berthelette's dedication, however, Tuke's preface itself became historicized. Already in Speght's editions it is printed in black letter, like the Middle English text and not the rest of the introductory material, which is set in roman. And in Urry's edition the preface is included as one of the "Testimonies of Learned Men," a series of extracts verifying Chaucer's preeminence among English poets.[53] While Berthelette's dedication, thus, served to antiquate even the critical frame of his edition, Tuke's preface was treated in ways that identified it as contem-

---

[52] Urry, ed., *The Works of Geoffrey Chaucer, compared with the Former Editions, and many valuable MSS* (London: Bernard Lintot, 1721), sig. e2ᵛ.

[53] Tim William Machan, "Speght's *Works* and the Invention of Chaucer," *Text* 8 (1996).

poraneous with the historical reception of Chaucer's *Works* and not with the current reading of them or, by implication, with their contemporary validity.

The most general issue here is the mutual interconnection between edited format and literary reputation. Inescapably, editions are historical constructions that emerge from literary, political, and economic forces, and the writers and works they construct can in turn influence these same forces. So long as the *Confessio* remained synonymous with Berthelette's edition, it could not contribute to the very forces that might motivate new editions and thereby invite new responses and audiences. Editorially speaking, Gower's poem and reputation remained trapped in a circle that would not be broken until the advent of philology in the nineteenth century, which complicated the reception of the *Confessio* in still other ways. If the reception history of Gower's *Confessio Amantis* is a shorter story than that of Chaucer's *Works*, it is in no small part because its printing history is as well.

Appendix:
Printed History of Latin Glosses in the *Confessio*

The history of the prose Latin glosses and their editorial treatment is long and complex in itself. As Macaulay describes the extant manuscripts, well over half of them have the glosses, and most of these have them incorporated in the columns of text and underscored or written in red.[54] For this reason, and because the Latin material in general figures meaningfully in the *Confessio*, it is widely considered today that Gower himself must have written the glosses.

They are not present at all, however, in the brief extracts printed by George Ellis in 1801 or by Rev. Henry John Todd in 1810.[55] Since in *The Works of the English Poets: From Chaucer to Cowper* Chalmers reprints Berthelette's 1554 edition, they do appear within the columns of text, though for perhaps merely typographical convenience the Chalmers edition, unlike Berthelette's, sets Latin poetry, Latin glosses, and Middle English text all in the same typeface—a roman font. In his new edition of 1857, Reinhold Pauli places the Latin poems in italics within the columns

---

[54] Macaulay, ed., *Works of John Gower*, 1:cxxxviii–clxvi.

[55] Ellis, ed., *Specimens of the Early English Poets*, 3 vols. (London: W. Bulmer, 1801); Todd, ed., *Illustrations of the Lives and Writings of Gower and Chaucer: Collected from Authentick Documents* (London: F. C. and J. Rivington, 1810).

of Middle English text but, apparently for the first time in the poem's printed history, literally marginalizes the glosses; he uses roman for the Middle English and a smaller variety of the same for the glosses. Pauli adopts this procedure even though he believes that the "Latin verses and the marginal Latin index are undoubtedly Gower's own composition" and claims to have restored both poems and glosses "to the shape in which they appear in" London, British Library MSS Harley 7184 and 3869. Despite this acknowledgment of authenticity and his testament to accuracy of layout, Pauli then observes that the glosses, "which in the old editions stand between and interrupt the text, have been placed in the margin, where they generally occur in the MSS. serving as a table of contents."[56] It should be noted that it is not true that in the manuscripts the glosses are "generally" marginal—though it may well have been true of the selection of copies to which Pauli had access. Further, in Harley 7184 the glosses occur *within* the body of the text, and in both manuscripts they are written in red. Henry Morley, who pays a glowing tribute to Pauli in his introduction and who evidently based his text on Pauli's, perhaps inferred from Pauli's procedure that the glosses were inconsequential and extended this judgment to the Latin poems as well, for without explanation and with the exception of part of the explicit of book VIII, he omits all of the glosses *and* the Latin poems in the selections he edited in 1889.[57]

Though Macaulay is highly critical of Pauli and dismissive of Morley,[58] he nonetheless and equally without explanation imitates the former's practice of marginalizing the glosses. His base manuscript (Oxford, Bodleian Library MS Fairfax 3) also in fact marginalizes them, as does one of the manuscripts (Oxford, Bodleian Library MS Bodley 902) that he collated throughout; the other two such manuscripts (Oxford, Corpus Christi College MS 67 and Bodleian Library MS 294), however, place the glosses, written in red, within the body of the text. It is presumably the influence of Macaulay's text, the only currently available scholarly edition, that has led editors of students' editions to omit the glosses entirely.[59]

---

[56] Pauli, ed., *Confessio Amantis of John Gower*, 3 vols. (London: Bell and Daldy, 1857), 1.xliv–xlv.

[57] Morley, ed., *Tales of the Seven Deadly Sins: Being the Confessio Amantis of John Gower* (London: George Routledge and Sons, 1889), pp. x–xi.

[58] Macaulay, ed., *Works of John Gower*, 1.clxix–clxx.

[59] See, for example, Russell Peck, ed., *Confessio Amantis* (New York: Holt, Rinehart and Winston, 1966); J. A. W. Bennett, ed., *Selections from John Gower* (Oxford: Clarendon Press, 1968); and Carole Weinberg, ed., *Selected Poetry* (Manchester: Carcanet, 1983). Though the glosses have not yet been translated, the intermittent Latin poems have. See Siân Echard and Claire Fanger, trans., *The Latin Verses in the* Confessio Amantis: *An Annotated Translation* (East Lansing, Mich.: Colleagues Press, 1991).

REVIEWS

MARK C. AMODIO, ed. *Oral Poetics in Middle English Poetry*. Albert Bates Lord Studies in Oral Tradition, vol. 13. New York: Garland Publishing, 1994. Pp. xii, 289. $45.00.

The central irony of medieval oral studies—the quest for spoken words among exclusively written sources—offers the best explanation for the seeming redundancy of the title *Oral Poetics in Middle English Poetry*, rather than, say, *Oral Poetics in Late-Medieval English Society*. Presenting a *Poetics* and a *Poetry* with no other context for *Oral*, the title signals a working premise of many of its eleven contributors: that we can find and evaluate orality solely by examining what *looks oral* in the poem at hand—and thus justify confining the inquiry to individual texts confronted in hermetic isolation.

In his introduction, Mark Amodio articulates several assumptions that crystallize the collection's strengths and weaknesses.

1. *Middle English poetry has been relegated to "the periphery of oral studies"* (p. 1). To the contrary, the first two essays of Amodio's book cite no fewer than fifty-three works that discuss Middle English orality, most of them published since 1980. Particularly in the realm of romance, current authors seldom raise serious questions of audience and style without addressing orality. Thomas Hahn's superlative introduction to *Sir Gawain: Eleven Romances and Tales* (1995), for example, offers major observations on the oral styles and presumed performance contexts of the Gawain poems. Only if one considers orality in terms of the oral-formulaic model developed by Parry and Lord can one argue persuasively that Middle English verse lies at "the periphery of oral studies."

2. *Middle English texts postdate the period of "high-context" orality, when poems were essentially re-created anew in performance by nonliterate artists. The mere presence of a textual passage that "looks oral" because it echoes the formularicity of* Beowulf *does not in itself constitute evidence of "an active oral poetics"* (p. 11). Here Amodio usefully separates Middle English orality from the Parry-Lord model.

3. *The unvaried metrical tradition of Old English poetry—which Amodio associates with "the oral tradition" {emphasis mine}—gives way to the "sudden appearance of different verse types following the Conquest"* (p. 12). *"Both before*

and especially after the Conquest, orality and literacy interact and intersect" (p. 21) *in complex ways, creating mixed modes best conceptualized on a continuum between orality and writing.* Amodio's recurrent phrase "the oral tradition" more than implies that there is only one form of pure poetic orality and that what is oral in Middle English verse derives from a unitary Anglo-Saxon orality. Yet the notion of one pure antecedent is unsustainable. Copious evidence of many kinds of oral performance—singing, reading, recitation, tale telling—in monastic, courtly, and popular settings leaves no warrant for making "the oral tradition" a useful point of departure. Many Old English oral traditions—as well as many oral traditions practiced by speakers of Welsh, Latin, and Old French—demonstrably influenced Middle English poetry. Having judged the Parry-Lord model inadequate to explain the variety of Middle English verse, Amodio returns to the fiction of a monolithic golden oral age from which Middle English literature slowly differentiates itself.

4. *Oral poetic techniques may survive in literature if scribes and poets use them "as a consequence of their experience with oral and oral-derived texts, whether they read, copied or took them down from dictation. Such conditioning occurred because the central affective, metonymic character of the oral tradition (something which insured its continued survival before the introduction of writing) does not vanish once the texts become encoded in manuscripts"* (p. 19). Here, although Amodio again invokes *the* oral tradition, he signals the book's major strength. Building largely upon the observations of John Foley's *Immanent Art* (1991), the best essays invoke oralities not merely identifiable because they are formulaic and repetitive, but esthetically valuable in their own right because their repetitions and juxtapositions interact organically with the concerns and situations of a responsive audience.

The most important aspect of any vital oral tradition is indeed metonymy, but the crucial metonymic flow lies not within the text itself, or even between texts, but rather between the text and the community from which it comes and whose approval the poet must meet in a richly reflexive process through which poet and audience together shape texts that continually reshape themselves and their responses. Attuned to this cardinal fact of orality, researchers can find ways of assessing Middle English orality, most markedly in instances of *cultural or social translation*, through which a poet transforms a received text to suit another social milieu. If both poems survive, and if we can establish a social context for one or both, then close comparison makes it possible to say something about the orality of at least one text. Such comparisons do not, however, dominate this book, half of whose contributors confine themselves to what "looks oral" within a given text and sometimes offer broad generalizations about a posited audience.

A case in point is John Ganim's "The Devil's Writing Lesson," which brilliantly examines orality as an image by contrasting the treatments of orality and bookishness in Robert Mannyng's *Handlyng Synne*. For all that Ganim says about the poem's imagery, he overlooks evidence for its socially situated orality. Because *Handlyng Synne* is largely a translation of a more bookish work, the Anglo-Norman *Manuel de Pechiez*, close comparative reading can reveal much about Mannyng's orality. The authors of both works announce their audience and intent: the *Manuel* pointedly addresses the upper classes (*gent*) while Mannyng speaks to "lewde men. . . . That talys and rhymys wyl blethly here." Mannyng thus makes not only a linguistic but a social and contextual translation of his source, offering specific insights into the esthetics of an orally active stratum of the same regional society that produced the *Manuel*. Ganim fails to demonstrate that the orality he posits is either Mannyng's or oral, because he does not examine how Mannyng's French source treats the same tales.

Two contributors do, however, apply interesting comparative methodologies. A section of Amodio's introduction illustrates how Laȝamon's *Brut* re-oralizes Wace's Anglo-Norman original through a series of formulaic flourishes drawing upon the diction of native English traditions. Alexandra Hennessey Olsen examines ten texts of *Robert of Cysile*, arguing that both scribal transmission and oral recitation account for manuscript variations, and concluding that the orally derived variations, though more radical than the scribal, more often preserve a sense of semantic continuity.

Two essays on *The Canterbury Tales* represent the book's strongest efforts to resituate Middle English literature in its oral surroundings. Ward Parks, noted for close oral readings, asserts logically that Chaucer relies on many oral traditions. Parks is the contributor most attentive to questions of performance; this focus requires him to cite instances from recently observed oral traditions and to argue by analogy—a problematic but necessary step toward the reconstruction of vanished contexts, for the only fully recoverable oralities available to us are those currently practiced. Leslie K. Arnovick's reading of the various kinds of learned and folk oralities potentially at work in *The Franklin's Tale* offers substantial insights because she, too, ties Chaucer's poem to specific modes of oral discourse present in his milieux.

The masterpiece of the collection is Nancy Bradbury's "Literacy, Orality, and the Poetics of Middle English Romance," which begins by unintentionally calling most of the remaining essays into question: "Regarding the oral survivals in medieval romance as one literary device among others . . . seems an inadequate response to the argument for the special significance even of residual orality" (p. 41). She moves on to make compelling arguments for memorization as a major component of medieval orality—both by citing medieval testimony and by examining variant texts in which memorization provides the best explanation of certain transpositions. She continues with comparisons revealing differences between texts obviously copied from written originals and those that carry the marks of memorization. Bradbury ends by using the concept of metonymy to demonstrate how the formulas of *Gamelyn* and the Robin Hood poems, long derided as signs of hackwork, can be read on their own terms as devices integral to structuring organic and sometimes complex wholes. Bradbury's is the only essay that seriously considers the crucial question, What is at stake in searching for oral effects in works that survive only in writing?

The remaining essays either argue from oversimplified schemas that oppose orality and writing (e.g., Dave Henderson's examination of "traditional" and "nontraditional" heroes in three Middle English poems) or sidestep the avowed purpose of the book by treating orality merely as a literary theme (Seth Lerer's "The Romance of Orality").

Two strengths—1) the occasional insistence that oral verse be read on its own metonymic terms and 2) the close comparative methods sometimes used to help establish what those terms may be—make this an important collection despite the failings of some of its parts. Indeed, by juxtaposing thoughtful comparative and contextual approaches with reductionist schemas, Amodio's book demonstrates the major point of its best essays: until we recognize that the ultimate metonymy of oral verse is social and that late-medieval English societies used writing and orality in thickly interwoven ways, literary approaches to orality will remain trapped in oversimplified intratextuality. "Pure oral performance" is simply unrecoverable, but textual variation responding to specific aural and social contexts offers a path to partial, often substantial insight.

CARL LINDAHL
University of Houston

DENISE NOWAKOWSKI BAKER. *Julian of Norwich's* Showings: *From Vision to Book*. Princeton, N.J.: Princeton University Press, 1994. Pp. xi, 215. $29.95.

Denise Baker's study is that kind of very useful and informative book in which the reading of an author is genuinely deepened and broadened by being related to contemporary traditions and patterns of thought and feeling. As the subtitle *From Vision to Book* suggests, Baker's interpretation of the *Showings* finds its focus in the evidence for an accumulative, layered composition of the text, as Julian's book is changed and expanded to match her developing understanding of her original visions, her "maturation . . . from a visionary into a theologian." Even more valuable, however, for modern readers untutored in theology will be the interpretation of Julian's text in the light of medieval theology, because this helps place what is boldly innovative in the thinking of this early and great woman writer in our language.

Baker's first chapter seeks to locate within the tradition of affective spirituality Julian's prayer for the three gifts or graces: "mind of Christ's passion," physical illness, and a third request for the three metaphorical wounds of contrition, compassion and "wylfulle langgynge to God." These are interesting pages, making a case for the very origins of the book—and, behind that, of what Julian wished to see and "saw"—in meditative traditions. This is built upon in the second chapter ("From Visualization to Vision"), where Baker suggests that what is described in Julian's more figurative, corporeal showings represents an amalgam of that devotional art produced with such flair in late-medieval East Anglia. Having tried myself to make a case for this, I appreciate the scruple with which Baker deploys what remains somewhat uncooperative evidence. Her identification of elements of the fifth and sixth showings with the iconographical motif of the Throne of Grace does link vision and visual arts suggestively. There is also some acute literary criticism of Julian's ways of seeing: she reads her visions like a picture rather than a story, ignoring the other personages who traditionally clutter the picture, so as to focus on Christ's experience. This makes its own supporting case for a susceptibility to the visual arts, which Julian then uses on her own terms.

The three following chapters locate within the context of medieval theological traditions Julian's "alle shalle be wele" theodicy, the "Lord and Servant" parable and her understanding of original sin, and her chapters on the Motherhood of Jesus. Julian's notion of the "godly wille" that never assented to sin may be seen to challenge the notion of the depraved will, which is evidently crucial to the doctrine of original sin. Whereas orthodoxy looks back to the causes of evil in seeking to lay blame, Julian concentrates less on Adam's transgression than Christ's reparation, seeing personal sin as a playing out of the "fortunate fall" in the individual's life, with beneficial consequences quite exceeding the initial culpability. Unusually optimistic about the large number of the elect, Julian can hence see predestination as a comfort more than a terror. Guided by a showing, Julian distinctively declines to attribute wrath to God, or a desire for retribution. Even more arrestingly, Julian declines to attribute disobedience to Adam, who is represented more as inadvertently separated from God than rebelling against him, with sin ensuing from the separation rather than causing it. Her emphasis is on the promise of restoration, on mankind's legacy of weakness rather than on ancestral guilt.

Baker's discussion of the theological context for Julian's understanding of the Motherhood of Jesus also provides a very readable synthesis and clarification. Theologians—while asserting the equality of men and women before God—constructed a gendered model of the essential self which denied that the part characterized as female (the lower reason) contained the image of God. As a consequence of the Fall the self is in any case a deformed image. For Augustine the higher reason is masculine, and therein he situates the *imago Dei*, whereas St. Bernard moves the *imago Dei* from the mind to the will, which, Baker suggests, may have been a stimulus to Julian's thinking. Baker sees Julian as challenging the contradiction between the Church's acceptance of the equality of male and female souls on the one hand and the symbolic difference of their bodies on the other. Women's spiritual equality enables Julian to reject their corporeal inequality, as this was suggested by theological discourse, which constructed the female figuratively as carnality, or by scientific theory, which identified the corporeal with the female. While maintaining the hierarchical division of the essential self into "substance" and "sensuality," Julian declines to attribute gender to either part, and so values the sensuality as the nexus between the spiritual and corporeal that sensuality is seen as the locus of Christ's presence in the individual, hence giving due value to the bodily and the female. Rather than holiness involving a suppression of the female and bodily aspects of the self, holiness for Julian involves sensuality reunited with the substance. After this, Baker's final chapter usefully addresses Julian's "re-visions": the relation between her developing insights and the structure and language of her book.

Baker's account of the possible theological influences and connections is set out fairly and clearly, and her study will be of use to all but the most specialist readers. Despite the abstruseness of some of the material, the book is written with exceptional clarity in good English—something worth congratulating in modern academe. Baker guides her reader towards an informed understanding of how Julian of Norwich, without controverting theological orthodoxy, extends its understandings by the transformative shifts of emphasis that her visions and revisions enable her and her readers to see.

BARRY WINDEATT
Emmanuel College, Cambridge

HELEN BARR. *Signes and Sothe: Language in the* Piers Plowman *Tradition.* Piers Plowman Studies, vol. 10. Cambridge: D. S. Brewer, 1994. Pp. x, 188. $63.00.

Those who welcomed Helen Barr's admirable edition of *Pierce the Plowman's Crede, Richard the Redeless, Mum and the Sothsegger,* and *The Crowned King* (in *The Piers Plowman Tradition* [London: J. M. Dent; Rutland, Vt.: Charles E. Tuttle Co., 1993]) will also welcome the present volume, although surely not at its exorbitant price. Building on its predecessor's careful textual work, it explores far more fully than its predecessor could how these highly political poems relate with each other and with the poem that inspired them, *Piers Plowman.* As its inclusion in a series much concerned with linguistic matters implies, it treats the poems' distinctive use of language. But it comes at a time when we tend to explain such use politically, and Ms. Barr superbly does just this. Her findings will likely long dominate discussion of these poems.

Barr presents these findings in five main sections. The first, "Locating Tradition," argues the usefulness of the label "*Piers Plowman* tradition" as applied to these four poems in particular. The second, "Reading Tradition," explores the poems' concern with "right reading" in relation to the various kinds of wrong reading practiced by certain established institutions. The third, central section, "Signes and Sothe," considers the poems' "call for a transparent, monosemic use of language" (p. 53) in relation to their liking for the kinds of wordplay that characterize *Piers Plowman.* The fourth sec-

173

tion, "'Signes of the times': Contesting Sothe," considers how *Pierce the Plowman's Crede* and *Mum and the Sothsegger* respond to ecclesiastical measures that increasingly sought to control what might and might not be discussed. And the fifth, "Legal Fictions," considers the poems' sometimes pervasive legal diction and how this helps define a truth-telling poetic. As Barr points out (pp. 93–94), it would be easy to dwell on the incompatibility between the poems' mission to speak the truth unequivocally and their playful verbal texture. She is more concerned to reconcile these features, however, by considering how these poems finally try to demonstrate "a right use of the manipulation of linguistic resources" (p. 168).

The above sketch does little justice to the intricacy of Barr's argumentation and none at all to her penetrating discussion of the individual texts. But it can suggest something of her approach. She shows well how the poems she is mainly concerned with developed from the kind of reforming discourses represented by *Piers Plowman* but in times when the significance of such discourses was changing. As is well known, in the earliest of these poems, *Pierce the Plowman's Crede*, the result is overtly Lollard. Barr goes well beyond previous commentators, however, in the degree to which she also decodes the slightly later *Mum and the Sothsegger* as Lollard in its sympathies. She also shows well how the other two poems, while not themselves dealing with issues the Lollards made their own, deploy a discourse very similar to that of the Lollards. And she suggestively touches on what could happen when counterdiscourses resembling those of these poems give rise to further counterdiscourses—in the poem R. H. Robbins entitled *Defend us from all Lollardry*, for example, which Barr plausibly suggests exists in discursive symmetry with *Pierce the Plowman's Crede* (p. 111).

Given that Barr does such a good job of considering the Lollard resonances of these works, one might regret that she has not more fully considered what her findings imply about the interests and identities of the poems' early authors and readers—she does not repeat her earlier suggestion that *Richard the Redeless* and *Mum and the Sothsegger* come from a parliamentary clerk, for example (*Piers Plowman Tradition*, p. 17). As she points out, the poems she is primarily discussing are not in the least interested in upsetting the secular status quo; rather, they are marked by what she terms a "stalwart support for a hierarchically maintained society directed by a strong secular power" (p. xi). They contain nothing that would necessarily have come across as threatening to the kind of readers who seem to have sponsored alliterative poetry, therefore, and a lot that might have

174

appealed to them. But apart from the *Crowned King* the poems also all belong to the years before Oldcastle's 1413 rebellion had made it all too easy for the church to associate Lollardy with civil as well as religious dissent. Had laypersons in the upper echelons of society been able to continue thinking of Lollardy in terms resembling those deployed in these poems, the English reformation might have belonged to the fifteenth rather than the sixteenth century. Oldcastle helped destroy this possibility.

As we learn more about Lollard discourse and the discourses immediately adjacent to it we will doubtless want to qualify some of Barr's findings. At present, however, her book leaves little room for criticism. It may be worth noting that for this reader at least her section on "Legal Fictions" seemed in places inadequately assimilated to its present context. And rhetorically her discussion is sometimes less forceful than it might be: it is too often propelled by the observation that something is "interesting," for example (as in pp. 10, 17, 19, 65, 127, 129, 130, 163). There are some other minor flaws. It is not easy to find one's way around the volume's bibliography of primary sources, which at one point abandons all pretense at alphabetization. It also seems odd in a work so concerned with locating a *Piers Plowman* tradition to find no reference to the first chapter of Helen C. White's *Social Criticism in Popular Religious Literature of the Sixteenth Century* (New York: Macmillan Co., 1944). But all such criticisms fade into insignificance beside Barr's discussion as a whole, which obviously grows from wide reading as well as a good deal of hard thinking. We may well wish that the volume were more affordable. But we should be very grateful to Barr for having written it.

CHRISTINA VON NOLCKEN
University of Chicago

ANNE CLARK BARTLETT. *Male Authors, Female Readers: Representation and Subjectivity in Middle English Devotional Literature.* Ithaca, N.Y., and London: Cornell University Press, 1995. Pp. xii, 212. $32.50.

Feminist scholars of the past two decades have enriched the discipline by making accessible medieval women's writings as well as engaging the issue of female representation in canonical texts. A few—such as Elizabeth Robertson, Bella Millett, Jocelyn Wogan-Browne, and now Anne Clark

Bartlett—have ventured into the less glamorous territory of devotional literature; yet this is undoubtedly where the richest vein of information concerning gender and reception is yet to be mined, including material evidence of female textual communities, manuscript transmission, devotional trends, literacy and Latinity, and, as Bartlett argues, "representation and subjectivity." Given the evidence for female ownership of manuscripts including male-authored works like the *Speculum devotorum* and *Contemplations on the Dread and Love of God*, it is perhaps surprising that no enterprising scholar has attempted a full-length study to address Bartlett's central concern: "Why were these texts, whose antifeminism ranges from the subtle to the vociferous, so popular among female readers? What did reading these works *do* to women?" (p. 2). Bartlett's response demonstrates just how fruitful a theoretically informed and interdisciplinary methodology can be.

Bartlett's intellectual eclecticism is learned, sensible, and convincing. In negotiating the space between representation and subjectivity, Bartlett constructs authorship and reception in the "complex dynamism" of reading in medieval textual communities, "each with its own cultural authorities, reading strategies, and levels and definitions of competence" (p. 2). Rather than presenting the transmission and reception of devotional literature as an authoritative, hierarchical, or static process, Bartlett deftly explores the tensions, inconsistencies, and polyvalence of devotional works that appeared in codices assimilating a variety of genres (courtly romances, prayers, antifeminist diatribes) and thus discourses of female representation. Three kinds of "counterdiscourses" in devotional literature challenge misogynist representations of women, each transmitting its own "cluster of social and cultural conventions" from which to "regender" female identity (p. 3). The conventions of courtly romance, monastic epistles of spiritual friendship, and narrative of nuptial and Passion contemplation offered women a variety of roles and rhetorical strategies from which to experience and establish a sense of identity. The reading process, by the material conditions of book production and conventions of authorship and reading in the Middle Ages, is "heteroglossic," occurring in the dynamic interplay of cultural and institutional voices.

Chapter 2 offers a fascinating case study of how textual transmission in a gendered reading culture necessarily destabilizes even the most authoritative devotional work: Aelred of Rievaulx's *De institutione inclusarum*. Bartlett illustrates how Aelred, writing in the twelfth century for an anchoress, identifies unbridled speech with female sexuality, ultimately encouraging the eradication of both. In exploring such issues, Aelred raises his own sexuality in the familiar mode of spiritual autobiography or confession, encouraging his devout female friend to construct her own spiritual identity according to a distinctly masculine ascetic ideal, informed by the repudiation of masculine desire. Bartlett then demonstrates how two fifteenth-century Middle English versions of Aelred's *Rule* offer alternatives for female self-fashioning, appropriately rejecting for wider female audiences "all aspects of the masculine 'hermeneutics of desire' that the Latin text introduces" (p. 50). In her examination of emendations and alterations in these later manuscripts, Bartlett diagrams how a devotional work can be modified to both meet and shape "social and cultural shifts in the perception of gender and sexuality" (p. 51).

Chapter 3 explores how the discourse of courtesy—circulated through the romance genre, literature of courtly love, and conduct manuals—was assimilated into devotional texts, offering female readers an empowering set of literary conventions that challenged clerical misogyny. Despite the androcentric underpinnings of courtesy literature and romance, which ultimately assert male identity and patriarchal order, their combined discourses support an image of female readers as "active and desiring lovers rather than as passive objects of male desire. . . . Christ becomes the acquiescent partner, submitting to the requests of the female lover" (p. 69). Although a sustained exploration of how this counterdiscourse influenced Margery Kempe's *Book* is outside the scope of her argument, Bartlett raises the issue, pointing the way for further research and profitable application of her study's methods. Similarly, Bartlett's exploration of the "discourse of familiarity," grounded in the Latin epistle of spiritual friendship but revised to express a spiritual equality and intellectual engagement between the devout woman and her religious advisor, will encourage us to rethink our assumptions about male/female relations from the cloister.

Perhaps the most original, and sure to be controversial, chapter in *Male Authors, Female Readers* is Chapter 5, which focuses on the discourse of Passion and/or nuptial contemplation. Women's writing about ecstatic union incurred the disgust and incredulity of late-medieval spiritual experts, who increasingly attempted to control and discern the validity of such experiences through a doctrine of *discretio spirituum* (most recently considered in the context of gender and authority by Rosalynn Voaden). In her highly original discussion of "how medieval women routinely and enthusiastically blurred the semiotic boundaries between physical and allegorical love," Bartlett turns to medieval theories of female sexual desire to locate representations of female spiritual love in devotional literature in the broader cultural context of medieval medical and scientific lore. Bartlett's reading strategy firmly places Margery Kempe, whose literalistic erotic spirituality undermines her status as a genuine mystic for many, in a powerful devotional tradition that acknowledged the power of female sexuality.

Finally, the author generously makes available her own preliminary "Descriptive List of Extant Books owned by Medieval English Nuns and Convents," an invaluable tool for scholars who now recognize that gendered reading can only be constructed convincingly in a historical continuum from material evidence; however intellectually exciting a highly theorized discussion of a medieval text might be, the most compelling arguments for reception will acknowledge manuscript redaction and transmission, book ownership, and evidence of actual reading habits, such as manuscript annotations. Bartlett's book is required reading for scholars of medieval devotional, mystical, and women's literature, but her innovative methodology for exploring the thorny problems of reading and reception in a manuscript culture should interest medievalists in a variety of disciplines.

DENISE L. DESPRES
University of Puget Sound

JUDITH BRONFMAN. *Chaucer's "Clerk's Tale": The Griselda Story Received, Rewritten, Illustrated.* Garland Studies in Medieval Literature, vol. 11. New York and London: Garland Publishing, 1994. Pp. xiv, 162. $28.00.

Judith Bronfman's study of the Griselda story ranges over seven centuries of retellings that reformulate Griselda in poems, plays, tracts, ballads, operas, novels, short stories, illustrations, and, mainly in this century, criticism. Many readers will be surprised at the number of imaginative reinventions of Griselda. Even in the twentieth century, the story has been adapted for the stage—with one sadomasochistic dramatization having Walter desire a wife "strong enough to stand a good beating" (p. 75); it has been retold in black dialect, anthologized in *A Selection from the World's Greatest Short Stories* under the heading "The Origin of the Modern Love Story," and parodied in *Ellery Queen's Mystery Magazine* in an adaptation that recasts

Walter as a "rich Midwesterner and Griselda as a New York showgirl" who murders him (p. 79). Bronfman is interested in the seemingly inexhaustible interpretive potential of the Griselda story, which since Boccaccio's rendering of it in the *Decameron* has inspired widely different responses from both its readers and its redactors. Bronfman's book documents the diverse manifestations of the Griselda story in criticism on Chaucer's *Clerk's Tale*, and in adaptations and illustrations of the story itself.

Readers interested in retellings of the Griselda story will find this work a valuable resource. Bronfman is an enthusiastic collector of Griselda stories and allusions; the book identifies nearly sixty dating from the Renaissance to 1985, and includes in an appendix a transcription of a sixteenth-century Griselda ballad, written in sonnet stanzas. Bronfman also clearly enjoys retelling versions that develop a new theme or a new facet in the characters or give the tale a new setting. Many readers, however, will be dissatisfied by the very limited analyses that Bronfman offers in her surveys both of criticism on Chaucer's *Clerk's Tale* and of retellings of the Griselda story, and by the omission of any discussion of her methodology.

The book's usefulness is hampered by Bronfman's conception of her study. She sets up a twofold project in her introduction: 1) "to look at the story from a long view, starting from its sources in the fourteenth century and then moving into the recent flood of critical interpretations"; and 2) to examine rewritings as works comparable to criticism "for the views that they have taken of the tale" (p. 4). Her aim is to provide a "broader perspective from which to view" questions that she sees arising from conflicting interpretations of *The Clerk's Tale* (p. 5):

Is it part of a "marriage group"? Or does it belong with the other three rhyme royal tales? . . . Is it about wifely behavior? Or is it a "personality clash" between the Clerk and the Wife of Bath? Is it about rulership and politics? . . . Is there one interpretation that is right or are there many interpretations, equally right? (pp. 4–5)

The book's most likely readers will not be interested in these questions because they have already been variously answered in complex and thoughtful ways, and because Bronfman's formulations of recurring issues in *Clerk's Tale* criticism are too simple. Lacking a more ambitious critical agenda, Bronfman shows that the story is an "infinitely malleable narrative" (p. 128), the point she makes in her conclusion. Unfortunately, she can achieve this aim merely by summarizing or describing what is different about a version without being systematic. Bronfman never inquires into the elements that make Chaucer's or Petrarch's or Boccaccio's version of the Griselda story so malleable, nor does she consider in any analytic way how authors have exploited that malleability.

The book is divided into five chapters, the first three of which are concerned with interpretive issues that have occupied scholars of *The Clerk's Tale*. Chapter 1, "The Story Before Chaucer," retells Boccaccio's final tale of the *Decameron*, briefly reviews the search for a folktale source, and traces the tale's transmission from Boccaccio to Petrarch to the French translators. The next two chapters, "The Marriage Group and the Allegorical Griselda" and "The Clerk's Tale as Religious Tale and Political Commentary," discuss some of the different kinds of *Clerk's Tale* criticism. These two chapters do not attempt to be comprehensive or evaluative but merely suggestive of the opposing interpretations of *The Clerk's Tale* and trends in criticism. Some errors and frequent imprecision will make scholars wary of Bronfman's reliability. For example, Bronfman does not identify the then sixty-year-old Boccaccio as the intended recipient of Petrarch's Griselda story; she notes that Petrarch made the story available to a wider audience "when he translated it into a Latin prose letter to a young man" (p. 16). Citing J. Burke Severs's edition of *Le Livre Griseldis*, Bronfman claims incorrectly that this anonymous French translation omits Petrarch's "religious moral" (p. 17), which it translates fully. She also incorrectly attributes Mary Carruthers's argument in "The Lady, the Swineherd, and Chaucer's Clerk" to John Fisher, citing his introduction to *The Clerk's Tale* in his edition of Chaucer's collected works (p. 25).

The real heart of the book is chapter 4, "Chaucer's Tale Rewritten," which is organized into sections by century, and almost exclusively focuses on Griselda stories in English. The discussions of the works are brief, usually consisting of one to two paragraphs in which Bronfman identifies the author, title, genre, and date of publication or performance, and includes a brief description—sometimes a summary—of what distinguishes a particular work. Two-thirds of the chapter is devoted to nineteenth- and twentieth-century versions. The chapter title is misleading; not all retellings are based on Chaucer's *Clerk's Tale*, and it is often not clear which source an author has used. Bronfman does not discuss any of the versions in terms of how it handles its source. The material in this chapter would be better organized as bibliographic entries than as an essay, even when Bronfman singles out a few particularly interesting versions for longer treatment of one to three pages.

The fifth chapter, "Griselda Illustrated," is more of a sampling than a survey of visual renderings of the tale. The book reproduces twenty-five illustrations (one in color) taken from six works in different media, dating from the late fourteenth to the nineteenth century. Bronfman does not discuss her criteria for choosing these illustrations rather than others or indicate the variety and quantity of Griselda illustrations available to her. Yet the pictures are inherently interesting, and Bronfman points out their many significant details. Teachers of *The Clerk's Tale* may find the four reproductions of manuscript illuminations useful in the classroom.

Although this book has serious flaws, it will serve a diverse audience. Teachers of *The Clerk's Tale* will find new ways to talk about the tale's odd appeal. *Clerk's Tale* scholars with different critical projects will be grateful to Bronfman for locating versions of the Griselda story and uncovering records of ones no longer extant. Indeed, most of the stories she documents are poised on the edge of oblivion. These stories may offer insights into such important topics as the fundamental elements of the Griselda story, changing reading practices, social values, and the relationship between literary conventions and ideology.

Amy W. Goodwin
Randolph-Macon College

Peter Brown. *Chaucer at Work: The Making of the* Canterbury Tales. London and New York: Longman, 1994. Pp. xi, 186. £28.00 cloth, £10.99 paper.

Peter Brown's *Chaucer at Work: The Making of the* Canterbury Tales emerges out of classroom praxis and perhaps most usefully serves teachers trying to help students gain more sophisticated entries into the Chaucerian universe. By seeking to re-create the poet's writing processes, it gives readers insight into "the crucial thought patterns and priorities which shaped Chaucer's compositions" (p. 3). Pointing to key passages in the *Tales* to explore central interpretive problems, Brown introduces readers to complex issues of source study and intertextuality, engaging them in an exploratory process that emphasizes close reading and attention to significant detail. His method has some affinity with Charles A. Owen, Jr.'s approach in "Crucial Passages in Five of *The Canterbury Tales*: A Study in

Irony and Symbol," which argues that certain passages in Chaucer's work "are in a sense symbolic of the whole work" (Edward Wagenknecht, ed., *Chaucer: Modern Essays in Criticism*, p. 252); and with V. A. Kolve's *Chaucer and the Imagery of Narrative: The First Five Canterbury Tales*, which centers on symbolic or "iconographic images" that are "discovered *within* the images one forms in attending to the narrative action itself" (p. 61).

Adapting these critical approaches for exploratory purposes, Brown selects meaningful "chunks" of texts or memorable images from Chaucer's sources or other contemporary materials, provides sufficient contextual discussion to highlight relevant issues, juxtaposes them with passages from Chaucer's text, and invites the reader to assess the significance of the poet's modifications. His approach helps readers understand how much Chaucer's compositional method depends on subtle modulations of conventional materials—often a difficult concept for those convinced that artists work from *ex nihilo* originality.

After an introductory chapter explaining the book's rationale and methodology, each succeeding chapter deals with a single tale—seven in all, plus *The General Prologue*. Brown draws on a rich variety of scholarly and critical materials; he moves comfortably through the very diverse materials he selects for juxtaposition: Geoffrey of Vinsauf's directions for describing a beautiful woman and his lament upon the death of Richard I; zodiacal illustrations of the reign of Saturn and his children; a dialogue between God and Noah from the Wakefield cycle; an illumination of the Annunciation; passages from Jerome's *Adversus Joviniam* and Dante's *Convivio*; Richard Rolle's translation of Psalm 13; a fifteenth-century Crucifixion showing soldiers dicing for Jesus's garments at the foot of the cross; and the opening lines of *Patience* by the *Gawain*-poet. One surprising lapse occurs early in the introduction: John of Gaunt is identified as the father—rather than the uncle—of Richard II (p. 3).

Two examples will illustrate Brown's method. To address the significance of the pilgrimage framework in *The General Prologue*, he places Chaucer's choice of setting against three contemporary backdrops: *A Mirror to Men and Women*, which treats pilgrimage as a metaphor for the spiritual journey of human life; a manuscript image of a pilgrim about to set sail for his spiritual destination; and a Lollard attack on the abuses that often characterized late-fourteenth-century pilgrimages. After exploring each of these in its own context, Brown invites readers to assess how much impact the pilgrimage controversy had on the opening lines of *The Canterbury Tales*. In discussing January from *The Merchant's Tale* Brown begins by showing how—as with Alisoun in *The Miller's Tale*—Chaucer constructs characters that are "facades concealing other creations of great antiquity" and thus are "the expression of a body of ideas" (p. 123). Noting that Chaucer's techniques for characterization can be considerably more complex than simply playing off conventional materials, Brown introduces calendar images of January portrayed as the two-faced god of antiquity who—in medieval depictions—becomes a solidly prosperous two-faced man, looking back on the past and forward to the future and intent on indulging himself in the seasonal activities of eating and drinking. The lavishness of January and May's wedding feast thus highlights how Chaucer draws on nature myths to enrich his portrayal of January.

A number of formatting elements enhance the book's usefulness: questions precede and follow discussion of the text, helping to focus the reader's attention on relevant issues and guiding teachers interested in using this material with their students; an annotated bibliography at the end of each chapter functions as a ready resource for those wishing to meander further down the interpretive pathways the book has traced; a detailed index makes specific information easily accessible.

Brown sees Chaucer's artistic purposes—entertaining his audience and encouraging dialogue on contemporary issues—as closely linked with the social milieu that gave him patronage. Although Brown's discussion—by virtue of the texts and images he selects—unavoidably leans more heavily in some directions than in others, he strives to facilitate analysis, to point toward fruitful avenues for exploration rather than to strain after definitive readings. In the spirit of Chaucer's own distaste for authoritative guides, Brown eschews the role of master-interpreter and presents his readers with a method that is adaptable to other passages and tales. Overall, his work helps students move quickly beyond the "roadside drama" approach and the focus on "realistic" detail; it directs them toward more contextual critical analysis. Readable and imaginative, it is a user-friendly resource for anyone seeking to better understand Chaucer's compositional methods and to deepen acquaintance with a poet who prefers "open-ended debate rather than conclusive moral teaching" (p. 10).

LILLIAN M. BISSON
Marymount University

MICHAEL A. CALABRESE. *Chaucer's Ovidian Arts of Love*. Gainesville, Fla.: University Press of Florida, 1994. Pp. x, 170. $29.95.

Chaucer's Ovidian Arts of Love presents a close reading of Chaucer's *Troilus*, *The Wife of Bath's Prologue*, and the *Retraction*. Professor Calabrese reads these texts against the textual tradition he calls the "medieval Ovid," a tradition that encompasses Ovidian texts in context, an "extending web of scholastic and poetic texts, treatments and testimonies" (p. 3). In Calabrese's terms, it is Ovid-the-love-poet—the author of the *Ars Amatoria*, the *Remedia Amoris*, the *Heroides*, and the *Amores*—that Chaucer studied and rewrote. In addition, Calabrese focuses as well on Ovid's "civic perils"— especially his exile, understood in the Middle Ages as imperial punishment for the lascivious content of the *Ars Amatoria*. The Ovidian commentary tradition, with its interest in the ethical interpretation of an author's "life" as well as "art," offered Chaucer a "model of the life of a lascivious poet who had to answer for his crimes" (p. 21).

Calabrese posits that Chaucer, as a vernacular poet alongside Boccaccio and Jean de Meun, confronted the contradictory nature of medieval responses to Ovid's love poetry. Ovidian amatory texts were simultaneously central to the canon and to vernacular poetics yet frequently condemned for their seductive dangers, a condemnation that elides rhetorical and erotic appeal. Calabrese briefly analyzes an anonymous fourteenth-century poem, the *Antiovidianus*, as an example of a countertradition to the ethical recuperation of Ovid's art and life in the conventional *accessus*. For Calabrese, it is this contradictory response to Ovidian art and life, rhetoric and desire, that Chaucer negotiates in the erotic machinations of the *Troilus*, through the subject position of the Wife of Bath, and in the authorial self-consciousness of the *Retraction*.

In two chapters at the center of the book, Calabrese reads Chaucer's *Troilus* as a vernacular narrative exploration of the *Ars Amatoria* and the *Remedia Amoris*. In this schema, Pandarus becomes identified as the quintessential Ovidian advisor, especially evident in his deployment of letter writing for erotic ends. This Ovidian Pandarus follows the blueprint of the *Ars* in books 1–3 of the *Troilus* and shifts to the *Remedia* in books 4–5. Criseyde is a "competent Ovidian" (p. 48) who "can play the game of love and can play it in specifically Ovidian terms" (p. 66); Diomede, a "textbook Ovidian lover" (p. 71). Troilus is the amateur lover whose ignorance of Ovid—and consequent lack of rhetorical polish—means that he "cannot see the world as fiction" (p. 63), a handicap that leads to his loss of Criseyde and his death. Indeed, Calabrese sees the trajectory of Troilus's desire as paradigmatic of the "scorned women in the *Heroides*" (p. 48). In Calabrese's reading, the end of the *Troilus* evokes the *Tristia* and its author's awareness that "fortune can change powerfully and tragically when one takes game for earnest" (p. 73). Chaucer's exploration of Ovidian art and amatory rhetoric results in a repudiation of eroticism: "he redefines love and points his readers away from the protean, rhetorical world to the Trinity, unchanging and eternal, asking them to learn what Troilus only glimpses after death and what Ovid, an exile and a pagan, could never learn" (p. 79).

The Wife of Bath represents the next step in Calabrese's view of Chaucer's evolving Ovidianism. In his analysis of the *Prologue* Calabrese finds a "neo-Ovidian art of love" (p. 87) in the Wife's rhetorical manipulation of her husbands. The Wife, Chaucer's "greatest Ovidian scholar" (p. 80), employs Ovid against the "antifeminist texts that . . . form another part of the medieval Ovidian tradition" (p. 87). In this reading, the Wife's engagement with Ovidianism becomes a liberatory process, and Ovidian rhetoric becomes an enabling discourse in Chaucer's text that "works toward a code of marital affection that is beyond treachery and beyond claims to inherited power," which might lead to "marriage and a romantic world that are free of art and game" (p. 104). According to Calabrese's scheme, the final stage of Chaucer's Ovidianism is marked by the *Retraction* to *The Canterbury Tales*. Calabrese reads the *Retraction* against Ovid's poems of exile and concludes that Chaucer, a "Christian servant of the Word," finally renounces poetic fictions to avoid "banishment from his 'true home,' the divine kingdom" (p. 130).

This study directs Chaucerians toward a new and important appreciation of Ovid's amatory and exile poetry and it thereby outlines a distinct Chaucerian/Ovidian intertextuality. For instance, Calabrese convincingly demonstrates that Chaucer grafted an Ovidian discourse onto Boccaccio's *Filostrato* and used Ovidian rhetoric to construct the *Troilus* as an "art of love." The interpretive range of *Chaucer's Arts of Love*, however, would have been enriched by a more thorough engagement with scholarship and theory, especially in relation to gender and sexuality. While Calabrese acknowledges the significance of gender in studies of both Ovid and Chaucer, his own interpretive models for gender analysis remain entirely uninterrogated. In his introductory chapter he states, "Ovid provided Chaucer . . . with a series of studies of gendered discourse and identity" (p. 4). But instead of including the "fictions of gender" among the poetic fictions he analyzes, he accepts—and uncritically reiterates—traditional attitudes toward Criseyde and the Wife of Bath as threatening women whose use of Ovidian rhetoric (in Calabrese's version) enhances their self-determination. This view ignores the power relations that contextualize such representations of female "agency": the coercive bedroom scene in book 3 of the *Troilus* becomes a "night of bliss" in which "we find no game and no woe"

(p. 58). Criseyde's "betrayal" of Troilus is discussed as though she had the autonomy to live and love as she chose. The physicality of the Wife becomes an "expression of freedom" (p. 93), an approach that overlooks the physical abuse the Wife endures; her deafness alone is a reminder of the price her body pays for its expression of freedom. Indeed, Calabrese often fails to critique the terms of gendered discourse he himself has inherited from Ovid and Chaucer, evident in assertions such as "the Wife becomes what men fear most, the fully armed, nimble Amazon, wise through experience yet still skilled at the 'olde daunce'" (p. 87). More thorough engagement in feminist and queer theory might have allowed Calabrese to analyze effectively the constructed nature of gender, agency, and subjectivity in Chaucer and Ovid. Calabrese even overlooks scholarship on the "medieval Ovid," such as Warren Ginsberg's "Ovid and the Problem of Gender," or John Fyler's "Love and the Declining World: Ovid, Genesis, and Chaucer" (*Mediaevalia* 13 [1987]), which addresses these issues. Chaucerians have yet to explore fully the status of the medieval Ovid in Chaucer's poetry. Calabrese's approach to Ovid outlines some important aspects of the relationship between Ovidian and Chaucerian poetry, though his conclusions—that Troilus "points his readers . . . to the Trinity" or that Chaucer is finally a "Christian servant of the Word"—do not do justice to the complexities of that textual relationship.

Marilynn Desmond
SUNY Binghamton

William Calin. *The French Tradition and the Literature of Medieval England*. Toronto, Buffalo, and London: University of Toronto Press, 1994. Pp. xiv, 587. $29.95 paper.

William Calin's *The French Tradition and the Literature of Medieval England* stands alone as both a reference work to and critical account of the relationship between Francophone and Anglophone literatures in the Middle Ages. In both conception and execution, the book is unique—and uniquely useful—even though it covers a scholarly field much discussed during the last hundred and fifty years. What Calin offers is not a traditional source study that catalogues and paraphrases earlier texts, with claims to the scholar's attention only because they have influenced or been incorporated into the works therein privileged for analysis. Such source studies usually are organized in ways that distortingly inscribe the complex transtextuality of this multilingual, transnational literary environment; they either construct a single language area to consider (e.g., late-medieval English poetry) for reasons of cultural and disciplinary politics or, prompted by post-romantic notions of creativity, place authors at the center of what are essentially generic and thematic networks of texts. Calin's book avoids these unnecessary limitations, but not by ignoring the claims of textual specificity or authorial difference. In other words, his is not a conventional literary history of the period, biased toward the philological facticity of contextual issues (e.g., the biography of writers, problems of attribution, dates of composition, and questions of audience and transmission). Yet he has mastered a bewildering amount of scholarship devoted to such matters, many of which lie outside his official disciplinary purview as a *romaniste*, and frequently offers *en passant* worthy and trenchant opinions on them.

Like traditional source historians, Calin does privilege for analysis a series of texts (designated with necessary ambiguity as "the literature of medieval England") in reference to which another series of texts (the equally ambiguous "French tradition") is both constructed and discussed. In a very rough sense, then, this book is about "the literature of medieval England" as viewed through a comparatist lens (i.e., the "English" texts discussed are those that are connected in some fashion to "French" tradition). It is not a history of French literature *per se*; it is concerned only with those texts identified as "French" that bear on those designated as "English." The book is not a guide (or a complete one, at any rate) to what might be called "the literature of medieval France." And yet what I have just written is not a particularly helpful or accurate description, precisely because one premise of Calin's book is the disjunction between the use of English and French to designate different languages, on the one hand, and their use to describe what we now tend to view as "national" areas of cultural production, on the other.

As Calin reminds us, this disjunction is the result of two historical conditions: that "for three hundred years after the Conquest French was the language of the upper classes in England"; and that during this period and later, French was a language of great cultural prestige in England, with the result that "writing in English . . . was bathed in French ambiance and looked to the French in addition to Latin for order and inspiration" (p. ix). In short, any consideration of "the literature of medieval England" should take into account a considerable body of material produced in Britain but written in French—that is, what is ordinarily called Anglo-Norman literature—as well as the influence of texts in French written in France on English writers, particularly those of the late fourteenth century, writing in English. Like its author, this book transgresses established fields of specialization; the result is a conception of the subject much truer to the cultural production it attempts to describe, however much that conception may not fit the "national" model of literary study within whose limitations medievalists have traditionally been forced to labor.

A useful case in point is Anglo-Norman literature, a literary tradition ordinarily ignored politely by French and English specialists alike, with exceptions made for certain authors (e.g., Marie de France) or works (e.g., *Tristan*) deemed worthy of inclusion within one or the other national tradition. Calin's full discussion of this body of literature (the only worthy one since Dominica Legge's somewhat dry 1963 study) includes those authors often co-opted for "French" literature: Marie, Beroul, Thomas, and Wace. His treatment here partakes equally and fruitfully of analysis and appreciation; he is especially strong on later works (the seldom mentioned *Amadis et Ydoine* and *Ipomedon*) that he sees, rightly I think, as commenting on those of the so-called classic period through various self-referential and thematic means. In addition, his enthusiasm for hagiographic literature— usually neglected by French specialists, as he points out—rescues this fascinating body of narrative from the misjudgments of modern taste.

The book's second and most lengthy section addresses in new and important ways a question often broached in microstudies by the first generation of modern philologists (Kittredge, Lowes, and company) but then largely neglected as medieval English texts became reconstituted for "national" literary study. Calin's intention here is all-encompassing and sets an agenda his work alone cannot possibly fulfill:

. . . I wish to show that a number of crucial developments in Middle and Early Modern English—great mythical figures such as Auberon, Lancelot, and Arthur; the narrative technique of interlace; the mode of allegory, sacred and secular; literature as irony and satire or as disjunction and deferral; the dream vision and *dit amoureux*; the self-conscious pseudo-autobiographical narrator; the historical ideal of English chivalry and heroism—are derived from continental French masterpieces. (p. xii)

Calin recognizes that even his immense study must be incomplete. Microanalyses of source relations are out of the question, and he does not cover satiric and religious allegory (Deguilleville and Langland still await the comparatist technique), Lydgate, late courtly lyrics, or drama. Though he makes an exception for Malory, the book otherwise stops at about 1420, though Calin believes fifteenth-century English poetry does have its merits.

The separate chapters of this part of the book are necessarily somewhat cursory on occasion, as Calin tries to survey broadly generic and thematic issues. For example, only twenty-three pages can be devoted to the *Roman de la Rose*, which rates only twice as much space as the certainly far less important *Huon de Bordeaux*. The strongest chapters devoted to French authors or works influential on English ones are those on Deguilleville, Froissart, Chartier, and Machaut (a poet of special interest to Calin since his groundbreaking study of some two decades ago, *A Poet at the Fountain*). Calin avoids the worst pitfall of traditional source study: discussing only those texts or formal features actually reused by a later writer. Instead, these chapters offer coherent and informative accounts of the literary *oeuvres* in question. Machaut and Froissart provided materials and examples that Chaucer or Gower decided to reuse in some fashion; but they also created an atmosphere of broadly generic and thematic trends that conditioned the development of courtly poetry in England. As Calin points out, late-medieval court poetry begins in France and afterward flourishes in England; thus "the distinction made between Chaucer and the French and between English poets and their predecessors is largely one of perception, based upon differences in modern academic critical approaches" (p. 270). If Chaucer becomes less exceptional, less of a genius creating *ex nihilo* as a result, the gain for literary history is a clearer understanding of his place within a tradition that neither begins nor ends with him.

Calin's chapters on Chaucer, Gower, and Hoccleve offer a clear and in-sightful account of the ways in which that French tradition is passed on, modified, and even transformed by these three writers. To my satisfaction at least, Calin proves his thesis that Chaucer never "transcended" his French literary background, but simply added other elements (Tuscan, native English) to it. In the book's final section, he broaches various questions of literary merit, narrative technique, thematic classification, and intended audience long associated with medieval English verse romance. His aim here, as elsewhere in the book, is largely appreciative; the critical analyses presented successfully contest the common judgment that the English romances are not a continuation of French traditions and that they should be faulted for "lack of elegance and polish" (p. 495).

189

The French Tradition and the Literature of Medieval England is not only an immensely useful work of synthesis, the fruit of one scholar's enormous labor of pursuing complex and long-standing disputes and reading an incredibly long list of difficult primary sources. It is also a genially polemical book, for it argues convincingly that the field described as "the literature of medieval England" must be remapped to include works written in England but in French, even as those works thought to be "English" because of their language must be seen as part of an unbroken series of cultural connections reaching to continental France. If the task of the comparatist is to challenge the disciplinary separation of national literatures by showing how political boundaries are easily crossed by multicultural exchanges, then William Calin has succeeded in this well-written, extensively documented, and amazingly erudite study. His book should be read closely by all of us who think we have been specializing in "the literature of medieval England" but have hitherto neglected worthy texts and their interrelations.

R. BARTON PALMER
Clemson University

DAVID CHAMBERLAIN, ed. *New Readings of Late Medieval Love Poems*. Lanham, Md., New York, and London: University Press of America, 1993. Pp. v, 198. $44.50 cloth, $23.50 paper.

This slim volume consists of essays by seven authors on late-medieval courtly love poems written or translated into Middle English or Middle Scots. Almost a third of this book can be attributed to David Chamberlain, who in addition to writing the introduction has authored one essay, "Clanvowe's Cuckoo," and coauthored another with Susan Schoon Eberly, " 'Under the Schaddow of the Hawthorne Greene': The Hawthorn in Medieval Love Poetry." The remaining contributors and essays are Bryan Crockett, "Venus Unveiled: Lydgate's *Temple of Glas* and the Religion of Love"; Claire F. James, "*The Kingis Quair*: The Plight of the Courtly Lover"; Melissa Brown Tomus, "The Hope for 'Pleasaunce': Richard Roos' Translation of Alain Chartier's *La Belle Dame Sans Mercy*"; Cynthia Lockard Snyder, "*The Floure and the Leafe*: An Alternative Approach"; and Bonita Friedman, "In Love's Thrall: *The Court of Love* and Its Captives." As Chamberlain's useful

190

introduction makes clear, despite the book's varied authorship, the essays are conceived as a coherent collection, unified through the use of the same critical approach and through the authors' familiarity and agreement with each other's conclusions.

Chamberlain describes the approach as an "attempt to be historical criticism of a broad and sensitive kind, drawing on a wide range of cultural resources, religious, social, literary, and philosophical" (p. 2). The approach emphasizes "the texts themselves, their cultural context, and the literary tradition of the genre" (p. 2). It is especially interested in "careful analysis of imagery as a means to determining the presence of humor and irony" (p. 2), and in "the poems' likely meaning to their original audiences" (p. 2). Although the terms "patristic" and "exegetical" are rarely found in this volume, the approach described and utilized is of course patristic criticism. While the emphasis in the volume is on specific readings of specific texts, Chamberlain's statement that "all the coherences are intended to create a more substantial and convincing body of criticism" (p. 3), with each essay "contribut[ing] something to the persuasiveness of the others" (p. 3), makes clear the additional intent to make a contribution toward further understanding and acceptance of exegetical criticism. One value of this volume, then, is the opportunity it provides to see how patristic criticism of the nineties compares with its earlier versions. As Chamberlain rightly notes, to assess the usefulness of a critical approach, it is helpful to have several examples marshalled together.

Chamberlain's invitation to "test the validity" of his approach marks a clear difference in tone and emphasis in Chamberlain's description of patristic criticism from that of such earlier practitioners of the approach as its originator, who was also Chamberlain's teacher, D. W. Robertson, Jr. No longer stressing exegetical criticism as the *only* authentic approach, and no longer merely dismissing all other approaches as modern and therefore "wrong," Chamberlain clearly strives to present a criticism for the nineties, updated and stripped of some of the excesses of its earlier versions. He describes himself and the other contributors as "aware of the value of recent critical theory" (p. 2), and "sensitive to reader response theory . . . sign theory and semiotics, and culture theory" (pp. 2–3), although he tellingly limits this awareness to "medieval variants" of the theories. And he aligns his approach with recent literary reevaluation and greater appreciation of the quality of fifteenth-century poetry, most especially with those social historians who have shown an extraordinary taste among the secular audience of that time for instructive and devotional literature. In contrast to an

191

earlier emphasis on the serious nature of medieval secular literature at the expense of its more playful aspects, Chamberlain and his contributors stress "what scholars knew already, but may tend to forget, that medieval poetry deliberately appeals to *both* . . . 'ernest and game'" (p. 6), and point to the wit and humor of the poems.

For most readers of this volume, then, the "new" in its title will be seen to refer less to radical departures or challenges to accepted approaches to late-medieval love poems than to a more modest development of a well-tried approach. The readings are "new" in the sense that a sustained pattern of patristic criticism has not previously been applied to this body of poems. In Chamberlain's words: "They are new because language, literary tradition, social culture, and close reasoning have led necessarily to new interpretations" (p. 3). And they are new in the creditable ways Chamberlain seems to have tried to address criticism of the approach through the modifications outlined earlier, especially by his volume's emphasis on a kind of close reading that earlier patristic criticism was frequently justly accused of neglecting.

What is not new about these readings, then, are their basic and conservative assumptions. Despite Chamberlain's attempts to go beyond the limitations of earlier practitioners of his approach, his efforts are undermined by his failure to address questions recent theory has posed about these assumptions. For example, his emphasis on "the texts themselves" would seem to be a reversal of the initial impetus of patristic criticism to go "outside" the text in order to escape the strictures of a formalist and New Critical focus on "the text itself" at the expense of contextual reading. But an emphasis on "the text itself" in the nineties seems to belie the theoretical explorations that have taken place since patristic criticism began that raise serious questions about what the nature of a text might be, and that question the possibilities of separating a text from its intra- and intertextualities and contexts in a way that would allow us to know "the text itself."

While the emphasis is said to be on "the texts themselves," Chamberlain also stresses the intertextuality of the texts in his and his contributors' attempts to place them in their cultural and literary contexts. But despite Chamberlain's claim to have drawn on "a wide range of cultural resources, religious, social, literary and philosophical" (p. 2), the cultural and literary contexts to which he and his contributors refer are limited, homogenizing, and monolithic. Cultural texts indicated as a guide to reading late-medieval love poems turn out to be those allegories of the Church fathers, mythographers, and philosophers that support one tradition: that promulgated by the fathers of the medieval Roman Catholic Church. The contributors constantly exhort readers to acquire a "proper medieval understanding" (p. 99) (James), which equates medieval thought (Snyder), or medieval tradition (Friedman), with patristic thinking. These exhortations of course are part of a nostalgia all the contributors share for a past that is markedly different from the present, especially in its homogeneity of outlook, together with a desire for discernible authorial intentions, both of which are seen as recoverable in an unproblematic way that ignores questions recent theory has raised: about the nature of this nostalgia and desire, about diversities the tendency to totalize a "medieval mind" ignores, and about our ability to know and "recover" such pasts and intentions. Thus, when Crockett attempts to redeem Lydgate's *Temple of Glas* by referring readers to medieval Christian mythography, he does show how what seems tiresomely imitative, inconsistently religious, and prolix to some readers could be seen as an inventive, intellectual, and subtle allegory for others, but he cannot prove that one of these readings is the author's intention, that even if it were it should be privileged, or even that these different readings are respectively restricted to the twentieth and fifteenth centuries. Nor are these issues addressed. Similarly with James's essay on *The Kingis Quair*, which can be said to show that the poem can be read as an ironic treatment of the narrator's loss of reason and consequent fall, but which does not demonstrate that this reading is either the author's or the most "reasonable," especially since the latter issues are never addressed.

The initial essay by Eberly and Chamberlain, a reading of an image rather than a poem, might seem to be an exception to the above in the sense that the iconography of the hawthorn is traced through multiple traditions: pagan, horticultural, and mythographic, as well as through moral readings of selected medieval poems. The authors' purpose, however—to show what "hasty" or "less sophisticated" modern readers have missed, how certain medieval signs retain one constant meaning throughout the centuries—reveals the univocal emphasis and the limitations of the project, which does not address the issues it raises. Presenting us with an interesting compendium of negative associations of the hawthorn with carnal desire and spiritual sterility, the essay demonstrates that readers *can* find negative associations for the hawthorn, despite some strained reading when the authors insert "hawthorns" for the Middle English texts' "thorns": "Although none of the printed lyrics of the passion mentions the hawthorn specifically, probably many of the poets did envision their 'thorns' as the ubiquitous hawthorn" (p. 20). Even the authors' more solid readings, however, do not demonstrate what their assumption implies, that the hawthorn should most "reasonably" and often be read negatively. In fact, when the authors acknowledge a positive tradition as well in the pagan associations of the hawthorn with divinity and fecundity, which Christian tradition incorporated and "redirected . . . to . . . the Virgin" Mary (p. 24), they also reveal the way their practice seems simply to privilege negative associations over positive ones in an arbitrary way: "If the context celebrates Mary or Christ, the hawthorn probably serves as a reminder of sin redeemed. If the context is erotic or concupiscent, the hawthorn is a sign of the thorns of sin or folly" (p. 25). Why this arbitrary distinction should obtain is not explained.

Similar difficulties persist in the literary tradition Chamberlain privileges over the social and political conditions of the fifteenth century. Perhaps his dismissal of New Historicist criticism, as "not offering insights that alter our interpretations of the meaning of the six poems" (p. 3), is based on his unexplained sense that "this is a poetry that depends more on literary tradition than on contemporary social and political conditions" (p. 9). The literary tradition that is evoked for these poems is the genre of didactic writing, and moral readings of such "germinal" works as Boethius's *Consolation*, Alan of Lille's *Complaint of Nature*, and selected works of Chaucer. Thus, Snyder suggests that readers of *The Floure and the Leafe* should allow medieval values and imagery, "as seen best in Boethius, Gower, Walton" (p. 167), and Chaucer, to guide their interpretations of the poem; the originality of Chamberlain's essay on Clanvowe's Cuckoo and Brown's essay on *La Belle Dame Sans Mercy* is that the authors read each poem through the grid of moral and religious themes in the religious works of Clanvowe and Chartier; and Friedman refers readers of *The Court of Love* to a tradition of moralistic reading of Chaucer and Gower for the "proper response" to erotic love. References in both Chamberlain's and Snyder's readings of Chaucer's *Knight's Tale* point up the limitations of this treatment of literary tradition. In both cases the complexities of recent readings that might see that tale as problematizing its morality or gender relations are overlooked in favor of a view of the poem that sees *The Knight's Tale* as the locus of serious moral advice about the foolishness of love. This phenomenon is of course in keeping with Chamberlain's admission that though all the poems analyzed "deal solely with problems of amorous desire" (pp. 8–9), and though several poems are especially "relevant to modern gender theory" (p. 3), he and his contributors "do not see how gender implications can be understood until the authors' intentions, and likely audience responses, are explored more carefully" (p. 3). Why this should be so needs explanation. Gender criticism would seem to have been particularly apt in Brown's essay, which attempts at least in part to redeem the Lady in *La Belle Dame* by showing that humor and criticism in the poem are directed toward the Lover.

Each essay in this volume presents a patristic reading intended to promote acceptance and validity of the method. Chamberlain is to be commended for his attempts to present a more moderate and situated patristic practice. Until the theoretical issues his approach raises are addressed, however, it would appear that those who come to this volume with a belief in its assumptions will find the approach valid, while those who would like to be persuaded will require further proof.

BARRIE RUTH STRAUS
University of Windsor

JANE CHANCE. *The Mythographic Chaucer: The Fabulation of Sexual Politics.* Minneapolis and London: University of Minnesota Press, 1995. Pp. xxix, 378. $18.95 paper.

Mythographic criticism has much in common with "Robertsonian" or patristic analysis: both decode medieval literature by reference to a meta-literature. In the one case, the works of the Church fathers are used to articulate how words, images, and allusions communicate—often covertly—the Augustinian aesthetic goal of encouraging Christian charity among readers. In mythographic analysis, the parallel goal is the piercing of *integumentum*—the disclosure of hidden truth—and the method is similar in that medieval commentaries on pagan literature and philosophy supply a meta-level body of discourse that the critic uses to explain what underlying or hidden truths the given work holds.

Jane Chance's contributions to mythographic criticism are impressive, to say the least. Rooted in her *The Genius Figure in Antiquity and the Middle Ages* (1975) and numerous articles, her more recent volumes reflect the depth and range of her comprehension of mythographic interpretation and its tradition. In recent years, she has edited a collection of essays, *The Mythographic Art: Classical Fable and the Rise of the Vernacular in Early*

France and England (1990), and produced a sweeping historical survey, *Medieval Mythography: From Roman North Africa to the School of Chartres* (1994). The volume under review reprises some of the earlier articles and focuses the legacy of Chance's scholarship upon Chaucer, arguing that mythographic analysis reveals his "embarrassing secrets," mostly sexual, and perverse by traditional standards.

Although such a focus on sexual secrets is not typical of Chance's earlier work, nor of mythographic analysis generally, these secrets here supply a centralizing focus for the mythological references and allusions in Chaucer's works. Just as detractors of the patristic school are concerned that Christian charity can in some cases be too blithely imposed upon all of medieval literature, I am concerned that Chance's idea of Chaucer's "secrets" is more an *a priori* assumption than a notion derived from Chaucer's works. She does not document with certainty Chaucer's familiarity with mythographic materials, and her arguments are therefore punctuated by such necessary qualifiers as "may," "might," and "perhaps." Unfortunately, such qualifiers occasionally drift into seeming certainties without justification, as in references to Chaucer's knowledge of Theodulf of Orleans (pp. 100, 265).

This general concern notwithstanding, Chance gives us a number of readings that are complex, provocative, and in step with postmodern concerns with sexuality and the reading of "gaps." She opens with a discussion of the Man of Law and the Manciple as alter egos of Chaucer, reflections of his anxieties about what art might disclose about the artist and the consequent need for disguise. This introduction is Chance's justification that there are secrets to be found in Chaucer, although I do not find much that is secretive in the ensuing discussion of *The Book of the Duchess* and *The Legend of Good Women*, where the two works are related by the presence in each of a female figure who descends to the underworld (Alcyone and Alceste). Reading the Black Knight's arc of emotion against Alcyone's descent, and comparing these to mythographic commentary on descents of Hercules, Virgil's Aeneas, and Alceste, Chance explores implicit suggestions about love, identifying parallels among the various patterns of descent and ascent and their interrelations.

In the next chapter, Chance takes up deceit in love in her discussion of *The House of Fame*, comparing it with poetic deceit. She examines the poem's parodies of Dante's use of classical allusion and correlates "Geffrey" with Dante's viator and with the Dido of mythographic tradition, pausing to suggest that he may embody an acknowledgement of homosexuality. A chapter on *The Parliament of Fowls* follows, wherein Venus-in-the-temple is

196

assessed as a figure of alienated love marked by interruption and frustration, part of the poem's broader depiction of the plentitudinous love of Chartrean tradition. Though normally included in mythographic commentary, Hymen is here excluded from Nature's scene to signify lack of fulfillment, a view of love that Chance compares with similar views in *Envoy to Scogan* and *The Complaint of Mars*.

To Chance, Paris's choice of Venus over Juno or Athena is the centralizing myth of *Troilus and Criseyde*, and in close examinations of the invocations, astrological references, and mythological allusions of the poem, she argues that the choice is an infernal one. Along the way here, as elsewhere in this book, I find the discussion somewhat tendentious, when Pandarus, for example, is figuratively connected with Tantalus "by his proximity to the ripe fruit of Criseyde that he cannot 'eat'" (p. 136). Similarly, Pandarus is connected with Janus and his mythographic tradition because "the building of Troy and storming of walls in the myth remind us . . . of the god of gates" (p. 123). Other allusions are more carefully linked to the text (Oenone, for example, pp. 117–18), but this wide-ranging discussion of *Troilus* does not seem to justify its final claim that the "real significance" of the poem is that it is about "broken families, missing mothers, and impotent fathers" (p. 166). Chance reads deeply into the tradition that lies behind the *Troilus* and discloses much about this backdrop, but because of some strained argument she does not convince me that the backdrop overwhelms the surface of Chaucer's work as thoroughly as she suggests.

The Canterbury Tales also has much behind it that disturbs its surface in Chance's analysis, perhaps quintessentially so in the opening figure of Zephyrus, who is not only the gentle west wind but also a rapist and, as such, a reminder of the need for spiritual renewal of the English church. Subsequent discussions of select tales identify mythological allusions and explore ways in which mythographic commentary is subversive throughout: Chaucer "uses mythographic imagery to conceal the sexual politics of a character's situation within a tale that dramatizes the psychological moment of his or her own subjectivity" (p. 167). Chance discusses the Knight, Wife of Bath, Merchant, Franklin, Physician, and Pardoner, arguing ultimately that they are means whereby Chaucer explores and exposes his own "giltes," acknowledging them in the death-bed (?) confession of his *Retraction*: "pederasty and rape, impotence, illusion, failure, and desire" (p. 282).

Few will argue that such topics recur in the classical myths to which Chaucer and his narrators refer, or that Chaucer may have had secrets. In my reading, however, Chance goes too far along these lines in seeking a cohesive, even developmental, pattern in Chaucer's works. Like the Robertsonian who everywhere finds Christian charity, she finds dark secrets everywhere hidden. Chance's erudition and impressive scholarship are clearly apparent in this work (103 pages of notes and reference material) and they help her to raise some intriguing possibilities, but her arguments do not demonstrate that Chaucer's command of the mythographers was as deep as hers or that his secrets were as deep as the ones she finds.

MARK ALLEN
University of Texas at San Antonio

GEOFFREY CHAUCER. The Canterbury Tales *by Geoffrey Chaucer*. Trans. Ronald L. Ecker and Eugene J. Crook. Palatka, Fla.: Hodge and Braddock, 1993. Pp. x, 578. $17.95 paper.

In the world of publishing, I believe, a law states that the value of the interior of a book is inversely proportional to the claims on the exterior. This book makes a lot of claims on the cover. The front cover of this book is proudly emblazoned with the phrase "The first *complete* new translation in over half a century," and the back cover repeats that information, adding that this new translation includes a *faithful* rendering" of Middle English original prose and poetry into Modern English, "*line numbers* found in Robinson" and other editions of the original text, and "a *glossary* of people, places, and terms." Between the covers, however, the book does not quite deliver so much. It is a translation, and it does have a glossary and line numbers. But the quality is quite another matter. Let me just say as briefly as possible, few Chaucerians are going to be at all interested in this book.

First of all, the supporting apparatus is very weak; it is brief and, at times, incorrect. Aside from a table of contents and a two-page preface, which is mostly an introduction to the translators, the glossary is really the only apparatus, and it is not much more helpful than a dictionary. Throughout its five pages, there are disbursed 121 entries that are brief glosses of foreign language terms and phrases and proper nouns, some of which are accurate enough but not helpful for interpretation. For "Inn of Court," the gloss is "a law school." This seems a bit incomplete. For "Zephyrus," likewise, "Greek god of the west wind"; this is accurate but does not really help much for understanding the connection to fertility in the opening lines of *The General Prologue*. Finally, the gloss for Saint Augustine, "Christian philosopher (354–430 BC)," is a howler—something we expect to find in humorous collections of student exam answers.

As to the translation, most of it is serviceable enough. There is a clarity that shapes the lines, rough hewn though they be. For a brief sample, here are the opening lines:

> When April's gentle rains have pierced the drought
> Of March right to the root, and bathed each sprout
> Through every vein with liquid of such power
> It brings for the engendering of the flower. (lines 1–4)

While "gentle rains" and "engendering of the flower" may be as good as one can get, must we endure "sprout"? There is something in me that just does not want any sprouts with my Chaucer. Also, the meter makes for a bit of a bumpy ride:

> *The droughte of March hath perced to the roote*
> Of March right to the root, and bathed each sprout.

The translation goes pretty much this way throughout the entire book. Some of the rhymes are impressive, catchy even, and some are silly. Here are a few from *The Pardoner's Tale*:

> For my concern is only with collection
> And not with any sin that needs correction.
> . . . .
> "For which the end is death. Their god's the belly."
> O gut, O bag, O belly foul and smelly. (lines 403–4, 533–34)

The first couplet seems to me to capture the essence of the line well enough, although Chaucer's verb "to winne" instead of collection resonates much more ironically due to the context of the Pardoner's role in life and on the pilgrimage, but collection is not bad for a different irony. The much admired "O stinking cod" couplet rendered as "smelly belly" is just too silly to imagine the skilled preacher from Roncivale ever saying.

The other type of problem with bits of this translation, again stemming from the attempt to render Chaucer clear, is to actually lose part of the figurative language and on occasion to be simply incorrect. Two more lines from *The Pardoner's Tale* will illustrate the former problem. The Pardoner claims to "saffron" his speech with a few Latin terms, thus implying a host of associations of the spice (its expense and rarity, its color and sensuous taste) to the Pardoner's life style. In this translation the lines are thus: "A few words in the Latin tongue I say / To add a little spice to what I preach" (lines 343–44). Earlier in the Fragment, the Host responds to the Physician's tale in one of the most humorous malapropisms in *The Canterbury Tales*. He says that the tale has moved him so much that he almost had a "cardinacle." Again, the translators have rendered it clear: "I know you've caused this heart in me / To grieve till I am near a cardiac" (lines 312–13). Finally, to end where I began, I will cite another line from *The General Prologue* as an example of the will to clarify leading to error:

> When Zephyrus too with his sweet breath has blown
> Through every field and forest, urging on
> The tender shoots, and there's a youthful sun,
> His second half-course through the Ram now run. (lines 5–9)

Now, unless I have missed some news on the astronomical references in *The General Prologue* of late, I do believe that the sun has run through the *first*, not the second, half-course.

The more general and important question of whether to use translations at all is, of course, implied in any review of a translation, but that question cannot be answered by this book. The book is not wholly bad; it is just not very good. It might be useful as part of an exercise in translation; it might also be useful as a pony text for non-English majors in a major course in Chaucer, since no other translation available contains *The Parson's Tale* or the *Melibee*. However, unless one has to meet these specific needs, I would not recommend ordering this book.

JOHN MICHEAL CRAFTON
West Georgia College

JANET COWEN and GEORGE KANE, eds. *Geoffrey Chaucer: The Legend of Good Women*. Medieval Texts and Studies, vol. 16. East Lansing, Mich.: Colleagues Press, 1995. Pp. xi, 344. $95.00.

This is an extremely important work, and Colleagues Press is to be commended for undertaking a project of this sort. The edition is modeled after the Kane-Donaldson edition of *Piers Plowman* and is concerned almost exclusively with textual matters. The introduction includes manuscript descriptions and classifications, analysis of variants, slightly expanded reprints of two articles (Cowen's 1986 article on the final *-e*, and Kane's 1983 article on MS CUL Gg. 4.27), a three-page section explaining the treatment of the prologues, and a brief section on the choice of copy-text. The edition of *LGW* follows, with full MS collations against Tanner 346 as copy-text; following that is an edition of the Gg prologue, partially collated (the apparatus lists only the variants for lines where Gg has been emended). In their preface, the editors claim that the edition is an "experiment"—an attempt to apply the same principles used in the Kane-Donaldson edition to a text of much less complexity. They claim further, more problematically, that the edition is "open" in that it "present[s] the manuscript evidence fully" (p. vii).

There are obviously significant differences between this and the *Piers Plowman* edition. In addition to the much simpler manuscript situation in *LGW*, the object to be reconstructed is quite different. What "originality" means in the *LGW* edition is only what reading might account for all manuscript evidence (p. viii); i.e., an original reading is itself likely to be a scribal corruption of Chaucer's text—a text in and of itself not regarded (conventionally) as of the calibre of *Piers Plowman*. Consequently, the very language employed in the *Piers Plowman* edition is inapplicable here—e.g., the contrast between the original language and thought of a "great poet" vs. its scribal mismanagement. What I will be concerned with below are two specific issues: Kane's definition of a variant (what constitutes "full manuscript evidence"), and the status of the prologue in MS Gg.

Kane follows directly Greg's definition of copy-text, and the discussion on pages 143–45 is useful in noting the frequent blurring of the two terms, base text and copy-text. To Greg, the notion of copy-text related specifically to the difference between substantives (those elements of an author's text that could be recovered by textual criticism) and accidentals (those features, such as spelling and punctuation, that in most manuscripts are largely within the province of the scribe). An editorial copy-text in Greg's sense is a matter of convenience and provides presumptive authority only for accidentals; the editor is not bound to follow it on the matter of substantives, which must be analyzed according to textual critical principles. In part because of the simpler textual situation, the result of applying Greg's notion of copy-text is less dramatic here than in the *Piers* edition. Here, Tanner 346 exerts strong authority over all printed readings, and after the first ten lines (heavily emended and appearing much like the text of *Piers*), Kane emends this copy-text rather infrequently. Despite the theoretical distinction between copy-text and base text, for all practical purposes the Tanner MS functions as both.

Kane and Cowen note in the text all emendations in the copy-text, whether those are substantive or accidental deviations. The apparatus contains a record of all substantive variation, and selected accidental variation (spellings of proper names are generally recorded, since spelling variants quickly become substantive variants, e.g., *Priamus/Pryamis/Piramus*, line 939). Excluded are purely orthographical and morphological variants (*maked/maketh* is recorded, but *quod/quoth*, *wil/wol* are not). This at times seems a rather flexible definition of morphology, but it is the same one used by Manly-Rickert and consequently by the Variorum Chaucer. Scribes could change such things capriciously, and the pattern of variation gives no evidence of manuscript filiation: Parkes and Beadle note, in the recent facsimile of Gg, the scribe's two versions of a stanza he accidentally copies twice. But if accidentals are defined functionally as anything strictly within the province of the scribe, transpositions might also be considered accidentals (e.g., inversions such as *have I/I have*). Such variants are scrupulously recorded by Kane, and occasionally emended against copy-text; i.e., they are treated strictly as substantives. Many other examples of problems could be noted: the notes record such variants as *venym/wemyn* (where a mechanical error results in a substantive variant); but why *obeisaunce/obesiaunce? knyght/kynght? whiche/whch?* (p. 44). Some gray area is inevitable, but the issue is an important one for textual criticism. And in an edition such as this—one that is more valuable for textual-critical theory than for Chaucer studies—these issues might well have been discussed in full.

The decision to include theories of the final *-e* in this edition causes further discrepancies. On page 112 (in Cowen's revised article on metrics), the claim is made that the final *-e* is a matter of the "form of the poetry" and thus not "a feature of the spelling of the copy-text." And again, on page 143: "This [the final *-e*] is certainly not an accidental in Greg's sense, since it is an immediate feature of the artistic form of the poetry." I don't think this is correct; despite its metrical import, the final *-e* is a spelling variant—an accidental. That editors consider it a significant feature of the poem does not make it a substantive in a textual-critical sense: punctuation also seriously affects sense, but manuscript virgules (despite certain well-meaning claims) cannot be treated as textual-critical substantives either. What Greg meant by defining such things as accidentals is that they were in the province of the scribe or editor. Furthermore, if final -*e* is a substantive variant, then by all rights it should be recorded in Kane's editorial apparatus. It is not, implying, somewhat illogically, that a substantive is defined differently in the copy-text and in other manuscripts.

Kane notes that it is permissible to emend final -*e* without manuscript warrant in certain cases where the implied conventions require it. I cannot disagree with that. Yet in the final chapter, he claims that in the apparatus, readings that "authorize" such emendation are also recorded (p. 153). This does not make sense. There is no need to authorize such emendation with manuscript support, and this is precisely the kind of gratuitous appeal to manuscript readings that Kane polemicizes against (see, e.g., p. 42). Furthermore, individual spellings in individual manuscripts are meaningful primarily within the context of the spelling conventions of that manuscript. It is eclecticism of the very sort often criticized by Kane to suggest that whenever editorial metrical theories require a final -*e*, editors should search through all the manuscripts until they find one with the desired spelling. I frankly don't believe that Kane seriously maintains any of this. But the elevation of the significance of the final -*e* (perhaps a concession made to his coeditor) undermines the textual-critical logic.

The most serious objection I have to the edition concerns Kane's statements of the status of the Prologue in MS Gg. Kane defines what he calls G as containing a version of the Prologue that is Chaucer's own. Thus, like Robinson and like Skeat, Kane emends Gg's readings to produce an earlier text he calls "Prologue II"—itself a Chaucerian revision of "Prologue I," the version found in all other manuscripts. Yet what is this thing he calls G? Is it the manuscript Gg? The text contained in the manuscript Gg? Or is it a theoretical text of which the text in Gg is a corruption? Phrases such as "the text of G," "the text of the *Prologue* in G," "originality in G" (p. 141) imply that "G" is merely a manuscript that happens to contain a text. Yet "Prologue II" is repeatedly glossed parenthetically as "G"; i.e., G is now a text, one represented by readings in MS Gg. This is a question Kane never confronts directly.

Kane's polemical assumption that "all manuscripts are corrupt" seems innocent enough, but it is not, for it requires that Gg be a corruption of "something earlier," which then becomes another version of the Prologue. I have argued elsewhere (*PBSA* 1993), as has Seymour (*RES* 1986), that Gg should be considered a manuscript variant of what Kane here calls "Prologue I," *not* a variant of a separate prologue. (Both of these articles were following up suggestions in Kane's 1983 article reprinted here, although

Seymour is misrepresented in Kane's citation on page 124.) In other words, the version of the Prologue called "Prologue II" by Kane (and by various other names in Skeat and Robinson) was produced *in the actual production* of MS Gg, and the text in Gg is thus a product of MS Gg, not the source of its readings. The various reconstructions by Skeat, Robinson, and now by Kane of a version of some text "behind" MS Gg are editorial mirages—and from these, sensitive Chaucerian critics drink all too deeply.

One of the strengths of Kane's methods shown here is in the analysis of variants (pp. 20ff.) and subsequent manuscript groupings. The specific conclusions are not much different from those sketched out by Robinson, and more recently by Edwards and Shaner in the new Riverside. But the same problems found in the *Piers Plowman* edition recur. Kane here categorizes variants under more than thirty types of scribal error: omission of letters, transposition of letters, confusion of letters, homoeoarchy, homoeoteleuton, eyeskip, inducement of preceding copy, inducement of following copy, inducement of both preceding and following copy, etc. It is hard to imagine a variant that could not be described in these terms, and by isolating variants, Kane often obscures evidence of what may be the actual basis of scribal variation (see *PBSA* 1993). But there are no cross-references in the apparatus of the edition itself. Where Kane emends, which he does infrequently, one is left to wonder why. I do not see why Gg's "goddis forbode" is accepted against all other MSS's *god forbede* (line 10) (presumably adjusting Gg's spelling to that of the copy-text, Kane prints: "God[des] forb[o]de"). Nor can I find the line listed in the analysis of variants in the introduction. Doubtless numerous combinations of the thirty-plus categories of scribal error could account for this, but it is difficult to respond to arguments that are never articulated. It would have been of great service to readers here to note each line discussed in the introduction (such an index for the *Piers Plowman* edition was drawn up and partially printed by David Fowler).

The main value of this edition will be in the exposure of Kane's methods. The richness and complexity of the *Piers Plowman* edition has led some scholars to demand acceptance of its readings and methods as an article of faith. Here, however, the situation is quite different. There is no question of an ongoing revision or evolving text. Kane speaks of his edited text as hypothetical: "The text is . . . a hypothesis which . . . attempts to give the best explanation for existing data" (p. viii). But this hypothetical text (a post-Chaucer one, essentially the same as Manly-Rickert's O') is quite different from the hypothesized texts contemporary with Langland's production of *Piers*.

It may seem odd that an edition of this type is being produced now. Most of the textual evidence is available and so limited that anyone could put it on-line. I assume this is being done, but no one need wait for the largess of a well-heeled consortium. The principal texts can be simply scanned in from the Chaucer Society transcripts and corrected from readily available facsimiles (e.g., of Tanner, Bodley, Fairfax, Pepys, Gg, and Ff). The open edition the editors refer to might be much better represented by an electronic edition of this sort, supplemented by photographic facsimiles. The principal value of this edition is as a supplement to the monumental editorial work of Kane. Kane has been instrumental in demystifying the rhetoric of Middle English editors, both of Chaucer and of Langland. This edition provides a potential demystification of his own procedures, and the application of these methods to a text such as *LGW* may be a case less of breaking a butterfly on a wheel than of breaking the wheel on the butterfly. Kane's editorial work, in all its forms, must rank as one of the most important achievements of late-twentieth-century Middle English scholarship; and if the *LGW* edition does no more than help clarify those methods and procedures, it will prove well worth the expense.

JOSEPH A. DANE
University of Southern California

MARILYNN DESMOND. *Reading Dido: Gender, Textuality, and the Medieval Aeneid*. Minneapolis: University of Minnesota Press, 1994. Pp. xv, 296. $44.95 cloth, $17.95 paper.

Reading Dido is, insists its author, "intended to be provisional in every respect," and, of course, such efforts always are provisional whether or not their authors are as self-aware as Desmond. Within that inevitable limitation, however, *Reading Dido* is a triumph, an extraordinary achievement in (and for) classical philology, medieval studies, comparative literary analysis, women's studies, and reception theory. Informed as well by postcolonialism, cultural studies, and film theory, *Reading Dido* is a feminist analysis of the historical reception of Dido from Virgil's poetic renegotiation of earlier historical tradition in the *Aeneid* through Christine de Pizan's *Cité des dames*. Throughout, the texts and passages discussed are judiciously chosen and scrupulously translated (except for Middle English and Scottish texts,

205

which appear only in the original languages). Furthermore, Desmond's awareness of relevant cultural conditions, of reading practices, and of educational elites informs and contextualizes her analysis of texts. Finally, appropriate visual images from manuscript illuminations and early printed texts are abundantly (and handsomely) reproduced to enrich, to affirm, or to complicate the evidence from written texts.

Since this review will attempt to combine description and summary with richly deserved glowing praise, I shall quickly note my few criticisms. First, I hope that the next printing will provide an appendix of translations for the Middle English and Scottish materials; the sensible, straightforward translations of the Latin, Italian (although there is a small misunderstanding of the Italian on p. 95), and Old French texts should be matched even in the case of more accessible vernaculars, especially if a book like this is to receive the wide readership it deserves, beyond the realms of specialists. (As a comparatist in a classics department, I rarely have occasion to teach Chaucer, but when I last did, to undergraduates at Stanford ten years ago, I found that my breezy confidence that they would have no trouble with Middle English was misplaced.) Second, the section on Chaucer's *House of Fame* (pp. 128–51) is almost impenetrably encrusted with theoretical considerations, in contrast to the perfect integration of traditional and theoretical concerns (and of text, context, and theory) throughout the rest of the book. Third, infinitives are split whenever it is possible to split them.

Such trivial complaints aside, however, *Reading Dido* is brilliantly conceived and beautifully executed. Desmond begins with a passage from *La Jeune Née* of Hélène Cixous, who responds lyrically to Dido's plight with profound sympathy while refusing to share in her victimization. The Cixous passage leads to an introductory discussion of the "Gender and Politics of Reading Virgil," prefaced by quotations from, emblematically, Rachel Blau Du Plessis and Walter Ong, S.J. After rehearsing the connections between the *Aeneid*, on the one hand, and the canon, cultural imperialism, and colonialism, on the other, and after drawing attention to the still "intensely regulated homosocial masculinity of Virgil readership" (p. 10), Desmond shows how the consideration of gender and intertextuality makes it possible for the contemporary reader to use the Dido episode as an "opportunity to intervene in the gendered discourses of colonialism and the canon" (p. 13).

The first chapter covers the ancient fragments (Timaeus of Tauromenium), testimony (Pompeius Trogus *via* Justin's epitome), and commentary (Servius) that provide evidence for the tradition of the historical

Dido who lies behind the Virgilian fiction, a Dido who is not only a great leader, but who also heroically kills herself on a funeral pyre rather than violate a sacred vow to her murdered husband. The tension between the historical Dido and the fictional one comes into play throughout Desmond's study, since the "countermemory" of the heroic historical Dido periodically complicates the reception of the dominant Virgilian tradition of the pathetic and fallen Dido. The chapter goes on to provide a superb and unprecedented overview, from a feminist perspective, of the history of reading Virgil and of modern Virgil criticism. The next section, on Ovid's renegotiation of Virgil's Dido in *Heroides* 7, is without question the best published work to date on Ovid's *Heroides* and could alone justify this book with its sophisticated conflation of traditional philology and feminist theory. From Ovid, Desmond moves to an overview of the medieval Dido in the *Ovide moralisé*, the Carmina Burana, the *Roman de la Rose*, and *The Book of the Duchess*. The last section of this first chapter cites Macrobius (*Sat.* 5.17) on the two conflicting traditions of Dido's story and on the reasons for the success of the fictional over the historical version. Macrobius's point leads to Boccaccio's use of both traditions: the fictional in his misogynous *Genealogia*; the historical in *De claris mulieribus*, where "in Boccaccio's terms, Dido is essentially a credit to her sex because she has transcended its normative boundaries by refusing to perform as a sexual woman" (p. 62).

The second chapter explores "Dido as *Libido*" by tracking readings of Dido that result from homosocial arrangements of late antique and medieval academic cultures (p. 75). Desmond brilliantly brings together St. Augustine's account of his boyhood tears shed over Dido in *Confessions* 1.13 (where Dido's sorrows form his whole sense of the *Aeneid*) with, by contrast, his elaborate efforts in *De civitate dei* to erase Dido from Roman history, even to the point of quoting her speeches but attributing them to others (p. 79). Fulgentius reduces Dido to a personification of *libido*, a marginal figure in relation to the larger allegory of the "ages of man." Bernardus (so-called Silvestris) describes Dido as *libido* to be purged from the male body. By contrast, Dante's interest in Dido "illustrates how vernacular poets . . . even when they have extensive acquaintance with the allegorical model of reading the *Aeneid* as a philosophical text that depicts Dido as . . . *libido*, nonetheless betray their interest in Dido as a character detached from Virgil's text" (p. 98).

The third chapter considers Dido in the *Roman d'Eneas* as object of exchange in the feudal economy, on the one hand, and as anomalous woman leader, on the other, in a "hybrid discourse" that contrasts with "the masculinist vision of Bernard's commentary" (p. 118). In the *Histoire ancienne jusqu'à césar* interestingly, although the text emphasizes Dido's "regal beneficence" (p. 120), the manuscript illuminations nevertheless share the iconographic tradition of the illuminator of the *Eneas* in their emphasis on Dido's falling on the sword, an emphasis that sustains "the affective focus of the *Roman*" (p. 120). The fourth chapter continues the exploration of vernacular uses of Dido with a focus on "the Chaucerian gaze" in *The House of Fame* and in *The Legend of Good Women*. In *HF*, the narrator cannot bring himself to speak of love but "can certainly describe Dido's death" and therewith implicate "the viewer in the penetration of Dido's body." Ultimately, too, the narrator chooses not to retell *Heroides* 7, resisting the "opportunity to read like a woman" (p. 148). In *LGW*, Dido is domesticated to fit the pattern of courtly romance, with her political power and her passion diminished.

The fifth chapter shows how Gavin Douglas's *Eneados* becomes a countertext to Chaucer and Caxton, shaped by an antifeminist discourse that aligns the "Court of James IV with . . . the Italian humanists" in an effort at cultural imperialism. Douglas appropriates the *Aeneid* in order to claim "cultural preeminence" and to authenticate "Scottish identity in opposition to the English, who are symbolically feminized . . . by their identification with their pro-Dido translator Caxton and their pro-woman poet, Chaucer" (p. 194).

Desmond's book closes with its *pièce de résistance*, Christine de Pizan's appropriation of Dido in her project of "feminist self-fashioning" in the *Cité des dames*. Whereas in her *Mutacion de fortune* Christine is ambivalent towards Dido as representing the destruction of cities, in the *Cité* Dido, as "the most eminent of the city builders," becomes emblematic of the "textual city as a whole" (p. 218): "Dido effectively figures Christine's textual construction of her authorial self" (p. 223), coming close to a "modern concept of feminist writing" (p. 224). "Christine's reliance on Dido, especially on the countermemory represented by the historical Dido, makes Dido rather than Virgil the central figure in the textual drama. Dido thereby becomes the originary literary figure who engenders the late medieval feminist writer" (p. 224).

Desmond follows this breathtaking conclusion with an epilogue on "reading Dido" now as a means to "revise our understanding of gender, national identity, and literary history" (p. 227). Closing with Cixous's refusal to reenact Dido's victimization, Desmond empowers and challenges her readers to see ancient and medieval texts in important new ways, lest

Elizabeth Kirk, for example, connects Langland's innovative representation of the Passion of Christ and his Harrowing of Hell in passus 18 of the B text (totally *unlike* late-fourteenth-century accounts in the mystics or in the mystery plays) to his daring experiential theology, which heterodoxically disjoins the human from the divine in his narrative rendering of the Hypostatic Union. (That ancient doctrine, of course, had defined Christ with two natures, human and divine, but united in a single person.) By narrating the Passion and the Harrowing as witnessed by "discontinuous but complementary" (p. 23) observers therein, Langland distinguishes between the two natures of Christ and thus between the roles of Piers and Christ in the larger context of the poem. Experiential theology too informs Anna Baldwin's discussion of older and newer English medieval debt laws. She argues that remnants of the older debt law that had survived into Langland's day are transmogrified in the poem into metaphors for Old Testament bondage, whereas the new debt law—with its emphasis on personal responsibility—serves as a metaphor for New Testament freedom. If a palpable imperative of the poem is *redde quod debes*, then the movement from Dowel to Dobest corresponds to an unfolding awareness of the terms of the debt—not only as it relates to personal sin but especially to the urgency of others' needs. Another important theological, and scriptural, metaphor in *Piers Plowman*—this one from the C text at 17.48–50—is uncovered by M. Teresa Tavormina in the last of these opening four essays. She connects Liber Arbitrium's criticism of the corrupt fourteenth-century clergy in Langland's phrase "charite þat cheild is now" to the eschatological warning of Matthew 24:12: "And because iniquity hath abounded, the charity of many *shall grow cold*." Her survey of "Chilling-of-Charity" citations leads beyond Matthew to a *catena* of eschatological allusions in a variety of Middle English works, like the *Pricke of Conscience*, all of which interpret such spiritual frigidity as a Laodicean sign of the Last Days. But because the *eschaton* ushers in the finality of heaven as well as hell, she contrasts the metaphor of "charite þat cheild is now" (and its cognates, like the barren fig tree) with Langland's *hopeful* eschatological metaphors, such as the budding fig tree and the approach of summer, the *aestas*.

As the first of four interpretive essays focusing on Chaucer, Monica McAlpine's seems to have been enlisted by the editor as apologia for the act of interpretation itself and as an authenticating preamble to the three essays that follow. It is disconcerting to observe a talent as nimble as Professor McAlpine's finding it necessary to kick the stone against recent critical orthodoxies, which claim that the point of a poem like *The Nun's Priest's*

Tale is its brilliant pointlessness. McAlpine's way is to challenge that kind of response to the poem but also to keep at bay the reductionism of the naive theologizers on the one hand and the beast fabulists on the other. She insists that Chaucer's intention was to "thematize interpretation" (p. 83) (a poem should both mean and be?), especially in the final chase scene, which "climactically demonstrates what fiction can do . . . with delightful and dismaying *significances*" (p. 92).

All three interpretive essays that follow tacitly agree with McAlpine that "abstinence from interpretation is neither possible nor desirable" (p. 89). Mary Carruthers offers us a medieval pedagogy of memorization, inherited from Hellenistic times, which in effect serves as prolegomenon to interpretation. *The Knight's Tale*, in her view, is especially "memory-friendly" because the various fixed and sequential locations in the poem function as potent "picture-inventories" (p. 104) of qualities, stories, and themes: the "gathering-in of 'things' to meditate on" (p. 105). Kathryn L. Lynch is less tacit about meaning by explicitly featuring the word in the title of her essay: "The *Meaning* and Importance of Walls in Chaucer's Poetry." She argues that although from the perspective of *fuori le mura*, walls have served as preservers of civilization, from intramural perspectives they have also "signalled the contaminations and failures of civilization" (p. 108), not the least of which are linguistic contaminations. Chaucer poetically exploits the *ambages* resident in both the literal and figurative meaning of walls in *The Knight's Tale* and *The Manciple's Tale*, but even more fully in *Troilus and Criseyde*. In the latter work, there are two sieges, not only that of the city's walls but also the "love-siege" of Criseyde. Inside the walls too the perversion and violence of language such as we find in the chief characters intimate an "extramural violence that is not figurative but real" (p. 122). If Lynch sees fit to end her essay with the figure of Lucrece (from *The Legend of Good Women*) as the quintessential example of breach and violation, Carolyn Colette holds up the Virgin Mary as the paradoxical female exemplar of both humility and exaltation—especially when she functions in *The Canterbury Tales* as the source of authority for the speech of religious women, in particular the Prioress and the Second Nun. Colette's uncovering of the deeper theological significances of the seemingly commonplace Marian pieties in the respective tales is unerringly brilliant: the complex of meanings surrounding the Virgin's milk, for example, as well as her *active* participation in the Incarnation and her empowering of the speech of women and children. More the pity, then, to witness a lapse of judgment in the penultimate paragraph when, in her eagerness to cite the Virgin's

211

unique warrant for feminine speech free of male authority, Colette gratu-
itously indicts the usurious lord of *The Prioress's Tale* for tolerating, if not
supporting, the little boy's murder. That the text never mentions the "lord
of that contree" after line three does not impede her from accusing male
authority—any available male will do, apparently—of complicity in silencing voices from the margins.

The last four essays lead away from exclusive focus on Chaucer's works.
Mary Hamel argues that the lively description of historical and fictional sea
battles, like Actium and others, in the alliterative *Morte Arthure*, Chaucer's
"Legend of Cleopatra," et al. actually depends upon a topos of *descriptio
navalis pugnae* from premedieval models like Lucan and Vegetius, especially
the latter. Formulas like trumpet signals, exchange of missiles, hand-to-
hand fighting, and combatants falling into the sea, while serving to vivify
historical (and sometimes fictional) accounts, nevertheless appear as rhetorical constants in each *descriptio*. In the next essay, Paul Strohm offers us still
another forceful example of his social/narrative criticism by connecting the
truncated story of Perkyn's "revelry" in Chaucer's *Cook's Tale* to the complex issues of the Peasants' Revolt of 1381. Strohm contends that although
Perkyn's story is not an allegory of, nor even a reference to, the Rising,
nevertheless it "participates ontologically" (p. 168) in the wider meaning
of the Peasants' Revolt, especially so by virtue of the "representational
field" (p. 169) of images of revelry and revelrous behavior. Stepping a
century back into the thicket of the Baron's War of the mid-thirteenth
century, Thomas Heffernan examines the political motives for the attempted canonization of Simon de Montfort, Earl of Leicester, who was,
early on, the trusted ally (as well as brother-in-law) of Henry III but later
his chief nemesis. The enormity of de Montfort's rebellion, directed as it
was against the quasi-sacerdotal office of the king, could only have been
countered by baronial panegyrists who claimed the divine sanction of
sainthood for their man, a "sanctity" that manifested itself for more than a
decade after his death in putative miracles and pilgrimages. In the final
essay, Peggy A. Knapp takes us on an instructive semantic *giro* through the
various unfoldings of the word *thrift* from the fourteenth to the seventeenth centuries, beginning with its original denotation of "thrive" to its
modern connotation of "frugality." The history of the word, with its modulations and double entendres—from the "thrift" of feudal aristocratic lar-
gesse to the bourgeois "thrift" of post-Reformation economics—tells us
much about those two centuries that separated Chaucer from Shakespeare.

There is something uncannily appropriate about Edwards rounding off his collection with Peggy Knapp's essay on *thrift*, especially when we are made aware of its original medieval meaning, for *thriving*—better than any other commemorative word—sums up the manner of Robert Frank's half century of remarkable contributions to our profession. I refer not only to the *thrift* of his four books, nineteen articles, and various reviews, of his cofounding of the *Chaucer Review* and his thirty years of uninterrupted editorship thereof, of his almost forty years of professing medieval studies at the Pennsylvania State University, but also to the *thrift* of his humanity and wit. How many doyens of his stature would have attended the final plenary session of Chaucerians at Trinity College/Dublin in 1994 dressed in a T-shirt emblazoned with the line "Tehee! quod she, and clapte the wyndow to"?

RODNEY DELASANTA
Providence College

JESSE M. GELLRICH. *Discourse and Dominion in the Fourteenth Century: Oral Contexts of Writing in Philosophy, Politics, and Poetry.* Princeton, N.J.: Princeton University Press, 1995. Pp. xiv, 304. $39.50.

Gellrich's first ambitious book, *The Idea of the Book in the Middle Ages: Language Theory, Mythology, and Fiction* (Ithaca, N.Y.: Cornell University Press, 1985), ranged over nearly a thousand years in exploring the western medieval metaphor—or what Gellrich argued was the consummate western "mythology"—of "the book of creation." Inquiries into the medieval notions of "the written" have subsequently flourished, and for all their sharp differences from Gellrich's first book he may be credited with having helped formulate the topic as a central issue in studies of medieval literary and other narrative. Recent work has sought both a narrowing and a deepening of the political and social applications and implications of literacy— witness Steven Justice's *Writing and Rebellion: England in 1381* (Berkeley: University of California Press, 1994)—and also a larger investment of modern narratological or discourse theory in these concerns—witness the "New Philology" issue of *Speculum* (vol. 65, January 1990), and Gabrielle M. Spiegel's *Romancing the Past: The Rise of Vernacular Prose Historiography in Thirteenth-Century France* (Berkeley: University of California Press, 1993).

The title of Gellrich's new book reflects some of the shifts that have occurred in the decade since his first book. "Discourse," with its Foucauldian frame of reference, connotes the wide range of kinds of writing that Gellrich learnedly surveys: two philosophical writers, a half-dozen historical writers, two poets. "Dominion" bespeaks political agenda, although it nicely accommodates the epistemological hierarchies Gellrich describes as well, especially the preeminence of postures of orality in fourteenth-century texts in spite of the increasing incursions of literacy in the period. For from the idea of the book Gellrich has turned to the "idea of the voice," surveying a terrain of persistent adherence to the authority of orality "with *writing* on the defensive and in need of apology," as he states in his discussion of *Sir Gawain and the Green Knight* (p. 198), and elucidating the resulting narrative and philosophical strategies and their political implications in fourteenth-century England.

"Voice" remained the *sine qua non* of medieval authority even into the fourteenth century, Gellrich asserts. Yet, as he also argues, medieval claims of political and ideological dominion had always depended on the capacity of one kind of discourse, whether the written or some other symbolic system, to displace another without acknowledging its own mediating presence. Any highly self-conscious exploration of the rift between representation and oral presence would generate a weakening of royal or other overarching authority, a break from the past, a questioning of faith in what George Steiner calls "real presences." This formulation of medieval authority draws explicitly on Derrida's concept of "logocentrism"—the ideal, often sustained even in the face of powerful self-contradiction, of authentic, oral "presence" behind writing, hence of a coherent and unified prior or "interior" intention. This abstract issue is given blood and bones in Gellrich's inquiry into the intellectual and narrative strategies necessary in the fourteenth century for invoking "voice" in philosophy, historiography, and politics, and into the political implications of such invocations. Finally, just as his first book argued that the unifying mythology of the "book of creation" was in part undermined in the works of late-medieval nonclerical, vernacular poets, so his present survey concludes with a study of how and to what political effect vernacular poets undermine such invocations of an ideal of oral authority, using two works portraying the founding of political dominion: *Sir Gawain and the Green Knight* and Chaucer's *Knight's Tale*.

I would hazard that Derrida's concerns with logocentrism have rarely received so persuasive an application in cultural studies, including the most overt efforts by Derrida himself. Gellrich's success in this is due to his having simplified down to a few, working tenets Derrida's wandering, rap-idly self-scrutinizing and self-ironizing style; having determined flexible but clear political implications to those ideas in their fourteenth-century milieux; and having quickly submerged even these few overt Derridean concerns in the details and paradoxes of fourteenth-century texts and intel-lectual traditions, beginning with Augustine and the inherent authorita-tive claims of Latin (the language that, Gellrich argues, even well beyond the Middle Ages was alone in maintaining the authoritative illusion of a seamless identity between and continuous authority in both spoken pres-ence and written representation. For all other languages, Gellrich implies, this was a misalliance: clerical culture insured the triumph of an unques-tioned displacement of text for voice and voice for text only in Latin. (I first wondered whether graphic riddles in Latin, such as those I printed in *Speculum* 70 [1995]: 68–105, were exceptions to this claim of Latin's trans-parent orality; yet it occurred to me that here too Latin allowed one system of signification, the lexical, seamlessly to displace another—in this case the graphic, syllabic, and visual—thus supporting Gellrich's broader argument about medieval Latin's facility of systematic discursive displacement). Gell-rich's Derrida is the Derrida of *Of Grammatology*, with its critique of the ideal of presence in texts, not the Derrida of "Signature Event Context" (in *Limited Inc*) with its critique of oral as well as written discourse, still less the Derrida linked to Freudian and Lacanian theory who informs, if only rarely even there, the work of more insistently "theoretical" cultural and intellectual historians, such as Dominick LaCapra. The result is that Gell-rich locates a point of close connection between late-medieval and modern theoretical discourses without ever seeming to depart from the traditions and turns of thought of the medieval works he considers.

Not every procedure Gellrich uses to tie together this ambitious and complicated study is felicitous, but intriguing issues and perspectives are raised at every turn. Ockham is paired with Wyclif to show that both the "nominalism" and "realism" of these philosophers were predicated on ide-als of oral authenticity and presence. Ockham's writings, treated first, are least centrally and overtly concerned with the status and the political im-port of "the oral" in writing. Gellrich must chart Ockham's philosophical and political aversion to mediation in all forms to show that Ockham's final political support of Ludwig of Bavaria over Pope John XXII, and of monarchy over the papacy, is a logical extension of his view that the mind can know the world directly and materially through discourse, that a men-tal concept can signify knowledge of the world just as spoken language does. So too, the church requires a directly present leader, the king, not one whose power is the mediated interpretation of divine authority. The analysis of philosophy and theology in the context of linguistic modality roughly follows the path of Brian Stock's *The Implications of Literacy: Written Language and Models of Interpretation in the Eleventh and Twelfth Centuries* (Princeton, N.J.: Princeton University Press, 1983); Gellrich differs from Stock in pursuing the political vision resulting from such issues of modality—a focus made inevitable by the politically "engaged" philosophers Gellrich has chosen to study. Yet the fact that the political is immanently present in such philosophical elaborations in the fourteenth century is itself one of the recurrent implications of Gellrich's book: when traditions are confronted with new forces, the political interests of both are brought into view. Participation in the traditions and authority of orality is more than an inert condition of late medieval life; like textuality, it is a politically invested position.

Gellrich's acuity in treating philosophical and theoretical issues, medieval and modern, is next displayed in an anatomy of the philosophical paradoxes of Wyclif's critique of postlapsarian human institutions, including language, yet his adherence to an ideal of "real language" in Scripture. Gellrich admirably demonstrates the paradox of Wyclif's construction of a tyrannical and monolithic authority of the scriptural Word even while attacking religious institutions as tyrannical and monolithic. Central to Wyclif's "realism" and his political positions, Gellrich shows, is an ideal of spoken immediacy in Latin—a deeply traditional clerical posture that conflicts with Wyclif's attack on the inability to distinguish mediation from presence, such as the mistaken orthodox claim that the Eucharist actually *was*, rather than simply (as Wyclif argued) figured, incarnate God.

So much is persuasive as an account of the linkage between specific logocentric claims and specific political positions. When Gellrich turns to historical writing to ferret out oral postures and logocentrism in writing and their political implications, however, he defines the politics of chronicles too flatly and monovocally. Here the connection between the representation of orality in writing and a specific political ideology depends on a rather elusive piece of argumentation: that the use of "oral" postures and rhetoric by chroniclers during the first decades of the Hundred Years' War implies their adherence to another proposition, namely that just as the king's word ideally had the power to claim (French) territory, so their textual imitations of orality formalistically support the king's claim and authority. Gellrich also twice suggests a broader argument: establishing an oral presence in a chronicle subsumes and appropriates the "surplus" of textuality in the same way that, in an ideal of what may be called feudalism—whose historical reality was (Gellrich claims) fast declining in the fourteenth century—the "ruling nobility in either church or state" have the ability to appropriate the "surplus" of money, goods, and labor (pp. 138, 150). In fact Gellrich never considers English chroniclers' relation to the church; this would raise complicated questions of loyalty (or antagonism) to particular horizons of religious leadership: local religious houses, the national church, the church of Rome.

Other distinctions need to be made too. Not all fourteenth-century chroniclers, even among those Gellrich considers, took contemporary political history as their main concern, nor indeed did all write to please the king. It is worth recalling that English historical writing from the Norman Conquest on is distinguished by a *lack* of consistent, direct royal patronage (in contrast to France and Spain, for example). Among chroniclers in the reign of Edward III, Gellrich might have considered Adam of Murimuth, who supports Edward's claim to France not on the basis of the king's "word" but only after an exhaustive genealogical inquiry, the product of Adam's fine legal mind, which assembles and does detailed, literate justice to all the material on both sides of the question. Or Gellrich might have noted William of Pagula's *De speculo Edwardi tertii*, more a diatribe against Edward than a chronicle, although it qualifies as a topical political narrative, Gellrich's umbrella definition of chronicles (p. 123): after suggesting that Edward III might become another Edward II, William of Pagula spends much ink condemning Edward's "purveyances," his appropriations of goods in the name of supplying the army.

Of those historians Gellrich does consider, neither Ranulph Higden nor Thomas of Walsingham, both Benedictines, seem entirely to align their interests with those of the English crown and aristocracy. Indeed, Walsingham's account of the Good Parliament is so antiaristocratic and anti-Lancastrian that after Henry IV's accession, he severely censored his own work. Yet both abundantly invoke oral postures in their texts, at least the postures of speakers surrounded by books from which they draw their authority or with which they debate. In Higden's case, drawing on the structure of Vincent of Beauvais's chronicle (as also, slightly later, does John of Tynemouth in his mammoth, unedited chronicle, which Gellrich cannot be faulted for not examining), the work was constructed as a continuous compilation of, or, better, continuous dialogue between, variant historical authorities and Ranulph Higden himself, under the tag "R."

217

Aside from this personal voice, Higden also used a more powerful voice to define one of his work's overarching organizing principles: the prophecy of "a certain anchorite" from the eleventh century, found at the end of the first book, who describes a typology of conquests of England with that of the Scots still to come, hardly a species of oral authority that would give an English king comfort. Higden moreover notoriously criticizes in his own name Geoffrey of Monmouth's claims for King Arthur, which by the fourteenth century amounted to a direct assault on royal ideology. Yet Higden also provided abundant grist for those who would attack the papacy, such as the story from Gerald of Wales about the ethereal voice at the Constantine Donation declaring that with the temporal endowment of the church, "poison this day is cast into the church," a phrase that the Lollards reused when they drew from Higden, as they often did: an entire chronicle of the foibles of the popes was compiled from Higden by some Lollard (ed. E. W. Talbert, *JEGP* 41 [1942]). A Bakhtinian approach to Higden might suggest that too *many* "voices" is as detrimental to a unified ideology as too sharp a sense of the distance between texts and presence.

One may grant that a simplistic "chivalric" ideology is upheld in the oral self-presentation of the Chandos herald's *Vie du Prince Noir*. But when more complicated historians are used, and especially when these are professional religious, the specificity of Gellrich's political argument—for all the desirability of a specific political argument in formalist and poststructural criticism—is implausibly narrow. Even Froissart, and even before he departed England to accept French aristocratic patronage, may not be so supportive of English claims on France as Gellrich implies, nor indeed entirely unable to see beyond aristocratic prerogative. Gellrich stresses the battle of Crécy as a test case for English chroniclers' emphasis on oral postures and oral rhetoric as a way of underwriting the appropriating "word" of the king; when Froissart emphasizes the English slaughter at Caen on the way to Crécy from the innocent townspeople's point of view, a "truly horrible carnage," he too can hardly be seen as entirely monovocal in his social description.

The same criticism could be made about Gellrich's treatment of Adam Usk, who is offered as a simple propagandist against Richard II and for Henry IV, a view dismantled by Chris Given-Wilson, who has outlined some of Adam's conflicting political postures (Given-Wilson remarks that "Adam's chronicle reads like the work of a man for whom the clash of loyalties had become too acute"; *Chronicles of the Revolution, 1397–1400* [Manchester: Manchester University Press, 1993], p. 6). Notwithstanding

Gellrich's identifications of Adam's public, oral rhetoric in relation to his overt political agenda, the mode, form, and purpose of Adam's narrative is nothing if not wildly unstable. If at some moments the model of Adam's narrative is, as Gellrich observes, "the persuasion of rhetoric before a listening audience entirely attendant upon the new political party in office under Henry IV" (p. 171), at another Adam states, "God forbid that this record of my present foolishness should be seen in my lifetime" (ed. Edward Maunde Thompson [London: Henry Frowde, 1904], pp. 55–56).

Gellrich could have said much about that striking passage, with its play between present, performative voice (it is couched as Adam's will) and intimately private text. As his study stands, however, Gellrich attends only to passages in chronicles that support his view that among nonliterary writers, a "critique of language . . . is only implied or ignored" (p. 227). In contrast, his treatment of *Sir Gawain and the Green Knight* lavishly credits this poet with deliberately manipulating the unstable relation between oral and literate production of fourteenth-century alliterative verse, "keenly concerned with its own genre" (p. 200) and exploiting the incommensurability of letter and tongue as these are played out in the portrayals of the authority and dominion of Arthur's court, repeatedly bringing to focus a breach between what is told about Arthur's court versus what it is seen to be. If the historians are seen as never conscious of their ideological investments in oral or written postures, the poets Gellrich treats are seen as fully conscious of such investments.

Like all of Gellrich's textual interpretations, this reading of *Gawain* has the great value of attending seriously to the persistence of oral postures as at once a formal, theoretical, and political issue of considerable importance. Gellrich casts his vote with those placing *Gawain* and the other late-medieval alliterative poetry in a long oral tradition reaching back to pre-Conquest times; but he adds that, in its confrontation with the fourteenth-century textualization of this tradition, *Gawain* possesses a degree of awareness about the opaque "materiality" of language and the political uses of its modes that Gellrich denies other kinds of fourteenth-century narrative, and presumably other alliterative poetry. I suspect that few readers of this journal, or Gellrich's book, would be disposed to deny the poem such self-consciousness, although not all might agree with the political narrative that Gellrich traces through the poem's manipulation of such modes. Sustaining the alignment between textually inscribed orality and feudal dominion presented in the section on the chronicles, Gellrich argues that Gawain serves in the narrative as the mediating figure between "the older feudal ethos of the king and a newer social style" (p. 207), since Gawain bridges many moments where silently inscribed or commonly told knowledge is juxtaposed with present and speaking reality. The court's final reinterpretation of the girdle does not cancel out Gawain's different interpretation; rather, the simultaneous presence of both views reveals that object not as "signifying" at all in the common, logocentric, medieval philosophical sense, but instead "suppositing" "for itself directly as a sign" (p. 222), that is, presenting *sign-ness* with a degree of linguistic reflexivity that epitomizes the status of discourse in the poem.

All this makes straight the way for the concluding chapter on *The Knight's Tale* as a political lesson by way of a critique of logocentrism. Chaucer's parallels to the Derridean critique of presence in language were adumbrated nearly a decade ago by H. Marshall Leicester, Jr., whose work Gellrich does not adequately cite (Leicester's recent work on *The Knight's Tale* receives only one footnote, on an inconsequential disagreement with Donald Howard). The absence of any reference to Leicester's older essay "'Oure Tonges *Différance*': Textuality and Deconstruction in Chaucer" (in Laurie A. Finke and Martin B. Shichtman, eds., *Medieval Texts and Contemporary Readers* [Ithaca, N.Y.: Cornell University Press, 1987]) is equally surprising, since there Leicester broached a cultural basis, the "transitional" nature of the incursions of literacy in fourteenth-century culture, for Chaucer's anticipations (as Leicester saw it) of Derrida's critique of logocentrism.

Gellrich's significant departure from Leicester's concerns, of course, is his exploration of the specific political implications of narrative modality and poetic self-consciousness about it. Gellrich's identification of the political crisis of the Merciless Parliament of 1387 as a time when the king's "word" was overridden by trumped up referrals to "law" is apt, and his alignment of this period with the exploration of the limits of voiced authority in *The Knight's Tale* is highly suggestive. Indeed, another study not cited, Larry Scanlon's "The King's Two Voices: Narrative and Power in Hoccleve's *Regement of Princes*" (in Lee Patterson's *Literary Practice and Social Change in Britain, 1380–1530* [Berkeley: University of California Press, 1990]), explores somewhat similar issues in discussing Richard's deposition, when Richard was said to have proclaimed "that his Laws were in his mouth" (Article 33). Again, Gellrich's differences in approach from Scanlon are significant—Scanlon takes "voice" more in its narratological, Benevistean sense than in the sense that contrasts with "text"—but some acknowledgment of and articulation with these important, recent cultural approaches to medieval narrative would seem appropriate. (Gellrich might also have cited Paul Strohm's fine essay on Thomas Usk in the same volume, where at one point Strohm elaborates the political implications of Usk's *lack* of an oral posture in his text [p. 105].) The point is not that Gellrich's ambitious, wide-ranging study could or should have acknowledged all current critical parallels, but that its acknowledgments of relevant and recent literary criticism in the final chapters seem particularly thin.

I persist in thinking also that many of the splendid points Gellrich makes about the narrative of *The Knight's Tale* could be applied to at least some of the historical narratives. While Gellrich would deny Froissart, for example, a "split voice" that is conscious of the politics of voice—although he documents Froissart's mixtures of oral and textual postures—he grants Chaucer this capability of proving that the fiction of the Knight's narrative, "oral" voice cannot contain the disparities of perception it seeks to encompass, with the result that Chaucer teaches a subtle political lesson, while Froissart is merely symptomatic of courtly sycophancy. Gellrich's reading of Chaucer is careful and sure, and he convincingly shows that Chaucer sets up moments of political claims to dominion at points where the "presence" and referentiality promised by language is least possible; Gellrich's lengthy, final reading of Theseus's speech on the First Mover as a demonstration that language is a matter of substitutions and self-references is a tour de force, its dense logic more convincing on each rereading. Yet Gellrich's main contribution to what other Chaucerians may have at least partly noted and explored will remain the political and contextual implications he elucidates in such formalist and poststructuralist issues. Presenting that context as fully and fairly as possible is, therefore, of paramount importance to his endeavor, and this requires acknowledging wherever possible the full extent of self-consciousness about narrative modality in nonliterary and literary writers, as well as, perhaps, poets' sometimes unconscious participation in prevailing ideologies and interests.

In addition to closer attention to the narrative self-consciousness and social locations of chroniclers, I would have appreciated an interweaving of his theme with some consideration of material and historical connections between all or any of his writers: for example, the place of Ockham's works in late-medieval vernacular political debate, or Wyclif's intermittent ties to the Ricardian court and the adaptations of his "realism" in courtly vernacular writings, religious and other. So deeply and widely implicated is Gellrich's theme that I began to want an integrated cultural history rather than a monograph with a series of discrete, elegant case histories. Neither this nor any other qualification I have made, however, impeaches the book's value and suggestiveness. In its scope, its method, and much of its brilliantly acute textual analysis, this is a powerful contribution to our understanding of the politics of intellectual labor and narrative form in fourteenth-century England.

ANDREW GALLOWAY
Cornell University

MARTIN IRVINE. *The Making of Textual Culture: "Grammatica" and Literary Theory, 350–1100.* Cambridge Studies in Medieval Literature, vol. 19. Cambridge: Cambridge University Press, 1994. Pp. xix, 604. $59.95.

Martin Irvine argues that *grammatica*, the institution of medieval grammar, governs all textuality in the Latin Middle Ages. It produces the techniques and ideologies that shape academic reading, commentary, compilation, and composition. It constructs the terms in which knowledge is understood. Irvine stresses the intertextual assumptions of *grammatica* and arrogates to it enormous power and productivity:

As a discipline sustained by the dominant social and political institutions of medieval Europe, *grammatica* functioned to perpetuate and reproduce the most fundamental conditions for textual culture, providing the discursive rules and interpretative strategies that constructed certain texts as repositories of authority and value. (p. 2)

In *grammatica*, the *litteratus*, the learned, the cleric, "was consistently gendered as masculine and socially empowered" (p. 2). These are, I think, plausible and powerful arguments.

This volume looks at late classical and early medieval treatises as well as poetic commentaries that expound and use the techniques of *grammatica*. A second volume is projected to cover the later Middle Ages. Here, Irvine moves through the textual theories of Clement of Alexandria, Augustine, and Origen to what he claims is the essentially "grammatical" political culture of the Carolingian and Anglo-Saxon periods. He thus includes materials that do not always appear in histories of Latin textual theory. As part of his avowed project to argue for the wide-ranging generative powers of medieval grammatical culture, Irvine concludes the book by considering some Anglo-Saxon poems. The book is hugely comprehensive, drawing on a wide bibliography and some materials available only in manuscript. It is a very useful reference work.

Nevertheless, the book is not always rigorous in its detail or in its larger arguments. Irvine seems to imply, for instance, that the Aristotelian notion of "ordinary" or "dominant" (*kyrios*) language is equivalent to the much cruder notion of "proper" (*proprius*) language, which was to dominate *grammatica* in the Middle Ages and long after (pp. 104–7). On the other hand, he remarks of the *Phaedrus* that Plato's "attempt to rewrite textuality and subvert textual memory by philosophical recollection was not successful": the remark echoes the bland tone rather than the content of his claim that the *Phaedrus* is "replete with irony, humor, and self-parody" (pp. 29, 26).

Irvine claims repeatedly that what distinguishes his book from other scholarship on medieval *grammatica* is his focus on the forms of cultural power located in the discipline. He sees *grammatica* as the first bastion of clerical hegemony. He foregrounds the first art of the trivium, as against the modern (and medieval) scholars who have emphasized other disciplines. He sees *grammatica* as a site of medieval hermeneutic control and semantic surveillance. He comments at length on its "technologies of authority— literacy, normative latinity, knowledge of a literary canon, the scribal arts, book production" (p. 306). Sometimes it all sounds rather homogenous. Although Irvine notes the interpretive innovations of Augustine, Isidore, and the Carolingian *De literis colendis*, he places enormous stress on their reproduction of ideologies already inscribed into *grammatica* (pp. 169–71, 185, 210–13, 241–43, 305–13). But he is surely substantially right.

However, Irvine's ideological analysis of medieval textual culture and *grammatica* ends up reproducing some rather traditional versions of both. They are seen as institutionally clerical, religiously orthodox, wedded to textual and disciplinary authority. This seems reductive in each case. The accusation leveled against some other Foucault-derived work seems relevant here: Irvine's analysis of the cultural power of *grammatica* allows for few sites of resistance or difference. Can it be true that authoritative *grammatica* controls "the entire textual culture of church and monastery" (p. 306; also p. 460)?

Even in the book, after all, there is evidence for alternative valuations of *grammatica*: the low pay customarily awarded to the late classical grammarian, Martianus Capella's jokey insinuation that a full exposition of *grammatica* might be boring, or the traditional cataloguing of medieval libraries, with the Scriptures first and the grammarians and poets last (according to Irvine, a "purely conventional rather than qualitative" judgment, p. 337; see also pp. 53, 63). The presence of more ambivalent attitudes toward *grammatica* might after all render Irvine's case more intriguing. Exemplary in this respect is Robert Kaster's innovative study of the pivotal and yet insecure position of the grammarian as "middleman" in late antique society (*Guardians of Language: The Grammarian and Society in Late Antiquity* [Berkeley: University of California Press, 1988], p. 7; also pp. 50–64, 104–6, 125). It is possible that medieval *grammatica* was well established but also in some situations denigrated or ignored. This might have enabled some of its work to be contested. But it might have enabled some of its work to occur unobserved and even unpoliced.

More important, Irvine's analysis of "allegorical grammar," the commentary practices of the grammarians, seems to be divided between two contradictory positions. On the one hand, Irvine claims that the Middle Ages takes the radical view that all commentary (and thus all language?) "allegorizes": "Servius's commentary reveals that . . . all commentary is allegorical, a rewriting of the text in the form of a supplement ('other-speaking')" (p. 133). On the other hand, Irvine's views about the ideological orientation of grammatical commentary lead to rather different conclusions. For Irvine also sees commentary as textual control and surveillance, reading and writing dependent on a "cultural encyclopedia embedded within the system of knowledge in each epoch that regulate[s] interpretive possibilities." And this grammatical surveillance hides what it is doing. It "obscures its textual status by presenting itself not as a secondary discourse but as the decoding of a prior encoding," as a "univocal, zero degree . . . nonfigurative, blank form of writing" (p. 246). Irvine's very cogent emphasis on the commentary's *presentation* of itself as textual decipherment may push him back toward a more traditional version of the allegorizing commentary—a less overtly figured discourse commenting on a highly figured one.

This is what is implied by the familiar examples of "allegorical grammar" that Irvine cites from Servius—Tityrus read as Virgil, the *Eclogues* and the *Aeneid* read as extended figures for Roman political history, book 6 of the *Aeneid* read in terms of ethics. It is also implied by Irvine's apparent separation of lexical or grammatical commentary from the category of "allegorical grammar" (pp. 120–21, 133): this should not be necessary, if all commentary is "allegorical" and all poetic allusions to the cultural encyclopedia are "allegories." Here Irvine himself seems to have succumbed to the illusion of degree-zero decipherment. Elsewhere Servius's remark that the "poetic art" is not an "open" one ("per legem artis poeticae aperte non potest ponere") allows Irvine to conclude: "Servius suggests [that] much of Vergil's narrative is allegorical, that is, not expressed openly" (p. 135). Irvine often seems to imply, in other words, that a degree of opacity is what differentiates a text from its "allegorical" commentary.

More important still, however, Irvine's determination to identify the ideological drive of medieval *grammatica* leads him to take a very circumscribed view of the varied productivity of *grammatica* in medieval writing. He plays down, for instance, the possibility that some grammarians did not consider all poetry to be amenable to tight semantic control. Servius often comments on the more rhetorical and open-ended aspects of Virgil's writing, noting, for instance, that Virgil departs from historical truth "per artem poeticam." But is Irvine correct to gloss Servius's term "poetical" as "allegorical," a term that for Irvine means highly troped and subject to interpretive control according to the cultural encyclopedia (p. 135)? Similarly, when Servius says "aut poetice dictum est aut secundum philosophorum altam scientiam," Irvine's translation implies that to write "poetically" is the same as writing "allegorically," "according to the deep science of the philosophers."[1] But for Servius these are surely two opposed possibilities. As Servius observes elsewhere, Virgil has a number of agendas, not all of which tally with "philosophy": Virgil "mingles poetical fictions with philosophy and offers as many popular views as things provided by truth and the natural order" (p. 140, my translation).

Irvine is certainly aware that the grammatical project involves a prolonged meditation on the possibility that there are many ways of saying things and that to say them differently might change them, even irrecuperably. Such an awareness must in some contexts have reflected back on the grammatical commentary itself. Under the heading "semiotic anxiety" he himself explains that

commentary and exegesis have a problematic status in relation to the texts which are being interpreted: exegesis, itself another text, can never exhaust the possibilities for meaning, never reach closure. (p. 265)

Also,

[1] P. 138. Other dubious translations in this section *alone* might include "ut plerique . . . scripserunt," p. 137, line 14; "alii distinctione mutata dicunt," p. 139, line 12; "publicam," p. 139, line 29; p. 140, lines 34–35.

all interpretation posits a meaning which can only be revealed in another or supplementary discourse. The terms "exegesis" and "enarratio" . . . are based on parallel etyma—a "leading out of" the text, "from the *narratio*." (p. 245)

The use of commentary techniques in all kinds of medieval composition has been well documented from an early period of the Middle Ages, most recently in Rita Copeland's *Rhetoric, Hermeneutics, and Translation* (Cambridge: Cambridge University Press, 1991). The notion of a "zero-degree" language of commentary was always potentially under question, even in the Middle Ages. And it was *grammatica* that taught the techniques for recognizing and practicing the figures of language. Due to his emphasis on the ideological unity of medieval *grammatica*, however, Irvine does not pursue the implications of the "leading out" of commentary practice.

Some of the poetic texts that Irvine mentions—the *Dream of the Rood* and *The Battle of Brunanburh* in MS Cambridge, Corpus Christi 173—illustrate his arguments about the ideological control exercised through medieval *grammatica* very well. But what about the biblical epics of which Irvine notes, "the very change in form . . . itself constitutes an interpretative act" (p. 370)? In book 2 of Avitus's *De spiritalis historiae gestis*,[2] for instance, the interplay of theological commentary and epic poetics around the subject of the devil's powerlessness, envy, and malice has exhilarating and unorthodox effect. Here Satan is split between outwardly directed aggression and the sorrow that he represses inwardly; the text affirms his heroism by a verbal allusion to Aeneas doing the same before his men (*De . . . gestis*, 2.85; *Aeneid* 1.209). Later on, Satan's speech stopped by weeping recalls that of personified Rome in Sidonius's panegyric to the Emperor Avitus (line 118; *De . . . gestis*, 2.117). Satan admits with orthodox theologians that his power "is perishing." But then he reasserts himself with a finer discrimination, raising the much-debated specter of the devil's "power": "not totally has my power perished: a large part retains its own force and can be said to have the special power of causing harm" (*De . . . gestis*, 2.94–96). But the poetic model for Satan here must be Juno in the *Aeneid* with her divine and effective malevolence toward the Trojans—even though she knows that she is powerless over their ultimate destiny. Indeed, the verbal echo of "si nequeo" in Satan's "if I cannot climb back up to the locked skies, let the skies be locked to them too" (*De . . . gestis* 2.108–9)

---

[2] *The Fall of Man. De spiritalis historiae gestis libri I–III*, ed. Daniel J. Nodes (Toronto: Toronto Pontifical Institute of Mediaeval Studies, 1985). I thank Michael Lapidge for commenting on this review.

takes us directly to the climax of Juno's rebellious speech in book 7: "If I cannot change the will of Heaven, I shall release Hell" (*Aeneid* 7.312). Such are the more exotic products of medieval *grammatica*.

NICOLETTE ZEEMAN
King's College, Cambridge

JEAN JOST, ed. *Chaucer's Humor: Critical Essays*. Garland Studies in Humor, vol. 5. New York and London: Garland Publishing, 1994. Pp. xlix, 477. $62.00.

This collection of critical essays was commissioned for the series Garland Studies in Humor. It follows a predetermined pattern in drawing its materials from a variety of sources: extracts of diverse length from books; articles previously published in critical anthologies or in scholarly journals; and articles solicited specifically for this volume. In addition to selecting and inviting contributions, the editor has written a general introduction and a historical survey of responses to Chaucer's humor, from the sparse comments of his contemporaries and immediate successors to the work of those early-twentieth-century critics who first engaged Chaucer's comic genius as a topic worthy of serious scholarly investigation. The reader is also provided a chronology of the major events in Chaucer's life, an annotated select bibliography, and an index.

Chaucer would seem to be an apt choice for inclusion in the series, since he can lay claim to having originated an essentially English style of humor. He was the first writer to exploit fully the comic possibilities of a fictional first-person narrator whose personality and circumstances jostle intriguingly with those of his creator; he was the first major author to naturalize the Old French fabliau form in English; and he was a tirelessly inventive experimenter with literary parody, the mock heroic, and burlesque misappropriation of the complex inventory of devices documented in the rhetorical handbooks of his time. Chaucer's works are so pervaded by humor that it is easier to note its absence than its presence: in the prose treatises, for example, or in the rhyme-royal Canterbury tales, although, as with *The Monk's Tale*, even in these groups individual works may be given a humorous cast by the circumstances of their narration within a fictional context. There is a problem in separating Chaucer the humorist from

Chaucer the poet, and two articles in this collection, Charles Owen's "Chaucer's Witty Prosody in *General Prologue*, Lines 1–42" and Alan Gaylord's "Chaucer's Dainty 'Dogerel': The 'Elvyssh' Prosody of *Sir Thopas*," posit a connection between Chaucer's humor and his exuberant displays of technical virtuosity.

The abundance and variety of the material available for investigating Chaucer's humor is well documented in "The Idea of Humor," an excerpt from *On Rereading Chaucer* in which Howard Rollin Patch identifies numerous sources of Chaucerian humor and attempts a definition of its characteristic qualities. Despite the title, Thomas Garbáty's "Chaucer and Comedy" is written in much the same spirit, and surveys a comparable range of texts and humorous *loci* with insight and evident enjoyment. After such a start it is disappointing to discover that most of the thirteen interpretive essays that comprise the main body of the collection do not mention *HF* or *PF*, the role of the narrator in these or other poems, characterization in *GP*, the figure of the Wife of Bath in her *Prologue*, or of Pandarus in *TC*, link passages in *CT*, or the multiple instances of Chaucer's quirky engagement with rhetoric and with the popular narrative genres of the late-medieval literary tradition. None of them deal significantly with any of these texts or topics, whose place is usurped by what rapidly establishes itself as a pervasive concern with comedy. Two essays in the introductory segment signal this shift in emphasis, Paul Ruggiers's "A Vocabulary for Chaucerian Comedy" and Derek Pearsall's *"The Canterbury Tales* II: Comedy."

Humor I understand to mean a predisposition of the mind, an amused and detached response to experience including, in the case of an author, literary experience. Comedy is a traditional literary genre, but with its own special significance for the Middle Ages, which applied the term to what little it knew of classical comedy, to the clerical twelfth-century Latin *comoedia*, and later to such popular narratives in the comic mode as the fabliaux, but applied it also to a variety of Christianized texts that relate very tenuously to the classical comedic tradition. From the perspective of audience response there is clearly common ground between the humorous and the comic, and if an author finds a particular kind of comedy congenial in the way that it presents experience of life, his decision to write in that mode may illustrate something of his own sense of humor. Ruggiers's essay is particularly valuable for defining two types of traditional comedy in Chaucer, "tales of license," as illustrated by *The Miller's Tale* and others dealing with adultery, and "unmaskings," as illustrated particularly in such nonsexual tales as those of the Friar and Summoner. Pearsall discusses both groups, and the two essays between them establish the canon of Canterbury tales from which an idea of Chaucerian humor might be derived.

Neither author suggests that any work designated a comedy in the Middle Ages is necessarily humorous, or that any explication of any aspect of a Chaucerian comedy in some way contributes to our understanding of Chaucer's humor. But such assumptions seem to govern a number of the remaining contributions. Whatever their value in articulating the nature and range of medieval comedy, discussions of the comedic structure of Chaucer's religious tales and of *TC* tell us next to nothing about Chaucerian humor. Daniel Pigg's new article, "The Semiotics of Comedy in Chaucer's Religious Tales," and "Felicity and Mutability: Boethian Framework of the *Troilus*," extracted from John Steadman's *Disembodied Laughter*, cannot be meaningfully integrated with the essays by Owen and Gaylord, and this fundamental uncertainty of purpose is not helped by the editor's dubious classification of these pieces as examples, respectively, of "religious," "tragic," "lyric," and "poetic" subspecies of "Generic Humor." Two articles on *The Merchant's Tale*, while addressing a text of crucial importance in understanding Chaucer's humor, also strike me as noncontributive. In "Chaucer's May, Standup Comics, and Critics," Susan Hagen draws some comparisons between the techniques of standup comedy and the Merchant's performance as they engage antifeminist sentiment. The parallels are real, but the circumstances of standup comedy necessarily dictate a less equivocal relationship between performer and audience than that operative in *CT*. The essay oversimplifies the effects of Chaucer's narrative strategies, and posits a response to the tale that has already been absorbed and transcended by its more perceptive critics. Similarly reductive is Frederick Jonassen's "Rough Music in Chaucer's *Merchant's Tale*," which marshals an inordinate weight of evidence to argue that the description of January's wedding music contributes to a sometimes suggested link between the tale and the charivari, a boisterous peasant ritual intended to humiliate partners in an unsuitable or disordered marriage.

Most of the remaining essays concentrate on the *Miller's* and *Shipman's Tales*. They attempt to define something of Chaucer's attitude toward comedy, and by implication the nature of his humor. Alfred David's "The Comedy of Innocence," taken from *The Strumpet Muse*, stresses *The Miller's Tale*'s festive escape from the eternal into a temporal world momentarily accepted as ultimate reality. William Woods's "Metamorphic Comedy: *The Shipman's Tale*" explores the tale's transformation of moral values, including those associated with ideas of fall and atonement, into commercial values. Robert Hanning's "'Parlous Play': Diabolic Comedy in Chaucer's *Canterbury Tales*" discusses *NPT* and several comedies of unmasking in tracing manifestations of the devil as trickster and as subverter of the creative force of divine providence, roles attributed to him particularly in medieval religious drama. By contrast, in "Chaucer's Creative Comedy: A Study of the *Miller's Tale* and the *Shipman's Tale*," Booker Thro argues that the essence of Chaucerian comedy in these two tales is to invest the most inventively duplicitous characters with powers that mimic divine creativity.

Three essays remain to be discussed. They are the least conventional in their approach and in the texts chosen for study, and the most interesting in what they have to offer for understanding humor. In "Chaucer, Freud, and the Political Economy of Wit: Tendentious Jokes in the *Nun's Priest's Tale*," James Goldstein comments on Chaucer's enigmatically offhand reference to the slaughter of Flemish artisans during the Peasants' Revolt of 1381. In relating tendentious jokes to the class and gender hierarchies of Chaucer's political unconscious, Goldstein accounts for a joke that untypically misfires for a modern audience, and relates it to other aspects of the tale: the frame description of the widow's rural subsistence economy, the tale's antifeminist sentiments, and its narrative contours. In "Paradoxicum Semiotica: Signs, Comedy, and Mystery in Fragment VI of the *Canterbury Tales*" John Crafton finds humor in the juxtaposition of the *Physician's* and *Pardoner's Tales* as they reflect language theories associated respectively with extreme Realism and Nominalism. In much lighter vein, but with an equally confident grasp of the pertinent history of ideas, Judith Tschann's "The Mind Distended: The *Retraction*, *Miller's Tale* and *Summoner's Tale*" looks at two scatalogical tales from the perspective of their final revocation and with reference to Saint Augustine's theory of time, and discovers that a fart can make time human, can be a reminder of death while ecstatically asserting life, and in its spatial and temporal configuration in cartwheel or shot-window can provide insight into the narrative process.

There are obviously a number of essays in this collection that amply repay reading or rereading, but the overall uncertainty of purpose does not inspire confidence in the editor's control and critical judgment in selecting and organizing her materials, and a similar impression is created by her handling of the introductory matter. To suppose that there is much profit in a painstaking account of six Canterbury tales acknowledged to be without significant humorous intent is to misjudge the nature of the probable readership for an anthology of this kind. The summary of contents tries to create an ordering framework for the diverse contributions, but folding an inflated tire would be an easier undertaking. There is no apparent rationale for classifying "Metamorphic Comedy" as "Social Theory" and "Diabolic Comedy" as "Generic Humor," and David's essay, also classed as "Social Theory," is as much indebted to Bakhtinian theory as Jonassen's. In its failure to impose a satisfactory sense of order, the Summary is open to the same objections as the materials it summarizes. Describing the individual essays as "incisive," "compelling," "rich," "intriguing," "perceptive," "delightful," or "classical" and "erudite" exhausts the vocabulary of subjective appreciation, but is no substitute for reasoned critical assessment. The section on "Comic Categorization" makes a braver attempt than the volume as a whole to capture the manifold varieties of Chaucerian humor, but it frequently anticipates what is said by contributors, or by other critics quoted in the annotated bibliography, it asserts rather than demonstrates the humor of the situations selected for commentary, and it is marred by pervasive errors of fact. The Nun's Priest does not "counteract" Harry Bailly's innuendoes that he is a treadfowl, since that occurs in the epilogue to his tale; the person so accused before the Nun's Priest tells his tale is the Monk. In this tale Chauntecleer has seven wives (not twenty); he does not "feather" them on a tree branch; and the fox is named Russell, not Reynard. The bribe to Morpheus in *BD* is a feather bed, not a pillow; *Lenvoy de Chaucer a Bukton* does not "humorously invite the Wife of Bath to read the poem"; Alla in *MLT* is not a Sultan; and the Second Nun is not the narrator of the tale of the *clergeon* who sings with his throat cut. There is only one unbridled horse in *RvT*, not two, and to describe the clerks in this tale ("I is thyn awen clerk, swa have I seel") as "suave" would be an in-joke in any other context, but contributes here to the reader's sense of the gap between the author and any intimate familiarity with Chaucer's text.

A book dealing sensitively and comprehensively with Chaucer's humor would have been a welcome addition to Chaucer scholarship, but the volume here reviewed falls far short of these ideals. This collection of essays as a whole amounts to rather less than the sum of its individual parts.

ROY J. PEARCY
London

EBBE KLITGÅRD. *Chaucer's Narrative Voice in* The Knight's Tale. Copenhagen: University of Copenhagen, Museum Tusculanum Press, 1995. Pp. 111. $30.00.

Ebbe Klitgård's discussion of Chaucer's "narrative voice" in *The Knight's Tale* is derived from an unusually narrow focus on the tale's "style and rhetoric," to the exclusion of psychological, dramatic, historical, institutional, philosophical, or cultural influences, contexts, intentions, or effects of any kind. His purpose is to establish the "uniqueness" of Chaucer's narrative voice. The book is presumably an unexpanded master's thesis (mentioned in the text) or possibly a doctoral dissertation: most of its arguments are made through references to the arguments and conclusions of other critics rather than to evidence from *The Knight's Tale* itself.

In chapter 1 Klitgård reviews the major twentieth-century critical approaches to Chaucer, rejecting, on the one hand, the "cult" of the Knight-as-persona critics (all ultimately descended from Kittredge's dramatic theory) as unhelpfully ironic and/or reductive, and rejecting also, on the other hand, the more recent ideological approaches (patristic, Marxist, feminist, Freudian) as reductive and New Historicism as text-external and therefore also irrelevant to his purpose. Instead, to aid in the search for Chaucer's narrative voice, Klitgård chooses Seymour Chatman's narrative communication model, which distinguishes three personages on the sending end (the real author, the implied author, and the narrator) and three at the receiving end (the narratee, the implied audience, and the real audience). Chaucer has a strong authorial presence in all his works, Klitgård argues, and behind the narrators in all of them, the implied authors speak with one, recognizable, consciously displayed voice.

In chapter 2 Klitgård moves from Chaucer criticism generally to *Knight's Tale* narration. He argues that the Knight as persona is present only briefly in the tale's frame. Other than that, the Chaucerian "educated voice" narrates, and he cites with approval those critics (C. David Benson, David Lawton, Leonard M. Koff) who focus on Chaucer's writing techniques: structure, diction, tone of voice, imagery, and speech. In chapter 3, arguing partly by contrast with the *Teseida*, Klitgård establishes the narrator's stance as detached with regard to the love story (unusual for a Chaucer narrator), and self-conscious with regard to his own story-telling. Chaucer's narrative strategy throughout *The Knight's Tale* is achieved, he says, through a "complex balance" of three contrasts in narrative style: seriousness vs. humor, high style vs. realism, involvement vs. distance. He then offers as complementary to his own approach the "structuring principles" of Paul T. Thurston, V. A. Kolve, and Derek Brewer.

In chapter 4 Klitgård shows that Chaucer's self-conscious narrator sometimes works contrary to his apparent intentions; occasionally he even loses "control" and goes too far. In chapter 5 Klitgård traces out the humor/ realism/distance side of the paired contrasts set up in chapter 3 and points out passages where Chaucer's voice fails or loses control. In chapters 6 and 7 Klitgård traces out the seriousness/high style/involvement side of the chapter 3 contrasts, first for the pagan deities (handled as a dream vision), and then for the philosophical passages, again pointing out the Chaucerian narrator's inconsistencies and lapses. During the Boethian speeches in books 1 and 4, the "narrative design foregrounds Stoic values, . . . but the narrative voice shows their inadequacy" (p. 99). Klitgård then concludes with a summarizing chapter.

I found the book somewhat puzzling. First, there is the question of audience. Is it intended for scholars or for students? On the one hand, it assumes the reader will possess substantial knowledge of Chaucerian scholarship of the past fifty years as well as "familiarity with such background as provided in J. A. Burrow's *Medieval Writers and Their Work*" (p. 10). On the other hand, there is no index, there are a disconcerting number of typos and punctuation errors, at least twice (pp. 66, 103) the reader is referred to the wrong internal page number, and critics' opinions rather than quotations from *The Knight's Tale* are constantly put forward as proofs. On the scholarship, Klitgård displays knowledge of a wide and varied selection. His suggestion of a complex balancing throughout *The Knight's Tale* of the paired contrasts set forth in chapter 3 (seriousness/high style/involvement vs. humor/realism/distance) seems to me interesting and somewhat familiar, in that didn't Charles Muscatine suggest a similar contrast throughout *The Canterbury Tales* in *Chaucer and the French Tradition* (1957)? Likewise, I wish that Klitgård, before debunking Theseus (pp. 96–98, 104–5), had come across the 1947 article by Henry J. Webb, the "first modern assassin of the duke's character" according to H. Marshall Leicester, Jr., in *The Disenchanted Self* (1990), another book I wish Klitgård had come across in his research, because it contains a major (ca. 160 pp.) and most enlightening reading of *The Knight's Tale*.

All in all, Klitgård's book is strongest on the different types of critical approaches. The neglect of many, perhaps most, *Knight's Tale* commentators to deal specifically with Chaucer's poetry (structure, diction, syntax, imagery, variation between concrete and abstract, meter, pace, variations in scope . . .) distresses him, as it does me. Perhaps as a result, it does seem to me that he goes too far in devaluing commentators who focus instead on cultural context, psychology, social class, history. . . . I guess I don't understand why we can't have both. Why we can't *do* both. Doesn't a critic need both kinds of evidence—text-internal and text-external—in order to make a truly persuasive case?

For example, Klitgård himself, in spite of striving to focus on Chaucer's narrative voice, finds no significant difference between Palamon and Arcite; discussing their prayers, for example, he does not mention the fact that Arcite's is structured rationally, divided into logical parts, whereas Palamon's is written in an emotionally associative style. Chaucer's narrative voice uses this same contrast in describing the two young men en route to their respective temples to pray: Arcite is described in rational, straightforward syntax; Palamon, in syntactically convoluted, repetitive phrases. In Chaucer's culture this kind of contrast was considered highly significant. Again, discussing the descriptions of the temples of the gods, Klitgård does not mention the fact that Chaucer's narrative voice structures Venus's and Mars's in the form of lists, whereas Diana's is in the form of story summaries. In Chaucer's culture this too was a meaning-filled contrast.

Thus, even when focusing narrowly on language use, in order to find out what is actually there in the language the poet was using, the critic still needs all the text-external help she or he can get, whether from history or culture or literary or linguistic theory or all of these. I was delighted to see Klitgård's insistence on the importance of zooming in on Chaucer's use of language, in my opinion a much neglected area. Confronting a poet's language is the most demanding task the literary critic faces, or more commonly, doesn't face. Klitgård's book certainly faces in the right direction.

Lois Roney
St. Cloud State University

Erik Kooper, ed. *Medieval Dutch Literature in its European Context*. Cambridge Studies in Medieval Literature, vol. 21. Cambridge: Cambridge University Press, 1994. Pp. xv, 327. $64.95.

The precocious urban cultures of the Low Countries, and most particularly of Flanders, should prove to be of compelling interest to students of

Chaucer and his "age." Court cultures in Hainault, Brabant, and Holland made contact with England through ties of marriage and diplomatic exchange; mercantile and artisanate cultures of the great Flemish cities were carried to and into England through the wool trade (a trade closely tied to the fortunes and financing of the Hundred Years' War). Flanders is chosen by Chaucer as the birthplace of his own Sir Thopas and as the setting for *The Pardoner's Tale*. Bruges forms the hub of the complex religious and mercantile *rekenynge* elaborated through *The Shipman's Tale*, a business Chaucer knew first hand through his quayside work in London (1374–86). Flanders, for Chaucer, was more familiar than anywhere in Britain west of Somerset and north of Yorkshire; it can be considered, in many respects, as part of his "native" ground.

Medieval Dutch Literature in its European Context is a collaborative effort of some twenty scholars currently working in Holland and Belgium. The volume thus represents a bold attempt to bring the medieval textual cultures of the Low Countries, as perceived through the disciplinary traditions of those countries, to an English-speaking audience. Not everything can run smoothly in such a genuinely pioneering effort; Cambridge University Press, editor Erik Kooper, and series editor Alastair Minnis are much to be commended for riding out evident difficulties of *translatio*. The general impression of the volume, and hence of the academic culture that underpins it, is of a traditional philology with a penchant for formalist analysis (which nonetheless shows itself cognizant of new developments in Britain and North America). Cognizance does not, of course, imply approval, or even thorough comprehension: the volume's introduction sounds a defensive note in recognizing the absence of "two approaches, very prominent in American publications in particular," namely "women's studies and deconstruction." These, Kooper argues, "have not made many converts among the *medioneerlandici*" (p. 4). "Deconstruction" is here employed (as often in England) as a code word for any kind of literary theory minted since 1966. And "women's studies" is here allied with deconstruction as a strange cultic exercise (which, if left to flourish, might lead to dancing at airports). Limited interest in "women's studies" might not be unrelated, of course, to the limited appearance of women as contributors to this volume. Essays are loosely grouped by topic (the book is not the product of strong editorial design) and the essayists tend to argue more openly with fellow critics than is usually the case in Britain, Canada, or the (exceptionally polite, at least in print) U.S. Readers will have to work harder than they might normally care to in mining material from this collection, but their efforts will be handsomely rewarded: the volume contains much that is fascinating, plus some true treasures of discovery.

Walter Prevenier, a professional historian, gets things off to a good start in discussing how the Low Countries came, by the fifteenth century, to be more intensively urbanized than anywhere else in the world: up to 36 percent of the population of Flanders and 45 percent of Holland lived in cities. Prevenier is particularly good on the political and commercial advantages gained (then as now) by a culture negotiated between Germanic (Dutch, German) and Romance (French) traditions. Frits van Oostrom, having insisted that the French/Dutch divide can nowhere be simply assimilated to a distinction between nobility and other estates, offers further subtle exploration of these linguistic axes. Dutch writers in Holland, he argues, received little encouragement while their homeland was governed by absentee French-speaking rulers from Hainault: but the coming of the House of Bavaria (1358) established a thriving court culture at the Hague that encouraged Dutch as well as German writing. This Germanified Dutch court culture, open to Bohemian influences, was to produce a figure who seems—in his choice of literary models, career trajectory, and Italian travels—fascinatingly reminiscent of both Chaucer and Gower. This writer, Dirc Potter, is accorded a chapter to himself later in the book that, through sheer dullness and unpruned repetition, dissolves such fascination like the morning dew.

Wim van Anrooij gives a good account of the "Reses de Pruce," those heroic journeys against the infidel undertaken by European Christian chivalry once the Holy Land lay too securely under infidel control. French and English knights, kept busy by the Hundred Years' War, tended to miss out here (although they did hurry eastward during truces and vacations). Chaucer's Knight, of course, had "reysed" in "Pruce" (l. 53–54); it is instructive to consider his *General Prologue* portrait in conjunction with the *Ehrenreden*, short poems in praise of the lives and careers of German (and Dutch) knights. Further opportunity for cross-cultural speculation is provided by Frank Willaerts's brilliant chapter on *hovedans*, fourteenth-century dance songs from the Rhine and Meuse area. Willaerts brings us directly from highly technical discussion of dance terminology to sites in Chaucer and Gower that suggest the presence of Dutch and German musicians: he explains, for example, why "pipers of the Duche tonge" should show up in *The House of Fame* and why (following Caxton's edition of 1483) they should be playing "hove-daunces" rather than (as the *Riverside Chaucer* has it) "love-daunces" (lines 1234–35). He then etymologizes the names of

John of Gaunt's minstrels—"Smeltes (< MHG *smeltz*, 'lard')," etc.—by way of ascertaining their Flemish, Dutch, or Rhineland provenance (p. 177). Four scholars combine to introduce a short treatise on vernacular poetics by Jan van Boendale (secretary to the aldermen of Antwerp). This proves to be something of a *De vulgari eloquentia* in reverse: for whereas Dante adopts Latin by way of pleading the superiority of the vernacular, Boendale employs the vernacular to assert that only the Latin-literate *gramarijn* is capable of true eloquence. Boendale's treatise, thoughtfully translated here by Erik Kooper, bristles with resentment at the productions of *ioculatores* and minstrels; hence and otherwise, it joins the European-wide effort to establish the vernacular author as a figure worthy of esteem and remuneration. Ria Jansen-Sieben also strives to construct an argument of more than local interest in tracing the evolution of the cookery-book (by the sixteenth century) out of ancient medical literature and medieval dietetics. She hence comes to consider physicians as cooks (pp. 263–65) and cooks as physicians (pp. 265–67), vocational shifts of particular pertinence for *The Canterbury Tales*.

Other chapters concern themselves with the Middle Dutch Charlemagne romances (apparently written from memories of performance), Reynaert the fox, and the Middle Dutch voyage of St. Brendan. There is an interesting glimpse of the so-called *Lancelot Compilation* (preserved in Royal Library of the Hague MS 129 A 10), which sees a compiler (also the principal scribe) attempting to forge a framed collection from diverse Arthurian materials. J. D. Janssens explains how and why the names "Walewein" and "Iwein" proved popular in Flanders before Chrétien de Troyes (or even Geoffrey of Monmouth) got busy; Joris Reynaert tantalizes us with Hadewich, a mid-thirteenth-century mystic whose songs conflate courtly, religious, and erotic registers. Reynaert argues for Hadewich as a "pre-beguine" (p. 221): if women within the convent are to be seen as brides of Christ, then religious women beyond it might imagine themselves as "*mistresses* of God" (p. 221).

Thom Mertens begins his chapter by observing that some seventy to eighty percent of late-medieval manuscript production in the Low Countries is dedicated to religious prose; he then castigates Dutch literary scholars for neglecting it and outlines the particular skills that will be needed for analysis of *devotio moderna* manuscripts. These manuscripts, small meditational handbooks prepared for private and personal use, present formidable difficulties when viewed as a corpus, since such a corpus "cannot be dealt with by author, by text or by manuscript" (p. 230). What

Mertens is asking for might be imagined as a rolling equivalent of the York Manuscripts Conferences, supervised by Anne Hudson. Lollard specialists might indeed benefit from acquainting themselves with this corpus, which forms such a fascinating contemporary counterpart to Lollardy: an attempt to revive the common life of the apostles, to revive the monastic spirit of the early Middle Ages, and to encourage brothers and sisters through the production of spiritual "testaments."

Erik Kooper's volume, which contains a useful bibliography of translations and an excellent four-column chronology, instructively complements the (predominantly) English-based collaboration edited by Caroline Barron and Nigel Saul, *England and the Low Countries in the Late Middle Ages* (Stroud: Alan Sutton, 1995). It certainly deepens the fascination of this shifting, densely populated bloc of European territories, native ground to anxieties and fantasies that will flower through Bosch and Brueghel and so inaugurate, some might say, the ego's era.

DAVID WALLACE
University of Pennsylvania

MICHAEL P. KUCZYNSKI. *Prophetic Song: The Psalms as Moral Discourse in Late Medieval England.* Middle Ages Series. Philadelphia: University of Pennsylvania Press, 1995. Pp. xxx, 292. $36.95.

This is a solid work of careful scholarship that makes an important, albeit limited, contribution both to our understanding of Psalmic reception and imitation in the later Middle Ages and, more generally, to our growing appreciation of the model character of biblical texts for medieval writers. As such, it takes us further down the exciting and challenging pathway pioneered by scholars like Beryl Smalley, A. J. Minnis, and Judson B. Allen.

A hallmark of the book is Kuczynski's close attention to, and citation of, numerous works in manuscript and his appended editions of two previously unpublished Middle English texts, "The Direccioun of a Mannys Lyfe" (a treatise concerning temptation) and "The Remnant of My Thoughts" (a meditation on Psalm 75:11). The book also includes four illustrative plates taken from different psalters, each of which Kuczynski

238

comments upon and incorporates into his larger discussion of the Psalmic "rhetoric of exegesis" (to echo a phrase he borrows from James O'Donnell).

This rhetoric, as Kuczynski explains, involves both interpretation and imitation. Biblical interpreters (preeminent among them, Saint Augustine in his *Enarrationes in Psalmos*) conveyed to others their own "often emotional readings of the Psalms" (p. xxiv) in the form of commentaries and homilies. This exegetical tendency to extend the language of the Psalms into one's own discourse was supported in the schools by a complementary grammatical and rhetorical tradition of biblical *imitatio*. As a result, Kuczynski argues convincingly, Middle English writers were moved by "an irresistible impulse to amplify, and (they hoped) thereby to clarify, the meaning of David's inspired poetry" (p. 217).

That meaning, according to Kuczynski, was primarily the moral teaching that derived from interpreting the Psalms not as autonomous lyrics but as prophetic utterances "caught up inextricably with the biography of David" (p. xx). As "both just King and murderer, *Beatus vir* and adulterer," David enjoyed a special status as "God's supreme prophet" (p. xxi), sometimes speaking in the persona of Christ, sometimes voicing the praise or penitential sighs of the Church. David's words could thus be appropriated by every Christian.

As Kuczynski emphasizes, "Middle English authors introduce David most often as an *exemplum* of compunction or penitential humility, citing and commenting on the Psalms in order to induce a humble attitude in their readers" (p. 84). As a person whose personal sin and repentance had definite public consequences, David taught the Middle Ages the "essential relationship between the renewal of the individual soul and the reform of society itself" (p. xvii). Kuczynski therefore focuses in particular on how the language of the Psalms influenced "the shape of moral discourse in late medieval England" (p. xv) and provided Middle English moralists with a "language of ethics" (p. xvii) that was both public and private, personal and social, devotional and ideological.

Dividing his study into three parts, Kuczynski first considers the Psalms as they were interpreted in the light of David's biography and prophetic status. Second, under the heading of "Psalm Discourse," he examines the use of Davidic language in three devotional and didactic prose treatises and in the poetic paraphrases and imitations of Richard Maidstone, Thomas Brampton, and John Lydgate. Third, in a section entitled "Psalm Ideology," he deals with the use of the Psalms in the reformist rhetoric of Lydgate's *Defence of Holy Church*, of the Lollard interpolations of Richard Rolle's *Psalter*, and of Langland's *Piers Plowman*.

In embarking on the "vast ocean" of his topic—the Psalms and moral discourse—Kuczynski had to set his course selectively. By and large, he made conservative choices. Although he uses Dante's *Commedia* powerfully to illustrate the "close relationship between David's *humilitas* and the use of poetic authority" (p. 29) and, following R. A. Shoaf, briefly suggests Davidic patterns in the alliterative *Morte Arthure*, he generally avoids treating works in which there is arguably a Psalmic deep-structure and deals instead with more obvious cases of Psalmic influence: Middle English translations and paraphrases of, and commentaries on, the Psalms themselves. The major exception to this rule is his sensitive treatment of Psalmic intertextuality in *Piers Plowman*.

As Kuczynski acknowledges, he also made a conscious decision to emphasize depth at the expense of breadth. As a result, he is able to offer close and patient (sometimes almost fussy) readings of a few neglected or virtually unknown works that he regards as representative. Because of his study of the relevant manuscripts, he is able, moreover, to challenge some of the views of previous textual scholars, such as Carleton Brown and Dorothy Everett.

As valuable as this close-grained scholarship no doubt is, one cannot help but wonder whether Kuczynski's relatively limited selection of examples best serves to support the larger claims of his major thesis. Given his emphasis on the dual, public/private nature and ethical thrust of Psalmic discourse, it is surprising how little attention he pays to Middle English homilies—all the more so because fourteenth-century clergymen associated the outbreak of the Black Death with the pestilence that David first incurred through sin and then averted through his confession of guilt and penitential practice (cf. 2 Samuel 24). Similarly, Kuczynski omits treatment of the role of "the prophete David" in Chaucer's *Parson's Tale* and in popular penitential handbooks, such as *The Prick of Conscience*. Medieval morality plays, too, go undiscussed, even though, as Kuczynski intimates, the Psalms have a "subtextual prominence" in them (p. xxiv). Nor does Kuczynski explore the admonitory function of David in mirrors for princes. Perhaps these regrets, however, only serve to indicate the value of Kuczynski's study, which has with love and learning charted a course for others to follow across the "vast ocean" of the Psalms and the literature inspired by David's prophetic song.

Ann W. Astell
Purdue University

CLARE A. LEES, ed. *Medieval Masculinities: Regarding Men in the Middle Ages.* Medieval Culture Series, vol. 7. Minneapolis and London: University of Minnesota Press, 1994. Pp. xxv, 193. $44.95 cloth, $17.95 paper.

The study of masculinity—or *masculinities*, in keeping with the notion that manliness is constructed in a variety of ways across time and according to place—often elicits the quip, "Isn't that redundant?" History, after all, is *his* story.

This collection of essays, the first of its kind in medieval studies, takes this question very seriously. Thelma Fenster argues in her preface that while the study of women in history and literature has often been shaped by gender, "the relationship between a man's gender and his acts remains to be examined. Women have been treated as material and local, whereas men have remained untouchable and unreachable" (p. x). As the ten essays illustrate, concentrating on masculinity, particularly on the question of how it is represented and reproduced, can shape our reading in fruitful and sometimes unexpected ways. More important, *Medieval Masculinities* demonstrates forcefully that no single, monologic male identity in medieval Western Europe can be posited; taken together, the essays effectively calibrate differences in representation from one genre or discourse or time or place to another.

Before I touch on individual essays, a word on contemporary men's studies is in order. There is a core group of texts, written mainly by sociologists and psychologists in the U.S., Great Britain, and Australia, that constitutes the "first wave" of research in men's studies. All of the leading scholars concerned with the study of masculinity take as their premise the cultural constructedness of male identity; many take a psychoanalytic approach. However, their relationship to feminism is often problematic: some scholars cite feminist scholarship in an extremely selective way; others ignore it altogether. The overall effect has been to downplay or deemphasize the activist agenda of feminism and feminist scholarship. Moreover, by stressing object-relations theory (best exemplified by Nancy Chodorow's *The Reproduction of Mothering*) at the expense of other psychoanalytic models, some scholars of masculinity have perpetuated a "blame the mom" attitude. The essays in *Medieval Masculinities* avoid these and other epistemological problems that sometimes characterize the academic study of masculinity; they do so by historicizing masculinity, grounding its effects and symptoms in specific events, trends, and texts. (Indeed, treatments of masculinity by literary scholars are usually superior to this nascent discipline's foundational texts.)

In the first essay, "The *Herrenfrage*: The Restructuring of the Gender System, 1050–1150," Jo Ann McNamara focuses on the early twelfth century in Western Europe, a time of "broad social changes, complicated by the ideological struggle between celibate and married men for leadership of the Christian world, [which] precipitated a masculine identity crisis" (p. 3). She dubs this crisis the *Herrenfrage*. General and assertive in its claims rather than demonstrative, this essay creates a context for the essays that follow.

Clare R. Kinney emphasizes the importance of "continuous and ultimately equivocal renegotiation" of "chivalric manhood" (p. 47) in "The (Dis)Embodied Hero and the Signs of Manhood in *Sir Gawain and the Green Knight*." The green girdle suggests how manliness is not necessarily stable and fixed; the adoption of the girdle by the court at the end of the poem illustrates how a dominant class can control its own representation.

In "Men and *Beowulf*," Clare Lees takes up the history of *Beowulf* scholarship as it has shaped our understanding of Anglo-Saxon manliness in the poem; she performs admirable readings of key texts by J. R. R. Tolkien, James W. Earl, and Gillian Overing. Lees then goes on to develop a reading of her own, in which she argues that *Beowulf* "is as much about the limits of aggression in this male aristocratic heroic world as it is about its successes" (p. 144). The poem is by no means an unequivocal celebration of violence; rather, while it "naturalizes gender and thereby promotes masculinism" (p. 146), it also reveals the tensions—and costs—inherent in any attempt to fulfill a society's ideals of masculinity.

Stanley Chojnacki ("Subaltern Patriarchs: Patrician Bachelors in Renaissance Venice") argues that "changes in the social order led to changes in the range of gender identity among both women and men" (p. 73) in fifteenth-century Venice. Gender was not necessarily polarized as masculine versus feminine, but slid along a scale that depended on a number of factors. The unmarried male patrician held a very ambiguous place in society, for bachelorhood denied him any real claim to authority, and relegated him to certain restricted private and public offices. At the same time, Chojnacki is quick to stress, the unmarried Venetian fully enjoyed the privileges of class and gender.

Christopher Baswell, in "Men in the *Roman d'Eneas*: The Construction of Empire," argues that "the *Eneas* created a space in which [Angevin] aristocratic readership could examine manhood and heroism for its own time, and imagine the old dangers and new pressures under which its concept of manhood labored, and the new forms into which it was struggling to emerge" (p. 149). This version of the story of Troy both shaped and reflected a new ideal of kingship in twelfth-century France, one that was based less on feudal violence and more on the consolidation of power through judicial regulation and patrilineal descent.

Medieval Masculinities suggests some directions for future studies in the subject, both by what it addresses and what it does not. Only a few of the essays mention male violence against other men—a topic that most feminist literary scholars have shunned, and that those working in men's studies have approached with caution. And while the historical and material situation of men *qua* men in the Middle Ages deserves full investigation, there are other approaches to the subject; for example, the new study of masculinity allows us to look at the social formation of the self in ways that feminist scholarship by itself cannot. Finally, several of the essays in *Medieval Masculinities* reveal that we have yet to develop the appropriate vocabulary for talking about men in the Middle Ages. We may find that we need to go far afield in search of useful theoretical frameworks for the study of masculinity; for example, *Screening the Male: Exploring Masculinities in Hollywood Cinema* (edited by Steven Cohan and Ina Rae Hark) is one text that can contribute to theorizing the subject of medieval masculinity in a new and rewarding way.

Some of the essays in this collection are based on papers given at a 1990 conference at Fordham University, "Gender and Medieval Society: Men." In addition to the essays noted above, the collection includes the following: Vern Bullough, "On Being a Male in the Middle Ages"; John Coakley, "Friars, Sanctity, and Gender: Mendicant Encounters with Saints, 1250–1325"; Louise Mirrer, "Representing 'Other' Men: Muslims, Jews, and Masculine Ideals in Medieval Castilian Epic and Ballad"; Harriet Spiegel, "The Male Animal in the Fables of Marie de France"; and Susan Mosher Stuard, "Burdens of Matrimony: Husbanding and Gender in Medieval Italy."

KATHLEEN COYNE KELLY
Northeastern University

TIM WILLIAM MACHAN. *Textual Criticism and Middle English Texts.* Charlottesville and London: University Press of Virginia, 1994. Pp. x, 250. $40.00.

Machan's project is an ambitious one: "to articulate the textual and cultural factors that characterize Middle English works as Middle English and to

243

indicate the ways in which these factors are relevant to the textual criticism, editing, and concomitant interpretation of those works" (pp. 3–4). His aim is not to provide a practical manual for editors, but to reassess— and also to challenge—the theoretical assumptions underlying traditional editorial approaches to Middle English works.

The main theme of a complex argument is that until recently the editing of medieval vernacular works has been dominated by a powerful "humanist" tradition of textual criticism—"lexical" (seeing the work as essentially a verbal construct), "idealist" (giving the intended work priority over its specific documentary realizations), and equating the authorial with the authoritative text. Machan argues, from an examination of "the construction of author, work, and text within the discourse of late Middle English manuscripts" (p. 85), that there are problems in applying this approach to Middle English works. The work is characteristically treated as "a nonlexical, not self-contained *res* inseparable from the supplements of others" (p. 165). Its *verba* (words, rhymes, etc.) are a less important feature than its *res* (content); it may be modified or expanded during textual transmission; and its documentary realizations in manuscripts of varying content and layout further modify its meaning for the medieval reader. Textual authority in this period was normally the prerogative of the Latin *auctores*, and late Middle English literature in general reflects the anxiety of vernacular writers about their dubious authorial status; "to equate the authoritative text with the authorial one is to grant them the very quality that their own desires indicate they did not have" (p. 135). Machan suggests that a genuinely historical edition of a medieval work might entail reconstructing the work behind a particular document rather than the authorially intended text behind several documents (p. 184), taking into account the social and cultural framework within which it would have been read, and giving greater attention than at present to the bibliographical codes involved in its documentary realization.

Machan's exploration of this difficult topic makes effective use of both modern and late-medieval critical theory, as well as original research on the primary texts; but there are some unresolved tensions and unevennesses in his analysis that prevent it from being as convincing as it might have been.

In particular, there is an underlying tension between the broad rhetorical thrust of his argument, which sharply opposes the humanist concepts of author, work, and text to those reflected in the "discourse of late Middle English MSS," and his recognition of the actual variety of the cultural situation he is describing. This tension comes to the surface in the final chapter, where he is discussing how Chaucer should be edited. The problem here is that Chaucer, of all late Middle English writers, comes closest to having the status of an *auctor*, and more than once (at the end of *Troilus and Criseyde*, and in his lines to Adam the scribe) emphasizes the lexical and self-contained nature of his poetry, and his concern to protect it from unwanted scribal alteration. Machan, however, argues that his "authorial self-consciousness . . . despite the intrinsic merits of his poetry, provides no broadly historical reason for valorizing his particular texts in the face of overwhelming contextual evidence to the contrary" (p. 182). It is hard to see how this position can be justified; it is one thing to argue that Chaucer's attitude to his work was not shared by the writers and scribes who followed him, but another to claim that it is historically unsound to edit his works according to his expressed wishes. Why should Machan take this view? Because of Chaucer's affinity with post-Renaissance attitudes? Although he protests that "my intention in this book has not been to demonize humanism or traditional textual criticism" (p. 183), the language he sometimes uses about them is sufficiently loaded to suggest that he is finding it a struggle:

Humanist textual criticism has . . . come to define the perimeters of textual criticism in general and the discursive field of Middle English in particular, largely because its totalizing positions, in a maneuver entirely consistent with humanist ideology, were articulated and institutionalized in such a way that subsequent critics have taken them at face value. (p. 178)

The quality of Machan's argument can also be variable. Where he is on his academic home ground (as in his discussions of poets' attitudes to the *auctores* in late Middle English poetry, or of the textual history of Chaucer's *Boece*), the argument is generously illustrated and confidently and convincingly handled; but some of his main generalizations are supported only by limited and ambiguous examples. For instance, to illustrate the late Middle English concept of the relationship between work and text, he compares two lyrics, the "punctuation poem" on priests beginning "Trvsty. seldom to their ffrendys vniust," and the "ivy" carol "Ouer all gatis that I haff gon," which links the letters of the spelling IVE with "Jhesus name," the "wurthy wyffe" Mary, and "Emanuell." Machan notes that the effect of the former depends on the exact reproduction of its punctuation in the MS; but that in the MS text of the latter, in spite of its theme, the word "ivy" is spelt with final *y* (rather than *e*) throughout. He argues that the punctuation poem is exceptional, a "novelty," and that the carol text, with its disregard for orthographic detail even where it is thematically significant, is more representative of the late Middle English concern for *res* rather than *verba*: "The text of the carol is an inherently imperfect realization of a work that requires writer and reader to supplement through graphic correspondence and mystical significance" (p. 176). But there is no reason to assume, as Machan does, that the manuscript text of the carol is the poet's autograph (as its earliest editors, M. R. James and G. C. Macaulay, commented, "The transcript is careless and the spelling bad"); and in any case the communication of the poem's message depends not (as in the punctuation poem) on the manuscript layout but on its rhyme scheme, which confirms both the poet's spelling of the word and the intended phonetic values of its individual letters (*quy/I, V/trewe, E/be*). It could be argued that *both* poems offer evidence for an increased late Middle English awareness of orthographic detail, and that the only difference between them is one of genre: the former is designed primarily for readers, the latter (as a carol) for listeners. A similar objection could be raised to Machan's use of the manuscript layout of the "Harley Lyrics," where the scribe sometimes ignores the elaborate formal structure of the poems, as a further illustration of the medieval subordination of *verba* to *res*. Since the content of these lyrics is often (as he says of *De Clerico et Puella*) "insubstantial," other explanations need to be considered; an alternative, and perhaps more likely, possibility is that the layout reflects a culture in which the formal structure of poetry was still perceived primarily through the ear rather than through the eye.

This is not to say that Machan's use of illustrations invalidates his arguments, only that they do not always do full justice to his case. His argument is less forceful than it might be partly because he concentrates mainly on late Middle English writers (particularly Chaucer) whose concepts of author, work, and text *can* be assimilated to post-Renaissance models without too much difficulty, partly because it tends to slip into a "totalizing" view of medieval literary production and transmission that is no more than a mirror image of the humanist approach to textual criticism that he is attacking. His thesis would carry more conviction if he had drawn on a wider range of Middle English works to demonstrate his points (the evidence is certainly there), and explored the possible exceptions to it more fully. Nevertheless, his book makes a substantial contribution to the developing literature on the special problems of editing medieval works, and anyone professionally interested in the editing of Middle English texts will find it worth consulting.

They should be warned, however, that the documentary realization of this particular work makes fewer concessions than might have been expected to the convenience of its scholarly readers. The book is attractively printed and laid out, but the proofreading shows numerous signs of "negligence and rape," and it is exasperatingly difficult to consult the Notes on the Text, which are relegated to the back of the book, and not keyed by a running header to either page numbers or chapters (Why do academic publishers still do this? Does nobody ever complain?).

BELLA MILLETT
University of Southampton

GAYLE MARGHERITA. *The Romance of Origins: Language and Sexual Difference in Middle English Literature.* Philadelphia: University of Pennsylvania Press, 1994. Pp. xvi, 214. $34.95 cloth, $14.95 paper.

Professor Margherita remarks early on in her preface that this is not "a book about 'women in medieval literature'" (p. xii), and indeed it is not. It does not at all seek to relive or re-create a feminine "experience," but is an attempt rather to look at a diverse group of well-known Middle English texts, with a view to uncovering, dissecting, and clarifying a whole series of discursive practices, linguistic formations that will shed light on very broad theoretical issues in historicity itself, and in particular, on the relationship between history and literary representations.

She begins by restating for us what she sees as the operative assumptions of present-day "historicist" readings of medieval literature, "specifically the assumption that only two readings of the past are possible, and that these readings cannot really speak to each other in any meaningful way. Either the medieval period is irreducibly different and 'other,' or it is fundamentally the same, linked to our own historical context by philosophical, linguistic, and/or psychic 'universals' that resist any historical specification" (p. ix). But faced with this apparently intractable schism between the claims of "alterity" on the one hand, and "human Nature"—or some other originary "fantasy" of your own choice—she decides upon a course that will shed light not only on the nature of this split but on the "natures" of many other things as well: literary representation, canonicity, the presentation of the feminine, and, ultimately, the ways in which we can re-view the contours and features of poems as heavily studied and remarked upon as *Troilus and Criseyde* and *Sir Gawain and the Green Knight*.

This course is to use the insights and heuristic frameworks provided by such modern theoretical inventions as deconstruction and psychoanalytical theory, basically Lacanian in its cast, to reinterrogate our own notions of historicity and our own creation and sustenance of originary myths in order to show the series of texts under scrutiny as repositories of historical "traces" of various kinds, traces that will in the end bring Margherita back to where she started in the preface, namely, to a way of re-seeing the historicist positioning not only of medieval literature as an object of study but also of the field of medieval studies as well. Let me assure you at the outset that this trip is well worth the taking, especially with Gayle Margherita as your guide.

The itinerary goes like this: aside from the preface and an introductory chapter called "The Psychic Life of the Past," and an intriguing afterword entitled "The Medieval Thing," the study consists of six chapters devoted to medieval texts. The first three of these are devoted to literary items that, though by no means "unknown," are certainly left relatively uncovered by modern critical commentary: "Margery Kempe and the Pathology of Writing," "Body and Metaphor in the Middle English *Juliana*," and the provocatively entitled "Women and Riot in the Harley Lyrics." The lyrics analyzed in this last chapter are also included in an appendix, where they are even translated for us by the author, as are all of the quotations from medieval texts used in the body of the book, except for those taken from Chaucer; all of which hints at a hoped-for audience ranging beyond the confines of the Medieval Academy membership itself, a hope that I share with the author, though my sanguinity in the matter is somewhat constricted. In the second half of the study, Margherita deals with, in succession, "Originary Fantasies and Chaucer's *Book of the Duchess*," "Historicity, Femininity, and Chaucer's *Troilus*," and "Father Aeneas or Morgan the Goddess," which, of course, deals with *Sir Gawain and the Green Knight*.

While it might seem to some readers that the real meat of any study arranged in this way is bound to be found in the second half of the book, and while indeed no reader's assumptions about the relative esthetic preeminence of Chaucer and the *Gawain*-poet are going to be challenged here, there are real merits in a careful scrutiny of the chapters on Kempe, *Juliana*, and the Harley lyrics. Taken together with the excellent, pointed, and marvelously compact introduction ("The Psychic Life of the Past"), they provide us with an orientation to the "problem of origins," attested to

248

in Margherita's view by "the scholarly obsession with the philological, generic, exegetical, and archaeological beginnings of medieval literary texts" (p. 2). They also introduce us to the author's overarching interpretive framework—"Throughout this project, I argue that history as an epistemological category is inseparable from the problematics of representation, or, more specifically, from fantasy and figuration" (p. 3)—and the means by which she proposes to conduct her argument: "In exploring this assumption, I rely heavily on psychoanalytic theory as the critical discourse that speaks most precisely to problems of memory, fantasy, and tropological substitution. This methodological foundation allows me to insert sexual difference into the dialectic of past and present, as a disruptive third term that breaks up the narcissistic mirroring of traditional criticism" (p. 3).

By starting her study of texts with the *Book of Margery Kempe*, Margherita enables herself to wade right into a work that many eminent scholars have in the past dismissed as pathological, and which for some, like Caroline Bynum, has embodied, along with other mystical writings, a redeployment of feminine imagery in the service of the usurpation of the patriarchal hierarchies of traditional theology—a usurpation achieved by linguistic means, that is, by a use of language that simply calls into question the foundational soundness of the works of her male predecessors. But for Gayle Margherita, Margery Kempe's language moves beyond that purpose, in that "it challenges the very conditions of meaning within the Christian signifying system" (p. 15). And this is only the first of many places that call out for a figural linkage to the Wife of Bath.

Similarly, both the specular use of the female body, exquisitely tortured for our delectation in *Juliana*, and the rape that is implicit in the scenario of the *pastourelle* figure sets forth for us a continuation of a split between the material and maternal origins represented by the feminine and the textual and verbal origins—from the Word on down through the many words of the theologians—of masculine myths of originary status. The result is that the *Juliana* deconstructs its apparent ideological intentions: "Intended as an ideological affirmation of Christianity and the English language, *Juliana* inadvertently unmasks the figural likenesses it seeks to create" (p. 60), though the exclusion of the poem from the Middle English canon could be attributed to many reasons—of many different sorts—besides "its failure to repress the ideological agenda of figuration" (p. 60). Much the same sense of things can also be seen operating within the Harley lyrics studied here, but they also function importantly for the development of the argument in this book by focusing our attention on the question of "loss," which will of course provide us with a bridge to *The Book of the Duchess*: "An exploration of the problem of loss is vital to any understanding of the lyric voice and the lyric event in the Middle Ages, since most medieval lyric poems are staged as an attempt to come to terms with absence or privation" (p. 63).

The link between the first half of the book and the second can be made no clearer than Margherita makes it near the beginning of the chapter on *The Book of the Duchess*. She believes, rightly I think, that she has shown forcefully and cogently that "Margery Kempe's insistence on the materiality of figurative language, the hagiographer's failure [in *Juliana*] to separate . . . body from metaphor, and the lyricist's inability to transcend the prurience of his own tropes all point to a larger failure to embrace the metaphysical dualism which canonical texts seem to affirm." But she goes on to observe, "I say 'seem' because, while the works of Chaucer and the *Gawain*-poet appear to have contained and transcended the problematics of origin and materiality, poems such as *The Book of the Duchess*, *Troilus and Criseyde*, and *Sir Gawain and the Green Knight* in fact succeed only in allegorizing their own failure to 'master matter'" (p. 83). The following out of the promise of this last sentence is perhaps most original with respect to *The Book of the Duchess*, but even in the other two poems, Margherita's readings, guided by the carefully crafted principles and examples developed up to this point in the book, will yield insights even to those who might have thought they had explored every avenue toward the explication of these much-read and much-taught "classics."

The fifth chapter, "Historicity, Femininity, and the *Troilus*," begins with a masterfully compact discussion of "historicity" in Chaucer, grounded in the work of recent critics and theorists (chief among them, not surprisingly, being Lee Patterson), and then opens into a reading of the poem that begins with the outburst of elegiac feeling at its onset: all the weeping, all the multiplied "sorwe." But this only leads Margherita back to her main concerns: "Through the narrator's identification with Oedipus, mourning for the lost past leads to an awareness of another, prior loss: the loss of the referential world or of the real necessitated by one's entry into language" (p. 109). The reading of *Troilus*, like the reading of *Sir Gawain* that follows it, is of a complexity that cannot be fairly described in such a brief review, especially in the sections suggestively subtitled "Criseyde Disfigured," and the twins "Historical Innocence: What Chaucer Knew" and "Sexual Innocence: What Troilus Knew." But the complexity can be sampled: "The need to keep the poem innocent of history parallels the need to keep

Troilus innocent of sexuality" (p. 125); and especially, "Courtly language, like Troilus himself, knows and yet doesn't know. Disavowing both its origin and the 'fyn of his entente,' the lover's metaphoric discourse becomes stagnant and absolute, except at those uncanny moments when the encrypted lost object returns to efface boundaries and restore forgotten knowledge" (p. 127).

And the same delicious and rewarding subtlety is present at all points in the reading of *Sir Gawain*, which toward the end comes to this point: "The poem leaves us in a state of epistemological ambivalence: should we celebrate the self-referential text, that is, take our pleasure in the fetish that veils an absence, or should we identify rather with Gawain's melancholic lament over 'the lathe and the losse' that the poem has revealed?" (p. 149). This dilemma brings Margherita right back to the plight of the medievalist herself: "Gawain thus becomes a type of the medievalist traumatized by historical difference and lack, who is not altogether certain that the romance text, the green girdle, is sufficient to cover over this originary absence. For that matter, 'theory' itself is often spoken of in our field as a kind of rhetorical dalliance, a fetishistic deferral of the medievalist's linear and epic journey back into the past" (p. 149–50).

This is the place the book brought us to in the first place, and the point to which it constantly returns, even before the summary of the argument attempted in the afterward. As analytical discourse, as sensitive poetic reading, as historical theorizing, and as a glimpse into the historical state of our profession, this book more than merits our attention; it deserves our thorough consideration, our debate with its premises and its conclusions, and, ultimately, our applause.

PAUL THEINER
Syracuse University

CAROL M. MEALE, ed. *Readings in Medieval English Romance*. Cambridge: D. S. Brewer, 1994. Pp. 238. $53.00.

Developed from papers at the 1992 conference on "Romance in Medieval England," the essays here assembled illustrate four important lines of inquiry for romance studies. None of these essays will redirect the field, but many are valuable contributions to the historical positioning, codicology, genre study, and thematic analysis of Middle English romances.

Romance's concerns resonate surprisingly with more overtly historical texts in John Scattergood's "*The Tale of Gamelyn*: The Noble Robber as Provincial Hero." Scattergood's juxtaposition of the much-maligned *Gamelyn* with legal records, letters, sermons, and complaints amply illustrates the work's contemporary engagements and its preservation of a "provincial voice" (p. 160) that is "not so much from the greenwood as from the backwoods, resistant to a centralism it mistrusts" (p. 178). Colin Richmond's "Thomas Malory and the Pastons" finds Malory's cadences and behaviors mirrored in the writing and lives of the Paston circle, and works these into a larger argument about the literary texture of chivalric life—its persistent tendency to dramatize and fictionalize itself. Less convincing in its attempt to find the historical place of romance is Diane Speed's "The Construction of the Nation in Medieval English Romance," which claims a postcolonial identity for *Havelok* by asserting that it (and similar romances) fulfill the functions described by Homi Bhabha, Timothy Brennan, Benedict Anderson, and others for the postcolonial novel. Speed's inspiration is perhaps to resist the dichotomy that modernists tend to assert between postcolonial complexity and a misapprehended medieval simplicity, but her attempt to align romances with novelistic realism and secularism does not serve the cause well. *Havelok* is not much like a novel; indeed, its distinctive premodernity might substantially revise postcolonial theorists' versions of literary history. A more successful attempt to situate romances in their historical moment is Arlyn Diamond's "Unhappy Endings: Failed Love/Failed Faith in Late Romances." Taking the romances to be artifacts of their times, Diamond argues that the genre's shift from twelfth-century "social optimism" to "the pessimism of Chaucer's period" indicates "a loss of faith in the social structures within which such narratives were generated" (pp. 71, 81). The point is not new, but it is eloquently illustrated here.

Two essays investigating audiences are John J. Thompson's "The *Cursor Mundi*, the 'Inglis tong,' and 'Romance'" and Carol Meale's "'gode men / Wiues maydnes and alle men': Romance and Its Audiences." Thompson argues from a range of evidence that the *Cursor Mundi* reaches out to French and Latin readers as well as to English speakers, and answers the Fourth Lateran Council's call for lay education by positioning its stories on a continuum with heroic secular tales. Meale restricts her inquiry into romance's audience to manuscript production, wills, and other historical records. She provides much interesting evidence concerning the circulation of romance texts, while recognizing that such evidence remains subject to interpretation. Given this situation, codicology cannot yet claim priority over other kinds of evidence for determining the audiences of romance.

Three essays on the styles and themes of particular works are the most traditional in the collection. Maldwyn Mills compares diverse manuscript versions of one work in "*Sir Isumbras* and the Styles of the Tail-rhyme Romance." The striking differences among the manuscripts illustrate, Mills argues, significant stylistic choices he characterizes as "terse," "climactic," "confrontational," "repetitive," "clipped," "expansive," and "laconic" (pp. 8–12). An underlying question, in my view, is whether the sensitivity to nuance belongs more to the modern critic than to the medieval editor. One way to test this out might be to look for sustained stylistic tendencies across each manuscript. J. A. Burrow in "The Uses of Incognito: *Ipomadon A*" makes this romance cohere pleasingly by arguing that Ipomadon's disguises and refusals to claim the honor he is due partake of a "curious honorific calculus" in which honor may be accumulated "undiminished, or perhaps one should say unconsumed, by praise" (pp. 30–31). Donna Crawford's "'Gronyng wyth grysly wounde': Injury in Five Middle English Breton Lays" argues that in these lays "the cost of social restoration" (p. 40) is registered in wounded bodies: the rape in *Sir Degarré*, for example, produces the hero at the expense of his mother's victimization. According to Crawford, when such wounding yields such rewards, the lays are striving to make palatable the idea that social order is only achievable through violence.

Three essays on the romance genre rightly insist on its provisional and expansive quality. A. S. G. Edwards gets into some trouble (as I have myself) by attempting to discern the genre's edges. His "Gender, Order and Reconciliation in *Sir Degrevaunt*" argues that *Degrevaunt* is "a fairly unusual contribution even to such a portmanteau form" (p. 54), but the unusual features he cites can be amply illustrated from the genre: conversations between women are important in the romances (French and English) of Tristan, Ywain, and Ipomedon; the domestic sphere of women's courtesy is complementary to the masculine sphere of prowess from *Eneas* through the *Romance of Horn* and the works of Chrétien de Troyes; engagement with contemporary issues, I have argued, characterizes insular romances whether or not they contain marvels; and the "denial of patriarchal authority" (p. 60) when Melidor seeks to marry Degrevant against her father's wishes instantiates the genre's persistent rejection of arranged marriages in favor of consensual ones. Jocelyn Wogan-Browne takes on the easier job of arguing against boundaries rather than for them in "'Bet . . . to . . . rede on holy seyntes lyves . . .': Romance and Hagiography Again." Her study of the legend of St. Clement (in an unpublished Anglo-Norman version) sustains her contention that we should not consider romance and hagiography to be "fixed oppositions" (p. 84); her suggestion that we should "treat romance and hagiography as forms of exemplary biography" (p. 85) is plausible so long as we recognize that the ideologies exemplified in each case are quite different. Thorlac Turville-Petre's "*Havelok* and the History of the Nation" argues that medieval writers thought of Havelok as a figure of history rather than of romance, noting that *Havelok*'s attention to "legal practices and social institutions" (pp. 122–23) and to the nation and nationalism are primary concerns of historical writing. Turville-Petre stops short of attempting to reclassify *Havelok* as a historical text, effectively arguing that romance is sufficiently capacious to encompass historical figures and political concerns.

The high standard of this collection, its impeccable editing, and the range of texts and approaches its contributors consider make *Readings in Medieval English Romance* a welcome addition to romance studies.

SUSAN CRANE
Rutgers University

A. J. MINNIS, ed. *Late-Medieval Religious Texts and Their Transmission: Essays in Honor of A. I. Doyle*. York Manuscripts Conferences: Proceedings Series, vol. 3. Cambridge: D. S. Brewer, 1994. Pp. ix, 198. $63.00.

Ian Doyle has made enormous contributions to the study of Middle English manuscripts, not only through his many publications, but perhaps even more through the advice and information he has given to so many who have consulted him. In acknowledgement of my own debt to him over many years, I am delighted to review this volume written in his honor, in which contributors frequently refer to his generous help. The eleven papers here, first given at a conference in York in 1991, are all of value, and if I concentrate my comments on just a few of them, that is simply a reflection of my own narrower range.

Bella Millett's "*Mouvance* and the Medieval Author," an examination of the issues confronting her as editor of *Ancrene Wisse*, was of particular interest to me. The fluidity of some medieval texts, constantly adapted over a period of time for new circumstances and new audiences, presents problems for the editor who wishes to produce a definitive text. *Ancrene Wisse* was copied over three centuries, primarily as a practical work with a particular function, and therefore it was constantly reshaped to meet new needs. It appears that the author himself took part in this process of textual change, and that the revisions in the Cleopatra and Corpus manuscripts are probably authorial. But even the more extensive revisions in Corpus are far from systematic, sometimes lack coherence, and in any case were not taken into the mainstream textual tradition. To make proper sense of the Corpus version, an edition must relate the state of the text to the overall development of the work; it must, in other words, represent the *mouvance* of the text. Millett considers the practical solutions for the editor of *Ancrene Wisse*, for which transcriptions of nearly all the texts have been printed: to print one version and relegate all variants to a dustbin at the foot of the page misrepresents the textual situation; but electronic hypertext requires more resources than are available. She therefore proposes to exclude later scribal variants and to list only the early variants which are possibly authorial. This is sensible in the short term, but sooner or later I believe an editor of a text of this importance will have to find the resources necessary for a hypertext edition, for that is the only fully acceptable solution.

In "The Outspoken *South English Legendary* Poet," O. S. Pickering points to the routine style of the *South English Legendary*, with its self-contained couplets and its simple vocabulary and syntax, and contrasts a number of passages written in quite a different style. Here the verse is fluid and overflows the boundaries of the couplet; the comments are witty, pungent, ironic, often learned, making use of extraordinary comparisons, such as the man who forgets all about fasting being likened to the bloodhound who loses the scent of game in the pleasant odors of springtime. Pickering identifies this style as that of a reviser who worked throughout the collection, and probably wrote whole lives as well as the *Southern Passion* with its extraordinarily sharp attack on those who defame women. It is good to rescue a buried poet from the rubble of the *South English Legendary*.

John J. Thompson focuses attention on the religious texts in Lincoln Cathedral Library MS 91, one of two manuscripts copied by Robert Thornton, best known for their collections of romances. Thompson looks for clues as to how Thornton assembled these texts, for whom he intended his volumes, and the appeal that some of the shorter pieces in particular might

255

have had for his family. Paying special attention to prose works by Hilton and Rolle, he makes the interesting observation that other collections of metrical romances do not choose to include this religious prose material. He might, though, have emphasized rather more that the inclusion of romances together with religious verse within the same volume is a feature of English collections from the Auchinleck manuscript onwards.

Sue Powell presents a valuable account of the genesis of the *Lay Folks' Catechism* and its later dissemination and adaptations. This work was written by John Gaytrige in about 1357 in order to instruct the laity in the articles of the faith. Powell considers the significance of the differences from the Latin text that precedes it in Archbishop Thoresby's Register, and examines the many later copies and adaptations, including the version printed by Caxton in his *Quattuor Sermones*.

In "Meddling with Makings and Will's Work," Ralph Hanna III takes a close look at *Piers Plowman* B 12.16–28, where Will defends himself from Ymaginatif's rebuke that "þow medlest þee wiþ makynges" instead of saying his psalter. Will replies that "making" (writing poetry) is his solace, and Hanna compares this with the rules for hermits that recommend alternating psalm-reading with manual labor, in order to avoid the grave danger of *vana imaginatio*. He shows that Will's formulation speciously evades the option of manual labor, and puts in its place precisely the indulging of vain imaginings that is the writing of his poem. *Piers Plowman* thus becomes a self-promoting violation of that silence that should characterize one "in habite as an heremite." Hanna announces that this discussion is part of a longer study of the revisions in the C Text, particularly the autobiographical passages.

There is no space here to discuss the other essays in the detail they deserve. Vincent Gillespie considers another aspect of *Piers Plowman*, looking at the special place accorded to the Pater Noster in the devotional life, and the particular significance of Patience's offer of the third petition, *fiat voluntas tua*, to Haukyn. Alan J. Fletcher traces the affiliations of Sidney Sussex, Cambridge, MS 74, noting the variety of Lollard and orthodox material both there and in other manuscripts to which the two main scribes contributed, and raising interesting questions about the supervision of centers that produced Lollard texts. Meanwhile Anne Hudson sorts out the organization of Wycliffe's Latin sermons in Trinity College, Cambridge, MS B.16.2. Jocelyn Wogan-Browne considers the accounts given in vernacular saints' lives, particularly those of St. Margaret, of the way they might be transmitted to their textual communities; while A. S. G.

thing—that somehow the essence of a chair is reflected or contained in the sound of the word 'chair'" (p. 2). But, as Myles points out, realist thinkers as diverse as Socrates, Augustine, Boethius, and Dante saw the relationship between word and thing as conventional. Consequently, Chaucer's examination of the relationship between word and deed in such places as *The General Prologue* to *The Canterbury Tales*, the proem to book 2 of *Troilus and Criseyde*, and the lyric poem "Lak of Stedfastnesse" does not serve to classify him as an antirealist. Moreover, Myles suggests, critics who have placed Chaucer among the nominalists have mistakenly equated nominalism with "post-Saussurian language theory" (p. 14). This assertion leads Myles to a critique of the "major misunderstandings" of ten scholars who have sought to explain Chaucer's poetry in nominalist terms, beginning with Robert Jordan's *Chaucer's Poetics and the Modern Reader* (Berkeley: University of California Press, 1987) and including Russell Peck's influential article, "Chaucer and the Nominalist Questions" (*Speculum* 53 [1978]: 745–60), as well as studies by John Gardner, P. B. Taylor, and Rodney Delasanta.

While Myles is concerned with all aspects of Chaucer's realism, he pays particular attention to the ethical dimension of the poet's philosophical allegiances. For Chaucer, as for most thinkers of the Middle Ages, "the will is the ethical center of the speech act" (p. 27). In support of his portrait of Chaucer as an ethical realist, Myles provides an extended survey of medieval and modern theories of intentionality. Here, Myles finds a high degree of consistency between medieval thinkers, such as Boethius and Duns Scotus, and modern ones, such as Paul Ricoeur and John Searle, in seeing linguistic utterances as intentional mental acts. It is against this extended tradition of thinking about intentionality that Myles places Chaucer's frequent probing of the "entente" and "entencioun" of his characters; like both ancient and modern thinkers, Chaucer is interested in "how the intending subject relates to the world, and how the world relates to the intending subject" (pp. 40–41). This interest, Myles asserts, accounts for the peculiar psychological depth and verisimilitude of Chaucer's characters.

Myles further relates Chaucer's theory of intentionality to a "Judeo-Christian semiological metaphysics" in which the world can be understood as the tangible manifestation of God's intentions. This metaphysical realism implies an epistemological realism as well, for such a world is knowable in some degree (p. 55). Language is an important and pervasive metaphor in this realist tradition. God's expression of His intentions through His acts of creation and through the scripture serves as a paradigm for man's expression of his will through the spoken and written word. In this sense, language serves as the vehicle for attaining knowledge and understanding in both the divine and the human realms.

This is not to say, however, that the three-way relationship between the intentions of the subject, the words that express those intentions, and the objects toward which the words are directed is unproblematic. In fact, Chaucer is frequently concerned with abuses of language, in which words do not match either intentions or things. For this reason, Myles devotes the final two chapters of his study to *The Friar's Tale*, which conveys in a particularly pointed way the potential disparities between intentions, words, and deeds. Myles observes that "throughout the *Friar's Tale*, attention is called again and again to the semantic process itself" (p. 95). This attention to semantics is especially evident in the double meaning of many of the Summoner's utterances, which include such theologically weighted words as "rentes," "maisters," "profit," and "fruyt." The Summoner's devious construction of these words exposes his "entente" and ultimately serves to align him with the devil. Moreover, the Summoner's willingness to disregard the intentions of the carter, who wishes for the devil to carry off his recalcitrant horse, shows that he is even less scrupulous than the devil. For the devil, at least, waits for intentions to match words before carrying the Summoner off to hell. Thus, in Myles's reading, *The Friar's Tale* affirms Chaucer's realism in its ethical, metaphysical, and epistemological dimensions by unmasking the work of a fraud who would pervert the natural relationship between intention, word, and deed.

Chaucerian Realism joins the ranks of only a handful of sustained, book-length studies of the philosophical implications of Chaucer's poetry, and for this reason it represents an important contribution to the field. In particular, Myles's careful scholarship and his attempt to provide a historical context for Chaucer's discourse on language and intention should exercise a healthy influence on subsequent studies in this area. The one area where *Chaucerian Realism* falls short, however, is in fulfilling the lofty ambitions of its title. If, as the title suggests, realism is central to Chaucer's art and to his representation of psychologically complex characters, one would expect its influence to be felt well beyond *The Friar's Tale*. Yet Myles offers only passing comments on characters who seem to cry out for careful examination under the light of his thesis, including Criseyde, Troilus, Griselda, Dorigen, and the narrator of *The Canterbury Tales*. Myles's hurried conclusion, just over two pages in length, cuts off discussion at its most interesting point and thereby calls attention to the unnecessarily restricted scope of his study. In the end, then, one can only hope that Myles will extend the valuable insights of his thesis into other areas of Chaucer's poetry in subsequent studies.

WILLIAM WATTS
Butler University

BARBARA NEWMAN. *From Virile Woman to WomanChrist: Studies in Medieval Religion and Literature*. Middle Ages Series. Philadelphia: University of Pennsylvania Press, 1995. Pp. vi, 355. $39.95 cloth, $18.95 paper.

In a field all but nonexistent twenty years ago but already becoming crowded with competition, Barbara Newman has written the most wide-ranging and thoroughly researched study to date of women's religious literature of the Middle Ages. Ranging across time (formally 1100–1500, but in fact drawing on material from late antiquity forward), regional and linguistic borders (particularly German, French, Italian, and English, in addition to Latin), and genres (especially spiritual treatises and hagiography, but also romance and courtly literature), Newman provides enough examples to sink an armada of skeptics who would dismiss medieval female piety as somehow unrepresentative of high medieval culture. The range of examples is itself dazzling, and students of religious and feminist history will treasure this book not least for its extensive bibliography and appendices (the first a catalogue of spiritual treatises, the second a glossary of religious women, both fully annotated). But to prodigious learning and careful scholarship Newman adds other potent critical weapons: acute analytical powers, a willingness to make well-supported judgments, and best of all a writer's gift for being both clear and engaging because she herself is so thoroughly engaged with her subject. In short, *From Virile Woman to WomanChrist* is not only good scholarship but a good read.

The terms of her title refer to seemingly opposed feminine spiritual ideals: the virile woman or *virago*, who through chastity escapes the weakness of her sex to become an "honorary male," and the womanChrist, Newman's term for the millennial goddess figure whose revolutionary power attests to female superiority. While the "from . . . to" form of the title may imply some theory of linear progress, in fact the two opposing ideals often appear simultaneously, thus requiring more carefully articulated explanations, which Newman's meticulous readings provide. What the title should suggest is the remarkable variety of female responses to the Christian calling played out against the "overwhelmingly masculine face" of the medieval Catholic church. Indeed, what is most stimulating about Newman's work is its insistence on a richly diverse "range of female voices" in the Middle Ages: "No universal discourse, no programmatic *écriture féminine* can encompass the commanding speech of Birgitta and Catherine of Siena, the subtle tones of Hadewijch and Julian, the impassioned cries of Angela and Mechthild, the fiery tongue of Na Prous Boneta. But each voice, whether strident or meek, struggled mightily to rise above the background noise of 'the fathers' clamoring for silence" (p. 245).

The first two chapters focus in different ways on that "background noise." "Flaws in the Golden Bowl: Gender and Spiritual Formation in the Twelfth-Century," examines forty-five spiritual treatises on the religious life, works Newman classifies as "literature of formation," especially gender formation. Looking beyond the "casual misogyny" and "ritual praise of women" that litters these texts, Newman compares works addressed to a female versus male audience, observing that those addressed to women focus on preventive measures against the loss of virginity. Since female virginity is "not a state to be achieved but a condition to be preserved," treatises designed for nuns lack the dynamism apparent in those composed for monks, which typically emphasize the common life, ardent monastic friendships, and the active quest for spiritual growth. Chapter 2, "Authority, Authenticity, and the Repression of Heloise," a detailed refutation of the various attacks on the authenticity of Heloise's letters, though skillful, may prove a bit tedious for some readers (but then the attacks themselves are tedious, as Newman shows, since they are often based on *a priori* notions of gender as narrow as those of medieval misogynists); but her treatment of the reception of Heloise by medieval and Renaissance writers is a useful reminder that for Chaucer and Jean de Meun, Heloise was a fully authorized scholar, an *auctor* in her own right, albeit an antifeminist one, which may be why Christine de Pizan, who had every reason to know Heloise's letters, omits her from the City of Ladies.

The heart of the volume contains its three most dazzling chapters, beginning with "'Crueel Corage': Child Sacrifice and the Maternal Martyr in Hagiography and Romance," a stunning exploration of the "tragically alienating experience of motherhood." Those tempted to sentimentalize medieval maternity by insisting, for example, that Chaucer portrays Griselda as a bad mother for sacrificing her children must perforce think twice about medieval family values in light of Newman's study of the maternal martyr who sacrifices her children for what the culture dictates is a higher good. Newman traces the shift from child sacrifice as a "paternal project carried out against a mother's protests," as in some versions of the Abraham-Isaac story, to a new form of "equal opportunity heroism" in which mothers rise to the challenge of abandoning their children in response to a divine calling or command. The extraordinary range of Newman's examples demonstrates the attraction and versatility of the ideal of the maternal martyr, urging us to view Griselda and other well-known representatives of the type in the light of numerous less-known figures, ranging from Sarah, Clytemnestra, and Perpetua to the host of medieval widows and fugitive wives for whom love of their children represents "a powerful but essentially selfish emotion" to be resisted. Newman relates medieval maternal feeling (or lack of it) to social practices such as wet-nursing, oblation, and fosterage, which worked against mother-child bonding, and religious ideals that encouraged a displacement of mother-love from biological family to others—whether the divine family or social outcasts in the local community. Painful though some of this material may be to modern sensibilities, Newman's respect for difference encourages the same in her audience.

Chapter 4, "On the Threshold of the Dead: Purgatory, Hell, and Religious Women," explores the role of "purgatorial piety" in the religious practice and literature of medieval women. Serving as intercessors for the dead brought prestige and power to religious women otherwise barred as agents from the most common systems of spiritual exchange, such as celebrating mass or fighting in crusades. Newman views purgatory as a "condition of suffering," showing how and why religious women, trading on the currency of their own pain and abjection, could become co-redemptors with Christ in the divine economy. She also traces in some female visionary writing a recurrent strain of anxiety and doubt concerning the need for damnation and the very existence of hell. Encouraged by their own capacity to suffer and their absolute confidence in a loving God, some visionaries, of whom Julian of Norwich is only the most well known, struggled mightily to circumvent if not challenge divine justice.

Chapter 5, "*La mystique courtoise*: Thirteenth-Century Beguines and the Art of Love," focuses on the mystical works of Hadewijch, Mechthild, Marguerite Porete, and the French author of the relatively unknown guide to the beguinal life, *Règle des Fins Amans* (ca. 1300). Both the rule's title and Newman's term "mystique courtoise" point to what she argues is the distinguishing feature of this literature, namely a dialectical joining of the "two great systems of medieval desire," the religious bridal mysticism as developed by Bernard of Clairvaux with the secular, troubadour topoi of *fine amour*. Purposely fusing the two loves that Robertsonian exegetes believe to have been strictly separated, the great beguine writers construct a dynamic mystical love affair in which rapture and abjection, subject and object, and feminine and masculine roles shift constantly "in an endless to and fro of loving." Mystical experience is by definition indescribable, but these "artists of desire" never stop trying, providing as they go a rich study of gender and sexuality.

The final two essays in the collection are more narrow in their focus and perhaps in their appeal. "WomanSpirit, WomanPope" treats the "thoroughly aberrant" thirteenth-century Guglielmites and later millennial figures who worshipped certain holy women as the Holy Spirit incarnate and awaited their return to establish a female papacy. Equally odd, and impenetrable besides, is the Renaissance treatise studied in the final chapter, Cornelius Agrippa's "On the Nobility and Superiority of the Female Sex." Though surprisingly popular in its own day, readers will have to decide for themselves whether this odd blend of occult theology and evangelical humanism serves "Renaissance feminism," as Newman argues, or the self-fashioning of a literary parlor game.

The emphasis in these final chapters on claims to female superiority suggests a teleological argument never quite explicit but occasionally breaking through, especially in the order of chapters and the title itself. Newman's meticulous readings of religious texts and practices are persuasive precisely because they resist any simple master narrative of linear progression. Furthermore, the material of the final chapters is by Newman's own account bizarre and unrepresentative, and it hardly contributes to what Newman describes at least once as "a progress from 'virile woman to womanChrist'" (p. 17). A book that otherwise succeeds so well in giving the lie to simple systems of binary classification should not succumb, even in its final moments, to the old temptation. Yet the excitement of following the turns of these magnificent essays more than offsets this slip.

LINDA GEORGIANNA
University of California, Irvine

ANN ELJENHOLM NICHOLS. *Seeable Signs: The Iconography of the Seven Sacraments, 1350–1544*. Woodbridge, Suffolk: Boydell Press, 1994. Pp. xvii, 412. $89.00.

While many recent books seem to have been ripped untimely from doctoral dissertations, this one is unquestionably a product of a much longer gestation. The conviction and the confidence that inform the argument of this book are the result of many years of exploration and thought, and the argument is all the more persuasively presented as a result. It comes along at an appropriate moment, when the study of devotionalism and spirituality in late medieval England is a growth industry, and larger works such as Eamon Duffy's *The Stripping of the Altars* are building successfully upon the foundations laid by many shorter studies in the past decade or so. Unlike Duffy's work, however, this one chooses a very limited corpus of materials—39 East Anglian baptismal fonts (and a handful from elsewhere) on which are portrayed the seven sacraments.

The book begins with an 89-page inventory of seven-sacrament art on the continent and in Britain, in which the author tersely describes and dates, at least tentatively, all the examples. While the sinewy prose is not boring, the piling-on of information does make the inventory a somewhat daunting reading experience and, as in my case, can lead to several false starts for the faint of heart. In the second chapter, "Dead Signs: The Lollard Challenge," the argument begins, and the pace accelerates and never falters. The essence of the argument is that the iconographical display of the sacraments on the baptismal fonts represents concise and pointed theological arguments for the validity of the sacraments so as to refute Lollard contentions that they were of "no value in the form used by the church."

The argument continues, relentlessly, through a two-part chapter on (1) literary treatments of the sacraments and (2) the theology of the fonts. Here Nichols argues forcefully that the manuscript and iconographic sources are primarily Carmelite, specifically the second volume (*De Sacramentis*) of Thomas Netter's response to Wyclif, *Doctrinale Fidei Catholicae*. A fourth and final chapter describes, in exhaustive detail, the iconography of each sacrament still extant on each of the fonts (and relevant stained glass), insofar as possible fitting each into the context of her main argument. Throughout these chapters Nichols contrasts continental and insular iconography to make her point that while art prevails in the continental works, theology prevails in the insular works. The book contains a postscript in two parts, the first on collateral dating of the fonts, the other on the persons responsible for creating the images they contain (dismissing former and facile theories on this subject). An appendix describes, explores, and explains the eight subjects found on the octagonal fonts. The book ends, finally, with a "Font Gazeteer"—"designed for more or less independent use"—which provides the locations and descriptions of fonts that are extant, including their present condition, and those that are now lost. (In this Gazeteer is a glossary that ought to be at the beginning of the book!)

What Nichols calls "the Lollard/Carmelite connection" is, as she admits, only "an attractive paradigm to explain the earliest fonts, to hypothesize that the specific link between donor and artisan was a reverend master of theology who knew the 'truth' of the sacraments, and if not a Carmelite himself, at least knew the 'order' of Netter's illustrated work" (p. 128). This and the larger argument, that the fonts are a response to East Anglian Lollardy, are beyond proof. About that Nichols is admirably forthright. Nevertheless, she argues with conviction, and she deploys the available evidence with great skill. If one leaves the book not entirely convinced by Nichols's speculations, one at least feels that they have a solid basis and that there is a substantial likelihood they might be true.

The extensive range of sources used in the argument—literature, art (especially in manuscripts), and historical documents—is quite remarkable, all the more so because Nichols uses them so adeptly. The two-line autobiography on the dust jacket tells us that Nichols is a professor of English, leading to the expectation that she will be most comfortable with literary sources. While that is the case, her handling of other source materials is hardly less assured and comfortable. Luckily for her, Nichols has had (apparently) free access to the unpublished study of later English Gothic manuscripts by Kathleen Scott, and she appropriately defers (as we all do) to the commanding knowledge of the field that Scott generously shares, while we await the publication of her major study.

Accompanying the text are 97 plates, all in black-and-white; the varying quality is surely a result of difficult conditions for photography *in situ*, though in some cases one does wonder whether better use of artificial lighting might not have produced sharper results. While the lack of color may cause some to groan, the fact that so many of the subjects are sculptural makes it a matter of less concern. Also, given the terms of the argument, that lack—even in the manuscript illuminations, windows, and paintings—is less serious than one might expect. (Plate 27 of a wing of the Roger van der Weyden altarpiece at the Koninklijk Museum voor Schoone Kunsten, Antwerp, is in some ways more informative than the color postcard I purchased there on a recent visit.)

This is a book that should be read, for its substance and for its methodology, by students working in all related areas. Surely, both its content and its handling of source materials will prove of value for all who wish to proceed with the difficult and intriguing task of exploring the spiritual needs, exercises, understandings, obligations, and satisfactions of the faithful in that fascinating period before and after the Reformation, before and

265

after the introduction of the printing press into England. For that, as well as for an exceedingly skillful presentation of a very controversial argument, we owe Ann Nichols a great debt of gratitude.

GEORGE R. KEISER
Kansas State University

JAMES J. PAXSON. *The Poetics of Personification*. Literature, Culture, Theory Series. Cambridge: Cambridge University Press, 1994. Pp. xii, 210. $49.95.

This book is more ambitiously theorized than its title might initially suggest. Writing explicitly in the tradition of Paul de Man's *Allegories of Reading*, and making considerable use of the narratologies of Gérard Genette and Paul Ricoeur, Paxson applies poststructuralist hermeneutics and phenomenology to the allegorical practices of canonical texts that (with the exception of Spenser's *Faerie Queene*) have more usually attracted traditional literary historical approaches. His project takes as its special focus the moments when the discursive operations of personification within allegorical narrative serve less to "clarify meaning and reduce uncertainty than to complicate meanings and raise uncertainty" (p. 165).

After a preliminary and wide-ranging survey of the history of personification theory from Cicero and Quintilian to the present day, Paxson proceeds to construct his own taxonomy of personification and its associated tropes. Examining in detail the question of what, in the various manifestations of personification, gets translated into whom, he is less interested in the deployment of "local rhetorical ornament" than in the specifically prosopoetic transformations that "give face"—and, even more important, voice—to an abstraction or inanimate object, producing a figural character which may subsequently be projected into, or engender, an allegorical narrative (pp. 39–42). Paxson's succeeding chapters offer sophisticated analyses of Prudentius's *Psychomachia*, Chaucer's *House of Fame* and *Parliament of Fowls*, *Piers Plowman*, and *The Faerie Queene*. Laying particular emphasis on the relationship between the prosopoetic process and the narrative unfolding of allegory, he outlines the various ways in which figures of personification may be understood as "textual encodings of phenomenal illusion" (p. 113).

Although his primary interest lies in the workings of personification in pre-seventeenth-century allegorical narratives, it is a twentieth-century model of allegory that determines Paxson's readings. His analyses are based on de Man's notion that literary texts tend to generate figurations of their own textuality—"allegories" of the self-referentiality of language that emphasize the limits of its ability to redescribe an external, material reality. He is consequently most interested in those textual moments when the narrative invention of a personification character puts into question the control of a work's internal narrative voice over the version of reality that the text strives to make present. Paxson's reading of the *Psychomachia*, for example, emphasizes Prudentius's disruption of his work's own internal decorum: having segregated his personifications from his representations of human figures, the author's unexpected introduction of the silent human figure of Job alongside the personified and voluble virtue of Patience results in his text's sly deconstruction of the "medieval ontology of created beings" (p. 81). Discussing *Piers Plowman*, Paxson suggests that the regular slippage of Will's narrative between different diegetic levels (as Will dreams and wakes, or dreams within his dreams) puts into question the transcendent significance of any of its personifications. This "self-undoing" tendency is reinforced by the way in which the poem draws attention to its own devices: the personification *Anima*, having told Will that it can also be called *Mens* or *Memoria* or *Racio*, becomes the signified for many other signifiers—as "personification personified," its appearance in the narrative offers a suggestively nominalist interrogation of the work's proliferating personifications (pp. 136–38).

Paxson takes a look at other metanarratives of personification in his reading of *The Faerie Queene*, claiming that "the governing poetic code for Spenserian personification is the narrativization of the trope as it comes into or goes out of existence" (p. 139). For example, Spenser's narration of the disrobing of Duessa foregrounds the "making and unmaking of the personification figure's semiotic constitution" (p. 152); alternatively, in the beheading of Errour, the narration "undoes" what was "never 'factual' or material in the first place" (p. 154). Given the cumulative thrust of his close readings, Paxson's observation that "literary personification is a code-specific *langue* that cannot impel, at the point of specific textual instantiation, the narrative of its own making without the narrative of its own unmaking" (p. 165) is fairly predictable, as is his insistence that, since moments of "metapersonification" imply a self-reflexive, self-conscious text offering its own "simulacrum of human consciousness," the totality of the allegorical narrative may itself be considered a "personification figure" (p. 164).

Paxson's alignment of the prosopoetic practice of canonical medieval and early modern allegories with de Man's suggestion that prosopopoeia is the "master-trope of poetic discourse" can seem programmatic as he discovers in these texts the workings of "the kind of genuine [sic] allegory described in current literary theory" (p. 5). It should be emphasized, however, that his study also digresses interestingly from its own master-narrative to offer suggestive insights into other aspects of the workings of personification. In discussing earlier writings on the trope, Paxson addresses the implications of Quintilian's claim that it portrays "the emotions of children, women, nations, and even of voiceless things," noting that, in giving human face and voice to Otherness, personification is informed by a culturally specific predetermination of what constitutes "humanity" (pp. 49–50). This observation might have become the starting point for a more historicized analysis of "what gets transformed into whom" than the book ultimately delivers. To his credit, Paxson concedes the ahistoricizing tendencies of his poetics in his final chapter, which contains a short, provocative meditation on some of the questions one might ask about the cultural contexts from which the texts that make extensive use of personification arise. His final pages also briefly confront the possibility that there may be something highly revealing in the desire of twentieth-century critics (like himself) to champion prosopopoeia as a kind of supertrope, conferring upon it "the power to call into question *all* mimetic creation" (p. 166).

Although Paxson's close readings of particular allegorical texts are always interesting, and although he lays out his main thesis with some subtlety, this book does have its *longeurs*. The fine distinctions between different categories of personification figures explored so carefully in his second chapter do not consistently inform Paxson's later discussions of individual works, and the algebraic formulae with which he describes the various manifestations of personification in relation to a narrative domain are pretty impenetrable. The reader may regret in particular that the less productive amplifications of Paxson's descriptive poetics leave him no room to elaborate upon his own most interesting ideas.

CLARE R. KINNEY
University of Virginia

SANDRA PIERSON PRIOR. *The Pearl Poet Revisited*. Twayne's English Authors Series, vol. 512. New York: Twayne Publishers, 1994. Pp. xi, 161. $23.95.

Instructors of fourteenth-century English poetry have long been in need of a handbook that introduces students, specifically undergraduates, to the language, versification, literary environment, and cultural background of the *Pearl*-poet. The publication of Sandra Pierson Prior's *The Pearl Poet Revisited* meets this need admirably. The first-time reader, for whom this book is intended, will benefit most from the attention given in each chapter to basic details and anticipated needs, but discussion of the individual poems is scholarly and comprehensive enough to reward advanced readers and specialists as well.

As one would expect, a number of useful aids are conveniently laid out for the student. The front of the book contains a chronology of important dates beginning in the early fourth century with Eusebius's *The History of the Church* and concluding in 1864 with Richard Morris's publication of *Early English Alliterative Poems*. At the back appears a select but descriptive bibliography that encompasses editions and translations; bibliography and reference; background in language, literature, and history (the least satisfactory or complete set of entries); and a section on critical studies, ranging from general studies to critical works on the individual poems. While by no means exhaustive, the critical bibliography is adequate for the audience intended.

For many readers the first chapter, entitled "The Pearl Poet and His Time and Place," will prove the most valuable and most frequently cited. In addition to supplying general information pertaining to the poet and the fourteenth-century literary scene, Prior makes pointed remarks about the poet's dialect, about the life of the manuscript, and about the illustrations that accompany it. Inasmuch as she believes emphatically in the centrality of versification to the efficacy of this poet's art, she devotes considerable time and space to a discussion of his linguistic skill and the power of his verse to generate realism and a sense of action. Her attention to this aspect of his verse is instructive and clearly articulated; unfortunately, there are no concrete examples cited or analyzed at this juncture to illustrate exactly how this poet creates vivid effects, nor is the reader referred to specific passages that would apply.

With the *Pearl*-poet, of course, the student is deprived of biographical information pertaining both to his social class and his education or to any certain means of mapping his poetic development. Prior addresses this problem by adducing evidence to support composition of the poems in the late fourteenth century. Her discussion touches on the social, political, economic, and theological conditions of the period, the extent to which cultural issues are reflected in these poems, and the important difference that existed at this time between the court culture and the middle class or mercantile one. Based on the forms of the poems, their language, and their level of learning, Prior concludes that the audience for these poems had to be a court one. In this and in the succeeding chapters, Prior is generous and balanced in her notes, indicating areas of dispute among scholars and apprising readers of responsible opposing views. To the credit of the book, Prior does not hesitate to identify or advance her own views, however controversial. She insists, for instance, that the *Pearl*-poet stands apart from most social and political issues of his time and place even though he wrote in a language that drew upon three older traditions (Anglo-Saxon, Celtic, and Continental) and during a milieu that witnessed the beginnings of an urban culture, an anglicized ruling class, and an English political identity. This flies in the face of recent approaches to the poet and to late medieval poetry in general and allies itself with Muscatine's assessment of the poet in his *Poetry and Crisis in the Age of Chaucer*, a view which has been challenged of late, especially in discussions of *SGGK*. In her chapter on *SGGK*, Prior confronts these new approaches head on. She questions the legitimacy of much recent feminist, cultural, and New Historicist criticism on the grounds that these approaches impose the same violence on the integrity of the text as Robertsonianism does. These approaches, she says, also allegorize the poem, "but not to find its religious message; instead they extract morals about oppression and analyze the relations between women and men, rulers and ruled, and rich and poor" (p. 93). It is not that *SGGK* is unconcerned with the various relationships in a court but that the critics of these schools resort to what she terms "a reductive moralizing tendency that lacks even the historical authenticity of the Robertsonian approach" (p. 93). For many, myself included, this view may prove too dismissive and insensitive to the kinds of valuable questions and insights these critical approaches pose.

For each poem, Prior wisely chooses to offer her own reading rather than a conflation of critical views. This strategy gives each chapter a greater coherence and allows the student to follow one approach in its entirety. Her familiarity with and knowledge of each poem is evident in the excellent plot summary contained in each chapter and in the development she provides of major themes. In her analysis of each poem we get the kind of close reading of vital passages that students will find illuminating and thought-provoking. With respect to *Cleanness*, for example, she shows us that the poem is less about sexual purity and more about the nearly hopeless relationship between a terrifying, angry creator and his repulsively wicked creatures. She develops the relationship between God's anger and human nature and behavior throughout, culminating in a penetrating account of the Incarnation sequence. In the chapter on *Patience*, she suggests that the lesson for Jonah and the poet's audience is to stop concentrating on the distant apocalypse and instead bring God's kingdom into the present. This well may state the central concern of the poet in all of his poems and, if so, he may be understood as more committed to social, political, and religious controversies in the fourteenth century than this book and several other studies allow.

For me, the most sustained and impressive chapter is the one on *Pearl*. Prior begins by showing how *Pearl* is both typical of a dream vision and untypical (it is not a personification allegory). Then she focuses on the points of controversy between the Maiden and the dreamer without burdening students with a technical analysis of the theological and philosophical issues involved. Consistent with her overall thesis, emphasis falls on the versification and language peculiar to each speaker because so much of what happens, she says, depends upon the poet's craft. Most readers will appreciate her extensive handling of the central symbol of the pearl but some may quarrel with her assessment of the dreamer. At the outset she closes the gap between the poet/narrator who crafts the poem and relates the dream and the dreamer who dreams it by separating them only by time and perspective. After implying a definite growth in the dreamer's understanding and insight, however, she denies that he progresses from his earthbound self to any significant self-enlightenment. We do not see him change his heart or his thinking, she says. If one leaves the dreamer too benighted, however, it not only undervalues the concerns and serious questions of the dreamer, but also may reopen the gap between the poet/narrator and the dreamer that the journey of the poem seeks to narrow.

Interpretive differences aside, *The Pearl Poet Revisited* is a well-written and reliable introduction to the poems and I will not hesitate to recommend it to my students.

JIM RHODES
Southern Connecticut State University

WILLIAM A. QUINN. *Chaucer's "Rehersynges": The Performability of* The Legend of Good Women. Washington, D.C.: Catholic University of America Press, 1994. Pp. x, 253. $55.95.

Chaucer's "Rehersynges" assumes that Chaucer performed *The Legend of Good Women* for a court audience and makes its object the recovery (insofar as that is possible) of that performance. To this end, Quinn distinguishes between texts as objects to be read and as scripts to be performed. While Chaucer made a comparable distinction—witness his prayer that none "myswrite" the *Troilus* or "mysmetre [it] for defaute of tonge" and that it be understood wherever it is read "or elles songe"—his formulation of it does not imply, at least not in the lines cited, that hearing produces a different understanding from reading. In contrast, Quinn assumes that written texts are inherently more indeterminate than oral utterances. Since he views public readings as dramatizations of a script, he treats a performance as an intentional interpretation that diminishes indeterminacy. Authorial performances produce authoritative interpretations; they, not texts, are the proper object of scholarly inquiry.

One need not appeal to Derrida to doubt the oral necessarily less indeterminate than the written, for just as a performance could settle the question, say, of whether or not the praise of good women in *The Legend of Good Women* is intended to be earnest or ironic, so a performance could so change its registers, so vary its voice, as to guarantee indeterminacy. Still, the burden of proof falls on those who suppose indeterminacy the goal of a script or a text, given that auditors and readers must and quite unconsciously do presuppose that statements make sense in order to decode them. Unfortunately, this linguistic fact does not permit the conclusion that a Chaucerian performance would have clearly expressed what he meant, for the disparities in social status and political power between Chaucer and his court audience must have insured, at least upon occasion, a need either to obscure or to defuse some of the implications of his text (as in Alceste's lectures on proper kingship). As Donald Howard (among others) pointed out, in all probability this need is one of the sources of Chaucer's self-disparaging persona in his texts (scripts), texts that always exceed their demeanor.

Quinn supposes that Chaucer created some of his works primarily as scripts for performing; others, as texts for readers. Chaucer's court poetry belongs in the former category; the Tales of Canterbury, in the latter. (Quinn even ventures, in passing, the hypothesis—shades of the rhyme-royal *Knight's Tale*—that there were two versions of the *Troilus*, an original script for performance and a rewritten text for reading.) Surely, Quinn is right to judge Chaucer's first-person narratives, those dream visions we traditionally suppose Chaucer read at court, generally his most scriptlike. Still, one hesitates to assume oral performance merely from its ostensible marks—most notably, a first-person narrator and direct address to an audience—since they are often aped by texts written solely for armchair consumption. Chaucer's most pronounced mimicry of these marks is found in *The Tale of Sir Thopas*, a parody of the minstrel's art intended, you will no doubt agree, for a readerly book. There is, of course, no denying that Chaucer's court audience must have influenced his rhetoric, but to what end? Just as the *Prologue* to *The Tale of Melibee* raises the possibility that the distinction between oral and written narratives was for Chaucer one without a difference—within three lines it refers to telling and writing the tale—so it insists on distinguishing the significance of a text from its rhetoric. Where a gap is assumed between sense and significance, not every variation in the letter's performance will be supposed to vary the "sentence." At the same time, we ought not to imprison ourselves in Chaucer's idealizations by concluding that his texts/scripts can only have the significance his theory and intention assign them.

The immediate difficulty for twentieth-century readers with settling issues of interpretation by appealing to Chaucer's performative voice is that it is now audible only at the House of Fame. Quinn's solution—he is aware of its circularity—is to use textual moments that have a pronounced tone to determine Chaucer's performative voice and that voice to determine in turn the tone of the text's less distinct moments. Not unlike a New Critical textual reading, this procedure relies upon the supposition that the performance is all of a piece. Those moments in the text that seem to Quinn so tonally distinct as to be definitive are invariably comic passages, passages where in Quinn's judgment Chaucer could not have meant what he says without being fatuous. The difficulty with determining the dominant tenor of a performance from its wit is that speakers are frequently prepared to momentarily disrupt even high seriousness with comedy. It is possible, to say the least, that the jokes adjacent to the pathos in the *Legend* may have been intended more as comic relief than as signs that the pathos is mock. Still, the possibility that Quinn is championing—that Chaucer performed the poem strictly for laughs—must be entertained.

Less easily entertained is the broad tenor of the comedy Quinn assigns to Chaucer's performance, for it ignores altogether what we believe we know

273

(not without reason) about the likely character of the other determinant of that performance, its audience. Thus, Quinn imagines that when Chaucer addresses the daisy in the second person, declaring her the light of his life, he would have gestured, as with a wink, to the lady in question and that she, embarrassed but charmed, would have blushed. So much for any supposition that the preoccupation in the *Troilus* with Criseyde's reputation reflects fourteenth-century values. Why did more than one great lady declare after John of Gaunt made an honest woman of Katherine Swynford that she would never darken her door? Surely, it was not just an issue of class. We are to believe (with Quinn, assisted by Sheila Delany) that when Chaucer described the battle of Actium, with the trumpets going up, the grapple hooks going in, the guns going out, he did so with a bump and grind that pronounced this language sexual innuendo. One must (stuffily) protest: Richard's court was not the modern academy. Was Christine de Pizan just pretending to be offended by Reason's talk of "coilles" and "viz" in the poem Chaucer is being indicted for having translated? Why did Chaucer apologize so anxiously for his fabliaux if his romances were already a churl's "harlotrie"?

There is of course profit in deconstructing the fabliau-romance binary, to find not only that the former were written for the same social class (the same audience or the same occasion) as the latter, but also that the latter were always already fabliaux. But this must remain a deconstruction based in the indeterminacy of language, not a denial that there was a court culture, that it saw itself as refined and sophisticated, that it pictured itself in the Wilton Diptych and the frontispiece to Corpus Christi College MS 61, fr. Surely, Chaucer assigned his fabliaux to churls in part because sophisticated aristocrats will put up with vulgarity from churls that they won't accept from courtier-poets, precisely because such vulgarity confirms distinctions in culture and class. Ultimately, the difficulty with Quinn's reading of Chaucer's performance of the *Legend* is that it removes all complexity from the poem by denying the conflict in values between Chaucer and his court audience that was both the poem's occasion and its preoccupation.

To my mind, the dimension of Quinn's argument that most compels rethinking the *Legend* (as one who has written on the *Legend* I am myself burdened with preconceptions) is his use of the script-text distinction to explain the differences in the two *Prologues*: he judges G a revision intended to turn script into text. He correctly notes in G not only a decrease in first-person utterance and in direct address but also a transformation of the two into the "impersonality" of the third person, as when F's "ye lovers that kan make of sentement" becomes G's folk who have reaped the corn of making. This proposition hardly is the simple and sufficient explanation, the Occam's razor, he would like it to be. It does nothing, for instance, to explain the presence in F, the absence in G, of the "ye of day" etymology and the god of Love's sun-crown. What is necessary is a double-edged razor: we need to suppose a significant change in audience accompanied the change in presentational mode Quinn has theorized. If we assume that F was a script (or script-like text: "yive it the quene") sensitively designed for presentation to a particular audience, a court invested in the ideology of love, and G a text designed for an audience either less committed to or less able to enforce that ideology, we do perhaps approach a sufficient explanation.

Finally, whatever one may think of the particular performative interpretation of the *Legend* Quinn proposes, the challenge to which *Chaucer's "Rehersynges"* contributes, that of rethinking Chaucer's relation to the oral and written, is welcome and invigorating.

DONALD W. ROWE
University of Wisconsin, Madison

ELIZABETH L. RAMBO. *Colonial Ireland in Medieval English Literature.* Selinsgrove, Penn.: Susquehanna University Press; London and Toronto: Associated University Presses, 1994. Pp. 166. $32.50.

This compact study surveys references to Ireland and the Irish in Middle English texts and asks how far they reflected and influenced English attitudes, from 1166, when Diarmait Mac Murchada sought the assistance of Henry II in his territorial quarrels, to the end of the fifteenth century. During this period England began to establish her claim to rule Ireland, and Middle English evidence is chosen as likely to indicate something of the attitudes of the laity, not just of the clerical elite. This is the first extended study of this particular topic, and is of considerable interest for the way it shows that a variety of views of Ireland were current before harsher colonial attitudes set in from the sixteenth century. The surviving Middle English evidence, though not large, is scattered; it has been marshalled usefully, and Rambo does not press points beyond what the evidence will bear.

The introduction includes a sketch of the historical background to English-Irish relations in the period, relying heavily on volume 2 of *A New History of Ireland* and principally on Otway-Ruthven's *A History of Medieval Ireland*, 2nd ed. (1967), as "the most concise and coherent source" (p. 126 n. 21). Ireland was convenient as a source of new feudal territories, revenue and troops, and a base for launching rebellions against the crown. Heavier settlement was to come later. Four subsequent chapters divide the evidence into chronicles and historical poems, romances, saints' lives, and visions of the otherworld and other religious and didactic writings. Hiberno-English writings are largely ignored on the assumption that the attitudes of English (initially Anglo-Norman) residents in Ireland are likely to be different from those of residents in England, "more informed, perhaps, if often less sympathetic" (p. 16).

England's claim to the right to rule Ireland was given spurious chronicle support in the stories of the British king Gurguint permitting Spanish exiles to settle in Ireland and of Arthur's victory over the Irish King Gillomar (Geoffrey of Monmouth onwards). The Irish are portrayed as "'wild,' and 'barbarous,' treacherous, cruel, and (occasionally) heretical" (p. 47), deserving conquest in the name of retribution, or civilization, or even charity—those universal calls of the colonizers. Irish skill in music and the Patrician absence of snakes constituted minor benefits.

Romance Ireland sports giants and the original Stonehenge, "Eotinde Ring," transferred to Salisbury Plain by Merlin, and much magic, as befits an otherworldly island "in þe vttermeste endes of the world" (Higden/ Trevisa). Echoes of Viking colonization survive alliteratively, linking "Orkkenaye and Irische kynges," for example, or in Irish figures with Norse names in *King Horn*.

Anglo-Saxon alertness to English and continental indebtedness to the early Irish church fades postconquest. Of the multitudes of Irish saints, fewer than a handful retained a firm place in English story and hagiography: Cuthbert, Brigid, Brendan, and Patrick. Ireland's otherworldly associations strengthened the visionary appeal of Fursey, Tundale, the voyage of Brendan, and accounts of St. Patrick's Purgatory, though only Higden/ Trevisa preserved Fursey's Irish origin, and it is hard to say what a fifteenth-century English audience would have made of the Irish names and references retained in *Tundale*.

Further Irish gleanings include references to ribald, chattering, and drunken priests in Mirk's *Festial*, *The Owl and the Nightingale*, and *Piers Plowman*, and to two Irish pilgrims—Gilemichel the cripple, whose healing prompts Edward the Confessor's founding of Westminster Abbey, and the Richard who befriends Margery Kempe in Venice. It is tantalizing to have this little company juxtaposed; speculation about their significance is appropriately circumscribed.

A chapter of conclusions considers the generical weight of this evidence, chronicles often purveying an "official history" for the politically influential; romances blurring history and story for a wider clientele; religious and didactic works supporting church interests. Saints Aidan and Columkille, for instance, virtually disappear from Middle English hagiography, despite their importance in the formation of the early English church. The Anglo-Norman and later medieval English church saw themselves as reformers of the church in Ireland, not its debtors.

English alienation from Ireland and the Irish—linguistic, social, political, ecclesiastical, and geographical—is reflected in recurrent images of Ireland as otherworld island, mysterious and dangerous; a wasteland, largely uninhabited, except for the "wild Irish," or at least uncultivated; like America or Australia later, a land of unused potential or a place of exile. "[T]he colonization of Ireland was a significant step in England's colonization of the New World" (p. 120).

Rambo's work is based on her thesis from the University of North Carolina at Chapel Hill, 1990. It could have been updated more carefully for publication. For instance, her discussions of St. Patrick's Purgatory would have been helped by reference to *The Medieval Pilgrimage to St. Patrick's Purgatory: Lough Derg and the European Tradition*, ed. Michael Haren & Yolande de Pontfarcy (Enniskillen, 1988); and *St. Patrick's Purgatory*, EETS, o.s., vol. 298 (1991). The account of the ME versions in the *Manual of the Writings in Middle English* (cited p. 99) has been corrected in *Notes and Queries*, n.s., vol. 35 (1988): 436–37, and it should be noted (p. 88) that the preliminary stories about St. Patrick in the *South English Legendary* derive from the *Legenda Aurea* (see *Leeds Studies in English* 21 [1990]: 119–40).

The volume suffers from its share of typos (e.g., Seigfried for Siegfried Wenzel, Margary for Margery Kempe) and solecisms ("The main exception in romances are . . ."). It has an oddball manner of citing manuscripts (pp. 26, 54), and repeated quotations turn out with different readings (pp. 48 and 72) and lineations (pp. 34 and 66). The unfortunate abbreviations "2d" and "3d ed" make some books in the bibliography look like twopenny dreadfuls. But this is a welcome volume, generally well produced, with a bibliography and index, useful for tracking down references to Ireland and the Irish in Middle English texts.

ROBERT EASTING
Victoria University of Wellington

ANNE ROONEY. *Hunting in Middle English Literature.* Cambridge: D. S. Brewer, 1993. Pp. 213. $59.00.

Anne Rooney has written a short but detailed study of hunting in Middle English texts. Her project is to analyze and categorize Middle English representations of the hunt, which she argues evolved along different lines from those in continental Europe. Beginning with a discussion of the English hunting manuals and a survey of the relevant literary models—classical, biblical, and European—Rooney goes on to classify and describe the hunting motifs in a variety of Middle English texts. She concludes her book with a chapter each on the two most extensive literary treatments of the hunt in Middle English poetry: *The Book of the Duchess* and *Sir Gawain and the Green Knight.*

There is no questioning the thoroughness of Rooney's research on the hunt. She brings together in one study a wealth of motifs that have rarely been considered together and manages to correct misconceptions created by previous scholars. Rooney is thus able to add to our knowledge of the distinctive paths taken by this particular facet of English culture. For example, she points to the Middle English hunting manuals' focus on terminology as opposed to actual hunting practices and the manuals' excessive concern for categorizing animals and types of hunts, a concern that Rooney says "serves no practical purpose" other than "to divide the elite who know it from those who do not" (p. 18).

In several respects, however, this book's methodology is flawed, while its contribution to our understanding is limited by the narrowness of the task Rooney has set for herself. First, there is Rooney's operative assertion that the hunt in Middle English literature developed its own peculiar features. Whereas Rooney makes a case for certain differences, I do not think she establishes a clear linguistic and cultural distinction between England and the continent. For one thing, in this period many "English" writings, that is, texts that were produced in England, were written in a dialect of French. As Rooney herself mentions, the earliest extant "English" hunting manual, the brief treatise by Twiti, exists in both Anglo-Norman and Middle English versions (p. 8). In addition, there is much that English and continental literature shared—not just sources and traditions, but actual stories, such as the legends of Tristan, "the most famous of all hunters in medieval literature" (p. 86). This is not to say that Rooney is incorrect in asserting the differences between continental and English traditions, only that these have to be more carefully laid out and cannot be presented as a simple distinction between English and French. An approach that does for the hunt what Susan Crane does for romance, namely an examination of the emergence of what Crane calls an "'insular' body of works,"[1] would have been a sounder way to proceed, I think.

There are moments in her book when Rooney gives us a taste of just this kind of contribution. For example, she points to a marked preference for English terminology over French, especially in Edward, Duke of York's early-fifteenth-century treatise, *The Master of Game*. In addition to this keenness "to preserve the integrity of the native English hunting vocabulary" (p. 13), Edward deviates from his French source in another way: in paying less attention to the practical aspects of hunting technique and more to "the social status of the noble hunter" (p. 12). Given the author's royal blood and his participation in the wars with France, it would have been worthwhile to pursue these aspects of Edward's hunting treatise. Could the preference for English be a part of the movement, attributed by John H. Fisher to the Lancastrian house, of defining English identity through the English language?[2] If the English nobility were seeking to separate themselves from the French, why the continued attraction to French courtly forms and practices? Even Edward, while privileging things English in his treatise, takes as his authority a French manual by a French nobleman: Gaston Phoebus's *Le Livre de la Chasse*. *The Master of Game*, in fact, is not just derived from Gaston's work—it is a direct translation.

As for Rooney's full discussions of the hunt in *The Book of the Duchess* and *Sir Gawain and the Green Knight*, they too suffer from a skewed methodology and an overly narrow focus. Rooney reads the hunt in *The Book of the Duchess* as representing the "figure of worldly bliss," which she says is "the most pervasive metaphorical use of the hunt in Middle English literature" (p. 145). But the *ubi sunt* tradition, which the "figure of worldly bliss" draws upon, is itself hardly an exclusively English topos, although it might be the case that it held an especially strong attraction for English authors. Rooney's examples seem to suggest that this is so, but again one would have wished for a more extended exploration of this feature and of how exactly it came to be an "English" concern.

The chapter on *Sir Gawain and the Green Knight* is stronger than the one

---

[1] Susan Crane, *Insular Romance: Politics, Faith, and Culture in Anglo-Norman and Middle English Literature* (Berkeley and Los Angeles: University of California Press, 1986), p. 1.

[2] John H. Fisher, "A Language Policy for Lancastrian England," *PMLA* 107 (1992): 1168–80.

on *The Book of the Duchess*, in part no doubt because, as Rooney says, the *Gawain*-poet gives us "the best known and most fully developed" hunting scenes in Middle English literature. Making careful reference to the poet's models in the hunting manuals and setting his poem in the context of other texts in the alliterative tradition, Rooney is able to provide a good context for reading the hunts in *Gawain*. Even so, here too the readings seem a bit thin and unsatisfying. She points out, for example, that in part *Gawain* is working with the narrative "structure of the seduction motif" (p. 186), but she might have gone further into the values and assumptions behind such a motif. Since *Gawain*, like other alliterative poems, uses the hunt as much for the glory and pleasure of the sport itself, Rooney would have done well to ground her discussion in the context of a chivalric culture that so valued and ritualized hunting.

In short, Rooney had two possible avenues for exploring the hunt in Middle English literature: a poetic consideration that would have focused on figural and metaphoric uses of the hunt, with probably some reference to theoretical work in allegory, metaphor, metonymy, and punning; or a more historical evaluation, especially of the linguistic and cultural kind, that would have examined the hunt as a primarily aristocratic sport, one that developed some distinctive features in England. One or the other of these approaches would have added to our understanding of Middle English literature and culture—both would have made a substantial contribution. To have done neither is to have lost a real opportunity.

SANDRA PIERSON PRIOR
Columbia University

GILLIAN RUDD. *Managing Language in* Piers Plowman. Piers Plowman Studies, vol. 9. Cambridge: D. S. Brewer, 1994. Pp. xiv, 246. $63.00.

The first paragraph of the introduction gives a concise expression of this book's chief concerns:

"Managing Language in *Piers Plowman*" focuses upon those sections of the poem which explore not only how "words manifestly force the understanding" but also illustrate how the confusion which language can create can be employed to lead mankind towards different appreciations of understanding and away from the desire for "innumerable controversies." In *Piers Plowman* the quest for salvation provides a framework for Langland's illustration of how our reactions to language and knowledge interact to shape, if not actually dictate, the sort of understanding we achieve. (p. ix)

Given that focus, Rudd concentrates on passus 8–14 of the B text (the C version is discussed where it differs from B).

Rudd's investigation combines interpretive readings of the poem with information drawn from various other medieval texts (favorites are Augustine, Balbus' *Catholicon*, Henry of Ghent, Robert of Basevorn, and the mystics). Her basic thesis is that Langland employs two fundamentally different but complementary kinds of "discourse": one rational, discursive and "deductive"; the other affective, employing images, parables and figures, and "emotive." The former Rudd associates with *scientia*, the latter with *sapientia*. Neither discourse is in itself capable of adequately expressing the "logos"—the transcendent Referent which is the object of understanding and toward which language strives. Langland is acutely aware of these limitations; he engages each discourse so as to glean, and to validate, what it has to offer, at the same time revealing its limits and defects.

In a short review one can but sketch the book's development. Part 1 (chapters 1 to 5) sets out the distinction the author would draw between *scientia* and *sapientia*, *verbum* and *logos*; considers the sources from which teachers might derive authority; presents Reason as the defining human faculty; and argues that Ymaginatif in passus 12 both defends and qualifies its power. Part 2 (chapters 6 to 9) considers the "academic" or scholastic approach to understanding in passus 8–10 and 13 (the Doctor); this mode is useful (Will achieves enough expertise to employ its knowledge and techniques against his own teachers), but at the same time its limitations are revealed (chiefly through criticisms of the teachers implicit in context and their inability to adapt their lessons suitably to Will's needs). Part 3 (chapters 10–15) explores the role of "affective" learning and vivid personal experience (the three-part inner dream of passus 11 and the figure of Haukyn in 13–14). The affective mode is not to be substituted for the rational (Will needs what he has learned "scholastically" to interpret what he learns experientially) or accepted without scrutiny; rather, "deductive" and "affective" discourse must be allowed to modify each other. The final part (chapters 16–17) concludes that Langland has deliberately managed language in the poem, not to question whether transcendent Truth exists, but rather to instill a less inadequate understanding of it by stimulating

Will and the reader to question and explore, to consider a plurality of interpretations achieved through both rational and affective modes.

This book has many virtues. It is clearly presented and argued. Despite its subject, it approaches *Piers* as a fourteenth-century text, resisting temptations to argue that Langland finally regarded "language" as meaningless, "understanding" as impossible, or "authority" as a radically corrupt construct. It employs a rich array of other medieval sources to inform its discussion and generally uses them to good effect: e.g., while quoting extensively from mystical writers, Rudd never suggests that Langland was particularly interested in mysticism or "contemplation" but rather explores various ideas about kinds of "knowing" and understanding.

A reviewer must nevertheless express reservations about the author's handling of the philosophical and theological context. There are, for example, terminological gaffes to peeve the purist ("to merit redemption") and places where quotations seem misapplied to the argument (Henry of Ghent on science, pp. 22–23, or Nicholas of Cusa on *simplex intellectualitas*, p. 177). Sometimes Rudd seems not to understand a concept (e.g., in saying that reason is concerned only with "temporal matters" (p. 56), that synderesis was regarded simply as an orientation of the *will* (pp. 129–32), that almsgiving is explicitly Christian (p. 136). Her usage of *logos* (especially in chapters 1, 16, 17) is evocative but is not "medieval" and never goes beyond positing a vaguely metaphorical relationship between the *Logos* and human language. The impression that Rudd is not fully in control of such material is intensified by the fact that, when she herself translates Latin, there are usually errors. Some of these are slips in rendering mood, tense, number, or individual words (e.g., p. 172; cf. pp. 35, 37, 74, 181–83); others more seriously distort the sense of the original (e.g., pp. 7, 10, 11, 19, 22–23, 75, 127). Balbus's *Catholicon*, which must have been used in a heavily abbreviated black-letter edition, seems to have been particularly troublesome (the Latin text itself seems misquoted at, e.g., pp. 7, 19–20).

Much of the book consists of close reading of the poem, and readers will likely find much of this interesting and stimulating even when it covers ground already well trodden (e.g., chapter 17 on the Pardon scene and the conclusion of passus 7). But this reader sometimes found himself objecting to Rudd's interpretation of the text: e.g., that Study is undercut by her criticisms at passus 10.182–84 (p. 82); that Will's teachers fail him because they do not use the appropriate language (e.g., p. 91); that the Doctor of passus 13 represents excessive desire for knowledge (rather than an abuse and perversion of "knowledge," p. 100); that passus 13.117 "stresses introspection" (p. 147). And for me the most unsatisfactory reading was of the Haukyn episode in passus 13–14 (chapter 12), which leads to a final comment.

One might ask if an investigation of the "problem of language" in the poem should not focus less on "knowing" and more on "choosing." Though the book several times acknowledges that *Piers* concerns the will, choice, and action, it nevertheless focuses on "insight and knowledge" (p. 199). Thus, for example, Will "misunderstands" Holy Church in passus 1 because pupil and teacher employ different modes of discourse (p. 13). Such a reading externalizes Will's moral failing as a problem of language badly managed. Rudd's discussion of the Friars' exemplum in passus 8 (p. 130) or of Haukyn do not, it seems to me, address what for Langland was the crucial problem: the failure of the will to choose what the mind knew to be "right" and the devastating consequence that one had continually to rise from sin and, through penance and "satisfaction," strive to reorient the dispositions (the *affectus*) to choose the "good," in imitation of Dowel, *id est Christus*.

JOSEPH S. WITTIG
University of North Carolina, Chapel Hill

JOYCE E. SALISBURY. *The Beast Within: Animals in the Middle Ages.* New York and London: Routledge, 1994. Pp. ix, 238. $55.00.

The fact that modern science and philosophy have still no clear "test of humanity" testifies to modern man's uncertainty as to what makes us "human."[1] Joyce E. Salisbury takes this profound insecurity as the starting point for her fascinating historical study of how people saw animals and themselves in the Middle Ages.

As the main representatives of the two differing views of the human-animal relationship covered by her study she chooses the fourth-century Church father St. Augustine and the early-thirteenth-century chronicler Gerald of Wales—two figures who, at the same time, also approximately mark the temporal limits of her project. Thus, for St. Augustine in the

---

[1] See, for example, Andrew N. Rowan's "The Human–Animal Interface," in M. H. Robinson and L. Tiger, eds., *Man and Beast Revisited* (Smithsonian Institute Press, 1991), pp. 279–89.

fourth century, the gulf between human beings and animals was obvious and unbridgeable, whereas the tales of "shape shifters" reported by Gerald of Wales are taken by Salisbury to illustrate the increasing "blurring of borders" between the two originally distinct categories of "human" and "animal."

In the main part of her study, Salisbury underpins her initial thesis by analyzing the relationship between animals and human beings in terms of animals as property, food, and sexual objects. She bases the first part of her analysis (chapters 1 to 3) on a wide range of medieval legal texts (both secular and clerical) and convincingly illustrates how human attitudes towards animals changed over the centuries from the assertion of an unquestioned (qualitative) difference in nature to a position that sees human beings and animals as being different only by degree. Thus, for example, increasingly severe punishments for bestiality are seen as becoming necessary in order to maintain the formerly unquestioned separation of humans and animals by means of legal prescriptions.

Salisbury's attempt, from chapter 4 onwards, to prove that the same development took place in the area of literature and manuscript-illustrations, however, is more problematic. Not only do we find considerable variation in the number of texts that have been handed down, but the selection of representative texts is also far from straightforward. St. Augustine, for example, may very well illustrate the prevailing early-medieval theological opinion. However, Gerald of Wales's *The Journey through Wales/ The Description of Wales*, which Salisbury uses to illustrate the thirteenth-century attitude and to contrast it with St. Augustine's point of view, belongs to an entirely different category of texts, with an orientation toward relating the "curiosa" rather than clarifying the relationship between human beings and animals from a philosophical-theological vantage point—as St. Augustine did. Consequently, we find a somewhat motley selection of texts, which are all rather one-sidedly examined for further evidence to support Salisbury's initial statement. The fact that the same procedure that yielded clear and highly relevant results with legal texts does not work convincingly when applied to literary texts in the widest sense of the word is not primarily the fault of the author, but may equally well be blamed on the fragmentary way in which the literature of the Middle Ages has been handed down to us.

Yet in spite of these theoretical inconsistencies in the second part of Salisbury's study, the book remains a brave and fascinating exploration of an area that has so far been rather neglected by both historical and literary critics. *The Beast Within* provides extremely valuable information on the legal and cultural background of the human-animal relationship and, as a companion to Beryl Rowland's specific studies on Chaucer's use of animals, may prove invaluable to all those Chaucerians who wish to track down the "bestis greete and smale."

THOMAS M. HONEGGER
University of Zürich

CORINNE J. SAUNDERS. *The Forest of Medieval Romance: Avernus, Broceliande, Arden.* Cambridge: D. S. Brewer, 1993. Pp. xiii, 235. $63.00.

Over the past two decades the scenery of medieval narrative has attracted increasing critical attention. Whether this development suggests a rising ecological consciousness on the part of the latest generation of scholars, let the forest judge. Still, Corinne J. Saunders's book is one of few to discuss this key topic in any depth. Forests pervade medieval romances, and are integral to their plots. They become, as Saunders notes, the natural landscape of the knight errant, his essential habitat. This elegant volume traces their evolution through Shakespeare's *Midsummer Night's Dream* and *As You Like It*.

The Forest of Medieval Romance stresses the roots of the forest of romance that lead back to classical epic and the *hyle* of the Neoplatonic philosophers, though historical and biblical connections are also explored. The first chapter comments succinctly on these diverse origins with special reference to French, English, and to some extent German evidence, first surveying the complex physical character of the medieval European forest, its inhabitants, and the rise of aristocratic hunting practices and forest law. Biblical wilderness settings are recognized as sources of the idea of the wild as a place of exile and vision. By contrast, Plato and his successors, Chalcidius in particular, associated the wood with primordial chaos. Saunders's second chapter plunges into the treatment of the forest in Latin literary tradition—Virgil's *Aeneid*, Ovid's *Metamorphoses*, and Statius's *Thebaid* in particular—and the *romans d'antiquité* that adapted Virgil's and Statius's epics to twelfth-century tastes. Chapter 3 traces the varied forests of twelfth-century romance—through the Breton lays of Marie de France, especially *Equitan*, *Chevrefoil*, and *Bisclavret*, the romances of Chrétien de

285

Troyes, and the *Tristan* romances of Beroul and Thomas, supplemented by *Tristramssaga*. The first section of chapter 4 characterizes the forest in the *contes* of *Aucassin and Nicolette, Jehan et Blonde, Le Vair Palefroi,* and *La Fille du Comte de Ponthieu*, before going on to the noncyclic prose *Lancelot* and the prose *Tristan*. A separate chapter discusses the Vulgate cycle in relation to Merlin in the *Vita Merlini*, with special reference to the *Queste del Saint Graal*. For students of the age of Chaucer, the central chapter is the sixth, where Saunders investigates forest settings in *Sir Orfeo, Launfal, Sir Gawain and the Green Knight*, and Chaucer's *Book of the Duchess, Knight's Tale*, and *Wife of Bath's Tale*. The demonic huntsman of *The Friar's Tale* also makes an appearance here. Chapter 7 leads the reader out of the age of Chaucer into the undergrowth of Malory's *Morte Darthur*, while chapter 8 probes the ways that Spenser and Shakespeare rewrote the forest of medieval romance in a Renaissance context.

It can be seen from this summary that *The Forest of Medieval Romance* is built around a chronologically organized series of analyses of key texts. It does not claim to be a comprehensive reference on the subject—"that were an impossible!"—though it should rank as essential reading for those interested in the role of the forest in medieval literature. What it does trace is the evolution of the forest as a specialized landscape adapted by romancers to their own literary purposes.

Without question, the chapter on the fourteenth century rests on the insights of the preceding chapters. For Saunders, the late works she discusses envision the forest as "ambiguous," teeming with the contrasting possibilities evoked by earlier writers. Within a single romance as compact as *Sir Orfeo* or *Sir Launfal*, contrasting ideas of the forest may be developed, and the plot may even turn upon the shift from one convention to another. Saunders sees this happening in *Sir Orfeo*, as the protagonist exchanges his own view of the wilderness as a place of penance and exile for the fairy court's playful view of wilderness as a courtly hunting preserve. This discussion by itself demonstrates the merit of an awareness of the multifaceted literary tradition of the forest for readers of fourteenth-century English literature. Equally valuable are Saunders's extended discussion of the elaborately detailed forest of *Sir Gawain and the Green Knight* and the contrasting woods of Chaucer's *Knight's Tale* and *Wife of Bath's Tale*. Overall, she sees the romances of the age of Chaucer becoming self-referential and self-conscious in their approaches to the forest. (For the late-twentieth-century critic these are almost invariably high compliments.) In both *Gawain* and Chaucer, Saunders detects a tension between realistic description and the strong symbolic value of the forests through which the characters pass.

For this reader, the astuteness of Saunders's evaluations of the diverse forests of the romances was an outstanding feature of the book. Centering a study of this length entirely on one scenic element of a particular genre is not an easy task, even when the genre and the scenic element both extend as far as the eye can see. The dearth of explicit descriptive language in many romances makes the task more challenging still, as Saunders notes herself (p. 48). To maintain interest in the theme, to differentiate Avernus from Brocéliande and from Arden over time, places heavy demands on the ingenuity and good sense of the author. *The Forest of Medieval Romance* contrives to maintain the reader's interest, thanks to the perceptive analytical skills and broad-based scholarship evident throughout the volume.

It can sometimes seem as if the forest of romance goes on forever. In these circumstances, omissions are inevitable if the book is not to go on forever likewise, or consume all the remaining trees on the planet. This reviewer does not propose to go on listing Saunders's omissions at any length, but a few items were especially regretted. While pursuing the trail that connects classical epic and the romance, Saunders neglects the vernacular epic tradition, where some of the best forests are to be found. The wintry landscapes of exile that the Old English poets reveled in describing, where Grendel and his mother prowl, may arguably be peripheral to the discussion, though Saunders finds them useful on p. 150, when she comes to *Sir Gawain and the Green Knight* and notes its connections to *The Wanderer* and *The Seafarer* as evidence for continuity in the alliterative tradition. The Ardennes of *Renaut de Montauban*, with its exiled, outlaw knights, might have merited some attention. Omitting this reference has the effect of uprooting Shakespeare's Arden, just as leaving out *Huon de Bordeaux* effectively orphans Shakespeare's Oberon. This problem will crop up as long as medieval literary studies continue to be specialized along the lines of the three traditional "matters" of Rome, Britain, and France. Saunders is commendable in her attention to the first two of these massive bodies of literature, and it seems unfair to fault her in any way for slighting the third. It does have something notable to contribute to the discussion, however. Perhaps this might help to make a case for the "continuity of epos" that William Calin notes in *A Muse for Heroes* (Toronto: University of Toronto Press, 1983), p. 3.

More pertinent to Chaucer are the necessary economies practiced in chapter 6. It would have been delightful to see Saunders attempt an analysis of *Sir Thopas*, and to find out how the conventions she identifies play out in an overtly parodic context. This would have been especially valuable since she considers that chivalric conventions seem so often to be undercut in fourteenth-century works, Chaucer's most of all. The comic possibilities of the romance forest demand discussion; both Chaucer and Malory do exploit these comic possibilities, each in their own way. (Further attention to the comic potential of the motif might require backtracking to the robber-infested wilds of Apuleius's *Golden Ass* in the section on the classical tradition, though that, I suppose, would open the door to its horde of Greek ancestors, which used to be called "romances" and have now been renamed "novels" by their editors, to make them the more marketable.) I was a bit surprised not to find any mention of Chaucer's Yeoman, or of Chaucer's own service as Forester of North Petherton. Overall, Saunders portrays Chaucer as a critic of the romance as a genre, "offering a critique of the empty clichés and tropes of metrical romance and dismissing the conventionality of which the forest forms a part" (p. 155). The possibility that Chaucer is playing might be worth additional consideration.

Certain sins of omission also plague the biblical section of chapter 1. Saunders here examines the landscapes of Exodus, Nebuchadnezzar's madness, John the Baptist, and of Jesus's temptation. The wilderness of Exodus was, it should be emphasized, a place of vision as well as suffering, as the Burning Bush and Mount Sinai both testify; multiple meanings emerge early in the history of the theme, rather complicating its history. To these should be added the landscapes of exile in which David and Judas Maccabeus, both later to enter European chivalric mythology as Jewish Worthies, wander, fight, and suffer. Maurice Keen noted the importance of the Hebrew Bible (in Latin or French translation) to knights of the twelfth and thirteenth centuries more than ten years ago, but it remains too often neglected by specialists in medieval chivalric literature. Elijah's flight to the wilderness and his mystical experience there (of the "still, small voice") helped to set the precedent for John the Baptist's activities, and would also have rewarded examination.

None of these lacunae detract from the value of what is here: an inspired and painstaking foray into a large and tangled field of study. Saunders proves herself a sagacious guide to this important topic; her work will be essential to future research in this field, and should inspire applications and responses for some time to come.

This is a well-produced book with an accurate index—both increasingly uncommon features that merit some mention here.

J. R. GOODMAN
Texas A&M University

Larry Scanlon. *Narrative, Authority, and Power: The Medieval Exemplum and the Chaucerian Tradition.* Cambridge Studies in Medieval Literature, vol. 20. Cambridge: Cambridge University Press, 1994. Pp. xii, 378. $64.95.

In this substantial, ambitious, wide-ranging, and provocative book there is much that deserves a warm welcome. It invites us to reimagine the Chaucerian tradition with exemplarity as a guiding concept, which means acknowledging the part played in it by the relationship of words to power. It thus suggests that the creation of a "literary" tradition in English crucially depended on certain political assumptions—a dependence which, to speak personally, I now recognize that I underestimated in my *Medieval to Renaissance in English Poetry.* Scanlon defines this English literary tradition as one of anticlericalism, or at least laicism, so that "what is usually seen as the transition from the medieval to the humanist might be more fruitfully understood as one from clerical to lay" (p. 54)—the transition being a paradoxical outcome of "the Church's broad-based attempts to increase its control of secular life" (p. 137). (This is in keeping with other recent explorations of anticlericalism in late medieval culture, notably by Wendy Scase in the same series of Cambridge Studies in Medieval Literature; it is a pity that Scanlon does not place his work in relation to such developments or even mention them.) Another of the book's merits, one comparatively rare in work by medievalists, is its awareness of the shaping of medieval studies by modernity, as in "the modernist ideal of an anti-didactic Chaucer, and the more general modern conviction that narrative and didacticism are antithetical" (p. 217), and the reciprocal shaping of modernity by the very laicization of spiritual authority that is the book's theme. All this is admirable and illuminating; but other parts of Scanlon's book are less satisfactory. In general, and not by accident, most of the illumination comes in chapters 1 and 6–12, which focus on texts in English, by Chaucer, Gower, Hoccleve and Lydgate, and on the relations among them; and most of what is unsatisfactory comes in chapters 2–5, which deal with Latin texts and with theoretical issues. I shall take up first what I think is wrong with the book, and then return to what I think is right.

For me a major obstacle, not overcome before chapter 7, was the slipperiness of the central concept, that of exemplum itself. Scanlon writes, "I offer a new definition: an exemplum is a narrative enactment of cultural authority" (p. 34), and while I grasp what these words mean I have real difficulty in grasping what difference they should make to anyone's understanding of exempla or exemplariness. The statement illustrates the book's tendency to become a self-absorbed conceptual dance: the abstracting power of a discourse adapted from Cultural Studies is always threatening to dissolve the specificity of its subject matter. (An example that caught my eye: in two dizzying paragraphs in chapter 9, *power* is repeated 14 times, *transgression/ive(ness)* 10 times, and *authority/ize(d)* 7 times.) Scanlon never discusses the rhetorical nature of the exemplum, which, like the proverb, serves to convey individual "truths" opportunistically rather than to endorse a whole doctrinal system; thus he seems surprised to find that in a collection of religious exempla one attaches sacred value to an "institutionally sanctioned" person while the next attaches it to a form "independent of the person dispensing it" (p. 76). That is exactly what might be expected of exempla. Nor does he show interest in the intellectual ingenuity with which narratives are applied to exemplary purposes, an aspect of exempla to which John Burrow has called attention, and with which modern readers especially need help. The tendency toward abstraction is at its strongest in chapter 3, "*Auctoritas* and *Potestas*," where the political theory of the Roman republic and empire, patriarchy, voice and text, deconstruction and Derrida, modernism and postmodernism, medieval and Renaissance, humanism and laicism, swirl and eddy, carrying the reader higher and higher on the feathers of thought until the ever-enlarging conspectus produces vertigo and (in my case) the sullen resistance of Geoffrey in the eagle's claws. This chapter may represent what the author needed to settle for himself in order to handle his subject, but its usefulness for his readers is not obvious.

One part of Scanlon's argument is that "authority is not some pure given," as, in his view, medievalists generally take it to be, "but an ideological structure that must be produced and maintained" (p. 26); it cannot be detached from history, and for him this means that it cannot be detached from power relationships. The common distinction between the sermon exemplum and the public exemplum is invalid, for both are "narratives employed by clerics to persuade lay audiences" (p. 58). The Church is "the ideological apparatus of the medieval ruling class" (p. 69) and the clerical tradition is "one part of the ruling class producing conceptions of power for the other" (p. 86); thus, predictably, "Through the sermon exemplum, the Church attempted to establish its ideological authority among subordinate classes it had previously ignored. Through the public exemplum, it attempted to extend its authority at court" (p. 58). What I find striking here is the assumption that *what* was taught by exempla was unimportant compared with the struggle for authority that they served. An analogous argument would be that what English professors have to say is insignificant compared with the "ideological authority" they gain by teaching, writing books, and reviewing them; but I don't see Scanlon's book in this way, nor I suppose does he. The struggle for authority was a reality in the Middle Ages as now, but to suppose that it was the only reality, and that, for example, religious belief and doctrine were always subordinate to this struggle, is grossly reductive. Here there is no attempt to imagine religious belief as experience, no entry into that late-medieval interpenetration of the material and the spiritual that scholars as various as Caroline Bynum, Eamon Duffy, Miri Rubin and Sarah Beckwith have been opening up for us, nothing but the relentless reduction of religion to politics.

Narrative, Authority, and Power would claim, I think, to be part of what Scanlon calls a "return to history" (p. 216), but until he reaches Chaucer his history, like that of some other New Historicists, is little more than materialist theory untouched by historical imagination. Part of its argument, particularly in discussion of John of Salisbury and Aegidius Romanus in chapter 4, is directed against an outmoded Whig idea of constitutional development, and this produces repeated statements of truths less surprising than they are evidently thought to be: "John does not expose the ideological diffusion at the heart of the royal ideal in order to democratize it" (p. 101); "Aegidius shows no interest at all in constitutional restraint" (p. 114); "The privileging of the royal will which informs this notion of tyranny is antithetical to modern constitutionalism" (p. 115); even (about *The Parson's Tale*) "There is nothing democratic about this text" (p. 19). At the same time, though, Scanlon evidently assumes that "progressive" and "regressive" retain the force that Whiggery and Marxism confer on them; he states that Aegidius's commitment to monarchy is tied to "medieval power relations in their most regressive and fundamental form, the heritability of nobility" (p. 111). What would it be like really to believe in "the heritability of nobility"? That is a question no more asked than what it would be like really to believe in medieval Catholicism, and as a result nobility, like religion, remains a central blankness. Scanlon takes for granted that "class" and "ruling class" are terms of such precision and transcendent validity that they can be used for the objective analysis of medieval and late-antique cultures that imagined their own structures in very different terms. We evidently know better—a glaring instance of the "presentism" (p. 228) against which he elsewhere protests. In Boethius's Fortune and her wheel, he writes, "an aristocratic class can at once recognize the flux of historical existence, and affirm its own privilege as a locus of stability beyond such flux" (p. 125). The second part of this statement is so odd that I wonder whether Scanlon can mean what he seems to be saying, for such privilege is precisely what Boethius has lost, and the argument of *Consolation* III pr. 6 and met. 6—one that in some form descended to John Ball—is that *nobilitas* has no meaning as privilege, only as something common to all human beings through their divine origin. Elsewhere Scanlon takes up Genius's discussion of *gentilesse* in Gower's *Confessio Amantis*, and notes its relation to Aegidius Romanus (but not to Boethius, or to Chaucer); it seems strange that he never confronts in more general terms the internalizing transvaluation of *nobilitas/gentilesse* found in the tradition of thought flowing from Boethius through Jean de Meun and Dante, a transvaluation dependent for its potency on pervasive belief in what it denies, "the heritability of nobility."

Finally, it must be said that some of what is wrong with chapters 2–5 has to do not just with the triumph of theory over imagination but, more pedestrianly, with inaccuracies in translation from Latin. These range from simple grammatical errors such as "most honorable Cato" for *honestissimos Catones* (p. 132) to fundamental misunderstandings such as "the blood of a tyrant is more pleasing to God than the host" for *nulla fere sit Deo acceptior hostia tyranni sanguine* (p. 121).

It is a pleasure to return to the book's merits. The two chapters on *The Canterbury Tales* are splendidly illuminating. When reread by Scanlon as exempla supporting a laicization of spiritual authority, *The Friar's Tale* and *The Summoner's Tale* are like old pictures newly cleaned, and the scatological comedy of the latter in particular emerges as far sharper and more powerfully directed. *The Clerk's Tale* too, envisaged as belonging to "the improvised genre of laicized hagiography" (p. 176), takes on new dimensions. The pathos evoked by Grisilde is seen as affirming "the spiritual integrity of lay existence" (p. 179), but Scanlon's interpretation also gets beyond an exclusive focus on the scandal of female suffering, and recognizes that a central interest in the tale is male power, which includes its own kind of suffering, the pathos of unlimited authority. In defining the tale's movement toward the possibility of incest as "purely ideological" (p. 188), solely a matter of Walter's ability to ensure complete control over his daughter as an item of exchange, Scanlon is more confident than I of the possibility of separating the political from the erotic; but this remains a brilliant new reading of a work that one might have supposed exhausted by recent critical attention. On *The Pardoner's Tale* I find Scanlon less interesting, largely

because here he is less closely engaged with specific textual effects—
though he does note perceptively how the personified Death of 6.675 "is
not death considered in itself, but death as human beings have named it, as
'men clepeth' it" (p. 201). The conception of exemplariness enables him to
approach both *Melibee* and *The Monk's Tale* seriously and productively, and
he has some appropriately sharp comments on how earlier criticism of *The
Monk's Tale*, obsessed with the notion of a necessary antithesis between
narrative and didacticism, "was less concerned with reading the tale than
with finding reasons not to read it" (pp. 216–17). A study of *The Nun's
Priest's Tale* ought perhaps to be the culminating achievement of a rereading of Chaucer as exemplary, but here Scanlon is disappointing. He struggles to make the tale a serious exemplum of lay sovereignty, and this leads
him to argue that "authority in this narrative has a single shape. It is
patriarchal and monarchical; its position is occupied by Chauntecleer"
(p. 234), and that "in a social world where authority has a single shape, the
displacement of Chauntecleer can have no other result but anarchy"
(p. 241). Such an undoing of Chaucer's mock-heroic treatment of exemplariness does not seem to me to be a necessary consequence of Scanlon's
approach. He is right to question the widespread conception of *The Nun's
Priest's Tale* as a kind of Chaucerian quintessence, which would imply that
Chaucer's attitude toward moral teaching in poetry must *always* be ironic;
but this tale surely *does* mock the lay appropriation of clerical authority, and
if its attribution to the Nun's Priest has any significance at all it is likely to
be that his clerical status provides him with a detached (or privileged)
standpoint from which to ironize the lay concerns with politics and marriage on which the tale focuses.

Whatever one's detailed disagreements, Scanlon's readings of Chaucer
form valuable contributions to the scholarly conversation, opening up new
perspectives, redressing balances, revealing new significance in details, and
collectively demonstrating that something of fundamental importance in
Chaucer's work has been overlooked—its lay emphasis. The chapters on
Gower, Hoccleve, and Lydgate are less exciting in themselves, but bring
out convincingly the role of these neglected poets in establishing a
Chaucerian tradition that institutionalized poetic authority in a form that
still survives. Scanlon is surely right to argue that "modern literary ideals
are closer to those of the later Middle Ages than they have usually cared to
admit" (p. 323), and in his later pages he has some thought-provoking
suggestions about how Lydgate's conception of tragedy looks forward to
that supposed to be peculiar to the English Renaissance. *Narrative, Author-*

293

ity, and Power is worth careful reading; I would not willingly reread chapters 2–5, but I shall go back to the rest of the book with interest and in the expectation of further enlightenment.

A. C. SPEARING
University of Virginia

M. C. SEYMOUR, gen. ed. *Authors of the Middle Ages: English Writers of the Late Middle Ages*, vol. 1, nos. 1–4. Brookfield, Vt.: Ashgate Publishing, 1994. Pp. v, 248. $72.50.

This volume contains four essays that focus chiefly on the biographical facts about several medieval English authors, Sir John Mandeville (by M. C. Seymour), John Trevisa (David C. Fowler), William Langland (Ralph Hanna III), and Thomas Hoccleve (J. A. Burrow). Each sixty-page essay surveys the life and provides a bibliography and (except in the case of Mandeville) a list of sources that document the life. Each essay also has been published separately in paperback.

Seymour's opening contribution first examines the "facts" about Mandeville's identity, then the "fictions." In the facts category are issues Seymour takes up one by one and draws conclusions about—the French versions of the *Travels*, date of original composition, provenance, nationality of the author, what the book says about Egypt and the Holy Land, its geography, and its orthodoxy. His conclusions are that the unknown author was a native French-speaker who wrote the book ca. 1357 in a large Continental library, an ecclesiastic, a fluent reader of Latin (but someone ignorant of Arabic and Greek), a curious reader of others' narratives about the world (including those that supported his belief in circumnavigation), and, finally, "a man who had never travelled to the lands he describes" (p. 27). Many students of Mandeville would agree with most of Seymour's determinations, although his review of opinion on some issues could have more clearly noticed contrary voices (e.g., Metlitzki's arguments for Mandeville's familiarity with Egypt). Seymour next turns to the "fictions"—certain interpolations made in various versions of the book, apocryphal works attributed to Mandeville/Jean de Bourgogne, de Bourgogne's reported epitaph, and other later accretions to the complex Mandeville legend. In the first part of the essay Seymour is given to saying that "Mandeville" is "false" for

294

alleging this or that (e.g., "his claim to have used an astrolabe on his journeys is worthless" [p. 24]), but in the rest of it (from p. 25 on) he acknowledges that "Mandeville" is a character and a narrator created by the author (which allows us, I believe, to understand that the astrolabe is there as an icon of the far traveller). Seymour plausibly suggests that the author of the *Travels* might have been a contemporary French translator and anthologizer of travel writings, Jean le Long, who for various reasons, a number of which Seymour discusses, made "Mandeville" appear to be English. That is why Sir John Mandeville is included in this volume on English writers.

Fowler's investigation of what is known about the life of Trevisa treats Trevisa's origins, his time at Oxford, his installation as Vicar of Berkeley, his years in Gloucestershire, and his writings. His links to Wyclif and his associations with other learned men at Quenehalle, Oxford, are carefully detailed, as are the library resources that may have supported Trevisa in his translations of the Bible and other works.

Hanna's essay on Langland returns us to the kinds of problems Seymour encountered in examining the author of "Mandeville." Of the four contributors, Hanna is the most thoughtful concerning the difficulties of saying much with certainty about the lives of medieval authors. We are not really sure who "William (or Robert) Langland" was or whether he wrote *Piers Plowman* (or some of it, or some versions of it), but Hanna reviews dates and locations of manuscripts of *Piers* as one way of establishing some information about "Langland." He also believes that "from the poem one can extract further bits of information, all in some way or another subject to scholarly contention, which form a represented biography" (p. 149); these bits draw our attention to seven matters that seem important in charting the poet's life: the Malvern Hills area, the poet's grammar school and university education, the interrupted quality of that education, his eclectic and undirected reading (and fascination with particular topics), his "fall" into concubinage or matrimony, his status as an itinerant clerical bedesman (or hermit), and his being "a man tall and emaciated" (pp. 149–56). Hanna's appendix 10, on the readership of *Piers Plowman*, is a valuable list of identifiable provenances, copies containing names of owners or readers, references to the poem in wills and inventories, and literary appropriations (pp. 166–68). Hanna ends with a selective bibliography "slanted toward the general goals of the series 'Authors in the Middle Ages,'" divided thus into studies concerned with authorship, the poet's life, manuscripts, and editorial matters. Hanna's hesitation about trying to discern "Langland's" life from his poetry is a reaction others have had in recent decades: only four of the fifteen authorship studies he lists appeared in the last fifty years, and only five of the seventeen concerned with the poet's life come from that period.

Burrow's life of Hoccleve moves chronologically, drawing upon the sixty existing documentary sources and Hoccleve's poetry. Although he admits that the autobiographical passages in the poetry are "not above suspicion," Burrow believes that the poems reveal much about their author, and that they and the documents "provide enough for a literary biography of some substance to be compiled" (p. 189). His discovery of the possibility that Hoccleve may have thought of his home as his office and his office as his home (pp. 195–96)—like Hanna's observation that "we do not yet understand the situations in which persons might employ either multiple or non-hereditary names in this period" (p. 136)—sharply reminds us how careful we ought to be in composing biographies of fourteenth-century figures. Burrow is cautious in this regard, and so, even after ferreting out all he can from the poetry and the records, he concludes that ultimately we do not know much about Hoccleve's social and private life (p. 217). Yet the two surviving manuscript collections of his poems, "gathered, ordered, and copied by the poet himself," were a new thing, and inasmuch as they "testify to the poet's direct involvement in the propagation of his writings as a distinct and individual literary achievement" (p. 219), they may constitute the most important fact about Hoccleve's life.

This volume of these four lives shows us how little we know about Hoccleve and Trevisa and about those who created Mandeville and Will, less at least than our times have made us want to know about writers. As aware as we have become that authors are not their personae, and that subjectivity clouds definitions of selves, we still give in to urges to know what we can of the lives of medieval people. There are certainly more records about and self-reference in writings by medieval figures from later in the period, which is perhaps why Seymour's series begins where it does (and why it may have increasing difficulty going earlier in time). The volume does not state an aim for the series or predict future contents, but there are plenty of reasons to justify starting the series with these four late-medieval English literary figures not named Geoffrey Chaucer. The volume describes no particular audience for itself, but it is probably both ourselves and our students (though a lot of them won't be able to read the untranslated OF and Latin quoted; only Burrow translates non-English material). The volume and series are further signs, I think, of the resurging interest in the biographies of medieval people (notably, of late, Chaucer); and they also can be viewed as anti-interpretive contributions to medieval literary study, positivist efforts at finding light and weight—definite facts about a writer's life, lists of tangible manuscripts—in a still murky, unrooted poststructuralist moment.

CHRISTIAN ZACHER
Ohio State University

LYNN STALEY. *Margery Kempe's Dissenting Fictions.* University Park, Penn.: Pennsylvania State University Press, 1994. Pp. xiii, 224. $35.00 cloth, $16.95 paper.

It may not be *The General Prologue* to *The Canterbury Tales*, but there is now a widely shared impression that the *Book of Margery Kempe* gives evidence of more than one voice. But before I continue, I should, as the British say, declare an interest: about twenty years ago, in a *Medium Ævum* article (vol. 44, 1975, pp. 145–50), I identified a second voice in the *Book* with that of the second scribe, whole role, for all of its ambiguity, was clearly more than that of an amanuensis, and suggested that he worked as a virtual coauthor of the work. Though he certainly brought his own agenda to the task, I suggested, he and Margery Kempe did not work at cross-purposes, and one way to investigate new topics—like the interaction of gender and spirituality—is to consider the nature and effect of their dialogue, and the extent to which they complemented or opposed each other's ideas and inclinations.

Now Lynn Staley has read the *Book* differently, attending to the presence of a voice which is not that of the protagonist, but insisting that it, and the implied judgments that it occasions, are the artful products of the same person, whom she calls "Kempe." "Just as we commonly distinguish between Will, the layabout, and Langland, the author, or between the pilgrim Geoffrey and the poet Chaucer, so in this study I draw a distinction between Margery, the subject, and Kempe her author" (p. 3), she writes, preparing the way for the fictionalized treatment which she believes emerges from "Kempe's" treatment of "Margery." The second scribe she describes as "a true witness of the Lord's grace as it is manifested throughout the life of Margery Kempe" (p. 34), which seems to mean that he is really "Kempe's" creation, though she allows him a limited degree of autonomy, including the ability "to shift attention from her ["Margery's"] role as a social critic to Margery's status as a holy woman" (p. 35), a shift presumably agreeable to "Kempe," whose "use of the trope of the second scribe indicates her fundamental understanding of the terms of the genre in which she worked" (p. 37).

These are the terms under which Staley discusses the relationship between "Kempe" and "Margery," a relationship which I can only describe as somewhat delicate: "Kempe constructs for her protagonist, Margery, an image of a 'holy woman' that serves as a screen for a penetrating analysis of contemporary English society" (p. 85), she remarks. (Actually she also has argued that it was the second scribe who constructed that "image," but since the second scribe is equally "Kempe's" fictive creation it comes to much the same thing.) This distinction makes it possible for Staley to address even such topics as "the image of ecclesia" with only limited reference to the *Book*'s record of Margery Kempe's meditative experiences—"as I have reiterated, the *Book* is not 'about' . . . religious experience" (p. 102), she writes—and though she does examine some of the literary sources and devout practices present in the *Book*, she does so, for the most part, without really plumbing their religious implications. In doing so, however, Staley takes up the *Book*'s sense of community, and in doing so touches what may well be her most useful and interesting contribution.

It is with some of the ramifications in her treatment of community in chapter 4, "The English Nation," that Staley produces both real insight, and also some unnecessary problems. Foremost among these is the attitude towards Wycliffism which she believes "Kempe" to reveal. "Kempe" uses "Margery," she argues, "in a way that evinces her sensitivity to the whole range of issues that had accrued around the Lollardy heresy and that suggests her sympathies for what might loosely be called Lollard views" (p. 127). But there is a certain amount of special pleading in all of this: as a whole, the *Book of Margery Kempe* is, if anything, distinctly anti-Lollard in sentiment, though given its use of the vernacular, its resolute attitude towards ecclesiastical corruption, and its evident regard for women's spirituality it is hardly a model of convention, even though each of these topics (like almost everything else in the *Book*) can quite easily be found elsewhere in the period. But the somewhat artificial splitting of "Margery" and "Kempe" has the effect of simplifying, and even setting aside, the evident and lively religious concerns that the *Book* everywhere reveals. What is central to this text, after all, is less Wyclif's teachings than Margery Kempe's (not "Margery's") complex religious faith, a faith in which meditation and utterance play major roles.

298

The "Margery"/"Kempe" distinction presented in this study thus has the effect of separating off Margery Kempe's evident religiousness from the more secular, and more contemporary, concerns of the critic. What really seems to be postulated here is less an authorial voice than an outside observer, admiring of "Margery" as a person but less inclined than she might be to excuse those who oppose her, and keenly aware, as "Margery" is not, of the attitudes that lie behind her difficulties (sometimes, however, as in her attitudes towards Jews [p. 70 ff.], "Kempe" betrays her own limitations). For the most part, "Kempe" is less a Chaucer- or Langland-the-poet-like character, than an approved modern critic, familiar with recent critical (and some theoretical) developments, and sensitive to a fault. In the current state of criticism this is, perhaps, no very bad thing, particularly if one wants to resolve some of the complexities and tensions that are evident in the text. But it is not finally convincing (for one thing, the terms of fiction are different in Chaucer and Langland, so that the analogy seems somewhat forced), and it clearly limits (or in the case of the treatment of Lollardy, further complicates), the sort of religious questions that the *Book* may reasonably be taken to entertain.

I noted earlier that one of this study's advantages is the attention it pays to a sense of community that appears often in the *Book*, but which has never before been examined with the imaginative seriousness which is evident here. It is not necessary to accept the "Margery"/"Kempe" distinction to appreciate the usefulness of this approach, and Staley's treatment throughout—even setting aside the whole matter of Lollardy—is clearly one of the most important contributions she has made. As her concluding consideration describes, the way Margery Kempe (she says "Kempe") reveals "activities associated with what are human attempts at unity (sexual, social or spiritual) is a sign of her self-conscious and highly strategic use of language as a means of suggesting both similarity and difference. What distinguishes the true moment of joining from the false or superficial is the charity that transcends the barriers of sex, language or age and makes of two one through the love of Christ" (198). This is a welcome and interesting reading, though religion in general, and faith in particular, play a far more important role in exactly this process than Staley is prepared to allow. Still, this perceptive concern for the role of community will suggest something of the good insight this study can and does realize in its often insightful consideration of individual topics.

JOHN C. HIRSH
Georgetown University

Martin Stevens and A. C. Cawley, eds. *The Towneley Plays.* 2 vols. Early English Text Society, s.s., vol. 13. Oxford: Oxford University Press, 1994. Pp. xlviii, 733. $78.00.

Professors Cawley and Stevens have presented us with a much needed scholarly edition of *The Towneley Plays.* For years, scholars have had to make do with the George England and Alfred W. Pollard EETS edition from 1897 (which itself reprints much of the introduction to the Surtees Society edition of 1836) or, for a small portion of the cycle, Professor Cawley's *The Wakefield Pageants in the Towneley Cycle.* The Cawley and Stevens edition is a complete text, with textual notes and a bibliography that offers reasonable coverage of important scholarship up through 1989 (although there is also a reference to Spector's 1991 edition of *The N-Town Play*). Furthermore, the pair are an appropriate choice to edit the cycle, having previously overseen the facsimile text edition (1976).

The editors' introduction is valuable to scholars in giving a brief but accurate description of the manuscript's history that considerably extends those in earlier editions. The editors helpfully reprint primary materials or refer readers to articles where they can be found. Perhaps too unequivocally, the editors associate the manuscript with Wakefield and strongly suggest that it was compiled and performed there. They point to internal evidence that associates at least a few of the plays with this Yorkshire town and are at some pains to place the burden of proof on those who would argue for other venues. They do not address the question of how late-medieval Wakefield would have supported such a cycle. They do, however, acknowledge that many of the texts in the cycle are based on plays from York and elsewhere. As a result, the editors consistently distinguish the Towneley plays from the Wakefield plays—the latter being only those written in the Wakefield Master's characteristic thirteen-line stanza—a practice that suggests their view of the manuscript as the record of an eclectic cycle, probably compiled by a single redactor who drew upon numerous sources for the cycle's dramatic texts.

Professors Cawley and Stevens make some editorial departures from previous editions, most notably in their treatment of stanzaic forms. In addition to regrouping the predominant stanzaic form of *Pharaoh* as a twelve-line stanza (as opposed to England and Pollard's treatment of it as eight and four) to more accurately reflect the manuscript, the editors take the nine-line Wakefield stanza to be a compressed form of a short-lined thirteener (an editorial practice that distinguishes this edition from Cawley's previous text of the Wakefield Master's plays). Their reasons for doing so are, however, cogent and well argued. The editors point to the Wakefield stanza's similarity to that found in several other pageants in the Towneley Cycle, to previous inconsistent applications of editorial logic, to the writing of this characteristic form as a thirteener by the main scribe, and to its similarity to stanzaic forms in other medieval plays. The text itself is an accurate transcription where I have had a chance to check it against a facsimile of the MS.

This is, of course, a scholarly edition, and priced out of the comfortable grasp of most students. This makes it somewhat surprising that the editors insert a list of *dramatis personae* at the start of every play. These are not in the manuscript, although England and Pollard included them in their edition. These cast lists would seem to be a departure from the editors' stated intention of providing "the first text of the full Towneley cycle based exclusively on the MS since the Surtees text of 1836" (p. xxxii). Such lists seem appropriate enough in an edition intended for actors or directors, but that seems an unlikely audience for this book, and it is not a consistent practice in other recent Early English Text Society editions of early drama.

The volume of notes is distinguished by brief but helpful introductory essays at the beginning of each play. The editors usually focus on such major issues as versification, borrowing, staging, and critical approach. The notes themselves are not above offering a reading of problematic or difficult lines (perhaps more than some readers would like), but do an excellent job of pointing to allusions (especially proverbial material), and the editors are careful to point to and sometimes include striking parallels from York and elsewhere. They also supply a helpful glossary of names as an aid to help scholars trying to locate particular characters.

Unlike Spector's recent edition of *The N-Town Play*, Cawley and Stevens do not attempt an analysis of the language of the manuscript. Such an analysis would be helpful, especially when the provenance of individual plays (as well as the cycle as a whole) continues to be a matter of dispute. They do, however, provide a full glossary including "such grammatical information as may be needed for a linguistic or dialect study of the text" (2.657); they also occasionally discuss dialectical matters in their notes.

Despite a few idiosyncrasies in presentation and interpretation, I can safely recommend the Cawley and Stevens edition of *The Towneley Plays*. The stage is now set for an inexpensively priced, modern spelling edition of all or part of the Towneley Cycle, perhaps along the lines of Richard Beadle's and Pamela King's *York Mystery Plays*. To end on a sad note: this undergraduate edition will not be a task undertaken by Professor Cawley, who regrettably passed away in 1993. This Early English Text Society edition is, however, a worthy testament to his scholarly achievements, as well as to the more than able editorial work of Martin Stevens.

VICTOR I. SCHERB
University of Texas at Tyler

SIEGFRIED WENZEL. *Macaronic Sermons, Bilingualism, and Preaching in Late-Medieval England*. Recentiores: Later Latin Texts and Contexts Series. Ann Arbor: University of Michigan Press, 1994. Pp. ix, 361. $52.50.

This book answers many questions and raises others of a controversial nature, because the author puts forward arguments that call into question the influential theories advanced by Owst and Lecoy de la March regarding the delivery of macaronic sermons.

A high proportion of the sermons surviving in England from the period 1350 to 1450 contain mixtures of English and Latin. Wenzel argues that the texts as we have them represent the way in which they were delivered. This draws attention to the linguistic competence of both the preachers and of the congregations who heard the sermons. Sometimes there is very little mixing of Latin and English, perhaps just a piece of vernacular glossing (e.g., "habeatis internum dolorem, an inderlych sorwe in herte," p. 15). Sometimes a whole sentence of a Latin text is translated into English. Elsewhere we find Latin expressions stitched into a sermon whose main language is English. To all these differing types of linguistic mixture the author applies what he felicitously calls "taxonomic rigor" (p. 29), and presents full analyses of every type according to his classification. The material is complicated, and so is the taxonomy, and readers will have to be as painstaking in their attention to this book as the author himself. Fortunately, the introductory chapters are helped by the inventories of manuscripts and sermons, which make up Appendix A.

Forty-three sermons are classified as "fully macaronic." These are sermons that contain "a significant amount of English material embedded in the Latin context" (p. 29). Sermons of this type form the most important part of the analysis and are to be found in thirteen separate manuscripts,

which "belong to three different kinds or types of late-medieval manuscripts: the notebook, the miscellany, and the sermon collection" (p. 60).
None of them contains macaronic sermons exclusively nor "any explicit
statement that would tell us for whom or for what purposes the material
was collected" (p. 63). Stylistic analysis shows that they were deliberately
constructed in macaronic register, and the controversial question as to the
form in which they were actually delivered has to be addressed. The exemplars on which these extant sermons are based have disappeared, and with
them the answer to this question.

Wenzel discards the explanation that a preacher composing a sermon in
Latin would switch to English because he was unfamiliar with a technical
term in Latin: ". . . rather their switching is a random phenomenon for
which all-encompassing causes, whether linguistic, stylistic, or psychological are hard to find" (p. 101). The explanation he advances is that the
preachers deliberately switched between English and Latin for rhetorical
effect, and the condition in which they survive suggests that they were
written for perusal by clerical readers. The base language was English, with
a mixture of Latin. In other words these sermon writers are to be regarded
as "functionally and fluently bilingual" (p. 112), and their sermons were
delivered macaronically. Wenzel's thesis contradicts the long-held opinion
that sermons for the clergy were preached in Latin, and those for the laity
in English. He presumes that the laity would have been comfortable and
informed while listening to sermons containing a mixture of English and
Latin.

This theory makes us think about contemporary remarks concerning the
laity's command of Latin. One thinks of a sermon preached by Archbishop
Richard FitzRalph "in processione Londoni facta pro rege" (dated 1346–
47?) in which he says that he will deliver the sermon in English rather than
do everything twice, in Latin and then in English, because the "insipiditas"
of the lay members of the congregation would prevent them from compre-
hending the Latin, or at least, leave them ignorant of parts of the address.
This seems to suggest that the laity in this particular congregation would
not have made sense of Latin. Hence, we may ask what such a congregation
would have made of a fully macaronic sermon. The fact that FitzRalph
spoke to the laity in English and the clergy in Latin seems to demonstrate
the validity of the traditional view that the linguistic register was not
normally mixed. But the picture is not totally clear. Wenzel cites a command from the Statutes of the Carthusian order: "In dispositione facientis
sermonem sit loqui latine vel vulgariter vel mixtim," which he translates

"Let it be up to whoever gives the sermon to speak Latin or vulgar *or in a mixture*" (his italics, p. 123). Wenzel rightly admits to uncertainty "to what extent this admittedly very isolated disposition could have influenced non-Carthusian preaching, or conversely might reflect preaching in other orders." Later he seems surer: "The quotation from the Carthusian statutes about mixed sermons fairly clinches the case for macaronic preaching at least by monastic preachers or to monastic audiences" (p. 125). Much depends on the ambiguous significance of the adverb "mixtim," which means "mixedly," or "in combination." It could mean "macaronically" in this instance, but I think that we should bear in mind the cautionary words of FitzRalph about what a lay audience could be expected to grasp, especially in the light of Wenzel's final claim that the Latin in fully macaronic sermons "formed a tool that would have been totally serviceable and effective in teaching and moving its audience" (p. 129).

This book is a substantial and original contribution to our understanding of an important type of sermon which has never before been subjected to such detailed analysis. It is an important compendium of the genre in its own right, offering a very useful set of three macaronic sermons edited in Latin, translated into exquisite English, with the macaronic elements highlighted, which form three of the appendices. The final appendix presents a statistical table of sermons, the total number of words in each, the number of English words, and the number of switches. From every point of view, it is an illuminating and thought-provoking work that is essential reading for scholars of medieval preaching.

T. P. DOLAN
University College Dublin

MURIEL WHITAKER, ed. *Sovereign Lady: Essays on Women in Middle English Literature*. Garland Medieval Casebooks, vol. 11. New York and London: Garland Publishing, 1995. Pp. xviii, 220. $36.00.

Garland's emergence as a serious press devoted to the important work of new translations, collections of interesting scholarly essays, and full-length critical studies in medieval literature has been undermined by this particular collection, which is in the Garland Medieval Casebooks series. Professor Whitaker's choice of essays suggests, if not a disregard for timely and rigorous research, then an indifference to even the formalities of writing, as many of these essays have somehow come through the editing process without a thesis of any kind. I am disappointed in these essays given that their range of topics suggests a mine of ideas about women in Middle English literature and women who write literature in the medieval period. Perhaps my disappointment is aggravated by the knowledge that the other casebooks seem to be examples of more up-to-date research, the essays more coherent in and of themselves, and the collections more cohesive as a group. For example, the collection titled *Discovering New Worlds: Essays on Medieval Exploration and Imagination* grew out of a conference held in 1989; the collection of essays published within the Garland Studies in Humor series titled *Chaucer's Humor* derives eight of its essays from scholars connected to NEH seminars on this and related topics. These situations do not assure coherence but they often help.

The essays in Whitaker's collection, on the other hand, "began as seminar papers" (Preface) in various medieval courses she taught at the University of Alberta. There is nothing inherently wrong with this approach, but the essays bear the marks of what is both good and bad about graduate papers. For example, Laura Watson's essay, "The Disposal of Paston Daughters," is a fascinating look into the private lives of the Paston women, but much of what Watson relates about marriage arrangements has been said before and her essay simply fades into observation after observation without suggesting a way to read these letters. It might be interesting, for example, to examine how the subjection of the Paston women's desires in marriage makes a difference to a culture that also consciously elevates women's desires in courtly literature. Carol Everest's essay, "'Paradys or Helle': Pleasure and Procreation in Chaucer's 'Merchant's Tale,'" arguing that medieval reproductive theory supports Chaucer's point that January cannot conceive a child (*The Merchant's Tale*)—"The state of May's sexual satisfaction" combined with "the doctrine of the two seeds . . . provid[es] evidence against May's pregnancy until she engages in more satisfactory intercourse with a younger lover" (pp. 64–65)—makes an interesting but, to my mind, minor point, the evidence for which is overwhelming without being altogether instructive. Each piece of evidence illustrates the very same idea rather than advancing her argument. These (and other) essays have no sustaining argument.

At the other end of the scale is Professor Whitaker's essay, "The Artists' Ideal Griselda," which seems to have more than one thesis—her preface notes that this essay is part of a larger study—and thus runs in more directions than a mere essay can sustain. She begins by suggesting that "Griselda's terrible and undeserved sufferings impose on the author the obligation of providing either directly or through the mouths of characters some justification for telling the tale" (p. 86), and notes that "Chaucer's representation of Griselda is based on a medieval aesthetic theory that equated beauty and goodness" (p. 87); but it is her discussion of "costume" and its symbolism and her analysis of paintings and sculptures of Griselda that leads her to note that Griselda becomes an "iconic rather than a realistic figure" (p. 91). After what seems like a few false starts, Whitaker settles into a discussion of how various historical ideals of women are reflected in art (but not fourteenth-century art). The commentary and photographs of paintings she presents are interesting as a register of the artists' idealized forms of both Walter and Griselda from the mid-eighteenth century through the late nineteenth century. But in what way does this line of investigation lead us to an understanding of the literary Griseldas? And why focus on Chaucer's version almost exclusively? In other words, why is this essay in a collection about women in Middle English literature? This would be a worthwhile project if her connections to the literature were more tightly woven and her goal more clearly defined. And it seems a shame that she could not or did not benefit from one of Garland's own publications, *Chaucer's* Clerk's Tale: *The Griselda Story Received, Rewritten, Illustrated*, a detailed and comprehensively illustrated study by Judith Bronfman (1994). On the other hand, the corollary relationship that Whitaker suggests between the figures of Griselda and the Virgin Mary represents a potentially fascinating line of investigation. One can imagine comparing literary descriptions of Griselda to literary descriptions, paintings, and sculptures of the Virgin Mary from the fourteenth century that would reveal some interesting facets of either or both characters: for example, Mary's unwavering patience under the stern demands of Archangel Michael, her resilience when her son is "taken" from her by his Father's demands, and so on. But this is not the way Whitaker goes.

Several of the essays appear to have been written several years ago and, I suspect, were not updated for this collection. For example, Elaine Filax's essay, "A Female I-deal: Chaucer's Second Nun," is an example of the almost-too-old-to-be-useful criticism that seems to pervade the volume. There is nothing wrong with using older criticism as a starting point, and indeed we can all point to seminal works that must be given credit for our more current understandings of a piece of literature. However, when an essay's dependence on articles from the 1970s is almost two-to-one over reliance on work from the 1980s (and nothing from the early 1990s), one begins to wonder if the work itself is dated. My numbers do not consider the material (a number of articles and books) from before 1970. The fact that she uses Robinson's 1957 edition suggests that the essay was written at least ten years ago. This is unacceptable scholarship in an academic world that, for good or ill, publishes hundreds of Chaucer articles every year. Finally, I must admit that I cannot figure out what Filax is arguing when she says, "As we work through to the Second Nun's Prologue and Tale, we will find not only the inevitable traces implied in the generic and visual absence of the Second Nun's representation, but the solid physical, representative presence of the female body, and the not so surprising communicatory webs that it both disrupts and sustains" (p. 134).

Even an essay that uses current criticism can fall short of real insight, of course. Pamela Farvolden's essay, " 'Love Can No Frenship': Erotic Triangles in Chaucer's 'Knight's Tale' and Lydgate's *Fabula duorum mercatorum*," works with newer materials (Benson's edition, criticism up through the early 1990s) and though her central argument—that the "felaweshipe" between Palamon and Arcite is the focus of the tale rather than the relationship between either of the men and Emelye—is clear, it has also been done before, for the most part by the people she herself quotes. Her contribution, not an insubstantial one, is the comparison with Lydgate's work, but I would like to see a further examination of the effects of Chaucer's and Lydgate's different approaches. The relationship between the male characters is clearly privileged in each work, but Chaucer seems to suggest that the forces of heterosexual desire will inevitably overpower the male "felaweshipe" and Lydgate seems to think the woman is simply expendable. This places the female character who "affirms the ideal of male friendship and confirms her role as the passive cementer of male bonds" (p. 36) in rather different positions that warrant discussion.

Some of the more successful essays include Arlette Zinck's "A Vindication of the Feminine in the *Showings* of Julian of Norwich," in which the author argues that "ultimately, it is not Julian's theology or her use of the God-as-mother image, but rather the changes in Julian's self-image as revealed in the two versions of the text that provide the most optimistic feminist statement" (p. 171). She has a clear sense of her own argument and executes a careful, text-based working out of it. Sr. Juliana Dusel suggests in "The Bride of Christ Image in the *Ancren Riwle*" that the imagery of anchoress as lover and spouse of the courtly knight-Christ pervades the manual not only because it is an effective teaching tool but also because it ameliorates the harshness of the instructions to the three young women.

Many of the essays in this collection expose their own weaknesses: they are inadequate as registers of rigorous scholarly inquiry and conscious critical methods; they are insufficiently focused; and, regrettably, they don't lead us to new or newer insights about the literature.

FAYE WALKER
University of Houston

BOOKS RECEIVED

Abou-El-Haj, Barbara. *The Medieval Cult of Saints: Formations and Trans-formations*. Cambridge: Cambridge University Press, 1995. Pp. xviii, 456. $90.00.

Adcock, Fleur, ed. and trans. *Hugh Primas and the Archpoet*. Cambridge Medieval Classics, vol. 2. Cambridge: Cambridge University Press, 1994. Pp. xxii, 129. $39.95.

Alford, John, ed. *From Page to Performance: Essays in Early English Drama*. East Lansing, Mich.: Michigan State University Press, 1995. Pp. ix, 266. $32.95.

Arn, Mary-Jo, ed. Fortunes Stabilnes: *Charles of Orléans's English Book of Love: A Critical Edition*. Medieval and Renaissance Texts and Studies, vol. 138. Binghamton, N.Y.: Medieval and Renaissance Texts and Studies, 1994. $45.00.

Bartlett, Anne Clark, with Thomas Bestul, Janet Goebel, and William F. Pollard, eds. *Vox Mystica: Essays on Medieval Mysticism in Honor of Valerie Lagorio*. Cambridge: D. S. Brewer, 1995. Pp. xiv, 235. $71.00.

Baswell, Christopher. *Virgil in Medieval England: Figuring the* Aeneid *from the Twelfth Century to Chaucer*. Cambridge Studies in Medieval Litera-ture, vol. 24. Cambridge: Cambridge University Press, 1995. Pp. xviii, 438. $60.00.

Blanch, Robert J., and Julian N. Wasserman. *From* Pearl *to* Gawain: *Forme to Fynisment*. Gainesville, Fla.: University Press of Florida, 1995. Pp. 207. $39.95.

Boenig, Robert. *Chaucer and the Mystics:* The Canterbury Tales *and the Genre of Devotional Prose*. Lewisburg, Penn.: Bucknell University Press, 1995. Pp. 231. $37.50.

Boitani, Piero, and Anna Torti, eds. *Interpretation: Medieval and Modern.* J. A. W. Bennett Memorial Lectures, 8th ser., Perugia, 1992. Cambridge: D. S. Brewer, 1993. Pp. viii, 212. $53.00.

Bond, Gerald A. *The Loving Subject: Desire, Eloquence, and Power in Romanesque France.* Middle Ages Series. Philadelphia: University of Pennsylvania Press, 1995. Pp. vii, 276. $38.95.

Burnley, David, and Matsuji Tajima. *The Language of Middle English Literature.* Annotated Bibliographies of Old and Middle English Literature, vol. 1. Cambridge: D. S. Brewer, 1994. Pp. viii, 280. $71.00.

Camargo, Martin, ed. *Medieval Rhetorics of Prose Composition: Five English* Artes Dictandi *and Their Tradition.* Medieval and Renaissance Texts and Studies, vol. 115. Binghamton, N.Y.: Medieval and Renaissance Texts and Studies, 1995. Pp. xiv, 256. $25.00.

Carpenter, Jennifer, and Sally-Beth MacLean, eds. *Power of the Weak: Studies on Medieval Women.* Urbana and Chicago: University of Illinois Press, 1995. Pp. xix, 227. $39.95 cloth, $14.95 paper.

Carruthers, Leo, ed. *Heroes and Heroines in Medieval English Literature, Presented to André Crépin.* Cambridge: D. S. Brewer, 1994. Pp. xi, 172. $53.00.

Chaucer, Geoffrey. *The House of Fame.* Ed. Nicholas R. Havely. Durham Medieval Texts, vol. 11. Durham: University of Durham, Department of English, 1994. Pp. 216. £10.00 paper.

Chaucer, Geoffrey. *A Variorum Edition of the Works of Geoffrey Chaucer. Vol. 2. The Canterbury Tales. Part 7. The Summoner's Tale.* Ed. John F. Plummer III. Norman and London: University of Oklahoma Press, 1995. Pp. xxviii, 242. $47.50.

Cherchi, Paolo. *Andreas and the Ambiguity of Courtly Love.* Toronto, Buffalo, and London: University of Toronto Press, 1994. Pp. xv, 194. $50.00.

Davidson, Clifford, ed. *The Iconography of Heaven.* Early Drama, Art, and Music Monograph Series, vol. 21. Kalamazoo, Mich.: Western Michigan University, Medieval Institute Publications, 1994. Pp. xi, 206. $15.00 paper.

Deschamps, Eustache. *L'art de dictier*. Ed. and trans. Deborah M. Sinnreich-Levi. Medieval Texts and Studies, vol. 13. East Lansing, Mich.: Colleagues Press, 1994. Pp. viii, 151. $28.00.

Dronke, Peter, ed. and trans. *Nine Medieval Latin Plays*. Cambridge Medieval Classics, vol. 1. Cambridge: Cambridge University Press, 1994. Pp. xxxv, 237. $54.95.

Edwards, Robert R., and Vickie Ziegler, eds. *Matrons and Marginal Women in Medieval Society*. Woodbridge, Suffolk: Boydell Press, 1995. Pp. xi, 127. $53.00.

Ellis, Roger, and Ruth Evans, eds. *The Medieval Translator, 4*. Medieval and Renaissance Texts and Studies, vol. 123. Binghamton, N.Y.: Medieval and Renaissance Texts and Studies, 1994. Pp. x, 256. $24.00.

Evans, Murray J. *Rereading Middle English Romance: Manuscript Layout, Decoration, and the Rhetoric of Composite Structure*. Montreal and Kingston, London, and Buffalo: McGill-Queen's University Press, 1995. Pp. xx, 203. $44.95.

Frank, Roberta, ed. *The Politics of Editing Medieval Texts*. Papers Given at the Twenty-seventh Annual Conference on Editorial Problems, University of Toronto, November 1991. New York: AMS Press, 1993. Pp. xiv, 181. $29.50.

Frantzen, Allen J., and David A. Robertson, eds. *Essays in Medieval Studies*, vol. 11. 1994 Proceedings of the Illinois Medieval Association. Chicago: Illinois Medieval Association, 1995. Pp. ii, 149. $10.00.

Friedman, John B. *Northern English Books, Owners, and Makers in the Late Middle Ages*. Syracuse, N.Y.: Syracuse University Press, 1995. Pp. xxvi, 423. $39.95.

311

Gaunt, Simon. *Gender and Genre in Medieval French Literature*. Cambridge Studies in French, vol. 53. Cambridge: Cambridge University Press, 1995. Pp. x, 372. $64.95.

Geary, Patrick J., gen. ed. *Historical and Religious Writers of the Latin West*. Peter Abelard and Honorius Augustodunensis. Authors of the Middle Ages Series, vol. 2, nos. 5–6. Brookfield, Vt.: Ashgate Publishing, 1995. Pp. vii, 183. $54.95.

Guerin, M. Victoria. *The Fall of Kings and Princes: Structure and Destruction in Arthurian Tragedy*. Figurae: Reading Medieval Culture Series. Stanford: Stanford University Press, 1995. Pp. xi, 336. $39.50.

Hallissy, Margaret. *A Companion to Chaucer's* Canterbury Tales. Westport, Conn., and London: Greenwood Press, 1995. Pp. xiv, 333. $49.95.

Harley, Marta Powell, ed. The Myrour of Recluses*: A Middle English Translation of* Speculum Inclusorum. Madison, N.J. and Teaneck, N.J.: Fairleigh Dickinson University Press, 1995. Pp. xxxiii, 90. $26.50.

Heffernan, Carol Falvo. *The Melancholy Muse: Chaucer, Shakespeare and Early Medicine*. Duquesne Language and Literature Series, vol. 19. Pittsburgh: Duquesne University Press, 1995. Pp. xiv, 185. $48.00.

Knittel, Frank, and Grosvenor Fattic, eds. *A Critical Edition of the Medieval Play* Mankind. Lewiston, N.Y.; Queenston, Ontario; and Lampeter, Dyfed, Wales: Edwin Mellen Press, 1995. Pp. 152. $79.95.

Laird, Edgar, and Robert Fischer, eds. *Pèlerin de Prusse on the Astrolabe: Text and Translation of his* Practique de Astralabe. Medieval and Renaissance Texts and Studies, vol. 127. Binghamton, N.Y.: Medieval and Renaissance Texts and Studies, 1995. Pp. 114. $20.00.

Larrington, Carolyne. *Women and Writing in Medieval Europe: A Sourcebook*. London and New York: Routledge, 1995. $17.95 paper.

Law, Vivien. *Wisdom, Authority, and Grammar in the Seventh Century: Decoding Virgilius Maro Grammaticus*. Cambridge: Cambridge University Press, 1995. Pp. x, 170. $49.95.

McKenna, Steven R. *Robert Henryson's Tragic Vision*. American University Studies. English Language and Literature Series, vol. 171. New York: Peter Lang, 1994. Pp. 221. $39.95.

McKitterick, Rosamund, ed. *The New Cambridge Medieval History, Vol. 2: c. 700–c. 900*. The New Cambridge Medieval History. Cambridge: Cambridge University Press, 1995. Pp. xxxi, 1082. $95.00.

Maddox, Donald, and Sara Sturm-Maddox, eds. *Literary Aspects of Courtly Culture: Selected Papers from the Seventh Triennial Congress of the International Courtly Literature Society, 1992*. Cambridge: D. S. Brewer, 1994. Pp. 360. $69.00.

Marx, C. W. *The Devil's Rights and the Redemption in the Literature of Medieval England*. Cambridge: D. S. Brewer, 1995. Pp. x, 184. $53.00.

Minnis, A. J. *Oxford Guides to Chaucer: The Shorter Poems*. Oxford: Clarendon Press, 1995. Pp. xiii, 578. $72.00.

Mooney, Linne R. *The Index of Middle English Prose: Handlist XI, Manuscripts in the Library of Trinity College, Cambridge*. Cambridge: D. S. Brewer, 1995. Pp. xxxviii, 251. $81.00.

Muir, Lynette R. *The Biblical Drama of Medieval Europe*. Cambridge: Cambridge University Press, 1995. Pp. xxiii, 320. $60.00.

Netzer, Nancy. *Cultural Interplay in the Eighth Century: The* Trier Gospels *and the Making of a Scriptorium at Echternach*. Cambridge Studies in Paleography and Codicology, vol. 3. Cambridge: Cambridge University Press, 1994. Pp. xvi, 258. $64.95.

Newhauser, Richard G., and John A. Alford, eds. *Literature and Religion in the Late Middle Ages: Philological Studies in Honor of Siegfried Wenzel*. Medieval and Renaissance Texts and Studies, vol. 118. Binghamton, N.Y.: Medieval and Renaissance Texts and Studies, 1995. Pp. ix, 414. $25.00.

Nicolaisen, W. F. H., ed. *Oral Tradition in the Middle Ages.* Medieval and Renaissance Texts and Studies, vol. 112. Binghamton, N.Y.: Medieval and Renaissance Texts and Studies, 1995. Pp. vi, 231. $24.00.

Ohler, Norbert. *The Medieval Traveler.* Trans. Caroline Hillier. Woodbridge, Suffolk: Boydell Press, 1989. Pp. xv, 245. $45.00.

Pratt, Karen, ed. *Shifts and Transpositions in Medieval Narrative: A Festschrift for Elspeth Kennedy.* Cambridge: D. S. Brewer, 1994. Pp. xxi, 206. $53.00.

Rex, Richard. *"The Sins of Madame Eglentyne" and Other Essays on Chaucer.* Newark, Del.: University of Delaware Press, 1995. Pp. 201. $35.00.

Rushing, James A., Jr. *Images of Adventure: Ywain in the Visual Arts.* Middle Ages Series. Philadelphia: University of Pennsylvania Press, 1995. Pp. xiv, 300. $39.95.

Salda, Michael N., and Jean E. Jost, eds. *Chaucer Yearbook: A Journal of Late Medieval Studies,* vol. 2 (1995). Cambridge: D. S. Brewer, 1995. Pp. 218. $53.00.

Schultz, James A. *The Knowledge of Childhood in the German Middle Ages, 1100–1350.* Middle Ages Series. Philadelphia: University of Pennsylvania Press, 1995. Pp. xx, 318. $38.95.

Seymour, M. C. *A Catalogue of Chaucer Manuscripts, Vol. 1: Works Before the Canterbury Tales.* Brookfield, Vt.: Ashgate Publishing, 1995. Pp. x, 171. $67.95.

Simpson, James. *Sciences and the Self in Medieval Poetry: Alan of Lille's Anticlaudianus and John Gower's* Confessio Amantis. Cambridge Studies in Medieval Literature, vol. 25. Cambridge: Cambridge University Press, 1995. Pp. xii, 321. $59.95.

Smith, Lesley, and Jane H. M. Taylor, eds. *Women, the Book, and the Godly.* Cambridge: D. S. Brewer, 1995. Pp. xiii, 191. $53.00.

Smith, Susan L. *The Power of Women: A Topos in Medieval Art and Literature.* Philadelphia: University of Pennsylvania Press, 1995. Pp. xv, 294. $44.95.

Stevens, Martin, and Daniel Woodward, eds. *The Ellesmere Chaucer: Essays in Interpretation.* San Marino: Huntington Library, 1995; and Tokyo: Yushodo Co., 1995. Pp. xvi, 363. $75.00.

Stevick, Robert D., ed. *One Hundred Middle English Lyrics.* Rev. ed. Urbana and Chicago: University of Illinois Press, 1995. Pp. liii, 194. $14.95 paper.

Taavitsainen, Irma. *The Index of Middle English Prose. Handlist X: Manuscripts in Scandinavian Collections.* The Index of Middle English Prose, vol. 10. Cambridge: D. S. Brewer, 1994. Pp. xxvii, 46. $45.00.

Tavormina, M. Teresa. *Kindly Similitude: Marriage and Family in* Piers Plowman. Piers Plowman Studies 11. Cambridge: D. S. Brewer, 1995. $71.00.

Utz, Richard J., ed. *Literary Nominalism and the Theory of Rereading Late Medieval Texts: A New Research Paradigm.* Mediaeval Studies, vol. 5. Lewiston, N.Y.; Queenston, Ontario; and Lampeter, Dyfed, Wales: Edwin Mellen Press, 1995. Pp. 256. $90.00.

Wada, Yoko, ed. and trans. *"Temptations" from* Ancrene Wisse. Vol. 1. Kansai University Institute of Oriental and Occidental Studies. Sources and Materials Series, vol. 18. Suita, Osaka: Kansai University, 1994. Pp. cxii, 135. $45.00.

Weisl, Angela Jane. *Conquering the Reign of Femeny.* Chaucer Studies, vol. 22. Cambridge: D. S. Brewer, 1995. Pp. ix, 133. $53.00.

Wetherbee, Winthrop, ed. and trans. *Johannes de Hauvilla*, Architrenius. Cambridge Medieval Classics, vol. 3. Cambridge: Cambridge University Press, 1994. Pp. xxxii, 276. $59.95.

Wilhelm, James J., ed. *Gay and Lesbian Poetry: An Anthology from Sappho to Michelangelo.* Garland Reference Library of the Humanities, vol. 1874.

New York and London: Garland Publishing, 1995. Pp. xii, 330. $50.00 cloth, $19.95 paper.

Wilkins, Nigel. *Music in the Age of Chaucer*. Second Edition, with *Chaucer Songs*. Chaucer Studies, vol. 1. Cambridge: D. S. Brewer, 1995. Pp. xiv, 210. $71.00.

Windeatt, Barry, ed. *English Mystics of the Middle Ages*. Cambridge: Cambridge University Press, 1994. Pp. xi, 311. $59.95.

Zink, Michel. *Medieval French Literature: An Introduction*. Trans. Jeff Rider. Medieval and Renaissance Texts and Studies, vol. 110. Binghamton, N.Y.: Medieval and Renaissance Texts and Studies, 1995. Pp. xii, 171. $25.00 cloth, $8.00 paper.

An Annotated Chaucer Bibliography
1994

Compiled and edited by Mark Allen and Bege K. Bowers

Regular contributors:

Bruce W. Hozeski, *Ball State University* (Indiana)
George Nicholas, *Benedictine College* (Kansas)
Martha S. Waller, *Butler University* (Indiana)
Marilyn Sutton, *California State University at Dominguez Hills*
Larry L. Bronson, *Central Michigan University*
Glending Olson, *Cleveland State University* (Ohio)
Winthrop Wetherbee, *Cornell University*
Elizabeth Dobbs, *Grinnell College* (Iowa)
Faye Walker, *Houston, Texas*
Masatoshi Kawasaki, *Komazawa University* (Tokyo, Japan)
William Schipper, *Memorial University* (Newfoundland, Canada)
Daniel J. Pinti, *New Mexico State University*
Erik Kooper, *Rijksuniversiteit te Utrecht*
Cindy L. Vitto, *Rowan College of New Jersey*
Richard H. Osberg, *Santa Clara University* (California)
Margaret Connolly, *University College, Cork* (Ireland)
Juliette Dor, *Université de Liège* (Belgium)
Mary Flowers Braswell, Theresa Kemp, and Elaine Whitaker, *University of Alabama at Birmingham*
Denise Stodola, *University of Missouri, Columbia*
Cynthia Gravlee, *University of Montevallo* (Alabama)
Gregory M. Sadlek, *University of Nebraska at Omaha*
Cynthia Ho, *University of North Carolina, Asheville*
Richard J. Utz, *University of Northern Iowa*
Thomas Hahn, *University of Rochester* (New York)
Rebecca Beal, *University of Scranton* (Pennsylvania)

Stanley R. Hauer, *University of Southern Mississippi*
Mark Allen, Gail Jones, and Connie Sabo-Risley, *University of Texas at San Antonio*
Brian A. Shaw, *University of Western Ontario*
Joyce T. Lionarons, *Ursinus College* (Pennsylvania)
John M. Crafton, *West Georgia College*
Robert Correale, *Wright State University* (Ohio)
Bege K. Bowers, *Youngstown State University* (Ohio)

Ad hoc contributions were made by the following: Paul R. Thomas, *Brigham Young University*; James McNelis, *University of Washington*; Andrew Lynch, *University of Western Australia*; and Jesús Luis Serrano Reyes, *Córdoba*.

The bibliographers acknowledge with gratitude the MLA typesimulation provided by Terence Ford, Director, Center for Bibliographical Services of the MLA; postage from the University of Texas at San Antonio, Division of English, Classics, and Philosophy; and assistance from the library staff, especially Susan McCray, at the John Peace Library, University of Texas at San Antonio.

This bibliography continues the bibliographies published since 1975 in previous volumes of *Studies in the Age of Chaucer*. Bibliographical information up to 1975 can be found in Eleanor P. Hammond, *Chaucer: A Bibliographic Manual* (1908; reprint, New York: Peter Smith, 1933); D. D. Griffith, *Bibliography of Chaucer, 1908–53* (Seattle: University of Washington Press, 1955); William R. Crawford, *Bibliography of Chaucer, 1954–63* (Seattle: University of Washington Press, 1967); and Lorrayne Y. Baird, *Bibliography of Chaucer, 1964–73* (Boston: G. K. Hall, 1977). See also Lorrayne Y. Baird-Lange and Hildegard Schnuttgen, *Bibliography of Chaucer, 1974–1985* (Hamden, Conn.: Shoe String Press, 1988).

Additions and corrections to this bibliography should be sent to Mark Allen, Bibliographic Division, New Chaucer Society, Division of English, Classics, and Philosophy, University of Texas at San Antonio, San Antonio, Texas 78249-0643 (FAX: 210-691-5366; E-MAIL: MALLEN @LONESTAR.JPL.UTSA.EDU). Authors are urged to send annotations for articles, reviews, and books that have been or might be overlooked.

Classifications

319

Abbreviations of Chaucer's Works

ABC	*An ABC*
Adam	*Adam Scriveyn*
Anel	*Anelida and Arcite*
Astr	*A Treatise on the Astrolabe*
Bal Compl	*A Balade of Complaint*
BD	*The Book of the Duchess*
Bo	*Boece*
Buk	*The Envoy to Bukton*
CkT, CkP, Rv–CkL	*The Cook's Tale, The Cook's Prologue, Reeve–Cook Link*
ClT, ClP, Cl–MerL	*The Clerk's Tale, The Clerk's Prologue, Clerk–Merchant Link*
Compl d'Am	*Complaynt d'Amours*
CT	*The Canterbury Tales*
CYT, CYP	*The Canon's Yeoman's Tale, The Canon's Yeoman's Prologue*
Equat	*Equatorie of the Planetis*
For	*Fortune*
Form Age	*The Former Age*
FranT, FranP	*The Franklin's Tale, The Franklin's Prologue*
FrT, FrP, Fr–SumL	*The Friar's Tale, The Friar's Prologue, Friar–Summoner Link*
Gent	*Gentilesse*
GP	*The General Prologue*
HF	*The House of Fame*
KnT, Kn–MilL	*The Knight's Tale, Knight–Miller Link*
Lady	*A Complaint to His Lady*
LGW, LGWP	*The Legend of Good Women, The Legend of Good Women Prologue*
ManT, ManP	*The Manciple's Tale, The Manciple's Prologue*
Mars	*The Complaint of Mars*
Mel, Mel–MkL	*The Tale of Melibee, Melibee–Monk Link*
MercB	*Merciles Beaute*
MerT, MerE–SqH	*The Merchant's Tale, Merchant Endlink–Squire Headlink*

MilT, MilP, Mil–RvL	*The Miller's Tale, The Miller's Prologue, Miller–Reeve Link*
MkT, MkP, Mk–NPL	*The Monk's Tale, The Monk's Prologue, Monk–Nun's Priest Link*
MLT, MLH, MLP, MLE	*The Man of Law's Tale, Man of Law Headlink, The Man of Law's Prologue, Man of Law Endlink*
NPT, NPP, NPE	*The Nun's Priest's Tale, The Nun's Priest's Prologue, Nun's Priest Endlink*
PardT, PardP	*The Pardoner's Tale, The Pardoner's Prologue*
ParsT, ParsP	*The Parson's Tale, The Parson's Prologue*
PF	*The Parliament of Fowls*
PhyT, Phy–PardL	*The Physician's Tale, Physician–Pardoner Link*
Pity	*The Complaint unto Pity*
Prov	*Proverbs*
PrT, PrP, Pr–ThL	*The Prioress's Tale, The Prioress's Prologue, Prioress–Thopas Link*
Purse	*The Complaint of Chaucer to His Purse*
Ret	*Chaucer's Retraction {Retractation}*
Rom	*The Romaunt of the Rose*
Ros	*To Rosemounde*
RvT, RvP	*The Reeve's Tale, The Reeve's Prologue*
Scog	*The Envoy to Scogan*
ShT, Sh–PrL	*The Shipman's Tale, Shipman–Prioress Link*
SNT, SNP, SN–CYL	*The Second Nun's Tale, The Second Nun's Prologue, Second Nun–Canon's Yeoman Link*
SqT, SqH, Sq–FranL	*The Squire's Tale, Squire Headlink, Squire–Franklin Link*
Sted	*Lak of Stedfastnesse*
SumT, SumP	*The Summoner's Tale, The Summoner's Prologue*
TC	*Troilus and Criseyde*
Th, Th–MelL	*The Tale of Sir Thopas, Sir Thopas–Melibee Link*
Truth	*Truth*
Ven	*The Complaint of Venus*
WBT, WBP, WB–FrL	*The Wife of Bath's Tale, The Wife of Bath's Prologue, Wife of Bath–Friar Link*
Wom Nob	*Womanly Noblesse*
Wom Unc	*Against Women Unconstant*

322

Periodical Abbreviations

AdI	*Annali d'Italianistica*
AEB	*Analytical and Enumerative Bibliography*
AJGLL	*American Journal of Germanic Linguistics and Literatures*
Anglia	*Anglia: Zeitschrift für Englische Philologie*
Archiv	*Archiv für das Studium der Neueren Sprachen und Literaturen*
BAM	*Bulletin des Anglicistes Médiévistes*
CE	*College English*
ChauR	*Chaucer Review*
ChLB	*Charles Lamb Bulletin*
Cithara	*Cithara: Essays in the Judaeo-Christian Tradition*
CLAJ	*College Language Association Journal*
CLS	*Comparative Literature Studies*
CMat	*Critical Matrix: The Princeton Journal of Women, Gender, and Culture*
Comitatus	*Comitatus: A Journal of Medieval and Renaissance Studies*
Connotations	*Connotations: A Journal for Critical Debate*
CRCL	*Canadian Review of Comparative Literature/ Revue Canadienne de Littérature Comparée*
CrSurv	*Critical Survey*
CSR	*Christian Scholar's Review*
DAI	*Dissertation Abstracts International*
EA	*Etudes Anglaises: Grand-Bretagne, Etats-Unis*
EIC	*Essays in Criticism: A Quarterly Journal of Literary Criticism* (Oxford, England)
ELH	*Journal of English Literary History*
ELN	*English Language Notes*
ELR	*English Literary Renaissance*
ELWIU	*Essays in Literature* (Macomb, Ill.)
EMS	*English Manuscript Studies 1100–1700*
English	*English: The Journal of the English Association* (London, England)

ES	*English Studies*
ESC	*English Studies in Canada*
Exemplaria	*Exemplaria: A Journal of Theory in Medieval and Renaissance Studies*
FCS	*Fifteenth-Century Studies*
Florilegium	*Florilegium: Carleton University Papers on Late Antiquity and the Middle Ages*
HJR	*Henry James Review*
HLB	*Harvard Library Bulletin*
HLQ	*Huntington Library Quarterly: A Journal for the History and Interpretation of English and American Literature*
InG	*In Geardagum: Essays on Old and Middle English Language and Literature*
JBAL	*Journal of British and American Literature* (Komazawa University)
JEGP	*Journal of English and Germanic Philology*
JLSTL	*Journal of Literary Studies/Tydskrif Vir Literaturwetenskap*
JRMMRA	*Journal of the Rocky Mountain Medieval and Renaissance Association*
KSJ	*Keats-Shelley Journal: Keats, Shelley, Byron, Hunt, and Their Circles*
LeedsSE	*Leeds Studies in English*
Linguistics	*Linguistics: An Interdisciplinary Journal of the Language Sciences*
MA	*Le Moyen Age: Revue d'Histoire et de Philologie*
MÆ	*Medium Ævum*
M&H	*Medievalia et Humanistica: Studies in Medieval and Renaissance Culture*
MedPers	*Medieval Perspectives*
MLQ	*Modern Language Quarterly*
MLR	*Modern Language Review*
MP	*Modern Philology: A Journal Devoted to Research in Medieval and Modern Literature*
MS	*Mediaeval Studies* (Toronto, Canada)
N&Q	*Notes and Queries*
NewComp	*New Comparison: A Journal of Comparative and General Literary Studies*

NM	*Neuphilologische Mitteilungen*
PLL	*Papers on Language and Literature: A Journal for Scholars and Critics of Language and Literature*
PMLA	*Publications of the Modern Language Association of America*
PoeticaT	*Poetica: An International Journal of Linguistic Literary Studies*
PQ	*Philological Quarterly*
ProverbiumY	*Proverbium: Yearbook of International Proverb Scholarship*
PVR	*Platte Valley Review*
QJS	*Quarterly Journal of Speech*
Raritan	*Raritan: A Quarterly Review*
RBPH	*Revue Belge de Philologie et d'Histoire/Belgisch Tijdschrift voor Filologie en Geschiedenis*
RenQ	*Renaissance Quarterly*
RES	*Review of English Studies*
RMSt	*Reading Medieval Studies*
RPLit	*Res Publica Litterarum: Studies in the Classical Tradition*
SAC	*Studies in the Age of Chaucer*
SB	*Studies in Bibliography: Papers of the Bibliographical Society of the University of Virginia*
SELIM	*SELIM: Journal of the Spanish Society for Mediaeval English Language and Literature*
SHR	*Southern Humanities Review*
SiM	*Studies in Medievalism*
SLJ	*Southern Literary Journal*
SMELL	*Studies in Medieval English Language and Literature*
SoRA	*Southern Review: Literary and Interdisciplinary Essays* (Adelaide, Australia)
SP	*Studies in Philology*
Speculum	*Speculum: A Journal of Medieval Studies*
SSF	*Studies in Short Fiction*
SSL	*Studies in Scottish Literature*
StHR	*Stanford Humanities Review*

325

Text	*Text: Transactions of the Society for Textual Scholarship*
TRev	*Translation Review*
YWES	*Year's Work in English Studies*

Bibliographical Citations
and Annotations

Bibliographies, Reports, and Reference

1. Allen, Mark, and Bege K. Bowers. "An Annotated Chaucer Bibliography, 1992." *SAC* 16 (1994): 311–94. Continuation of *SAC* annual bibliography (since 1975); based on 1992 *MLA Bibliography* listings, contributions from an international bibliographic team, and independent research. A total of 404 items, including reviews.

2. Allen, Valerie, and Lucinda Rumsey. "Middle English: Chaucer." *YWES* 73 (1992): 150–70. A discursive bibliography of Chaucerian scholarship and research published in 1992; divided into four categories: general, *CT*, *TC*, and other works.

3. Bowers, Bege K. "Chaucer Research, 1993: Report No. 54." *ChauR* 29 (1994): 207–25. The 1993 report of the Committee on Chaucer Bibliography and Research; lists 371 Chaucer studies.

4. Burnley, David, and Matsuji Tajima. *The Language of Middle English Literature*. Annotated Bibliographies of Old and Middle English Literature, no. 1. Woodbridge, Suffolk; and Rochester, N.Y.: D. S. Brewer, 1994. viii, 280 pp. An annotated bibliography of 1,335 studies, arranged chronologically (1865–1900) within three broad categories: Early Middle English, Later Middle English, and dissertations. Includes studies in which "linguistic description has been used to cast light upon the function of language for literary effect." Annotations range from a brief sentence to lengthy paragraphs. Excludes studies that pertain primarily to Chaucer, but the subject index lists thirty-seven items in which Chaucer's works are a significant concern. Also includes a descriptive introduction and an author index.

5. Watts, William H., and Richard J. Utz. "Nominalist Perspectives on Chaucer's Poetry: A Bibliographical Essay." *M&H* 20 (1994): 147–73. Surveys and evaluates scholarly work on Chaucer and nominalist—especially Ockhamist—philosophy, using four categories: epistemology, universals versus particulars, poetic structure, and relation of human to divine. Chaucer's awareness of and interest in the nominalist controversy is clear, but critics must not assume a specific relationship between Chaucer and nominalism or "over-philosophize" Chaucer.

See also nos. 21, 33, 43, 49.

Recordings and Films

6. *The Book of the Duchess*. ANZAMRS Readings, no. 2. Provo, Utah: Chaucer Studio, 1988. Audio cassette; 59 min. Dir. T. L. Burton. Recorded at the Fourteenth Australian and New Zealand Association for Medieval and Renaissance Studies (ANZAMRS) Conference, University of Sydney. Readers include Francis de Vries, Mary Dove, Diane Speed, Gary Simes, David May, Andrew Lynch, Tom Burton, and Kevin Magarey.

7. *The Franklin's Tale*. NCS Readings, no. 7. Provo, Utah: Chaucer Studio, 1990. Audio cassette; 56 min. Dir. T. L. Burton. Recorded at the Seventh International Congress of the New Chaucer Society, University of Kent. Readers include A. C. Spearing, Mary-Ann Stouck, Tom Burton, William Cooper, Jr., Harvey De Roo, Paul R. Thomas, and Emerson Brown, Jr.

8. *The Friar's Tale*. NCS Readings, no. 5. Provo, Utah: Chaucer Studio, 1990. Audio cassette; 54 min. Dir. Alan T. Gaylord. Recorded at Dartmouth College. Read by Alan T. Gaylord.

9. *The General Prologue*. Occasional Readings, no. 8. Provo, Utah: York Productions, 1990; jointly published with Chaucer Studio, 1994. Audio cassette; 57 min. Dir. Paul R. Thomas. Recorded at Brigham Young University. Read by Paul R. Thomas.

10. *The Merchant's Tale*. NCS Readings, no. 3. Provo, Utah: Chaucer Studio, 1988. Audio cassette; 81 min. Dir. T. L. Burton. Recorded at the Sixth International Congress of the New Chaucer Society, Simon Fraser University. Readers include Emerson Brown, Jr., Bennett J. Lamond, Robert Worth Frank, Jr., D. Thomas Hanks, Jr., Tom Burton, Richard Firth Green, Paul R. Thomas, Susan Crane, John Burrow, and Jane Chance.

11. *The Pardoner's Tale*. Occasional Readings, no. 12. Provo, Utah: Chaucer Studio, 1994. Audio cassette; 57 min. Dir. Joseph Gallagher. Recorded at Simon Fraser University. Read by Joseph Gallagher.

12. *The Parlement of Foules*. ANZAMRS Readings, no. 1. Provo, Utah: Chaucer Studio, 1986. Audio cassette; 79 min. Dir. T. L. Burton. Recorded at the Thirteenth Australian and New Zealand Association for Medieval and Renaissance Studies (ANZAMRS) Conference, University of Melbourne. Readers include Francis de Vries, Kevin Magarey, John Gray, Michael Wright, Margaret Singer, Greg Waite, Stephanie Hollis, Rosemary Greentree, Andrew Lynch, Forrest Scott, and Mary Dove.

13. *The Prioress's Tale: Two Readings*. NCS Readings, no. 8. Provo, Utah: Chaucer Studio, 1990. Audio cassette; 32 min. Dir. T. L. Burton.

Recorded at Campion College, University of Regina (side one), and at the Seventh International Congress of the New Chaucer Society, University of Kent (side two). Read by Thomas Rendall (side one) and Michelle Matthews (side two).

14. *Sir Thopas: Two Readings*. NCS Readings, no. 2 Provo, Utah: Chaucer Studio, 1988. Audio cassette; 24 min. Dir. T. L. Burton. Recorded at the Sixth International Congress of the New Chaucer Society, Simon Fraser University. Readers include Bennett J. Lamond (monologue); and Bennett J. Lamond, Robert Worth Frank, Jr., Richard Firth Green, and Paul R. Thomas (dramatization).

15. *Specimens of Middle English Pronunciation*. Occasional Readings, no. 11. Provo, Utah: Chaucer Studio, 1994. Audio cassette with accompanying booklet; 61 min., 18 pp. Dir. and read by Alex Jones. Recorded at the University of Sydney. Includes the booklet *How to Pronounce Middle English*. Readings feature *GP* 1–42; *Piers Plowman* Prologue (B-version); *Sir Gawain and the Green Knight* 691–810; *HF* 1110–200; and *FranT* 709–1260.

16. *The Summoner's Tale*. NCS Readings, no. 6. Provo, Utah: Chaucer Studio, 1990. Audio cassette; 48 min. Dir. T. L. Burton. Recorded at the Seventh International Congress of the New Chaucer Society, University of Kent. Readers include Harvey De Roo, Paul R. Thomas, Tom Burton, Thomas Rendall, Maldwyn Mills, R. A. Shoaf, Priscilla Martin, Emerson Brown, Jr., Mary-Ann Stouck, and Joseph Gallagher.

Chaucer's Life

17. Yatzeck, Elena. "Godwin's *Life of Chaucer*: Making Virtue of Necessity." *ChLB* 84 (1993): 126–35. Yatzeck reads Godwin's *Life of Chaucer* as an extension of Godwin's social philosophy, which combines necessity and human perfectibility. Godwin reconstructs Chaucer's life and makes generalizations about medieval life to encourage readers to recognize the process of social formulation.

See also nos. 45, 51.

Facsimiles, Editions, and Translations

18. Dane, Joseph A. "The Presumed Influence of Skeat's *Student's Chaucer* on Manly and Rickert's *Text of the Canterbury Tales*." *AEB*, n.s., 7

(1993): 18–27. Collates versions of the epitaph on Chaucer's tomb to challenge assumptions underlying the *Chaucer Variorum*'s choice of the Hengwrt manuscript as a base text. While Hengwrt may be close to Chaucer's original, the "movement" from Skeat to Hengwrt in the Manly-Rickert collations does not support the notion.

19. Dor, Juliette, with Guido Latré. "Douleurs et joies du traducteur de textes médiévaux." In Christine Pagnoulle, ed. *Les gens du passage*. L³— Liège Language and Literature. Liège: Université de Liège, 1992, pp. 85–91. Discusses problems of translating medieval texts, especially *CT* and *Sir Gawain and the Green Knight*, treating problems of cultural distance and reception as well as linguistic aspects.

20. Edmonds, David, electronic ed., and Lou Burnard, technical consultant. Electronic edition of *The Riverside Chaucer*. Oxford Electronic Text Library. Oxford and New York: Oxford University Press, 1992. 42 pp.; 2 computer disks. SGML-encoded version of the texts of *The Riverside Chaucer* (*SAC* 11 [1989], no. 11), without notes or other apparatus, readable on a personal computer or Macintosh. See also no. 292.

21. Fischer, Andreas, and Roland Lüthi. "Der deutsche Chaucer: Eine bibliographische Übersicht mit Kommentar." *Archiv* 231 (1994): 44–58. An annotated bibliography of thirty German translations of Chaucer's works published between 1826 and 1992, with additional commentary that notes patterns of reception.

22. Matsushita, Tomonori, ed. *Chaucer's* Canterbury Tales: The Knight's Tale. Tokyo: Matsushita, 1994. xii, 288 pp. Edition of *KnT* with modern English translation, pronunciation guide, and glossary.

23. Robinson, Peter M. W. "Redefining Critical Editions." In George P. Landow and Paul Delany, eds. *The Digital Word: Text-based Computing in the Humanities*. Cambridge, Mass., and London: MIT Press, 1993, pp. 271–91. Critiques print-based critical editions of *CT* and *Piers Plowman*, arguing that they are based on spelling- and punctuation-normalized texts that disguise so-called accidentals and may confuse the difference between accidentals and substantive variants. Recommends production of electronic editions and describes efforts to do so with *WBP*.

24. Wynne-Davies, Marion, ed. *Geoffrey Chaucer: The Tales of the Clerk and the Wife of Bath*. Routledge English Texts. London and New York: Routledge, 1992. viii, 210 pp. An edition of *WBPT* and *ClPT*, based on the Hengwrt manuscript. The introduction and critical commentary address the social context of the works, discussing Griselda and the Wife as accurate reflections of the medieval status of women. The edition includes

bottom-of-the-page glosses and a glossary, brief notes indicating sources and some manuscript variants, and a selected bibliography. See also no. 352.

See also no. 41.

Manuscripts and Textual Studies

25. Fisher, John H. "Historical and Methodological Considerations for Adopting 'Best Text' or 'Usus Scribendi' for Textual Criticism of Chaucer's Poems." *Text* 6 (1994): 165–80. Since no authorial text of *CT* or *TC* is available for a best-text edition, a combination of the habits or "uses" of the earliest scribes, with spelling normalized to accord with *Equat*, should be used to produce an edition. Fisher exemplifies such an editorial process for a brief section of *WBP*.

26. Kendrick, Laura. "Les 'bords' des *Contes de Cantorbéry* et des manuscrits enluminés." *BAM* 46 (1994): 926–38. Explores wordplay involving French and Anglo-Norman *bords* that may have authorized the use of the borders of medieval illuminated manuscripts for visual jesting, contestation, and derision. Considers the verbal "borders" of *CT* in relation to this tradition.

27. McClellan, William. "The Transcription of the 'Clerk's Tale' in MS HM140: Interpreting Textual Effects." *SB* 47 (1994): 89–103. Three important omissions (including omission of *ClP*) strip the HM140 text of *ClT* of its "Canterbury" context. Whether these were deliberate excisions or a consequence of problems in production cannot be demonstrated conclusively.

28. Machan, Tim William. "Chaucer's Poetry, Versioning, and Hypertext." *PQ* 73 (1994): 299–316. A clear-text, eclectic edition provides convenience and coherence for the reader by presenting a text (such as Chaucer's) as the artist's completed product. But current interest in "versioning"—seeing the text as a process by comparing versions and formulating a sense of historical constitution—can be accommodated on computers via hypertext, which keeps open interpretive possibilities closed by traditional theory.

29. ———. *Textual Criticism and Middle English Texts*. Charlottesville: University of Virginia Press, 1994. x, 250 pp. Machan identifies and defines specific cultural and textual factors particular to Middle English works. He argues that textual criticism, in its evolutionary approach, is

331

consonant with source-and-analogue criticism. Today's standard texts develop from earlier ones.

30. Pearsall, Derek. "The Uses of Manuscripts: Late Medieval English." *HLB*, n.s., 4:4 (1993–94): 30–36. Surveys problems with critical editions that distort readers' ideas of medieval literature and indicates directions for the scholarly study of manuscripts. The article refers repeatedly to manuscripts of Chaucer and of Langland.

31. Ramsey, Roy Vance. *The Manly-Rickert Text of the* Canterbury Tales. Lewiston, N.Y.; Queenston, Ontario; Lampeter: Edwin Mellen, 1994. xxii, 691 pp. Defends the Manly-Rickert (M-R) text of *CT* and its apparatus against "false and demeaning" impressions in recent discussions and editions. In separate chapters, Ramsey (1) critiques the methods of editors from Urry to the *Chaucer Variorum*; (2) explains the method and chronology of M-R; (3) surveys the practices of late-medieval scribes and book production; (4) suggests the existence of a complex variety of *CT* texts ca. 1400; (5) argues for the influence of these texts on post–1400 manuscripts; (6) explores the production of post–1400 manuscripts; and (7) examines the production of Hengwrt and its value. Using M-R data throughout his discussion, Ramsey concludes that M-R must be used in conjunction with the best-text manuscript (Hengwrt) to produce an edition that closes the gap between the *Variorum* and classroom texts.

See also nos. 18, 77, 84, 110, 249.

Sources, Analogues, and Literary Relations

32. Anderson, David. "The Italian Background to Chaucer's Epic Similes." *AdI* 12 (1994): 15–38. Argues that Chaucer's similes cannot be explained in terms of imitation of Dante and Boccaccio or direct imitation of classical models. Instead, following the example of Dante and Boccaccio, Chaucer practiced a "poetics of vernacularization," imitating the "well-articulated model of the rhetorical form" of the simile as defined in the Italian tradition of Ciceronian rhetoric.

33. Arden, Heather M. The Roman de la Rose: *An Annotated Bibliography*. New York and London: Garland, 1993. xxx, 385 pp. An annotated bibliography focusing on *The Roman de la Rose*, divided into five broad categories: the text of the poem; other works by or attributed to Jean de Meun; modern critical studies; influence; and miscellaneous. Arden provides an overview of the work's literary history, sources, allegorical mean-

ing, and poetic technique, plus an author and subject index. A total of 794 items—82 indexed to Chaucer and 26 to *Rom*.

34. Calabrese, Michael A. *Chaucer's Ovidian Arts of Love*. Gainesville: University Press of Florida, 1994. x, 170 pp. Examines Chaucer's uses of Ovid, assessing the former's perception of the ancient poet, tracing Ovidian reception in the Middle Ages, and exploring Chaucer's reflection of Ovid's struggles with life and art. *TC* and *WBPT* display Chaucer's "evolving treatment" of the Ovidian art of love—from the "skepticism" shown by Pandarus and Criseyde to the "celebration" shown by the Wife. Chapter 5 considers the relation between Chaucer's "Ovidianism" and his conception of himself as a poet, especially as reflected in *ParsT* and *Ret*. Unlike the permanently exiled Ovid, Chaucer found a spiritual escape from gaming.

35. Calin, William. *The French Tradition and the Literature of Medieval England*. Toronto: University of Toronto Press, 1994. xvi, 587 pp. Surveys medieval English responses to and assimilations of Anglo-Norman and continental French literature, with separate sections on (1) Anglo-Norman romance and hagiography; (2) major continental French narratives and authors, including *Huon of Bordeaux*, *The Prose Lancelot*, the *Roman de la Rose*, Guillaume Deguilleville, Machaut, Froissart, and Chartier; (3) appropriations and adaptations by Chaucer, Gower, and Hoccleve; and (4) French influence on English verse and prose romances. The section on Chaucer (pp. 273–370) concentrates on *BD*, *LGWP*, *RvT*, *MerT*, *WBPT*, *PardPT*, *FranT*, and *ManT*.

36. Hamel, Mary. "The *Descriptio Navalis Pugnae* in Middle English Literature." In Robert R. Edwards, ed. *Art and Context in Late Medieval English Narrative: Essays in Honor of Robert Worth Frank, Jr.* (*SAC* 18 [1996], no. 85), pp. 149–62. Critics have attributed Chaucer's description of naval warfare in the Legend of Cleopatra to his knowledge of contemporary battles. Hamel argues instead that Chaucer, like other medieval writers and even historians, drew the elements of his description from a common literary or rhetorical topos. The details of these battles seem realistic because the topos itself was "based on actual practice."

37. Rudd, Niall. *The Classical Tradition in Operation: Chaucer/Virgil, Shakespeare/Plautus, Pope/Horace, Tennyson/Lucretius, Pound/Propertius*. Toronto: University of Toronto Press, 1994. xii, 186 pp. Chaucer drew on two classical sources, Virgil's *Aeneid* and Ovid's *Heroides*, to illustrate two themes. In *HF*, complex characterizations of Venus, Aeneas, and Dido illustrate different meanings of Latin *fame*; in *LGW*, Dido's queenliness is emphasized to support the theme of female faithfulness.

38. Van Buuren, A. M. J. "Dirc Potter, a Medieval Ovid." In Erik Kooper, ed. *Medieval Dutch Literature in Its European Context.* Cambridge Studies in Medieval Literature, no. 21. Cambridge: Cambridge University Press, 1994, pp. 151–67. The Dutch writer Potter (d. 1428) followed a career similar to Chaucer's and also translated the Old French *Melibee.* Van Buuren discusses Gower's and Chaucer's uses of Ovid and analyzes Potter's *Der minnen loep (The Course of Love)* for its use of Ovid's *Heroides* and medieval commentaries.

39. Anderson, Judith. "The 'Covert Vele': Chaucer, Spenser, and Venus." *ELR* 24 (1994): 638–59. Spenser's depictions of the Bower of Bliss and the Temple of Venus (*The Faerie Queene* 2 and 4) are indebted to *PF* and, to a lesser degree, *Th* for explicit references and more general personal and cultural allusions.

See also nos. 83, 134–36, 145, 152, 153, 160, 163, 169, 174, 175, 177, 179, 189, 192, 196, 199, 202, 203, 212, 218, 228, 235, 247, 254, 255, 262, 265–68, 270, 275–78, 280, 286, 287.

Chaucer's Influence and Later Allusion

40. Aronstein, Susan. "Cresseid Reading Cresseid: Redemption and Translation in Henryson's *Testament.*" *SLJ* 21:2 (1994): 5–22. Aronstein shows how Henryson, influenced by late-fifteenth-century attitudes toward women, especially prostitutes, returns the story of Criseyde to its pre-Chaucerian misogynistic purpose. The article examines the story's literary history and its participation in the debate about women; considers Chaucer's ambiguous attitude toward Criseyde; and shows how Henryson suppresses such ambiguities to eliminate the danger of sympathetic misreadings.

41. Binns, J. W. "Wenceslas Clemens' Homage at the Tomb of Chaucer, 1636." *MÆ* 62 (1993): 289–92. Records a Latin poem written by Clemens upon visiting Chaucer's tomb. The poem indicates that Clemens was familiar with Chaucer through Sir Frances Kynaston's Latin version of *TC* 1–2.

42. Bloom, Harold. "Chaucer: The Wife of Bath, the Pardoner, and Shakespearean Character." In Harold Bloom. *The Western Canon: The Books and School of the Ages.* New York, San Diego, and London: Harcourt, 1994, pp. 105–26. Appreciative criticism of Chaucer and his contribution to Western literary tradition, especially his anticipation of Shakespeare as a

comic ironist and creator of self-conscious characters. Focuses on *CT*—in particular, the Falstaffian vitality of the Wife of Bath and the Iago-like genius of the Pardoner, the "first nihilist, at least in literature."

43. Boswell, Jackson Campbell, and Sylvia Wallace Holton. "References to Troilus, Criseyde, and Pandarus." *ChauR* 29 (1994): 93–109. Catalogues thirty-one previously unlisted references to Troilus, Criseyde, and Pandarus published 1475–1640. Part of a work in progress: an updating of the *Short-Title Catalogue of Books Printed . . . 1475–1640* and of Caroline Spurgeon's *Five Hundred Years of Chaucer Criticism and Allusion, 1357–1900*.

44. Classen, Albrecht. "Hoccleve's Independence from Chaucer: A Study of Poetic Emancipation." *FCS* 16 (1990): 59–81. Surveys the reception of Hoccleve's poetry and argues that its "autobiographical self-presentation" underlines its differences from Chaucer's influential precedent. Hoccleve also introduces innovative themes and topics: madness, alienation, and various biographical and topical concerns.

45. Dane, Joseph A. "Who Is Buried in Chaucer's Tomb?—Prolegomena." *HLQ* 57 (1994): 99–123. Discusses variants in editorial and antiquarian reports of the Latin inscription engraved on Chaucer's tomb and the verses "about the ledge" of the tomb. Suggests that the "snowy tablet" supposedly fixed by Surigone to a pillar near the tomb on which the Latin epitaph appeared is Leland's metaphor for the page of his own book and that the otherwise unknown "Hickeman" to whom Commaunder attributes the inscription results from a misreading of a blackletter copy of Foxe.

46. Easting, Robert. "Another Echo of Chaucer's *Troilus* in *The Kingis Quair.*" *N&Q* 38 (1991): 161. *The Kingis Quair* 668–89 echoes *TC* 3. 1361–63.

47. Evans, Dansby. "Chaucer and Eliot: The Poetics of Pilgrimage." *MedPers* 9 (1994): 41–47. Similarities in the depiction of character, in the pilgrimage topos, and in the reworking of source material suggest Chaucer's influence on *The Waste Land*. Evans explores Eliot's academic and scholarly familiarity with Chaucer.

48. Fisher, Judith L. *"The Canterbury Tales* in Charles Knight's *Old England*: Conservative Reform in Popular Publishing." *PoeticaT* 39–40 (1994): 155–77. Examines the iconography of nineteenth-century engravings of select Canterbury pilgrims published by Knight. The postures, details, and styles in the engravings reflect assumptions about social order, as well as Knight's program of educating his readership.

335

49. Johnson, James D. "Identifying Chaucer Allusions, 1981–1990: An Annotated Bibliography." *ChauR* 29 (1994): 194–203. An annotated list of thirty-seven items, intended as an update of Caroline Spurgeon's *Five Hundred Years of Chaucer Criticism and Allusion, 1357–1900*.

50. Kindrick, Robert L. *Henryson and the Medieval Arts of Rhetoric*. Garland Studies in Medieval Literature, no. 8. New York and London: Garland, 1993. xiii, 345 pp. Summarizes fundamental information about Henryson and surveys his use of and familiarity with the medieval rhetorical arts (*ars poetriae, ars dictaminis*, and *ars praedicandi*). Kendrick mentions Chaucer throughout as a source and model for the Scots poet, and the volume includes a comparison of Henryson's "Taill of Schir Chanteclair and the Foxe" to its source, *NPT*, to demonstrate Henryson's skill with rhetorical abbreviation.

51. Kraman, Cynthia. "Four Poems by Cynthia Kraman." *Paris Review* 35:127 (1993): 38–41. Includes two poems—"Chaucer at Aldgate" and "Chaucer at Park House"—that fictionalize moments in Chaucer's life.

52. Lau, Beth. "Keats's Markings in Chaucer's *Troilus and Criseyde*." *KSJ* 43 (1994): 39–55. Argues that Keats marked the British Library copy of *TC* once owned by Charles Cowden Clarke. The markings indicate Keats's concerns with burgeoning love and with Criseyde's character as developed in books 1–3, but they "do not provide definitive evidence of Keats's reaction" to the poem, which he probably later reread.

53. Maley, Willy. "Spenser's Irish English: Language and Identity in Early Modern Ireland." *SP* 91 (1994): 417–31. Spenser's Irish English was modeled both on Chaucer's language and on an archaic dialect of English that survived in Elizabethan Ireland. The "Old English peasantry" in Spenser's Ireland spoke a form of English similar to Chaucer's.

54. Patterson, Lee. "Court Politics and the Invention of Literature: The Case of Sir John Clanvowe." In David Aers, ed. *Culture and History, 1350–1600: Essays on English Communities, Identities, and Writing* (SAC 18 [1996], no. 70), pp. 7–41. During the reign of Richard II, love poetry such as Clanvowe's *Book of Cupid* was a means whereby courtiers could interrogate the "power, patronage and lordship" of the fetishized court. Patterson considers Clanvowe's allusions to Chaucer in this light.

55. Steele, Elizabeth. "Chaucer and Henry James: Surprising Bedfellows." *HJR* 13 (1992): 126–42. Tallies parallels between James's *The American* and Chaucer's *TC*, including aspects of characterization (James "splits" Chaucer's major characters), plot, and diction.

56. Tintner, Adeline R. "*Daisy Miller* and Chaucer's 'Daisy' Poem: *The*

Prologue to the Legend of Good Women." *HJR* 15 (1994): 10–23. Daisy Miller was modelled on "another martyr to love": Alceste of *LGWP*. Tintner documents James's familiarity with Chaucer and his imitations of Chaucerian diction. She reads Daisy as an inexpert, desperate lover similar to the victims of love in *LGW*.

57. Watson, Nicholas. "Outdoing Chaucer: Lydgate's *Troy Book* and Henryson's *Testament of Cresseid* as Competitive Imitations of *Troilus and Criseyde.*" In Karen Pratt, ed. *Shifts and Transpositions in Medieval Narrative: A Festschrift for Elspeth Kennedy*. Woodbridge, Suffolk; and Rochester, N.Y.: D. S. Brewer, 1994, pp. 89–108. The relation of Lydgate and Henryson to Chaucer is anxious and competitive; their retellings of *TC* help canonize Chaucer but also subvert "his authority by criticizing or outdoing him." Lydgate associates Chaucer with Criseyde's falsity and "stands with Guido against Chaucer." Henryson acknowledges that Chaucer is one among many who have fictionalized the story, especially the character of Criseyde.

See also nos. 17, 120, 284.

Style and Versification

58. Rusch, Willard, J. "When Rhymes Go Bad: Recontextualizing Chaucer's Rhymes with the Mid Front Long Vowels." *AJGLL* 6 (1994): 1–50. Studies of Chaucer's rhymes have traditionally assumed that textual criticism and historical phonology together could recover lost information about the pronunciation of his verse. The rhymes, however, possess their own unique written properties. Rusch notes connections between the traditional view and Derrida's critique of spoken versus written language.

59. Shoaf, R. A. "The Play of Puns in Late Middle English Poetry: Concerning Juxtology." In Jonathan Culler, ed. *On Puns: The Foundation of Letters*. Oxford: Basil Blackwell, 1988, pp. 44–61. Considers four Chaucerian puns as devices for "delaying, interrupting, or otherwise frustrating closure," comparing them with single examples from *Sir Gawain and the Green Knight* and *Piers Plowman*. Chaucerian examples come from *TC*, *FranT*, *MilT*, and *GP*.

60. Wimsatt, James I. "Rhyme/Reason, Chaucer/Pope, Icon/Symbol." *MLQ* 55 (1994): 17–46. Using the linguistic theories of Charles Pierce, Wimsatt proposes that "the function of rhyme in Chaucer's poetry . . . is to help organize the sounds to create a sign independent of a particular verbal sense" (p. 18). Sound in poetry is carried in two registers, one a

symbolic meaning and the other a "phonetic icon." Although undertaken by William K. Wimsatt, comparison of Chaucer's and Pope's rhyming is invalid because "the standards that are alleged to hold for Pope's work do not fit Chaucer's" (p. 34).

See also nos. 32, 150, 271.

Language and Word Studies

61. Cannon, Christopher David. "The Making of Chaucer's English: A Study in the Formation of a Literary Language." *DAI* 54 (1994): 4100A. Though hailed as an innovator by his successors and subsequent critics, Chaucer adapted existing traditions in innovative ways. "Colloquial" and "aureate" styles had already been developed in English, but he juxtaposed them. He was less the inventor of literary English than a brilliant figure in its tradition.

62. De la Cruz, Juan Manuel. "The Modals Again in the Light of Historical and Cross-Linguistic Evidence." In Francisco Fernandez, Miguel Fuster, and Juan Jose Calvo, eds. *English Historical Linguistics, 1992* (*SAC* 18 [1996], no. 87), pp. 145–56. The co-occurrence of modals of the type *I shall may go* and participial modal constructions of the type *I have wold* in Chaucer's *Bo* helps us understand the practical absence of them in post-Medieval English. Through a three-hundred-year process, the bulk of English verbs separated from the modals.

63. Diller, Hans-Jürgen. "Emotions in the English Lexicon: A Historical Study of a Lexical Field." In Francisco Fernandez, Miguel Fuster, and Juan Jose Calvo, eds. *English Historical Linguistics, 1992* (*SAC* 18 [1996], no. 87), pp. 219–34. Studying four families of emotion words (wrath, anger, annoyance, grief) in the Chaucer canon, Diller draws several conclusions: the introduction of emotion words from French and their rivalry with native English words deserve close scrutiny; semantic study of emotion words is inextricably intertwined with their stylistic and cultural study; and such study may bring a new perspective to the question of whether emotions are universal or culture-specific.

64. Fisher, John H. "A Language Policy for Lancastrian England." *PMLA* 107 (1992): 1168–80. Argues that English became the official language of England in the fifteenth century as the result of "deliberate, official policy." Dissemination of Chaucer's works and those of his followers suggests that the poet was chosen as the "cynosure" of a conscious move-

ment to promote English letters, sponsored by Henry V, Henry Beaufort, and Thomas Chaucer and carried forth by John Lydgate and Thomas Hoccleve.

65. Kanno, Masahiko. "Chaucer's Sense of Originality." *Studies in Foreign Languages and Literature* (Aichi University) 30 (1994): 45–66. Chaucer frequently uses familiar words or phrases that at first seem insignificant or trivial; examined closely, however, they reflect unexpected humor. Chaucer excels at molding new science out of old books.

66. Knapp, Peggy A. "Thrift." In Robert R. Edwards, ed. *Art and Context in Late Medieval English Narrative: Essays in Honor of Robert Worth Frank, Jr.* (SAC 18 [1996], no. 85), pp. 193–205. Both the world and the language with which we try to render it intelligible are in constant flux. Tracing changes in the word *thrift* from pre-Chaucerian times through Shakespeare, Knapp stresses the necessity for developing strategies of capturing meaning through language and the impossibility of capturing it entirely. On the one hand, literary uses of language seem to reflect social and linguistic history; on the other, they seem to subvert it. Chaucer's uses of *thrift* reflect both the feudal sense of propriety and the emerging Renaissance sense of frugality, as well as the tension between the two senses. Knapp discusses Chaucer's uses of the word in *TC* and *CT*.

67. Rothwell, W. "The Trilingual England of Geoffrey Chaucer." *SAC* 16 (1994): 45–67. Examines the relations among Latin, French, and English in late-medieval England, using evidence from documents of the twelfth–fourteenth centuries, the *Chaucer Life-Records*, and Chaucer's works. Argues that the Latin of the time was often influenced by French structures, reflecting use of oral and written Latin as a lingua franca. Examines the close relations in vocabulary and word formation between French and English, demonstrating their common differences from Parisian French. Such evidence suggests that traditional study of English language history is based on simplistic models of development.

68. Van Gelderen, Elly. "Arguments Without Number: The Case of *it* and *het*." *Linguistics* 30 (1992): 381–87. In Chaucer's Middle English usage and in modern Dutch usage, *it* and *het* are "defective in number."

See also nos. 4, 15, 53, 58, 59, 87, 151, 170, 201, 217, 245, 281, 285.

Background and General Criticism

69. Acker, Paul. "The Emergence of an Arithmetical Mentality in Middle English Literature." *ChauR* 28 (1994): 293–302. Looks for evi-

dence that certain medieval writers were aware of the newly emerging "arithmetical mentality." Because of his work at the Customs House, Chaucer was much more aware than most writers. He knew counting boards and algorisms, the ancestor of modern arithmetic. Gower seems to have known little arithmetic, and Langland seems to have considered it "euil."

70. Aers, David, ed. *Culture and History, 1350–1600: Essays on English Communities, Identities, and Writing*. Detroit: Wayne State University Press, 1992. 213 pp. Six essays by various hands explore and critique the notion of a steady rise of individualism underlying the traditional historical periodization of the Middle Ages and Renaissance. Human identities in all times are functions of humans interacting in groups. The essays assess the roles of various groups and the identities they produce: court culture, the church, the theater, and women. The volume closes with the editor's critique of historicism in medieval and Renaissance studies. For an essay that pertains to Chaucer, see no. 54. See also no. 289.

71. Amodio, Mark C., ed. *Oral Poetics in Middle English Poetry*. Albert Bates Lord Studies in Oral Tradition, no. 13. New York and London: Garland, 1994. xii, 289 pp. Eleven essays by different hands define and explore the complex relationship between the emerging Middle English literate tradition and its receding oral ancestor in the centuries following the Norman Conquest. Three essays relate to Chaucer; see nos. 211, 231, and 232.

72. Astell, Ann W. *Job, Boethius, and Epic Truth*. Ithaca, N.Y.; and London: Cornell University Press, 1994. xvi, 240 pp. In the Middle Ages, Job was regarded as a figure comparable to the heroes of classical epic, prompting allegorical readings of Job that parallel allegorical readings of works by Homer, Virgil, and Boethius. Astell traces the tradition of treating Job and Boethius as "moral analogues"—from philosophical tradition and commentary, through various romances and saints' lives, to Milton's epic narratives. Considers Jobian allusions and patterns in *TC*, *ClT*, and *MLT*.

73. Baswell, Christopher. "Talking Back to the Text: Marginal Voices in Medieval Secular Literature." In Charlotte Cook Morse, Penelope Reed Doob, and Marjorie Curry Woods, eds. *The Uses of Manuscripts in Literary Studies: Essays in Memory of Judson Boyce Allen* (*SAC* 18 [1996], no. 110), pp. 121–30. Medieval habits of reading characteristically produce "a voicing and an inscription of that voicing" (p. 123), allowing for a fluidity of margin and text, reader and author. Geffrey's position as author and glossed

text in *LGWP* and the Wife's position as text and speaker in *WBP* exemplify this process.

74. Blamires, Alcuin. "Questions of Gender in Chaucer, from Anelida to Troilus." *LeedsSE* 25 (1994): 83–110. Examining Chaucer's construction of gender roles and role reversals in light of contemporary medieval texts, Blamires argues that Chaucer manipulated gender stereotypes. The poet ingeniously contrived Troilus and Anelida to confound specific medieval gender expectations.

75. Bland, Cynthia Renee. "John of Cornwall's Innovations and Their Possible Effects on Chaucer." In Charlotte Cook Morse, Penelope Reed Doob, and Marjorie Curry Woods, eds. *The Uses of Manuscripts in Literary Studies: Essays in Memory of Judson Boyce Allen* (*SAC* 18 [1996], no. 110), pp. 213–35. John of Cornwall's *Speculum grammaticale* uses English as well as Latin sentences for examples, and such vernacular pedagogy seems to have been widely established by the late fourteenth century. The unidiomatic phrase "conservatyf the soun" (*HF* 847) may indicate that Chaucer learned Latin from "teaching grammars" that included materials in English.

76. Bloch, R. Howard. *Medieval Misogyny and the Invention of Western Romantic Love*. Chicago and London: University of Chicago Press, 1991. ix, 298 pp. Explores the scriptural roots of medieval attitudes toward women, focusing on how various kinds of abstraction and aestheticizing led to fundamentally misogynistic contradictions. Examines French romances, lays, and lyrics for the ways they elevate women to debase them. A section on *PhyT* (pp. 101–12) argues that Chaucer's praise of Virginia assaults her in ways similar to Appius's lustful gaze. See also no. 296.

77. Boffey, Julia. "English Dream Poems of the Fifteenth Century and Their French Connection." In Donald Maddox and Sara Sturm-Maddox, eds. *Literary Aspects of Courtly Culture: Selected Papers from the Seventh Triennial Congress of the International Courtly Literature Society* (*SAC* 18 [1996], no. 106), pp. 113–21. Examines the provenance and contents of several fifteenth-century manuscripts, arguing that such compilations reflect interest in Chaucer's dream poems, acquaintance with a range of English and French texts, and a "lively awareness of current subjects of literary debate" or quarrel.

78. Boyd, Beverly. "Chaucer's Audience and the Henpecked Husband." *Florilegium* 12 (1993): 177–80. Chaucer's frequent references to nagging wives and henpecked husbands have less to do with his personal views than with his awareness of audience; women as well as men could

share the misogynistic joke because in Pauline theory the shrew was "some other woman."

79. Brewer, Derek. "The Couple in Chaucer's Fabliaux." In Flemming G. Andersen and Morten Nøjgaard, eds. *The Making of the Couple: The Social Function of Short-Form Medieval Narrative: A Symposium*. Odense: Odense University Press, 1991, pp. 129–43. Surveys views on sex and marriage in Chaucer's works and argues that his fabliaux reflect human desires to escape from and to re-create the couple. The brevity of the fabliau limits the possibilities of readers' identification with the characters and thereby creates the "essential ambivalence of comedy." Fabliaux also capitalize on the contradiction implicit in the orthodox view of sex in marriage: it is both enjoyable and sinful.

80. Burger, Glenn. "Queer Chaucer." *ESC* 20 (1994): 153–70. Queer theory, by emphasizing provisionality, enables us to think of sexuality and culture differently; it provides a means for gay/lesbian/bi- readers to engage Chaucer. Contemporary constructions of sex, gender, and sexuality can be used as conditions of agency and potentiality to investigate premodern representations of sexualities.

81. Carruthers, Leo, ed. *Heroes and Heroines in Medieval English Literature: A Festschrift Presented to André Crépin on the Occasion of His Sixty-Fifth Birthday*. Woodbridge, Suffolk; and Rochester, N.Y.: D. S. Brewer, 1994. xi, 172 pp. Fourteen essays on heroism and anti-heroes in *Beowulf* and in other Old English poetry, *Sir Gawain and the Green Knight*, and the works of Dunbar, Malory, and others. Includes three essays on Chaucer; see nos. 146, 153, and 174.

82. Desmond, Marilynn. *Reading Dido: Gender, Textuality, and the Medieval Aeneid*. Medieval Cultures, no. 8. Minneapolis and London: University of Minnesota Press, 1994. xvi, 296 pp. Surveys understandings of Dido—e.g., historical, Virgilian, Ovidian—and examines what her medieval presentations tell us about intertextual relations, gender attitudes, and the "reading positions" of various authors including Chaucer, Gavin Douglas, Christine de Pizan, and a variety of commentators on Virgil and Ovid. Chaucer "reads Dido as a loveless male narrator of classical stories." In *HF*, Geffrey's ekphrastic viewing of her enables the author to explore the politics of the gaze; in *LGW*, Chaucer attempts a less tentative representation of female sexuality, although it is based ultimately in heterosexual binarism.

83. Economou, George D. "Chaucer." In Carl Woodring and James Shapiro, eds. *The Columbia History of British Poets*. New York: Columbia

University Press, 1994, pp. 55–80. Surveys Chaucer's works and their reception, emphasizing his innovation and experimentation. Introduced by a brief section on Chaucer's reading, discussions of each of his major works summarize the sources Chaucer used and his adaptations of them.

84. Edwards, A. S. G. "The Chaucer Portraits in the Harley and Rosenbach Manuscripts." *EMS* 4 (1993): 268–71. Argues that the portrait of Chaucer in Rosenbach MS 1083/30 was most likely copied from Harley MS 4866 in the early eighteenth century for John Murray. Both manuscripts are of Hoccleve's *Regement of Princes*.

85. Edwards, Robert R., ed. *Art and Context in Late Medieval English Narrative: Essays in Honor of Robert Worth Frank, Jr.* Cambridge: D. S. Brewer, 1994. xiv, 205 pp. Twelve essays by different hands address the "poetic art that emerges in late medieval English narrative out of multiple historical contexts." Treating Langland, Chaucer, and other late-medieval poets, the collection includes an introduction by the editor and a bibliography of Frank's works. Seven essays pertain directly to Chaucer; see nos. 36, 66, 104, 138, 155, 172, and 241.

86. Evans, Ruth, and Lesley Johnson, eds. *Feminist Readings in Middle English Literature: The Wife of Bath and All Her Sect.* London and New York: Routledge, 1994. x, 257 pp. Ten essays by various hands, including an introduction by the editors, plus previously published pieces by Mary Carruthers (with a new afterword), Sheila Delany, and Susan Schibanoff. Topics include Christine de Pizan, Margery Kempe, *Piers Plowman*, cycle drama, virginity literature, and several Chaucerian tales. Includes suggestions for further reading. For newly published essays that pertain to Chaucer, see nos. 128, 183, 202, and 216.

87. Fernandez, Francisco, Miguel Fuster, and Juan Jose Calvo, eds. *English Historical Linguistics, 1992.* Amsterdam and Philadelphia: Benjamins, 1994. viii, 388 pp. Twenty-nine papers read during the Seventh International Conference on Historical Linguistics, Valencia, Spain, 21–26 September 1992. The papers range from general interest to phonology and writing, morphology and syntax, lexicology and semantics, varieties of English, and studies of individual texts. Two papers relate to Chaucer; see nos. 62 and 63.

88. Fuog, Karin Edie Capri. "'I Mene This by Myself': Defining the Self of 'The Kingis Quair.'" *DAI* 55 (1994): 959A. Although Renaissance scholars have tended to deny subjectivity in medieval literature, medievalists have shown that Chaucer develops it. So does the author of "The Kingis Quair," an important but generally neglected work.

89. Gallacher, Patrick J. "Chaucer and the Rhetoric of the Body." *ChauR* 28 (1994): 216–36. Chaucer's system of corporeal signs and gestures suggests a continual praise and blame of the flesh. Movement (or lack thereof) in *CT* is associated with sickness and health; the body is treated as subject and object, as an "affective medium of values," and as "naturalistic and exemplary."

90. Godden, Malcolm, Douglas Gray, and Terry Hoad, eds. *From Anglo-Saxon to Early Middle English: Studies Presented to E. G. Stanley*. Oxford: Clarendon Press, 1994. viii, 233 pp. Eleven essays by various authors, assessing materials from the eighth to the fourteenth century. Most essays pertain to the development of language and literary forms; Chaucer mentioned *passim*.

91. Harwood, Britton J., and Gillian R. Overing, eds. *Class and Gender in Early English Literature: Intersections*. Bloomington: Indiana University Press, 1994. xiii, 156 pp. Although criticism on gender and class has suggested their mutual exclusion, this collection of eight essays focuses on their intersections. Three articles on Old English examine the elegies, *Judith*, and the *Exeter Book*, while those on Middle English include one essay on Middle English popular romances, two on Langland's *Piers Plowman*, one on Chaucer's *HF*, and one on his *PardT*. For essays pertaining to Chaucer, see nos. 221 and 262. See also no. 316.

92. Hill, Ordelle G. *The Manor, the Plowman, and the Shepherd: Agrarian Themes and Imagery in Late Medieval and Early Renaissance English Literature*. Selinsgrove, Penn.: Susquehanna University Press, 1993. 257 pp.; illus. Traces the changing reception of the literary images of the plowman and the shepherd from the thirteenth to the sixteenth century. In the fourteenth century, the plowman begins to shift from representing such values as hard work and thrift to appearing as a figure of discontent and shiftlessness. By contrast, the pastoral figure begins to gain in status and, by the sixteenth century, takes the plowman's place in literary prominence. Chapter 3 examines the literary responses to changing agrarian conditions as seen in Gower, Chaucer, and the poetic followers of Langland. Hill argues that Chaucer responds to agrarian themes by transforming and incorporating the learned classical tradition of Virgil's *Georgics* in *CT*. See also no. 318.

93. Irvine, Martin. "'Bothe Text and Gloss': Manuscript Form, the Textuality of Commentary, and Chaucer's Dream Poems." In Charlotte Cook Morse, Penelope Reed Doob, and Marjorie Curry Woods, eds. *The Uses of Manuscripts in Literary Studies: Essays in Memory of Judson Boyce Allen* (*SAC*

18 [1996], no. 110), pp. 81–119. Various practices of writing and formatting texts clarify how authors imagined writing and how readers received vernacular texts. Using models from cultural studies, editorial theory, semiotics, and traditions of medieval commentary, Irvine argues that Chaucer's dream poems reproduce the metatextual and metalingual consciousness represented by the interplay of text and gloss in a manuscript culture.

94. Jost, Jean E., ed. *Chaucer's Humor: Critical Essays*. Garland Studies in Humor, no. 5. Garland Reference Library of the Humanities, no. 1504. New York and London: Garland, 1994. xliv, 477 pp. Nineteen essays by various hands, plus an introduction. Nine of the pieces are previously published works or excerpts by Howard Patch, G. K. Chesterton, Paul G. Ruggiers, Thomas A. Garbáty, Derek Pearsall, Alfred David, Alan T. Gaylord, A. Booker Thro, and John M. Steadman. Jost introduces the volume with an interpretive description of Chaucer's humor and groups the essays as reception, theory, and genre studies; she also contributes a historical survey of responses to Chaucer's comedy. For other essays not previously published, see nos. 140, 141, 150, 207, 209, 217, 225, 240, and 251.

95. Justice, Steven. *Writing and Rebellion: England in 1381*. New Historicism Series, no. 27. Berkeley, Los Angeles, and London: University of California Press, 1994. xiv, 289 pp. New Historical exploration of the relations between late-medieval vernacular literacy and the insurgency of 1381 (Peasants' Revolt). Focuses on six brief texts concerning leaders of the revolt, treating their production, implications, and relations with contemporary writings and political conditions. Separate chapters consider attempts of the rebels to re-create written culture; Wycliffite influences; the role of *Piers Plowman* in the uprising; definition of classes through writing; and attitudes toward these issues in Gower, Chaucer, and Langland. The treatment of Chaucer concentrates on fragment 7 of *CT*, especially *NPT*.

96. Kang, Ji-Soo. "Poetic Closure in the Works of the *Gawain*-Poet." *DAI* 55 (1994): 274A. Discusses tensions between disorder and coherence in the conclusions of *Sir Gawain and the Green Knight*, *Pearl*, *Cleanness*, and *Patience*, contrasted to conclusions of works by Chaucer.

97. Kawasaki, Masatoshi. "Time-Consciousness in Chaucer." *JBAL* 29 (1994): 11–24 (in Japanese). Exploring the meaning of time in medieval English literature, Kawasaki suggests that there are two time dimensions in Chaucer, relating them to Chaucer's doubleness or ambiguity.

98. Kelly, Henry Ansgar. *Ideas and Forms of Tragedy from Aristotle to the Middle Ages*. Cambridge Studies in Medieval Literature, no. 18. Cam-

345

bridge: Cambridge University Press, 1993. xvii, 257 pp. Identifies classical and medieval uses and understandings of "tragedy." For Aristotle, tragedy was a serious story, although one that might end happily. The notion of "irretrievable misfortune" came to dominate the late-classical use of the term. Lost and then reclaimed in the Middle Ages, the term was understood variously by Boethius, Isidore of Seville, Averroes, John of Salisbury, Dante, and others. Some of them were influenced by classical uses, but most exhibit new fusions of ideas. Late-medieval definitions varied from country to country, with Chaucer's legacy leading to Shakespeare and solidifying into the modern sense. Comments on *TC* and *MkT*.

99. King, Laura Severt. "Sacred Eroticism, Rapturous Anguish: Christianity's Penitent Prostitutes and the Vexation of Allegory, 1370–1608." *DAI* 54 (1994): 3757A. Among the handful of converted whores, Mary Magdalene is best known in late-medieval writing through the homily *De Maria Magdalena* (which Chaucer translated) and the Digby play. These works reveal remarkably literal physicality in which carnal desire appears to merge with spiritual, as reflected in *BD*, *LGW*, *Pity*, and *ShT*.

100. Lee, Monika H. "Conceptions of Truth in Fourteenth-Century English Poetry." *ELWIU* 21 (1994): 152–65. Like many other medieval English poets, Chaucer was much concerned with the nature of truth, especially in *FranT* and *TC*. The late Middle Ages still showed a "vestigial orality" in approaching the subject.

101. Leland, John L. "The Abjuration of 1388." *Medieval Prosopography* 15 (1994): 115–38. Those compelled to abjure the court in 1388, while less well known than the companions of Richard II who faced charges of treason, can be studied collectively as typical members of Richard's court. They include an older group, friends of Richard's father and mother, "more courtiers than warriors"; and a younger group, predominantly masculine and military.

102. Lerer, Seth. "Cluster on Chaucer." *PMLA* 107 (1992): 1139–41. Comments on Chaucer's reception and introduces the essays in the cluster. See nos. 64 and 220.

103. Lynch, Andrew. " 'Be War, Ye Wemen': Problems of Genre and the Gendered Audience in Chaucer and Henryson." In Hilary Fraser and R. S. White, eds. *Constructing Gender: Feminism in Literary Studies*. Nedlands, West Australia: University of Western Australia Press, 1994, pp. 19–38. When linked to issues of genre, the manner of constructing a female audience in *FranT*, *LGW*, and Henryson's *Testament* may destabilize narrative closures and thereby offer moral instruction to women.

104. Lynch, Kathryn L. "Partitioned Fictions: The Meaning and Importance of Walls in Chaucer's Poetry." In Robert R. Edwards, ed. *Art and Context in Late Medieval English Narrative: Essays in Honor of Robert Worth Frank, Jr.* (*SAC* 18 [1996], no. 85), pp. 107–25. From the dream visions through *CT*, Chaucer never abandoned his fascination with walls and "enclosed fictions." On the one hand, walls function metaphorically, representing such forces as the rise and fall of civilization. On the other, they create enclosed spaces corresponding to the enclosed fictions, or tales within tales, that define the structure and meaning of Chaucer's later works. Lynch examines *KnT*, *ManT*, *LGW*, and *TC*.

105. McDevitt, Mary Katherine. " 'With a Worde, of the Mayden Spoke': Medieval Marian Poetics." *DAI* 54 (1994): 3430A. As bearer of the Word, teacher, muse, and pilgrims' guide, Mary provides a feminine model of poetics for Dante, Chaucer, and Lydgate.

106. Maddox, Donald, and Sara Sturm-Maddox, eds. *Literary Aspects of Courtly Culture: Selected Papers from the Seventh Triennial Congress of the International Courtly Literature Society, University of Massachusetts, Amherst, USA, 27 July–1 August 1992.* Cambridge: D. S. Brewer, 1994. 360 pp. Thirty-four essays in English and French by various hands, arranged under five categories: (1) Configuring the Feminine; (2) Lyric Voice, Poetic Style: From Troubadours to Rhetoriqueurs; (3) Amor: Ethos and Affect; (4) Fictions of Identity and Alterity; and (5) Culture and Historiography: Perspectives and Appraisals. For essays that pertain to Chaucer, see nos. 77, 210, 270, 272, and 275.

107. Madsen, Deborah L. *Rereading Allegory: A Narrative Approach to Genre.* New York: St. Martin's Press, 1994. 177 pp. Defines allegory by structural features of plot rather than by content, surveying theory and history of the genre from the classics to contemporary criticism. Briefly considers *BD* and *PF* as allegories.

108. Margherita, Gayle. *The Romance of Origins: Language and Sexual Difference in Middle English Literature.* Philadelphia: University of Pennsylvania Press, 1994. xvi, 214 pp. Six essays that treat literature as "another kind of history" by "problematizing the question of history both within and around medieval literature." Challenging historicist approaches, the essays are deconstructive, psychoanalytic, and feminist, concerned with questions of literary origins and their relations with sexual difference and canonicity. Individual essays consider Margery Kempe, the Middle English *Juliana*, the Harley lyrics, *Sir Gawain and the Green Knight*, *BD*, and *TC*. See nos. 258 and 279.

347

109. Meale, Carol M., ed. *Readings in Medieval English Romance*. Cambridge: D. S. Brewer, 1994. viii, 238 pp. Twelve essays, by various authors, from the Third Conference on Romance in England, held March–April 1992 at the University of Bristol. Topics include generic definition, textual transmission, audience reception, romance and emergent nationalism, genre and gender, and the relationships between historical events and their representation in literature. Chaucerian works mentioned throughout include *ClT*, *CkT*, *FranT*, *MilT*, *RvT*, *Th*, *WBT*, *PF*, *TC*, and the Dido and Thisbe portions of *LGW*. One essay pertains directly to Chaucer; see no. 157.

110. Morse, Charlotte Cook, Penelope Reed Doob, and Marjorie Curry Woods, eds. *The Uses of Manuscripts in Literary Studies: Essays in Memory of Judson Boyce Allen*. Studies in Medieval Culture, no. 31. Kalamazoo, Mich.: Medieval Institute Publications, 1992. xvii, 338 pp. Includes six essays pertaining directly to Chaucer. See nos. 73, 75, 93, 130, 203, and 245. See also no. 333.

111. Myles, Robert. *Chaucerian Realism*. Chaucer Studies, no. 20. Cambridge: D. S. Brewer, 1994. xiii, 153 pp. Countering the modern critical view of Chaucer as a nominalist or antirealist, Myles finds Chaucer a realist in many senses of the term: "a foundational realist, an epistemological realist, an ethical realist, a semiotic and linguistic realist, and an author capable of creating psychologically real characters." Topics include medieval understandings of realism, intentionality, and semiological metaphysics, as well as medieval and modern understandings of modes of presentation. Myles demonstrates his argument primarily in terms of Chaucer's deliberate play with three-level semantics in *FrT*, the very subject of which is intentionality. Gives some attention to *Bo*, *ClT*, *GP*, *ManT*, *MerT*, *NPT*, *PardT*, *ParsT*, *Ret*, *Rom*, *Sted*, *SumT*, *TC*, and *WBT*.

112. Nilsen, Don L. F. "Geoffrey Chaucer's Humor." *InG* 15 (1994): 77–84. Reprises the opinions of a host of scholars on Chaucer's humor: its sources, characteristics, and influences on later writers.

113. North, John David. "Astrological Structures in the Poetry of Geoffrey Chaucer." In Graziella Federici Vescovini and Francesco Barocelli, eds. *Filosofia, scienza e astrologia nel Trecento europeo: Biagio Pelucani Parmense*. Percorsi della scienza storia testi problemi, no. 2. Padua: Poligrafi, 1992, pp. 95–104. Surveys Chaucer's works for evidence of his knowledge and acceptance of astronomy and astrology. Argues that he uses astrological allegory as a structural device in his poetry.

114. Odegard, Margaret. "'Alas, Alas, That Ever Love Was Sin!': Mar-

riages Moral and Immoral in Chaucer." In Nicholas J. Karolides, Lee Bur-
ress, and John M. Kean, eds. *Censored Books: Critical Viewpoints*. Metuchen,
N.J., and London: Scarecrow Press, 1993, pp. 144–58. Describes the "host
of moral issues for high school readers to consider" in *MilT* and *WBPT* and
argues for an ethic of inclusion rather than exclusion in selecting books.

115. Pask, Albert Kevin. "The Emergence of the English Author: Pre-
scripting the Life of the Poet in Early Modern England." *DAI* 55 (1994):
578A. Pask develops a distinct genre from Foucault's formulation of an
"author-function": the life-and-works narratives that emerge in the historical perceptions of readers of Chaucer, Sidney, Spenser, and Donne.

116. Paxson, James J. *The Poetics of Personification*. Literature, Culture,
Theory, no. 6. Cambridge: Cambridge University Press, 1994. xii, 210 pp.
Defines and analyzes personification as fundamental to literature and human consciousness. Surveys the history and theory of the device and examines its roles in works by Prudentius, Chaucer, Langland, and Spenser,
applying various modern critical theories, including narratology, phenomenology, semiotics, and deconstruction. The chapter on Chaucer considers
HF and *PF* as works whose personifications are projections of the narrator,
who phenomenologically loses self through the projections. The loss of self
is similar to, or a form of, sloth or *accedia*.

117. Pinti, Daniel J. "Dialogism, Heteroglossia, and Late Medieval
Translation." *TRev* 44–45 (1994): 16–23. Examines Gavin Douglas's *Eneados* as a work in which Mikhail Bakhtin's notions of dialogism and heteroglossia help illuminate medieval translation practice. Encourages application of such an approach to medieval translators, including Chaucer.

118. Purdon, Liam O., and Cindy L. Vitto, eds. *The Rusted Hauberk:
Feudal Ideals of Order and Their Decline*. Gainesville, Fla.: University Press
of Florida, 1994. xxi, 338 pp. Twelve essays examine the decline of the
feudal ideal, an ideal that may never have existed in practice. Exploring
interactions between literature and sociohistorical data, contributors out-
line various gaps between feudal ideals and realities: conflicting loyalties,
power struggles, treachery, and the exclusion of women and other groups
from feudal benefits. See nos. 143 and 159.

119. Sabadash, Deborah Margaret. "Worlds Upside-down: Inversive
Structures in Late Medieval Literature." *DAI* 55 (1994): 561A. Expands
Curtius's topos through Bakhtinian theories of textual dialogue and the
carnivalesque to reveal the rich variety of a wide sampling of medieval
texts, including *CT*.

120. Scanlon, Larry. *Narrative, Authority, and Power: The Medieval Ex-*

emplum and the Chaucerian Tradition. Cambridge Studies in Medieval Literature, no. 20. Cambridge: Cambridge University Press, 1994. xii, 378 pp. Late-medieval English exempla and exemplum collections have political and ideological significance. Vernacular exempla are "narrative enactment[s] of cultural authority" that appropriate the authority of exemplary sermons and imitate the political goals of the *Fürstenspiegel*, or Mirrors of Princes. Such "Chaucerian" uses of exempla as those in *CT*, Gower's *Confessio Amantis*, Lydgate's *Fall of Princes*, and Hoccleve's *Regement of Princes* claim "moral and cultural authority" and support secular claims for power over the church. Chaucer's efforts at textual complexity are "always conditioned" by his political goal of promoting the sharing of power between the crown and the aristocracy. Following the Ellesmere order of *CT*, Scanlon traces patterns of relations between textual complexity and political moralization in *FrT*, *SumT*, *ClT*, *PardT*, *Mel*, *MkT*, *NPT*, and *ParsT*.

121. Stanbury, Sarah. "Women's Letters and Private Space in Chaucer." *Exemplaria* 6 (1994): 271–85. Chaucer's accounts of women who write and read letters in *TC*, *MerT*, and *MLT* reveal female privacy and autonomy to be sites of profound anxiety concerning the control of domestic space, women's actions, and women's bodies.

122. Taylor, Paul Beekman. "Chaucer's Names." *NM* 95 (1994): 243–48. Chaucer's use of the name Geffrey in his poetry contains a humorous and self-reflexive impact, although reference to his ancestral name Malyn does not.

123. Tobias, Sheila, and Lynne S. Abel. "Scientists and Engineers Study Chaucer and Wordsworth: Peer Perspectives on the Teaching of Poetry." *English Education* 22 (1990): 165–78. Reports on a 1988 pedagogical experiment designed to explore differences between scientific and humanistic study and the implications of such differences for the teaching of poetry. Poetic language is a "code" not unlike mathematics, although it lacks methods of proof.

124. Tolan, John. *Petrus Alfonsi and His Medieval Readers*. Gainesville: University Press of Florida, 1993. xv, 288 pp. Surveys the life and works of Petrus Alfonsi and the reception of his two major works: the anti-Jewish *Dialogi contra Iudaeos* and his collection of tales and wisdom literature, *Disciplina clericus*. Tolan briefly mentions *Mel* as evidence of Chaucer's regard for Petrus as an authority, an attitude widely reflected in the *Disciplina*'s popularity as a preachers' handbook and a source of proverbs and tales.

125. Walker, Sue Sheridan. *Wife and Widow in Medieval England*. Ann

Arbor: University of Michigan Press, 1993. x, 221 pp. Eight historical and legal essays by various hands, including two of potential value to Chaucer studies, especially treatments of *WBPT*: Barbara A. Hanawalt, "Remarriage as an Option for Rural Widows in Late Medieval England"; and Richard M. Helmholz, "Married Women's Wills in Later Medieval England."

126. Weisl, Angela Jane. "Gender and Genre in Chaucer's Romance." *DAI* 55 (1994): 1556A. Chaucer explores the limits of romance and extends them so that *TC*, *KnT*, *SqT*, *Th*, *WBT*, and *FranT* become "poems about narrative."

127. Winick, Stephen D. "Proverbial Strategy and Proverbial Wisdom in *The Canterbury Tales*." *ProverbiumY* 11 (1994): 259–81. Challenges B. J. Whiting's (1934) intuitive definition of proverbs and offers an ethnographic definition, focusing on "strategies" of performance of the proverbs in *CT* and *TC* and the utility of proverbs in effecting "normalization, valorization, and stigmatization." Proverbs are widely used in *CT*, but *MerT* provides the "most complete statement" of Chaucer's view concerning the applications and misapplications of "received wisdom": one should choose a course of wisdom by carefully considering options and their implications.

128. Wogan-Browne, Jocelyn. "The Virgin's Tale." In Ruth Evans and Lesley Johnson, eds. *Feminist Readings in Middle English Literature: The Wife of Bath and All Her Sect* (*SAC* 18 [1996], no. 86), pp. 165–94. The early Middle English "Letter on Virginity" and the "Katherine Group" saints' lives critique male desire and the violation of female will, challenging conventions of courtly love. In *WBP*, *SNT*, and *PhyT*, Chaucer's use of "virginity material" exposes the "self-construction" of patriarchy, but "less canonical texts of virgin lives" may have more to offer.

129. Wood, Charles Roger. "Narrativity, Allusion, and the Peasants' Revolt of 1381 According to Froissart, Chaucer, and Paine." *DAI* 55 (1994): 1572A. Froissart's *Chroniques* have shaped subsequent perceptions of the uprising of 1381. Although Chaucer refers to it only once, his placement of the simile in *NPT* is significant. Edmund Burke and Thomas Paine took opposing eighteenth-century views. Rhetorical analysis reveals how the revolt took shape in human consciousness.

130. Woods, Marjorie Curry. "In a Nutshell: *Verba* and *Sententia* and Matter and Form in Medieval Composition Theory." In Charlotte Cook Morse, Penelope Reed Doob, and Marjorie Curry Woods, eds. *The Uses of Manuscripts in Literary Studies: Essays in Memory of Judson Boyce Allen* (*SAC*

351

18 [1996], no. 110), pp. 19–39. Medieval rhetorical textbooks and school commentaries illuminate Chaucer's attention to literal meaning. Discussions of such devices as amplification and abbreviation help explain interrelations and conflicts between poetical structures and individual narratives.

131. Wynne-Davies, Marion. "'He Conquered Al the Regne of Femenye': Feminist Criticism of Chaucer." *CrSurv* 4:2 (1992): 107–13. Surveys feminist criticism of Chaucer from 1977 forward, focusing on representative works rather than aiming to be exhaustive. Briefly contrasts Emelye of *KnT* with Alisoun of *MilT*.

132. Yuasa, Nobuyuki. "The Art of Naming: A Study of Fictional Names as an Element of Style in Chaucer, Spenser, and Shakespeare." *PoeticaT* 41 (1994): 59–83. Comments on the names of selected characters, including the names of Chaucer's *CT* pilgrims and some of the characters in the tales. Compared with Spenser's and Shakespeare's names, "Chaucer's fictional names are rather limited in kind and number," although they are often ironic.

The Canterbury Tales—General

133. Andreas, James R. "'Wordes Betwene': The Rhetoric of the Canterbury Links." *ChauR* 29 (1994): 45–64. Drawing from Geoffrey of Vinsauf and Mikhail Bakhtin on the "rhetoric of the utterance," Andreas stresses the importance of Chaucer's links between tales in the development of characters, authors, audience, and still more stories. The links exist in temporal time and demonstrate the characters making their own choices.

134. Bennett, Helen T. "Pope Gregory's *Liber Regulae Pastoralis* and Chaucer's *Canterbury Tales*." *MedPers* 9 (1994): 24–40. Bennett argues that the pilgrimage frame of *CT* was influenced by Gregory's *Liber*, particularly in presenting "a range of human types" and in suiting pastoral care to individual exigencies. The *Liber* has particular applications to Chaucer's Reeve, Franklin, Summoner, Pardoner, and Parson. The Parson's "if gold ruste" is indebted to Gregory, not the French analogues.

135. Braswell, Mary Flowers. "Chaucer's 'Court Baron': Law and *The Canterbury Tales*." *SAC* 16 (1994): 29–44. Chaucer's office as Justice of the Peace necessitated his close familiarity with the forms and styles of court proceedings available to us in the records of the "Court Baron." Braswell notes in such records the frequency of figures similar to Chaucer's Host, Miller, Reeve, and Cook. Cases in the records are marked by the types of

ambiguities and indeterminacies we see in Chaucer's depictions of his characters, and such court records include testimonies called "tales."

136. Brown, Peter. *Chaucer at Work: The Making of the* Canterbury Tales. London and New York: Longman, 1994. xii, 186 pp. An "interactive" introduction to *CT* designed for classroom use. Provides for *GP* and select tales contextual materials from sources and analogues, rhetorical and visual traditions, and contemporary resources, guiding students in their considerations of how Chaucer adapted or responded to such materials. For *GP*, Brown focuses on pilgrimage, the Parson and the Pardoner, the Host and the narrator; for *KnT*, Boccaccio's *Teseida* and the imagery of Saturn and imprisonment; for *MilT*, rhetorical *effictio* and the Noah mystery plays; for *WBPT*, antifeminism and *gentilesse*; for *MerT*, the iconography of the seasons and gardens; for *FranT*, patience and imagery of hell; for *PardPT*, the "sins of the mouth" and gambling; and for *NPT*, rhetorical tradition and imagery of the Fall.

137. Buffoni, Franco. *I racconti de Canterbury: Un'opera unitaria*. I Saggi di Testo a fronte, no. 2. Milan: Guerini, 1991. 214 pp. Focuses on *Mel* as the central and unifying section of *CT*, reading it as an expression of Chaucer's preference for unvarnished moralism over poetry. See also no. 298.

138. Collette, Carolyn P. "Chaucer's Discourse of Mariology: Gaining the Right to Speak." In Robert R. Edwards, ed. *Art and Context in Late Medieval English Narrative: Essays in Honor of Robert Worth Frank, Jr.* (*SAC* 18 [1996], no. 85), pp. 127–47. Collette examines the tradition of Mariology in relation to *PrPT* and *SNPT*. In their *Prologues*, the Prioress and the Second Nun invoke the Virgin "as a figure of virtuous female power and speech." In their *Tales*, however, women and children die struggling to be heard. Religious truth inspires the faithful to speak, but it cannot assure that they will be accepted or heard.

139. Crane, Susan. *Gender and Romance in Chaucer's* Canterbury Tales. Princeton, N.J.: Princeton University Press, 1994. viii, 233 pp. Romance is the medieval genre that most clearly dramatizes gendered identity, focusing on "courtship, marriage, lineal concerns, primogeniture, and sexual maturation." Chaucer's *KnT*, *WBT*, *SqT*, *FranT*, and *Th* reflect and confront the ideologies of gender implicit in romance tradition. These tales depict masculine identity and its objectification of the feminine, feminine mimicry of such objectification, and parallels between gender opposition and other oppositions such as authority and submission, familiarity and exoticism, justice and mercy, public and private. Men's magic and women's magic also differ in Chaucer's romances, and his adventures of love suggest

a kind of cross-gendering in which men manifest "feminine pliancy" to errancy and accident.

140. Hanning, Robert W. "'Parlous Play': Diabolic Comedy in Chaucer's *Canterbury Tales*." In Jean E. Jost, ed. *Chaucer's Humor: Critical Essays* (*SAC* 18 [1996], no. 94), pp. 295–319. Hanning examines the allusions to demons and devils in *CT* and compares them with the devil figure in late-medieval English religious drama. In both contexts, the devil is a tricker of humans who is tricked by God; a "spirit of inversion" who seeks to distort the "salvific Truth-telling function of the Word of God."

141. Pigg, Daniel F. "The Semiotics of Comedy in Chaucer's Religious Tales." In Jean E. Jost, ed. *Chaucer's Humor: Critical Essays* (*SAC* 18 [1996], no. 94), pp. 321–48. Pigg traces a pattern in the Ellesmere order of *CT*, beginning with how the narrators circumscribe the religious comedy of *MLT* and *ClT* by keeping their plots earthbound. *PhyT* is a "transitional . . . refiguring" that leads to the more spiritual accounts of *PrT* and *SNT*. The sequence constitutes "the poet's contemplation of religious comedy."

142. Portnoy, Phyllis. "Beyond the Gothic Cathedral: Post-Modern Reflections in *The Canterbury Tales*." *ChauR* 28 (1994): 279–92. The ending of *CT* is intentionally ambiguous to leave the choice of a final meaning—if there *is* one—to the reader. The most characteristically "Chaucerian" reading of the ending is also the most modern: to choose not to make a choice is to make certain that one does not choose amiss.

143. Roney, Lois. "Chaucer Subjectivizes the Oath: Depicting the Fall from Feudalism into Individualism in the *Canterbury Tales*." In Liam O. Purdon and Cindy L. Vitto, eds. *The Rusted Hauberk: Feudal Ideals of Order and Their Decline* (*SAC* 18 [1996], no. 118), pp. 268–98. In Chaucer's three most noble, most feudal tales, the meaning of the characters' oaths is subjectively conditioned by their makers—reflecting a decline from the feudal ideal that oaths could be objectively understood. The subjectivity of oaths is demonstrated in conflicting interpretations of the "brotherhood oath" of Palamon and Arcite in *KnT*; in the neglect of intention in Dorigen's "rash promise" in *FranT*; and in the escalated fulfillment of Griselda's "obedience oath" in *ClT*.

144. Shynne, Gwanghyun. "Chaucerian Textuality: The Politics of Allegory in 'The Canterbury Tales.'" *DAI* 54 (1994): 3046A. Examines *CT* in light of medieval discourses on allegory and of modern theories (exegetical, deconstructive, Bakhtinian), considering framework, prologues, and tales, especially *WBT*, *PardT*, and *CYT*. Also discussed are *ParsT*, *Ret*, *Th*, *MkT*, *FrT*, *SumT*, *ManT*, and *ShT*.

145. Sylvester, Louise. "'What Amounteth Al This Wit?': The Aims of Chaucer's *Canterbury Tales* and Boccaccio's *Decameron*." *NewComp* 11 (1991): 137–57. Chaucer's borrowings from *Decameron* are more often poetic strategies and individual episodes than complete plots. The wife in *ShT* echoes Peronella in *Decameron* 7.2; *MilT* reflects *Decameron* 2.4 more than *RvT* does 9.6. Generally, Chaucer extends Boccaccio's realism and his exploration of the relations between writers and characters.

146. Wimsatt, James I. "Type Conceptions of the Good Knight in the French Arthurian Cycles, Malory and Chaucer." In Leo Carruthers, ed. *Heroes and Heroines in Medieval English Literature: A Festschrift Presented to André Crépin on the Occasion of His Sixty-Fifth Birthday* (*SAC* 18 [1996], no. 81), pp. 137–48. In the prose *Tristan* and Malory's *Morte d'Arthur*, no single knight embodies all attributes of the courtly ideal. Similarly, Chaucer's complete depiction of the idealized knight is created through the description of the *GP* Knight in combination with characters in *KnT*, *SqT*, and *FranT*.

See also nos. 19, 23, 26, 31, 66, 79, 89, 119, 120, 132.

CT—The General Prologue

147. Eisner, Sigmund. "The Ram Revisited: A Canterbury Conundrum." *ChauR* 28 (1994): 330–43. Reviews critical opinion about the date on which the pilgrims started for Canterbury and concludes that it was Easter Saturday, 18 April 1394. The term "Ram" refers both to the constellation Aries (thus confirming the date) and to the sign Aries, balancing the Libra sign at the pilgrimage's end "in order to encompass both man's and mankind's lifetime."

148. Greenwood, M. K. "Chaucer's Clerk in the General Prologue to the *Canterbury Tales*." *BAM* 45 (1994): 847–69. Bakhtinian approach to the sketch of the Clerk: there is an intricate dialogue between the latter and the narrator. The facts behind the story and the way it is told reveal much about Chaucer's complex personality.

149. Olmert, Michael. "Chaucer's Little Lotteries: The Literary Use of a Medieval Game." *Arete: The Journal of Sport Literature* 2:1 (1984): 171–82. Briefly surveys the practice of drawing lots in ancient history, the Bible, medieval literature, and Chaucer's works, focusing on the *GP* "lottery" to select who will tell the first tale.

150. Owen, Charles A., Jr. "Chaucer's Witty Prosody in *General Pro-*

logue, Lines 1–42." In Jean E. Jost, ed. *Chaucer's Humor: Critical Essays* (*SAC* 18 [1996], no. 94), pp. 261–70. Close reading of rhythm, rhyme, and syntax discloses the wry control of the opening of *GP*.

151. Rowland, Beryl. "How to Pronounce Berwick: A Curious Paradigm of Chaucer's Bishop Bradwardine." *Florilegium* 11 (1992): 116–23. While we cannot be sure of Chaucer's pronunciation of "Berwyk" (*CT* 1.792), one manuscript version of Bradwardine's memory treatise may suggest the loss of medial [w].

See also nos. 9, 15, 59, 92, 136, 146, 181, 214, 215, 232, 246, 248.

CT—The Knight and His Tale

152. Boyd, Beverly. "The Prayer of Chaucer's Emelye to Diana." *RPLit* 17 (1994): 147–52. Considers Emelye's prayer in *KnT* in light of both Boccaccio's *Teseida* and the fertility symbolism in Chaucer's tale, concluding that the prayer should be understood in terms of Diana's various mythological powers, while the answer should be understood in terms of her role as goddess of childbirth.

153. Brewer, Derek. "Chaucer's Knight as Hero and Machaut's *Prise d'Alexandrie*." In Leo Carruthers, ed. *Heroes and Heroines in Medieval English Literature: A Festschrift Presented to André Crépin on the Occasion of His Sixty-Fifth Birthday* (*SAC* 18 [1996], no. 81), pp. 81–96. Like Peter of Cyprus, celebrated in Machaut's *Prise*, Chaucer's Knight is a hero, his lists of battles showing him to be a Crusader-knight virtuous in devotion to duty. Chaucer deemed the knightly ideal possible in his contemporary world.

154. Brimer, Alan. "'The Knight's Tale': Against Synthesis." *JLSTL* 6 (1990): 333–56. This Bakhtinian discussion of *KnT* argues that the "flaws" perceived by earlier critics result from misguided efforts at finding homogeneity in the poem. As a product of a complex literary culture, *KnT* reflects the culture's "heteroglossia" and cannot be reduced to a single coherent reading. The poem's multiplicity reflects equivocal understandings in Chaucer's time of such crucial concepts as mercy, tyranny, and love.

155. Carruthers, Mary. "Seeing Things: Locational Memory in Chaucer's Knight's Tale." In Robert R. Edwards, ed. *Art and Context in Late Medieval English Narrative: Essays in Honor of Robert Worth Frank, Jr.* (*SAC* 18 [1996], no. 85), pp. 93–106. Carruthers explores the role of memory, one of the five divisions of classical rhetoric, in composing and understanding medieval poetry. Works such as *Sir Gawain and the Green*

Knight and Chaucer's *KnT* are "memory-friendly" because images associated with well-defined places help both poet and audience construct a mental diagram of the poem.

156. Clogan, Paul M. "Lydgate and the *Roman Antique*." *Florilegium* 11 (1992): 7–21. While the *Siege of Thebes* can be read in terms of Lydgate's anxiety about his relationship to *KnT*, its combination of narrative and moralizing is principally influenced by developments within the tradition of the *roman antique*. Lydgate's work is closer generically to the historiographic tradition than to chivalric romance.

157. Diamond, Arlyn. "Unhappy Endings: Failed Love/Failed Faith in Late Romances." In Carol M. Meale, ed. *Readings in Medieval English Romance* (*SAC* 18 [1996], no. 109), pp. 65–81. Examines the intersection of gender, genre, and history in *Sir Gawain and the Green Knight* and *KnT* to argue that "the inversion or refusal of generic conventions, enabled by the self-conscious use of a rich tradition of courtly narratives, points to a loss of faith in the social structures within which such narratives were generated." Also mentions *TC*, *MilT*, and *RvT*.

158. Harley, Marta Powell. "Chaucer's Use of the Proserpina Myth in 'The Knight's Tale' and 'The Merchant's Tale.'" In Elizabeth T. Hayes, ed. *Images of Persephone: Feminist Readings in Western Literature*. Gainesville, Fla.: University Press of Florida, 1994, pp. 20–32. In alluding to the triple goddess Diana-Lucina-Proserpina to characterize Emily in *KnT* and May in *MerT*, Chaucer "simultaneously represents female assertiveness . . . and vulnerability." However, he allows the potential to depict female pain to dissipate, never transcending "antifeminist clichés."

159. Jost, Jean E. "Potency and Power: Chaucer's Aristocrats and Their Linguistic Superiority." In Liam O. Purdon and Cindy L. Vitto, eds. *The Rusted Hauberk: Feudal Ideals of Order and Their Decline* (*SAC* 18 [1996], no. 118), pp. 49–76. Chaucer's primary representatives of aristocracy, the Knight and the Squire, reveal differing assumptions about acting within their social stations. Both exhibit confidence through linguistic security, but the Knight's epic reality and narrative control contrast with the Squire's "rambling," fantastic diversions, which lack coherence and order.

160. Noguchi, Shunichi. "Prayers in Chaucer's *Knight's Tale*." *PoeticaT* 41 (1994): 45–50. Compared with their Boccaccian originals, the prayers in Chaucer's *KnT* are more symmetrical and more concerned with promises to perform duty or to offer sacrifice.

161. Sherman, Mark A. "The Politics of Discourse in Chaucer's *Knight's Tale*." *Exemplaria* 6 (1994): 87–114. The discourse of *KnT* displays the

357

Knight's ideological desire to construct a boundary between a stable Christian cosmos and the restless eros of unregulated tale-telling by establishing a political and narrative paradigm for the other pilgrims to follow.

See also nos. 22, 104, 126, 131, 136, 139, 143, 146, 267.

CT—The Miller and His Tale

162. Breeze, A. C. "Chaucer's *Miller's Tale*, 3770: *Viritoot.*" *ChauR* 29 (1994): 204–206. Proposes that "upon the viritoot," often glossed as "to be astir," actually means "fairy toot," a common topological expression from southwest England. This second meaning suggests that Gervase the smith, speculating on why the angry Absolon has appeared to him in the middle of the night, is comparing the latter to a "nocturnal sentinel, on the lookout."

163. Calabrese, Michael. "The Lover's Cure in Ovid's *Remedia Amoris* and Chaucer's *Miller's Tale.*" *ELN* 32:1 (1994): 13–18. Edward Schweitzer has linked the scene of Absolon's kissing the "naked ers" with medieval medical cures of lovesickness. However, the episode may also draw on Ovid's proposal in *Remedia Amoris* that desperate lovers may be cured by witnessing the naked bodies and excretory functions of women.

164. Dane, Joseph A. "The *Syntaxis Recepta* of Chaucer's 'Prologue to the Miller's Tale,' Lines 3159–61." *ELN* 31:4 (1994): 10–19. Chaucer's phrase is traditionally interpreted, "Yet for all the oxen in my plough, I would not take upon me more than enough [i.e., be overly suspicious]." A more accurate reading, however, is "I would not take upon me more than the oxen in my plough can handle."

165. Leicester, H. Marshall, Jr. "Newer Currents in Psychoanalytic Criticism and the Difference 'It' Makes: Gender and Desire in the *Miller's Tale.*" *ELH* 61 (1994): 473–99. With its richness subverting fabliau conventions, *MilT* glitters with multiple significations. Alison, the central figure, is both sexy and presexual, both Medusa and "bryd" (in multiple and homonymous senses). Unlike the traditional old cuckold, John is trustful, caring, almost parental. Absolon, like the Miller in loving music and drama, combines the vindictive and the childlike. The Miller works his audience to achieve a discharge of laughter.

166. Lochrie, Karma. "Women's 'Pryvetees' and Fabliau Politics in the *Miller's Tale.*" *Exemplaria* 6 (1994): 287–304. *MilT* constructs cuckoldry as a transaction between men that governs our reading of both the tale and

the interaction between Miller and Reeve. The homosocial exchange of female sexuality is a secret concealed in cuckoldry but revealed in the masculine economy of storytelling.

167. Pigg, Daniel. "The Carpenter's 'Ernest of Game': A Reevaluation of Noah's Flood." *InG* 15 (1994): 41–53. Through the character of John the Carpenter, Chaucer parodies not the mystery plays but their credulous audiences, who conflated past and present and often confused illusion with reality.

168. Woods, William F. "Private and Public Space in *The Miller's Tale.*" *ChauR* 29 (1994): 166–78. In *MilT*, the house and the space around it symbolize both the tale itself and the principal characters. The top floor represents the "heavenly" sphere where the flood is predicted and awaited; the middle, or "earthly," level is Alison's bedroom; and the lower, street level is where all the punishments take place. Each male character seeks his private space with Alison at his own level and is "rewarded" accordingly.

See also nos. 59, 109, 114, 131, 136, 145, 186, 251.

CT—The Reeve and His Tale

169. Beidler, Peter G. "Chaucer's *Reeve's Tale*, Boccaccio's *Decameron*, IX, 6, and Two 'Soft' German Analogues." *ChauR* 28 (1994): 237–51. Chaucer's *RvT* contains sufficient close parallels with Boccaccio's story of Pinuccio and Niccolosa to suggest that the latter might have been a source for the former. Two German versions of the cradle-trick story, although more similar in general story lines, are consistently inexact in their specifics.

170. Smith, Jeremy. "The Great Vowel Shift in the North of England, and Some Forms in Chaucer's *Reeve's Tale*." *NM* 95 (1994): 433–37. Some northernisms in *RvT* have been dismissed as quasi-northern or as scribal misreadings. However, these forms are genuine attempts by post-Shift southern scribes to reflect a pre-Shift northern pronunciation.

171. Yager, Susan. "'A Whit Thyng in Hir Ye': Perception and Error in the *Reeve's Tale*." *ChauR* 28 (1994): 393–404. The "whit thyng" the miller's wife sees in the dark bedroom is not her husband's nightcap. Instead, the term is taken from medieval philosophy, wherein objects are first judged by color. On closer inspection, they become human and take form. The "white thing" is often subject to human error. Thus, *RvT*, like

other stories in the first fragment, explores "the limitations of human perception."

See also nos. 35, 109, 134, 145, 166.

CT—The Cook and His Tale

172. Strohm, Paul. "'Lad with Revel to Newegate': Chaucerian Narrative and Historical Meta-Narrative." In Robert R. Edwards, ed. *Art and Context in Late Medieval English Narrative: Essays in Honor of Robert Worth Frank, Jr.* (*SAC* 18 [1996], no. 85), pp. 163–76. The language and imagery with which the Cook denounces Perkyn's revelry in *CkT* evoke the rhetoric with which contemporary writers denounced the so-called Peasants' Revolt of 1381. Perkyn's revelry may seem "innocuous" to readers today, but "the imagery of revelry carried a heavy symbolic freight in the later fourteenth century." Through narrative containment, Chaucer and contemporary chroniclers imposed closure on events that threatened the dominant social order.

See also no. 109.

CT—The Man of Law and His Tale

173. Bracken, Christopher. "Constance and the Silkweavers: Working Women and the Colonial Fantasy in Chaucer's 'The Man of Law's Tale.'" *CMat* 8:1 (1994): 13–39. Cast as a discussion among four participants (Reductio, Thea, Ceres, and Cassandra), this closet drama explores relations among power, gender, trade, religion, and their representation in *MLT*. The characters are, loosely, representatives of different but nonconflicting critical schools, discussing how (and whether) patriarchy speaks through the poem, its kinds of commodification and repression, parallels between matters related to women and Islam, and the applicability of *MLT* to the modern world.

174. Dor, Juliette. "*Humilis exaltetur*: Constance, or Humility Rewarded." In Leo Carruthers, ed. *Heroes and Heroines in Medieval English Literature: A Festschrift Presented to André Crépin on the Occasion of His Sixty-Fifth Birthday* (*SAC* 18 [1996], no. 81), pp. 71–80. The suffering of Custance in *MLT* echoes Innocent III's description of human life in his *De*

miseria condicionis humane; the tale's end, which indicates that Custance's humility will ultimately be rewarded, draws from the pseudosource of the uncompleted companion volume to the pessimistic *De miseria*.

175. Harty, Kevin J. "Chaucer, the Liturgy (Again), and Constance's Ever-Increasing Pathos: *The Man of Law's Tale* II (B¹) 846–47." *SSF* 31 (1994): 489–90. Although other allusions to the liturgy of Holy Week have been found in *MLT*, an allusion previously unnoted occurs when Constance is set adrift with her infant son, another instance of Chaucer's adding to the pathos of Constance's situation.

176. Hendrix, Laurel L. "'Pennance Profytable': The Currency of Custance in Chaucer's *Man of Law's Tale*." *Exemplaria* 6 (1994): 141–66. The Man of Law erases distinctions among spiritual, linguistic, and monetary exchange by trying to turn Custance and Christ into signs that can be circulated and traded for profit, raising the question of whether his tale is "true coining."

177. Hurd, Myles R. "Chaucer and the Imagery of Woe: The Blind Briton and the Veiled Child in the 'Man of Law's Tale.'" *CLAJ* 34:1 (1990): 99–107. Presented differently than in Trevet, the scenes of the blind Briton and the blindfolded Maurice in *MLT* emphasize the helplessness of humankind and the help of God. The emphasis is consistent with Innocent III's *De miseria condicionis humane* and with the characterization of Custance.

178. Moore, Roger E. "Nominalistic Perspectives on Chaucer's 'The Man of Law's Tale.'" *Comitatus* 23 (1993): 80–100. In *MLT*, God's remoteness and arbitrariness and the "extreme limitations on human rationality" reveal a nominalistic background that contrasts with Custance's faith.

179. Pelen, Marc M. "Providence and Incest Reconsidered: Chaucer's Poetic Judgment of His Man of Law." *PLL* 30 (1994): 132–56. The narratives of Trevet and Gower turn the story of Constance into a secular moral fable. Similarly, "the Man of Law exposes himself to Chaucer's irony . . . : it is this transcendent freedom from the moral content of the legend that the Man of Law has sought to deny, but which Chaucer pursues in an emphatic Ovidian departure from his two immediate models."

180. Rose, Christine M. "The Provenance of the Trevet *Chronicle* (fMS Eng 938)." *HLB*, n.s., 3:4 (1992–93): 38–55. The existence of a fifteenth-century Middle English translation of Trevet's *Chronicle* indicates that one may have been available to Chaucer and Gower in the fourteenth century.

181. Umland, Sam. "Chaucer's Man of Law and Boethian 'Bad Fortune.'" *PVR* 21 (Winter 1993): 17–33. In the *GP* sketch and in *MLPT*,

Chaucer characterizes his Man of Law as one who does not recognize Divine design behind the pattern of natural events, eternal law behind natural law. The Man of Law errs in focusing on temporal events, failing to perceive Boethian "endes of thynges" that are part of Divine plan.

See also nos. 72, 121, 141, 210.

CT—The Wife of Bath and Her Tale

182. Breuer, Horst. "Narrative Voices in Chaucer's *Wife of Bath's Prologue*." In Wilhelm G. Busse, ed. *Anglistentag 1991 Düsseldorf: Proceedings*. Tübingen: Niemeyer, 1992, pp. 418–27. Tallies devices in *WBP* whereby Chaucer sought to "criticize and belittle his own creation": blasphemy, intrusions of male discourse, contradiction, and various forms of distortion and exaggeration. But the Wife's "loud, polemical voice . . . carries the day."

183. Carruthers, Mary. Afterword to "The Wife of Bath and the Painting of Lions." In Ruth Evans and Lesley Johnson, eds. *Feminist Readings in Middle English Literature: The Wife of Bath and All Her Sect* (*SAC* 18 [1996], no. 86), pp. 39–44. Comments on the rhetorical ontology of the Wife of Bath. The character is a figure of power who "continues to bother" because she is not silenced in the text, compelling readers to wish to respond.

184. Cuesta, Julia Fernández. "A Pragmatic Approach to the Wife of Bath's Tale." *SELIM* 3 (1993): 103–16. Pragmatic analysis suggests that the Wife of Bath in *WBP* and the loathly lady in *WBT* flout the "Quality and Quantity maxims of the Cooperative Principle" and the "maxim of Tact" of the "Politeness Principle." Targets of Chaucer's satire, the two characters seek to "manipulate rather than cooperate."

185. Dauby, Hélène. "Sens et Structure de *The Wife of Bath's Tale*." In Danielle Buschinger, ed. *Sammlung—Deutung—Wertung: Ergebnisse, Probleme, Tendenzen und Perspektiven philologischer Arbeit. Mélanges de littérature médiévale et de linguistique allemande offerts à Wolfgang Spiewok à l'occasion de son soixantième anniversaire par ses collègues et amis*. [Amiens]: Université de Picardie, Centre d'Etudes Médiévales, 1988, pp. 57–62. Examines the pace of *WBT* as an example of the loathly hag story and reads in it echoes of several other Canterbury narratives.

186. Elliott, Ralph. "Chaucer's Garrulous Heroine: Alice of Bath." *SMELL* 4 (1989): 1–30. Considers the Wife of Bath's "colloquial, conver-

sational idiom as a key to her character," examining details of diction, syntax, and imagery, and comparing her with Alison of *MilT*.

187. Justman, Stewart. "Trade as Pudendum: Chaucer's Wife of Bath." *ChauR* 28 (1994): 344–52. Although Chaucer does not satirize the three estates in *CT* (there is no high nobility; clerical offenders do not reflect on the church; the peasantry does not speak), he does attack the middle class and its values through the Wife of Bath, who represents the "town" and its illicit values.

188. Robinson, Carol L. "Celluloid Criticism: Pasolini's Contribution to a Chaucerian Debate." *SiM* 5 (1993): 115–26. Pasolini's reading of the Wife of Bath as "a rebellious heretic who is yet a sexual and clownish bully" challenges more sympathetic "readings" of the Wife rather than re-creating her Chaucerian self-presentation. The film *I racconti di Canterbury* is not a "faithful adaptation" of *CT* but a series of "critical 'essays'" colored by Pasolini's deep-seated misogyny.

189. Root, Jerry. "'Space to Speke': The Wife of Bath and the Discourse of Confession." *ChauR* 28 (1994): 252–74. Root draws on selected primary and secondary sources to illustrate that *WBP* was influenced by the doc-trine of mandatory confession decreed by the Fourth Lateran Council of 1215.

190. Spearman, Alan. "'How He Symplicius Gallus . . .': Alison of Bath's Name-Calling, or 'The Taming of the Shrewed.'" *ChauR* 29 (1994): 149–62. The Wife's changing of the name Sulpicius Gallus to Symplicius Gallus (3.643) allows her to poke fun at one of her antifeminist "authori-ties" as well as to link this man to another antifeminist *gallus*, the cook in *NPT*. She indicates that a man who holds such antifeminist attitudes is a fool and—like other male authorities challenged by *WBP*—not worthy of respect.

191. Van, Thomas A. "False Texts and Disappearing Women in the *Wife of Bath's Prologue and Tale*." *ChauR* 29 (1994): 179–93. Although *WBP* and *WBT* seem more disparate than similar, they are not. The pair-ing of the two allows Alison to make a statement about how to love well and how to be happy.

192. Vance, Sidney. "Contending with the Masculinist Traditions: *Sun-diata*'s Sogolon and the Wife of Bath." In Sandra Ward Lott, S. G. Hawkins, and Norman McMillan, eds. *Global Perspectives on Teaching Liter-ature: Shared Visions and Distinctive Visions*. Urbana, Ill.: National Council of Teachers of English, 1993, pp. 101–8. Observes parallels between *WBT* and the narrative of the matriarch Sogolon in the African (Mandingo) epic

Sundiata. Each includes a quest, a knowledgeable old hag, shape-shifting, and a version of rape. Such parallels enable us to "engage in a dialogue with an African text that narrates another woman's heroic confrontation with a system that would use her and other women."

193. Wurtele, Douglas. "The 'Double Sorwe' of the Wife of Bath: Chaucer and the Misogynist Tradition." *Florilegium* 11 (1992): 179–205. The Wife's pain and anxiety in regard to clerical pronouncements on the sinfulness of carnal pleasure in marriage and on the superiority of virginity to the married state suggest that she is reacting chiefly to the dominant "rigorist" school of thought on these topics (e.g., Jerome, Bromyard) rather than to a more "liberal" attitude espoused in some Victorine and Chartrist thought.

194. Yamamoto, Dorothy. "'Noon Oother Incubus but He': Lines 878–81 in the *Wife of Bath's Tale*." *ChauR* 28 (1994): 275–78. Lines 878–81 of *WBT* have been glossed incorrectly to suggest that while an incubus would get a woman pregnant, a friar would cause only dishonor. In fact, the tradition of the incubus is much darker, for this individual, associated with evil, had the power not only to impregnate but also to hurt severely or even to kill the intended victim and the victim's family. Comparatively, friar damage seems relatively minor.

See also nos. 23–25, 34, 35, 42, 73, 109, 114, 125, 126, 128, 136, 139, 144, 233.

CT—The Friar and His Tale

195. Hartman, Michael Oscar. "Laughing at the Devil: Satan as a Humorous Figure in Middle English Literature." *DAI* 55 (1994): 559A–60A. Although Old English poetry always depicts Satan as supernaturally powerful (while doctrinally powerless), late Middle English works show him as comic, the boaster who must fail—as in the mystery cycles followed by the morality plays. In Chaucer's *FrT*, the summoner seems more evil than the fiend does. Renaissance treatments vary.

See also nos. 8, 111, 144.

CT—The Summoner and His Tale

196. Hanks, D. Thomas, Jr. "'Savour,' Chaucer's 'Summoner's Tale,' and Matthew 5:13." *ELN* 31:3 (1994): 25–29. The lord in *SumT* speaks of "the

salt of the erthe and the savor," usually taken as a reference to Matthew 5:13. Yet no Bible known to Chaucer uses the word "savor" (Latin *sapor*) in this passage. Instead, Chaucer may have drawn the phrase from Gower's *Vox clamantis* 3.1997–98.

197. Kanno, Masahiko. "Some Notes on the *Summoner's Tale*." *Bulletin of the Aichi University of Education (Humanities)* 43 (1994): 1–13. Friar John is guilty of the sin of gluttony, which he discusses. Diction relating to foodstuffs recurs throughout *SumT*, as does "in-and-out" imagery, culminating in scatological diction that reflects John's degraded state of mind.

198. Saito, Isamu. "Chaucer's Kneeling Friar." *PoeticaT* 41 (1994): 51–58. The two references to kneeling in *SumT* help create irony. The friar's kneeling in the first half of the tale "forecasts" his "spiritual downfall" in the last scene.

See also nos. 16, 134, 144, 251.

CT—The Clerk and His Tale

199. Bronfman, Judith. *Chaucer's* Clerk's Tale: *The Griselda Story Received, Rewritten, Illustrated.* New York: Garland, 1994. xiv, 162 pp.; illus. Studies the origin and development of the Griselda story from the fourteenth through the twentieth century. Surveys topics including the Italian and French sources before Chaucer; twentieth-century critical interpretations of *ClT* that read the *Tale* as allegory, religious exemplum, or political commentary; literary rewritings of the story by such diverse writers as John Lydgate, Christine de Pizan, John Phillips, Thomas Dekker, Maria Edgeworth, Elizabeth Barrett Browning, and Oscar Hammerstein; and artistic representations as seen in twenty-five plates that retell the story. An appendix includes the text of "A Most Pleasant Ballad of Patient Grissell."

200. Figueroa, Fernando Luis. "Woven Words: A Semiology of Clothing in Medieval Texts." *DAI* 54 (1994): 3022A. Explores the figural significance of the veil, the earthly body of Christ, as projected in the garments of the *Pearl* maiden and of Griselda in *ClT*.

201. Finnegan, Robert Emmett. "'She Should Have Said No to Walter': Griselda's Promise in *The Clerk's Tale*." *ES* 75 (1994): 303–21. Examines implications of Griselda's problematic promise of obedience (which she should have rescinded once she realized that it meant consent to the murder of her children) from the perspective of theologians and religious

writers such as Aquinas and Wycliffe. Concludes with a study of *tempten*, *assaien*, and *assaillen*.

202. Johnson, Lesley. "Reincarnations of Griselda: Contexts for the *Clerk's Tale*." In Ruth Evans and Lesley Johnson, eds. *Feminist Readings in Middle English Literature: The Wife of Bath and All Her Sect* (*SAC* 18 [1996], no. 86), pp. 195–220. Literary and historical contexts modify the presentation of the Griselda story in its many versions, reflecting a broad range of views on women and marriage. Chaucer's version raises questions about the exemplary value of Griselda in religious and political contexts, challenging the way her story had traditionally been told. Nonetheless, the responses of the Host and the Merchant contribute to her "continuing life" as "an icon of the ideal wife."

203. Morse, Charlotte Cook. "What to Call Petrarch's Griselda." In Charlotte Cook Morse, Penelope Reed Doob, and Marjorie Curry Woods, eds. *The Uses of Manuscripts in Literary Studies: Essays in Memory of Judson Boyce Allen* (*SAC* 18 [1996], no. 110), pp. 263–303. Manuscript rubrics variously identify the genre of Petrarch's story as *mythologia*, *fabula*, and *historia* (perhaps the least constricting choice). Some rubrics emphasize Griselda's wifely virtues of obedience and fidelity, while others single out womanly patience and steadfastness (often associated with martyrdom rather than conjugal subordination).

See also nos. 24, 27, 72, 109, 141, 143, 148.

CT—The Merchant and His Tale

204. Boenig, Robert. "January's Trumpets." *ELN* 32:1 (1994): 19–23. The instruments that January uses to solemnize his wedding in *MerT* are trumpets, the only instrument capable of making "loud mynstrancye."

205. Field, Rosalind. "January's 'Honeste Thynges': Knighthood and Narrative in the *Merchant's Tale*." *RMSt* 20 (1994): 37–49. Considers January's social status and asks why *MerT* concerns a knight. Examines portrayal of January's household, finding him well-bred but lacking gentility; *MerT* is thus more firmly situated in the debate about "gentilesse." Also argues that part of *MerT*'s satire focuses on the idea of privacy: it is in private that January is ridiculed, whereas his public image is maintained.

206. ———. "'Superfluous Ribaldry': Spurious Lines in the *Merchant's Tale*." *ChauR* 28 (1994): 353–67. Certain ribald but spurious lines added to the pear-tree episode and printed by Caxton in 1478 helped to shape

readers' attitudes toward Chaucer for three centuries, until Tyrwhitt removed them in 1775. The lines are probably the work of a scribe who had read Chaucer attentively (for they have a "Chaucerian" flavor), acting as "tabloid journalist" and providing a coarse and stereotypical ending to a dark tale.

207. Hagen, Susan K. "Chaucer's May, Standup Comics, and Critics." In Jean E. Jost, ed. *Chaucer's Humor: Critical Essays* (*SAC* 18 [1996], no. 94), pp. 127–43. Compares the narrative strategy of *MerT* with the techniques of standup comedy. The narrator of *MerT* holds up for ridicule the socially sanctioned convention of marriage between young women and old men, while at the same time affirming conventional attitudes about the sexual appetites of women. Our laughter at January implies our complicity in his misogyny.

208. Jager, Eric. "The Carnal Letter in Chaucer's Earthly Paradise." Chapter 6 in Eric Jager. *The Tempter's Voice: Language and the Fall in Medieval Literature*. Ithaca, N.Y., and London: Cornell University Press, 1993, pp. 241–98. In *MerT*, Chaucer presents a version of the Edenic Fall that emphasizes the roles of language and writing in seduction. Especially in the pear-tree episode, the Merchant's "dark vision" dramatizes Augustinian commentary on the Fall as an abuse of signs, implicating Chaucer's own fiction. But *ParsT* and *Ret* encourage transcendence of the Fall.

209. Jonassen, Frederick B. "Rough Music in Chaucer's *Merchant's Tale*." In Jean E. Jost, ed. *Chaucer's Humor: Critical Essays* (*SAC* 18 [1996], no. 94), pp. 229–58. Briefly surveys the carnivalesque folk tradition of charivari in medieval literature and assesses *MerT* in light of it, especially the description of the marriage between January and May, the musical imagery, and the inexpressibility topos.

See also nos. 10, 35, 121, 127, 136, 158.

CT—The Squire and His Tale

210. Fyler, John M. "Chaucerian Romance and the World Beyond Empire." In Donald Maddox and Sara Sturm-Maddox, eds. *Literary Aspects of Courtly Culture: Selected Papers from the Seventh Triennial Congress of the International Courtly Literature Society* (*SAC* 18 [1996], no. 106), pp. 257–63. *MLT* and *PrT* "recoil from the otherness of Islam and of medieval Jewry," but *SqT* treats the Mongols with "toleration and an engaged sympathy."

The xenophobia of the first two *Tales* indicates that they should be read ironically; *SqT* is Chaucer's metaphor for the "difficulty of bridging gaps."

See also nos. 126, 139, 146, 159, 257.

CT—The Franklin and His Tale

211. Arnovick, Leslie K. "Dorigen's Promise and Scholars' Premise: The Orality of the Speech Act in the *Franklin's Tale*." In Mark C. Amodio, ed. *Oral Poetics in Middle English Poetry* (*SAC* 18 [1996], no. 71), pp. 125–47. In light of linguistic, legal, and folkloric traditions, Dorigen's speech to Aurelius in the garden—a moment of dialogue within the larger dialogue of the pilgrims—does not constitute a promise. Rashly made promises were not considered legally binding contracts, and Chaucer's folk audience would have known this.

212. Cook, Robert. "Chaucer's *Franklin's Tale* and 'Sir Orfeo.'" *NM* 95 (1994): 333–36. *FranT* was influenced by *Sir Orfeo*, especially in the illustrations produced for Aurelius's benefit by the Clerk of Orleans.

213. Coss, P. R. "Literature and Social Terminology: The Vavasour in England." In T. H. Aston et al., eds. *Social Relations and Ideas: Essays in Honour of R. H. Hilton*. Cambridge: Cambridge University Press, 1983, pp. 109–50. Coss surveys Continental and English historical and literary uses of the term "vavasour" to demonstrate its varying meanings. Applied to Chaucer's Franklin, the term might convey an "old-fashioned air," but such connotations must be drawn from literary rather than social contexts.

214. Green, Joe. "Chaucer's Genial Franklin." *PVR* 21 (Winter 1993): 6–16. In *GP*, *Sq–FranL*, and *FranP*, Chaucer characterizes the Franklin as obsessed "with appearances and good feeling." *FranT* manifests these obsessions and exposes the teller's "superficial understanding of 'gentilesse.'"

215. Jonassen, Frederick B. "Carnival Food Imagery in Chaucer's Description of the Franklin." *SAC* 16 (1994): 99–117. Documents the medieval traditions of the Land of Cockaigne and the Battle of Carnival and Lent, suggesting that they underlie the reference to the seasonal cycle of meat and fish in the Franklin's *GP* sketch. Such traditions adumbrate the Renaissance carnivalesque tradition theorized by Bakhtin.

216. Riddy, Felicity. "Engendering Pity in the *Franklin's Tale*." In Ruth Evans and Lesley Johnson, eds. *Feminist Readings in Middle English Literature: The Wife of Bath and All Her Sect* (*SAC* 18 [1996], no. 86), pp. 54–71. Examines the sexual politics of *FranT*, arguing that its fundamental ideas

of "gentilesse" and "pitee" reflect an aristocratic, masculinist hierarchy. The courtly setting entails this hierarchy, which dominates the tale, but Dorigen's complaint and the closing unanswered question enable readers to dissent against such assumptions about class and gender.

See also nos. 7, 15, 35, 59, 100, 103, 109, 126, 134, 136, 139, 143, 146.

CT—The Physician and His Tale

217. Crafton, John Micheal. "*Paradoxicum Semiotica*: Signs, Comedy, and Mystery in Fragment VI of the *Canterbury Tales*." In Jean E. Jost, ed. *Chaucer's Humor: Critical Essays* (*SAC* 18 [1996], no. 94), pp. 163–86. Chaucer's comedy is a "function of the inherent paradoxes of language, particularly as articulated by Freud," and the humor of *CT* depends on the audience's awareness of the slippage between truth and language. The paired opposition of *PhyT* and *PardT* caricatures the respective extremes of realism and nominalism, affirming a moderate conceptualism.

218. Pelen, Marc M. "Murder and Immortality in Fragment VI (C) of the *Canterbury Tales*: Chaucer's Transformation of Theme and Image from the *Roman de la Rose*." *ChauR* 29 (1994): 1–25. Although *PhyT* and *PardT* may seem to bear little relationship to each other, a thematic unity rooted in the *Roman de la Rose* links the two tales. Raison's exemplum contains ideas and images of sexual violence and natural generation that Chaucer seems to have borrowed and opposed in his pilgrims' *Tales*.

See also nos. 76, 128, 141, 267.

CT—The Pardoner and His Tale

219. Bitterling, Klaus. "Goon A-Blakeberyed." *NM* 94 (1993): 279–86. Explains *PardT* 6.406 to mean "to be damned" in light of the figurative associations of brambles with sins and the picking of fruit with spiritually dangerous activity, corroborated in exegetical commentary and other medieval literature.

220. Burger, Glenn. "Kissing the Pardoner." *PMLA* 107 (1992): 1143–56. Reads the kiss between the Pardoner and Host at the end of *PardT* as a challenge to "the repressive binaries of a hermeneutical model

based on heterosexual reproduction." The Pardoner inverts dominant ideology, and the kiss brings to readers' consciousness its own participation in the "politics of inversion and perversion." For a response and reply, see Anne Barbeau Gardiner, "The Medieval Kiss" (*SAC* 17 [1995], no. 198); and Glenn Burger, "The Medieval Kiss: Reply" (*SAC* 17 [1995], no. 196).

221. Frantzen, Allen J. "*The Pardoner's Tale*, the Pervert, and the Price of Order in Chaucer's World." In Britton J. Harwood and Gillian R. Overing, eds. *Class and Gender in Early English Literature: Intersections* (*SAC* 18 [1996], no. 91), pp. 131–48. Through his sexual ambiguity and his exposure of the illusory nature of social hierarchy, the Pardoner is a "double threat." Through him, Chaucer "provisionally negates" the model of the three estates and also "demonstrates, through the fates of the three men and the Pardoner himself, the gratuitous but deeply satisfying destruction of those who depart from the order it dictates."

222. Hoerner, Fred. "Church Office, Routine, and Self-Exile in Chaucer's Pardoner." *SAC* 16 (1994): 69–98. Reads *PardPT* psychoanalytically and in light of Max Weber's theory of charisma, commenting on how words and details of the Pardoner's performance reflect his attraction to salvation and his fearful distortion of it. Institutionalized and rhetorically routinized, the performance inverts the methods of genuine charismatic transformation, perverting rather than converting the Pardoner and threatening the other pilgrims, especially the Host, a figure of corporation and institutionalization.

223. Ireland, Richard W. "Chaucer's Toxicology." *ChauR* 29 (1994): 74–92. Chaucer's use of poison in *PardT* and *ParsT* indicates more than a cursory knowledge of the law and lore associated with it. In *PardT*, poison—affiliated with Envy and Jealousy and with the devil—serves to darken both the characters and the plot line. The Parson's use of poison—associated with contraception and abortion—reveals a tension between contemporary civil and common laws.

224. Kruger, Steven F. "Claiming the Pardoner: Toward a Gay Reading of Chaucer's *Pardoner's Tale*." *Exemplaria* 6 (1994): 115–39. Through a historically situated investigation of the Pardoner's possible homosexuality and its relation to language in *PardPT*, modern readers can resist Chaucer's (possibly) homophobic intentions, reclaiming and even celebrating the Pardoner's disruption of the heterosexual constructions of medieval society.

See also nos. 11, 35, 42, 134, 136, 144, 217, 218.

CT—The Shipman and His Tale

225. Woods, William F. "Metaphoric Comedy in the *Shipman's Tale*." In Jean E. Jost, ed. *Chaucer's Humor: Critical Essays* (SAC 18 [1996], no. 94), pp. 207–28. The conversion of all to "mercantile exchange" underlies a comic displacement of roles in *ShT*. The merchant and the monk switch roles, and the wife paradoxically gains a sense of self-worth, a comic transformation of her economic and sexual dependency.

See also nos. 99, 144, 145.

CT—The Prioress and Her Tale

226. Despres, Denise L. "Cultic Anti-Judaism and Chaucer's 'Litel Clergeon.'" *MP* 91 (1994): 413–27. England's implementation of the Fourth Lateran Council's legislation of 1215, two anti-Judaism sermon exempla from medieval manuscripts, and the "child-as-Host" motif suggest how the "ideology of bodily and social purity could become salient for the fourteenth-century audience" of Chaucer's *PrT*. Members of Chaucer's pilgrim-audience experience a "miracle of wholeness" in the same manner as would the audience of the sermon exempla.

227. Koretsky, Allen C. "Dangerous Innocence: Chaucer's Prioress and Her Tale." In Derek Cohen and Deborah Heller, eds. *Jewish Presences in English Literature*. Montreal and Kingston: McGill-Queen's University Press, 1990, pp. 10–24. Chaucer uses the anti-Semitism of *PrT* to depict pernicious innocence.

228. Orsten, Elisabeth M. "Madame Eglentyne in Her Day and Ours: Anti-Semitism in *The Prioress's Tale* and a Modern Parallel." *Florilegium* 11 (1992): 82–100. The Prioress's combination of pious sentiment, moral blindness, and indifference to official church doctrine can be paralleled in a 1985 attempt, in an Austrian village, to defend and preserve an anti-Semitic legend about the murder of a three-year-old and the local cult that grew up around it.

229. Pigg, Daniel F. "Refiguring Martyrdom: Chaucer's Prioress and Her Tale." *ChauR* 29 (1994): 65–73. *PrT* expresses the notion of spiritual, or "white," martyrdom popular in the Middle Ages. Unlike physical martyrdom, white martyrdom was a mental act, often involving the preservation of virginity. Through the character of the little boy, the Prioress sug-

gests her own struggle with evil and chastity, thereby adding complexity to her own voice as a pilgrim.

230. Rudat, Wolfgang E. H. "Gender-Crossing in the *Prioress' Tale*: Chaucer's Satire on Theological Anti-Semitism?" *Cithara* 33:2 (1994): 11–17. Chaucer satirizes the anti-Semitism and sexual restrictiveness of the medieval church by presenting the serpent-Satan as a representation of Judaic reproduction denied the celibate Prioress. Rudat suggests the Prioress terminated an earlier unwanted pregnancy in an action underlying the murder and disposal of the little clergeon in her tale.

See also nos. 13, 18, 141, 210.

CT—The Tale of Sir Thopas

231. Lerer, Seth. "'Now Holde Youre Mouth': The Romance of Orality in the *Thopas–Melibee* Section of the *Canterbury Tales*." In Mark C. Amodio, ed. *Oral Poetics in Middle English Poetry* (*SAC* 18 [1996], no. 71), pp. 181–205. *Th* and *Mel* pose an oral-literate opposition. *Th* is a parody of rambling orality, more concerned with its narrator than with its protagonist; constant interruptions and stereotypical devices direct the audience's attention away from the story. In *Mel*, however, the narrator recedes behind the action of the story, and Prudence not only reads but also quotes from literary sources, matching quotation to situation appropriately.

232. Parks, Ward. "Oral Tradition and the *Canterbury Tales*." In Mark C. Amodio, ed. *Oral Poetics in Middle English Poetry* (*SAC* 18 [1996], no. 71), pp. 149–79. The tension between literacy and orality—evident throughout *CT*—can be seen in *GP*, where a literate and learned Chaucer positions himself as the mere recorder of oral performance. *Th* satirizes the English metrical romance, a genre deeply rooted in orality, when Chaucer places oral-derived styles and formulas in a textual setting. The narrator of *Th* repeatedly fails to organize narrative formulas into a coherent tale, and stock themes set up expectations that the story never fulfills.

See also nos. 14, 39, 109, 126, 139, 144, 234.

CT—The Tale of Melibee

233. Daileader, Celia R. "The *Thopas–Melibee* Sequence and the Defeat of Antifeminism." *ChauR* 29 (1994): 26–39. *WBT* and *Mel* contain com-

parable female characters who use discourse to challenge the antifeminist patristic tradition. The plot in both tales—the transformation of a misguided male by a knowledgeable woman—points to a more "peaceful" world where women will have the upper hand.

234. Riehle, Wolfgang. "Aspects of Chaucer's Narratorial Self-Representation in *The Canterbury Tales*." In Herbert Foltinek et al., eds. *Tales and "Their Telling Difference": Zur Theorie und Geschichte der Narrativik, Festschrift zum 70.* Geburtstag von Franz K. Stanzel. Heidelberg: Universitätsverlag, 1993, pp. 133–47. Two tales in *CT* define Chaucer's role as an "implied author" and reflect his double vocation as a poet and diplomat. *Th* is a "brilliant example of his mastery as a poet"; *Mel* expresses his "ideological premises," anticipating the closing of the Canterbury fiction and providing a means to assess other tellers and their characters.

See also nos. 124, 231.

CT—The Monk and His Tale

235. DiMarco, Vincent. "Nero's Nets and Seneca's Veins: A New Source for the *Monk's Tale?" ChauR* 28 (1994): 384–92. Suggests that the sources for Nero's fishing nets of golden thread and for the cutting of both of Seneca's arms as he lies in the bathtub come from the unedited *Alphabetum narrationum*, ca. 1308.

236. Herold, Christine. "The Unfortunate Iconography of Chaucer's Wayward Monk." *ELN* 31:4 (1994): 5–10. The Monk's bald head and gleaming eyes recall medieval representations of Fortuna and her victims.

237. Marzec, Marcia Smith. "'I Wol Yow Seyn the Lyf of Seint Edward': Evidence for Consistency in the Character of Chaucer's Monk." *InG* 15 (1994): 85–95. To show that a love for hunting does not preclude piety, the worldly Monk of *GP* invokes Edward the Confessor, who was often portrayed as a celibate Christian as well as a passionate hunter. Because of Edward's dual interests, the Monk's pursuit of venery might be viewed more favorably.

238. Zatta, Jane Dick. "Chaucer's Monk: *A Mighty Hunter Before the Lord." ChauR* 29 (1994): 111–33. *MkT* makes a political statement reflecting Richard II's tyrannous activities during the latter years of his reign. The stories of misgovernment suggest a later date of composition for the work. The character of the Monk is based on Nimrod, himself an "unholy

hunter," a "tyrant-priest," more concerned for his own personal wealth (as supposedly was Richard) than for common profit.

See also nos. 98, 144.

CT—The Nun's Priest and His Tale

239. Fehrenbacher, Richard W. "'A Yeerd Enclosed Al About': Literature and History in the *Nun's Priest's Tale*." *ChauR* 29 (1994): 134–48. With the introduction of "Jakke Straw" into *NPT*, Chaucer returns to the English setting of the early Canterbury stories. By alternating styles in the peasant passages and the chicken passages, he both addresses the historical turmoil of the day and, ultimately, retreats from it. Such vacillation reflects the unwillingness of Chaucer's contemporaries to take seriously the voice of the third estate.

240. Goldstein, R. James. "Chaucer, Freud, and the Political Economy of Wit: Tendentious Jokes in the *Nun's Priest's Tale*." In Jean E. Jost, ed. *Chaucer's Humor: Critical Essays* (*SAC* 18 [1996], no. 94), pp. 145–62. Offers a Freudian analysis of the antifeminist and political jokes in *NPT*. The opening frame concerning the widow and the allusion to the rebellion of 1381 suggest that the "repression of the class interests of the exploited" is "a symptom of the political unconscious of the text."

241. McAlpine, Monica E. "The Triumph of Fiction in the Nun's Priest's Tale." In Robert R. Edwards, ed. *Art and Context in Late Medieval English Narrative: Essays in Honor of Robert Worth Frank, Jr.* (*SAC* 18 [1996], no. 85), pp. 79–92. Critical studies of *NPT* fall primarily into two groups: allegorical, or interpretive readings, versus mock-epic, or "noninterpretive" readings, based on the premise that the poem has "no meaning except its escape from meaning." Focusing on elements such as fable, debate, biblical motifs, and narratorial commentary, McAlpine argues that the *Tale* transcends both allegorical and mock-epic readings. *NPT* explores the value and limitations of narrative, ultimately affirming the value of fiction and transforming satire into "a vision of human reality."

242. Paley, Karen Surman. "'Al the Revers Seyn of This Sentence': The Enigma of Dream Interpretation in Chaucer's 'Nun's Priest's Tale.'" *Dreaming* 4 (1994): 205–12. The fact that Chauntecleer defies his dream and still escapes harm "raises serious questions about the validity of dream interpretation, leaving the reader with a sense that dreams mean whatever we want them to."

243. Wauhkonen, Rhonda. "The Authority of Text: Nicholas of Lyra's Judaeo-Christian Hermeneutic and *The Canterbury Tales*." *Florilegium* 11 (1992): 141–59. The hermeneutic method in Nicholas of Lyra's *Postilla* gave new richness to the understanding of the biblical *sensus literalis*, expanding it to include parabolic senses and typology, and fostered more interactive reading. Similar principles seem to govern Chaucer's hermeneutics, especially in *NPT*, which focuses on problems of adequate interpretation of and response to texts.

See also nos. 50, 95, 129.

CT—The Second Nun and Her Tale

244. Fields, Peter. "Chaucer's Cecile as Christian-Humanist Disputer of the Sacred." *InG* 15 (1994): 29–39. Cecilia is a humanist who represents the changing medieval world view. Her religion is personal rather than evangelical and is grounded in the practical. She does not perform miracles, nor do any supernatural powers vanquish her enemies or save her from death.

See also nos. 128, 138, 141, 245, 267.

CT—The Canon's Yeoman and His Tale

245. Fyler, John M. "Nimrod, the Commentaries on Genesis, and Chaucer." In Charlotte Cook Morse, Penelope Reed Doob, and Marjorie Curry Woods, eds. *The Uses of Manuscripts in Literary Studies: Essays in Memory of Judson Boyce Allen* (*SAC* 18 [1996], no. 110), pp. 193–211. Medieval commentaries on the confusion of language introduced through the Tower of Babel (Genesis 10–11) illuminate the motif of linguistic disintegration that runs through *SNT*, *CYT*, and *ManT*. The associations of Nimrod with pride, magic, fire, and idol worship underlie the characterization of the alchemist in *CYT*.

See also no. 144.

CT—The Manciple and His Tale

See nos. 35, 104, 144, 245.

CT—The Parson and His Tale

246. Brooke, Christopher. "Chaucer's Parson and Edmund Gonville: Contrasting Roles of Fourteenth-Century Incumbents." In David M. Smith, ed. *Studies in Clergy and Ministry in Medieval England*. Purvis Seminar Series; Borthwick Studies in History, no. 1. York: University of York, 1991, pp. 1–19. Explores the life of Edmund Gonville—cleric, shrewd land agent, and man of affairs—and Chaucer's depiction of the Parson. Despite his considerable financial successes, Gonville was like the Parson in that he did not rent out his benefice.

247. Hamilton, Christopher T. "Poet Versus Priest: Biblical Narrative and the Balanced Portrait in English Literature." *CSR* 23 (1993): 145–58. Chaucer's and Langland's depictions of clergy are rooted in the "biblical topos of contrastive portraits for emulation and rejection," reflecting the medieval belief that church reform depended on the renewal of the clergy. Chaucer's Parson and Langland's Will counterpoint the poets' vice-ridden clergymen. By the time of Henry Vaughn, poets had come to see themselves as crucial to reform.

248. Hirsh, John C. "*General Prologue* 526: 'A Spiced Conscience.'" *ChauR* 28 (1994): 414–17. Although often glossed erroneously as "hypocritical," the word "spiced," as applied to the Parson's conscience, indicates an individual whose soul is touched suddenly and profoundly by religion, "as spices might do the palate."

249. Owen, Charles A., Jr. "What the Manuscripts Tell Us About the *Parson's Tale*." *MÆ* 63 (1994): 239–49. Although most critics agree that Chaucer intended *ParsT* and *Ret* to conclude *CT*, early manuscript history indicates that *ParsT* may have been an independent work, a *Treatise on Patience*, for which *Ret* would serve as a fitting conclusion.

See also nos. 34, 134, 144, 208, 223.

CT—Chaucer's Retraction

250. Braswell-Means, Laurel. "Antiquarian or Bibliographer? The Dilemma of Thomas Frognall Dibdin." *SiM* 4 (1992): 105–12. Cites Dibdin's views on the authenticity of Chaucer's *Ret* to illustrate the former's development as a critical bibliographer.

251. Tschann, Judith. "The Mind Distended: The *Retraction, Miller's Tale*, and *Summoner's Tale*." In Jean E. Jost, ed. *Chaucer's Humor: Critical*

Essays (*SAC* 18 [1996], no. 94), pp. 349–78. Like *Ret*, the farts in *MilT* and *SumT* remake something for their recipients. On the highest level of abstraction, they combine to remake time from the "end" perspective of death.

See also nos. 34, 144, 208, 249.

Anelida and Arcite

See no. 74.

A Treatise on the Astrolabe

252. Hager, Peter J., and Ronald J. Nelson. "Chaucer's *A Treatise on the Astrolabe*: A 600-year-old Model for Humanizing Technical Documents." *IEEE Transactions on Professional Communication* 36 (1993): 87–94. *Astr* shows how technical writers can "judiciously incorporate into their writing such central rhetorical components as coherent structure, appropriate content, accurate and precise descriptions, personable tone, effective metadiscourse, and varied sentence structure and length." The work shows how Chaucer merged his "logico-rational" and "humanistic" selves.

Boece

See no. 62.

The Book of the Duchess

253. Butterfield, Ardis. "Pastoral and Politics of Plague in Machaut and Chaucer." *SAC* 16 (1994): 3–27. Reads *BD* and Machaut's *Jugement dou Roy de Navarre* as "counter pastorals"—works that both disturb the superficial idealization of pastoral poetry and replicate the social tension latent in the form, a social tension that also reflects contemporary effects of the plague. Machaut presents the plague directly in his work and obliquely explores its social impact. Even more obliquely, *BD* confronts the social upheaval of the Black Death in the relations of the Black Knight and the narrator.

377

254. Connolly, Margaret. "Chaucer and Chess." *ChauR* 29 (1994): 40–44. The references to chess in *BD* are confused because Chaucer seems not to have had any firsthand knowledge of the game, his source being not a proper handbook but the *Roman de la Rose*. Applying the chess metaphor from Jean de Meun to a dissimilar situation in *BD*, Chaucer adds to the ambiguity in the character of the Dreamer.

255. Crane, Susan. "Froissart's *Dit dou Bleu Chevalier* as a Source for Chaucer's *Book of the Duchess*." *MÆ* 61 (1992): 59–74. Despite traditional misconceptions of their relative chronology and a lack of specific verbal echoes, the "structural and thematic parallels" of *BD* and Froissart's *Dit dou Bleu Chevalier* indicate Chaucer's dependence on Froissart. Their common features include "emblematic descriptions, representations of service and patronage, and articulations between court occasions and commemorative writing."

256. Hardman, Phillipa. "The *Book of the Duchess* as a Memorial Monument." *ChauR* 28 (1994): 205–15. Cruxes in *BD*—how it can function both universally and individually, why it was composed some years after Blanche's death—can be better understood by placing the poem in the context of tomb sculpture. At the time Chaucer was writing, Henry Yevele was sculpting Blanche's monument, and parallels in methodology can be discerned between fourteenth-century tomb-sculpting techniques and Chaucer's poem.

257. ———. "Chaucer's Man of Sorrows: Secular Images of Pity in the *Book of the Duchess*, the *Squire's Tale*, and *Troilus and Criseyde*." *JEGP* 93 (1994): 204–27. The portrait of the Man in Black of *BD* reflects a traditional *imago pietatis*, the Man of Sorrows. So, to a lesser degree, do the Falcon of *SqT* and Criseyde.

258. Margherita, Gayle. "Originary Fantasies and Chaucer's *Book of the Duchess*." In Gayle Margherita. *The Romance of Origins: Language and Sexual Difference in Middle English Literature* (*SAC* 18 [1996], no. 108), pp. 82–99. In *BD*, rhetorical insufficiency (especially Alcyone's) is linked to the gap left by Blanche. These lacks pose for the narrator, the Black Knight, and the poet a "fetishistic dilemma" that Chaucer explores: a tension between the impulse to recuperation and fascination with loss. The "wholeness" of the poem is illusory, leaving space for the uncanny, subverting the masculine with an implied feminine, and maintaining a "sexual undecidability." See also *SAC* 17 [1995], no. 229.

259. Stone, Gregory B. "Chaucer's Evening Sickness." In Gregory B. Stone. *The Death of the Troubadour: The Late Medieval Resistance to the Re-*

naissance. Philadelphia: University of Pennsylvania Press, 1994, pp. 143–98. Deconstructs *BD* as an example of a work that resists the Renaissance impulses to individualism and the rise of narrative. In *BD*, lyricism is asserted by the failure of narrative to console, and individualism is undercut by recurrent verbal play on oneness and evenness—e.g., Alcyone as "all-is-one"; Octovyen as "octo-even"; and the narrator's "evening" sickness. Stone focuses on the "arithmetical discourse" of the poem.

See also nos. 6, 35, 93, 99, 107.

The Equatorie of the Planetis

See also no. 25.

The House of Fame

260. Breeze, Andrew. "The Bret Glascurion and Chaucer's *House of Fame*." *RES*, n.s., 45 (1994): 63–69. Chaucer's harpist, Glascurion (*HF* 1208), is Gwydion, son of Dôn. Various sound changes can account for Chaucer's "hearing" of Glascurion, suggesting a lost tale about Gwydion known to Chaucer and his audience.

261. Delany, Sheila. *Chaucer's* House of Fame: *The Poetics of Skeptical Fideism*. Gainesville: University Press of Florida, 1994. xiv, 134 pp. A paperback reprint of the 1972 study, with a descriptive foreword by Michael Near.

262. Harwood, Britton J. "Building Class and Gender into Chaucer's *Hous*." In Britton J. Harwood and Gillian R. Overing, eds. *Class and Gender in Early English Literature: Intersections* (*SAC* 18 [1996], no. 91), pp. 95–111. An analogy between gender and class applied to *HF* reveals that Lady Fame assumes a typical paternal role in naming the tidings that exit the House of Rumor. Although Chaucer's source is Ovid, he divides Fame's house along strict class lines—the house of twigs and the palace—suggesting that the poem's "historical conflicts . . . are reflected in its own contradictions" and that "gender and class . . . unite."

263. Schoeck, R. J. "*The Hous of Fame* Revisited." *Connotations* 3:2 (1993–94): 110–14. Treating *HF* as a performance piece enables us to better recognize its humor.

264. Vankeerbergen, Bernadette C. "Chaucer's *House of Fame*: A Journey

into Skepticism." *MedPers* 9 (1994): 158–69. Elements of the poem—dream vision, narrator's self-mockery, genre, satire, absence of authority—contribute to uncertainty of interpretation. That the "mechanics of uncertainty" inhere in all of these elements reinforces skepticism as the poem's major theme.

See also nos. 15, 37, 75, 82, 93, 116.

The Legend of Good Women

265. Delany, Sheila. *The Naked Text: Chaucer's* Legend of Good Women. Berkeley: University of California Press, 1994. xi, 259 pp. Analyzes *LGW* as an under-appreciated work, using an eclectic combination of approaches derived from semiotic, historicist, and feminist theories. *LGWP* and the separate legends are coherent but not organic; they combine in their recurrent Pauline/Augustinian orthodoxy and in their concerns with poetic language and such contemporary political topics as Lollardy and crusading. Exploring issues of art, philosophy, and history, Delany compares *LGW* to works of Ovid, Boccaccio, and Christine de Pizan, emphasizing its sexual wordplay, Orientalism, and representations of gender and class.

266. Minnis, Alastair J. "Repainting the Lion: Chaucer's Profeminist Narratives." In Roy Eriksen, ed. *Contexts of the Pre-Novel Narrative: The European Tradition.* Approaches to Semiotics, no. 114. Berlin and New York: Mouton de Gruyter, 1994, pp. 153–83. Chaucer's adjustments of his source materials in *LGW* produce narratives in which "Marriage, whether secured or desired, motivates and ennobles all the deaths for love." Experimenting with creating archetypically false men, Chaucer idealizes female dedication to "wyfhod," and though such a notion is reductionist by modern standards, it underlies Chaucer's earnest—if often humorous—endeavor to celebrate women.

267. Quinn, William A. *Chaucer's Rehersynges: The Performability of* The Legend of Good Women. Washington, D.C.: Catholic University of America Press, 1994. x, 253 pp. Explores the humor and "tonal delights" of *LGW*, examining the poem as a script for oral performance, and argues that the F version was written for oral presentation; the G version, a revision, for manuscript publication. Quinn reads each of the legends for "pseudo-sacrilegious" humor, considering relations to sources, rhetorical embellishments, and comic themes. He conjectures about emphases Chaucer may have employed in performance and explores the comic range

of the legends, from slapstick to "smarmy cynicism." Quinn concludes by examining how *KnT*, *PhyT*, and *SNT* preserve "significant manifestations of Chaucer's own rehearsals."

See also nos. 35–37, 56, 73, 82, 93, 99, 103, 104, 109.

The Parliament of Fowls

268. Hill, Ordelle G., and Gardiner Stillwell. "A Conduct Book for Richard II." *PQ* 73 (1994): 317–28. In *PF* 316–18, Chaucer alludes to Alain de Lille's discussion of love, the main points of which are Nature's law of love and humans' unnatural violation of it (with implicit references to the homosexuality of Richard's great-grandfather Edward II). *PF* thus served as a conduct book to prepare the young Richard II for marriage, although ironically he was never to know the fatherhood Dame Nature endorses.

See also nos. 12, 39, 93, 107, 109, 116.

Troilus and Criseyde

269. Andretta, Helen Ruth. "Chaucer's 'Troilus and Criseyde': A Poet's Response to Ockhamism." *DAI* 54 (1994): 3429A–30A. Although recent criticism tends to classify Chaucer as an Ockhamist/nominalist, a close study of his most philosophical poem, *TC*, indicates that his thought was traditional and scholastic.

270. Boitani, Piero. "*In Gentil Hertes Ay Redy to Repaire*: Dante's Francesca and Chaucer's Troilus." In Donald Maddox and Sara Sturm-Maddox, eds. *Literary Aspects of Courtly Culture: Selected Papers from the Seventh Triennial Congress of the International Courtly Literature Society* (*SAC* 18 [1996], no. 106), pp. 135–52. Examines intertextual relations among the opening of *TC* 3, its sources in Boethius and Boccaccio, Dante's *Inferno*, and Guido Guinizelli's canzone, "Al cor gentile rempaira sempre amore." Chaucer's modifications of his predecessors and Troilus's apotheosis reflect the poet's conviction that human sensual love is analogous to the "love by which the cosmos is ruled."

271. Bradbury, Nancy Mason. "Gentrification and the *Troilus*." *ChauR* 28 (1994): 305–29. In *TC*, Chaucer uses not only sophisticated, upper-

class materials but also lower-class matter that has "moved 'upward' into the most prestigious and learned layers of medieval discourse." This "gentrification" can best be seen in Chaucer's use of legends, charms, curses, oaths, and proverbs.

272. Collette, Carolyn. "Criseyde's Honor: Interiority and Public Identity in Chaucer's Courtly Romance." In Donald Maddox and Sara Sturm-Maddox, eds. *Literary Aspects of Courtly Culture: Selected Papers from the Seventh Triennial Congress of the International Courtly Literature Society (SAC 18 [1996], no. 106), pp. 47–55. Criseyde's status as a widow and her self-conscious concern with her "honour" and "estat" help characterize her as someone "concerned with maintaining herself and her household as independent units." Her inconstancy is a rational response to her social and political context.

273. Downes, Jeremy. "'Streght to My Matere': Rereading Chaucer's *Troilus and Criseyde.*" *Journal of Narrative and Life History* 3:2–3 (1993): 155–78. A psychoanalytic analysis suggesting parallels between the "scopophilic" instinct represented in *TC* and the "extreme intertextuality" of the poem. Both are forms of the Oedipal complex whereby Criseyde, although she is finally unknowable, is for both Troilus and the narrator a "happy substitute" for the mother; Pandarus and Lollius are approving fathers.

274. Garcia Martinez, Isabel. "Destiny, Fortune and Predestination in *Troilus and Criseyde.*" *SELIM* 1 (1991): 134–42. Briefly surveys medieval attitudes toward destiny and suggests the difficulty of being certain what Chaucer's attitude was.

275. Haruta, Setsuko. "The End of an Adventure: *Sir Gawain and the Green Knight* and Chaucer's *Troilus and Criseyde.*" In Donald Maddox and Sara Sturm-Maddox, eds. *Literary Aspects of Courtly Culture: Selected Papers from the Seventh Triennial Congress of the International Courtly Literature Society (SAC* 18 [1996], no. 106), pp. 353–60. Chaucer, in *TC*, and the Gawain poet "understate" the prowess of their heroes and emphasize the negative aspects of courtly love. The heroes fail to realize their chivalric ideals— Troilus, because he is vulnerable to Criseyde's inconstancy; and Gawain, because (Criseyde-like) he fails to stay loyal.

276. Heinrichs, Katherine. "Mythological Lovers in Chaucer's *Troilus and Criseyde.*" *JRMMRA* 12 (1991): 13–39. Mythological lovers alluded to in *TC* were associated in medieval letters with *amor stultus*, foolish love. Allusions to Oenone, Tereus and Procne, Orpheus and Eurydice, and Myrrha help characterize the love of Troilus and Criseyde as foolish, thereby foreshadowing the message of the epilogue.

277. Holloway, Julia Bolton. "'The Asse to the Harpe': Boethian Music in Chaucer." In Michael Masi, ed. *Boethius and the Liberal Arts: A Collection of Essays*. Utah Studies in Literature and Linguistics, no. 18. Berne: Peter Lang, 1981, pp. 175–86. Surveys the history and iconography of the "asinus ad liram" topos and examines its use in Boethius's *Consolation of Philosophy*, Juan Ruiz's *Libro de buen amor*, and *TC*. Pandarus inverts Philosophy's use of the topos.

278. Klassen, N. "Optical Allusions and Chaucerian Realism: Aspects of Sight in Late Medieval Thought and *Troilus and Criseyde*." *StHR* 2:2–3 (1992): 129–46. Surveys the late-medieval science of optics, focusing on Alhazan, Grosseteste, Bacon, Ockham, and their links between optics and epistemology. In Boccaccio's *Filostrato*, sight is merely a convention of courtly literature, but Chaucer's optical references in *TC* add theological and philosophical depth to the conventional use.

279. Margherita, Gayle. "Historicity, Femininity, and Chaucer's *Troilus*." *Exemplaria* 6 (1994): 243–69; reprinted in Gayle Margherita. *The Romance of Origins: Language and Sexual Difference in Middle English Literature* (*SAC* 18 [1996], no. 108), pp. 100–28. Challenges historicist criticism on the grounds that it is caught between reality and representation, and argues that *TC* explores this problem in the tension between history and romance. The poem "begins as a drama of loss, and then proceeds to show how this essentially historicist problem becomes, through displacement, a problem of sexual difference." Troilus "is a victim of feminine and material instability"; Criseyde is "victimized by male fantasies." Knowing "more than the courtly system can or will allow," Criseyde is a figure of feminine historicism.

280. Miyares, Rubén Valdés. "Chaucer's Criseyde and Eurydice." *SELIM* 2 (1992): 142–53. Explores Chaucer's understanding of the Orpheus and Eurydice myth to argue that Criseyde's reference to Eurydice (*TC* 4.791) is the poet's way of "lending voice" to a classical figure who, like Criseyde, was the object of barter.

281. Nakao, Yoshiyuki. "A Note on the Affectivity of Criseyde's *Pite*." *PoeticaT* 41 (1994): 19–43. Charts use of "pite" in Chaucer's works and argues that, as applied to and by Criseyde in *TC*, it signals transitions in her affections and enables the audience to view her both critically and empathetically.

282. Pedersen, Frederik. "Did the Medieval Laity Know the Canon Law Rules on Marriage? Some Evidence from Fourteenth-Century York." *MS* 56 (1994): 111–52. Witnesses' statements and other court documents con-

cerning marriage litigation in the Northern Province (including the dioceses of York, Lincoln, Chester, and others) indicate that many lay people would have known the stipulations of canon law well enough to recognize that the exchange of vows and sexual union of Troilus and Criseyde constituted a valid marriage.

283. Schoeck, R. J. "Chaucerian Irony Revisited: A Rhetorical Perspective." *Florilegium* 11 (1992): 124–40. In *TC*, ironic effects are achieved through a rich exploration of a variety of rhetorical devices that create a complicated interplay between speaker, subject, and audience.

284. Storm, Melvin. "The Intertextual Cressida: Chaucer's Henryson or Henryson's Chaucer?" *SSL* 28 (1993): 105–22. Chaucer's moral judgment of Troilus may be uncertain, and his judgment of Criseyde is definitely uncertain. Readers have attempted to clarify these judgments by appeals outside the text to law and theology; however, reading Henryson's *Testament* as a continuation of Chaucer with close attention to the intertextual connections makes clear that both Troilus and Criseyde are ameliorated.

285. Yager, Susan. "'As She That': Syntactical Ambiguity in Chaucer's *Troilus and Criseyde*." *PQ* 73 (1994): 151–68. "As [s]he that" appears most frequently—twenty-five of forty-three occurrences throughout Chaucer's work—in *TC*, with twenty of these instances clustered in *TC* 4 and 5. Although in some of these passages the phrase clearly means "for" or "because," it usually signals ambiguity, mirroring the doubleness and doubt of this portion of the narrative and undermining the reader's ability to interpret characters' behavior.

See also nos. 34, 40, 41, 43, 46, 52, 55, 57, 59, 66, 72, 74, 98, 100, 104, 109, 121, 126, 257.

Lyrics and Short Poems

See nos. 286, 287.

Pity

See no. 99.

Venus

286. Phillips, Helen. "*The Complaint of Venus*: Chaucer and de Graunson." In Roger Ellis and Ruth Evans, eds. *The Medieval Translator, 4*. Medi-

eval & Renaissance Texts & Studies, no. 123. Binghamton, N.Y.: Medieval & Renaissance Texts & Studies, 1994, pp. 86–103. Compares the diction of Chaucer's *Ven* with that of its sources (three of Otto de Graunson's ballades) to explore how Chaucer reconceived "what de Graunson had written for a male speaker as an expression of a woman's feelings." The speaker of the poem is presented as a translator and, like other Chaucerian narrator-translators, is feminine or feminized. Includes the text of *Ven* and its sources.

287. Scattergood, John. "Chaucer's *Complaint of Venus* and the 'Curiosite' of Graunson." *EIC* 44 (1994): 171–89. John Shirley's comments about the relationship of *Ven* to court scandal have been misconstrued, disguising the poem's connection to Otto de Graunson's *Cinq ballades*. Chaucer used five ballades to realize Graunson's "curiosite" (intricate workmanship), exploring the diminishing not of love but of composition. In *Ven*, memory, though diminished, consoles.

Chaucerian Apocrypha

288. Jost, Jean E. "From Southwark's Tabard Inn to Canterbury's Cheker-of-the-Hope: The Un-Chaucerian *Tale of Beryn*." *FCS* 21 (1994): 133–48. *Beryn* lacks several typical Chaucerian characteristics: a "courtly demeanor and value system," idealism, verbal wit, and sophisticated characterization. Neither prologue nor tale rises above slapstick or the "mundane reality of life."

See no. 206.

The Romaunt of the Rose

See no. 33.

Book Reviews

289. Aers, David, ed. *Culture and History, 1350–1600: Essays on English Communities, Identities, and Writing* (*SAC* 18 [1996], no. 70). Rev. Barbara A. Hanawalt, *SAC* 16 (1994): 143–45.

290. Baltzer, Rebecca A., Thomas Cable, and James I. Wimsatt, eds.

The Union of Words and Music in Medieval Poetry (*SAC* 15 [1993], no. 86). Rev. Beverly K. Evans, *SAC* 16 (1994): 145–49.

291. Benson, Larry D., gen. ed. *The Riverside Chaucer* (*SAC* 11 [1989], no. 11). Rev. Juliette Dor, *MA* 100 (1994): 144–45.

292. ———, gen. ed.; David Edmonds, electronic ed.; Lou Burnard, tech. consultant. *The Riverside Chaucer*. CD-ROM Electronic Version (*SAC* 18 [1996], no. 20). Rev. Whitney Bolton, *Computers and the Humanities* 27:5–6 (1993–94): 403–5.

293. Biscoglio, Frances Minetti. *The Wives of the* Canterbury Tales *and the Tradition of the Valiant Woman of Proverbs 31:10–31* (*SAC* 17 [1995], no. 128). Rev. Priscilla Martin, *SAC* 16 (1994): 158–60.

294. Blake, Norman, ed. *The Cambridge History of the English Language: Volume II, 1066–1476* (*SAC* 16 [1994], no. 67). Rev. Terence Odlin, *SAC* 16 (1994): 160–63.

295. Blamires, Alcuin, ed., with Karen Pratt and C. W. Marx. *Woman Defamed and Woman Defended: An Anthology of Medieval Texts* (*SAC* 16 [1994], no. 68). Rev. Elaine Tuttle Hansen, *SAC* 16 (1994): 163–66.

296. Bloch, R. Howard. *Medieval Misogyny and the Invention of Western Romantic Love* (*SAC* 18 [1996], no. 76). E. D. Blodgett, *CRCL* 20 (1993): 233–38.

297. Bowers, John M., ed. *The* Canterbury Tales: *Fifteenth-Century Continuations and Additions* (*SAC* 16 [1994], no. 6). Rev. Stephan Kohl, *SAC* 16 (1994): 166–68.

298. Buffoni, Franco. *I racconti de Canterbury: Un'opera unitaria* (*SAC* 18 [1996], no. 137). Rev. David Wallace, *MÆ* 63 (1994): 137–39.

299. Cable, Thomas. *The English Alliterative Tradition* (*SAC* 15 [1993], no. 67). Rev. Françoise Le Saux, *MA* 100 (1994): 311–12.

300. Carruthers, Mary J. *The Book of Memory: A Study of Memory in Medieval Culture* (*SAC* 14 [1992], no. 65). Rev. Anne Hudson, *MÆ* 61 (1992): 107–9; Beryl Rowland, *ELN* 31:2 (1993): 75–77.

301. Copeland, Rita. *Rhetoric, Hermeneutics, and Translation in the Middle Ages: Academic Traditions and Vernacular Texts* (*SAC* 15 [1993], no. 97). Rev. Martin Camargo, *QJS* 80 (1994): 237–39; Sarah Kay, *MÆ* 61 (1992): 109–10; Glending Olson, *MP* 91:3 (1994): 339–42; Douglas Robinson, *CRCL* 21 (1994): 520–28.

302. Dane, Joseph A. *The Critical Mythology of Irony* (*SAC* 17 [1995], no. 82). Rev. Lillian R. Furst, *CLS* 31 (1994): 180–81.

303. Davidson, Linda Kay, and Maryjane Dunn-Wood. *Pilgrimage in the Middle Ages: A Research Guide* (*SAC* 16 [1994], no. 132). Rev. Mary Baine Campbell, *SAC* 16 (1994): 172–74.

304. Dean, James M., and Christian Zacher, eds. *The Idea of Medieval Literature: New Essays on Chaucer and Medieval Culture in Honor of Donald R. Howard* (*SAC* 16 [1994], no. 79). Rev. A. J. Minnis, *SAC* 16 (1994): 175–78.

305. Doane, A. N., and Carol Braun Pasternack, eds. *Vox intexta: Orality and Textuality in the Middle Ages* (*SAC* 15 [1993], no. 26). Rev. Thomas N. Hall, *AEB* n.s., 7 (1993): 30–39.

306. Dor, Juliette, ed. *A Wyf Ther Was: Essays in Honour of Paule Mertens-Fonck* (*SAC* 16 [1994], no. 83). Rev. Ebbe Klitgård, *ES* (1994): 482–83; A. A. McDonald, *RBPH* 72 (1994): 741–43.

307. Emmerson, Richard K., and Ronald B. Herzman. *The Apocalyptic Imagination in Medieval Literature* (*SAC* 16 [1994], no. 137). Rev. Kathryn Kerby-Fulton, *SAC* 16 (1994): 189–92.

308. Fleming, John V. *Classical Imitation and Interpretation in Chaucer's Troilus* (*SAC* 14 [1992], no. 259). Rev. Robert R. Edwards, *CLS* 30 (1993): 295–98.

309. Frese, Dolores Warwick. *An Ars Legendi for Chaucer's* Canterbury Tales: *A Reconstructive Reading* (*SAC* 15 [1993], no. 150). Rev. John M. Fyler, *Speculum* 69 (1994): 474–76.

310. Frantzen, Allen J. Troilus and Criseyde: *The Poem and the Frame* (*SAC* 17 [1995], no. 254). Rev. Russell A. Peck, *SAC* 16 (1994): 197–99; James R. Sprouse, *SoRA* 59:4 (1994): 124–26.

311. Gittes, Katharine S. *Framing the* Canterbury Tales: *Chaucer and the Medieval Frame Narrative Tradition* (*SAC* 15 [1993], no. 102). Rev. Kathryn McKinley, *ELN* 32:1 (1994): 74–77; A. C. Spearing, *M&H* 20 (1993): 228–33; Christian K. Zacher, *Speculum* 69 (1994): 481–82.

312. Glowka, Arthur Wayne. *A Guide to Chaucer's Meter* (*SAC* 15 [1993], no. 68). Rev. James M. Dean, *Speculum* 69 (1994): 482–83.

313. Hanawalt, Barbara A., ed. *Chaucer's England: Literature in Historical Context* (*SAC* 16 [1994], no. 89). Rev. Peggy A. Knapp, *MP* 92:1 (1994): 87–88.

314. Hanly, Michael G. *Boccaccio, Beauvau, Chaucer:* Troilus and Criseyde: *Four Perspectives on Influence* (*SAC* 14 [1992], no. 261). Rev. H. L. Spencer, *RES*, n.s., 45 (1994): 412–13.

315. Hansen, Elaine Tuttle. *Chaucer and the Fictions of Gender* (*SAC* 16 [1994], no. 90). Rev. Cheryl Glenn, *CE* 56 (1994): 324–30; Evelyn S. Newlyn, *Women's Studies International Forum* 16 (1993): 305–6; David J. Wallace, *Speculum* 69 (1994): 156–58.

316. Harwood, Britton J., and Gillian R. Overing, eds. *Class and Gen-*

der in Early English Literature: Intersections (SAC 18 [1996], no. 91). Rev. Ruth Evans, Medieval Feminist Newsletter 18 (1994): 228–30.

317. Hertog, Erik. Chaucer's Fabliaux as Analogues (SAC 15 [1993], no. 38). Rev. Thomas D. Cooke, Speculum 69 (1994): 493–95.

318. Hill, Ordelle G. The Manor, the Plowman, and the Shepherd: Agrarian Themes and Imagery in Late Medieval and Early Renaissance English Literature (SAC 18 [1995], no. 92). Rev. John Micheal Crafton, SAC 16 (1994): 207–10; Robert Lambdin, SoRA 59:3 (1994): 116–18.

319. Hines, John. The Fabliau in English (SAC 17 [1995], no. 130). Rev. Michael Baron, English 43 (1994): 189; M. P. Kuczynski, MÆ 63 (1994): 331–32.

320. Jankofsky, Klaus P., ed. The South English Legendary: A Critical Assessment (SAC 16 [1994], no. 254). Rev. Karen A. Winstead, SAC 16 (1994): 210–13.

321. Kinney, Clare Regan. Strategies of Poetic Narrative: Chaucer, Spenser, Milton, and Eliot (SAC 16 [1994], no. 97). Rev. Bridget Gellert, RenQ 47 (1994): 971–73.

322. Kiser, Lisa J. Truth and Textuality in Chaucer's Poetry (SAC 15 [1993], no. 113). Rev. Anne Rooney, RES, n.s., 45 (1994): 552–53; A. C. Spearing, M&H 20 (1993): 228–33.

323. Kruger, Steven F. Dreaming in the Middle Ages (SAC 16 [1994], no. 101). Rev. John M. Ganim, JEGP 93 (1994): 246–49; Kathryn Lynch, SAC 16 (1994): 215–19.

324. Lerer, Seth. Chaucer and His Readers: Imagining the Author in Late-Medieval England (SAC 17 [1995], no. 50). Rev. John M. Bowers, MÆ 63 (1994): 332–33.

325. Lomperis, Linda, and Sarah Stanbury, eds. Feminist Approaches to the Body in Medieval Literature (SAC 17 [1995], no. 103). Rev. Kathleen Ashley, SAC 16 (1994): 219–24.

326. McAlpine, Monica E. Chaucer's Knight's Tale: An Annotated Bibliography, 1900–1985 (SAC 15 [1993], no. 5). Rev. Alan T. Gaylord, Speculum 69 (1994): 211–14.

327. Mandel, Jerome. Geoffrey Chaucer: Building the Fragments of the Canterbury Tales (SAC 16 [1994], no. 147). Rev. Catherine Batt, MLR 89 (1994): 966–76; Leo Carruthers, EA 47 (1994): 72–73; Vincent DiMarco, Speculum 69 (1994): 831–33; Ebbe Klitgård, ES 75 (1994): 481–82; Dieter Mehl, SAC 16 (1994): 224–26.

328. Mann, Jill. Geoffrey Chaucer: Feminist Readings (SAC 15 [1993], no. 117). Rev. Patricia Shaw, SELIM 2 (1992): 188–96.

329. Meale, Carol M., ed. *Women and Literature in Britain, 1150–1500* (*SAC* 17 [1995], no. 105). Rev. Jennifer Summit, *Medieval Feminist Newsletter* 17 (1994): 18–21.

330. Minnis, A. J., ed. *Chaucer's* Boece *and the Medieval Tradition of Boethius* (*SAC* 17 [1995], no. 220). Rev. M. Gibson, *MÆ* 63 (1994): 132–33.

331. ————, and A. B. Scott, eds., with David Wallace. *Medieval Literary Theory and Criticism, c. 1100–c. 1375: The Commentary Tradition* (*SAC* 12 [1990], no. 98). Rev. A. Bravo, *SELIM* 1 (1991): 154–57.

332. ————, and Charlotte Brewer, eds. *Crux and Controversy in Middle English Textual Criticism* (*SAC* 16 [1994], no. 17). Rev. Susan E. Deskis, *AEB*, n.s., 7 (1993): 148–50; Douglas Moffat, *SAC* 16 (1994): 226–29.

333. Morse, Charlotte Cook, Penelope Reed Doob, and Marjorie Curry Woods, eds. *The Uses of Manuscripts in Literary Studies: Essays in Memory of Judson Boyce Allen* (*SAC* 18 [1996], no. 110). Rev. Caroline D. Eckhardt, *SAC* 16 (1994): 229–31.

334. Morse, Ruth. *Truth and Convention in the Middle Ages: Rhetoric, Representation, and Reality* (*SAC* 15 [1993], no. 121). Rev. Winthrop Wetherbee, *MÆ* 61 (1992): 110–12.

335. Neuse, Richard. *Chaucer's Dante: Allegory and Epic Theater in* The Canterbury Tales (*SAC* 15 [1993], no. 158). Rev. Cheryl Glenn, *CE* 56 (1994): 324–30.

336. Nolan, Barbara. *Chaucer and the Tradition of the Roman Antique* (*SAC* 16 [1994], no. 30). Rev. James M. Dean, *SAC* 16 (1994): 231–35; John M. Ganim, *JEGP* 93 (1994): 409–11; Derek Pearsall, *MP* 92:2 (1994): 227–28; Barry Windeatt, *MÆ* 63 (1994): 136–37.

337. Patterson, Lee. *Chaucer and the Subject of History* (*SAC* 15 [1993], no. 124). Rev. Valerie Allen and Ares Axiotes, *RES*, n.s., 45 (1994): 410–12; James W. Earl, *Raritan* 12 (1993): 120–30; Rubén Valdés Miyares, *SELIM* 2 (1992): 202–8; Paul A. Olson, *JEGP* 93 (1994): 251–54; James I. Wimsatt, *M&H* 20 (1993): 247–52.

338. Pearsall, Derek. *The Life of Geoffrey Chaucer: A Critical Biography* (*SAC* 16 [1994], no. 5). Rev. Thomas H. Bestul, *Speculum* 69 (1994): 871–73; Leo Carruthers, *EA* 47 (1994): 72; Martha Driver, *MLR* 89 (1994): 967–69; Sumner Ferris, *SAC* 16 (1994): 235–41; Jill Mann, *MÆ* 63 (1994): 130–32; Thomas L. Wright, *SHR* 28 (1994): 297–98.

339. ————, ed. *Studies in the Vernon Manuscript* (*SAC* 15 [1993], no. 29). Rev. Emerson Brown, Jr., *SAC* 16 (1994): 241–45.

340. Richmond, Velma Bourgeois. *Geoffrey Chaucer* (*SAC* 16 [1994], no.

112). Rev. Stephen A. Barney, *Speculum* 69 (1994): 1259; Michael D. Cherniss, *SAC* 16 (1994): 252–54; Thomas L. Wright, *SHR* 28 (1994): 297–98.

341. Rooney, Anne. *Hunting in Middle English Literature* (*SAC* 17 [1995], no. 111). Rev. W. Martin, *MÆ* 63 (1994): 336–37.

342. Rudat, Wolfgang E. H. *Earnest Exuberance in Chaucer's Poetics: Textual Games in the* Canterbury Tales (*SAC* 17 [1995], no. 137). Rev. Peter Fields, *InG* 15 (1994): 99–103.

343. Ruud, Jay. *"Many a Song and Many a Leccherous Lay": Tradition and Individuality in Chaucer's Lyric Poetry* (*SAC* 16 [1994], no. 321). Rev. Liam Purdon, *SAC* 16 (1994): 257–60; John Scattergood, *MÆ* 63 (1994): 135–36.

344. Shoaf, R. A., ed., with the assistance of Catherine S. Cox. *Chaucer's* Troilus and Criseyde: *"Subgit to Alle Poesye": Essays in Criticism* (*SAC* 16 [1994], no. 309). Rev. William Watts, *SAC* 16 (1994): 260–63.

345. Simons, John, ed. *From Medieval to Medievalism* (*SAC* 16 [1994], no. 168). Rev. Carolyn P. Collette, *SAC* 16 (1994): 263–66.

346. Spearing, A. C. *The Medieval Poet as Voyeur: Looking and Listening in Medieval Love-Narratives* (*SAC* 17 [1995], no. 117). Rev. Leo Carruthers, *EA* 47 (1994): 322–23; Roy M. Liuzza, *SAC* 16 (1994): 271–75; Gayle Margherita, *PLL* 30 (1994): 187–92.

347. Stillinger, Thomas C. *The Song of Troilus: Lyric Authority in the Medieval Book* (*SAC* 16 [1994], no. 314). Rev. Caron Ann Cioffi, *SAC* 16 (1994): 282–93.

348. Strohm, Paul. *Hochon's Arrow: The Social Imagination of Fourteenth-Century Texts* (*SAC* 16 [1994], no. 119). Rev. David Lorenzo Boyd, *Medieval Feminist Newsletter* 17 (1994): 21–22; John Scattergood, *SAC* 16 (1994): 293–96.

349. Volk-Birke, Sabine. *Chaucer and Medieval Preaching: Rhetoric for Listeners in Sermons and Poetry* (*SAC* 15 [1993], no. 133). Rev. Richard J. Utz, *Anglia* 112 (1994): 203–6.

350. Wimsatt, James I. *Chaucer and His French Contemporaries: Natural Music in the Fourteenth Century* (*SAC* 15 [1993], no. 45). Rev. Robert Boenig, *Speculum* 69 (1994): 273–75; Ardis Butterfield, *MÆ* 63 (1994): 133–35; Jane H. M. Taylor, *RES*, n.s., 45 (1994): 551–52.

351. Windeatt, Barry. *Troilus and Criseyde* (Oxford Guides to Chaucer) (*SAC* 16 [1994], no. 320). Rev. John M. Ganim, *Speculum* 69 (1994): 1297–99; Karla Taylor, *SAC* 16 (1994): 297–99.

352. Wynne-Davies, Marion, ed. *Geoffrey Chaucer: The Tales of the Clerk and the Wife of Bath* (*SAC* 18 [1996], no. 24). Rev. Jean E. Jost, *SAC* 16 (1994): 299–303; C. Hardman, *RMSt* 20 (1994): 111–14.

Author Index—Bibliography

Moffat, Douglas   332
Moore, Roger E.   178
Morse, Charlotte Cook   73, 75, 93,
   110, 130, 203, 245, 333
Morse, Ruth   334
Myles, Robert   111

Nakao, Yoshiyuki   281
Nelson, Ronald J.   252
Neuse, Richard   335
Newlyn, Evelyn S.   315
Nilsen, Don L. F.   112
Noguchi, Shunichi   160
Nøjgaard, Morten   79
Nolan, Barbara   336
North, John David   113

Odegard, Margaret   114
Odlin, Terence   294
Olmert, Michael   149
Olson, Glending   301
Olson, Paul A.   337
Orsten, Elisabeth M.   228
Overing, Gillian R.   91, 221, 262,
   316
Owen, Charles A., Jr.   150, 249

Pagnoulle, Christine   19
Paley, Karen Surman   242
Parks, Ward   232
Pask, Albert Kevin   115
Pasternack, Carol Braun   305
Patch, Howard   94
Patterson, Lee   54, 337
Paxson, James J.   116
Pearsall, Derek (A.)   30, 94, 336,
   338, 339
Peck, Russell A.   310
Pedersen, Frederik   282
Pelen, Marc M.   179, 218
Phillips, Helen   286

Pigg, Daniel (F.)   141, 167, 229
Pinti, Daniel J.   117
Portnoy, Phyllis   142
Pratt, Karen   57, 295
Purdon, Liam (O.)   118, 143, 159,
   343

Quinn, William A.   267

Ramsey, Roy Vance   31
Rendall, Thomas   13, 16
Richmond, Velma Bourgeois   340
Riddy, Felicity   216
Riehle, Wolfgang   234
Robinson, Carol L.   188
Robinson, Douglas   301
Robinson, Peter (M. W.)   23
Roney, Lois   143
Rooney, Anne   322, 341
Root, Jerry   189
Rose, Christine M.   180
Rothwell, W.   67
Rowland, Beryl   151, 300
Rudat, Wolfgang E. H.   230, 342
Rudd, Niall   37
Ruggiers, Paul G.   94
Rumsey, Lucinda   2
Rusch, Willard J.   58
Ruud, Jay   343

Sabadash, Deborah Margaret   119
Saito, Isamu   198
Scanlon, Larry   120
Scattergood, John   287, 343, 348
Schibanoff, Susan   86
Schoeck, R. J.   263, 283
Scott, A. B.   331
Scott, Forrest   12
Shapiro, James   83
Shaw, Patricia   328
Sherman, Mark A.   161

396

Index